We listened.

Let's face it: born into a learning environment rich in information technology, where speed of delivery and visually dynamic presentation are expected, the student world has changed. It's not enough to provide helpful information that few writing students read or study. We want you to be engaged! So we did our homework. We gathered students like you for surveys and focus groups, and we observed you attending class, working, and studying. Instructors reviewed our content and design at every stage and helped shape every page of this book.

McGraw-Hill conducted in-depth ethnographic research of student learning to explore what makes students' reading and learning experience more engaging, memorable, effective, lasting, and enjoyable. We then interviewed instructors to identify their biggest challenges and how a completely different kind of text could serve as a solution to those challenges.

Students showed us they wanted more portable texts with innovative visual appeal, interactive pedagogy, an integrated approach, and relevant content designed according to the way they learn. Instructors told us they wanted a way to engage their students without compromising on high-quality content.

More current, more portable, more captivating, plus a rigorous and innovative research foundation adds up to: more learning. When you meet students where they are, you can take them where you want them to be.

About *argument!*

Argument! marries solid instruction in critical reading and analysis, argument, and research strategies with a visually engaging and dynamic design. Through the use of current, captivating features along with a visually stimulating design, *argument!* helps students learn more.

This text will teach you how to read with a critical eye, how to think about and respond to the ideas of others, and ultimately how to craft your own effective, relevant, and engaging arguments. You will learn how to acknowledge and respond to the complex arguments (both visual and textual) that exist all around you and how to enter into those debates with your own strong and thoughtful voice.

We understand that you live in a visual world and learn in multiple ways. No longer does a simple "textbook" suffice. After all, you have instant access to information, to history . . . to the world. You can watch a video of an event on YouTube five minutes after it has happened. You can research a topic by contacting special interest groups and experts on Facebook. You are part of a global society that moves quickly and watches itself while doing it. You are engaged with the world around you in ways that were unheard of even a few years ago and you expect educators to keep up.

WHAT TO LOOK FOR:

- Diagrams, charts, boxes, and visuals that pop from the page and become a thousand words that did not have to be written. Visuals do not decorate; they document, illustrate, and reinforce the textual content.
- Visual content reinforces the textual content and makes the learning experience more memorable and thus the content more memorable for students during writing assignments and exams.
- Scholarship that meets students where they are: information is segmented in shorter chunks because evaluation of students' study habits shows that they prefer information in this format and retain it better.
- Portability. Students prefer a book they can always take with them. Research shows they will study more from it.

Our research confirms that students like you want a visually engaging book and will study longer and more effectively from a book designed this way. That's exciting for us, but even better for you: you'll retain content better, use writing to learn and to share what you know, be better prepared for your other college classes, and become more likely to succeed and advance in the workplace. We have listened to your call for change. Our hope is that you come away from *argument!* with a new sense of your own place in the visual and vibrant world around you!

argument!

VICE PRESIDENT, EDITORIAL **Michael Ryan**

PUBLISHER **David S. Patterson**

SENIOR SPONSORING EDITOR **Christopher Bennem**

DIRECTOR OF DEVELOPMENT **Dawn Groundwater**

DEVELOPMENTAL EDITOR **Craig Leonard**

EDITORIAL COORDINATOR **Zachary Norton**

EDITORIAL COORDINATOR **Jesse Hassenger**

EXECUTIVE MARKETING MANAGER **Allison Jones**

SENIOR PRODUCTION EDITOR **Carey Eisner**

DESIGN MANAGER **Cassandra Chu**

INTERIOR DESIGN **Maureen McCutcheon**

COVER DESIGNER **Linda Beaupre**

PHOTO RESEARCHER AND ART EDITOR **Sonia Brown**

SENIOR PRODUCTION SUPERVISOR **Louis Swaim**

PERMISSIONS COORDINATOR **Marty Moga**

COMPOSITION **10/12 Sabon by Lachina Publishing Services**

PRINTING **45# Influence Gloss, World Color Press Inc.**

FRONT COVER **Loungepark**

BACK COVER **ColorBlind Images**

FOLDOUT: (LEFT TO RIGHT): **Stockbyte/PunchStock; 2007 Getty Images; Nick White/Getty Images; Stockbyte/PunchStock**

CREDITS: **The credits appear at the end of the book and are considered an extension of the copyright page.**

ISBN: 978-0-07-338401-6

MHID: 0-07-338401-1

Library of Congress Cataloging-in-Publication Data

Messenger, Erica
    Argument! / Erica Messenger, John Gooch, Dorothy U. Seyler.—1st ed.
       p. cm.
    ISBN-13: 978-0-07-338401-6 (pbk. : alk. paper)
    ISBN-10: 0-07-338401-1 (pbk. : alk. paper)
1. English language—Rhetoric. 2. Persuasion (Rhetoric) 3. Critical thinking. 4. College readers. 5. Report writing. I. Gooch, John. II. Seyler, Dorothy U. III. Title.
    PE1408.M5173 2010
    808'.042—dc22

                                                                                              2009047272

www.mhhe.com

Knowing how important writing is to you in school and on the job, the authors of *argument!* developed features to help you read, write, and respond to complex arguments. The readings and assignments focus on fresh and contemporary topics of our increasingly global and visual world.

ARGUMENT! INCLUDES:

Innovative design: Research-based and instructor- and student-tested, our "M-series" design delivers course content in ways you learn it best.

Seeing the Argument: Through the use of visual elements—photographs, advertisements, bumper stickers, Web sites, etc.—this feature demonstrates how to acknowledge and respond to complex arguments that exist all around us.

Try It!: This feature asks you to think about what you've just read and apply it to various types of exercises that include readings, writing, questions, and collaborative exercises.

Good Advice: As the name implies, this feature offers advice on important aspects of the writing process—things every writer should know.

Did You Know?: This feature appeals to the curious minded by answering questions like: Who was Stephen Toulmin? or Who was Aristotle?

Anthology of 65 Contemporary Arguments: Drawn from a wide variety of genres including magazine and journal articles, Web sites, blogs, political cartoons, advertisements, photographs, YouTube videos, and Facebook pages, this anthology presents a wide range of arguments on the issues that matter today.

Student Writing: You learn best by not only studying the writing of great writers, but also studying the writing of your peers. Student writing samples are presented to demonstrate how to put principles into practice.

Online Learning Center: Get interactive and visit our award-winning multimedia resource, Catalyst 2.0, at www.mhhe.com/argument where you will find interactive tutorials on writing arguments, avoiding plagiarism, visual rhetoric, and more.

Making Connections: Appearing at the end of each chapter, this feature presents a list of what you should have learned, followed by an exercise that requires all of the skills covered in the chapter.

Brief Contents

PART ONE

[reading arguments critically]

chapter 1

Reading Arguments with a Critical Eye

chapter 2

Responding Critically to the Arguments of Others

PART TWO

[writing arguments]

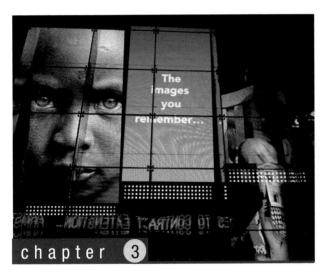

chapter 3

The Basics of Argument

chapter 4

Writing Effective Arguments

chapter ⑤

More about Argument: Induction, Deduction, Analogy, and Logical Fallacies

chapter ⑥

The Refutation Essay

chapter ⑦

The Position Essay

chapter 8

The Causal Essay

chapter 9

The Problem/Solution Essay

PART THREE

[writing a researched argument]

chapter 10

Planning the Researched Argument

Evaluating and Utilizing Sources

Drafting and Revising the
Researched Argument

Documenting Sources
(MLA, APA, and More)

PART FOUR

[an anthology of contemporary arguments]

chapter 20

Enduring Controversies in a New Age: Abortion, Animal Rights, Capital Punishment, and Health Care

chapter 21

Marriage and Gender Roles: Changing Attitudes vs. Traditional Values

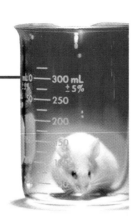

chapter (22)

Arguing About Science: Policy, Politics, and Culture

chapter (23)

Competing Perspectives on the American Economic and Financial Crisis

reading arguments with a critical eye

chapter 1

What Does an Argument Look Like?

Many everyday arguments are easy to spot. Most readers can sense when an author has intentionally chosen words and images to convince them to adopt a certain position or stance. The cover of *The Economist* from the week before the 2008 U.S. election, for example, can clearly be seen as an argument. It presents an opinion about which candidate in the 2008 presidential election should be victorious, and it uses both text and effective visual design to make its opinion clear.

Similarly, most readers would easily identify the words of Ron Paul, representative from Texas, spoken to Congress in 2002 as an argument:

> There are economic reasons to avoid this war. We can do serious damage to our economy. It is estimated that this venture into Iraq may well cost over a hundred billion dollars. Our national debt right now is increasing at a rate of over $450 billion yearly, and we are talking about spending another hundred billion dollars on an adventure when we do not know what the outcome will be and how long it will last. What will happen to oil prices? What will happen to the recession that we are in? What will happen to the deficit? We must expect all kinds of economic ramifications.

(To read Paul's entire speech, visit http://en.wikisource.org/wiki/Arguments_Against_a_War_in_Iraq.)

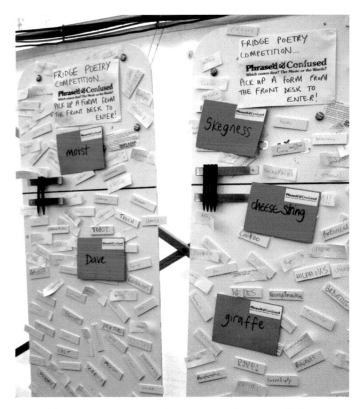

Although these examples seem rather straightforward, other everyday arguments are harder to spot. Consider this example of "refrigerator" poetry. Is this an argument? You might claim that this poem was written primarily to entertain and to present one person's emotional perspective, not to present an argument. This is true—to a degree. However, this poet has made specific choices about what words to use, what visuals to use, the physical setting of the work, and about how his or her audience should read the material. Even writing primarily designed to entertain, such as a blog entry, a social networking post, or even highway graffiti, says to readers: Do it my way! Think about these ideas as I would! Believe what I believe!

Surely the argument made by this artist is more subtle than the one made by the editors of *The Economist*. The ideas about life and experience that appear in works we label "expressive" are often more subtle than the points we meet head-on in an overt argument. Still, expressive writing gives us new ways of seeing the world. Perhaps, then, we need to recognize that writing strategies and purposes spread along a continuum; they often overlap and do not fit into neat categories. Oftentimes, one image or piece of writing has several different purposes. Typically, however, if you look hard enough, an argument of some sort is being made.

Recognizing Purpose in Everyday Arguments

Many pieces of communication that we don't think of as arguments still contain subtle elements of persuasion. For example, comedian Denis Leary's humorous

The cover of the July 21, 2008, issue of *The New Yorker* magazine depicts Barack Obama (who some conservatives were criticizing as being sympathetic to Muslims and ultimately anti-American) in Muslim garb and fist-bumping his military-clad and rifle-toting wife, Michelle, as an American flag burns in the White House fireplace. According to many, the cover is clearly satire. However, Obama's presidential campaign issued a statement saying, "*The New Yorker* may think, as one of their staff explained to us, that their cover is a satirical lampoon of the caricature Sen. Obama's right-wing critics have tried to create. But most readers will see it as tasteless and offensive. And we agree."

As you examine the cover of *The New Yorker* presented here and compare it to the cover of *The Economist* presented earlier in the chapter, what are some of the first things you notice? What ideas are suggested by the very different images? Do you think that the editors clearly have differing points of view? Do you agree that many readers will view *The New Yorker* cover as an insult rather than as satire? What makes each of these pieces an argument rather than a record of an event? For what audience(s) might each piece be targeted? How do you know?

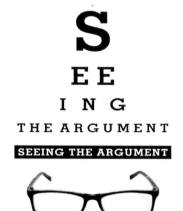

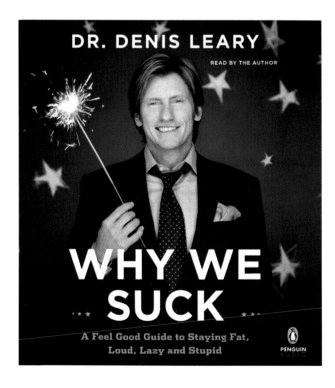

book *Why We Suck: A Feel Good Guide to Staying Fat, Loud, Lazy, and Stupid* has the primary purpose of entertaining its readers, but it can also be seen as an attempt at making a fairly serious argument about the current state of American society and its citizenry.

Although it may be fairly easy to identify a text's primary purpose (to entertain, to explain information, or to argue for or against an issue), it is often more challenging to recognize the more subtle intentions of an author. Most texts have more than one purpose and most, in fact, attempt to persuade their readers to accept the positions and opinions of their authors.

Much more about recognizing an argument's purpose will be covered in Chapter 4. For now, keep in mind that every piece of communication, whether written, visual, or even oral, has at least one clear and distinct purpose.

Understanding Audience in Everyday Arguments

Just as every argument has a clear purpose (to persuade its readers), so too does it have an intended audience. An author must understand the needs of her readers if she hopes to connect with them and persuade them to accept her position. An author who writes without

Can you think of other examples of texts with multiple purposes? Or can you think of something not typically considered an argument that actually is one? Find an everyday text, examine the continuum below, and decide where your piece might fall along it. Might your text actually include elements of all three purposes?

IMPLICIT ARGUMENT

PRIMARY PURPOSE: EXPRESSIVE
(to evoke feeling or provide humor)

Author is expressing an emotional viewpoint, but guides the reader's experience by making specific choices about what is presented and how.

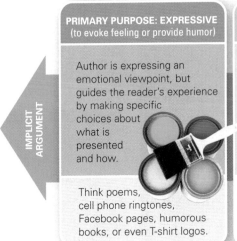

Think poems, cell phone ringtones, Facebook pages, humorous books, or even T-shirt logos.

PRIMARY PURPOSE: EXPOSITORY
(to impart information)

Author provides information but still has a distinct point of view on events, details, or facts that is evident in the choices he or she makes.

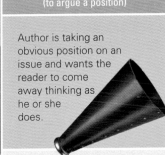

Think textbooks, newspaper articles, product labels, true-life crime books, or even the nightly news.

PRIMARY PURPOSE: PERSUASIVE
(to argue a position)

Author is taking an obvious position on an issue and wants the reader to come away thinking as he or she does.

Think political speeches, television ads, newspaper editorials, sermons, or college research essays.

EXPLICIT ARGUMENT

considering her audience runs the risk of alienating and offending readers who are not ready to accept the proposed position, or wasting time and energy "preaching to the choir," or trying to convince readers who already agree with the proposed position.

Much more about analyzing audience needs, values, and expectations will be covered in Chapter 4.

For now, keep in mind that the success of an argument depends on the author's understanding of his or her audience.

Why You Need to Learn to Read and Write Arguments. Right Now.

Now that you've come to see the larger scope of argument and that it exists in practically every piece of communication, it's time to narrow our focus a bit. You can most likely expect that in your current course on argument—or critical thinking—you probably will not be asked to write a short story, personal narrative, poem, or t-shirt logo. You might, though, be asked to write a summary, critique, research essay, or analysis, so you will need to think about how those writing tasks connect to the world of argument. Regardless of what specific assignments your professor gives you, you can count on one thing: You will be asked to write!

Why work on your writing skills? Here are some good answers to this question:

1. The better writer you become, the better reader you will become.

Communication and writing skills are *the most important abilities* sought by employers. As evidence, you may want to consider the following article from *The New York Times*.

The New York Times
August 26, 2007
Young Workers: U Nd 2 Improve Ur Writing Skills

PHYLLIS KORKKI

A generation ago, employers were still lamenting the poor technical abilities of their entry-level workers. Well, that's not much of an issue anymore, thanks to the omnipresence of computers, cellphones and the Internet.

In a survey of 100 human resources executives, only 5 percent said that recent college graduates lacked computer or technology skills, according to Challenger, Gray & Christmas, the outplacement firm.

The problem now is more basic. Nearly half the executives said that entry-level workers lacked writing skills, and 27 percent said that they were deficient in critical thinking.

It seems that some young employees are now guilty of the technological equivalent of wearing flip-flops: they are writing company e-mail as if they were texting cellphone messages with their thumbs.

In response, employers are sending a message of their own: When you're in the office, put on those dress shoes and start spelling your words correctly, and in full.

http://www.mhhe.argument/from the author

GOOD ADVICE

You might be asking, "Won't my instructor be my audience?"

Yes, your instructor or TA is probably the actual audience for your paper. Your instructors read and grade your essays, and you want to keep their needs and perspectives in mind when you write. However, when you write an essay with only your instructor in mind, you might not say as much as you should or say it as clearly as you should, because you assume that your instructor knows more than you do and will fill in the gaps. This leaves it up to the instructor to decide what you are really saying, and she might decide that those gaps show that you don't understand the material. If you say to yourself, "I don't have to explain communism; my instructor knows more about that than I do," you could get back a paper that says something like "Shows no understanding of communism." That's an example of what can go awry when you think of your instructor as your only audience.

Thinking about your audience differently can improve your writing, especially in terms of how clearly you express your argument. The clearer your points are, the more likely you are to have a strong essay. Your instructor will say, "You really understand communism—you're able to explain it simply and clearly!" By treating your instructor *as an intelligent but uninformed audience*, you end up addressing her more effectively.

Source: The Writing Center at UNC Chapel Hill, www.unc.edu/depts/wcweb/handouts/audience.html

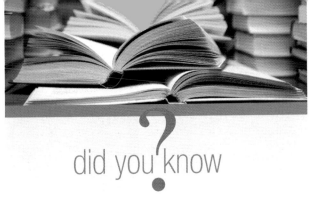

did you know

To participate fully in society and the workplace in 2020, citizens will need powerful literacy abilities that until now have been achieved by only a small percentage of the population.

Source: National Council of Teachers of English Standards for the English Language Arts
www.readfaster.com/education_stats.asp

2. The more confident a writer you become, the more efficiently you will handle written assignments in all of your courses.

3. The more you write, the more you will learn about who you are and what really matters to you. More colleges and universities are designing courses focused on critical thinking about personal values, ethics, and morals. Learning to write about your beliefs and to understand and accommodate the beliefs of others are great ways to be ready for future coursework in this area.

What You Can Expect from Your Writing Assignments

You are about to face a variety of writing assignments, each with its own specific audience and purpose. Pay close attention to each assignment sheet so that you will know what sort of writing your instructor expects. To help you learn the conventions of different types of writing for different audiences, this text includes a variety of argument forms: editorials, advertisements, articles from scholarly journals, photographs, book reviews, and of course, research essays.

While writing your own assignments, always think about what role you will play as the author and what that specific role calls for. Are you expected to be a student demonstrating knowledge, a citizen arguing for tougher drunk-driving laws, or a scholar presenting the results of research? Any writer—including you—will take on different roles when writing for different audiences and will use different strategies to reach each audience. There are many kinds of argument and many ways to argue successfully.

Why Read and Respond to the Work of Others?

If this is a text about *writing* arguments, why does it contain so many readings, you may wonder. There are good reasons for the collection of readings you find here:

1. College and the workplace will demand that you learn complex information and ideas through reading. This text will give you practice in reading more challenging works.

2. You will need to read to learn and to think critically about what you read. In the world of argument, your reading will serve as a basis for writing.

3. Your writing will be based in some way on one or more sources you have been assigned or that you have selected in response to an assignment. The focus of attention will shift from you to your subject, a subject others have debated before you. You will need to understand the issue, think carefully about the views of others on the issue, and only then develop your own response.

Critical Reading and the Contexts of Argument

In some contexts, the word *critical* carries the idea of harsh judgment: "The manager was critical of her secretary's long phone conversations." In other contexts, though, the term means "to evaluate carefully." When we speak of the critical reader or critical thinker, we have in mind someone who reads actively, who thinks about issues, and who makes informed judgments. Here is a profile of the critical reader or thinker:

Traits of the Critical Reader/Thinker

- **Focused on the facts.** Give me the facts and show me that they are relevant to the issue.
- **Analytic.** What strategies has the writer/speaker used to develop the argument?
- **Open-minded.** Prepared to listen to different points of view, to learn from others.
- **Questioning/skeptical.** What other conclusions could be supported by the evidence presented? How thorough has the writer/speaker been?
- **Creative.** What are some different ways of looking at the issue or problem?

- **Intellectually active, not passive.** Willing to analyze logic and evidence. Willing to consider many possibilities. Willing, after careful evaluation, to reach a judgment, to take a stand on issues.

Active Reading: Use Your Mind!

Reading is not about looking at black marks on a page—or turning the pages as quickly as you can. Reading means constructing meaning from the marks on the page and getting a message. We read with our brains, not our eyes and hands! This concept is underscored by the term *active reading*. To be an active reader, not a passive page-turner, follow these guidelines:

- **Understand your purpose in reading.** Do not just start turning pages to complete an assignment. Think first about your purpose. Are you reading for knowledge on which you will be tested? Focus on your purpose as you read, asking yourself, "What do I need to learn from this work?"

- **Reflect on the title before reading further.** Titles are the first words writers give us. Look for clues in the title that may reveal the work's subject and perhaps the writer's approach or attitude as well. The title "The Idiocy of Urban Life," for exam-

ple, tells you both subject (urban or city living) and the author's position (urban living is idiotic).

- **Become part of the writer's audience.** Not all writers have you and me in mind when they write. As an active reader, you need to join a writer's audience by learning about the writer, about the time in which the piece was written, and about the writer's expected audience. For the readings in this text, you are aided by introductory notes; be sure to study them.

- **Predict what is coming.** Look for a writer's main idea or purpose statement. Study the work's organization. Then use this information to anticipate what is coming. For example, when you read "There are three good reasons for requiring a dress code in schools," you know the writer will list three reasons.

- **Concentrate.** Slow down and give your full attention to reading. Watch for transition and connecting words that show you how the parts of a text connect. Read an entire article or chapter at one time—or you will need to start over to make sense of the entire piece.

- **Annotate as you read.** The more senses you use, the more active your involvement. That means marking the text as you read (or taking notes if the material is not yours). Underline key sentences, such as the writer's thesis. Then, in the margin, indicate that it is the thesis. For a series of examples (or reasons), label them and number them. When you look up a word's definition, write the definition in the margin next to the word. Draw diagrams to illustrate concepts; draw arrows to connect example to idea. Studies have shown that students who annotate their texts get higher grades. Do what successful students do.

- **Keep a reading journal.** In addition to annotating what you read, you may want to develop the habit of writing regularly in a journal or creating a reading blog online. A reading blog gives you a place to note impressions and reflections on your reading, your initial reactions to assignments, and ideas you may use in your next writing.

Understanding the Arguments of Others

Readers expect accurate, fair, and sensitive uses of sources. An inaccurate summary does not serve its purpose. A passage that is misquoted or quoted out of context makes readers question your credibility. So, after reading and annotating, develop your understanding of each source and the author's argument by

Whether you are reading print material or online, be sure to create a quiet atmosphere in which you can concentrate.

did you know

Rhetoric is one of the three ancient arts of discourse. From ancient Greece to the late nineteenth century, it was a central part of Western education, filling the need to train public speakers and writers to move audiences to action with arguments.

Source: www.wikipedia.org

doing a preliminary analysis that answers the following questions:

1. **What is the work's primary purpose? Does it combine purposes?** Remember that texts can be classified as expressive (evoking feelings), expository (imparting information), or persuasive (arguing for a position). We can also distinguish between a serious purpose and a humorous one, although humor can be used to advance a serious topic. However, purposes shade into one another. Arguments appeal to emotions, and passionate fiction can teach us about human life and experience. You may assume that a textbook's primary purpose is to give information, but keep in mind that textbooks can take a position on various conflicts within their field.

2. **What is the thesis, or the main idea of the work?** Often the best way to understand a text's thesis is to first ask, What is the subject? Then ask, What does the author assert about that subject, or want me to understand about that subject? Stating the thesis as a complete sentence will help you move

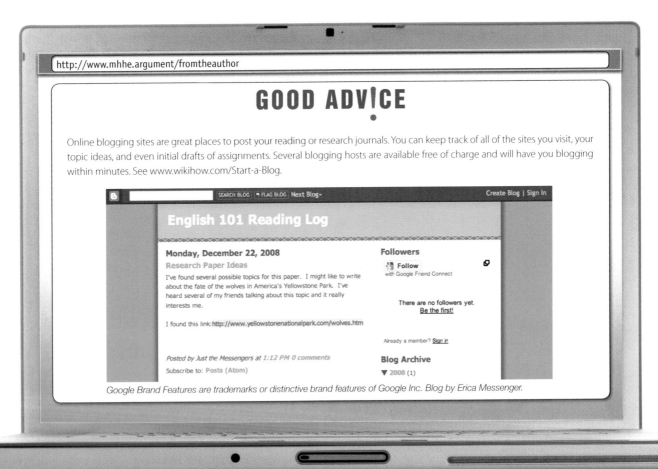

Read the following selection from the editors of the *Los Angeles Times*, noting the annotations that have been started for you. As you read, add your own annotations. Then write a journal or blog entry—four to five sentences at least—to capture your reactions to the following editorial.

Los Angeles Times
Editorial
December 20, 2008
Music Piracy: A New Tune
Lawsuits against music pirates too often miss their mark. So the major labels are changing tactics.

[handwritten: This topic is timely and looks interesting.]

[handwritten left margin: I should find out more about the RIAA as I conduct more research.]

[handwritten right margin: Prodigious = monstrous or huge]

After five years and about 35,000 lawsuits, the major record companies have ended their prodigious litigation campaign against music fans who shared songs online without the labels' permission. It's a welcome step for many reasons, not the least of which being that the suits were eroding the public's support for copyrights in general. But, as the Recording Industry Assn. of America, or RIAA, shifts to a less bare-knuckle approach to enforcing its rights, we hope it also will work harder to profit from an activity it can't seem to kill. *[handwritten: support]*

The major labels—Universal Music Group, Sony BMG Music Entertainment, Warner Music Group, and EMI Group—have been playing catch-up online almost since the MP3 format was developed. First they sued the start-ups that were distributing file-sharing software, only to see new ones emerge to replace them. In 2003, they went after individual file-sharers, stopping the growth of music sharing but not the slide in CD sales and overall music revenue. *[handwritten: opinions]*

The suits were a blunt instrument that inflicted too much damage on the wrong people. The industry's investigators couldn't match the Internet accounts that were active on file-sharing networks with the actual computer users. The RIAA wound up suing the account-holders, putting them at the mercy of law firms determined to extract compensation from someone—if not the defendants themselves, then their children, roommates or relatives. The pressure to settle was intense even on those who didn't infringe, given the high cost of defense attorneys and the risk of calamitous financial penalties.

[handwritten: update] Now, the RIAA says, it's working with the New York attorney general's office and as-yet-unnamed Internet service providers to deter piracy without threatening families with financial ruin. The ISPs can and should help the record companies deliver warnings to customers whose accounts were used for piracy; similar efforts on campuses and in other countries have put a real dent in bootlegging. The danger is that the new approach is no more precise than the lawsuits, so imposing automatic penalties on repeat offenders (which the RIAA favors) risks inflicting the same amount of collateral damage.

What's really amiss here is that, almost a decade after the original Napster introduced file sharing to the masses, the labels still haven't found a way to make money off that activity. The industry has become much more open in recent years to new business models, including those that let people consume music for free. File sharing is the last frontier. Now that the RIAA has called off its attack dogs, perhaps it can find a way to make money from file-sharers' enthusiasm for its products.

www.latimes.com/news/opinion/editorials/la-ed-riaa20-2008dec20,0,922164.story

from subject to assertion. You may find one or two sentences that state the work's thesis, but keep in mind that sometimes the thesis is implied, not stated.

3. **How is the thesis developed and supported?** Does the writer present a series of examples to illustrate the main idea? Or blend reasons and evidence to develop an argument? Does the writer organize chronologically? Set up a contrast pattern or make an analogy? Explain causes? Observing both the type of support and its organization will help you see how the parts fit together. When you know what it says, you can write a summary or begin to analyze or judge the work.

did you know
?

In 1967, Roland Barthes, a French literary critic, published an essay titled "Death of the Author" in which he argued that no aspect of the author's identity (political views, religious beliefs, psychological state, or other details) should be considered when analyzing a literary work and that the only true meaning in a piece of literature is whatever meaning that the reader finds in it.

Even now, scholars disagree about how important an author's experiences are in analyzing literary works.

In argumentative writing, however, the author's background, research methods, values, and education all play a major role in establishing credibility for readers.

Examining the Context of an Argument

Reading critically requires preparation. Instead of jumping into reading, begin by asking questions about the work's total context. You need to be able to answer the following four questions before—or while—you read.

Who Is the Author?

Key questions about the author include the following:

- **Does the author have a reputation for honesty, thoroughness, and fairness?** Read the biographical note, if there is one. Ask your instructor about the author. Learn about the author in a biographical dictionary or online. Try *Book Review Digest* (in your library or online) for reviews of the author's books.

- **Is the author writing within his or her area of expertise?** People can voice opinions on any subject, but they cannot transfer expertise from one subject area to another. A football player endorsing a political candidate is a citizen with an opinion, not an expert on politics.

- **Is the author identified with a particular group or set of beliefs?** Does the biography place the writer in a particular institution or organization? For example, a member of a Republican administration may be expected to favor a Republican president's policies. A Roman Catholic priest may be expected to take a stand against abortion. These kinds of details provide hints, but you should not assume what a writer's position is until you have read the work with care. Be alert to reasonable expectations, but avoid stereotyping a writer.

Who Is the Audience?

Knowing the intended audience can give you a clue about the work's depth and sophistication and a possible bias or slant.

- **Does the writer expect a popular audience, a general but educated audience, or a specialized audience that shares professional expertise or cultural, political, or religious preferences?** Often you can judge the expected audience by noting the kind of publication in which an article appears or the publisher of the book. For example, *Reader's Digest* is written for a mass audience; *Psychology Today, Science,* and *Newsweek* aim for a general but more knowledgeable reader. By contrast, articles in the *New England Journal of Medicine* are written by medical doctors and research scientists for a specialized audience.

Do you think this author is demonstrating bias? Why or why not? Will the intended audience accept this argument as credible or might the author risk losing credibility with his readers?

- **Does the writer expect readers who are likely to agree with the writer's views?** Some newspapers, magazines, and Web sites are usually liberal, whereas others are usually politically conservative. (Do you know the political leanings of your local paper?) The particular interests of the *Christian Science Monitor* or *Ms.*, for example, should be considered when you read articles from them. Remember that all arguments are slanted or biased—that is, they take a stand. That's OK. You just need to read with an awareness of a writer's particular background and interests.

What Is the Author's Purpose?

Is the piece informative or persuasive in intent? Designed to entertain or to be inspiring? Think about the title; read a book's preface to learn of the author's goals; pay attention to tone as you read.

What Are the Writer's Sources of Information?

Some questions to ask about sources include these: Where was the information obtained? Is it still valid? Are sources clearly identified? Be suspicious of writers who want us to believe that their unnamed "sources" are reliable. Pay close attention to dates. A biography of King George III published in 1940 may still be the best source; however, an article published in the 1980s urging the curtailing of county growth is no longer reliable.

try it !

Exercises: Examining the Context

1. What can you judge about the reliability or bias of the following?

   Consider author, audience, and purpose.

   a. An article on the Republican administration written by a former campaign worker for the Democratic presidential candidate.

   b. A discussion, published in *The Boston Globe,* of the Patriots' hope for the next Super Bowl.

   c. A letter to the editor about conservation written by a member of the Sierra Club. (What is the Sierra Club? Study some of its publications or check out its Web site to respond to this topic.)

   d. A column in *Newsweek* on economics. (Look at the business section of *Newsweek.* Your library has the magazine.)

   e. A 1948 article in *Nutrition Today* on the best diets.

   f. A biography of Benjamin Franklin published by Oxford University Press.

   g. A *Family Circle* article about a special vegetarian diet written by a doctor. (Who is the audience for this magazine? Where is it sold?)

   h. A pamphlet by Jerry Lewis urging you to contribute to a fund to combat muscular dystrophy.

   i. A discussion of abortion in *Ms.* magazine.

   j. An editorial in your local newspaper titled "Stop the Highway Killing."

2. Analyze an issue of your favorite magazine. Look first at the editorial pages and articles written by the staff, then at articles contributed by other writers. Answer these questions:

   a. Who is the audience of both staff writers and contributors?

   b. What is the purpose of each of the articles and of the entire magazine?

   c. What type of article dominates the issue?

   d. Describe the style and tone of the articles. How appropriate are the style and tone?

continued

3. Select one environmental Web site and study what it offers. The EnviroLink Network (www .envirolink.org) will lead you to many sites. Another possibility is the Nature Conservancy (www.tnc.org). Write down the name of the site you chose and its uniform resource locator (URL). Then answer these questions:

a. Who is the intended audience?

b. What seems to be the primary purpose or goal of the site?

c. What type of material seems to dominate the site?

d. For what kinds of writing assignments might you use material from the site?

Understanding an Author's Attitude and Tone

Critical readers read for implication and are alert to tone and nuance. When you read, think about not just *what* is said but *how* it is said. Awareness of the author's attitude will be helpful as you attempt to analyze his or her overall approach and style. Consider the following excerpt:

> What happened to the War on Drugs? Did Bush—the old man, not the son—think that we actually *won* that war? Or did he confuse the War on Drugs with the stupid Gulf War he's so proud of winning? Well, he never did understand "the vision thing."

First, we recognize that the writer's subject is the War on Drugs, an expression that refers to government programs to reduce drug use. Second, we understand that the writer does not believe that the war has been won; rather, we still have a drug problem that we need to address. We know this from the second sentence, the rhetorical question that suggests that Bush thought the drug problem had been solved, but the writer—like us—knows better.

What else do you observe in this passage? What is the writer's attitude toward George Bush? Note the writer's language. The former president is "the old man." He is proud of winning a "stupid" war. He, by implication, is stupid to think that he helped win the War on Drugs. And, finally, we are reminded of Bush's own words that he didn't have a vision of what he wanted to do as president.

How would you rewrite the passage to make it more favorable to Bush? Here is one version that students wrote to give the passage a positive attitude toward Bush:

> What has happened to the War on Drugs? Did some members of President George Bush's administration think that government policies had been successful in reducing drug use? Or did the administration change its focus to concentrate on winning the Gulf War? Perhaps, in retrospect, President Bush should have put more emphasis on the war against drugs.

The writers have not changed the assertion that the War on Drugs has not been won—yet they have greatly altered our outlook on the subject. This version suggests that the failure to win the drug war was the fault of Bush's administration, not of Bush himself, and that perhaps the failure is understandable given the need to focus attention on the Gulf War. In addition, references to the former president treat him with dignity. What is the difference in the two passages? Only the word choice.

Denotative and Connotative Word Choice

The students' ability to rewrite the passage on the War on Drugs to give it a positive slant tells us that, although some words may have similar meanings, they cannot always be substituted for one another without changing the message. Words with similar meanings have similar denotations. Often, though, words with similar denotations do not have the same connotations. A word's *connotation* is what the word suggests, what we associate the word with. The words *house and home*, for example, both refer to a building in which people live, but the word *home* suggests ideas—and feelings—of family and security. Thus the word *home* has a strong positive connotation. *House* by contrast brings to mind only a picture of a physical structure because the word doesn't carry any emotional baggage.

We learn the connotations of words the same way we learn their denotations—in context. Most of us living in the same culture share the same connotative associations of words. At times, the context in which a word is used will affect the word's connotation. For example, the word *buddy* usually has positive connotations. We may think of an old or trusted friend. But when an unfriendly person who thinks a man may have pushed in front of him says, "Better watch it, *buddy*," the word has a negative connotation. Social, physical, and language contexts control the connotative significance of words. Become more alert to the connotative power of words by asking what words the writers could have used instead.

Would you use the word *house* or the word *home* to describe this structure?

try it !

Exercises: Connotation

1. For each of the following words or phrases, list at least two synonyms that have a more negative connotation than the given word:

   a. child
   b. persistent
   c. thin
   d. a large group
   e. scholarly
   f. trusting
   g. underachiever
   h. quiet

2. For each of the following words, list at least two synonyms that have a more positive connotation than the given word:

   a. notorious
   b. fat
   c. politician
   d. old (people)
   e. fanatic
   f. reckless
   g. sot
   h. cheap

3. Select one of the words listed below and explain, in a paragraph, what the word connotes to you personally. Be precise; illustrate your thoughts with details and examples.

   a. nature
   b. mother
   c. romantic
   d. nerd
   e. playboy
   f. artist

4. Read the following paragraph and decide how the writer feels about the activity described. Note the choice of details and the connotative language that make you aware of the writer's attitude.

Needing to complete a missed assignment for my physical education class, I dragged myself down to the tennis courts on a gloomy afternoon. My task was to serve five balls in a row into the service box. Although I thought I had learned the correct service movements, I couldn't seem to translate that knowledge into a decent serve. I tossed up the first ball, jerked back my racket, swung up on the ball—clunk—I hit the ball on the frame. I threw up the second ball, brought back my racket, swung up on the ball—ping—I made contact with the strings, but the ball dribbled down on my side of the net. I trudged around the court, collecting my tennis balls; I had only two of them.

5. Write a paragraph describing an activity that you liked or disliked without saying how you felt. From your choice of details and use of connotative language, convey your attitude toward the activity. (The paragraph in Exercise 3 is your model.)

On Connotation

1. List all of the words you know for *human female* and for *human male.* Then classify them by connotation (positive, negative, neutral) and by level of usage (formal, informal, slang). Is there any connection between type of connotation and level of usage? Why are some words more appropriate in some social contexts than in others? Can you easily list more negative words used for one sex than for the other? Why?

2. Some words can be given a different connotation in different contexts. First, for each of the following words, label its connotation as positive, negative, or neutral. Then, for each word with a positive connotation, write a sentence in which the word would convey a more negative connotation. For each word with a negative connotation, write a sentence in which the word would suggest a more positive connotation.

   a. natural   d. free

   b. old   e. chemical

   c. committed   f. lazy

3. Each of the following groups of words might appear together in a thesaurus, but the words actually vary in connotation. After looking up any words whose connotation you are unsure of, use one word in each group correctly in a sentence. Briefly explain why the other two words in the group would not work in that sentence.

   a. brittle, hard, fragile

   b. quiet, withdrawn, glum

   c. shrewd, clever, cunning

   d. strange, remarkable, bizarre

   e. thrifty, miserly, economical

Recognizing Tone

Closely related to a writer's attitude is the writer's tone. We can describe a writer's attitude toward the subject as positive, negative, or (rarely) neutral. *Attitude* is the writer's position on, or feelings about, his or her subject. The way that attitude is expressed—the voice we hear and the feelings conveyed through that voice—is the writer's *tone*. Writers can choose to express attitude through a wide variety of tones. We may reinforce a negative attitude through an angry, somber, sad, mocking, peevish, sarcastic, or scornful tone. A positive attitude may be revealed through an enthusiastic, serious, sympathetic, jovial, light, or admiring tone.

We cannot be sure, however, that when a writer selects a light tone, the attitude must be positive. Humor columnists such as Dave Barry often choose a light tone to examine serious social and political issues. When we consider the subject, we recognize that the light and amusing tone actually conveys a negative attitude.

Analyzing an Author's Tone

We have begun the process of understanding attitude by becoming more aware of context and connotation and more alert to tone. Tone is created and attitude conveyed primarily through word choice and sentence structure but also through several other techniques.

Analyzing for Tone: Word Choice

In addition to responding to a writer's choice of connotative language, observe the *level of diction* used. Are the writer's words typical of conversational language or of a more formal style? Does the writer use slang words or technical words? Is the word choice concrete and vivid or abstract and intellectual? These differences help to shape tone and affect our response to

did you know?

One-third of 500,000 = 22? There are almost half a million words in our English language—the largest language on earth, incidentally—but a third of all our writing is made up of only twenty-two words.

Source: www.readfaster.com/education_stats.asp#readingstatistics

what we read. A politician's word choice may be very formal and abstract, using terms such as *commitment*, *sustainability*, and *economic recovery*. Another style, the technical, will be found in some articles in this text. The social scientist may write that "the child . . . is subjected to extremely punitive discipline," whereas a nonspecialist might write, more informally, that "the child is given beatings or other forms of punishment."

One way to create an informal style is to choose simple words: *given* instead of *subjected to*. To create greater informality, a writer can use contractions: *we'll* for *we will*.

Analyzing for Tone: Sentence Structure

The eighteenth-century satirist Jonathan Swift once said that writing well was a simple matter of putting "proper words in proper places." Writers need to think not just about the words they choose but also about their arrangement into sentence patterns. Studying a writer's sentence patterns will reveal how they affect style and tone. When analyzing these features, consider the following questions:

1. **Are the sentences generally long, or short, or varied in length?**
   Are the structures primarily

   - *Simple* (one independent clause)

     In 1900 empires dotted the world.

   - *Compound* (two or more independent clauses)

     Women make up only 37 percent of television characters, yet women make up more than half of the population.

   - *Complex* (at least one independent and one dependent clause)

     As nations grew wealthier, traditional freedom wasn't enough.

Sentences that are both long and complex create a more formal style. Long compound sentences joined by *and* do not increase formality much because such sentences are really only two or more short, simple patterns hooked together. On the other hand, a long "simple" sentence with many modifiers will create a more formal style. The following example, from an essay on leadership by Michael Korda, is more complicated than the sample compound sentence above.

- *Expanded simple sentence:*

  [A] leader is like a mirror, reflecting back to us our own sense of purpose, putting into words our own dreams and hopes, transforming our needs and fears into coherent policies and programs.

Although many instructors struggle to rid student writing of fragments, professional writers know that the occasional fragment can be used effectively for emphasis. Science fiction writer Bruce Sterling, thinking about the "melancholic beauty" of a gadget no longer serving any purpose, writes:

Like Duchamp's bottle-rack, it becomes a found objet d'art. A metallic fossil of some lost human desire. A kind of involuntary poem.

The second and third sentences are, technically, fragments, but because they build on the structure of the first sentence, readers can add the missing words *It becomes* to complete each sentence. The brevity, repetition of structure, and involvement of the reader to "complete" the fragments all contribute to a strong conclusion to Sterling's paragraph.

2. **Does the writer seem to be using an overly simplistic style? If so, why?**
   Overly simplistic sentence patterns, just like overly simplistic words, can be used to show that the writer thinks the subject is silly or childish or insulting. In one of her columns, Ellen Goodman objects to society's oversimplifying of addictions and its need to believe in quick and lasting cures. She makes her point with reference to two well-known examples—but notice her technique:

   Hi, my name is Jane and I was once bulimic but now I am an exercise guru.

   Hi, my name is Oprah and I was a food addict but now I am a size 10.

   She uses a simplistic sentence style purposefully in order to make her point and her attitude clear for her reader.

Jonathan Swift is most remembered for works such as *Gulliver's Travels*, "A Modest Proposal," and "An Argument Against Abolishing Christianity."

3. **Does the writer use parallelism (coordination) or antithesis (contrast)?**

When two phrases or clauses are parallel in structure, the message is that they are equally important. Look back at Korda's expanded simple sentence. He coordinates three phrases, asserting that a leader does these three things:

- reflects back our purpose
- puts into words our dreams
- transforms our needs and fears

Antithesis creates tension. A sentence using this structure says "not this" but "that." Abraham Lincoln, in the Gettysburg Address, uses both parallelism and antithesis in one striking sentence:

> The world will little note nor long remember what we say here, but it [the world] can never forget what they did here.

Analyzing for Tone: Metaphors

When Korda writes that a leader is like a mirror, he is using a *simile*. When Lincoln writes that the world will not remember, he is using a *metaphor*—actually *personification*. Metaphors, whatever their form, make a comparison between two items that are not otherwise alike. The writer is making a figurative comparison, not a literal one. The writer wants us to think about some ways in which the items are similar. Metaphors state directly or imply the comparison; similes express the comparison using a connecting word; personification always compares a nonhuman item to humans. The exact label for a metaphor is not as important as

- recognizing the use of a figure of speech,
- identifying the two items being compared,
- understanding the point of the comparison, and
- grasping the emotional impact of the figurative comparison.

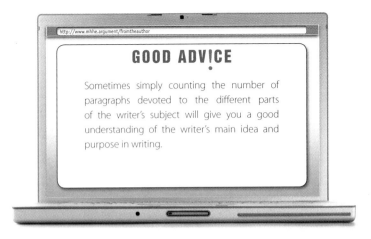

http://www.mhhe.argument/fromtheauthor

GOOD ADVICE

Sometimes simply counting the number of paragraphs devoted to the different parts of the writer's subject will give you a good understanding of the writer's main idea and purpose in writing.

Analyzing for Tone: Organization and Examples

Two other elements of writing, organization and choice of examples, also reveal attitude and help to shape the reader's response. When you study a work's organization, ask yourself questions about both placement and volume. Where are these ideas placed? At the beginning or end—the places of greatest emphasis—or in the middle, suggesting that they are less important? With regard to volume, ask yourself, What parts of the discussion are developed at length? What points are treated only briefly?

try it !

Exercise: Opening Up Metaphors

During World War II, E. B. White, the essayist and writer of children's books, defined the word *democracy* in one of his *New Yorker* columns. His definition contains a series of metaphors. Here is one in the series:

> [Democracy] is the hole in the stuffed shirt through which the sawdust slowly trickles.

We can open up or explain the metaphor this way: Just as one can punch a hole in a scarecrow's shirt and discover that there is only sawdust inside, nothing to be impressed by, so the idea of equality in a democracy punches a hole in the notion of an aristocratic ruling class and reveals that aristocrats are ordinary people, just like you and me.

Here are two more of White's metaphors on democracy. Open up each one in a few sentences.

> [Democracy is] the dent in the high hat.

> [Democracy is] the score at the beginning of the ninth.

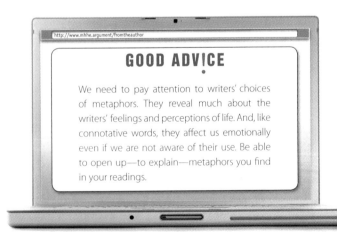

http://www.mhhe.argument/fromtheauthor

GOOD ADVICE

We need to pay attention to writers' choices of metaphors. They reveal much about the writers' feelings and perceptions of life. And, like connotative words, they affect us emotionally even if we are not aware of their use. Be able to open up—to explain—metaphors you find in your readings.

Analyzing for Tone: Repetition

Well-written, unified essays will contain some repetition of key words and phrases. Some writers go beyond this basic strategy and use repetition to produce an effective cadence, like a drum beating in the background, keeping time to the speaker's fist pounding the lectern. In his repetition of the now-famous phrase "I have a dream," Martin Luther King, Jr., gives emphasis to his vision of an ideal America. (Visit www.youtube.com and use the search term "I have a dream" in order to watch this historic speech.)

In the following paragraph a student tried her hand at repetition to give emphasis to her definition of liberty:

> Liberty is having the right to vote and not having other laws which restrict that right; it is having the right to apply to the university of your choice without being rejected because of race. Liberty exists when a gay man has the right to a teaching position and is not released from the position when the news of his orientation is disclosed. Liberty exists when a woman who has been offered a job does not have to decline for lack of access to day care for her children, or when a 16-year-old boy from a ghetto can get an education and is not instead compelled to go to work to support his needy family.

These examples suggest that repetition generally gives weight and seriousness to writing and thus is appropriate when serious issues are being discussed in a forceful style.

Analyzing for Tone: Hyperbole, Understatement, and Irony

Grace Lichtenstein chose *Playing for Money* as the title of her book on college sports. Now, college athletes do play, but presumably not for money. The title emphasizes that these games are serious business, not play, for the athletes, coaches, and colleges. The bringing together of words that do not usually go together—*play* and *money*—ironically underscores the problems in college athletics that Lichtenstein examines.

Analyzing for Tone: Visuals

Several visual techniques can be used within text to give special attention to certain words or ideas and ultimately help to create the author's tone:

SEEING THE ARGUMENT

Visual elements can also create irony in a text. Consider how this picture might communicate the same point that Grace Lichtenstein is making in her book *Playing for Money*. As you examine arguments around you, think about how visual elements play a role in communicating the author's tone.

- A writer can place a word or phrase in quotation marks and thereby question its validity or meaning in that context. Ellen Goodman writes, for example:

  I wonder about this when I hear the word "family" added to some politician's speech.

  Goodman does not agree with the politician's meaning of the word *family*, as she reveals in her essay, but we know this immediately from her use of quotation marks.

S
E E
I N G

THE ARGUMENT

SEEING THE ARGUMENT

Along with these textual techniques, visual elements in the work can also add to the author's style. Pictures, boxes, headings, color choices, fonts, and even the layout of the piece are all important elements of tone. Consider, for example, the following visual argument:

What can you determine about the author's attitude toward the product by looking at the visual elements of the ad? Notice the colors, the positioning of the images, and the special effects that are utilized. Remember to look at how visuals affect your own emotional reaction to an argument and how they can give you clues about the author's intended tone.

try it !

1. Name the techniques used in each of the following passages. Then briefly explain the idea of each passage.

   a. We are becoming the tools of our tools. (Henry David Thoreau)

   b. The bias and therefore the business of television is to *move* information, not collect it. (Neil Postman)

   c. If guns are outlawed, only the government will have guns. Only the police, the secret police, the military. The hired servants of our rulers. Only the government—and a few outlaws. (Edward Abbey)

   d. Having read all the advice on how to live 900 years, what I think is that eating a tasty meal once again will surely doom me long before I reach 900 while not eating that same meal could very well kill me. It's enough to make you reach for a cigarette! (Russell Baker)

   e. If you are desperate for a quick fix, either legalize drugs or repress the user. If you want a civilized approach, mount a propaganda campaign against drugs. (Charles Krauthammer)

   f. Oddly enough, the greatest scoffers at the traditions of American etiquette, who scorn the rituals of their own society as stupid and stultifying, voice respect for the customs and folklore of Native Americans, less industrialized people, and other societies they find more "authentic" than their own. (Judith Martin)

   g. Text is story. Text is event, performance, special effect. Subtext is ideas. It's motive, suggestions, visual implications, subtle comparisons. (Stephen Hunter)

   h. This flashy vehicle [the school bus] was as punctual as death: seeing us waiting at the cold curb, it would sweep to a halt, open its mouth, suck the boy in, and spring away with an angry growl. (E. B. White)

- Italicizing a key word or phrase also gives added emphasis.

  Dave Barry, in his essay on page 31 in chapter 2, uses italics for emphasis:

  Do you want appliances that are smarter than you? Of course not. Your appliances should be *dumber* than you, just like your furniture, your pets and your representative in Congress.

- Capitalizing words not normally capitalized has the same effect of giving emphasis. As with exclamation points, writers need to use italics or capitalization sparingly; otherwise, the emphasis sought through contrast will be lost.

making connections

let's review

After reading Chapter 1, you should understand the following:

- If you look hard enough, an argument of some sort is usually being made in any type of writing.

- Many pieces of communication that we don't typically think of as arguments still contain subtle elements of persuasion.

- An author must understand the needs of her readers if she hopes to connect with them and persuade them to accept her position.

- Any writer—including you—will take on different roles when writing for different audiences and will use different strategies to reach each audience. There are many kinds of argument and many ways to argue successfully.

- When we speak of the critical reader or critical thinker, we have in mind someone who reads actively, who thinks about issues, and who makes informed judgments.

- Reading critically requires preparation. Instead of "jumping into reading," begin by asking questions about the work's total context.

- When you read, think about not just *what* is said but *how* it is said. This awareness of an author's attitude will be helpful as you attempt to analyze his or her overall approach and style.

connect

With your class partner or in a small group, examine the following three paragraphs, which are different responses to the same event. First, decide on each writer's argument. Then describe, as precisely as possible, the tone of each paragraph, the writer's attitude, who you think the author might be, and within what context the paragraph might have been written. Discuss your conclusions with your classmates. What clues within the writing allowed you to draw these conclusions?

1. It is tragically inexcusable that this young athlete was not examined fully before he was allowed to join the varsity team. The physical examinations given were unbelievably sloppy. What were the coach and trainer thinking of not to insist that each youngster be examined while undergoing physical stress? Apparently they were not thinking about our boys at all. We can no longer trust our sons and our daughters to this inhuman system so bent on victory that it ignores the health—indeed the very lives—of our children.

2. It was learned last night, following the death of varsity fullback Jim Bresnick, that none of the players was given a stress test as part of his physical examination. The oversight was attributed to laxness by the coach and trainer, who are described today as being "distraught." It is the judgment of many that the entire physical education program must be reexamined with an eye to the safety and health of all students.

3. How can I express the loss I feel over the death of this wonderful boy? I want to blame someone, but who is to blame? The coaches, for not administering more rigorous physical checkups? Why should they have done more than other coaches have done before or than other coaches are doing at other schools? Jim, for not telling me that he felt funny after practice? His teammates, for not telling the coaches that Jim said he did not feel well? Myself, for not knowing that something was wrong? Who is to blame? All of us and none of us. But placing blame will not return Jim to me; I can only pray that other parents will not have to suffer so. Jimmy, we loved you.

responding critically to the arguments of others

chapter 2

Responding to Arguments

To understand how critical thinkers may respond to the arguments of others, let's examine the Gettysburg Address in the right column, Abraham Lincoln's famous speech dedicating the Civil War battlefield—and quite possibly the best example of succinct persuasive argumentation in our history. We can use this document to see the various ways writers respond—in writing—to the writing of others.

Responding to Content: What Does It Say?

Instructors often ask students to *summarize* or *paraphrase* their reading of a complex chapter, a supplementary text, a difficult poem, or a series of journal articles on library reserve. Frequently, report or critique assignments specify that summary and evaluation be combined. Your purpose in writing a summary is to show your understanding of the work's main ideas and of the relationships among those ideas. If you can put what you have read into your own words and focus on the text's main points, then you have command of that material. Here is one student's restatement of the main argument in Lincoln's address:

> Our nation was initially built on a belief in liberty and equality, but its future is now being tested by civil war. It is appropriate for us to dedicate this battlefield, but those who fought here have dedicated it better than we. We should dedicate ourselves to continue the fight to maintain this nation and its principles of government.

Sometimes it is easier to recite or quote famous or difficult works than to state, more simply and in your own words, what has been written. The ability to summarize or paraphrase reflects both reading and writing skills.

Writing Summaries

Preparing a good summary is not always as easy as it looks. A *summary* briefly restates, in your own words, the main points of a work in a way that does not misrepresent or distort the original. A good summary shows your grasp of main ideas and your ability to express them clearly. You need to condense the original while giving all key ideas appropriate attention. As a student, you may be assigned a summary to

The Gettysburg Address

Abraham Lincoln

Four score and seven years ago our fathers brought forth on this continent a new nation, conceived in liberty and dedicated to the proposition that all men are created equal. Now we are engaged in a great civil war, testing whether that nation, or any nation so conceived and so dedicated, can long endure. We are met on a great battlefield of that war. We have come to dedicate a portion of that field as a final resting place for those who here gave their lives that that nation might live. It is altogether fitting and proper that we should do this. But, in a larger sense, we cannot dedicate—we cannot consecrate—we cannot hallow—this ground. The brave men, living and dead, who struggled here have consecrated it far above our poor power to add or to detract. The world will little note nor long remember what we say here, but it can never forget what they did here. It is for us, the living, rather to be dedicated here to the unfinished work which they who fought here have thus far so nobly advanced. It is rather for us to be here dedicated to the great task remaining before us—that from these honored dead we take increased devotion to that cause for which they gave the last full measure of devotion; that we here highly resolve that these dead shall not have died in vain; that this nation, under God, shall have a new birth of freedom; and that government of the people, by the people, for the people shall not perish from the earth.

- show that you have read and understood assigned works,
- complete a test question,
- have a record of what you have read for future study or to prepare for class discussion, or

Many news sites and online newspapers use summaries to introduce articles or longer stories. You can easily identify these summaries because they are usually followed by a phrase such as "Read full story." Go online and find a summary of a current event. Does it follow the guidelines set up in this chapter? How and why might these summaries differ from the ones you will be asked to write for your college courses?

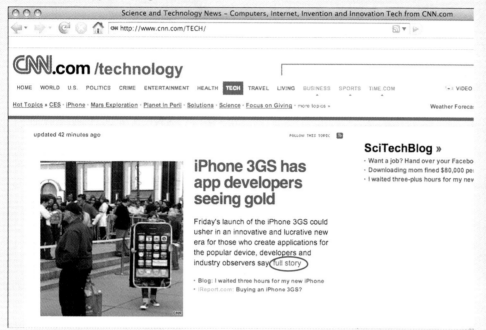

SEEING THE ARGUMENT

GOOD ADVICE

http://www.mhhe.argument/fromtheauthor

Guidelines for Writing Summaries

1. **Write in a direct, objective style, using your own words.** Use few, if any, direct quotations, probably none in a one-paragraph summary.
2. **Begin with a reference to the writer (full name) and the title of the work and then state the writer's thesis.** You may also want to include where and when the work was published.
3. **Complete the summary by providing other key ideas.** Show the reader how the main ideas connect and relate to one another.
4. **Do not include specific examples, illustrations, or background sections.**
5. **Combine main ideas into fewer sentences than were used in the original.**
6. **Keep the parts of your summary in the same balance as you find in the original.** If the author devotes about 30 percent of the essay to one idea, that idea should get about 30 percent of your summary.
7. **Select precise, accurate verbs to show the author's relationship to ideas.** Write "Jones argues," "Jones asserts," "Jones believes." Do not use vague verbs that provide only a list of disconnected ideas. Do not write "Jones talks about," "Jones goes on to say."
8. **Do not make any judgments about the writer's style or ideas.** Do not include your personal reaction to the work.

To practice reading and summarizing the content of sources, study the following article by Ellen Goodman and then analyze the summary attempts that follow.

Why might someone write in praise of snail mail? What does Goodman mean by "hyperactive technology"?

In Praise of a Snail's Pace
Ellen Goodman

Author of *Close to Home* (1979), *At Large* (1981), and *Keeping Touch* (1985), collections of her essays, Ellen Goodman has been a feature writer for *The Boston Globe* since 1967 and a syndicated columnist since 1976. The following column was published August 13, 2005.

CASCO BAY, Maine—I arrive at the island post office carrying an artifact from another age. It's a square envelope, handwritten, with a return address that can be found on a map. Inside is a condolence note, a few words of memory and sympathy to a wife who has become a widow. I could have sent these words far more efficiently through e-mail than through this "snail mail." But I am among those who still believe that sympathy is diluted by two-thirds when it arrives over the Internet transom.

I would no more send an e-condolence than an e-thank you or an e-wedding invitation. There are rituals you cannot speed up without destroying them. It would be like serving Thanksgiving dinner at a fast-food restaurant.

My note goes into the old blue mailbox and I walk home wondering if slowness isn't the only way we pay attention now in a world of hyperactive technology.

Weeks ago, a friend lamented the trouble she had communicating with her grown son. It wasn't that her son was out of touch. Hardly. They were connected across miles through e-mail and cell phone, instant-messaging and textmessaging.

But she had something serious to say and feared that an e-mail would elicit a reply that said: I M GR8. Was there no way to get undivided attention in the full in-box of his life? She finally chose a letter, a pen on paper, a stamp on envelope.

How do you describe the times we live in, so connected and yet fractured? Linda Stone, a former Microsoft techie, characterizes ours as an era of "continuous partial attention." At the extreme end are teenagers instant-messaging while they are talking on the cell phone, downloading music, and doing homework. But adults too live with all systems go, interrupted and distracted, scanning everything, multi-technological-tasking everywhere.

We suffer from the illusion, Stone says, that we can expand our personal bandwidth, connecting to more and more. Instead, we end up overstimulated, overwhelmed and, she adds, unfulfilled. Continuous partial attention inevitably feels like a lack of full attention.

But there are signs of people searching for ways to slow down and listen up. We are told that experienced e-mail users are taking longer to answer, freeing themselves from the tyranny of the reply button. Caller ID is used to find out who we don't have to talk to. And the next "killer ap," they say, will be e-mail software that can triage the important from the trivial.

Meanwhile, at companies where technology interrupts creativity and online contact prevents face-to-face contact, there are no e-mail-free Fridays. At others, there are bosses who require that you check your BlackBerry at the meeting door.

If a ringing cell phone once signaled your importance to a client, now that client is impressed when you turn off the cell phone. People who stayed connected 10 ways, 24-7, now pride themselves on "going dark."

"People hunger for more attention," says Stone, whose message has been welcomed even at a conference of bloggers. "Full attention will be the aphrodisiac of the future."

Indeed, at the height of our romance with e-mail, *You've Got Mail* was the cinematic love story. Now e-mail brings less thrill—"who will be there?" And more dread—"how many are out there?" Today's romantics are couples who leave their laptops behind on the honeymoon.

As for text-message flirtation, a young woman ended hers with a man who wrote, "C U L8R." He didn't have enough time to spell out Y-O-U?

Slowness guru Carl Honoré began *In Praise of Slowness* after he found himself seduced by a book of condensed classic fairy tales to read to his son. One-minute bedtime stories? We are relearning that paying attention briefly is as impossible as painting a landscape from a speeding car.

It is not just my trip to the mailbox that has brought this to mind. I come here each summer to stop hurrying. My island is no Brigadoon: WiFi is on the way, and some people roam the island with their cell phones, looking for a hot spot. But I exchange the Internet for the country road.

Georgia O'Keeffe once said that it takes a long time to see a flower. No technology can rush the growth of the leeks in the garden. All the speed in the Internet cannot hurry the healing of a friend's loss. Paying attention is the coin of this realm.

Sometimes, a letter becomes the icon of an old-fashioned new fashion. And sometimes, in this technological whirlwind, it takes a piece of snail mail to carry the stamp of authenticity.

With the "Good Advice" guidelines from page 25 in mind, read the following two summaries of Ellen Goodman's "In Praise of a Snail's Pace" (see pages 26–27). Then answer the question, What is flawed or weak about each summary? To aid your analysis, (1) <u>underline</u> or highlight all words or phrases that are inappropriate in each summary, and (2) put the number of the guideline next to any passage that does not adhere to that guideline.

SUMMARY ATTEMPT 1

I really thought that Goodman's essay contained some interesting ideas about modern technology. She talks about mailing a letter instead of using e-mail or text-messaging. She thinks it's better to do this when someone dies. Goodman says that we don't pay attention, and some people think cell phones should be turned off. But it would be hard for me to turn off my phone.

SUMMARY ATTEMPT 2

In Ellen Goodman's "In Praise of a Snail's Pace" (August 13, 2005), she talks about problems with today's use of electronic communication devices—not technical problems but how people feel about communicating this way. She is on vacation in Maine to slow down, and she starts by saying that she has used a letter rather than e-mail to send a sympathy message. She wonders if e-mail is appropriate for personal messages. She says our times are "connected and yet fractured." We don't pay attention to others and get into multi-tasking. We should turn off our phones and take time to look at flowers.

Although we can agree that the writers of these summaries have read and basically understood most of Goodman's essay, we can also find weaknesses in each summary. The second summary can be greatly improved by eliminating some details, combining some ideas, and refocusing on the main idea. Here is a much-improved version of summary 2:

continued

In Ellen Goodman's column "In Praise of a Snail's Pace" (syndicated August 13, 2005), she asserts that we need to slow down and give more personal attention to others. We have embraced modern communications technology, believing that this makes us more connected to others, but the connection is impersonal and distant. Many, along with Goodman,

see text-messaging and 24/7 electronic "connections" as interfering with the personal attention that makes relationships meaningful. She suggests that we turn off the electronic gadgets, slow down in our personal lives, and give the people who matter to us our full attention.

- explain the main ideas in a work that you will also examine in some other way, such as in a book review or a refutation essay.

When assigned a summary, pay careful attention to your word choice. Avoid judgmental words, such as "Brown then proceeds to develop the *silly* idea that . . ."

CliffsNotes, which provides summaries and analysis of hundreds of literary works and is the predecessor of today's SparkNotes, was started by a Nebraska native named Cliff Hillegass in 1958 in the basement of his home in Lincoln, Nebraska, with sixteen William Shakespeare titles. The term *Cliffs-Notes* has come into common usage as a noun for summaries like the original CliffsNotes books.

Writing Paraphrases

Although the words *summary and paraphrase* are sometimes used interchangeably, they are not exact synonyms. Summaries and paraphrases are alike in that they are both written responses to sources. They differ in how they respond and why.

Like a summary, a paraphrase is an objective restatement of someone's writing. But the purpose of a paraphrase is to clarify a complex passage or to include material from a source in your own writing.

When using sources for research, you will incorporate some of their information and ideas in your own paper, in your own words, and with proper documentation. Usually each paraphrased passage is fairly brief and is blended into your own thinking on the topic. Paraphrasing clearly and accurately—and documenting correctly—takes some practice. Much more discussion, together with examples and opportunities for practice, can be found in the section on research (see pages 38–42).

Paraphrase of the Passage by Russell

All that we can do, before we lose our loved ones and then face our own death, is to place value on the important ideas that mark humans as special creatures and give meaning to our lives. We must reject any fear of dying that would make us slaves to Fate and instead be proud of what we have accomplished. We must not be distressed by the powers of chance or blind luck. We must not let their control over much that happens to us keep us from maintaining a mind that is free, a mind that we use to think for ourselves. Keeping our minds free and embracing knowledge are ways to defy the powers of the universe over which we have no control. And so, even though we may at times grow weary of battling the blind forces of the universe, we continue to find strength in the interior world that we have shaped by our ideals.

Note, first, that the paraphrase is longer than the original (on page 29). The goal is to clarify, not to highlight main ideas only. Second, the paraphrase clarifies the passage by turning Russell's one long sentence into several sentences and using simpler language. When

Exercise: Paraphrase

When your purpose is to clarify a poem, a complex philosophical passage, or prose filled with figurative language, your paraphrase will be long, maybe longer than the original. Here is an example: first a passage from British philosopher Bertrand Russell's "A Free Man's Worship." As you read Russell's passage, underline words or phrases you find confusing. Then, as you read the paraphrase, look back to the original to see how the writer has restated Russell's ideas.

From "A Free Man's Worship"
Bertrand Russell

[F]or Man, condemned today to lose his dearest, tomorrow himself to pass through the gate of darkness, it remains only to cherish, ere yet the blow falls, the lofty thoughts that ennoble his little day; disdaining the coward terrors of the slave to Fate, to worship at the shrine that his own hands have built; undismayed by the empire of chance, to preserve a mind free from the wanton tyranny that rules his outward life; proudly defiant of the irresistible forces that tolerate, for a moment, his knowledge and his condemnation, to sustain alone, a weary but unyielding Atlas [someone bearing a heavy load, as Atlas did, holding up the sky on his shoulders], the world that his own ideals have fashioned despite the trampling march of unconscious power.

you can state a writer's ideas in your own words, you have really understood the writer's ideas.

When you are asked the question "What does it say?" think about whether you need a summary or a paraphrase. When an instructor asks you to state in your own words the meaning of Lincoln's long concluding sentence in the Gettysburg Address, the instructor wants a paraphrase. When an instructor asks you what an assigned essay is about, the instructor wants a summary.

The Analytic Response: How Is It Written?

Although many assignments call for some measure of summary or paraphrasing, most of the time you will be expected to do something with what you have read, and to simply summarize or paraphrase will be insufficient. Frequently you will be asked to *analyze* a work—that is, to explain the elements of structure and style that a writer has chosen. You will want to examine sentence patterns, organization, metaphors, and other techniques selected by the writer to convey attitude and give force to ideas. Developing your skills in style analysis will make you both a better reader and a better writer.

Many writers have examined Lincoln's word choice, sentence structure, and choice of metaphors to make clear the sources of power in his Gettysburg Address. (See, for example, Gilbert Highet's essay "The Gettysburg Address" in *The Clerk of Oxenford: Essays on Literature and Life* [New York: Oxford UP, 1954].) Analyzing Lincoln's style, you might examine, among other elements, his effective use of *tricolon*: the threefold repetition of a grammatical structure,

did you **?** know

Early in his "I have a dream" speech, delivered on the steps of the Lincoln Memorial, Dr. Martin Luther King, Jr., alludes to Abraham Lincoln's Gettysburg Address by saying "five score years ago."

Similarly, President Obama, in his 2008 victory speech in Chicago, Illinois, quoted Lincoln and echoed Dr. King as well. He said, "It's the answer that led those who have been told for so long, by so many, to be cynical and fearful and doubtful about what we can achieve . . . to put their hands on the arc of history and bend it once more toward the hope of a better day."

"The arc of history" is a direct reference to one of King's most riveting lines, spoken in Montgomery, Alabama, after the long and dangerous march from Selma in March 1965.

Consider how the settings and the references to Lincoln's and King's speeches played a role in the overall persuasiveness of this historic event. Also consider how both King's and Obama's choices might lend themselves to a comparative style analysis.

Source: http://opinion.latimes.com/opinionla/2008/11/echoes-of-king.html

with the three points placed in ascending order of significance.

Lincoln uses two effective tricolons in his brief address. The first focuses on the occasion for his speech, the dedication of the battlefield: "we cannot dedicate—we cannot consecrate—we cannot hallow. . . ." The best that the living can do is formally dedicate; only those who died there for the principle of liberty are capable of making the battlefield holy. The second tricolon presents Lincoln's concept of democratic government, a government "of the people, by the people, for the people." The purpose of government—"for the people"—resides in the position of greatest significance.

A second type of analysis, a comparison of styles of two writers, is a frequent variation of the analytic assignment. By focusing on similarities and differences in writing styles, you can see more clearly the role of choice in writing, and you may also examine the degree to which differences in purpose affect style. One student, for example, produced a thoughtful and interesting study of Lincoln's style in contrast to that of Martin Luther King, Jr., as revealed in his "I have a dream" speech:

> Although Lincoln's sentence structure is tighter than King's and King likes the rhythms created by repetition, both men reflect their familiarity with the King James Bible in their use of its cadences and expressions. Instead of saying "eighty-seven years

> ago," Lincoln, seeking solemnity, selects the biblical expression "four score and seven years ago." Similarly, King borrows from the Bible and echoes Lincoln when he writes "five score years ago."

Understanding Purpose and Audience in a Style Analysis

A style analysis is not the place for challenging the ideas of the writer. A style analysis requires the discipline to see how a work has been put together even if you disagree with the writer's views. You do not have to agree with a writer to appreciate his or her skill in writing. A style analysis may imply, or even express, a positive evaluation of the author's writing—but that is not the same as agreeing or disagreeing with the author's ideas.

If you think about audience in the context of your purpose, you should conclude that a summary of content does not belong in a style analysis. Why? Because we write style analyses for people who have already read the work. Remember, though, that your reader may not know the work in the detail that you know it, so you will need to give examples to illustrate the points of your analysis.

Just as you will be asked to do in your college writing assignments, Dave Barry wears many hats. He is primarily a humor columnist. For 25 years, however, he was a syndicated columnist whose work appeared in more than 500 newspapers in the United States and abroad. And in 1988 he won the Pulitzer Prize for Commentary.

Barry has also written a total of 30 books, although (according to him) virtually none of them contain useful information.

Barry also plays lead guitar in a literary rock band called the Rock Bottom Remainders, whose other members include Stephen King, Amy Tan, Ridley Pearson, and Mitch Albom. They are not musically skilled, but they are extremely loud.

Source: www.davebarry.com

did you know?

try it !

Read the following excerpt from an essay by Dave Barry. Use the questions that follow the essay to help you determine Barry's attitude toward his subject and to characterize his style.

In a Battle of Wits with Kitchen Appliances, I'm Toast
Dave Barry

Dave Barry has been a regular humor columnist for the *Miami Herald* from 1983–2004. A Pulitzer Prize winner in 1988, Barry has written several books, including *Dave Barry Slept Here* (1989). The following column appeared in March 2000.

Recently *The Washington Post* printed an article explaining how the appliance manufacturers plan to drive consumers insane.

Of course they don't *say* they want to drive us insane. What they *say* they want to do is have us live in homes where "all appliances are on the Internet, sharing information" and appliances will be "smarter than most of their owners." For example, the article states, you could have a home where the dishwasher "can be turned on from the office" and the refrigerator "knows when it's out of milk" and the bathroom scale "transmits your weight to the gym."

I frankly wonder whether the appliance manufacturers, with all due respect, have been smoking crack. I mean, did they ever stop to ask themselves why a consumer, after loading a dishwasher, would go to the office to start it? Would there be some kind of career benefit?

YOUR BOSS: What are you doing?
YOU (tapping computer keyboard): I'm starting my dishwasher!
YOUR BOSS: That's the kind of productivity we need around here!
YOU: Now I'm flushing the upstairs toilet!

Listen, appliance manufacturers: We don't *need* a dishwasher that we can communicate with from afar. If you want to improve our dishwashers, give us one that senses when people leave dirty dishes on the kitchen counter, and shouts at them: *"Put those dishes in the dishwasher right now or I'll leak all over your shoes!"*

QUESTIONS FOR READING AND REASONING

After reading this excerpt, how would you describe the essay's tone? Serious? Humorous? Ironic? Angry? Something else? Does a nonserious tone exclude the possibility of a degree of serious purpose? Explain your answer.

If, instead of a piece of writing, you were asked to write a style analysis of a Web site like the one shown here, you might choose to organize your essay around use of color, design layout, font choice, and graphic elements. In each case, your goal is to analyze the author's style and tone based on the choices he or she made about how to write, design, and organize the piece.

S E E I N G THE ARGUMENT

SEEING THE ARGUMENT

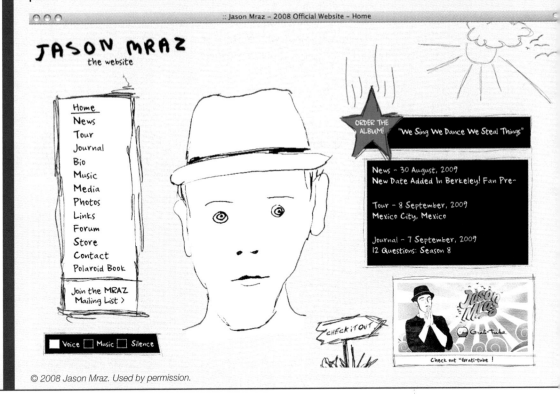

Planning a Style Analysis

First, organize your analysis according to elements of style, not according to the organization of the work. Scrap any thoughts of hacking your way through the essay, commenting paragraph by paragraph. This approach invites summary rather than analysis. It also means that you have not selected an organization that supports your purpose in writing.

You need to select those techniques you think are most important in creating the writer's attitude and to discuss them one at a time. If you were asked to write an analysis of an essay by famous satirist Dave Barry, for example, you might select his use of italics and quotation marks, his use of hyperbole, and his use of irony. These are three techniques that stand out in Barry's writing.

Drafting a Style Analysis

If you were to select and analyze the three elements of style mentioned above as being characteristic of Dave Barry's writing (italics and quotation marks, hyperbole, and irony), your essay might have a structure like this:

Paragraph 1: Introduction
1. Attention-getter
2. Author, title, publication information of article/book
3. Brief explanation of author's subject
4. Your thesis—stating that you will be looking at Barry's style

Paragraph 2: First body paragraph
Analysis of italics and quotation marks.

Paragraph 3: Second body paragraph
1. Topic sentence that introduces analysis of hyperbole
2. Three or more examples of hyperbole
3. Explanation of how each example connects to the author's thesis—that is, how the example of hyperbole works to convey attitude. This is your analysis; don't forget it!

Paragraph 4: Third body paragraph
Analysis of irony—with same three parts as in paragraph 3.

Paragraph 5: Conclusion
Restate your thesis: We can understand the author's point through a study of these three elements of his style.

GOOD ADV!CE

A Checklist for Revision of the Style Analysis

When revising and polishing your draft, use these questions to complete your essay:

- **Have I handled all titles correctly?**
- **Have I correctly referred to the author?**
- **Have I used quotation marks correctly when presenting examples of style?**
- **Do I have an accurate, clear presentation of the author's subject and thesis?**
- **Do I have enough examples of each element of style to show my readers that these elements are important?**
- **Have I connected examples to the author's thesis? That is, have I shown my readers how these techniques work to develop the author's attitude?**

try it !

To reinforce your understanding of style analysis, read the following essay by Ellen Goodman, answer the questions that follow, and then study the student essay that analyzes Goodman's style.

prereading }
questions }
What is Goodman's subject? Why is it incorrect to say that her subject is Thanksgiving?

Choosing Our Families
Ellen Goodman

Author of *Close to Home* (1979), *At Large* (1981), and *Keeping Touch* (1985), collections of her essays, Ellen Goodman has been a feature writer for *The Boston Globe* since 1967 and a syndicated columnist since 1976. She has won a Pulitzer Prize for distinguished commentary. The following column was published on November 24, 1988.

BOSTON—They will celebrate Thanksgiving the way they always do, in the Oral Tradition. Equal parts of food and conversation. A cornucopia of family. These are not restrained people who choose their words and pick at their stuffing. These are people who have most of their meals in small chicken-sized households. But when they come together, they feast on the sounds as well as tastes of a turkey-sized family.

Indeed, their Thanksgiving celebrations are as crowded with stories as their tables are with chairs. Arms reach indelicately across each other for second helpings, voices interrupt to add relish to a story. And there are

continued

always leftovers too enormous to complete, that have to be wrapped up and preserved.

But what is it that makes this collection of people a family? How do we make a family these days? With blood? With marriage? With affection? I wonder about this when I hear the word *family* added to some politician's speech like gravy poured over the entire plate. The meaning is supposed to be obvious, self-evident. It is assumed that when we talk about family we are all talking about the same thing. That families are the same. But it's not that simple.

For the past eight years, the chief defender of the American family has lived in the White House. But Reagan's own family has always looked more like our contemporary reality than his traditional image. There has been marriage and divorce among the Reagans, adoption and blending, and more than one estrangement. There is a mother, this holiday season, who hasn't talked to her daughter for more than a year. The man who will take his place as head of this family ideology has wrapped himself in a grandfatherly image. Yet Bush's family is also extended in ways that are common but not always comforting to other Americans.

As young people, George and Barbara Bush left home again and again, setting up temporary quarters in 17 cities. Now they have five children scattered in an equal number of states: Texas and Florida, Colorado, Virginia and Connecticut. Theirs, like many of ours, do not live at home, but come home, for the holidays.

We hold onto a particular primal image of families—human beings created from the same genetic code, living in the same area code. We hold onto an image of the family as something rooted and stable. But that has always been rare in a country where freedom is another word for mobility, both emotional and physical.

In America, families are spliced and recombined in as many ways as DNA. Every year our Thanksgiving tables expand and contract, place settings are removed and added. A guest last year is a member this year. A member last year may be an awkward outsider this year. How many of our children travel between alienated halves of their heritage, between two sets of people who share custody of their holidays?

Even among those families we call stable or intact, the ride to the airport has become a holiday ritual as common as pumpkin pie. Many parents come from retirement homes, many children from college, many cousins from jobs in other zip codes. We retrieve these people, as if from a memory hole, for reunions.

What then makes a family, in the face of all this "freedom"? It is said that people don't choose their parents. Or their aunts and uncles. But in a sense Americans do choose to make a family out of these people. We make room for them in our lives, choose to be with them and preserve that choice through a ritual as simple as passing seconds at a table.

All real families are made over time and through tradition. The Oral Tradition. We create a shared treasure trove of history, memories, conversation. Equal parts of food and conversation. And a generous serving of pleasure in each other's company.

QUESTIONS FOR READING, REASONING, AND WRITING

1. What is Goodman's attitude toward families; that is, what does she assert about families in this column? Is there one sentence that states her thesis? If so, which one? If not, write a thesis for the essay.

2. Characterize Goodman's style. Analyze her word choice, metaphors, sentence structure, organization, and use of the Reagan and Bush families as examples. How does each contribute to our understanding of her point?

3. Why are Goodman's metaphors especially notable? Open up—or explain—three of her metaphors.

Student Essay—A Style Analysis

GOODMAN'S FEAST OF STYLE

Alan Peterson

Thanksgiving is a time for "families" to come together, eat a big meal, share their experiences and each other's company. In her November 24, 1988, article "Choosing Our Families," which appeared on Thanksgiving Day in *The Washington Post*, Ellen Goodman asks the question, Who makes up these families? By her definition, a family does not consist of just blood relatives; a family contains acquaintances, friends, relatives, people who are "chosen" to be in this year's "family." An examination of Goodman's essay reveals some of the elements of style she uses to effectively ask and answer her question.

Introduction includes author, title, and date of article

Student's thesis statement

Goodman's clever organization compels the reader to read on. She begins by focusing on a Thanksgiving dinner scene, referring to families and households in terms of food. After setting the table by evoking the reader's memories of Thanksgivings past, Goodman asks the central question of her essay: "[W]hat is it that makes this collection of people a family" (49)? Goodman argues that the modern meaning of *family* has evolved so much that the traditional definition of *family* is no longer the standard. To clarify modern definitions, she provides examples of famous families: First Families. After suggesting that the Reagans have been the "chief defender of the American family" (49) for the last eight years, she points out that the Reagans, with their divorces, their adoptions, their estrangements, are anything but the traditional family they wish to portray. Rather, the Reagans represent the human traits that define the "contemporary reality" (49) of today's families. Next, President Bush's family is examined. Goodman points out that the Bushes' five children live in five different states, and that Barbara and George Bush, as young people, set up "temporary quarters in 17 cities" (50). She develops an answer to her question in the ensuing paragraphs. She observes that families today are disjointed, nontraditional, different from one another. She refers to families that are considered "stable or intact" (50) and shows how even those families can be spread out all over the country. In her closing paragraphs she repeats the question "What then makes a family?" Then, after another reference to Thanksgiving dinner, she concludes the article by stating her main point: "All real families are made over time and through tradition" (50). Goodman's organization—a question, some examples, several answers, and strong confirmation—powerfully frames her thesis.

Analysis of Goodman's organization

In an essay written about a theme as homespun as family and Thanksgiving celebrations, a reader would not expect the language to be too formal. Choosing her words carefully, Goodman cultivates a familiar and descriptive, yet not overly informal style. Early in the essay, Goodman uses simple language to portray the Thanksgiving meal. She refers to voices interrupting, arms reaching, leftovers that have to be wrapped up. Another effective technique of diction Goodman employs is the repetition of words and sounds. She points out that the Bushes, as young people, "left home again and again" (50). She defines the image we have of families as that of people created from the same "genetic code," living in the same "area code," and of cousins in "other zip codes" (50). Then, characterizing the reality of the configuration of today's American families, Goodman states: "A guest last year is a member this year," while a "member last year may be an awkward outsider this year" (50). An additional example of repetition appears in the first and last paragraphs. Goodman repeats the sentence fragment "Equal parts of food and conversation" (50). This informal choice of words opens and closes her essay, cleverly setting the tone in the beginning and reiterating the theme at the end.

Analysis of Goodman's word choice and repetition

Perhaps the most prevalent element of style present in Goodman's piece, and a dominant characteristic of her essay style, is her use of metaphors. From the opening sentences all the way through to the end, this article is full of metaphors. Keeping with the general focus of the piece (the essay appeared on Thanksgiving Day), many of the metaphors liken food to family. Her references include "a cornucopia of family," "chicken-sized households" and a "turkey-sized

Analysis of Goodman's metaphors

continued

family," people who "feast on the sounds as well as the tastes," and voices that "add relish to a story" (49). She imparts that a politician can use the word *family* like "gravy poured over the entire plate" (49). Going to the airport to pick up members of these disjointed American families has become "a holiday ritual as common as pumpkin pie" (50). Goodman draws parallels between the process of "choosing" people to be with and the simple ritual of passing seconds at the table. Indeed, the essay's mood emphasizes the comparison of and inextricable bond between food and family.

Ellen Goodman's "Choosing Our Families" is a thought-provoking essay on the American family. She organizes the article so that readers are reminded of their own Thanksgiving experiences and consider who is included in their "families." After asking "What is it that makes this collection of people a family?" Goodman provides election-year examples of prominent American families, then an explanation of "family" that furnishes her with an answer. Her word choice and particularly the repetition of words and sounds make reading her essay a pleasure. The metaphors Goodman uses link in readers' minds the images of Thanksgiving food and the people with whom they spend the holiday. Her metaphors underscore the importance she places on having meals with the family, which is the one truly enduring tradition for all people. Perhaps the most important food-and-family metaphor comes in the last sentence: "a generous serving of pleasure in each other's company" (50).

> Conclusion restates Goodman's position and student's thesis.

Works Cited

Goodman, Ellen. "Choosing Our Families." *Washington Post*. 24 Nov. 1988. Rpt. *Read, Reason, Write: An Argument Text and Reader*. 8th ed. Ed. Dorothy U. Seyler. New York: McGraw-Hill, 2008. 50–51.

The Evaluation Response: Does It Achieve Its Purpose?

Many critical responses to texts include some element of evaluation. Even when the stated purpose of an essay is "pure" analysis, the analysis implies a *judgment*. We analyze Lincoln's style because we recognize that the Gettysburg Address is a great piece of writing and we want to see how it achieves its power. On other occasions, judgment is the overtly stated purpose for close reading and analysis. The columnist who challenges a previously published editorial has analyzed the editorial and has found it flawed. The columnist may fault the editor's logic or lack of adequate or relevant support for the editorial's main idea. In each case the columnist makes a negative judgment about the editorial, but that judgment is an informed one based on the columnist's knowledge of language and the principles of good argument.

Part of the ability to judge wisely lies in recognizing each writer's purpose and intended audience. It would be inappropriate, for example, to assert that Lincoln's address is weakened by its lack of facts about the battle. The historian's purpose might be to record the number killed or to analyze the generals' military tactics. Lincoln's purpose and audience were much different. Observe how one student evaluates Lincoln's speech in light of its intended purpose and audience:

> As Lincoln reflected upon this young country's being torn apart by civil strife, he saw the dedication of the Gettysburg battlefield as an opportunity to challenge the country to fight for its survival and the principles upon which it was founded. The result was a brief but moving speech that appropriately examines the connection between the life and death of soldiers and the birth and survival of a nation.

These sentences establish a basis for an analysis of Lincoln's train of thought and use of metaphors, but this analysis, and its positive judgment, is grounded in an understanding of Lincoln's purpose, audience, and the context in which he spoke.

Combining Summary, Analysis, and Evaluation: The Critique or Review

Writing a good critique (or review) requires combining skills you have been working on: critical reading, accurate summary, analysis of style, and evaluation of the work—book, Web site, advertisement, essay, or film—in the context of the writer's or director's subject and

Movie reviews can be excellent examples of evaluative responses to the arguments of others. Take, for example, the following review of Michael Moore's movie *Sicko*. Reviewers typically attempt to establish and analyze relevant criteria (such as the quality of acting, for example) in order to evaluate how well the director or producers achieved their intended purpose for their intended audience. For the full text of this review, visit www.prospect.org/cs/articles?article=why_michael_moore_is_good_for_your_health.

Discuss the review with your peers. Who is the intended audience for this review? Do you think the author does a good job of providing relevant and necessary information to his readers?

Why Michael Moore Is Good for Your Health

The provocateur's new movie, *Sicko*, takes aim at our broken health care system -- and argues, in true patriotic fashion, that it represents a failing of America's own best principles and promise.

EZRA KLEIN | *June 22, 2007* | web only

Michael Moore poses for a portrait at the 60th International film festival in Cannes, southern France, on Monday, May 21, 2007. (Photo by the Associated Press.)

"Socialism kills!" roared the guy dressed up like Fidel Castro. The six nurses in miniskirts and high heels who flanked his wheelchair winked coquettishly and passed out literature meant to prove the point. An older woman behind me in line for the premiere of Michael Moore's *Sicko* softly clucked at them. "Ain't no nurse who could wear heels like that and be on her feet for 12 hours," she said.

But whether government-run medicine really kills, or in fact just turns our nurses into a cadre of propagandists in stilettos, is actually a bit beside the point. Contrary to its billing, *Sicko* is not a movie about health care policy. It does not spend time examining inefficiencies, or incentive structures, or public-private hybrids. It does not offer a methodologically rigorous cross-national comparison of health care systems. (Its portrayal of Cuba is, indeed, absurdly rosy.) That's not its point.

Its point, of course, is to arouse passion, to force debate, and on that, it succeeds. A few hours before, I'd been on Larry Kudlow's TV show, ostensibly to discuss health care and Moore's new movie. "I hate it," barked Kudlow. "Michael Moore's movie *Sicko* calls for socialized medicine." He hadn't seen it, of course, but felt perfectly comfortable assuming, and judging, its arguments.

S E E I N G THE ARGUMENT

SEEING THE ARGUMENT

intended audience. Let's look again at steps in the writing process as they apply to writing a critique.

Knowing Your Audience

Try to imagine writing your critique for a larger audience, not just for your instructor. Try not to focus on this assignment as writing to be graded. Rather, think about why we turn to reviews: What do readers want to learn? They want to know if they should read the book or see the film. Your job is to help readers make that decision.

Understanding Your Purpose

Your purpose, then, is to provide clear, accurate information and a fair evaluation of both the material covered (or not covered) and the presentation of that material. Balance is important. You do not want most of your review to be summary, with just a few sentences of evaluation "stuck on" at the end. You also do not want a detailed summary of the work's beginning followed by skimpy coverage of the rest. This lack of balance may suggest to readers that you have not read or seen the entire work. And when reviewing a novel or movie, do not explain the entire plot. You do not want to give away the ending!

Establishing a General Plan

First, study the work carefully. Be sure that you can write a complete and accurate summary, even if you need to leave some of the plot details or main points out of your review. Second, the analysis part of your review or critique needs two elements: comment on the work's structure and special features plus discussion of the writer's (or director's) style.

As you study the work, consider these questions:

- How is the work put together?
- For a nonfiction book, how many chapters or sections are there, and what does each cover?
- Does the book contain visuals? An index?
- For a film, how does the story unfold? What actors are in the lead roles? What special effects are used?
- For an advertisement, how does the author use color or fonts to persuade the reader? What types of textual techniques are used?

These are the kinds of questions readers expect a review to answer. Your analysis of style needs to be connected to the work's intended audience. For example, if you are evaluating a biography, consider these questions:

- Is it informally written or heavily documented with notes and references?
- What is the level of formality of the book?
- What is the age level or knowledge level of the author's expected audience? Films are rated for age groups. Books can also be rated for age and level of knowledge of the subject. Web sites might be targeted to a specific gender or audience.

Your summary and analysis can point the way to a fair and sensible evaluation. If, for example, you have many problems understanding a book aimed at a general audience, then it is fair to say that the author has not successfully reached his or her audience. If, on the other hand, you selected a Web site to critique that was designed for specialists or for a group with a particular interest, then your reading challenge is not relevant to a fair judgment. All it allows you to do is point out that the Web site is tough going for a nonspecialist (or that a movie sequel, for another example, is hard to follow in

spots for those who did not see the original film). Your evaluation should include an assessment of content and presentation. Did the book or film fulfill its intended purpose? Was it as thorough as you expected in the light of other works on the same or a similar topic?

Drafting the Critique or Review

There is no simple formula for combining summary, analysis, and evaluation in a review or critique. Some instructors simplify the task by requiring a two-part review: summary first and then analysis and evaluation. If you are not so directed, then some blending of the three elements will be expected. Often reviews begin with an opening that is both an attention-getter and a broad statement of the work's subject or subject category. (This is a *biography* of Franklin; this is a *female action-hero* film.) An evaluation (in general terms) usually completes the opening paragraph. Then the reviewer uses a summary–analysis–evaluation pattern, providing details of content and presentation and then assessing the work.

The Research Response: How Does It Help Me Understand Other Works, Ideas, and Events?

Frequently, especially in your research writing courses, you will read not to analyze or evaluate but rather to use the source as part of learning about a particular subject. Lincoln's address is significant for the Civil War historian both as an event of that war and as an influence on our thinking about that war. The Gettysburg Address is also vital to the biographer's study of Lincoln's life and to the literary critic's study of famous

As you read the following critique of Malcolm Gladwell's book *Outliers*, make your own annotations. Notice if, where, and how effectively the author addresses Gladwell's purpose and intended readers, summarizes the work, analyzes Gladwell's style, and provides an overall evaluation of the text. Do you think this is an effective critique? Discuss your annotations with your classmates and instructor.

The New York Times
David Leonhardt
November 28, 2008
Chance and Circumstance

In 1984, a young man named Malcolm graduated from the University of Toronto and moved to the United States to try his hand at journalism. Thanks to his uncommonly clear writing style and keen eye for a story, he quickly landed a job at *The Washington Post*. After less than a decade at the *Post*, he moved up to the pinnacle of literary journalism, *The New Yorker*. There, he wrote articles full of big ideas about the hidden patterns of ordinary life, which then became grist for two No. 1 best-selling books. In the vast world of nonfiction writing, he is as close to a singular talent as exists today.

Or at least that's one version of the story of Malcolm Gladwell. Here is another:

In 1984, a young man named Malcolm graduated from the University of Toronto and moved to the United States to try his hand at journalism. No one could know it then, but he arrived with nearly the perfect background for his time. His mother was a psychotherapist and his father a mathematician. Their professions pointed young Malcolm toward the behavioral sciences, whose popularity would explode in the 1990s. His mother also just happened to be a writer on the side. So unlike most children of mathematicians and therapists, he came to learn, as he would later recall, "that there is beauty in saying something clearly and simply." As a journalist, he plumbed the behavioral research for optimistic lessons about the human condition, and he found an eager audience during the heady, proudly geeky 90s. His first book, *The Tipping Point*, was published in March 2000, just days before the NASDAQ peaked.

These two stories about Gladwell are both true, and yet they are also very different. The first personalizes his success. It is the classically American version of his career, in that it gives individual characteristics—talent, hard work, Horatio Alger–like pluck—the starring role. The second version doesn't necessarily deny these characteristics, but it does sublimate them. The protagonist is not a singularly talented person who took advantage of opportunities. He is instead a talented person who took advantage of singular opportunities.

Gladwell's latest book, *Outliers*, is a passionate argument for taking the second version of the story more seriously than we now do. "It is not the brightest who succeed," Gladwell writes. "Nor is success simply the sum of the decisions and efforts we make on our own behalf. It is, rather, a gift. Outliers are those who have been given opportunities—and who have had the strength and presence of mind to seize them."

He doesn't actually tell his own life story in the book. (But he lurks offstage, since he does describe the arc of his mother's Jamaican family.) Instead, he tells other success stories, often using the device of back-to-back narratives. He starts with a tale of individual greatness, about the

continued

Beatles or the titans of Silicon Valley or the enormously successful generation of New York Jews born in the early 20th century. Then he adds details that undercut that tale.

So Bill Gates is introduced as a young computer programmer from Seattle whose brilliance and ambition outshine the brilliance and ambition of the thousands of other young programmers. But then Gladwell takes us back to Seattle, and we discover that Gates's high school happened to have a computer club when almost no other high schools did. He then lucked into the opportunity to use the computers at the University of Washington, for hours on end. By the time he turned 20, he had spent well more than 10,000 hours as a programmer.

At the end of this revisionist tale, Gladwell asks Gates himself how many other teenagers in the world had as much experience as he had by the early 1970s. "If there were 50 in the world, I'd be stunned," Gates says. "I had a better exposure to software development at a young age than I think anyone did in that period of time, and all because of an incredibly lucky series of events." Gates's talent and drive were surely unusual. But Gladwell suggests that his opportunities may have been even more so.

Many people, I think, have an instinctual understanding of this idea (even if Gladwell, in the interest of setting his thesis against conventional wisdom, doesn't say so). That's why parents spend so much time worrying about what school their child attends. They don't really believe the child is so infused with greatness that he or she can overcome a bad school, or even an average one. And yet when they look back years later on their child's success—or their own—they tend toward explanations that focus on the individual. Devastatingly, if cheerfully, Gladwell exposes the flaws in these success stories we tell ourselves.

The book's first chapter explores the anomaly of hockey players' birthdays. In many of the best leagues in the world, amateur or professional, roughly 40 percent of the players were born in January, February, or March, while only 10 percent were born in October, November, or December. It's a profoundly strange pattern, with a simple explanation. The cutoff birth date for many youth hockey leagues is January 1. So the children born in the first three months of the year are just a little older, bigger, and stronger than their peers. These older children are then funneled into all-star teams that offer the best, most intense training. By the time they become teenagers, their random initial advantage has turned into a real one.

At the championship game of the top Canadian junior league, Gladwell interviews the father of one player born on January 4. More than half of the players on his team—the Medicine Hat Tigers—were born in January, February, or March. But when Gladwell asks the father to explain his son's success, the calendar has nothing to do with it. He instead mentions passion, talent, and hard work—before adding, as an aside, that the boy was always big for his age. Just imagine, Gladwell writes, if Canada created another youth hockey league for children born in the second half of the year. It would one day find itself with twice as many great hockey players.

Outliers has much in common with Gladwell's earlier work. It is a pleasure to read and leaves you mulling over its inventive theories for days afterward. It also, unfortunately, avoids grappling in a few instances with research that casts doubt on those theories. (Gladwell argues that relatively older children excel not only at hockey but also in the classroom. The research on this issue, however, is decidedly mixed.) This is a particular shame, because it would be a delight to watch someone of his intellect and clarity make sense of seemingly conflicting claims.

For all these similarities, though, *Outliers* represents a new kind of book for Gladwell. *The Tipping Point* and *Blink*, his second book, were a mixture of social psychology, marketing and even a bit of self-help. *Outliers* is far more political. It is almost a manifesto. "We look at the young Bill Gates and marvel that our world allowed that 13-year-old to become a fabulously successful entrepreneur," he writes at the end. "But that's the wrong lesson. Our world only allowed one 13-year-old unlimited access to a time-sharing terminal in 1968. If a million teenagers had been given the same opportunity, how many more Microsofts would we have today?"

After a decade—and, really, a generation—in which this country has done fairly little to build up the institutions that can foster success, Gladwell is urging us to rethink. Once again, his timing may prove to be pretty good.

speeches or of the Bible's influence on English writing styles. Thus Lincoln's brief speech is a valuable source for students in a variety of disciplines; it becomes part of their research process. Able researchers study it carefully; analyze it thoroughly; place it in its proper historical, literary, and personal contexts; and use it to develop their own arguments.

Arguments made by authors, especially experts in a particular field, can be valuable sources for students in a variety of disciplines. As you research for your own projects and papers, you will need to respond to the arguments of others as part of your research pro-

cess. Able researchers study their sources carefully, analyze them thoroughly, place them in their proper historical, literary, and personal contexts, and then use them to develop their own arguments.

While writing research essays in future classes, for example, you will be asked to respond to the research and opinions of other writers. You will need to annotate the texts, make your own notes, and possibly even write short-response essays detailing and analyzing their perspectives, opinions, and assertions so that you can make good decisions about their usefulness to your own project.

did you know?

Despite the fact that it is often referred to as the speech that changed a nation, according to many scholars, Lincoln's Gettysburg Address was considered less than a complete success at its 1863 unveiling.

The audience had just heard Edward Everett, a well-known orator of the time, give a 2-hour speech on the significance of the war and the honor of those who had fallen. In sharp contrast, Lincoln's seven-sentence speech, which never mentioned any names or the issue of slavery, seemed to take the audience by surprise.

Although the ceremony was attended by nearly 15,000 people (including the governors of 6 of the 24 Union states), there was little, if any, applause when the president finished delivering his 272-word speech.

In fact, the speech was so brief that it even caught photographers (who needed extensive set-up time) off-guard. As a result, there are no confirmed photos of the speech being given.

Sources: www.wikipedia.org, www.bellaonline.com/articles/art22873.asp

The only confirmed photo of Abraham Lincoln at Gettysburg (circled), taken about noon, just after Lincoln arrived and some three hours before he spoke. To Lincoln's right is his bodyguard, Ward Hill Lamon.

Read the following article from MedicalNewsToday.com and consider how (or if) you might use this as a source for your own argument. Might this article be a useful research tool for certain topics or issues? Try to list any essay topics that come to mind as you read the article. Then make a note of what other types of sources you would try to find to assist with your research if you were writing an essay on each issue.

Medical News Today
May 29, 2007
Grim Warning for America's Fast Food Consumers Offered by "Supersize Me" Mice Research

It's research that may have you thinking twice before upgrading to the large size at your favorite fast food joint. Saint Louis University research presented in Washington, D.C., shows the dangers of high-fat food combined with high fructose corn syrup and a sedentary lifestyle—in other words, what may be becoming commonplace among Americans.

Brent Tetri, M.D., associate professor of internal medicine at Saint Louis University Liver Center, and colleagues studied the effects of a diet that was 40 percent fat and replete with high fructose corn syrup, a sweetener common in soda and some fruit juices. The research was presented at the Digestive Diseases Week meeting.

"We wanted to mirror the kind of diet many Americans subsist on, so the high fat content is about the same you'd find in a typical McDonald's meal, and the high fructose corn syrup translates to about eight cans of soda a day in a human diet, which is not far off with what some people consume," says Tetri, a leading researcher in nonalcoholic fatty liver disease, which can lead to cirrhosis and, ultimately, death. "But we were also keeping the mice sedentary, with a very limited amount of activity."

The study, which lasted for 16 weeks, had some curious results, says Tetri.

"We had a feeling we'd see evidence of fatty liver disease by the end of the study," he says. "But we were surprised to find how severe the damage was and how quickly it occurred. It took only four weeks for liver enzymes to increase and for glucose intolerance—the beginning of type II diabetes—to begin."

And unlike other studies, the mice were not forced to eat; rather, they were able to eat whenever they wanted—and eat they did. Tetri says there's evidence that suggests fructose actually suppresses your fullness, unlike fiber-rich foods, which make you feel full quickly.

The take-home message for humans is obvious, he says.

"A high-fat and sugar-sweetened diet compounded by a sedentary lifestyle will have severe repercussions for your liver and other vital organs," he says. "Fatty liver disease now affects about one of every eight children in this country. The good news is that it is somewhat reversible—but for some it will take major changes in diet and lifestyle."

Article adapted by Medical News Today from original press release.
www.medicalnewstoday.com/articles/71966.php

let's review

After reading Chapter 2, you should understand the following:

- There are multiple ways to respond to the writing of others, including responding to content (summaries and paraphrases); analyzing style; evaluating; and connecting to research.

- A good *summary* shows your grasp of main ideas and your ability to express them clearly. Like a summary, a *paraphrase* is an objective restatement of someone's writing, but the purpose of a paraphrase is to clarify a complex passage or to include material from a source in your own writing.

- Frequently you will be asked to *analyze* a work—that is, to explain the elements of structure and style that a writer has chosen. You will want to examine sentence patterns, organization, metaphors, and other techniques selected by the writer to convey attitude and give force to ideas.

- Many critical responses to texts include some element of evaluation. Even when the stated purpose of an essay is "pure" analysis, the analysis implies a judgment. You may be asked to combine summary, analysis, and evaluation while writing a critique.

- Frequently, especially in your research writing courses, you will read not to analyze or evaluate but rather to use sources as part of learning about a particular subject so that you can then incorporate sources into your own work.

connect

Read the article below and review the discussion questions that follow. Then form a peer group and discuss how you might respond to the piece. How might you respond to the content? How might you analyze the writer's style? How might you evaluate the piece? Might you use this as part of a larger research project? Write up notes about your discussion and be prepared to share your ideas with the class.

Beware of Facebook Danger

Alyson Waite

May 10, 2006

The popular Facebook Web site, which connects peers and classmates, also gives predators an opportunity to find unsuspecting victims. Facebook permits access to anyone with a legitimate university e-mail address. Students, professors, graduate assistants, landscapers, and electricians—all people at the university—have a legitimate university e-mail address. In other words, every employee or student at this university can view the information posted on an individual's personal page.

When I began working on the campus, I discovered how accessible the Web site was. Older male colleagues would log onto the Web site and "check out" random women they met or saw on the campus. If they saw a woman wearing sorority letters, they searched the sorority until a picture of the woman appeared. By simply clicking on the photo, they gained access to the woman's personal information. I trust my colleagues, but I doubt every person with a university e-mail address is as trustworthy.

continued

Facebook is a danger to students. Almost every woman I know reveals her residence on the Web site. Some mistakenly believe because viewing one's page is limited to others at their university, it is safer than other blog-type Web sites that have open access. However, a predator would be more likely to know and pursue someone local. Online predators abduct and abuse kids they meet on the Internet every day. Why would it be any different on a college campus?

Even scarier, people can post photos of others on their accounts and label their names. This is a problem for athletes who find themselves facing penalties because fans post questionable photos of them. These photos may or may not be valid, but athletic administrators and coaches—who also have university e-mail addresses—can easily search athletes' names and access the photos.

Worst of all, Facebook exposes the insecurity of some college students. By posting intimate details and graphic photos, they portray themselves as potential victims.

I admit when I was a naive freshman, I created a Facebook account. I posted my biographical information, my hobbies, my residence, and a link to my personal photographs. Because I used Facebook primarily to chat with friends and link to old high school classmates, I did not see the potential dangers. In fact, I thought it was a great opportunity to catch up with old friends and create relationships with acquaintances. If I met people, I plugged in their names and learned about their personalities. A friend of mine even referred to the Web site as "the stalker pages."

Students use Facebook to boast about their drinking habits, their relationships, and their opinions. Friends can publicly comment on one another's pages. When students have new and attractive photos of themselves—often half-naked vacation photos—they immediately attach them to their homepages. When Facebook users change their photos, their friends are informed of the updates as soon as they log on.

In addition to exposing photos, students post their instant messenger screen names, which link to more information. People often use away messages to inform their friends of where they are. To predators, this is another tool. There are only so many McKeldin libraries in College Park.

I encourage all students with a Facebook account to reassess what information they choose to expose online. The Internet can be a powerful tool, but it can also be a dangerous source for criminals and perverts. In addition, employers have caught on to the Facebook obsession and often find ways to check the profiles of potential employees for implicating information and photographs.

My Facebook days are over.

Alyson Waite is a junior public relations major.

SOURCE: http://media.www.diamondbackonline.com/media/storage/paper873/news/2006/05/10/Opinion/Beware.Of.Facebook.Danger-2325542.shtml

RESPONDING TO CONTENT

1. What is Waite's subject? What was her purpose for writing?

2. Does she acknowledge that there are possible advantages to having a Facebook account? How does she dismiss these?

3. What disadvantages of having an account does she mention?

4. How might you summarize Waite's essay?

ANALYZING THE AUTHOR'S STYLE

1. What is the author's primary strategy for conveying attitude? What is Waite's attitude toward Facebook? What examples and word choice help to convey her attitude?

2. Do you enjoy and appreciate the strategy Waite uses? Or does it bother you? If you appreciate it, what makes it clever? If you are bothered, why?

EVALUATING

1. Do you think that this is an effective essay? Why or why not?

2. What criteria might you use to evaluate this piece?

RESEARCHING

1. Might you find this essay useful in writing a future research essay? Why or why not?

2. What information might you annotate as useful or interesting?

3. What types of sources might you try to find to further your research on this topic?

The
images
you
remember....

the basics
of argument

chapter 3

Even everyday communications like Facebook profiles can be viewed as arguments.

When you begin to understand the basics of argument, you will start to look at the world around you in a new way. Facebook profiles, T-shirt logos, newspaper editorials, Web sites, and even junk mail all possess elements of persuasion. Have you ever considered how your own daily communications are actually arguments or attempts at persuading an audience? Look at any Facebook, MySpace, or similar web blog and think about what the author is trying to communicate to the world. Is there a purpose to the page? Is there an intended audience? If you can begin to look at even the most familiar forms of communication as arguments, you will soon begin to realize that arguments are everywhere.

Characteristics of Argument

Argument Is Conversation with a Goal

When you enter into an argument (as speaker, writer, or reader), you become a participant in an ongoing debate about an issue. Since you are probably not the first to address the issue, you need to be aware of the ways that the issue has been debated by others and then **seek to advance the conversation**, just as you would if you

http://www.mhhe.argument/fromtheauthor

GOOD ADVICE

In this section we will explore the processes of thinking logically and analyzing issues to reach informed judgments. Mature people do not need to agree on all issues in order to respect one another's good sense, but they do have little patience with uninformed or illogical statements masquerading as argument. (Just ask Judge Judy how frustrating this can be.) As you learn to read, respond to, and write arguments, you will need to take other opinions and logical opposing points of view (often called counterarguments) into account. After all, there are always more than two sides to every argument!

Judge Judy, the famously impatient TV judge, has learned to recognize illogical arguments in her courtroom.

Arguments are all around us, and each one has a specific goal or purpose. For example, when you read a bumper sticker, you are entering into an argument, like it or not. Look at the bumper stickers here. What argument is each one making to its readers? Have you seen other bumper stickers that clearly present an argument? Discuss these and any others you have seen with your classmates. As you do, speculate about the reason bumper stickers were invented. Do you think they are an effective way to communicate an argument? Why or why not?

WELCOME TO AMERICA NOW SPEAK ENGLISH

IF YOU CAN READ THIS THANK A TEACHER, IF YOU CAN READ THIS IN ENGLISH, THANK A VET

S

EE

ING

THE ARGUMENT

SEEING THE ARGUMENT

were having a casual conversation with friends about going to a movie. Once the time of the movie is set, the discussion turns to whose car to take or where to meet. If you were to just repeat the time of the movie, you would add nothing useful to the conversation. Also, if you were to change the subject to a movie you saw last week, you would annoy your friends by not offering useful information or showing that you valued the current conversation. Just as with a conversation about a movie, you want your argument to stay focused on the issue, to respect what others have already contributed, and to make a useful addition to everyone's understanding of the issue.

Argument Takes a Stand on an Arguable Issue

A meaningful argument focuses on a debatable issue. We usually do not argue about facts. "Professor Jones's American literature class meets at 10:00 on Mondays"

is not arguable. It is either true or false. We can check the schedule of classes to find out. (Sometimes, however, the facts change; new facts replace old ones.) We also do not debate personal preferences for the simple reason that they are just that—personal. If the debate is about the appropriateness of boxing as a sport, for you to declare that you would rather play tennis is to fail to advance the conversation. You have expressed a personal preference, interesting perhaps, but not relevant to the debate.

Argument Uses Reasons and Evidence

Some arguments merely look right. That is, conclusions are drawn from facts, but the facts are not those that actually support the assertion, or the conclusion is not the only or the best explanation of those facts. To shape convincing arguments, we need more than an array of facts. We need to think critically, to analyze the issue, to see relationships, to weigh evidence. We

S
E E
I N G
THE ARGUMENT
SEEING THE ARGUMENT

Arguments incorporate the values of their writers and try to appeal to the values of their readers. The famous "got milk?" campaign attempts to appeal to specific values both visually and with text. Look at the ads here. What values does the milk industry seem to believe are important to their customers? Do you think these two ads are targeted at different audiences? If so, what makes you think so?

need to avoid the temptation to argue from emotion only, or to believe that just stating our opinion is the same thing as building a sound argument.

Argument Incorporates Values

Arguments are based not just on reason and evidence but also on the beliefs and values we hold and think that our audience may hold as well. In a reasoned debate, you want to make clear the values that you consider relevant to the argument. For example, many people disagree about whether boxing should be banned as a sport.

A writer against a ban on boxing might argue that boxing teaches children about the importance of discipline, persistence, and motivation in sports. (The writer thinks these things are worthwhile, which gives us insights into the values she holds.)

A writer for a ban on boxing might argue that fighters are promoting vicious and injury-producing violence to children in order to make money. (These points give us insights into the things this writer values or believes worthwhile.)

Argument Recognizes the Topic's Complexity

Much false reasoning (the logical fallacies discussed in Chapter 5) results from a writer's oversimplifying an issue. A sound argument begins with an understanding that most issues are complicated. The wise person approaches ethical concerns such as abortion or euthanasia or public policy issues such as tax cuts or trade agreements with the understanding that there are many philosophical, moral, and political perspectives that complicate discussions of these topics. Recognizing an argument's complexity may also lead us to an understanding that there can be more than one "right" position. The thoughtful arguer respects the views of others, seeks common ground when possible, and often chooses a conciliatory approach.

The Shape of Argument

The Aristotelian Model

One of the best ways to understand the basics of argument is to reflect on what the Greek philosopher Aristotle describes as the three "players" in any argument:

Even seemingly straightforward issues like vegetarianism can be complex and politically charged. Be sure that you understand the debate before you attempt to enter into it.

Does the author of this ad seem to understand and appreciate the complexity of this issue? Why or why not? Does this affect your reaction to this argument? Why do you think this author chose to handle the argument in this manner? What values does the author seem to hold?

Feeding kids meat is child abuse

FIGHT THE FAT • GO VEG

- the writer (or speaker),
- the argument itself, and
- the reader (or audience).

Aristotle called the logic of the argument the *logos*—the assertion and the support for that assertion. A successful argument needs a logical and convincing logos. An argument also implies an audience, those whose views we want to influence. Aristotle called this part of argument *pathos*. Good arguers need to be alert to the values and attitudes of their audience and to appeal effectively to their emotions. However, Aristotle also explains that part of our appeal to an audience rests in the logos, our logic and evidence. An argument that is all emotional appeal will not move thoughtful audiences.

Finally (and for Aristotle the most important of the three players) is the writer/speaker, or *ethos*. No argument, Aristotle asserts, no matter how logical, no matter how appealing emotionally, will succeed if the audience rejects the arguer's credibility, the writer's "ethical" qualities. As members of the audience, we need to believe that the arguer is a person of knowledge, honesty, and goodwill.

We argue in a specific context of three interrelated parts. We present support for a concrete assertion, thesis, or claim to a specific audience whose demands,

did you **?** know

Aristotle, one of the most famous of the Greek philosophers, a student of Plato and a teacher of Alexander the Great, was also one of the earliest to recognize the power of visuals in the creation of meaning.

In his famous work *De Anima*, or *On the Soul*, he states,

> " . . . the soul never thinks without an image."

Source: http://classics.mit.edu/Aristotle/soul.3.iii.html

expectations, and character we have given thought to when shaping our argument. And we present ourselves as informed, competent, and reliable so that our audience will give serious attention to our argument. Your

GOOD ADV!CE

For an argument to be its most persuasive, it should use all three of Aristotle's players:

LOGOS—Argument Being Made

The reader should be persuaded because the assertion being made is logical and well-supported.

ETHOS—Writer/Speaker

The reader should be persuaded because the writer/speaker is ethical and credible on this subject.

PATHOS—Readers/Listeners

The reader should be persuaded because the writer understands her audience's needs, values, and expectations.

If one or more elements is lacking, the writer runs the risk that his or her readers will not find the argument convincing.

Read the following argument made by Steve Jobs, founder and CEO of Apple, during a speech to a senior team of a company. Does it successfully use all three of Aristotle's players? Does he possess credibility on this subject? Does his assertion seem logical? Does he understand to whom he is addressing his argument?

Killing bad ideas isn't that hard—lots of companies, even bad companies, are good at that. . . . What is really hard—and a hallmark of great companies—is that they kill a lot of good ideas. . . . For any single good idea to succeed, it needs a lot of resources, time, and attention, and so only a few ideas can be developed fully. Successful companies are tough enough to kill a lot of good ideas so those few that survive have a chance of reaching their full potential and being implemented properly.

Source: http://blogs.bnet.com/bnet1/?p=680

did you know

Despite the fact that rhetoricians have used his model as the basis for much of their work for decades, Stephen Toulmin (b. 1922) never intended to become one of the leading theorists in the field of rhetoric and writing.

In fact, he began his career as a philosopher and maintained a focus on ethics and moral reasoning for most of his career.

As of 2007, he was Luce Professor of Multiethnic and Transnational Studies at the University of Southern California School of International Relations.

Sources:
www.willamette.edu/cla/rhetoric/courses/argumentation/Toulmin.htm
www.giffordlectures.org/Author.asp?AuthorID=269

audience evaluates *you* as a part of their evaluation of your argument. Lose your credibility and you lose your argument.

The Toulmin Model

British philosopher Stephen Toulmin adds to what we have learned from Aristotle by focusing our attention on the basics of the argument itself. First, consider this definition of argument: An argument consists of evidence and/or reasons presented in support of an assertion or claim that is either stated or implied. Here are two examples:

CLAIM: We should not go skiing today

EVIDENCE: because it is too cold.

EVIDENCE: Because some laws are unjust,

CLAIM: civil disobedience is sometimes justified.

The basics of a complete argument, Toulmin asserts, are actually a bit more complex than these examples suggest. Each argument has a third part, which is not stated in the preceding examples. This third part is the glue that connects the support—the evidence and reasons—to the argument's claim and thus fulfills the logic of the argument. Toulmin calls

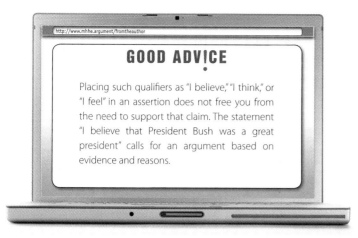

this glue an argument's *warrants*. These are the principles or assumptions that allow us to assert that our evidence or reasons—what Toulmin calls the *grounds*—do indeed support our claim. Look again at the sample arguments to see what warrants must be accepted to make each argument work:

CLAIM: We should not go skiing today.

EVIDENCE: It is too cold.

ASSUMPTIONS (WARRANTS): When it is too cold, skiing is not fun; the activity is not sufficient to keep one from becoming uncomfortable.

AND:

"Too cold" means whatever is too cold for me.

Collaborative Exercise: Building Arguments

With your class partner or in small groups, examine each of the following claims. Select two, think of one statement that could serve as evidence for each claim, and then think of the underlying assumptions that complete each of the arguments.

1. Professor X is not a good instructor.

2. Americans need to reduce the fat in their diets.

3. Tiger Woods is a great golfer.

4. Physical education classes should be graded pass/fail.

5. College newspapers should be free of supervision by faculty or administrators.

CLAIM: Civil disobedience is sometimes justified.

EVIDENCE: Some laws are unjust.

ASSUMPTIONS (WARRANTS): To get unjust laws changed, people need to be made aware of the injustice. Acts of civil disobedience will get people's attention and make them aware that the laws need changing.

Assumptions play an important role in any argument, so we need to be sure to understand what they are. Note, for instance, the second assumption operating in the first argument: The temperature the speaker considers uncomfortable will also be uncomfortable for her companions—an uncertain assumption. In the second argument, the warrant is less debatable, for acts of civil disobedience usually get media coverage and thus dramatize the issue.

The Language of Claims and Support

What kinds of statements function as claims and as support? Philosopher Stephen Toulmin was particularly interested in the strength or probability of various arguments. Some kinds of arguments are stronger than others because of the language or logic they use. Other arguments must, necessarily, be heavily qualified for the claim to be supportable. Toulmin developed terminology to provide a strategy for analyzing the degree of probability in an argument and to remind us of the need to qualify some kinds of claims. You have already seen how the idea of warrants, or assumptions, helps us think about the glue that presumably makes an argument work. Additional terms and concepts from Toulmin help us analyze the arguments of others and prepare more convincing arguments of our own.

Types of Claims

A *claim* is what the argument asserts or seeks to prove. It answers the question, What is your point? In an argumentative speech or essay, the claim is the speaker's or writer's main idea or thesis. Although an argument's claim follows from reasons and evidence, we often present an argument—whether written or spoken—with the claim stated near the beginning. We can better understand an argument's claim by recognizing three types of claims: claims of fact, claims of value, and claims of policy.

Claims of Fact

Although facts usually support claims, we do argue over some facts. Historians and biographers may argue over what happened in the past, although they are more

Support: Facts, inferences, judgments, or a combination of these, used as evidence or grounds for a claim

Claims: Debatable assertions

This billboard makes a claim. What is it? Who is making it?

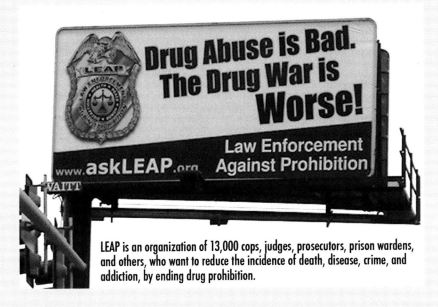

LEAP is an organization of 13,000 cops, judges, prosecutors, prison wardens, and others, who want to reduce the incidence of death, disease, crime, and addiction, by ending drug prohibition.

These statistics, which show the homicide rate during the War on Drugs in America, could be used as support for the claim made by the billboard above.

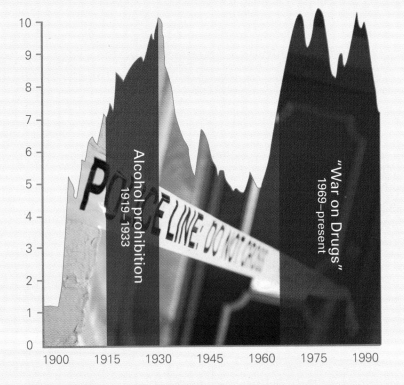

Murder in America
Homicides per 100,000 population
1900–1997 (FBI Uniform Crime Reports)

Drug War Facts, 6th ed., p. 21. www.drugwarfacts.org.

SEEING THE ARGUMENT

likely to argue over the significance of what happened. Scientists also argue over the facts, over how to classify an unearthed fossil, for example, or whether the fossil indicates that the animal had feathers.

CLAIM: The small, predatory dinosaur *Deinonychus* hunted its prey in packs.

This claim is supported by the discovery of several fossils of *Deinonychus* close together and with the fossil bones of a much larger dinosaur. Their teeth have also been found in or near the bones of dinosaurs that have died in a struggle.

Assertions about what will happen are sometimes classified as claims of fact, but they can also be labeled as inferences supported by facts. Predictions about a future event may be classified as a claim of fact:

CLAIM: The United States will win the most gold medals at the 2014 Olympics.

CLAIM: I will get an A on tomorrow's psychology test.

What evidence would you use today to support each of these claims?

Claims of Value

These include moral, ethical, and aesthetic judgments. Assertions that use such words as *good* or *bad*, *better* or *worse*, and *right* or *wrong* are claims of value. The following are all claims of value:

CLAIM: *Family Guy* is a better show than *The Simpsons*.

CLAIM: *Adventures of Huckleberry Finn* is one of the most significant American novels.

CLAIM: Cheating hurts others and the cheater too.

CLAIM: Abortion is wrong.

Claims of Judgment

Judgments are opinions based on values, beliefs, or philosophical concepts. (Judgments also include opinions based on personal preferences, but we have already excluded these from argument.) Judgments concern right and wrong, good and bad, better or worse, and *should* or *should not*:

CLAIM: No more than twenty-six students should be enrolled in any English class.

CLAIM: Cigarette advertising should be eliminated, and the federal government should develop an antismoking campaign.

To support the first judgment, we need to explain what constitutes overcrowding, or what constitutes the best class size for effective teaching. If we can support our views on effective teaching, we may be able to convince the college president that ordering more desks for Room 110 is not the best solution for the increased enrollment in English classes. The second

SEEING THE ARGUMENT

Visuals can be an effective way to express claims of judgment (for example, whether something is good or bad, effective or ineffective, ethical or unethical, or should be left as it is or should be changed). What judgment is being expressed by the author of this photo? Does this image make an argument? If so, is it an effective one?

judgment also offers a solution to a problem, in this case a national health problem. To reduce the number of deaths, we need to reduce the number of smokers, by encouraging smokers either to quit or not to start. The underlying assumption: Advertising does affect behavior.

GOOD ADVICE

As you evaluate and form your own judgments, be aware that ethical and moral judgments (those based on personal standards) may be more difficult to support because they depend not just on definitions and established criteria but on values and beliefs as well. If taking another person's life is wrong, why isn't it wrong in war? Or is it? These are difficult questions that require thoughtful responses rather than snap judgments.

try it!

Exercise: Judgments

Go to your favorite Web site or pick up your favorite magazine. As you read through the content, compile a list of three claims of judgment. For each judgment listed, generate one statement of support, either a fact, an inference, or another judgment. Then state the warrant (underlying assumption) required to complete each argument.

Claims of Policy

Finally, claims of policy are assertions about what should or should not happen, what the government ought or ought not to do, how to best solve social problems. Claims of policy debate, for example, college rules, state gun laws, and U.S. aid to Africans suffering from AIDS. The following are claims of policy:

CLAIM: College newspapers should not be controlled in any way by college authorities.

CLAIM: States should not have laws allowing people to carry concealed weapons.

CLAIM: The United States must provide more aid to African countries where 25 percent or more of the citizens have tested positive for HIV.

Claims of policy are often closely tied to judgments of morality or political philosophy, but they also need to be grounded in feasibility. That is, your claim needs to be doable, to be based on a thoughtful consideration of the real world and the complexities of public policy issues.

Support for Claims

Grounds (Reasons, Data, or Evidence)

The term *grounds* refers to the reasons and evidence provided in support of a claim. Although the words *data*, *reasons*, and *evidence* can also be used, *grounds* is the more general term because it includes logic as well as examples or statistics. We determine the grounds of an argument by asking, "Why do you think that?" or "How do you know that?" When writing your own arguments, you can ask yourself these questions and answer them by using a *because* clause:

CLAIM: Smoking should be banned in restaurants

GROUNDS: *because* secondhand smoke is a serious health hazard.

CLAIM: Pete Sampras was a better tennis player than Andre Agassi

GROUNDS: *because* (1) he was ranked number one longer than Agassi,

(2) he won more tournaments than Agassi, and

(3) he won more major tournaments than Agassi.

Let's consider what types of evidence are sometimes used as grounds for arguments and which are most effective and reliable.

Facts

Facts are statements that are verifiable. Factual statements refer to what can be counted, measured, or confirmed by reasonable observers or trusted experts and are often used as grounds for researched arguments.

- There are 26 desks in Room 110.
- In the United States, about 400,000 people die each year as a result of smoking.

These are factual statements. We can verify the first by observation—by counting. The second fact comes from medical records. We rely on trusted record-keeping sources and medical experts for

GOOD ADVICE

Support for claims of value often include other value statements. For example, to support the claim that censorship is bad, arguers often assert that the free exchange of ideas is good and necessary in a democracy. The support is itself a value statement. The arguer may believe, probably correctly, that most people will more readily agree with the support (the free exchange of ideas is good) than with the claim (censorship is bad).

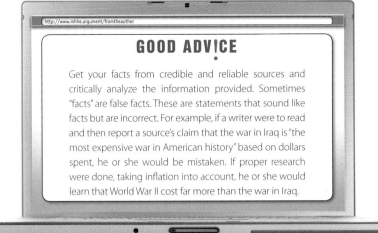

S
E E
I N G
THE ARGUMENT
SEEING THE ARGUMENT

verification. By definition, we do not argue about the facts. Usually. Sometimes "facts" change, as we learn more about our world. For example, only in the last thirty years has convincing evidence been gathered to demonstrate the relationship between smoking and various illnesses of the heart and lungs.

Inferences

Inferences are opinions based on facts. Inferences are the conclusions we draw from an analysis of facts. If a proper and logical analysis is done, inferences can provide logical grounds for arguments.

- There will not be enough desks in Room 110 for upcoming fall-semester classes.
- Smoking is a serious health hazard.

Predictions of an increase in student enrollment for the coming semester lead to the inference that most English classes scheduled in Room 110 will have several more students than last year. The dean should order new desks. Similarly, we infer from the number of deaths that smoking is a health problem; statistics show more people dying from tobacco-related illnesses than from AIDS, murder, or car accidents, causes of death that get media coverage but do not produce nearly as many deaths.

Inferences vary in their closeness to the facts supporting them. That the sun will rise tomorrow is an inference, but we count on its happening, acting as if it is a fact. However, the first inference stated above is based not just on the fact of 26 desks but on another inference—a projected increase in student enrollment— and on two assumptions. The argument looks like this:

CLAIM: There will not be enough desks in Room 110 for upcoming fall-semester classes.

FACT: There are 26 desks in Room 110.

INFERENCE: There will be more first-year students next year.

The billboard shown here is an example of a claim of policy. But is simply making this claim enough to create an actual policy? The clear answer is no. In order to make a solid argument for a policy change, an audience member would expect this claim to be backed with evidence and convincing, logical support. What types of sources might this group use to support their claim that gay and lesbian couples should have equal protection, just as married couples do? Why do you think they used Coretta Scott King's quote here? Does it help their argument? If so, how?

ASSUMPTIONS:
1. English will remain a required course.
2. No additional classrooms are available for English classes.

This inference could be challenged by a different analysis of the facts supporting enrollment projections.

Read the following article and then complete the exercise that follows. This exercise tests both careful reading and your understanding of the differences among facts, inferences, and judgments.

Paradise Lost
Richard Morin

Richard Morin, a journalist with *The Washington Post*, writes a regular Sunday column titled "Unconventional Wisdom," a column presenting interesting new information from the social sciences. The following article was Morin's column for July 9, 2000.

Here's my fantasy vacation: Travel back in time to the 1700s, to some languid South Pacific island paradise where ripe fruit hangs heavy on the trees and the native islanders live in peace with nature and with each other.

Or at least that was my fantasy vacation until I talked to anthropologist Patrick Kirch, one of the country's leading authorities on the South Pacific and director of the Phoebe Hearst Museum of Anthropology at the University of California at Berkeley.

The South Seas islands painted by Paul Gauguin and celebrated by Robert Louis Stevenson were no Gardens of Eden, Kirch writes in his riveting new history of the South Pacific, *On the Road of the Winds.* Many of these islands witnessed episodes of environmental depredation, endemic warfare and bloody ritual long before seafaring Europeans first visited. "Most islands of the Pacific were densely populated by the time of European contact, and the human impact on the natural ecosystem was often disastrous—with wholesale decimation of species and loss of vast tracts of land," he said.

Kirch says we can blame the French for all the loose talk about a tropical nirvana. "French philosophers of the Enlightenment saw these islands, especially Tahiti, as the original natural society where people lived in a state of innocence and food fell from the trees," he said. "How wrong they were."

French explorer Louis Antoine de Bougainville visited Tahiti for two weeks in 1769 and thought he discovered a paradise awash in social tolerance and carefree sex. Bougainville's breathless description of Tahiti became the basis for Jean Jacques Rousseau's concept of *l'homme naturel*—the noble savage.

Savage, indeed. Even as Bougainville poked around their craggy volcanic island, Rousseau's "noble savages" were busy savaging each other. The Tahitians were in the midst of a bitter civil war, complete with ritual sacrifice to their bloodthirsty war god, Oro. On Mangaia in the Cook Islands, Kirch discovered ovens and pits filled with the charred bones of men, women, and even children.

And forget that free-love nonsense. Dating, mating, and reproduction were tricky business throughout the South Seas several hundred years ago. To keep the population in check, the residents of tiny Tikopia in the Santa Cruz Islands practiced infanticide. Abortion also was common. And to "concentrate" their bloodlines, Kirch said, members of the royal class in Hawaii married their brothers and sisters. If they only knew . . .

Not all South Seas islands were little cesspools. On some of the smaller islands, early Polynesians avoided cultural collapse by adopting strict population control measures, including enforced suicide. "Some young men were encouraged to go to sea and not return," he said.

Perhaps the best example of the havoc wrought by the indigenous peoples of the South Pacific is found on desolate Easter Island, home of the monolithic stone heads that have gazed out from the front of a thousand travel brochures. Until recently, researchers believed that Easter Island's open, grassy plains and barren knife-point volcanic ridges had always been, well, grassy plains and barren ridges.

Not true, says Kirch. The island was once covered with dense palm and hardwood forests. But by the 1700s, when the first Europeans arrived, these forests had been burned by the islanders to clear land for agriculture, transforming lush groves into semi-tropical tundra. "On Easter Island, the ultimate extinction of the palm and other woody plants had a further consequence: the inability to move or erect the large stone statues" because there were no logs to use as rollers to move the giant heads from the quarries, Kirch writes.

The stone carvers' society collapsed, as did Easter Island culture. By the time Dutch explorer Jacob Roggeveen arrived on Easter Sunday in 1722, residents had taken to living in underground caves for protection from the social chaos that had enveloped their island home.

When viewed today, Kirch says, the monoliths remain an "imposing stone text that suggests a thousand human sagas." They also carry a lesson to our age, he argues—warning us "to achieve a sustainable relationship with our planet"—or else.

Label each of the following sentences as F (fact), FF (false fact), I (inference), or J (judgment).

_____ 1. In the 1700s native South Pacific islanders lived in peace and harmony.

_____ 2. It is foolish to romanticize life on South Sea islands.

_____ 3. French philosopher Rousseau based his idea of the noble savage on the Tahitians.

_____ 4. The stone statues on Easter Island suggest many stories.

_____ 5. In the past, noble Hawaiians married within their families.

_____ 6. Tahitians were savage people.

_____ 7. Some South Pacific islanders used to practice abortion and infanticide.

_____ 8. Easter Island has always had grassy plains and barren ridges.

_____ 9. Finding and using sustainable strategies will help preserve the environment.

_____ 10. People should not marry family members.

did you know

One of the world's most famous yet least visited archaeological sites, Easter Island is a small, hilly, now treeless island of volcanic origin. Located in the Pacific Ocean some 2,200 miles (3,600 kilometers) off the coast of Chile, it is considered to be the world's most remote inhabited island.

The island's most famous features are its enormous stone statues called *moai*, at least 288 of which once stood upon massive stone platforms called *ahu*.

There are some 250 of these ahu platforms spaced approximately one-half mile apart and creating an almost unbroken line around the perimeter of the island. Another 600 moai statues, in various stages of completion, are scattered around the island.

Consider how this subject might lead to an argumentative research essay. Could you speculate about the origins of these statues? Argue about their significance to our modern society?

Source: www.sacredsites.com/americas/chile/easter_island.html

To create an effective argument, you need to assess the potential for acceptance of your warrants and backing. Is your audience likely to share your values, your religious beliefs, or your scientific approach to issues? If you are speaking to a group at your church, then backing based on the religious beliefs of that church may be effective. If you are preparing an argument for a general audience, then using specific religious assertions as warrants or backing probably will not result in an effective argument.

Consider this ad for Abercrombie & Fitch. What claims is the author making about the product (jeans)? Who is the target audience? Based on what you know about this target audience, are they likely to share the values and beliefs this ad demonstrates? What types of backing might this audience expect in support of this claim?

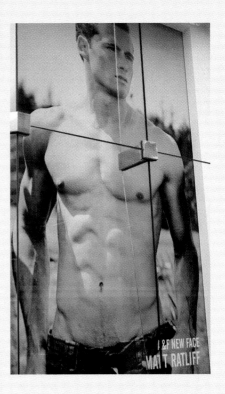

Or if additional rooms can be found, the dean will not need to order new desks. Note that inferences can be part of the support of an argument, or they can be the claim of an argument.

Warrants

Why should we believe that your grounds do indeed support your claim?

Your argument's warrants answer this question. They explain why your evidence really is evidence. Sometimes warrants reside in language itself, in the meanings of the words we are using. If I am *younger* than my brother, then my brother must be *older* than I am.

In many arguments based on statistical data, the argument's warrant rests on complex analyses of the statistics—and on the conviction that the statistics have been developed without error.

In some philosophical arguments, the warrants are the logical structures (often shown mathematically) connecting a sequence of reasons. Still, without taking courses in statistics and logic, you can develop an alertness to the good sense of some arguments and the dubious sense of others. You know, for example, that good SAT scores are a predictor of success in college. Can you argue that you will do well in college because you have good SATs? No. We can determine only a statistical probability. We cannot turn probabilities about a group of people into a warrant about one person in the group. In addition, SAT scores are only one predictor. Another key variable is motivation.

Here is an example of how a claim, grounds (or evidence), and a warrant work together in forming a logical argument:

CLAIM: Pete Sampras was a better tennis player than Roger Federer.

GROUNDS:
- He had a streak of 31 straight wins at Wimbledon.
- Sampras won his first major tournament at 19, while Federer didn't win one until 21.
- Federer is $18 million and 24 titles shy of Sampras' career records.

WARRANT: It is appropriate to judge and rank tennis players on these kinds of statistics. That is, the better player is the one who has the higher winning streak at Wimbledon, who won a major tournament earlier in his career, and who has won more and earned more than the other.

Backing

Standing behind an argument's warrant may be additional backing. Backing answers the question, How do we know that your evidence is good evidence?

You may answer this question by providing authoritative sources for the data (for example, the Census Bureau or the U.S. Tennis Association). Or you may explain in detail the methodology of the experiments performed or the surveys taken.

When scientists and social scientists present the results of their research, they anticipate the question of backing and automatically provide a detailed explanation of the process by which they acquired their evidence. In criminal trials, defense attorneys challenge the backing of the prosecution's argument. They question the handling of blood samples sent to labs for DNA testing, for instance. The defense attorneys want jury members to doubt the *quality* of the evidence, perhaps even to doubt the reliability of DNA testing altogether.

Qualifiers

Some arguments are absolute; they can be stated without qualification.

> If I am younger than my brother, then he must be older than I am.

Most arguments, however, need some qualification; many, in fact, need precise limitations. If, when playing bridge, I am dealt eight spades, then my opponents and partner together must have five spade cards—because there are thirteen cards of each suit in a deck. My partner probably has one spade but could have no spades. My partner possibly has two or more spades, but I would be foolish to count on it. When bidding my hand, I must be controlled by the laws of probability.

Look again at the smoking ban claim made earlier. Observe the absolute nature of both the claim and its support. If secondhand smoke is indeed a health hazard, it will be that in all restaurants, not just in some. With each argument we have to assess the need of qualification that is appropriate to a successful argument.

Sweeping generalizations often come to us in the heat of a debate or when we first start to think about an issue.

Having the ability to foresee and effectively rebut your audience's potential objections is a crucial part of crafting a successful argument. For example, protesters typically attend rallies fully expecting their opposition's arguments and have a plan for rebutting those counterarguments.

UNQUALIFIED CLAIM: Gun control is wrong because it restricts individual rights.

But, on reflection, surely you would not want to argue against all forms of gun control. (An unqualified assertion is understood by your audience to be absolute.) Would you sell guns to felons in jail or to children on the way to school? Obviously not. So, let's try the claim again, this time with two important qualifiers:

QUALIFIED CLAIM: Adults without a criminal record should not be restricted in the purchase of guns.

Others may want this claim further qualified to eliminate particular types of guns or to limit the number purchased or to regulate the process for purchasing. The gun-control debate is not about absolutes; it is about which qualified claim is best.

Counterarguments and Rebuttals

Arguments can be challenged. Smart debaters assume that there are people who will disagree with them. They anticipate the ways that opponents can challenge their arguments. When you are planning an argument, you need to think about how you can counter or rebut the challenges you anticipate. Think of yourself as an attorney in a court case preparing your own argument and a defense against the other attorney's challenges to your argument. If you ignore the important role of rebuttals, you may not win the jury to your side.

There are several effective ways of handling counterarguments. You may, in fact, partially concede certain facts. For example, if your opponent points out that marriage has a long history of being between a man and a woman (and attempts to use this to counter your argument that gay marriage should be legalized), you can acknowledge that this is a true statement without undermining your own argument. You can rebut the assertion, however, that this fact somehow supports the notion that marriage should continue to be viewed in this manner.

You may also want to use support (evidence, facts, data) to completely repudiate your opponent's counterargument. By bringing potential objections to the forefront and effectively negating them, you will strengthen your own credibility with your audience and will ultimately create a stronger argument.

Using Toulmin's Terms to Analyze Arguments

Terms are never an end in themselves; we learn them when we recognize that they help us to organize our thinking about a subject. Toulmin's terms can aid your reading of the arguments of others. You can see what's going on in an argument if you analyze it, applying Toulmin's language to its parts. Not all terms will be useful for every analysis because, for example, some arguments do not have qualifiers or rebuttals. But to recognize that an argument is without qualifiers is to learn something important about that argument.

First, here is a simple argument broken down into its parts using Toulmin's terms:

GROUNDS: Because Dr. Bradshaw has an attendance policy,

CLAIM: students who miss more than seven classes will

QUALIFIER: most likely (last year, Dr. Bradshaw did allow one student, in unusual circumstances, to continue in the class) be dropped from the course.

WARRANT: Dr. Bradshaw's syllabus explains her attendance policy,

BACKING: a policy consistent with the concept of a discussion class that depends on student participation and consistent with the attendance policies of most of her colleagues.

REBUTTAL: Although some students complain about an attendance policy of any kind, Dr. Bradshaw does explain her policy and her reasons for it the first day of class. She then reminds students that the syllabus is a contract between them; if they choose to stay, they agree to abide by the guidelines explained on the syllabus.

try it !

The argument in the example is brief and fairly simple. Let's see how Toulmin's terms can help us analyze a longer, more complex argument. Read actively and annotate the following essay while noting the existing annotations using Toulmin's terms. Then answer the questions that follow the article.

prereading questions} What are some good reasons to have zoos? What are some problems associated with them?

Let the Zoo's Elephants Go
Les Schobert

The author has spent more than 30 years working in zoos, primarily in care of elephants. He has been a curator of both the Los Angeles and North Carolina zoos. His argument was published October 16, 2005, in *The Washington Post*.

The Smithsonian Institution is a national treasure, but when it comes to elephants, its National Zoo is a national embarrassment. *Claim*

In 2000 the zoo euthanized Nancy, an African elephant that was suffering from foot problems so painful that standing had become difficult for her. Five years later the zoo has announced that Toni, an Asian elephant, is suffering from arthritis so severe that she, too, may be euthanized.

The elephants' debilitating ailments are probably a result of the inadequate *Grounds* conditions in which they have been held. The same story is repeated in zoos across the country.

When I began my zoo career 35 years ago, much less was known about elephants than is known today. We now understand that keeping elephants in *Backing* tiny enclosures with unnatural surfaces destroys their legs and feet. We have learned that to breed naturally and rear their young, elephants must live in herds that meet their social requirements. And we have come to realize that controlling elephants through domination and the use of ankuses (sharply pointed devices used to inflict pain) can no longer be justified.

Zoos must change the concept of how elephants are kept in captivity, *Claim* starting with how much space we allot them. Wild elephants may walk 30 miles a day.

A typical home range of a wild elephant is 1,000 square miles. At the National Zoo, Toni has access to a yard of less than an acre. Zoo industry standards allow the keeping of elephants in as little as 2,200 square feet, or about 5 percent of an acre.

Grounds

Some zoos have begun to reevaluate their ability to house elephants. After the death of two elephants in 2004, the San Francisco Zoo sent its surviving elephants to a sanctuary in California. This year the Detroit Zoo closed its elephant exhibit on ethical grounds, and its two surviving elephants now thrive at the California sanctuary as well.

Grounds

But attitudes at other zoos remain entrenched. To justify their outdated exhibits, some zoos have redefined elephant longevity and natural behavior. For example, National Zoo officials blame Toni's arthritis on old age. But elephants in the wild reproduce into their fifties, and female elephants live long after their reproductive cycles cease. Had she not been captured in Thailand at the age of 7 months, Toni, at age 39, could have had decades more of life as a mother and a grandmother. Instead, she faces an early death before her 40th birthday, is painfully thin and is crippled by arthritis.

Rebuttal to counter-argument

Claim qualified (options explained). Grounds

The National Zoo's other elephants face the same bleak future if changes are not made. A preserve of at least 2 square miles—1,280 acres, or almost eight times the size of the National Zoo—would be necessary to meet an elephant's physical and social needs. Since this is not feasible, the zoo should send its pachyderms to a sanctuary. One such facility, the Elephant Sanctuary in Tennessee, offers 2,700 acres of natural habitat over which elephants can roam and heal from the damage caused by zoo life. The sanctuary's soft soil, varied terrain, freedom of choice and freedom of movement have restored life to elephants that were suffering foot and joint diseases after decades in zoos and circuses.

The National Zoo has the opportunity to overcome its troubled animal-care history by joining progressive zoos in reevaluating its elephant program. The zoo should do right by its elephants, and the public should demand nothing less.

Claim restated. Warrant (states values).

QUESTIONS FOR READING

1. What is the occasion that had led to the writing of this article?

2. What is Schobert's subject?

3. State his claim in a way that shows that it is a solution to a problem.

QUESTIONS FOR REASONING AND ANALYSIS

1. What type of evidence (grounds) does the author provide?

2. What are the nature and source of his backing?

3. What makes his opening effective?

4. What values does Schobert express? What assumption does he make about his readers?

QUESTIONS FOR REFLECTING AND WRITING

1. Are you surprised by any of the facts about elephants presented by Schobert? Do they make sense to you, upon reflection?

2. Should zoos close down their elephant houses? Why or why not?

3. Are there any alternatives to city zoos with small elephant houses besides elephant sanctuaries?

Using Toulmin's Terms to Structure Your Own Arguments

You have seen how Toulmin's terms can help you to analyze and see what writers are actually doing in their arguments. You have also observed from both the short and the longer argument that writers do not usually follow the terms in precise order. Indeed, you can find both grounds and backing in the same sentence, or claim and qualifiers in the same paragraph, and so on. Still, the terms can help you to sort out your thinking about a claim you want to support. The following exercises will provide practice in your use of these terms to plan an argument.

EXERCISES: USING TOULMIN'S TERMS TO PLAN ARGUMENTS

Select one of the following claims, or one of your own if your instructor approves, and plan an argument, listing as many grounds as you can and paying attention to possible rebuttals of counterarguments. Expect your outline to be one to two pages.

   a. Professor X is (or is not) a good teacher.

   b. Colleges should (or should not) admit students only on the basis of academic merit.

   c. Americans need (or do not need) to reduce the fat in their diets.

   d. Physical education classes should (or should not) be graded pass/fail.

   e. Public schools should (or should not) have dress codes.

   f. Helmets for bicyclists should (or should not) be mandatory.

   g. Sales taxes on cigarettes should (or should not) be increased.

   h. All cigarette advertising should (or should not) be prohibited.

The images you remember...

making connections

let's review

After reading Chapter 3, you should understand the following:

- If you can begin to look at even the most familiar forms of communication as arguments, you will soon begin to realize that arguments are everywhere.

- Arguments take a stand on a debatable issue. Ask yourself whether a logical audience member, after reading your thesis, could take an opposing position. If not, your essay will most likely fall short of being a sound and effective argument.

- Arguments are based not just on reason and evidence but also on the beliefs and values we hold and think that our audience may hold as well.

- Much false reasoning (the logical fallacies discussed in Chapter 5) results from a writer's oversimplifying an issue. A sound argument begins with an understanding that most issues are terribly complicated.

- For an argument to be its most persuasive, it must use logos, ethos, and pathos. If one or more elements is lacking, the writer runs the risk that his or her readers will not find the argument convincing.

- The Toulmin model explains that an argument consists of evidence and/or reasons presented in support of an assertion or claim that is either stated or implied. It offers us a method by which to both read the arguments of others and construct our own logical arguments.

connect

Form a peer group and complete the exercise below, taking into account the characteristics of an argument, Aristotle's "players," and Toulmin's model.

Construct a claim of judgment regarding the problems caused by college students' drinking. Then support your claim using your knowledge and experience. You may also want to go online for some statistics about college drinking and health and safety risks. Drawing on both experience and data, can you effectively support your claim? What counterarguments might your opposition (those who disagree with your claim) assert? What might your rebuttals be? Develop an outline of your argument using the Toulmin terms. Be prepared to compare your outline to others in your class. Compare and evaluate the various types of claims and the sorts of support each group used to support their claims.

writing effective arguments

c h a p t e r 4

Much like Martin Luther King's famous "I have a dream" speech on the steps of the Lincoln Memorial, Barack Obama's 2009 inaugural speech may well be remembered as one of the most successful written arguments in history. As you read an excerpt from Obama's speech, think about the characteristics of argument discussed in the previous chapter. Why do you think Obama's writing is so successful? Do you recognize specific strategies or tools he uses in his writing? To watch Obama's historic speech, go to www.youtube.com and search using the keywords "Obama Inauguration."

Inaugural Address

Barack Obama

Forty-four Americans have now taken the presidential oath.

The words have been spoken during rising tides of prosperity and the still waters of peace. Yet, every so often the oath is taken amidst gathering clouds and raging storms. At these moments, America has carried on not simply because of the skill or vision of those in high office, but because We the People have remained faithful to the ideals of our forebears, and true to our founding documents.

So it has been. So it must be with this generation of Americans.

That we are in the midst of crisis is now well understood. Our nation is at war against a far-reaching network of violence and hatred. Our economy is badly weakened, a consequence of greed and irresponsibility on the part of some but also our collective failure to make hard choices and prepare the nation for a new age.

Homes have been lost, jobs shed, businesses shuttered. Our health care is too costly, our schools fail too many, and each day brings further evidence that the ways we use energy strengthen our adversaries and threaten our planet.

These are the indicators of crisis, subject to data and statistics. Less measurable, but no less profound, is a sapping of confidence across our land; a nagging fear that America's decline is inevitable, that the next generation must lower its sights.

Today I say to you that the challenges we face are real, they are serious and they are many. They will not be met easily or in a short span of time. But know this America: They will be met.

On this day, we gather because we have chosen hope over fear, unity of purpose over conflict and discord.

On this day, we come to proclaim an end to the petty grievances and false promises, the recriminations and worn-out dogmas that for far too long have strangled our politics.

We remain a young nation, but in the words of Scripture, the time has come to set aside childish things. The time has come to reaffirm our enduring spirit; to choose our better history; to carry forward that precious gift, that noble idea, passed on from generation to generation: the God-given promise that all are equal, all are free, and all deserve a chance to pursue their full measure of happiness.

In reaffirming the greatness of our nation, we understand that greatness is never a given. It must be earned. Our journey has never been one of shortcuts or settling for less.

It has not been the path for the faint-hearted, for those who prefer leisure over work, or seek only the pleasures of riches and fame.

Rather, it has been the risk-takers, the doers, the makers of things—some celebrated, but more often men and women obscure in their labor—who have carried us up the long, rugged path towards prosperity and freedom.

For us, they packed up their few worldly possessions and traveled across oceans in search of a new life. For us, they toiled in sweatshops and settled the West, endured the lash of the whip and plowed the hard earth.

For us, they fought and died in places like Concord and Gettysburg; Normandy and Khe Sanh.

Time and again these men and women struggled and sacrificed and worked till their hands were raw so that we might live a better life. They saw America as bigger than the sum of our individual ambitions; greater than all the differences of birth or wealth or faction.

This is the journey we continue today. We remain the most prosperous, powerful nation on Earth. Our workers are no less productive than when this crisis began. Our minds are no less inventive, our goods and services no less needed than they were last week or last month or last year. Our capacity remains undiminished. But our time of standing pat, of protecting narrow interests and putting off unpleasant decisions—that time has surely passed.

Starting today, we must pick ourselves up, dust ourselves off, and begin again the work of remaking America.

The basics of good writing are much the same for works as different as the personal essay, the argument, the Web page, the Facebook Group post, and the researched essay. Good writing is focused, organized, and concrete. Effective essays are written in a style and tone that are suited to both the audience and the writer's purpose. These are sound principles, all well known to you. But how, exactly, do you achieve them when writing your own arguments? This chapter will help you answer that question.

Know Your Audience

Too often students plunge into writing without thinking much about audience. They wrongly assume that their audience is only the instructor who has given the assignment, just as their purpose in writing is to complete the assignment and get a grade. These views of audience and purpose are likely to lead to poorly written arguments. First, if you are not thinking about readers who may disagree with you, you may not develop the best defense of your claim—which may need a rebuttal to possible counterarguments. Second, you may ignore your essay's needed introductory material on the assumption that the instructor, knowing the assignment, has a context for understanding your writing. To avoid these pitfalls, use the following questions to sharpen your understanding of audience.

Who Is My Audience?

If you are writing an essay for the student newspaper, your audience consists primarily of students, but do not forget that faculty and administrators also read the student newspaper. If you are preparing a letter-to-the-editor refutation of a recent column in your town's newspaper, your audience will be the readers of that newspaper—that is, adults in your town. Some instructors give assignments that identify an audience such as those just described so that you will practice writing with a specific audience in mind.

If you are not assigned a specific audience, imagine your classmates, as well as your instructor, as part of your audience. In other words, you are writing to many readers in the academic community. These readers are intelligent and thoughtful, expecting sound reasoning and convincing evidence. These readers also represent varied values and beliefs, as they are from diverse cultures and experiences. They may hold clear opinions about your topic, reject certain ideas based on value systems they were raised with, or automatically accept the validity of your claims based on their beliefs or experiences. Do not, however, confuse the shared expectations of writing conventions, sound reasoning, and accuracy in presenting data with shared beliefs. In order to identify and more clearly understand the values, positions, and beliefs of your intended readers, you may want to think about the following questions.

What Will My Audience Already Know about My Topic?

What can you expect a diverse group of readers to know? Whether you are writing on a current issue or a centuries-old debate, you must expect most readers to have some knowledge of the issues. Their knowledge

WHAT IS A COUNTERARGUMENT?

This, simply stated, is the argument that could be made against your position. Don't be fooled, however, into thinking a counterargument is simply the opposite of your position. Many counterarguments are subtle and more complex than you might first assume.

For example, the image here is designed to present a clear argument against drilling for oil in Alaska based on the claim that it would harm the natural habitat of animals. But is the counterargument simply that the drilling would not cause this harm? Or is it more complex than that? Might your opponent concede that some harm may come to the habitat of the polar bear, but that the increase in oil production is worth that sacrifice? Might she claim that not nearly as much harm will come to the native wildlife as many believe? Or might she even claim that this is simply a scare tactic created by those with an interest in maintaining our foreign oil dependence?

When considering potential objections to your argument, you need to analyze your opposition's position fully. What might he raise as potential questions or problems with your position? By fully understanding the complexity of your opponent's position, you will more effectively be able to refute or rebut his objections and ultimately strengthen your own argument.

try it !

Write the opening paragraph of a letter to each audience based on the scenario below. How might your letter differ based on these different potential lenders? Would you use different language? Include different details? Make different promises? Consider how the audience for your argument can completely change your strategy.

WHAT IF?

You decide that you need a new car. But you don't just want any car. You want a brand new, top-of-the-line hybrid. In order to borrow the money to purchase your dream ride, however, you must write a letter that argues why you want and need this vehicle rather than a less expensive model.

Your best friend, who doesn't own a car.

The local banker, whom you've never met.

Your mom, who worries about your safety.

Your uncle, who works for the Environmental Protection Agency.

does not free you from the responsibility of developing your support fully, though. In fact, their knowledge creates further demands. For example, most readers know the main arguments on both sides of the abortion issue. For you to write as if they do not—and thus to ignore the arguments of the opposition—is to produce an argument that probably adds little to the debate on the subject.

On the other hand, what some readers "know" may be little more than an overview of the issues from TV news—or the emotional outbursts of a family member. Some readers may be misinformed or prejudiced, but they embrace their views enthusiastically nonetheless. So as you think about the ways to develop and support your argument, you will have to assess your readers' knowledge and sophistication. This assessment will help you decide how much background information to provide or what false facts need to be revealed and dismissed.

Where Does My Audience Stand on the Issue?

Expect readers to hold a range of views, even if you are writing to students on your campus or to an organization of which you are a member. It is not true, for instance, that all students want coed dorms or pass/fail grading. And if everyone already agrees with you, you have no reason to write. An argument needs to be about a topic that is open to debate. So you will need to make these assumptions:

- Some of your audience will probably never agree with you but may offer you grudging respect if you compose an effective argument. If you know you hold an unpopular position, your best strategy will be a conciliatory approach (see page 76 for a discussion of the conciliatory argument).

- Some readers will not hold strong views on your topic and may be open to convincing if you present a good case.

- Those who share your views will still be looking for a strong argument in support of their position.

Your audience may cling not only to their positions on an issue, but also to their values, beliefs, and morals while reading your argument. In order to fully understand why your readers might hold their positions, you should attempt to uncover what they believe is important in the world. Oftentimes, these values are shaped by a reader's culture, personal experiences, and even religious beliefs. For example, many Americans have been raised to believe that patriotism is an extremely important value. If your argument attempts to challenge this value directly, like the political cartoon does (see page 72), you will need to address the obvious disconnect or you will risk alien-

SEEING THE ARGUMENT

What do you think the intended audience for this print ad values or believes? Understanding the values of your target readers can help you focus your argument and choose strategies that will be effective in persuading them to believe as you do.

ating your readers who do not believe as you do. If everyone already agrees with you, you have no reason to write. An argument needs to be about a topic that is open to debate.

As you read the cartoon, imagine how it might be received by various audiences—a soldier coming home from the war in Iraq, an anti-war protester on a college campus, a veteran's widow, and so on. Do you think every audience member would see the humor in this

Most readers already know the main arguments on both sides of the abortion debate and realize that the issue is not as simple as this poster would have you believe. Ignoring the prior knowledge and experience of your readers can not only insult their intelligence, but can also work against your own credibility.

Is this poster convincing in presenting a pro-life position? Would it convince someone who has traditionally held a pro-choice point of view to change his or her position? Or would it be viewed as an oversimplification of a complex and important issue?

S EE ING THE ARGUMENT

SEEING THE ARGUMENT

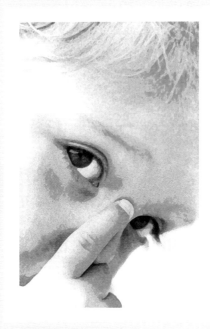

WHO WOULD KILL THIS CHILD?

argument? Might some audience members feel that the author is failing to understand their values and beliefs? Does this cartoon make a compelling argument in your mind?

How Should I Speak to My Audience?

Your audience will form an opinion of you based on how you write and how you reason. The image of argument—and the arguer—that we have been creating in this text's discussion is one of thoughtful claims defended with logic and evidence. However, the heated debate at yesterday's lunch does not resemble this image of argument. Sometimes the word *persuasion* is used to separate the emotionally charged debate from the calm, intellectual tone of the academic argument. Unfortunately, this neat division between argument and persuasion does not describe the real world of debate. The thoughtful arguer also wants to be persuasive, to win over the audience. And highly emotional presentations can contain relevant facts in support of a sound idea. Instead of thinking of two separate categories—argument and persuasion—think instead of a continuum from the most rigorous logic at one end to

www.russmo.com. Reprinted with permission.

extreme flights of fantasy on the other. Figure 4.1 suggests this continuum with different kinds of arguments placed along it.

| Rigorously objective language | Thoughtful, restrained language | A combination of reason and various clever strategies with language | Strong appeals to emotion |

figure 4.1 A Continuum of Argumentative Language

Where should you place yourself along the continuum in the language you choose and the tone you create? You will have to answer this question with each specific writing context. Much of the time you will choose "thoughtful, restrained language" as expected by the academic community, but there may be times that you will use various persuasive strategies. Probably you will not select "strong appeals to emotion" for your college or workplace writing. Remember that you have different roles in your life, and you use different voices as appropriate to each role. Most of the time, for most of your arguments, you will want to use the serious voice you normally select for serious conversations with other adults. This is the voice that will help you establish your credibility, your *ethos*.

http://www.mhhe.argument/fromtheauthor

GOOD ADV!CE

Irony or Sarcasm?

As you learned in Chapter 2, irony is a useful rhetorical strategy for giving your words greater emphasis by writing the opposite of what you mean. Many writers use irony effectively to give punch to their arguments. Irony catches our attention, makes us think, and engages us with the text. Sarcasm is not quite the same as irony. Irony can cleverly focus attention on life's complexities; sarcasm is more often vicious than insightful, relying on harsh, negative word choice. Probably in most of your academic work, you will want to avoid sarcasm, and you will want to think carefully about the effect of any strongly worded appeal to your readers' emotions. Better to persuade your audience with the force of your reasons and evidence than to lose them because of the static of mean language. But the key, always, is to know your audience and understand how best to present a convincing argument to them.

CONGRATULATIONS. YOU BROKE THE CODE. IF YOU PRESS THE ELEVATOR BUTTON 3 TIMES AFTER IT'S ALREADY BEEN PRESSED, IT GOES INTO "HURRY" MODE.

REALLY?

Sarcasm and stupidity meet at the elevator.

Understand Your Writing Purpose

There are many kinds of arguments. As you consider possible topics, think about what you would want to do with each topic—beyond writing convincingly in defense of your claim. Different types of arguments require different approaches or different kinds of evidence. Here are some useful ways to classify arguments:

- **Inductive argument or investigative paper such as those in the social sciences:** If you are given an assignment to collect evidence in an organized way to support a claim about a topic such as advertising strategies or violence in children's programming, then you will be writing an investigative paper, presenting evidence that you have gathered and analyzed to support your claim.

- **Claim of values or position paper:** If you are given the assignment to argue for your position on a topic such as euthanasia, trying juveniles as adults, or national identification cards, you need to recognize that this assignment calls for a claim of values. You will be writing a rather philosophical argument, presenting reasons in support of a complex, controversial issue. You will need to pay close attention to your warrants or assumptions.

- **A definition argument:** If you are asked to consider the qualities or traits we should look for in a president or professor, you are really being asked to define "a good president" or "a good professor." Some of your points may seem quite concrete—practical—to you, but your specifics are really tied to an ideal you imagine, and that ideal is best understood as a definition.

- **A problem/solution argument or claim of policy:** You are being asked to recommend solutions to a current problem, if you are asked to answer the broad question, What should we do about . . . ? What should we do about students' disruptive behavior? About gridlock on your town's streets? These kinds of questions ask for different types of answers than do questions about what traits make a good president or who are the greatest athletes.

- **A refutation or rebuttal of someone else's argument:** If you are given the assignment to find a letter to the editor, a newspaper editorial, or an essay in your textbook with which you disagree, you are being asked to prepare a refutation essay, a specific challenge to a specific argument. You will repeatedly refer to the work you are rebutting, so you will need to know that work thoroughly.

Understand at the beginning of your planning just what kind of argument you have chosen, and you will write more effectively.

Move from Topic to Claim to Possible Support

When you write a letter to the editor of a newspaper, you have chosen to respond to someone else's argument that has bothered you. In this writing context, you already know your topic and probably your claim as well. You also know that your purpose will be to refute the article you have read. In composition classes, the context is not always so clearly established, but you will usually be given some guidelines with which to get started.

Selecting a Topic

Suppose that you are asked to write an argument that is in some way connected to First Amendment rights. Your instructor has limited and focused your topic choice and purpose. Start thinking about possible topics that relate to freedom of speech and censorship issues. To aid your topic search and selection, use one or more invention strategies:

- **Map or cluster:** Connect ideas to the general topic in various spokes, a kind of visual brainstorming.

- **Brainstorm:** Make a list of ideas that come to mind. List absolutely everything and anything that crosses your mind.

- **Read:** In this case, look through the text for ideas, check out online chat rooms or Facebook groups, or conduct informal online research to learn about your topic.

- **Freewrite:** Write without stopping for 10 minutes. Do not edit yourself or correct errors. Just keep writing for the entire time.

Your invention strategies lead, let us suppose, to the following list of possible research questions or topics:

- Administrative restrictions on the college newspaper—should the administration have the right to tell reporters what they can or can't print?

- Hate speech restrictions or code—isn't hate speech exactly what the law was designed to protect?

- Deleting certain books from high school reading lists—can parents of underage students restrict their freedoms?

- Controls and limits on alcohol and cigarette advertising—if it's in the best interest of people, can speech be restricted?

- Restrictions on violent TV programming—should we restrict free speech in order to protect kids from violence?

All of the topics seem to have promise. Which one do you select?

Two considerations should guide you: interest and knowledge. First, your argument is likely to be more thoughtful and lively if you choose an issue that matters to you. You can also appreciate the usefulness of information and ideas on the topic. But unless you have time for study, you are wise to choose a topic about which you already have some information and ideas. To continue the example, let's suppose that you decide to write about television violence because you are concerned about violence in American society and you have given this issue some thought. It is time to phrase your topic as a tentative thesis or claim.

Drafting a Claim or Thesis

Good claim (or thesis) statements will keep you focused in your writing—in addition to establishing your main idea for readers. Give thought, then, both to your position on the issue and to the wording of your claim. Here are some claim statements to avoid:

- Claims using vague words such as *good* or *bad*.

  VAGUE: TV violence is bad for us.

  BETTER: We need more restrictions on violent TV programming.

- Claims in loosely worded two-part sentences.

  UNFOCUSED: Campus rape is a serious problem, and we need to do something about it.

  BETTER: College administrators and students need to work together to reduce both the number of campus rapes and the fear of rape.

- Claims that are not appropriately qualified.

  OVERSTATED: Violence on television is making us a violent society.

  BETTER: TV violence is contributing to viewers' increased fear of violence and insensitivity to violence.

- Claims that do not help you focus on your purpose in writing.

  UNCLEAR PURPOSE: Not everyone agrees on what is meant by violent TV programming.

  (Perhaps this is true, but more importantly, this claim suggests that you will define violent programming. Such an approach would not keep you focused on a First Amendment issue.)

  BETTER: Restrictions on violent TV programs can be justified.

  (Now your claim directs you to the debate over restrictions of content.)

Listing Possible Grounds

As you learned in Chapter 3, you can generate grounds to support a claim by adding a *because* clause after a claim statement. You can start a list of grounds for the topic on violent TV programming by simply freewriting about your topic and thinking of all of the reasons you feel the way that you do. You can also collect images, graphs, and even statistics that you find while doing preliminary research or reading on your topic. The most important thing is to keep a log or journal of your ideas so that you can return to them when you begin to draft your essay.

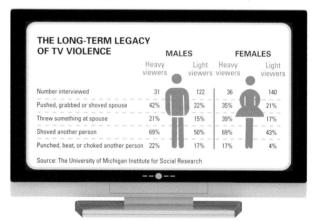

We need more restrictions on violent television programming *because*

1. many people, including children and teens, watch many hours of TV (I will need to get stats for this).

2. people are affected by the dominant activities/experiences in their lives.

3. there is a connection between violent programming and desensitizing and fear of violence and possibly more aggressive behavior in heavy viewers. (I will need to get detail of studies.) Maybe I could use this chart to help:

THE LONG-TERM LEGACY OF TV VIOLENCE

	MALES Heavy viewers	MALES Light viewers	FEMALES Heavy viewers	FEMALES Light viewers
Number interviewed	31	122	36	140
Pushed, grabbed or shoved spouse	42%	22%	35%	21%
Threw something at spouse	21%	15%	39%	17%
Shoved another person	69%	50%	69%	43%
Punched, beat, or choked another person	22%	17%	17%	4%

Source: The University of Michigan Institute for Social Research

4. society needs to protect young people. Everyone will agree with this, right?

You now have four good points to work on, a combination of reasons and inferences drawn from evidence, and even a potential visual for your essay.

Listing Grounds for the Other Side or Another Perspective

Remember that arguments generate counterarguments. Continue your exploration of this topic by considering possible rebuttals to your proposed grounds. How might someone who does not want to see restrictions placed on television programming respond to each of your points? Let's think about them one at a time:

We need more restrictions on violent television programming *because*

1. many people, including children and teens, watch many hours of TV.

   My opposition cannot really challenge this point on the facts, only on its relevance to restricting programming. The opposition might argue that if parents think their children are watching too much TV, they should turn it off. The restriction needs to be a family decision. How will I handle this?

2. people are affected by the dominant activities/ experiences in their lives.

   It seems common sense to expect people to be influenced by dominant forces in their lives. My opposition might argue, though, that many people have the TV on for many hours but often are not watching it intently for all of that time. The more dominant forces in our lives are parents and teachers and peers, not the TV. The opposition might also argue that people seem to be influenced to such different degrees by television that it is not fair or logical to restrict everyone when perhaps only a few are influenced by their TV viewing to a harmful degree. Do I agree with any of these points? Should I concede any of them?

3. there is a connection between violent programming and desensitizing and fear of violence and possibly more aggressive behavior in heavy viewers.

   Some people are entirely convinced by studies showing these negative effects of violent TV programming, but others point to the less convincing studies or make the argument that if violence on TV were really so powerful an influence, most people would be violent or fearful or desensitized. Can I find studies from really reputable sources that will convince even the biggest skeptics? How can I best present my statistics? Can I create an easy-to-read chart or graph?

4. society needs to protect young people.

   My opposition might choose to agree with me in theory on this point—and then turn again to the argument that parents should be doing the protecting. Government controls on programming restrict adults, as well as children, whereas it may only be some children who should watch fewer hours of TV and not watch adult cop shows at all. So what will my response be to this point?

Working through this process of considering opposing views can help you see

- where you may want to do some research for facts to provide backing for your grounds,
- how you can best develop your reasons to take account of typical counterarguments, and
- if you should qualify your claim in some ways.

Considering the Rogerian or Conciliatory Argument

Psychologist Carl Rogers asserts that the most successful arguments take a conciliatory approach. The characteristics of this approach include

- showing respect for the opposition in the language and tone of the argument,
- seeking common ground by indicating specific facts and values that both sides share, and
- qualifying the claim to bring opposing sides closer.

In their essay "Euthanasia—A Critique," Peter A. Singer and Mark Siegler provide a good example of a conciliatory approach. They begin by explaining and then rebutting the two main arguments in favor of euthanasia. After stating the two arguments in clear and neutral language, they write this in response to the first argument:

We agree that the relief of pain and suffering is a crucial goal of medicine. We question, however, whether the care of dying patients cannot be improved without resorting to the drastic measure of euthanasia. Most physical pain can be relieved with the appropriate use of analgesic agents. Unfortunately, despite widespread agreement that dying patients must be provided with necessary analgesia, physicians continue to underuse analgesia in the care of dying patients because of concern about depressing respiratory drive or creating addiction. Such situations demand better management of pain, not euthanasia.

In this paragraph, Singer and Siegler accept the value of pain management among dying patients. They go even further and offer a solution to the problem of suffering among the terminally ill—better pain management by physicians. They remain thoughtful in their approach and tone throughout, while sticking to their position that legalizing euthanasia is not the solution.

Consider how you can use this conciliatory approach to write more effective arguments. It will help you avoid overheated language and maintain your focus on what is doable in a world of differing points of view. After reading these examples, do you agree with the old expression "You can catch more flies with honey than with vinegar"?

This photograph represents a good example of conciliatory argument. In July 2009, controversy ensued when the Cambridge, Massachusetts Police arrested Harvard professor Henry Louis Gates outside his home in response to a neighbor's complaint. A neighbor had previously reported that "two black males with backpacks" were trying to gain entrance to the home. When the police arrived and asked Professor Gates to step outside his residence, he became incensed and began shouting. Sergeant James Crowley arrested Professor Gates for disorderly conduct—a charge that was quickly dropped. Gates, however, threatened legal action against police for their treatment of him.

In an attempt to resolve this conflict, President Obama asked Gates and Crowley to the White House "for a beer." What is the issue here? And what are the two sides of this issue? What are people supposed to see in this image? What is President Obama attempting to accomplish by bringing Gates and Crowley together? Is it important that they are talking out their differences while drinking beer? Why or why not?

S EE ING
THE ARGUMENT

SEEING THE ARGUMENT

Planning Your Approach

Now that you have thought about arguments on the other side, you decide that you want to argue for a qualified claim that is also more precise.

> My thesis:
>
> To protect young viewers, we need restrictions on violence in children's programs and ratings for prime-time adult shows that clearly establish the degree of violence in those shows.

This qualified claim responds to two points of the rebuttals. You haven't given in to the other side but have chosen to narrow the argument to emphasize the protection of children, an area of common ground.

Next, it's time to check some of the articles in your text, your library databases, or even go online to get some supporting data to develop Points 1 and 3. Your research might, for instance, help you find out that

- according to *USAToday*, "There are 2.73 TV sets in the typical home and 2.55 people" (www.usatoday.com/life/television/news/2006-09-21-homes-tv_x.htm)

- according to the American Academy of Child and Adolescent Psychiatry, by the time young people graduate from high school they have spent more time in front of the TV than in the classroom (www.aacap.org/cs/root/facts_for_families/children_and_watching_tv)

- according to the A. C. Nielsen Company, the average number of violent acts seen on TV by the time a child leaves elementary school is over 8,000 (www.csun.edu/science/health/docs/tv&health.html)

You may also find more images, charts, Web sites, or even videos that will help you illustrate and support your points more effectively.

GOOD ADVICE

Be sure to select reliable sources and then cite the sources you use. Citing sources is not only required and right; it is also part of the process of establishing your credibility and thus strengthening your argument. Remember to keep accurate records of each of your images and media files so that you can accurately cite them in your draft.

Finally, how are you going to answer the point about parents controlling their children? You might counter that in theory this is the way it should be—but in reality not all parents are at home watching what their children are watching, and not all parents care enough to pay attention. Furthermore, all of us suffer from the consequences of those children who are influenced by violence on TV, and therefore we, as a society, have a responsibility to protect our citizens. After all, these children grow up to become adults we have to interact with, so the problem is one for the society as a whole to solve, not individual parents. If you had not disciplined yourself to go through the process of listing possible rebuttals, you may not have thought through this part of the debate.

Organizing and Drafting Your Argument

So how will you set up your argument? After you have planned your tentative thesis, your potential claims, your possible support, and your rebuttals to counterarguments, it's time to decide how you will organize your essay. There are several approaches to argument organization. Your organizational plan should depend on what you think will be the most effective way of presenting your position to your audience. Will your reader expect you to immediately address obvious opposing points of view? Or should you lay out your entire position and present solid support before you refute your opponents' objections? Do you need to provide detailed background information about your topic before your reader can fully understand your position? These decisions, like all your writing choices, must be made by you according to your desired goals. Below are two possible organizations for the television violence essay. Which would you choose?

Plan 1: Organizing the Argument

Attention-getting opening (why the issue is important, current, etc.)

Claim statement (thesis)

Reasons and evidence in order from least important to most important

Challenge to potential rebuttals or counterarguments

Conclusion that reemphasizes claim

Plan 2: Organizing the Argument

Attention-getting opening

Claim statement (or possibly leave to the conclusion)

Arguments of opposing position, with my challenge to each

Conclusion that reemphasizes (or states for the first time) my claim

Now that you have chosen an organizational structure for your argument, it's time to get down to the work of actually composing, or drafting, your essay. Typically, writers follow a procedure that includes the following steps in the Good Advice box on page 79.

Revising Your Draft

If you have drafted at the computer, begin revising by printing a copy of your draft. Most of us cannot do

Drafting   Revising   Editing   Proofreading

an adequate job of revision by looking at a computer screen. Then remind yourself that revision is just that: re-vision. Your goal is to see your draft in a new way.

Try not to look at the grammar or spelling at this point. You will not be ready to polish the writing until you are satisfied with the argument. Look first at the total piece.

Do you have all the necessary parts: a claim, support, some response to possible counterarguments? Examine the order of your reasons and evidence. Do some of your points belong, logically, in a different place? Does the order make the most powerful defense of your claim? Be willing to move whole paragraphs around to test the best organization. Also reflect on the argument itself. Have you avoided logical fallacies? Have you qualified statements when appropriate? Do you have enough support? The best support for your argument?

Consider development: Is your essay long enough to meet assignment requirements? Are points fully developed to satisfy the demands of readers? One key to development is the length of your paragraphs. If most of your paragraphs are only two or three sentences, you have not developed the point of each paragraph satisfactorily. It is possible that some paragraphs need to be combined because they are really on the same subtopic. More typically, short paragraphs need further explanation of ideas or examples to illustrate ideas. Compare the following paragraphs for effectiveness:

First Draft of a Paragraph from an Essay on Gun Control

One popular argument used against the regulation of gun ownership is the need of citizens, especially in urban areas where the crime rate is higher, to possess a handgun for personal protection, either carried or kept in the home. Some citizens may not be aware of the dangers to themselves or their families when they purchase a gun. Others, more aware, may embrace the myth that "bad things only happen to other people."

Revised Version of the Paragraph with Statistics Added

One popular argument used against the regulation of gun ownership is the need of citizens, especially in urban areas where the crime rate is higher, to possess a handgun for personal protection, whether it is carried or kept in the home. Although some citizens may not be aware of the dangers to themselves or their families when they purchase a gun, they should be. According to the Center to Prevent Handgun Violence, from their Web page "Firearm Facts," "guns that are kept in the home for self-protection are 22 times more likely to kill a family member or friend

http://www.mhhe.argument/fromtheauthor

GOOD ADVICE

Guidelines for Drafting

- Try to write a complete draft of an essay in one sitting, so that you can "see" the whole piece.

- If you can't think of a clever opening, state your claim and move on to the body of your essay. After you draft your reasons and evidence, a good opening may occur to you.

- If you find that you need something more in some parts of your essay, leave extra space as a reminder that you will need to return to those paragraphs later.

- Try to avoid using a dictionary or thesaurus while drafting. Your goal is to get the ideas down. You will polish later.

- Learn to draft at your computer. Revising is so easy on a PC that you will be more willing to make significant changes. If you are handwriting your draft, leave plenty of margin space for additions or for directions to shift parts around.

than to kill in self-defense." The Center also reports that guns in the home make homicide three times more likely and suicide five times more likely. We are not thinking straight if we believe that these dangers only apply to others.

A quick trip to the Internet has provided this student with some facts to support his argument. Observe how he has referred informally but fully to the source of his information. (If your instructor requires formal MLA documentation in all essays, then you will need to add a Works Cited page and give a full reference to the Web page.)

Editing

After you make your changes and print another copy, you are ready to begin the editing process. As you read through this time, pay close attention to unity and coherence, to sentence patterns, and to word choice. Read each paragraph as a separate unit to be certain that everything is on the same subtopic. Then look at your use of transition and connecting words, both within and between paragraphs. Ask yourself, Have I guided the reader through the argument? Have I shown how the parts connect by using appropriate connectors such as *therefore, in addition, as a consequence,* and *also*?

Read again, focusing on each sentence, checking to see that you have varied sentence patterns and length. Read sentences aloud to let your ear help you find awkward constructions or unfinished thoughts. Strive as well for word choice that is concrete and specific, avoiding wordiness, clichés, trite expressions, and incorrect use of specialized terms. Observe how Samantha edited one paragraph in her essay "Balancing Work and Family":

Draft Version of Paragraph

Women have come a long way in equalizing themselves, but inequality within marriages do exist. One reason for this can be found in the media. Just last week America turned on their televisions to watch a grotesque dramatization of skewed priorities. On *The Bachelor*, a panel of women vied for the affections of a millionaire who would choose one of them to be his wife. This show said that women can be purchased. Also that men must provide and that money is worth the sacrifice of one's individuality. The show also suggests that physical attraction is more important than the building of a complete relationship. Finally, the show says that women's true value lies in their appearance. This is a dangerous message to send to both men and women viewers.

Edited Version of Paragraph

Although women have come a long way toward equality in the workplace, inequality within marriages can still be found. The media may be partly to blame for this continued inequality. Just last week Americans watched a grotesque dramatization of skewed priorities. On a popular television show called *The Bachelor*, a panel of women vied for the affections of a millionaire who would choose one of them to be his wife. Such displays teach us that women can be purchased, that men must be the providers, that the desire for money is worth the sacrifice of one's individuality, that physical attraction is more important than a complete relationship, and that women's true value lies in their appearance. These messages discourage marriages based on equality and mutual support.

Samantha's editing has eliminated wordiness and vague references and has combined ideas into one forceful sentence. If you have a good argument, you do not want to lose readers because you have not taken the time to polish your writing.

Word Choice and Tone

You have just been advised to check your word choice to eliminate wordiness, vagueness, clichés, and so on. Here is a specific checklist of problems often found in student papers with some ways to fix the problems.

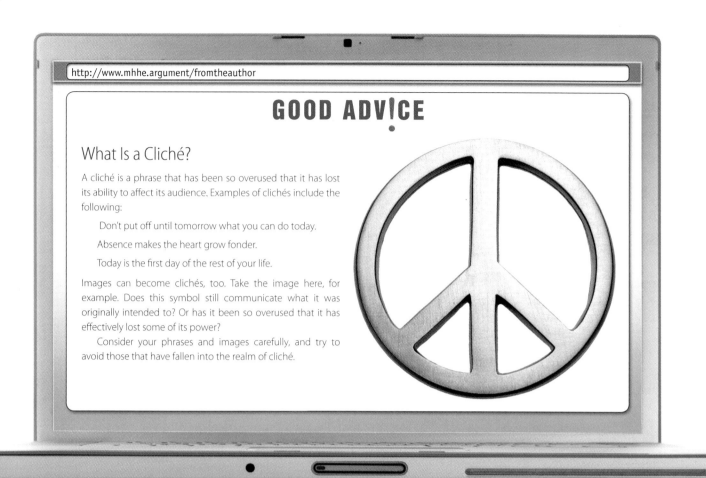

GOOD ADV!CE

What Is a Cliché?

A cliché is a phrase that has been so overused that it has lost its ability to affect its audience. Examples of clichés include the following:

> Don't put off until tomorrow what you can do today.

> Absence makes the heart grow fonder.

> Today is the first day of the rest of your life.

Images can become clichés, too. Take the image here, for example. Does this symbol still communicate what it was originally intended to? Or has it been so overused that it has effectively lost some of its power?

Consider your phrases and images carefully, and try to avoid those that have fallen into the realm of cliché.

- **Eliminate clichés.** Do not write about "the fast-paced world we live in today" or the "rat race." First, do you know for sure that the pace of life for someone who has a demanding job is any faster than it was in the past? Using time effectively has always mattered. Also, clichés suggest that you are too lazy to find your own words.

- **Avoid jargon.** Specialists of any kind have their own language. That's one meaning of jargon, and if the audience is other specialists, it can be appropriate. However, some nonspecialists fill their writing with heavy-sounding terms to give the appearance of significance. Watch for any overuse of "scientific" terms such as *factor* or *aspect*, and other vague, awkward language.

- **Avoid language that is too informal for most of your writing contexts.** What do you mean when you write, "*Kids* today watch too much TV"? Alternatives include *children, teens, adolescents*. These words are both less slangy and more precise.

- **Avoid nasty attacks on the opposition.** Change "those jerks who are foolish enough to believe that TV violence has no impact on children" to language that explains your counterargument

without attacking those who may disagree with you. After all, you want to change the thinking of your audience, not make them resent you for name-calling.

- **Avoid all discriminatory language.** In the academic community and the adult workplace, most people are bothered by language that belittles any one group. This includes language that is racist or sexist or reflects negatively on people because of age, disability, sexual orientation, or religious beliefs. Just don't use it!

Proofreading

You also do not want to lose the respect of readers because your paper is filled with "little" errors—errors in punctuation, mechanics, and word choice. Most readers will forgive one or two little errors but will become annoyed if they begin to pile up. So after you are finished rewriting and editing, print a copy of your paper and read it slowly, looking specifically at punctuation, at the handling of quotations and references to writers and titles, and at those pesky words that come in two or more versions: *to, too,* and *two; here* and *hear; their, there,* and *they're;* and so forth. Your

During the 2008 presidential campaign, attack ads like these were posted on multiple blogs and online sites, as well as worn on T-shirts. Do you think this strategy was wise? What are the risks involved in attacking your opponent in this way?

S
EE
ING
THE ARGUMENT

SEEING THE ARGUMENT

JOHN McCAIN
LIARLIAR

TRUST ME

rockhate.com

http://www.mhhe.argument/fromtheauthor

GOOD ADV!CE

A Checklist for Revision/Editing/Proofreading

☐ Have I selected an issue and purpose consistent with assignment guidelines?

☐ Have I stated a claim that is focused, appropriately qualified, and precise?

☐ Have I developed sound reasons and evidence in support of my claim?

☐ Have I used Toulmin terms to help me study the parts of my argument, including rebuttals to counterarguments?

☐ Have I taken advantage of a conciliatory approach and emphasized common ground with opponents?

☐ Have I found a clear and effective organization for presenting my argument?

☐ Have I edited my draft thoughtfully, concentrating on producing unified and coherent paragraphs and polished sentences?

☐ Have I eliminated wordiness, clichés, and jargon?

☐ Have I selected an appropriate tone for my purpose and audience?

☐ Have I used my word processor's spell checker and proofread a printed copy with great care?

computer spell checker can't tell if the wrong version has been used.

If instructors have found these kinds of errors in your papers over the years, then focus your attention on the specific kinds of errors you have been known to make. Use a glossary of usage in a handbook for problems with homonyms (words that sound alike but have different meanings), and check a handbook for punctuation rules. Take pride in your work and present a paper that will be treated with respect. The Good Advice box on page 82 contains a checklist of the key points for writing good arguments.

making connections

let's review

After reading this chapter, you should understand the following points:

- Effective essays are written in a style and tone that are suited to both the audience and the writer's purpose.

- Your readers may hold very clear opinions about your topic, reject certain ideas based on value systems they were raised with, or automatically accept the validity of your claims based on their beliefs or experiences.

- Different types of arguments require different approaches or different kinds of evidence.

- Two considerations should guide your topic choice: interest and knowledge. Your argument is likely to be more thoughtful and lively if you choose an issue that matters to you.

- Good claim (or thesis) statements will keep you focused in your writing—in addition to establishing your main idea for readers.

- There are several approaches to argument organization. Your organizational plan should depend on what you think will be the most effective way of presenting your position to your audience.

- Revision is just that: re-vision. Your goal is to see your draft in a new way.

- Editing focuses on issues such as unity and coherence, sentence patterns, and word choice.

- Proofreading focuses on "little errors" such as errors in punctuation, mechanics, and word choice.

connect

Individually or in a small group, read the following essay by Deborah Tannen and answer the questions that follow.

We Need Higher Quality Outrage

Deborah Tannen

University professor and professor of linguistics at Georgetown University, Deborah Tannen has written popular books on the use of language by ordinary people. Among her many books are You Just Don't Understand *(1990),* Talking from 9 to 5 *(1994),* I Only Say This Because I Love You *(2004), and* You're Wearing THAT? *(2006). The following article was published October 22, 2004, in the* Christian Science Monitor. *Even though it refers to former President Bush's campaign, think about its implications to our nation's most recent election. Do Tannen's arguments still apply?*

We need to ratchet up the level of opposition in our public and private discourse.

This statement may seem surprising, coming from someone who wrote a book, *The Argument Culture*, claiming that the rise of opposition is endangering our civil life. Why do I now say we need more? The key is what I call "agonism": ritualized opposition, a knee-jerk, automatic use of warlike formats.

Agonism obliterates and obfuscates real opposition. When there's a ruckus in the street outside your home, you fling open the window and see what's happening. But if there's a row outside every night, you shut the window and try to block it out. That's what's happening in our public discourse. With all the shouting, we have less, rather than more, genuine opposition—the kind that is the bedrock on which democracy rests.

Agonism grows out of our conviction that opposition is the best, if not the only, path to truth. In this view, the best way to explore an idea is a debate that requires opponents to marshal facts and arguments for one side, and ignore, ridicule, or otherwise undermine facts and arguments that support the other side.

Many journalists prize two types of agonism: One is the value of attack over other modes of inquiry, such as analyzing, integrating, or simply informing. The other is a seemingly laudable search for "balance," which results in reporting accusations without examining their validity.

Legitimate opposition is quashed when dissension from public policy is branded "hate speech" or unpatriotic. True hate speech stirs passions against members of a group precisely because of their membership in that group. Expressing passionate opposition to—even hatred for—the policies of elected officials is a legitimate, necessary form of engagement in public life. Candidates and individuals may differ—indeed, must differ—on public policy, such as whether invading Iraq enhanced or hampered American security. But questioning the patriotism of those who believe the invasion was a mistake quashes legitimate debate.

We can know others' policies, but we cannot know their motives. Accusing opponents of venal motives makes it easy to dismiss valid criticism. One can decry the fact that many of the contracts for rebuilding Iraq were awarded to Halliburton without claiming that the war was undertaken in order to enrich the company the vice president once led. One can argue that having received medals for heroic deeds in the Vietnam war does not equip John Kerry to execute the war in Iraq without seeking to discredit not only his, but all, Purple Hearts. One can argue that the president is using the Sept. 11 attacks to bolster his public profile without going so far as to claim (as does a message circulating on the Internet) that he played a role in authorizing those attacks. And one can validly defend the way the war was conducted without accusing one's critics of undermining the war efforts.

Agonism leads to the conviction that fights are riveting to watch. Together with ever-diminishing budgets and corporate demands for ever-greater profits, this conviction tempts TV producers to quickly assemble shows by finding a spokesperson for each side—the more extreme, the better—and letting them slug it out. This format leaves no forum for the middle ground, where most viewers are. The result is that the extremes define the issues, problems seem insoluble, and citizens become alienated from the political process.

A single-minded devotion to "balance" also creates the illusion of equivalence where there is none. For example, as shown repeatedly by journalist Ross Gelbspan as well as in a recent article by Maxwell and Jules Boykoff in the academic journal *Global Environment Change*, news coverage of global warming actually ends up being biased because news reports of scientists' mounting concern typically also feature prominently one of the few "greenhouse skeptics" who declare the concern bogus. This "balanced" two-sides approach gives the impression that scientists are evenly divided, whereas in fact the vast majority agree that the dangers of global climate change are potentially grave.

Take, too, the current bemoaning of negativity in the presidential campaign. Given the devotion to "balance," reports tend to juxtapose negative statements from both sides. But negativity comes in many forms. Attacks on an opponent's character distract attention from the issues that will be decided in the election. Attacks on an opponent's proposed and past policies are appropriate; we need more of such attention to policy.

The preoccupation with balance plays a role here, too. If the goal is only ensuring balance, then journalists can feel their work is done when they have reported accusations flung from each side, abnegating the responsibility to examine the validity of the attacks.

Ironically, while the press is busy gauging who's ahead and who's behind in the contest, significant opposition is left out. Martin Walker, of United Press International, notes that when President Bush addressed the United Nations last month, newspapers in every country other than our own—including our British allies and papers such as the French *Le Figaro*, which supported the invasion of Iraq—reported the event as a duel, with President Bush on one side and UN Secretary-General Kofi Annan or the international community on the other. The American press, whether they are supportive or critical of the president's speech, ignored the oppositional context and reported on his speech alone.

This downplaying of genuine opposition is mirrored in our private conversations. In many European countries, heated political discussions are commonplace and enjoyed; most Americans regard such conversations as unseemly arguments, so they avoid talking politics—especially with anyone whose views differ, or are unknown, lest they inadvertently spark a conflict or offend someone who disagrees.

As a result, we aren't forced to articulate—and therefore examine—the logic of our views, nor are we exposed to the views of those with whom we disagree. And if young people don't hear adults having intense, animated political discussions, the impression that politics has no relevance to their lives is reinforced. Surely this contributes to the woefully low voter turnout among young Americans.

The Yugoslavian-born poet Charles Simic has said, "There are moments in life when true invective is called for, when it becomes an absolute necessity, out of a deep sense of justice, to denounce, mock, vituperate, lash out, in the strongest possible language."

We have come to such a moment. Leaving aside invective, vituperation, and mockery, I believe that we need space for peaceful yet passionate outrage. The challenges we face are monumental. Among them are the spread of nuclear weapons, the burgeoning number of individuals and groups who see the United States as a threat, and the question of how far to compromise our liberties and protections in the interest of security.

On the domestic side, the challenges include the impending insolvency of Medicare and social security, the rising number of working Americans with no health insurance, and the question of whether the checks and balances provided by the three branches of government should be strengthened or weakened.

In the face of challenges of these proportions, we can no longer afford to have voices of true opposition muted by the agonistic din.

QUESTIONS FOR READING

1. What is Tannen's subject? Be precise.

2. What does the term *agonism* mean? What is the typical response to agonism?

3. What are the two types of agonism embraced by journalists?

4. What are the characteristics of "attack" journalism? What are the consequences of this approach to the news? What is the problem with the "balanced" approach to reporting the news?

QUESTIONS FOR REASONING AND ANALYSIS

1. Examine Tannen's examples of attack journalism. What makes them effective?

2. Analyze her two examples of balanced journalism. What makes them effective? Observe that the author does not state a presidential preference. Is it possible to infer her preference?

3. Analyze the author's conclusion—her last four paragraphs. Study her lists of problems and her word choice. Is this an effective ending? Does she drive home her point and get the reader's attention focused on the problem she has examined? Why or why not?

QUESTIONS FOR REFLECTING AND WRITING

1. Look again at Tannen's list of problems at the conclusion of her argument. Would you make the same list of problems that we need to be debating? If not, what would you add? Delete? Why?

2. Does Tannen's objection to the balanced approach to reporting make sense to you? Agree or disagree and defend your choice.

3. Which form of agonism might most distort issues for the public? Why? Defend your choice.

⚠ CAUTION

SLIPPERY SLOPE

more about argument: induction, deduction, analogy, and logical fallacies

chapter 5

"Ozy and Millie" www.ozyandmillie.org ©2007 D.C. Simpson

Reprinted by permission of Dana Claire Simpson, OzyAndMillie.com.

You can build on your knowledge of the basics of argument, examined in Chapter 3, by understanding some traditional forms of argument: induction, deduction, and analogy. It is also important to recognize arguments, like the one in the cartoon here, that do not work due to a logical error or flaw.

Induction

Induction is the process by which we reach inferences—opinions based on facts or on a combination of facts and less-debatable inferences. The inductive process moves from particular to general, from support to assertion. We base our inferences on the facts we have gathered and studied. In general, the more evidence, the more convincing the argument. No one wants to debate tomorrow's sunrise; the evidence for counting on it is too convincing. Most inferences, though, are drawn from less evidence, so we need to examine inductive arguments closely to judge their reasonableness.

The pattern of induction is easy to understand if you image the following scenario:

You have been assigned as the prosecuting attorney in a case against Mr. Jones. You are presented with his file which includes all of the evidence gathered against him. In court, you make the following argument:

"Ladies and gentlemen of the jury, the EVIDENCE is as follows:

- There is the dead body of Smith.
- Smith was shot in his bedroom between the hours of 11:00 p.m. and 2:00 a.m., according to the coroner.
- Jones was seen, by a neighbor, entering the Smith home at around 11:00 the night of Smith's death.
- A coworker heard Smith and Jones arguing in Smith's office the morning of the day Smith died.

- Smith was shot by a .32-caliber pistol.
- The .32-caliber pistol left in the bedroom contains Jones's fingerprints.

This evidence leads to a logical conclusion (CLAIM) that Jones killed Smith."

The facts are presented. The jury infers that Jones is a murderer. Unless there is a confession or a trustworthy eyewitness, the conclusion is an inference, not a fact. This is the most logical explanation; that is, the conclusion meets the standards of simplicity and frequency while accounting for all of the known evidence.

As you write your own arguments, you may want to try to organize your points around an inductive pattern of reasoning. You can build your case by pointing to logical and sound evidence and then reaching a logical and well-supported conclusion.

try it!

Collaborative Exercise: Induction
With your class partner or in small groups, find evidence (make a list of facts or find images in magazines or online) that could be used to support each of the following inferences:

1. Whole-wheat bread is nutritious.

2. Fido must have escaped under the fence during the night.

3. Sue must be planning to go away for the weekend.

4. Students who do not hand in all essay assignments fail Dr. Bradshaw's English class.

5. The price of Florida oranges will go up in grocery stores next year.

Examine how the advertisement here uses inductive reasoning to make its argument. Consider how the author chooses images and the placement of those images to provide points of support that allow the reader to reach the logical conclusion that watching movies on Sony televisions is just like being there, amidst the action. Does this conclusion (or inference) seem justified by the images the author chooses to include? Does the author need to directly state this conclusion or does the audience simply reach it by examining the evidence presented? Think about how you might use images in your own arguments to provide points of support.

Deduction

Although induction can be described as an argument that moves from particular to general, from facts (evidence) to inference (claim), deduction cannot accurately be described as the reverse. Deductive arguments are more complex.

Deduction is the reasoning process that moves the reader from a set of premises (or ideas) to the logical conclusion that must be true if the premises are true.

In other words, your job in using deductive reasoning is to provide your readers with premises that they can assume to be true and then show how your conclusion must be true based on those premises.

For example, suppose, on the way out of American history class, you have the following conversation with your classmate:

Wow. I never realized that Nelson Mandela is such a great leader.

Why do you think he is a great leader?

Well, because he performed with courage and a clear purpose in a time of crisis!

Hmm . . . I guess it is true that people who perform that way in a time of crisis are great leaders. And we just learned about how Mandela did perform with courage and purpose, so I guess you're absolutely right—he IS a great leader!

Your explanation of your claim rests on the fact that your reader believes (1) that people who perform with courage and conviction in a time of crisis are great leaders and (2) that Nelson Mandela performed this way. If your reader believes that both of these statements are true, she must accept that Mandela is a great leader. You have convinced her using deductive reasoning!

The two reasons (or statements your reader must assume are true) are called *premises*. The broader one, called the *major premise*, is written first and the more specific one, the *minor premise*, comes next.

MAJOR PREMISE: All people who perform with courage and a clear purpose in a crisis are great leaders.

MINOR PREMISE: Nelson Mandela is a person who performed with courage and a clear purpose in a crisis.

CONCLUSION: Nelson Mandela is a great leader.

PENGUINS ARE BLACK AND WHITE.
SOME OLD TV SHOWS ARE BLACK AND WHITE.
THEREFORE, SOME PENGUINS ARE OLD TV SHOWS.

GLASBERGEN

**Logic: another thing that
penguins aren't very good at.**

Reprinted by permission of Randy Glasbergen.

If these two premises are correctly, that is, logically, constructed, then the conclusion follows logically, and the deductive argument is *valid*.

But be careful! This does not mean that the conclusion is necessarily true. It does mean that if you accept the truth of the premises, then you must accept the truth of the conclusion, because in a valid argument the conclusion follows logically and necessarily.

When composing a deductive argument, your task will be to defend the truth of your premises. Then, if your argument is valid (logically constructed), readers will have no alternative but to agree with your conclusion. If your reader disagrees with your logically constructed argument, then he or she will need to show why one (or more) of your premises isn't true. In other words, your opponent's counterargument will seek to discredit one (or more) of your premises.

Reading and writing valid and true deductive arguments can be tricky. Some deductive arguments merely look right, but the two premises do not lead logically to the conclusion that is asserted. We must read each argument carefully to make certain that the conclusion follows from the premises.

Analogy

The *argument from analogy* is an argument based on comparison. Analogies assert that since A and B are alike in several ways, they must be alike in another way as well. The argument from analogy concludes with an inference, an assertion of a significant similarity in the two items being compared. The other similarities serve as evidence in support of the inference.

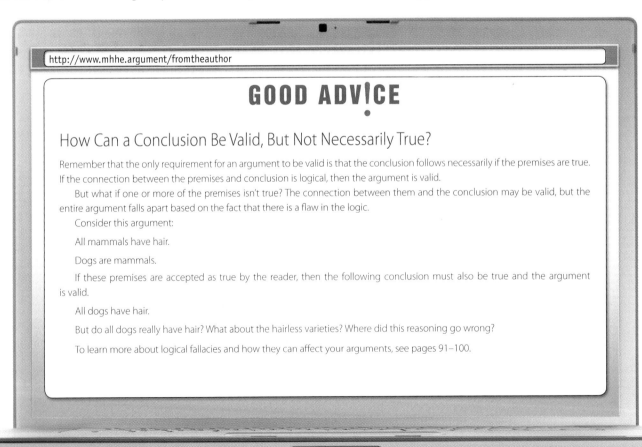

http://www.mhhe.argument/fromtheauthor

GOOD ADV!CE

How Can a Conclusion Be Valid, But Not Necessarily True?

Remember that the only requirement for an argument to be valid is that the conclusion follows necessarily if the premises are true. If the connection between the premises and conclusion is logical, then the argument is valid.

But what if one or more of the premises isn't true? The connection between them and the conclusion may be valid, but the entire argument falls apart based on the fact that there is a flaw in the logic.

Consider this argument:

All mammals have hair.

Dogs are mammals.

If these premises are accepted as true by the reader, then the following conclusion must also be true and the argument is valid.

All dogs have hair.

But do all dogs really have hair? What about the hairless varieties? Where did this reasoning go wrong?

To learn more about logical fallacies and how they can affect your arguments, see pages 91–100.

Exercises: Completing and Evaluating Deductive Arguments

Here is an example of a valid and true argument:

PREMISE: All Jesuits are priests.
PREMISE: No women are priests.
CONCLUSION: No women are Jesuits.

The first premise is true by definition; the term *Jesuit* refers to an order of Roman Catholic priests. The second premise is true for the Roman Catholic Church, so if the term *priest* is used to refer only to people with a religious vocation in the Roman Catholic Church, then the second premise is also true by definition. And if both premises are true, the conclusion must logically and necessarily follow.

Turn each of the following statements into valid deductive arguments. (You have the conclusion and one premise, so you will have to determine the missing premise that would complete the argument.) Then decide which arguments have premises that could be supported. Note the kind of support that might be provided. Explain why you think some arguments have insupportable premises.

1. Mrs. Ferguson is a good teacher (**CONCLUSION**) because she can explain the subject matter clearly (**FIRST PREMISE**).

2. Segregated schools are unconstitutional because they are unequal.

3. Michael must be a good driver because he drives fast.

4. The media clearly have a liberal bias because they make fun of religious fundamentalists.

Although analogy is sometimes an effective approach because clever, imaginative comparisons are often moving, analogy is not as rigorously logical as either induction or deduction. Frequently an analogy is based on only one, two, or possibly three points of comparison, whereas a sound inductive argument likely presents many examples to support its conclusion. Further, to be convincing, the points of comparison must be fundamental to the two items being compared.

Observe one student's argument for a county leash law for cats developed by analogy with dogs. Does it seem logical? Or does it fall short of being a convincing and logical argument?

- Cats are pets, just like dogs.

- Cats live in residential communities, just like dogs.

- Cats can mess up other people's yards, just like dogs.

- Cats, if allowed to run free, can disturb the peace (fighting, howling at night), just like dogs.

- Therefore, cats should be required to walk on a leash, just like dogs.

Does it necessarily follow that cats should be required to walk on a leash, just like dogs? If such a county ordinance were passed, would it be enforceable? Have you ever tried to walk a cat on a leash? In spite of legitimate similarities brought out by the analogy, the conclusion does not logically follow because the arguer is overlooking a fundamental difference in the two animals' personalities. Dogs can be trained to a leash; most cats (Siamese are one exception) cannot be so trained. Such thinking will produce sulking cats and scratched owners. But the analogy, delivered passionately to the right audience, could lead community activists to lobby for a new law.

Observe that the problem with the cat-leash-law analogy is not in the similarities asserted about the items being compared but rather in the underlying assumption that the similarities logically support the argument's conclusion. A good analogy asserts many points of comparison and finds likenesses that are essential parts of the nature or purpose of the two items being compared. The best way to challenge another's analogy is to point out a fundamental difference in the nature or purpose of the compared items. For all of their similarities, when it comes to walking on a leash, cats are not like dogs.

Arguments That Do Not Work: Logical Fallacies

As you can see, if one or more premises of an argument is shown to be untrue or illogical, the entire argument becomes suspect. Readers will not have faith in the conclusion you are reaching if your basic premises are not sound. A thorough study of argument needs to include a study of logical fallacies because so many arguments fail to meet standards of sound logic and good sense. Before examining specific types of arguments that do not work, let's consider briefly why people offer arguments that aren't sensible.

This advertisement below is a good example of an analogy. It claims that choosing a sexual partner is like choosing which jack to plug your phone into. An analogy is being made between the two items, which provides support for the argument that choosing the right sexual partner and sticking with that person will help you avoid getting AIDS.

try it!

Exercises: Analogy

Analyze the following analogies. List the stated and implied points of comparison and the conclusion. Then judge each argument's logic and effectiveness as a persuasive technique. If the argument is not logical, state the fundamental difference in the two compared items. If the argument could be persuasive, describe the kind of audience that might be moved by it.

a. College newspapers should not be under the supervision or control of a faculty sponsor. Fortunately, no governmental sponsor controls *The New York Times,* or we would no longer have a free press in this country. We need a free college press, too, one that can attack college policies when they are wrong.

b. Let's recognize that college athletes are really professional and start paying them properly. College athletes get a free education, and spending money from boosters. They are required to attend practices and games, and—if they play football or basketball—they bring in huge revenues for their "organization." College coaches are also paid enormous salaries, just like professional coaches, and often college coaches are tapped to coach professional teams. The only difference: the poor college athletes don't get those big salaries and huge signing bonuses.

c. Just like any business, the federal government must be made to balance its budget. No company could continue to operate in the red as the government does and expect to be successful. A constitutional amendment requiring a balanced federal budget is long overdue.

Causes of Illogic

Ignorance

One frequent cause for illogical debate is a lack of knowledge of the subject. Some people have more information than others, either from formal study or from wide-ranging experiences. The younger you are, the less you can be expected to know about or understand complex issues. On the other hand, if you want to debate a complex or technical issue, then you cannot use ignorance as an excuse for producing a weak argument. Rather, you will need to conduct solid research in order to be fully educated about your topic.

Egos

Ego problems are another cause of weak arguments. Those with low self-esteem often have difficulty in

debates because they attach themselves to their ideas and then feel personally attacked when someone disagrees with them. Usually the next step is a defense of their views with even greater emotion and irrationality, even though self-esteem is enhanced when others applaud our knowledge and thoughtfulness, not our irrationality. Try to remember that while good arguments often appeal to the emotions of the audience, they do not personally attack readers. You should be able to separate your (or your opponent's) argument from your own sense of worth or level of intelligence.

Prejudices

A third cause of irrationality is the collection of prejudices and biases that we carry around, having absorbed them ages ago from family and community. Prejudices range from the worst ethnic, religious, or sexist stereotypes to political views we have adopted uncritically (Democrats are all bleeding hearts; Republicans are all rich snobs), to perhaps less serious but equally insupportable notions (if it's in print, it must be right; if it's not meat and potatoes, it is not really dinner). People who see the world through distorted lenses cannot possibly assess facts intelligently and reason logically from them. For example, look at the sign above. Consider how this argument responds to deeply held prejudices about the issue of homosexuality. Might readers reject this author's point based on their own prejudiced point of view?

A Need for Answers

Finally, many bad arguments stem from a human need for answers—any answers—to the questions that deeply concern us. We want to control our world because that makes us feel secure, and having answers makes us feel in control. This need can lead to illogic

This poster attempts to make a case against teaching evolution. But is this argument grounded in a solid understanding of evolutionary theory? Might this argument be perceived by some readers as flawed due to the author's ignorance?

from oversimplifying problems or refusing to settle for qualified answers to questions.

The causes of illogic lead us to a twofold classification of bad arguments: logical fallacies that result from (1) oversimplifying the issue or (2) ignoring the issue by substituting emotion for reason.

Fallacies That Result from Oversimplifying
Errors in Generalizing

Errors in generalizing include overstatement and hasty or faulty generalization. All have in common an error in the inductive pattern of argument. The inference drawn from the evidence is unwarranted, either because too broad a generalization is made or because the generalization is drawn from incomplete or incorrect evidence. *Overstatement* occurs when the argument's assertion is an unqualified generalization—that is, it refers to all members of a category or class, although the evidence justifies an assertion about only some of the class. Overstatements often result from stereotyping, giving the same traits to everyone in a group. Overstatements are frequently signaled by words such as *all, every, always, never,* and *none.* In addition, assertions such as "children love clowns" are understood to refer to all children, even though the word *all* does not appear in the sentence. It is the writer's task to qualify statements appropriately, using words such as *some, many,* or *frequently.* Overstatements are discredited by finding only one exception to disprove the assertion. One frightened child who starts to cry when the clown approaches will destroy the argument.

The following reading is another example, from LiveScience.com. See if you can find the generalizations that are being made.

Why Teens Are Lousy at Chores

LiveScience Staff
May 17, 2005

Finally researchers have come up with a reason other than pure laziness for why teenagers can't shower *and* brush their teeth or unload the dishwasher *and* wipe down the counter.

Blame it on "cognitive limitations." Their brains can't multitask as well as those of the taskmasters.

Trust, however, that they'll grow out of it.

The part of the brain responsible for multitasking continues to develop until late adolescence, with cells making connections even after some children are old enough to drive, according to a new study in the May/June issue of the journal *Child Development.*

The frontal cortex, which starts just behind the eyes and goes back almost to the ears, figures out (or doesn't) what to do when a person is asked to juggle multiple pieces of information. Imagine, then, how "make your bed and bring the laundry down" might befuddle a 13-year-old.

In one of the study's tests, subjects between ages 9 and 20 were given multiple pieces of information, then asked to re-order the information to formulate an accurate response to a question. In another of several tests, they were asked to find hidden items using a high degree of strategic thinking.

The ability to remember multiple bits of information developed through age 13 to 15, the study found. But strate-

gic self-organized thinking, the type that demands a high level of multi-tasking skill, continues to develop until ages 16 to 17.

The notion is not entirely new. Brain imaging has suggested as much.

"Our findings lend behavioral support to that work and indicate that the frontal lobe is continuing to develop until late adolescence in a manner that depends upon the complexity of the task that is being demanded," said lead researcher Monica Luciana, an associate professor of psychology at the University of Minnesota.

Unfortunately the study did not reveal any solution to parents at their wits' end over the problem. But Luciana did offer this advice:

"We need to keep their cognitive limitations in mind, especially when adolescents are confronted with demanding situations in the classroom, at home, or in social gatherings."

Hasty or faulty generalizations may be qualified assertions, but they still oversimplify by arguing from insufficient evidence or by ignoring some relevant evidence. Here are examples:

- Lawyers are only interested in making money.

  (What about lawyers who work to protect consumers, or public defenders who take care of those unable to pay for a lawyer?)

- Political life must lead many to excessive drinking. In the last six months the paper has written about five members of Congress who either have confessed to alcoholism or have been arrested on DUI charges.

  (Five is not a large enough sample from which to generalize about *many* politicians. Also, the five in the newspaper are not a representative sample; they have made the news because of their drinking.)

Forced Hypothesis

The *forced hypothesis* is also an error in inductive reasoning. The explanation (hypothesis) offered to account for a particular situation is "forced," or illogical, because either (1) sufficient evidence does not exist to draw any conclusion or (2) the evidence can be explained more simply or more sensibly by a different hypothesis. This logical fallacy often results from failure to consider other possible explanations. You discredit a forced hypothesis by providing alternative conclusions that are more sensible or just as sensible as the one offered. Consider the following example:

- Professor Redding's students received either As or Bs last semester. He must be an excellent teacher.

  (The grades alone cannot support the conclusion. Professor Redding could be an excellent teacher; he could have started with excellent students; he could be an easy grader.)

Non Sequitur

The term *non sequitur,* meaning "it does not follow," could apply to all arguments that do not work, but the term is usually reserved for those arguments in which the conclusions are not logically connected to the reasons, those arguments with the glue missing. In a hasty generalization, for example, there is a connection between support (five politicians in the news) and conclusion (many politicians with drinking problems), just not a convincing connection. With the non sequitur there is no recognizable connection, because either (1) whatever connection the arguer sees is not made clear to others or (2) the evidence or reasons offered are irrelevant to the conclusion. For example:

- Donna will surely get a good grade in physics; she earned an A in her biology class.

  (Doing well in one course, even one science course, does not support the conclusion that the student will get a good grade in another course. If Donna is not good at math, she definitely will not do well in physics.)

Slippery Slope

The *slippery slope* argument asserts that we should not proceed with or permit A because, if we do, the terrible consequences X, Y, and Z will occur. This type of argument oversimplifies by assuming, without evidence and usually by ignoring historical examples, existing laws, or any reasonableness in people, that X, Y, and Z will follow inevitably from A. This kind of argument rests on the belief that most people will not want the final, awful Z to occur. The belief, however accurate, does not provide a sufficiently good reason for avoiding A. One of the best-known examples of slippery slope reasoning can be found in the gun-control debate:

- If we allow the government to register handguns, next it will register hunting rifles; then it will prohibit all citizen ownership of guns, thereby creating a police state or a world in which only outlaws have guns.

  (Surely no one wants the final dire consequences predicted in this argument. However, handgun registration does not mean that these consequences will follow. The United States has never been a police state, and its system of free elections guards against such a future. Also,

citizens have registered cars, boats, and planes for years without any threat of these belongings being confiscated.)

False Dilemma

The *false dilemma* oversimplifies an issue by asserting only two alternatives when there are more than two. The either–or thinking of this kind of argument can be an effective tactic if undetected. If the arguer gives us only two choices and one of those is clearly unacceptable, then the arguer can push us toward the preferred choice. Here is an example:

- The Federal Reserve System must lower interest rates, or we will never pull out of the recession.

S
EE
ING
THE ARGUMENT

SEEING THE ARGUMENT

Look at the following classic slogan used fairly often by political groups. How is this slogan engaging in the false dilemma fallacy? Does it lead the reader to believe that there are only two choices? Is this necessarily a logical claim?

America
Love It Or Leave It!

(Clearly, staying in a recession is not much of a choice, but the alternative may not be the only or the best course of action to achieve a healthy economy. If interest rates go too low, inflation can be triggered. Other options include the government's creating new jobs and patiently letting market forces play themselves out.)

Politicians often try to use this fallacy to their advantage in their campaigns.

False Analogy

When examining the shape of analogy, we also considered the problems with this type of argument. Remember that you challenge a false analogy by noting many differences in the two items being compared or by noting a significant difference that has been ignored.

did you know

The federal government's decision to raise the legal drinking age to 21 was, in the opinion of many, based at least partially on a post hoc fallacy. Read the following excerpt from President Reagan's statement that prompted most states to change their laws. Do you spot the logical fallacy?

> *Now, raising that drinking age is not a fad or an experiment. It's a proven success.*
> *Nearly every state that has raised the drinking age to 21 has produced a significant drop in the teenage driving fatalities. In the state of New Jersey, whose governor made it a very personal crusade for himself, the rate dropped by 26 percent; in Illinois, it has fallen 23 percent; in Michigan, 31 percent. And when the Commission on Drunk Driving submitted its report, it forcefully recommended that all 50 States should make 21 the legal drinking age.*

Source: President Ronald Reagan, 1984
www.madd.org/Parents/Parents/Research/View-Research
.aspx?research=22

Post Hoc Fallacy

The term *post hoc*, from the Latin *post hoc, ergo propter hoc* (literally, "after this, therefore because of it") refers to a common error in arguments about cause. One oversimplifies causation by confusing a time relationship with cause. Reveal the illogic of post hoc arguments by pointing to other possible causes:

- We should throw out the entire city council. Since the members were elected, the city has gone into deficit spending.

  (Assuming that deficit spending in this situation is bad, was it caused by the current city council? Or did the current council inherit debts? Or is the entire region suffering from a recession?)

Exercises: Fallacies That Result from Oversimplifying

1. Here is a list of the fallacies we have examined so far. Make up or collect from your reading, or from the Web, at least one textual or visual example of each fallacy.

   a. Overstatement   f. Slippery slope

   b. Stereotyping   g. False dilemma

   c. Hasty generalization   h. False analogy

   d. Forced hypothesis   i. Post hoc fallacy

   e. Non sequitur

2. Explain what is illogical about each of the following arguments. Then name the fallacy represented. (Sometimes an argument will fit into more than one category. In that case, name all appropriate terms.)

   a. Everybody agrees that we need stronger drunk-driving laws.

   b. The upsurge in crime on Sundays is the result of the reduced rate of church attendance in recent years.

   c. The government must create new jobs. A factory in Illinois has laid off half its workers.

   d. Steve has joined the country club. Golf must be one of his favorite sports.

   e. Blondes have more fun.

   f. You'll enjoy your Volvo; foreign cars never break down.

   g. Gary loves jokes. He would make a great comedian.

   h. The economy is in bad shape because of the Federal Reserve Board. Ever since it expanded the money supply, the stock market has been declining.

   i. Either we improve the city's street lighting, or we will fail to reduce crime.

   j. DNA research today is just like the study of nuclear fission. It seems important, but it's just another bomb that will one day explode on us. When will we learn that government must control research?

   k. To prohibit prayer in public schools is to limit religious practice solely to internal belief. The result is that an American is religiously "free" only in his own mind.

   l. Professor Johnson teaches in the political science department. I'll bet she's another socialist.

   m. Coming to the aid of any country engaged in civil war is a bad idea. Next we'll be sending American troops, and soon we'll be involved in another Vietnam.

   n. We must reject affirmative action in hiring or we'll have to settle for incompetent employees.

Fallacies That Result from Ignoring the Issue

There are many arguments that divert attention from the issue under debate. Of the six discussed here, the first three try to divert attention by introducing a separate issue or sliding by the actual issue; the following three seek diversion by appealing to the audience's emotions or prejudices. In the first three the arguer tries to give the impression of presenting an argument; in the last three the arguer charges forward on emotional manipulation alone.

Begging the Question

To assume that part of your argument is true without supporting it is to *beg the question*. Arguments seeking to pass off as proof statements that must themselves be supported are often introduced with such phrases as "the fact is" (to introduce opinion), "obviously," and "as we can see." Here is an example:

• Clearly, lowering grading standards would be bad for students, so a pass/fail system should not be adopted.

(Does a pass/fail system lower standards? No evidence has been given. If so, is that necessarily bad for students?)

You are said to be "begging the question" when you simply state that you are right because you are right. Consider how you might avoid this illogical reasoning in your own arguments.

Red Herring

The *red herring* debater introduces a side issue or some point that is not relevant to the debate:

• The senator is an honest woman; she loves her children and gives to charities.

(The children and charities are side issues; they do not demonstrate honesty.)

To further illustrate this fallacy, read the following article from *The Baltimore Sun*. Consider how the author brings the issue of a murder victim's family's suffering to the forefront of his argument that the death penalty should exist. But consider the red herring here.

Does the death of the murderer really put an end to the family's suffering? This appeal to the emotions of the reader acts as a distraction, or an effective red herring in this argument. Can you identify any other logical fallacies here that weaken this author's position?

To Murder Victims' Families, Executing Killers Is Justice

Gregory Kane
February 5, 2003

Frederick Anthony Romano remembers the night. More than 15 years later, he remembers it as if it happened within the last week. It was Sunday night, Nov. 1, 1987. Seventeen-year-old Romano had gone to bed. His mother, Betty Romano, was in the house with him and his father, Frederick Joseph Romano. Soon the father received a call from his son-in-law Keith Garvin, a Navy petty officer who had returned to his base in Oceana, Va. Garvin had called his wife, Dawn Garvin, to let her know he had arrived back safely. But there was no answer.

After two calls to his daughter's house, Frederick J. Romano headed to the newlywed couple's White Marsh apartment. He found his daughter beaten, tortured, mutilated and dead.

Frederick A. Romano remembers his mother's panic-filled voice as she talked to his father, of himself grabbing the phone only to hear his father tell him that his older sister had been hurt.

"But he knew she was dead," Frederick A. Romano said yesterday from his Harford County home. Yes, Frederick A. Romano—who prefers to be called just "Fred"—remembers it all. He remembers the man who murdered his sister and two other women—Patricia Antoinette Hirt and Lori Elizabeth Ward—and how he has waited for 15 years for one Steven Howard Oken to, in the younger Romano's words, "meet his maker."

Does the argument presented here highlight the complexity of and multiple perspectives on this important issue? Or does it attempt to divert attention to a more emotionally charged point?

"It's caused a lot of emotional problems for me and my mom and dad," Fred said. "They're on so many drugs to keep themselves calm, it's unbelievable."

That is a suffering death penalty opponents can't or won't understand. The pain of homicide victims' relatives never ends. It chips away at their souls and psyches year after depressing year. So what's the appropriate punishment for that? Death penalty opponents would have us believe that squirreling Oken away in a cell—where Frederick A. and Frederick J. Romano, Betty Romano and Keith Garvin would be among the taxpayers footing the bill for his housing and meals—is punishment enough. If the correctional system offered any college courses, the Romanos and Garvin would pay part of the cost if Oken wanted to take them.

Dawn Garvin never got to finish her education at Harford Community College. Capital punishment foes figure that's justice. Here's what death penalty advocates feel is justice. Execute Oken the week of March 17, as a Baltimore County judge ordered two weeks ago. After Oken is dead, death penalty advocates can then defy death penalty opponents to show us why and in what ways Oken's execution was not justice.

That's what it's about for Fred Romano. He doesn't buy into the closure argument some death penalty advocates make. (It's just as well. Death penalty opponents, ever noble with grief not their own, dismiss the notion of closure, too.) "It won't bring closure," Fred Romano said. "Dawn will never be back. I'm not looking for closure. That's a bad misconception on the part of some people. I want Oken to die for the murder of Dawn, Patricia Hurt and Lori Ward." This isn't even about revenge, another rallying cry of the anti-capital punishment crowd, who chide death penalty advocates for seeking vengeance. "It's justice," Fred Romano said. "It's not revenge." His wife, Vicki Romano, agreed, then elaborated. "Revenge would be going out and killing one of [the murderer's] family members," Vicki Romano said. "The death penalty isn't revenge. It's the law."

Fred Romano believes the man who's supposed to uphold that law, Maryland Attorney General J. Joseph Curran, has inserted himself squarely in the path of Oken's execution. Last week, Curran called for abolishing Maryland's death penalty. His reasons will appear in a separate column Saturday. Fred Romano called Curran after the announcement, to give the attorney general a piece of his mind. Curran, to his credit, called Fred Romano back and heard him out. Curran, Fred Romano said, asked him if he had a problem with a sentence of life without parole as opposed to the death penalty. His response was what you might expect from a guy who organized the Maryland Coalition for State Executions more than a year ago, and who's had the group's Web site (www.mc4se.org) up for two months. "My problem with it is that 10 years from now some other idiot will come along and say life without parole is too harsh," Fred Romano said. "Then they'll pass a bill granting them parole and then we'll have a bunch of murderers walking the streets." In Maryland's bleeding-heart liberal legislature, that's exactly what would happen.

Straw Man

The *straw man* argument attributes to opponents erroneous and usually ridiculous views that they do not hold so that their position can be easily attacked. We can challenge this illogic by demonstrating that the arguer's opponents do not hold those views or by demanding that the arguer provide some evidence that they do:

- Those who favor gun control just want to take all guns away from responsible citizens and put them in the hands of criminals.

    (The position attributed to proponents of gun control is not only inaccurate but actually the opposite of what is sought by gun-control proponents.)

Ad Hominem

One of the most frequent of all appeals to emotion masquerading as argument is the *ad hominem* argument (literally, argument "to the man"). Sometimes the debate turns into an attack on a supporter of the issue; other times, the illogic is found in name-calling. When someone says that "those crazy liberals at the ACLU just want all criminals to go free," or a pro-choice demonstrator screams at those "self-righteous fascists" on the other side, the best retort may be silence, or the calm assertion that such statements do not contribute to meaningful debate.

Common Practice or Bandwagon

To argue that an action should be taken or a position accepted because "everyone is doing it" is illogical. The majority is not always right. Peer pressure is a common use of this fallacy. Frequently when someone is defending an action as ethical on the ground that everyone does it, the action isn't ethical and the defender knows it isn't. The *bandwagon* argument is a desperate one. Here is an example:

- There's nothing wrong with fudging a bit on your income taxes. After all, the superrich don't pay any taxes, and the government expects everyone to cheat a little.

    (First, not everyone cheats on taxes; many pay to have their taxes done correctly. And if it is wrong, it is wrong regardless of the number who do it.)

Ad Populum

Another technique for arousing an audience's emotions and ignoring the issue is to appeal *ad populum*, or "to the people," to the audience's presumed shared values and beliefs. Every Fourth of July, politicians employ this tactic, appealing to God, mother, apple pie, and traditional family values. As with all emotional gimmicks, we need to reject the argument as illogical. Here is an example:

- Good, law-abiding Americans must be sick of the violent crimes occurring in our once godly society. But we won't tolerate it anymore; put the criminals in jail and throw away the key.

    (This does not contribute to a thoughtful debate on criminal justice issues.)

Reprinted by permission of Doug Savage.

Can you spot the straw man fallacy in this political cartoon? What is the author trying to accomplish by presenting President Bush in this light? Remember to be on the lookout for logical fallacies in everyday media. They are often effective because the reader isn't aware of their presence. If, however, the reader understands what the author is attempting to do, the logic of the entire argument falls apart. In writing your own academic arguments, you should always try to avoid these fallacies and logical errors. Otherwise, you risk alienating your audience and losing your credibility as an author.

S
EE
I N G
THE ARGUMENT

SEEING THE ARGUMENT

try it !

Exercises: Fallacies That Result from Ignoring the Issue

1. Here is a list of fallacies that result from ignoring the issue. Make up or collect from your reading (or from the Web) at least one example (either textual or visual) of each fallacy.

   a. Begging the question
   b. Red herring
   c. Straw man
   d. Ad hominem
   e. Common practice or bandwagon
   f. Ad populum

2. Explain what is illogical about each of the following arguments. Then name the fallacy represented.

   a. Gold's book doesn't deserve a Pulitzer Prize. She has been married four times.

   b. I wouldn't vote for him; many of his programs are basically socialist.

   c. Eight out of ten headache sufferers use Bayer to relieve headache pain. It will work for you, too.

   d. We shouldn't listen to Colman McCarthy's argument against liquor ads in college newspapers because he obviously thinks young people are ignorant and need guidance in everything.

   e. My roommate Joe does the craziest things; he must be neurotic.

   f. Since so many people obviously cheat the welfare system, it should be abolished.

   g. She isn't pretty enough to win the contest, and besides she had her nose "fixed" two years ago.

   h. Professors should chill out; everybody cheats on exams from time to time.

   i. The fact is that bilingual education is a mistake because it encourages students to use only their native language and that gives them an advantage over other students.

   j. Don't join those crazy liberals in support of the American Civil Liberties Union. They want all criminals to go free.

   k. Real Americans understand that free trade agreements are evil. Let your representatives know that we want American goods protected.

Consider the following article from the *New York* magazine. This reader is responding to a personal attack on Mariah Carey that was printed in the *New York Daily News*. It is clear that the ad hominem attack on Ms. Carey failed to succeed in persuading this reader and instead may have had the opposite effect by creating a sympathetic point of view. But does this writer himself engage in ad hominem attacks? Think about how these personal attacks on your opponent can hurt your credibility with your readers and ultimately weaken your argument.

« **DAILY Intel** »

Ad Hominem Attack on Mariah Carey in the 'Daily News'

3/18/08 at 12:45 PM | **3** | Comments

Mariah Carey, hurting.
Photo: Getty Images

Dude, *News* editorial board, what's with this 63-word diatribe today?

Cultural note: We see that the warbler Mariah Carey, who has already tied Elvis Presley as the second-place holder of the most No. 1 records, will soon, if her new hit ditty goes to the top of the charts, tie the Beatles as the first-place holder of the most No. 1 records ever.

Man.

That's — that's just wrong.

On so many levels.

Why, exactly, is it wrong, you guys? Because you're a bunch of mostly white old people who don't understand R&B? If you'll recall, your parents thought Elvis and the Beatles were trashy, too. We won't defend Mariah Carey's cultural relevance in comparison to those musical giants — though we do love her. But from now on, you're no longer allowed to wonder why young people think your newspaper is irrelevant.

Off the Charts [NYDN]

S
E E
I N G
THE ARGUMENT
SEEING THE ARGUMENT

⚠ CAUTION!

making connections

let's review

After reading this chapter, you should understand the following:

- You can build on your knowledge of the basics of argument, examined in Chapter 3, by understanding some traditional forms of argument: induction, deduction, and analogy.

- It is also important to recognize arguments that do not work due to a logical error or flaw.

- The inductive process moves from particular to general, from support to assertion.

- Although induction can be described as an argument that moves from particular to general, from facts (or evidence) to inference (claim), deduction cannot accurately be described as the reverse. Deductive arguments are more complex. *Deduction* is the reasoning process that moves the reader from a set of premises (or ideas) to the logical conclusion that must be true if those premises are true.

- When composing a deductive argument, your task will be to defend the truth of your premises.

- The *argument from analogy* is an argument based on comparison. Analogies assert that since A and B are alike in several ways, they must be alike in another way as well.

- A thorough study of argument needs to include a study of logical fallacies because so many arguments fail to meet standards of sound logic and good sense, many for the following reasons:

  - a lack of knowledge of the subject;

  - attaching yourself to your ideas and then feeling personally attacked when someone disagrees with you;

  - having prejudices and biases that come out in your arguments;

  - wanting to control your world by having answers to important questions, leading to oversimplifying problems or refusing to settle for qualified answers to questions; and

  - diverting attention from the issue under debate.

connect

ANALYZING LOGICAL FALLACIES

Examine the following letter to the editor of CollegiateTimes.com. If you think it contains logical fallacies, identify the passages and explain the fallacies.

Letter: Legalization of Drugs Would Solve Many Problems for Government

Stephen Heath
Law Enforcement Against Prohibition
February 8, 2005

In the column "Drug War Wastes Needed Resources" (*CT*, Feb. 4), the author is right on target when suggesting that state lawmakers should change priorities and reprioritize the fight against dangerous drugs. His views are echoed by a growing group of judges and police who believe the best way to deal with dangerous drugs is to legalize them and eliminate the criminal dealers. They have organized as Law Enforcement Against Prohibition (LEAP).

LEAP knows that criminal dealers are the ones who actively market dangerous drugs to minors and who conduct violence in the streets. These criminal dealers require that millions of valuable police hours be wasted in a futile attempt to control illegal drug flow. The only way to control in-demand drugs is to have them in a regulated market. This is how we deal with the risky and most commonly abused drug in America—alcohol.

Legalizing drugs will not solve all of the problems related to drug use and abuse. But we did not end Prohibition in 1934 because alcohol use was without risk. We did it because of the urgent need to put Al Capone and other criminal dealers out of business, as well as move the product into a market that could be easily monitored by authorities. We were then more able to help those who have problems with alcohol, while simultaneously respecting the privacy of those who use the drug responsibly.

It's time for an equally sensible change in policy for the 21st century. It's time to legalize drugs.

SOURCE: www.collegiatetimes.com/stories/4730

Analyze the following letter to the editor published in the Minnesota State University *Mankato Reporter* on May 2, 2006, by a university student. How effectively does the author make his case? How convincing is the evidence that he presents? Do you find this argument effective? What do you think he should have included in the letter? What should he have done differently? Try to answer these questions in detail to be prepared for class discussion.

Letter: Better Things to Worry about Than Smoking

Miles Haefner, Student

Tanner, your sarcastic article on smoking was on par. For real, smoking isn't good for you? I never would have guessed outside of the Target Market commercials, the fresh laws banning smoking in every public space, the constant berating smokers get from others on how disgusting they are. Seriously, I am sick of it. I am not a smoker. My whole family smokes or is addicted to nicotine in some way or another. But me on the other hand is lucky enough to have dodged the black lung bullet and maintained the somewhat healthy life. But does this mean I can look down upon Marlboro Men with a snide comment? Of f—ing course not! Last time I checked, smoking was legal. We aren't selling marijuana in blunt form to 16-year-olds via a cartoon camel. The companies are marketing within the realm of legal to make a profit like every other company on the face of our capitalistic "money, money, money" country.

So who the hell are you to yell at the tobacco companies who are trying to increase their bottom line? You got a problem with tobacco? Then don't smoke and teach your kids not to either! Wow those beer commercials during halftime at the Super Bowl are entertaining and sure made me laugh before I was 21. Those male stiffy help ya outty keep ya boney pills that bombard the airways sure are good also. Dick you got a new sense of pride? Well I'll be damned, I want a little of that pride too! But hey, if the pride lasts for more than 4 hours consult your physician so he can perform emergency surgery. You getting my point MNSU? Our land has more to worry about than whether or not we are smoking. Our baby boomers are notorious smokers and our country seems to be doing alright now. Perhaps instead we should worry about the ridiculous no child left behind, or the fact that more young people (yeah you future leaders) would rather sit on Facebook than read the newspaper to pass the time.

Smoking is as old as the human race in one way or another. Hell, my grandpa used nicotine and lived to 92 years old. Let's quit arguing over tobacco use and start to worry about the real social, economic or political problems that face our country. Let smokers be free and enjoy it as they may. You don't like it? Then quit working at the bar, quit going to the bar, quit bitching about smoke and quit being such a pansy. I'm sorry to all the people with effects from smoke like certain incurable diseases, but what are smokers supposed to do? They don't start with the intent to harm others or themselves. So let people make their own decisions and let's get passed this juvenile argument of cigarettes. We have more to worry and debate about.

SOURCE: http://media.www.msureporter.com/media/storage/paper937/news/2006/05/02/EditorialOpinionletters/Letters.To.The.Editor-2021758.shtml

Top Riding Mowers Under $1600

Popular Mechanics

TECHNOLOGY   SCIENCE   AUTOMOTIVE   HOME   OUTDOORS

Jay Leno
Drives The World's
Biggest Pickup

DEBUNKING
9/11
LIES

**Conspiracy Theories
Can't Stand Up To
The Hard Facts**

A growin
chorus of fring
groups say
a U.S. pl
brought dow
the tower
After a
in-dept
investigatio
PM answer
with the trut

ALSO IN THIS ISSUE

**NASCAR'S
HIGH-TECH SECRET**

**Wild Homebuilt
Computers**

**LONG-TERM CAR
TESTS:** Living With The
Nissan Titan, Scion xB
And Chrysler Pacifica

44 **DIY Tips:**
Fix Screen Doors,
Clean Up Your
Hard Drive,

the refutation essay

c h a p t e r 6

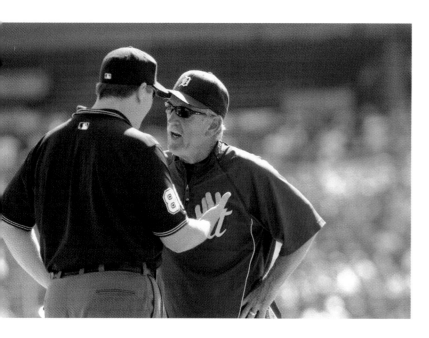

What Is a Refutation Essay?

To refute something is to prove it wrong, illogical, or erroneous. When your primary purpose in writing is to challenge someone's argument rather than to present your own argument, you are writing a *refutation*. This is, in fact, an important skill when it comes to almost any type of argumentation. After all, any argument has at least two sides, right? In order to write a persuasive refutation argument, you will need to fully understand why your opponent may hold certain beliefs and construct a plan to show why those beliefs or reasons are wrong. However, you must remember that simply disagreeing with your opponent is not enough. Your reader will expect you to present logical, clear, and solid evidence that your opponent is wrong, misinformed, or not seeing things clearly.

A good refutation demonstrates, in an orderly and logical way, the weaknesses of logic or evidence in the argument, or it both analyzes weaknesses and builds a counterargument. Refutations can challenge a specific written argument, or they can challenge a prevailing attitude or belief that is, in the writer's view, contrary to the evidence. The sample refutation, "Gender Games," shows the first purpose. It is annotated to show you how the author puts together his refutation. But first, let's look at the steps involved in preparing a good refutation essay.

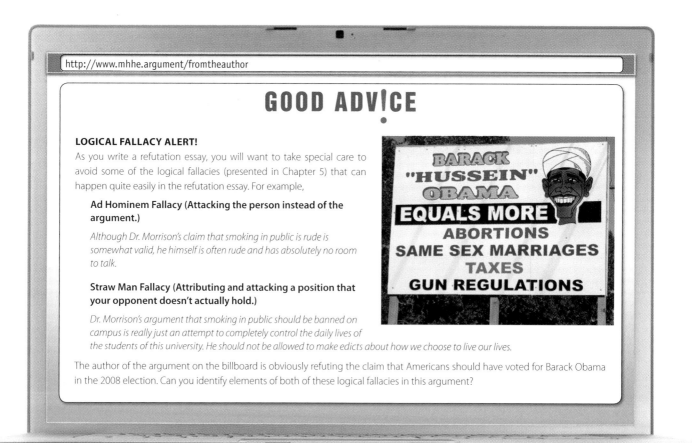

GOOD ADVICE

LOGICAL FALLACY ALERT!

As you write a refutation essay, you will want to take special care to avoid some of the logical fallacies (presented in Chapter 5) that can happen quite easily in the refutation essay. For example,

Ad Hominem Fallacy (Attacking the person instead of the argument.)

Although Dr. Morrison's claim that smoking in public is rude is somewhat valid, he himself is often rude and has absolutely no room to talk.

Straw Man Fallacy (Attributing and attacking a position that your opponent doesn't actually hold.)

Dr. Morrison's argument that smoking in public should be banned on campus is really just an attempt to completely control the daily lives of the students of this university. He should not be allowed to make edicts about how we choose to live our lives.

The author of the argument on the billboard is obviously refuting the claim that Americans should have voted for Barack Obama in the 2008 election. Can you identify elements of both of these logical fallacies in this argument?

Guidelines for Writing a Refutation Essay

- **Read accurately.** Make certain that you have understood your opponent's argument. If you assume the writer holds views that he or she does not, you may commit the straw man fallacy, attributing and then attacking a position that the person does not hold. Look up terms and references you do not know, and examine the logic and evidence thoroughly.

- **Pinpoint the weaknesses in the original argument.** Analyze the argument to determine, specifically, what flaws the argument contains. If the argument contains logical fallacies, make a list of the ones you plan to discredit. Examine the evidence presented. Is it insufficient, unreliable, or irrelevant? Decide, before drafting your refutation, exactly which elements of the argument you intend to challenge.

- **Write a strong thesis.** After analyzing the argument and deciding on the weaknesses to challenge, write a thesis that establishes your disagreement with the writer's logic, assumptions, or evidence, or a combination of these.

- **Draft your essay, making sure to include all of the following elements in your organizational plan:**

  a. *The opponent's argument.* Usually you should not assume that your reader has read or remembered the argument you are refuting. Therefore, toward the beginning of your essay, you need to state, accurately and fairly, the main points of the argument to be refuted.

  b. *Your thesis.* Make clear the nature of your disagreement with the argument you are refuting.

  c. *Your refutation.* The specifics of your counterargument will depend upon the nature of your disagreement. For example, if you are challenging the writer's evidence on the grounds that it is outdated, then you must present the more recent evidence to explain why the evidence used is unreliable or misleading. If you are challenging assumptions, then you must explain why each one does not hold up. If your thesis is that the piece is filled with logical fallacies, then you must present and explain each fallacy.

Read "Gender Games," study the annotations, and then answer the questions that follow.

> ## GOOD ADVICE
>
> Your essay's organization should be based on the needs of your reader, your intended purpose, and the visual elements or sources you will include. There is no one right way to organize a refutation essay. However, you must have a clear understanding of how you are structuring your argument and the effect that structure will have on your reader.

http://www.mhhe.argument/fromtheauthor

Gender Games

David Sadker

A professor emeritus at American University and teaching at the University of Arizona, David Sadker has written extensively on educational issues, especially on the treatment of girls in the classroom. He is the author of *Still Failing at Fairness* (2009). "Gender Games" appeared in *The Washington Post* on July 31, 2000.

Remember when your elementary school teacher would announce the teams for the weekly spelling bee? "Boys against the girls!" There was nothing like a gender showdown to liven things up. Apparently, some writers never left this elementary level of intrigue. A spate of recent books and articles takes us back to the "boys versus girls" fray but this time, with much higher stakes. [Attention-getting opening]

May's *Atlantic Monthly* cover story, "Girls Rule," is a case in point. The magazine published an excerpt from *The War Against Boys* by Christina Hoff Sommers, a book advancing the notion that boys are the real victims of gender bias while girls are soaring in school. [Claim to be refuted]

Sommers and her supporters are correct in saying that girls and women have made significant educational progress in the past two decades. Females today make up more than 40 percent of medical and law school students, and more than half of college students. Girls continue to read sooner and write better than boys. And for as long as anyone can remember, girls have received higher grades than boys. [Concession: What's right about opponent's argument]

But there is more to these selected statistics than meets the eye. Although girls continue to receive higher report card

continued

grades than boys, their grades do not translate into higher test scores. The same girls who beat boys in the spelling bees score below boys on the tests that matter: the PSATs crucial for scholarships, the SATs and the ACTs needed for college acceptances, the GREs for graduate school and even the admission tests for law, business, and medical schools.

First point of refutation

Many believe that girls' higher grades may be more a reflection of their manageable classroom behavior than their intellectual accomplishment. Test scores are not influenced by quieter classroom behavior. Girls may in fact be trading their initiative and independence for peer approval and good grades, a trade-off that can have costly personal and economic consequences.

The increase in female college enrollment catches headlines because it heralds the first time that females have outnumbered males on college campuses. But even these enrollment figures are misleading. The female presence increases as the status of the college decreases. Female students are more likely to dominate two-year schools than the Ivy League. And wherever they are, they find themselves segregated and channeled into the least prestigious and least costly majors.

Second point of refutation

In today's world of e-success, more than 60 percent of computer science and business majors are male, about 70 percent of physics majors are males, and more than 80 percent of engineering students are male. But peek into language, psychology, nursing and humanities classrooms, and you will find a sea of female faces.

Higher female enrollment figures mask the "glass walls" that separate the sexes and channel females and males into very different careers, with very different paychecks. Today, despite all the progress, the five leading occupations of employed women are secretary, receptionist, bookkeeper, registered nurse, and hairdresser/cosmetologist.

Add this to the "glass ceiling" (about 3 percent of Fortune 500 top managers are women) and the persistence of a gender wage gap (women with advanced degrees still lag well behind their less-educated male counterparts) and the crippling impact of workplace and college stereotyping becomes evident.

Even within schools, where female teachers greatly outnumber male teachers, school management figures remind us that if there is a war on boys, women are not the generals. More than 85 percent of junior and senior high school principals are male, while 88 percent of school superintendents are male.

Third point of refutation

Despite sparkling advances of females on the athletic fields, two-thirds of athletic scholarships still go to males. In some areas, women have actually lost ground. When Title IX was enacted in 1972, women coached more than 90 percent of intercollegiate women's teams. Today women coach only 48 percent of women's teams and only 1 percent of men's teams.

Fourth point of refutation

If some adults are persuaded by the rhetoric in such books as *The War Against Boys*, be assured that children know the score. When more than 1,000 Michigan elementary school students were asked to describe what life would be like if they were born a member of the opposite sex, more than 40 percent of the girls saw positive advantages to being a boy: better jobs, more money and definitely more respect. Ninety-five percent of the boys saw no advantage to being a female.

Fifth point of refutation

The War Against Boys attempts to persuade the public to abandon support for educational initiatives designed to help girls and boys avoid crippling stereotypes. I hope the public and Congress will not be taken in by the book's misrepresentations. We have no time to wage a war on either our boys or our girls.

Author concludes by stating his claim (thesis)

QUESTIONS FOR READING

1. What work, specifically, is Sadker refuting? What is the claim presented by this work?
2. What facts about girls does Sadker grant to Sommers?
3. What facts about girls create a different story, according to Sadker?

QUESTIONS FOR REASONING AND ANALYSIS

1. What is Sadker's claim? What is he asserting about girls?
2. What does Sadker think about the whole idea of books such as Sommers's?

Read the following refutation piece from *The Chronicle of Higher Education*'s Web site. What do you think about the refutation made by this author? Is it effective? What elements of a good refutation essay does this piece exhibit? Annotate this piece, noting the specific strategies the author uses to attempt to persuade his reader. What might this author do to make this piece even more persuasive?

Dear Dr. Brottman,

Although, in reading your article "Goth's Wan Stamina," I found your thoughts on the goth subculture very interesting (I have always been interested in subcultures of all kinds), I was a bit disturbed by your treatment of punk and skin culture in this article. To say that "skinheads have come and gone" is to completely ignore the continued vitality of the skinhead subculture in the United States and the United Kingdom and such currently active Oi! bands such as The Business, The Dropkick Murphys, and The Cockney Rejects.

Furthermore, the claim that "punk didn't last" only has the slightest bit of validity if you choose to completely ignore the hardcore movement of the 1980s and its continued effect on a variety of punk genres. Not to mention it was this movement that imparted the punk subculture with, in my opinion, its most important feature: the DIY ethic.

I am a punk and a student at the University of Chicago, where I am part of the school's hardcore punk group UxCxHxC Trix. One only needs to come to one of the shows or lectures (affectionately referred to as "The Common 'Core'") to see that each member of the group, though each with his or her own specific knowledge of a subgenre of the music, still identifies himself or herself as "punk" and is continuing to listen to the music and practice the ideology every day.

I play in a ska-core band (which, if you're unfamiliar, is a blend of ska and hardcore influenced by bands such as The Clash, Operation Ivy, and Choking Victim) called Alleyway Sex in my home town of Champaign–Urbana, IL. We have been active for over two years, putting on our own shows in basements or renting out venues, and booking any touring band who wants to come through town. Although some shows are definitely better attended than others, one only needs to come to one of our shows to see the prominence of the punk subculture in the area. In fact, we recently released a DIY compilation called *C/U In The Streets* featuring 28 songs by 14 local bands, ranging in musical genre from thrash to folk to ska to hardcore to hip-hop, but all identifying as punks. I noticed from the article that you are writing from Baltimore, Maryland. Well, I would encourage you, if you would like to learn more about the prevailing punk subculture, to come out to the Sidebar Tavern on June 20th, where my band will be continuing its East Coast tour, playing with Baltimore locals The Twats.

Finally, I would like to disagree with the claim that, unlike goth, punk is only for the young. I am a punk now, and I will continue to be a punk for the rest of my life. It's not about the fashion. I personally don't really dress punk, have never dyed or gelled up my hair, but I still fiercely identify with the subculture, not only through the music, but also through the DIY ethic, as I mentioned before. Both I and my friends at the University of Chicago have incorporated this aspect of our lives into our schoolwork (in fact, one of my friends [guitarist for two UxCxHxC bands, f*** Your Face and Gun, With Occasional Music] gave a lecture at Yale on the affinity of straight-edge with hardcore music), and I have no reason to think that we will not

continued

continue to do so in our daily lives after college, both personal and professional. While goth is simply a fashion, punk (and especially hardcore) has a true ideology that rings true (or should ring true) for both young and old.

Basically, I think you might find it of interest to re-examine the punk subculture here in America. If you have any questions, you can feel free to contact me via e-mail.

Up The Punks,
Mike Alleyway

Source: http://chronicle.com/forums/index.php/topic,38949.0/prev_next,next.html#new

Consider this billboard as a refutation argument. Its purpose is clearly to refute a claim that is often used when arguing against legalizing gay marriage: that it is against God's wishes and is forbidden by the Christian Bible. However, another author has chosen to refute the billboard's claim by painting "LIE" on it. Is either refutation argument providing enough evidence to persuade its intended audience? Will either argument persuade viewers to alter their beliefs? Remember that attempting to refute deeply ingrained or commonly held beliefs can be particularly difficult.

S
EE
ING
THE ARGUMENT

SEEING THE ARGUMENT

Image by Jesus Metropolitan Community Church, www.JesusMCC.org

Using Research in Refutation Arguments

If you were writing a researched essay that was attempting to refute a deeply ingrained, highly controversial, and commonly held notion or a notion that challenged a popular belief, what types of sources, visuals, and organizational strategies might you choose to utilize? How would understanding your audience's values and beliefs help you as you conducted your research?

Consider the following editorial from *Newsweek:*

The Case for Legal Late-Term Abortions:
Abortion wasn't an option for my parents, but raising my severely retarded brother nearly destroyed our family.

Jim Buie

Newsweek Web Exclusive

June 17, 2009

The murder of Kansas abortion provider Dr. George Tiller has intensified the national debate over late-term abortions. I have a special interest in this topic because I had a brother who was severely retarded. Though he lived well into adulthood, he never developed beyond an infantile state.

Abortion was not an option for my parents when Jon was born back in 1949. I doubt they would have chosen abortion even if it were an option. But in not having the right to choose abortion, there was also a heavy emotional price to be paid. They never had the chance to take a personal inventory and ask themselves honestly if they were capable of caring for a severely retarded child along with their four other children.

For anyone who believes life is precious, such a decision is bound to be wrenching. Whatever choice one makes is sure to be painful and deeply personal.

For the first three years of Jon's life, my parents tried to care for him at home. He would spend nearly all day screaming or rocking uncontrollably or banging his head out of frustration for what he couldn't do for himself. "Success" at the end of the day, as my mother described it, would mean coaxing the baby to swallow enough food to nourish himself.

Jon caused my family severe emotional distress in his early years. Both of my parents experienced nervous breakdowns. They could not face the reality that they could not care for him in their home and at the same time meet the needs of their healthy children. Years later, my uncle wrote a rather macabre story about how he was tempted to let the baby who was wreaking havoc in his beloved sister's home "accidentally" slip from his arms while swimming in the ocean and drown, so that the family's emotional collapse could be avoided.

Thankfully, he resisted that temptation. Instead, he searched far and wide for an institution that would take Jon. There were few such facilities in those days. He finally found a place 300 miles from my parents' home, and he persuaded (or perhaps bullied) my indecisive and not completely rational parents into doing what they needed to do to stabilize their family unit. Jon was 3 at the time; he lived at an institution until he died at 52 of heart failure.

Sending Jon away, no matter how caring the institution was, was a heart-wrenching decision. And yet my parents found a great sense of relief—finally, they were able to recover their emotional stability. My mother went on to lead a relatively happy, pro-ductive life, devoting it to helping children. She became an outstanding educator and North Carolina English Teacher of the Year in 1979.

My father, in his denial, prayed repeatedly for decades for a miracle cure to his namesake's Down syndrome. He'd visit Jon and come home expressing the false and unrealistic hope that "I believe he's better." For him, the stigma of having a severely retarded son was real, and I think he internalized the notion that he was a failure as a parent because he agreed to send his child away to be cared for at an institution. To dull his sadness and pain, he turned to beer and wine.

My sisters were 9, 7 and 1 at the time Jon was sent away—I had not been born yet. The irony is that if Jon, who was at the time my parents' only son, hadn't been severely retarded, I might not have been conceived. So in one sense, I owe my very life to him. My sister calls this "soul sacrifice"—Jon's soul was sacrificed so that another soul could have a more abundant life.

I cannot say that the option of a late-term abortion would have been the right one for my parents. But some of the arguments advanced by pro-life forces disturb me. There is a tendency to romanticize, sentimentalize and idealize life with a cute, forever-young Down-syndrome "angel child." Alaska Gov. Sarah Palin and her supporters are particularly adept at this. It's an argument I find off-putting, especially when it's espoused by people who have never been through the wringer trying to care for a child whose disability level is on the most severe end of the scale.

At the same time, it is very disturbing that until recently, the majority of Down-syndrome fetuses were aborted without expectant mothers receiving proper information or support. Widely differing degrees of disability exist in Down syndrome, some of which can be determined through ultrasound and diagnostic tests in the first trimester, obviating the need for a late-term abortion.

Pro-life and pro-choice forces have been going around and around on the issue of abortion for decades, without finding common ground. What seems to have been largely ignored by the mainstream media is that there was a meeting of the minds last fall when the Prenatally and Postnatally Diagnosed Conditions Awareness Act, sponsored by Sens. Ted Kennedy and Sam Brownback, was signed into law.

The measure provides that families receiving a prenatal or postnatal diagnosis of Down syndrome or other conditions are offered accurate and up-to-date information about the nature of the condition and are also connected

continued

with support services. In addition, a registry of parents willing to adopt children with disabilities is now being compiled and maintained. This law is something pro-life and pro-choice forces agreed on.

The late Dr. Tiller was one of three doctors in the nation to admit to performing late-term abortions. I do not feel qualified to judge whether the procedures he engaged in were ethical. The fact that he was quickly acquitted in March of misdemeanor charges speaks in his favor. And certainly the testimonials from former patients are persuasive.

With his murder, there is a very real danger that late-term abortions will end in this country—not after public deliberation, legislative debate and majority vote, but because anti-abortion absolutists on the fringe have intimidated and blacklisted doctors and successfully threatened violence against them. It's possible there won't be any doctors in the country willing to perform late-term abortions even if prenatal tests indicate severe retardation. In other words, domestic terrorism could win. That would be a travesty.

It would mean that parents like my own would no longer have a choice, and would instead be forced to endure the same harsh realities that were present in the 1950s.

If you were given the task of refuting the claim in this editorial, how might you go about it?

> The author of this article believes in the legality of late-term abortions so that people can choose this option under certain conditions or in certain instances. I want to refute this idea and persuade my readers that late-term abortions should be illegal under any circumstances.

As you write your researched essay refuting this common belief, you should consider the following questions:

- **What do my readers already know (or think that they know) about late-term abortions?** Where are they primarily getting their information? From magazines? Scholarly journals? Billboards? Television advertisements? Print ads? Friends? Their churches? Personal experience? Their teachers? It's very important to try to figure out what types

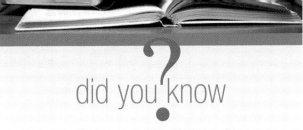

did you know

There are Facebook groups dedicated to many of the issues you may write about in your composition course. You can connect with other students from around the world, find links to important sources, and even conduct online interviews with renowned experts. Just use the Search feature and type the area or topic you would like to research.

of sources your readers may have been exposed to and how reliable or credible those sources seem. For example, if the author's position about late-term abortion is based on reading an article about Britney Spears in *People* magazine, you could call that position into question based on a lack of credible research. He or she would not have enough evidence to make such a claim regarding late-term abortions.

- **What values most likely cause my readers to feel the way they do on this subject?** Oftentimes, people base their positions on the values they hold, that is, what they consider worthwhile and important in the world. Values can be formed early in life due to family members' opinions, religious affiliations, or even peer influence. If you try to understand why writers feel the way they do, you can often figure out why they hold certain positions. This can also point out flaws in their logic or places where they are relying purely on emotional or value-driven arguments rather than logical ones. If, for example, you discovered that this writer was a libertarian who valued personal freedom and a lack of governmental interference over all else, might that alter the way you viewed her claim? It might open up the possibility that she is arguing out of very strong loyalty to individualism and may be ignoring important issues in the debate.

- **What types of evidence have informed their current opinions?** Are there compelling statistics that support this belief? Are there visuals that have helped to create or perpetuate stereotypes or preconceived notions? Are there vocal experts who have influenced public opinion? This question means that you will need to enter into the debate in a very real way. You will need to find out the current trends regarding the subject, whether it has been in the news recently, who the leading experts may be, and how valid the current research seems. For example, what if a recent study had been published revealing that a large percentage of women choosing the late-term option abort completely healthy and normal fetuses? Although the original author

Consider this visual refutation argument and the accompanying critique by a columnist for PoliticalIrony.com. The *National Review* cover satire was intended as a rebuttal to *The New Yorker* cover depicted in Chapter 1. This author, however, argues that it is an ineffective rebuttal and even claims that it presents a flawed argument. See if you can identify the flaws according to this author. Do you agree that this is a flawed rebuttal or refutation argument? Why or why not?

© Tribune Media Services, Inc. All Rights Reserved. Reprinted with permission. New Yorker *cover* © Condé Nast Publications, Barry Blitt 2008.

S
EE
ING
THE ARGUMENT

SEEING THE ARGUMENT

What I find ironic is that while the images in *The New Yorker* cover were completely false (Obama as a Muslim terrorist?), there is video of McCain singing "Bomb Iran," and Cindy McCain admitted to being addicted to pain killers (after she lied about it). So, the real cover contains falsehoods, while the fake cover contains truths.

What would be a more equivalent rebuttal would be depicting McCain collaborating with his Viet Cong captors to become a Manchurian candidate. In fact, I dare *The New Yorker* (or anyone) to publish such a cover. Then we'll see what kind of response that gets.

may not have cited this study, it would be relevant and could affect your ability to make a logical and informed refutation of her claim. You would need to somehow refute this study in order to be successful in your own essay. You cannot ignore expert opinions or data simply because the original author did not mention them. To do so would only hurt your refutation essay's credibility.

- **What types of evidence could I present that would be persuasive to my readers, given all of the above?** Will statistics or case studies work? Should I incorporate visuals that will counter ones they may have already seen? Are there respected experts who disagree with the common belief? Remember that evidence is the key to any successful argument. You must be able to present sound, logical, and credible evidence that refutes your opponent's original argument. Statistics and visuals can be effective ways to do this, as can quotes from reputable sources.

- **Where can I find sources?** Should I start with my library databases? Are there journal articles that present a new perspective on this debate? Should I first conduct a general Internet search to get an overall sense of the debate? Will youtube.com have videos that I can use? As with any research process, you will want to begin by surveying the current information on your issue. You will need to gather credible sources (whether from your library's database or some other online or print source) and try to determine which sources will help you the most. Do not ignore sources that seemingly disagree with you or that support the opposite position. These can be valuable in understanding the opposing point of view and ultimately how you can refute its assertions.

let's review

After reading this chapter, you should understand:

- A good refutation demonstrates, in an orderly and logical way, the weaknesses of logic or evidence in the argument, or it both analyzes weaknesses and builds a counterargument.

- So that you can construct an effective refutation, you must read the original piece accurately in order to attempt to pinpoint its weaknesses.

- Your thesis should establish your disagreement with the writer's logical assumptions or evidence, or a combination of these.

- A typical refutation essay includes three parts: the opponent's argument, your thesis, and your support for your refutation.

- When using research to support your refutation, you should always consider what sources your readers may have already consulted about your issue and what attitudes and values they may bring to the table as a result.

- You should attempt to find sources and visuals that will be particularly persuasive to your readers given their probable values, beliefs, and attitudes toward your subject.

connect

Read the following refutation essay. Individually or in a small group, answer the questions that follow and be prepared to discuss you answers with the class.

prereading questions } **Should police and airport security personnel use profiling to protect against terrorism? If profiling were used, would you be a suspect? Does how you answer the second question affect how you answer the first one?**

You Can't Fight Terrorism with Racism

Colbert I. King

A native Washingtonian, Colbert King has held a number of positions in the government, including special agent for the State Department, and in banking, including at the World Bank. King joined The Washington Post's *editorial board in 1990, began writing a weekly column in 1995, and became deputy editor of the editorial page in 2000. In 2003 he won a Pulitzer Prize for commentary. His column on fighting terrorism was published July 30, 2005.*

During my day job I work under the title of deputy editorial page editor. That entails paying more than passing attention to articles that appear on the op-ed page. Opinion writers, in my view, should have a wide range in which to roam, especially when it comes to edgy, thought-provoking pieces. Still, I wasn't quite ready for what appeared on the op-ed pages of Thursday's *New York Times* or Friday's *Post*.

A *New York Times* op-ed piece by Paul Sperry, a Hoover Institution media fellow ("It's the Age of Terror: What Would You Do?"), and a *Post* column by Charles Krauthammer ("Give Grandma a Pass: Politically Correct Screening Won't Catch Jihadists") endorsed the practice of using ethnicity, national origin, and religion as primary factors in deciding whom police should regard as possible terrorists—in other words, racial profiling. A second *Times* column, on Thursday, by Haim Watzman ("When You Have to Shoot First") argued that the London police officer who chased down and put seven bullets into the head of a Brazilian electrician without asking him any questions or giving him any warning "did the right thing."

The three articles blessed behavior that makes a mockery of the rights to which people in this country are entitled. Krauthammer blasted the random-bag-checks program adopted in the New York subway in response to the London bombings, calling it absurd and a waste of effort and resources. His answer: Security officials should concentrate on "young Muslim men of North African, Middle Eastern, and South Asian origin." Krauthammer doesn't say how authorities should go about identifying "Muslim men" or how to distinguish non-Muslim men from Muslim men entering a subway station. Probably just a small detail easily overlooked.

All you need to know is that the culprit who is going to blow you to bits, Krauthammer wrote, "traces his origins to the Islamic belt stretching from Mauritania to Indonesia." For the geographically challenged, Krauthammer's birthplace of the suicide bomber starts with countries in black Africa and stops somewhere in the Pacific Ocean. By his reckoning, the rights and freedoms enjoyed by all should be limited to a select group. Krauthammer argued that authorities should work backward and "eliminate classes of people who are obviously not suspects." In the category of the innocent, Krauthammer would place children younger than 13, people older than 60 and "whole ethnic populations" starting with "Hispanics, Scandinavians and East Asians . . . and women," except "perhaps the most fidgety, sweaty, suspicious-looking, overcoat-wearing, knapsack-bearing young women."

Of course, by eliminating Scandinavians from his list of obvious terror suspects, Krauthammer would have authorities give a pass to all white people, since subway cops don't check passengers' passports for country of origin. As for sweaty, fidgety, knapsack-bearing, overcoat-wearing young women who happen to be black, brown, or yellow? Tough nuggies, in Krauthammer's book. The age-60 cutoff is meaningless, too, since subway cops aren't especially noted for accuracy in pinning down stages of life. In Krauthammer's worldview, it's all quite simple: Ignore him and his son; suspect me and mine.

Sperry also has his own proxy for suspicious characters. He warned security and subway commuters to be on the lookout for "young men praying to Allah and smelling of flower water." Keep your eyes open, he said, for a "shaved head or short haircut" or a recently shaved beard or moustache. Men who look like that, in his book, are "the most suspicious train passengers."

It appears to matter not to Sperry that his description also includes huge numbers of men of color, including my younger son, a brown-skinned occasional New York subway rider who shaves his head and moustache. He also happens to be a former federal prosecutor and until a few years ago was a homeland security official in Washington. Sperry's profile also ensnares my older brown-skinned son, who wears a very short haircut, may wear cologne at times, and has the complexion of many men I have seen in Africa and the Middle East. He happens to be a television executive. But what the hell, according to Sperry, "young Muslim men of Arab or South Asian origin" fit the terrorist profile. How, just by looking, can security personnel identify a Muslim male of Arab or South Asian origin goes unexplained.

Reportedly, after September 11, 2001, some good citizens of California took out after members of the Sikh community, mistaking them for Arabs. Oh, well, what's a little political incorrectness in the name of national security. Bang, bang—oops, he was Brazilian. Two young black guys were London bombers: one Jamaican, the other Somalian. Muslim, too. Ergo: Watch your back when around black men—they could be, ta-dum, Muslims.

So while advocates of racial profiling would have authorities subject men and women of black and brown hues to close scrutiny for criminal suspicions, they would look right past:

- White male Oklahoma bomber Timothy McVeigh, who killed 168 people, including 19 children, and damaged 220 buildings.
- White male Eric Rudolph, whose remote-controlled bomb killed a woman and an off-duty police officer at a clinic, whose Olympic Park pipe bomb killed a woman and injured more than 100, and whose bombs hit a gay club and woman's clinic.
- White male Dennis Rader, the "bind, torture, kill" (BTK) serial killer who terrorized Wichita for 31 years.
- D.C.–born and Silver Spring–raised white male John Walker Lindh, who converted to Islam and was captured in Afghanistan fighting for the Taliban.
- The IRA bombers who killed and wounded hundreds; the neo-fascist bombers who killed 80 people and injured nearly 300 in Bologna, Italy; and the truck bombings in Colombia by Pedro Escobar's gang.

But let's get really current. What about those non-Arab, non-South Asians without black or brown skins who are bombing apartment buildings, train stations, and theaters in Russia. They've taken down passenger jets, hijacked schools, and used female suicide bombers to a fare-thee-well, killing hundreds and wounding thousands. They are Muslims from Chechnya, and would pass the Krauthammer/

continued

Sperry eyeball test for terrorists with ease. After all, these folks hail from the Caucasus; you can't get any more Caucasian than that.

What the racial profilers are proposing is insulting, offensive and—by thought, word and deed, whether intentional or not—racist. You want estrangement? Start down that road of using ethnicity, national origin, and religion as a basis for police action and there's going to be a push-back unlike any seen in this country in many years.

QUESTIONS FOR READING

1. What are Krauthammer's views on random searches? Who should be targeted? Who ignored?

2. What are Sperry's views? Who would he profile?

QUESTIONS FOR REASONING AND ANALYSIS

1. What is King's claim? Where does he state it?

2. How does the author refute the arguments of Krauthammer and Sperry? List his points of rebuttal, both practical and value-based.

3. In paragraphs 10 and 11, King lists those who would not be stopped based on profiling. What is effective about the list? How might Krauthammer and Sperry respond to King's list?

4. Woven into the careful quoting and specific examples are lines that create a hard-edged tone to King's refutation. Find these lines and explain their effect.

QUESTIONS FOR REFLECTING AND WRITING

1. Has King effectively refuted Krauthammer and Sperry? Why or why not?

2. Do you see any opportunities for visual arguments in this article? Where and how might you add visual information or support?

3. If you were going to write a researched argument on this topic, what types of sources would you want to utilize? Do you see any points that could be made stronger through the use of source material?

the position essay

chapter 7

We have already seen that arguments are all around us. They appear throughout our daily lives, sometimes without even being noticed. However, some arguments are obvious. Taking-a-position or taking-a-stand arguments appear not only in academic settings as formal essays, but also as editorials in newspapers, flyers for causes or candidates, blog entries on the Web, and even magazine articles. Authors who have clear points of view and who wish to convince their readers to adopt those points of view often use this straightforward type of argument to accomplish their goals. While the position paper is often perceived as the easiest type of argument to write due to its clear purpose, in fact, it can actually be one of the most difficult argument assignments. Review the following characteristics of this kind of argument and consider why this might be so.

Characteristics of a Position Argument

- A position argument is often more general, abstract, or philosophical than other types of arguments. It may not always ask its readers to take a specific action, but it may instead ask them to change their belief systems or to examine their values.

- It makes a claim about what is right or wrong, good or bad for us as individuals or as a society. Topics can vary from the abolishment of the IRS to the legalization of prostitution to the best ways to protect endangered species.

- A position essay is developed in large part by a logical sequencing of reasons supported by relevant facts.

- A successful position argument requires more than a forceful statement of personal beliefs and can often be weakened by appealing primarily to readers' emotions.

- In order to be successful, a position argument must take into account its readers' values, beliefs, and potential counterarguments or objections.

Writing a Position Essay

As you write a position essay, your primary goal will be to persuade your reader to accept your point of view as valid, worthwhile, and true. You are not simply explaining your opinion on a topic or issue. Rather, you are seeking a distinct and committed response from your audience. Even if your readers are already inclined to agree with you, you are still attempting to solidify their current position. If your readers hold a different position on the issue, you are asking them to think about the issue in a new way or possibly even to abandon their position in favor of yours. Some position essays even go so far as to call for a specific action from the reader. None of these are easy tasks. You will need to carefully plan, draft, and revise your essay in order to be persuasive. You may also need to conduct research on your topic and use visual elements as ways to persuade your readers. In addition to the guidelines for writing solid and effective arguments presented in Chapter 4, you can use the advice specific to writing position papers presented throughout this chapter.

Planning and Organizing the Position Essay

Before you can begin drafting your essay, you will need to spend some time thinking about your topic, your audience, your specific purpose, and your strategy. The following questions can help you begin your prewriting and planning activities.

- **What claim, exactly, do you want to support?** What do you want your audience to think, believe, do, or feel after reading your essay?

- **Who is your audience?** Will you attempt to persuade those who clearly disagree with you? Those who agree with you on some points and not others? (Consider all of the questions concerning your readers' expectations and values from Chapter 4.)

- **What (if any) background information might your readers need on your topic?** Will you need to explain the controversy? Give them statistics? Tell a story? Consider how much your audience will already know about your issue and how much you will need to provide for them in the beginning of your essay.

- **What grounds (evidence) do you have or might you need to support your claim?** You may want to make a list of the reasons and facts you could use to defend your claim. Where might you find evidence or sources? Will you need to conduct interviews? Do library research? Conduct a survey? Recall your own experiences? Use visuals to illustrate your main points? Consider all the ways you can support your claims and which ones will be most persuasive to your particular audience.

- **What personal values do you and your audience members hold that inform your positions?** Study your list of possible grounds and recognize the assumptions (warrants) and backing for your grounds. Do you hold certain core beliefs that cause you to feel the way that you do? How might your readers view your values and beliefs? Will they automatically accept them as valid and

WHAT IS A VALUE?

A value is any principle, standard, or quality that we believe is worthwhile or important. People often form their positions based on their personal values and belief systems. This means that in order to write a persuasive position essay, you must understand not only your own values but also the values of your readers and how those values affect their position on your topic.

For example, in 2007, thousands of people filled the streets in a small Louisiana town to protest the arrests of six African American students charged with beating a white classmate after nooses were hung from a schoolyard tree. (For more information on the Jena 6, go to www.abc.net.au/news/stories/2007/09/21/2040080.htm.)

What do you think the protester in the photo values? What does he believe is important? How do you know? How might you attempt to convince him that even in the face of this racially charged act, the beating of the white student was not justified? Do you think it would be difficult to write a paper that would convince him to adopt this position?

true? Now make a list of the grounds most often used by those whose views oppose your claim and a list of the values these readers might hold. This second list will help you prepare rebuttals to your readers' possible counterarguments (opposing points), but first it will help you test your understanding of and commitment to your position. If you find the opposition's arguments persuasive and cannot think how you would rebut them, you may need to rethink your position. Ideally, your two lists will not only confirm your views but also increase your respect for opposing views.

Counterarguments and Finding Common Ground

Discovering the counterarguments to your position is an important part of the writing process. This will allow you not only to more fully understand the complexity of your issue, but also to more effectively defend your position in the face of opposition. Writing an effective rebuttal to your readers' counterargument is one of the trickiest and most delicate tasks you must undertake as you construct your position paper. It's not as simple as finding a directly opposing position and then claiming it is wrong. Rather, it means that you will need to identify and attempt to truly understand your potential readers, the positions they may hold, and the values that inform those positions. Then you will need to identify what logical strategies you can use to overcome their potential objections to your position.

First and foremost, your readers must believe that you fully understand their position and that you are presenting it in a fair and accurate way. But how can you do this without undermining your own (often directly opposing) position?

LOGICAL FALLACY ALERT!

As you write a position essay, you will want to take special care to avoid the logical fallacies presented in Chapter 5 (Slippery Slope, Begging the Question, Bandwagon, Ad Populum) that can happen quite easily in this type of essay. Analyze the following visual arguments and see if you can match the logical fallacy to each.

circular reasoning works because

Slippery Slope Fallacy

Attention: Lunatic Atheists & their Lawyers
Anti-God is Anti-American
Anti-American is Treason
Traitors lead to Civil War
Rev. E. F. Briggs, PO Box 9066, Monongah, WV 26554

Begging the Question

LOVE IT OR LEAVE IT

Bandwagon Fallacy

McDonald's
OVER 99 BILLION SERVED

SAT 730 AM
COME HAVE BREAKFAST
WITH THE MUNCHKINS

Ad Populum Fallacy

The key to presenting your opponents' position is to always be fair but not to give their position any more weight than necessary. You should demonstrate that you understand the complexities of alternate positions and the reasons why readers may hold those views. You should never attack your opponents by insinuating that their position is ridiculous or unintelligent. This will only turn off your readers before they have had a chance to consider your points.

One strategy that might help you is to use conciliatory language in an attempt to find common ground with your readers. Showing that there are points of agreement (even if they are small) helps your readers feel open to your argument and will give you a

chance to then rebut the points on which your opinions differ.

For example, you might present your counterargument by raising a potential objection using conciliatory language (in order to point to common ground), and then immediately rebutting the objection by using a transitional word or phrase:

> <u>Admittedly</u>, there is evidence that mandatory vaccinations for children would help to eradicate specific diseases. <u>However</u>, when one considers all of the available statistics, the risks of these immunizations far outweigh any potential benefits.

The phrase *common ground* historically referred to the central place in many towns and villages made available to everyone and used for everything from trading or selling goods, to settling disagreements, to expressing opinions.

For example, one technique for anonymous trade between mutually suspicious parties was for the offerers to lay the goods (such as gold) in a clearing (the potential common ground), and then to hide in the forest with the gold in their plain sight, while armed with weapons in the event of treachery. Thus, the offers could be made to traders. The traders, who bore goods and who were also armed with weapons, would lay the trade goods in the clearing and take the gold back with them. This was a mechanism for trading between the Moors and the gold miners of Africa over a millennium ago, and also for trade with Sumatra (the isle of gold) and other islands of Southeast Asia. Now the term is typically used to mean a "foundation for mutual understanding."

Source: *Common ground* definition from http://encyclopedia.thefreedictionary.com/common+ground +(communication+technique)

Consider how you might use a conciliatory approach as you present your position. When the issue is emotion-laden or highly controversial, or when your readers might hold values very different from your own, the conciliatory approach can be an effective strategy. Conciliatory arguments use

- nonthreatening language,
- a fair expression of opposing views, and
- a statement of the common ground shared by opposing sides.

You may want to use a conciliatory approach in the following instances:

1. You know your views will be unpopular with at least some members of your audience.

2. The issue is highly emotional and the sides are entrenched, so you are seeking some accommodations rather than dramatic changes of position.

3. You will need to interact with members of your audience in the future and want to maintain a respectful relationship.

GOOD ADV!CE

Certain words and phrases can effectively set up a conciliatory rebuttal. Some words highlight specific points of agreement, while others point out the areas of opposition. These can be very effective in softening readers' attitude toward an argument that directly opposes their point of view. Try using these words as you construct your own counterarguments and rebuttal paragraphs.

Sample Conciliatory Words and Phrases to Introduce Counterarguments

Certainly	Obviously	Unquestionably
Assuredly	Admittedly	I will admit
I will concede the fact	Of course	Surely
While it is true	It seems clear	Without a doubt
Clearly	Undeniably	

Sample Transitional Words and Phrases to Introduce Rebuttals

However	Conversely	On the other hand
Nevertheless	Still	Yet
Even so	Regardless	Despite this fact

try it !

Draft a prewriting sheet or free-write a journal entry that answers each of the questions below. This will help you identify the potential counterarguments of your readers and will enable you to anticipate and effectively rebut those objections.

- What is my tentative thesis? What am I trying to convince my readers to do or believe?

- What specific beliefs, values, and experiences have helped to form my position on this issue? What do I believe is important regarding this issue?

- Who are my readers? What do they do? How old are they? Where do they live? Why do they care about this issue? What stake do they have in this debate? (Write down every characteristic you can think of regarding your potential audience.)

- What values and beliefs might my reader already hold that affect their current positions on this issue?

Why might they hold these values?

- What counterarguments or objections might my readers raise? Which of their points will be the most difficult to rebut? (Write down every possible objection and every possible rebuttal that you can think of—even if they sound far-fetched at this point.)

- Is there common ground between my readers' counterarguments and my own position? Are there things we can all agree on?

- Taking these counterarguments and points of common ground into account, how can I convince my readers to consider my points without offending them? Do I need to consider using a conciliatory approach?

Editorial Essay

The following sample essay illustrates a conciliatory approach. As you read, notice the highlighted elements of this approach. Does this writer do a good job of establishing common ground with the readers?

Editorial: Ultimately We Control Our Own Privacy Levels on Facebook

CT Editorial Board

February 19, 2009

Unbeknownst to many of the 175 million users worldwide, two weeks ago Facebook revised its terms of use, specifically giving itself permission to access users' account information even after they've deleted their accounts. This information included users' photos, wall posts, and personal information. When users caught wind of the changes in Facebook's terms, the backlash for Mark Zuckerberg was severe.

On Wednesday morning, Zuckerberg took to the Internet to clear up misconceptions among active users who were worried about the security of their information. On blog.facebook.com, Zuckerberg wrote that based on the feedback he had received regarding the changes, the Facebook team had decided to "return to our previous terms of use while we resolve the issues that people have raised."

While it's understandable that people are worried about their privacy and don't want people at Facebook to have access to their information—especially after their accounts have been deactivated—it is also ridiculous to assume that the information posted on Facebook on a daily basis is completely private, anyway.

Conciliatory language

Rebuttal

The Facebook team has always maintained that the users of Facebook own their information and control with whom they share it. And that is true, to a certain extent. However, whenever people access the Internet, they should always assume that they're taking a risk in regard to personal privacy and should accept whatever consequences arise as a result of personal decisions made on the Internet. It is up to us to decide what pictures we want to upload and have floating around the Internet. Similarly, the personal information we provide and the language we use to sign a friend's wall is also left to our discretion.

Conciliatory language

Transition to rebuttal

In a similar blog post from Monday evening, Zuckerberg attempted to better communicate to concerned users the idea behind Facebook's security. He calls out users, claiming that we want full ownership of our information so that we can control others' access to it at any given time, yet we also want to be able to use information that we receive from others, like phone numbers or e-mail addresses, for other services.

According to the blog, "There is no system today that enables me to share my e-mail address with you and then simultaneously lets me control who you share it with and also lets you control what services you share it with."

Facebook's decision to alter the terms of use understandably angered people because it made us feel like our privacy as users was being violated. However, rather than get hung up on specific wording, a more responsible option would be to closely monitor the information we upload and allow to be linked to us online. When signing up for Facebook a few years ago, few of us likely sat down and carefully read through the terms of use multiple times before deciding to become a member of the Web site. Few of us would have immediately noticed the difference between the original sentence in the terms of use reading, "Facebook could not claim any rights to original content that a user uploaded once the user closed his or her account," and the briefly updated version, "You may remove your User Content from the Site at any time. . . . [H]owever, you acknowledge that the Company may retain archived copies of your User Content." According to company spokesman Barry Schnitt's blog, within the next couple weeks, the Facebook team will be working on updating the terms of use in "simple language that defines Facebook's rights much more specifically."

This is good for users because in order to most responsibly take advantage of the Facebook applications, we need to know where we stand. We can't fully exercise our rights until we know what they are.

continued

It's safe to say that some of the people most upset about this are those who have may not have used Facebook responsibly and are now concerned about the repercussions of that one picture from that one party that one night falling into the hands of someone who was never an intended viewer.

You've heard it time and time again. Be careful what you put online. We all want our privacy and that's understandable. It's one thing to obviously not want your information floating around out there freely, but don't be naive.

We should never count on technology to be 100 percent secure. It is a manmade resource, after all.

Source: www.collegiatetimes.com/stories/13034

As you can see, this author anticipates that the readers' values and counterarguments to the thesis "whenever people access the Internet, they should always assume that they're taking a risk in regard to personal privacy and should accept whatever consequences arise as a result of personal decisions made on the Internet." The author recognizes that readers place a high value on their privacy, may be highly upset at Facebook for sharing their information, and may claim that Facebook falsely led them to believe that users had control over their own information. Would the essay have been as effective if the author had not addressed these concerns and instead simply made the argument that people should take responsibility for their own information online?

Drafting the Position Essay

There are several strategies that you can use as you begin to organize and draft your essay:

- **Begin with an opening paragraph or two that introduces your topic in an interesting way.** Possibilities include a statement of the issue's seriousness or reasons why the issue is currently being debated—or why we should go back to reexamine it. Some writers are spurred by a recent event that receives media coverage; recounting such an event can produce an effective opening. You can also briefly summarize points of the opposition that you will challenge in supporting your claim.

- **Decide where to place your claim (thesis) statement.** Your best choices are either early in your essay (in order to capture your readers' attention and clarify your essay's purpose) or at the end of your essay, after you have made your case. The second approach can be an effective alternative to the more common pattern of stating the claim early if you are attempting to use deductive reasoning or lead your reader through your argument point by point, ultimately reaching a logical and necessary conclusion.

- **Avoiding Thesis Traps.** Writing a clear and engaging argumentative thesis statement can be difficult. Sometimes, students fall into one of the following traps that, more often than not, result in ineffective theses. Be sure that you clearly understand your purpose, your audience, and your writing situation as you construct your thesis statement, so as to avoid these traps.
  The Rhetorical Question Trap. If your thesis is a question, then it is not really an argumentative thesis because it doesn't assert a clear position. You can, of course, use a question to forecast an upcoming point you would like to make (for example, "Isn't making money the whole point

To curb truancy, one Texas school system is requiring students to wear ankle monitors. If you were writing a position essay, would you support this program? What might be your opening line for your paper?

of going to college?"), but this won't be sufficient to make clear your position. Don't make your reader guess where you stand.

The Obvious Fact Trap. If your thesis announces a commonly accepted fact (for example, "Dogs are popular pets" or "Building a fuel-efficient car is important"), you don't have an argument at all. Accepted facts don't stir up reactions or emotions. And in the rare event that someone might disagree with you, your argument will be lackluster and uninspired. You will leave your audience thinking, "I already knew that," and you surely don't want that reaction.

The Personal Response Trap. Your thesis (and your entire argument) depends on much more than your personal opinion. Just because you love strawberry yogurt is not adequate support for the conclusion that it is the best flavor in the world. Be sure that your thesis doesn't simply make public your opinion on an event or issue ("I really liked the movie" or "My 1985 Toyota Corolla is my favorite car in the world"). You must approach your topic in a logical manner, and you must be able to provide clear and convincing support for your thesis. An academic argument cannot stand on the back of a personal opinion. It just can't.

The B-O-R-I-N-G Trap. You don't want your reader to put your essay down before they even get started, right? Your thesis is your chance to grab your readers' attention and excite them (or even fire them up) about your position. Don't blow this opportunity. Try to figure out how to use interesting and expressive nouns, adjectives, and verbs to express exactly what you want to say. Don't worry if you need two or even three sentences to state your thesis. Break the rules. Work it out.

Think about the differences between the following thesis statements. Which ones successfully avoid the thesis traps above?

- All kids should have chores.
- The overindulged and undermotivated teens of this give-it-to-me-now generation should be forced to put down their video game controllers, pick up the piles of stinking laundry on their bedroom floors, and actually contribute to society.
- All parents should require their teens to complete a lengthy list of chores before they are permitted any free time.
- I hated doing chores when I was growing up. Didn't you?

- **Organize evidence in an effective way.** Even if your thesis statement and main points are brilliant, your readers will not find your argument persuasive if they cannot follow it. If your essay seems jumbled or disorganized, or if you do not logically lead your reader from one point to the next, your essay will not be successful. There are several ways to organize a position essay. What is important is to have a clear organization plan and to stick to it. Here are three typical organizations for a position essay:

  - Move from the least important to the most important reasons, followed by rebuttals to potential counterarguments. This organizational plan allows readers to consider your most compelling points and your rebuttals to their objections last, which can increase their retention of these important points.

  - Another possibility is to organize by the arguments of the opposition, explaining why each reason fails to hold up. As you rebut each of your opponent's main points, you will also assert and support your own arguments and show how they are more logical than those typically offered by the opposition. This strategy can be particularly effective if you are writing about a highly controversial issue or to a highly resistant audience. By fairly presenting and effectively refuting each opposing point, you leave your readers no choice but to consider your position on the issue.

  - A third approach is to organize logically. That is, if some reasons require accepting other reasons, you want to begin with the necessary underpinnings and then move forward from those. This approach can be a bit difficult to plan, as many of your reasons will result from your presentation of other reasons. Use effective transitions between paragraphs (sometimes referred to as *metadiscourse*) to lead your reader from point to point. Be sure not to leave logical gaps or make sudden leaps from idea to idea.

- **Provide a logical defense of (or specifics in support of) each reason.** You have not finished your task by simply asserting several reasons for your claim. You also need to present facts or examples for (or a logical explanation of) each reason or rebuttal. For example, defending your views on capital punishment requires more than asserting that it is right or just to take the life of a murderer. Why is it right or just? Executing the murderer will not bring the victim back to life. Do two wrongs make a right? These are some of the questions skeptical readers may have unless you explain and justify your reasoning.

- **Provide adequate context for your relevant source materials.** Simply quoting another writer's opinion on your topic does not provide proof for your reasons. It merely shows that someone else agrees with you. Similarly, dropping quotations into your essay does not necessarily provide support for your ideas. In order to provide context for your

GOOD ADV!CE

George Boole is known as the inventor of Boolean logic, which is the basis of modern digital computer logic.

Conducting Research for Position Essays

Supporting your points with valid research is especially important when you are entering a debate about a highly controversial issue. Simply stating that you are right doesn't convince most readers. Consider conducting a basic keyword search in your library database as part of your prewriting process in order to learn what others are saying about your issue. From there, you can continue to search for relevant articles and even Web sites that will help you support your points. For example, if you are arguing that automated traffic control devices (ticket cameras) should not be legal, you could type the term "automated traffic ticket" into your library's database. Be sure, however, that you understand how your library database works. Unlike Google, which pulls up every possible lead related to all of the words in your search (and can often pull up completely useless material), most library databases use Boolean operators (AND, OR, NOT) to narrow searches to the most relevant and helpful materials. For example, if you type "state of iowa gay marriage legal" into Google, you will get hits, but if you type the same phrase into your library database, you may not (even if your library has many articles on your topic). This is because Boolean searches look for the exact phrase within the context of the articles. For a Boolean search, you would want to type "state of iowa AND gay marriage AND legal. For more information on Boolean operators and how they can affect your library searches, visit your campus library site or go to www.youtube.com/watch?v=vube-ZcJFk4.

quotes (as well as credible support for your argument), you should identify each quote's author, attempt to fully discuss the quote's significance, explain how it supports your claim, and then tie it back to your thesis. It is very important to put your sources (especially of direct quotes) into context for your readers so that they can fully understand the relationship between the author's words and your own. Read the following quote:

> I was called a terrorist yesterday.

If you were given nothing more than this, what guess would you make about the quote's author? Is he a good person? Is he a credible source? It's hard to tell, isn't it? Now read the full quote in the context of a student essay:

> In an interview on *Larry King Live*, Nelson Mandela, who spent over 27 years in prison after fighting for civil rights in South Africa and who was elected that country's first Black president in 1994, stated, "I was called a terrorist yesterday, but when I came out of jail, many people embraced me, including my enemies, and that is what I normally tell other people who say those who are struggling for

> liberation in their country are terrorists. I tell them that I was also a terrorist yesterday, but, today, I am admired by the very people who said I was one." The fact that Mandela, who is known as one of the most active civil rights advocates in the world could be called a terrorist by some supports my notion that terrorism, and in fact, the entire premise of "evil" is a subjective concept. After all, what is evil to one might just be necessary or even positive to another.

www.notable-quotes.com/t/terrorism_quotes.html

Does the quote make sense in this context? Would readers accept this as a credible and reliable source for an essay? Do you understand why this author chose this quote and how it supports his claim?

- **Use effective visuals to support your position.**

  - Oftentimes, a well-crafted or well-placed visual element can serve as excellent support for your argument. After all, people respond very differently to visuals than they do to text, even in academic essays. Visuals can help to clarify statistics, provide evidence of your claims, or even make effective use of irony or satire. These tasks can be more difficult to accomplish with text alone. There is a good reason for the old expression "a picture is worth a thousand words." Let's examine some of the types of visuals you might want to use as you draft your position essay. *Note:* Be sure to provide captions for each of your visual elements to explain its significance for your argument and to properly provide attribution according to your instructor's documentation guidelines. Visuals, like all sources, need to be cited!

Top 10 Global Markets for Fast Food Consumption

Market	Percent of Adult Population That Eats Fast Food at Least Once a Week
Hong Kong	61%
Malaysia	59%
Philippines	54%
Singapore	50%
Thailand	44%
China	41%
India	37%
United States	35%
Australia	30%
New Zealand	29%

Source: From *Consumers in Europe—Our Fast Food/Take Away Consumption Habits, 2nd Half, 2004.* ACNielsen, 2005. http://ie.nielsen.com/pubs/documents/EuroFastFoodDec04.pdf. The Nielsen Company. Reprinted with permission.

- Charts, graphs, and tables can help you to clarify difficult concepts or statistics for your readers. Consider learning how to create your own tables or graphs in a spreadsheet or word-processing program. For example, if, while asserting that many Americans don't seem to care about their health, you presented the table in the left column showing that 35% of American adults eat fast food at least once a week, you would be providing solid support for your claim.

- Photographs can help to support your claims by actually showing rather than telling your reader that something is occurring or should be changed. For example, if you were writing an essay arguing that your environmental group should receive funding to clean up the local river, might a photograph like the one in the bottom left column and taken by you help support your claim?

- Stock images, while often not as compelling as personal photos, can make a big impact on a reader. They can help to introduce a controversy and show readers a side of an issue they may not have considered before. These can be especially useful at the beginning of an essay to grab the readers' attention and create interest in your topic. For example, if you were writing an essay about eating disorders, imagine using the stock photo below in your introduction. Does it make an impact?

GOOD ADV!CE

A CHECKLIST FOR REVISION

☐ Do I have a clear statement of my claim? Is it qualified, if appropriate? Have I organized my argument, building the parts of my support into a clear and logical structure that readers can follow?

☐ Have I avoided logical fallacies?

☐ Have I presented and effectively rebutted my readers' potential objections to my argument?

☐ Have I found relevant facts and examples to support and develop my reasons?

☐ Have I used appropriate visuals that support and clarify my argument?

☐ Have I paid attention to appropriate word choice, including using a conciliatory approach if that is a wise strategy?

☐ Have I used the basic checklist for revision in Chapter 4 (see page 82)?

- **Maintain an appropriate level of seriousness for an argument of principle.** Of course, your word choice must be appropriate to a serious discussion, but in addition be sure your reasons are also appropriately serious. For example, if you are defending the claim that music CDs should not be subject to content labeling because such censorship is inconsistent with First Amendment rights, do not trivialize your argument by including the point that young people are tired of adults controlling their lives. (This is an issue for another paper.)

making connections

let's review

After reading this chapter, you should understand:

- Taking-a-position or taking-a-stand arguments appear not only in academic settings as formal essays, but also as editorials in newspapers, flyers for causes or candidates, blog entries on the Web, and even magazine articles.

- A position argument often makes a claim about what is right or wrong, good or bad for us as individuals or as a society. It may not always ask readers to take a specific action, but it may ask them to change their beliefs or to examine their values.

- A value is any principle, standard, or quality that we believe is worthwhile or important. People often form their positions based on their personal values and belief systems. This means that in order to write a persuasive position essay, you must understand not only your own values but also the values of your readers and how those values affect their position on your topic.

- Before you can begin drafting your essay, you will need to spend some time thinking about your topic, your audience, your specific purpose, and your strategy.

- Discovering the counterarguments to your position is an important part of the writing process. This will not only allow you to more fully understand the complexity of your issue, but also to more effectively defend your position in the face of opposition.

- The key to presenting your opponents' position is to always be fair but not to give their position any more weight than necessary. You should demonstrate that you understand the complexities of alternate positions and the reasons why your readers may hold those views.

- One strategy that might help you is to use conciliatory language in an attempt to find common ground with your reader.

- You will need to make important decisions about thesis placement, organization strategy, finding sources, and using visuals as you draft.

connect

Read the following position argument. Individually or with your classmates, analyze the argument being made. Use the questions at the end of the reading to guide your discussion.

Brain-Enhancing Drugs: Legalize 'Em, Scientists Say

Brandon Keim

December 10, 2008

If drugs can safely give your brain a boost, why not take them? And if you don't want to, why stop others?

In an era when attention-disorder drugs are regularly—and illegally—being used for off-label purposes by people seeking a better grade or year-end job review, these are timely ethical questions.

The latest answer comes from *Nature*, where seven prominent ethicists and neuroscientists recently published a paper entitled, "Towards a responsible use of cognitive-enhancing drugs by the healthy."

In short: Legalize 'em.

"Mentally competent adults," they write, "should be able to engage in cognitive enhancement using drugs."

Roughly seven percent of all college students, and up to 20 percent of scientists, have already used Ritalin or Adderall—originally intended to treat attention-deficit disorders—to improve their mental performance.

Some people argue that chemical cognition-enhancement is a form of cheating. Others say that it's unnatural. The *Nature* authors counter these charges: Brain boosters are only cheating, they say, if prohibited by the rules—which need not be the case. As for the drugs being unnatural, the authors argue, they're no more unnatural than medicine, education and housing.

In many ways, the arguments are compelling. Nobody rejects pasteurized milk or dental anesthesia or central heating because it's unnatural. And whether a brain is altered by drugs, education or healthy eating, it's being altered at the same neurobiological level. Making moral distinctions between them is arbitrary.

But if a few people use cognition-enhancing drugs, might everyone else be forced to follow, whether they want to or not?

If enough people improve their performance, then improvement becomes the status quo. Brain-boosting drug use could become a basic job requirement. Ritalin and Adderall, now ubiquitous as academic pick-me-ups, are merely the first generation of brain boosters. Next up is

continued

Provigil, a "wakefulness promoting agent" that lets people go for days without sleep, and improves memory to boot. More powerful drugs will follow. As the *Nature* authors write, "cognitive enhancements affect the most complex and important human organ and the risk of unintended side effects is therefore both high and consequential." But even if their safety could be assured, what happens when workers are expected to be capable of marathon bouts of high-functioning sleeplessness?

Most people I know already work 50 hours a week and struggle to find time for friends, family, and the demands of life. None wish to become fully robotic in order to keep their jobs. So I posed the question to Michael Gazzaniga, a University of California, Santa Barbara, psychobiologist and *Nature* article co-author.

"It is possible to do all of that now with existing drugs," he said. "One has to set their goals and know when to tell their boss to get lost!"

Which is not, perhaps, the most practical career advice these days. And University of Pennsylvania neuroethicist Martha Farah, another of the paper's authors, was a bit less sanguine.

"First the early adopters use the enhancements to get an edge. Then, as more people adopt them, those who don't, feel they must just to stay competitive with what is, in effect, a new higher standard," she said.

Citing the now-normal stresses produced by expectations of round-the-clock worker availability and inhuman powers of multitasking, Farah said, "There is definitely a risk of this dynamic repeating itself with cognition-enhancing drugs."

But people are already using them, she said. Some version of this scenario is inevitable—and the solution, she said, isn't to simply say that cognition enhancement is bad.

Instead we should develop better drugs, understand why people use them, promote alternatives and create sensible policies that minimize their harm.

As Gazzaniga also pointed out, "People might stop research on drugs that may well help memory loss in the elderly"—or cognition problems in the young—"because of concerns over misuse or abuse."

This would certainly be unfortunate collateral damage in the 21st-century theater of the War on Drugs—and the question of brain enhancement needs to be seen in the context of this costly and destructive war. As Schedule II substances, Ritalin and Adderall are legally equivalent in the United States to opium or cocaine.

"These laws," write the *Nature* authors, "should be adjusted to avoid making felons out of those who seek to use safe cognitive enhancements."

After all, according to the law's letter, 7 percent of college students and 20 percent of scientists should have done jail time—this journalist, too.

RESPONDING TO CONTENT

1. What is the writer's claim? Is it clear?

2. Is the claim qualified if necessary? Some claims of value are broad philosophical assertions: "Capital punishment is immoral and bad public policy." Others are qualified: "Capital punishment is acceptable only in crimes of treason."

3. What facts and sources are presented? Are they credible? Are they relevant to the claim's support?

4. What reasons are given in support of the claim? What assumptions are necessary to tie reasons to the claim? Make a list of reasons and assumptions and analyze the writer's logic. Do you find any fallacies?

5. Has the author considered the implications of his or her claim? For example, if you argue for the abolishment of a legal drinking age, you eliminate all underage drinking problems by definition. But what new problems may be created by this approach? Consider more car accidents and reduced productivity in school for openers.

6. Is the argument convincing? Does the evidence provide strong support for the claim? Has the writer demonstrated understanding of possible opposing positions? Has the writer effectively refuted or accommodated those positions without sacrificing his or her own position? Are you prepared to agree with the writer in whole or in part, or at the very least to consider the writer's position as valid?

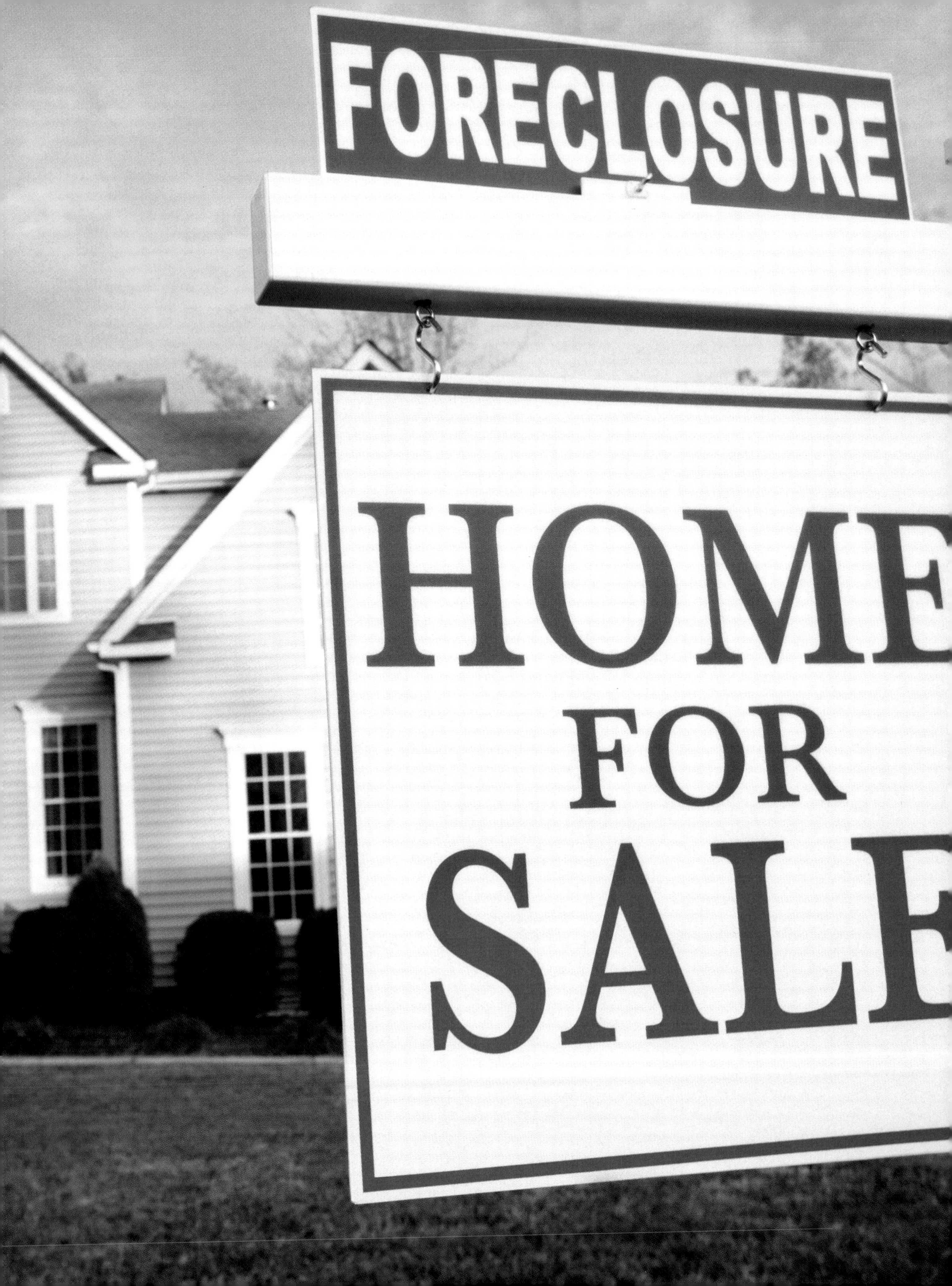
FORECLOSURE
HOME
FOR
SALE

the causal essay

WHAT'S TO COME

Autism Trend (1992–2005)
California Department of Education

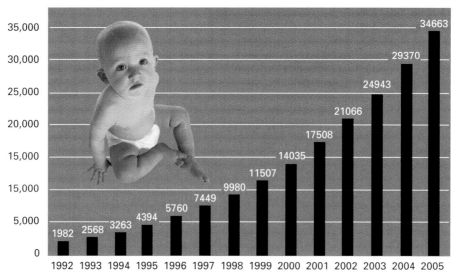

Reprinted by permission from the California Department of Education, CDE Press, 1430 N Street, Suite 3207, Sacramento, CA 95814.

What Is a Causal Essay?

This graph demonstrates the increase in the number of autism cases reported in California over the past decade. Writing a causal argument can help you and your readers speculate about and possibly determine why trends are occurring.

Because we want to know why things happen, arguments about cause abound. We want to understand past events (why did so many Americans buy houses in the early 2000s that they couldn't afford?). We want to explain current situations (why do some teenagers use drugs while others don't?). We want to predict the future (will the economy improve if taxes are cut?).

The answers to all three questions require causal arguments. In a causal essay, you will be expected to write an argument that asserts what you believe to be the main causes of the trend, event, or phenomenon and that supports your assertion with logical reasons and evidence.

Some specific terms related to the discussion of causation provide useful distinctions about why something has happened (or not happened). For example, a house fire is an **event.**

First, when looking for the cause of an event, we look for an **agent**—a person, a situation, another event that caused the event to take place. A lit cigarette dropped in a bed caused a house fire; the lit cigarette is the agent. But why, we ask, did someone drop a lit cigarette on a bed? The person, old and ill, took a sleeping pill and dropped the cigarette when he fell asleep. Where do we stop in this chain of causes?

Second, we learn that most events do not occur in a vacuum with a single cause. There are **conditions** surrounding the event, making the assigning of only one cause often difficult. For example, the man's age and health are conditions.

Third, we can also speak of **influences.** The sleeping pill certainly influenced the man to drop the cigarette and cause the fire. Some conditions and influences may qualify as *remote causes.*

Proximate causes are more immediate, usually closer in time to the event or situation. The man's dozing off with a lighted cigarette is a proximate cause of the fire.

Finally, we come to the **precipitating cause,** the triggering event—for example, the cigarette's igniting the combustible mattress fabric. Isolating a precipitating cause is usually necessary to prevent events from recurring, but often we need to go further back to determine remote causes or conditions, especially if we are interested in assigning responsibility for what has occurred.

You encounter causal arguments all the time. Every scientific research project you will either write or read hypothesizes about a possible cause and then attempts to support or reject it. Investigative journalists often write articles that probe for potential causes of incidents or trends in their communities. And whenever a monumental event occurs (9/11 or the economic recession of 2008, for example), many newscasters, pundits, and even laypeople attempt to make sense of it by investigating its possible causes. This type of argument can lead not only to a better understanding of the world around us, but also to remedies that allow for positive change. We must, after all, understand what is causing something before we can make effective changes.

Characteristics of Causal Arguments

Assigning cause is tricky business. Perhaps that is the first and most important point to make. Here are some other points about causal arguments.

- Causal arguments are similar in their purpose but vary considerably in their subject matter and structure. Some causal arguments are about a particular situation; others seek explanations for a general state of affairs. However, in either case there may be one or there may be several causes.

- Because some complex situations have long chains of causes, arguers about cause need to decide on their focus—based on their purpose in writing. While it may be simpler to determine the causes of a specific event (the house fire example in the Good Advice box), sometimes it gets a bit more complicated to find the causes of a trend or an ongoing phenomenon. Suppose, for example, your concern is global warming. Cows contribute to global warming. Factories contribute to global warming. Car emissions contribute to global warming. But do all of these contribute equally to the phenomenon? Your task as a writer is to determine which of all potential causes is the most likely or most plausible cause of the event, trend, or phenomenon. You do not need to present every potential cause. However, you must make it clear to your reader that while other possibilities exist,

did you know?

What Is a Trend?
A **trend** is a prevailing tendency over a period of time. For example, more mothers work today than in the 1950s. This is a social trend. You might speculate about why things have changed over time or why they have remained the same.

A **phenomenon** is an observable and unique occurrence. For example, you might wonder about why nearly 7 million people aged 35–54 currently have a Facebook page (www.scribd.com/doc/9713724/Facebook-Demographics-and-Statistics-2009).

An historical **event** is something that happened in the past and is well documented. As a result, historical events do not typically lead to effective and engaging causal essays.

your chosen cause is the most likely or reasonable. This, in effect, allows you to deal with counterarguments (possible objections) to your claim. (For more on counterargument in causal arguments, see page 142, later in this chapter.)

Recognizing Relationships in Causal Arguments

It can be tricky to identify the cause-effect relationship between two events or issues. Just because one event follows another does not necessarily mean that the first caused the second. For example, imagine eating strawberry yogurt at every meal for three days. At the end of the third day, you get a severe migraine headache. Could you logically argue that the strawberry yogurt was the cause of the headache? Possibly. There may very well be a causal relationship between the two. On the other hand, there may be no relationship between the two events at all. It would be up to you to prove the relationship exists. Simply demonstrating that one followed the other would not be sufficient evidence for your readers. As you construct your own causal essay,

try it!

From the following events or situations, select the one you know best and list as many conditions, influences, and causes—remote, proximate, precipitating—as you can think of. You may want to do this exercise with your class partner or in a small group. Be prepared to explain your causal pattern to the class.

1. Teen suicide

2. Decrease in the use of condoms by college students

3. Increase in the numbers of women elected to public office

4. High salaries of professional athletes

5. Increased interest in soccer in the United States

6. Comparatively low scores by U.S. students on international tests in math and science

This billboard for AAA presents a causal argument. For what cause-and-effect relationship is the author attempting to argue? Do you think it is a valid causal relationship? How do you feel about the use of visuals in this argument? Do they serve as logical support or do they have a different purpose?

you will need to pay special attention to causal relationships to ensure that you are not engaging in a post-hoc logical fallacy (see Chapter 5 for more on logical fallacies) or creating relationships that do not exist.

Mill's Methods for Investigating Causes

John Stuart Mill, a nineteenth-century British philosopher, explained some important ways of investigating and demonstrating causal relationships: commonality, difference, and process of elimination. We can benefit in our study of cause by understanding and using his methods.

1. **Commonality.** One way to isolate cause is to demonstrate that one agent is common to similar outcomes. For instance, 25 employees attend a company luncheon. Late in the day, 10 report to area hospitals, and another 4 complain the next day of having experienced vomiting the night before. Public health officials will soon want to know what these people ate for lunch. Different people during the same 12-hour period had similar physical symptoms of food poisoning. The common factor may well have been the tuna salad they ate for lunch.

2. **Difference.** Another way to isolate cause is to recognize one key difference. If two situations

are alike in every way but one, and the situations result in different outcomes, then the one way they differ must have caused the different outcome. Studies in the social sciences are often based on the single-difference method. To test for the best teaching methods for math, an educator could set up an experiment with two classrooms similar in every way except that one class devotes 15 minutes three days a week to instruction by drill. If the class receiving the drill scores much higher on a standardized test given to both groups of students, the educator could argue that math drills make a measurable difference in learning math.

But the educator should be prepared for skeptics to challenge the assertion of only one difference between the two classes. Could the teacher's attitude toward the drills also make a difference in student learning? If the differences in student scores are significant, the educator probably has a good argument, even though a teacher's attitude cannot be controlled in the experiment.

3. **Process of elimination.** You can develop a causal argument around a technique we all use for problem solving: the process of elimination. When something happens, we examine all possible causes and eliminate them, one by one, until we are satisfied that we have isolated the actual cause (or causes). When the Federal Aviation Administration investigates a plane crash, it uses this pro-

cess, exploring possible causes such as mechanical failure, weather, human error, and terrorism. Sometimes the process points to more than one cause or to a likely cause without providing absolute proof.

Planning and Drafting a Causal Argument

Before you begin drafting your causal argument, you will want to spend a significant amount of time working through your ideas. This type of argument is tricky, and writers can easily be led astray and end up attempting to solve a problem (which is a different type of argument). Other pitfalls include focusing too heavily on one cause while ignoring other important possible causes, creating false or illogical cause-and-effect relationships between events, and simply stating a cause without providing sufficient evidence to support its effects. There are, however, specific strategies for writing causal arguments that you can use, in addition to the guidelines for writing arguments presented in Chapter 4.

Planning the Causal Argument

As with all effective arguments, organized and strategic planning is key to causal arguments. In order to plan your essay, you should begin by asking yourself the following questions:

- **What are the focus and limits of your causal argument?** Do you want to argue for one cause of an event or situation? Do you want to argue for several causes leading to an event or situation? Do you want to argue for a cause that others have overlooked? Do you want to show how one cause is common to several situations or events? Diagramming the relationship of cause to effect may help you see what to focus on. For example:

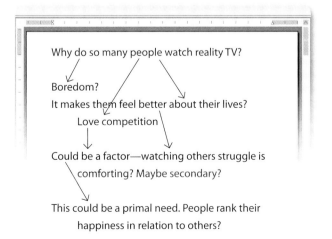

- **What reasons and evidence do you have to support your tentative claim?** Consider what you already know that has led to your choice of topic. A brainstorming list may be helpful. You may also want to conduct some initial research in order to find out what others have said about your issue. For example:

What do I know?

All of my friends watch tons of reality shows.

It seems to be a trend over the past decade or so. There are lots more than there used to be.

Many of them include competition of some kind.

The producers make them very (maybe overly) dramatic.

Some of them are not real at all.

Many of them include love relationships.

What will I need to find out?

How many shows are there now as compared to a decade ago?

How many people watch these shows?

What do other researchers say is causing this trend?

Are there surveys that ask people why they watch?

What types of needs are these shows fulfilling? What do they do for them?

Are certain types of shows more successful than others? If so, why?

Where can I find these answers?

- **How, then, do you want to word your thesis?** As we have discussed, wording is crucial in causal arguments. Can you make a firm and definite claim about a direct cause-and-effect relationship? Or should you present several possible causes and then argue that one is more likely than the others? Or might you argue that several factors are contributing to the effect in combination? The key is to make your claim clear to your reader. Do not overstate or understate the relationship you are attempting to support.

- **What, if any, additional evidence do you need to develop a convincing argument?** You may need to do some library or online research to obtain data to strengthen your argument. Readers expect relevant, reliable, current statistics in most arguments about cause. Assess what you need and

Consider the following options for integrating research into your causal argument. Which do you think would be more engaging, and ultimately more persuasive, to a reader? Why? What can visuals sometimes do more effectively for your argument than words?

OPTION A

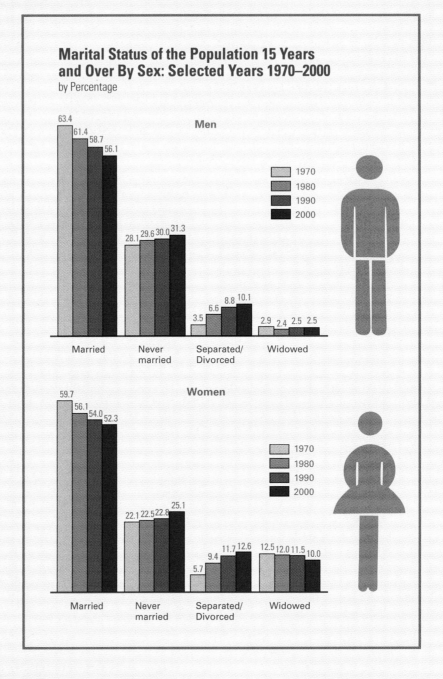

Marital Status of the Population 15 Years and Over By Sex: Selected Years 1970–2000
by Percentage

OPTION B

There were approximately 2,230,000 marriages in 2005—down from 2,279,000 the previous year, despite a total population increase of 2.9 million over the same period. Furthermore, the divorce rate in 2005 (per 1,000 people) was 3.6—the lowest rate since 1970, and down from 4.2 in 2000 and from 4.7 in 1990. (The peak was at 5.3 in 1981, according to the Associated Press.)

Jason Fields and Lynne M. Casper, America's Families and Living Arrangements: March 2000.
Current Population Reports, P20-537. Washington, DC: U.S. Census Bureau, Figure 4 (p. 10).
www.census.gov/prod/2001pubs/p20-537.pdf.

S
E E
I N G
THE ARGUMENT
SEEING THE ARGUMENT

then think about what sources will provide the needed information.

- **What assumptions (warrants) are you making in your causal reasoning?** Do these assumptions hold up to logical scrutiny? Will readers be likely to agree with your assumptions, or will you need to defend them as part of the development of your argument? For example, one reason that heavy TV watching has an effect on viewers is the commonsense argument that what we devote considerable time to has a significant effect on our lives. Will your readers be prepared to accept this commonsense reasoning, or will they remain skeptical, looking for stronger evidence of a cause-effect relationship?

Using Visuals in the Causal Essay

Oftentimes, causal essays depend heavily on the presentation of research and statistical data. After all, you must demonstrate that the trend or phenomenon is actually occurring before you can defend a specific cause (or causes). Visual representations such as charts and graphs can be very helpful in causal essays. Visuals allow your readers to quickly and easily understand trends, statistics, and complex information about cause-effect relationships.

Drafting the Causal Argument

As you begin to draft your argument, you will want to keep the following points in mind:

- **Begin with an opening paragraph or two that introduces your topic in an interesting way.** Look at the way Gregg Easterbrook begins his essay (Try It! on pages 143–145). Why does he present the controversy in this way rather than simply stating "I believe that television is a possible cause of autism"?

  This opening establishes the topic and Easterbrook's purpose in examining causes—that current research is supporting a hypothesis he made in the past. The statistics and research presented in these early paragraphs get the readers' attention. You may also want to use visuals in your introduction to grab your readers' interest and to present statistical data regarding your trend or phenomenon. Do not begin by announcing your subject. Avoid openers such as "In this essay I will explain the causes of teen vandalism."

- **Decide where to place your claim statement.** You can conclude your opening paragraph with it, or you can place it in your conclusion, after you have shown readers how best to understand the causes of the issue you are examining. Easterbrook uses a third technique—the implied

claim—to his advantage. He makes it clear to his readers what his position is throughout the essay without actually stating it outright. Be careful when using this technique, however. It is usually much safer to explicitly state your claim at either the beginning or end of your essay.

- **Present reasons and evidence in an organized way.** There are several effective strategies for organizing a causal essay:

  1. If you are examining a series of causes and begin with background conditions and early influences, then your basic plan will be time sequence. Readers need to see the chain of causes unfolding. Consider using appropriate terms and transitional words to guide readers through each stage in the causal pattern. Some transitional phrases that indicate a series of events include *at first, first of all, to begin with, in the first place, at the same time, for now, for the time being, the next step, in time, in turn, later on, meanwhile, next, then, soon, in the meantime, later, while, earlier, simultaneously, afterward, in conclusion, with this in mind.*

  2. Or you may choose to organize your essay by refuting the validity of other potential causes. If you are arguing for an overlooked or less-than-popular cause, begin with the familiar causes and show the flaws in each one (in other words, rebut each potential counterargument or alternate cause). Then present and defend your explanation of cause. This process-of-elimination structure works well when readers are likely to know what other causes have been offered in the past. You can also use one of Mill's other two approaches if one of them is relevant to your situation. That is, you can present the points of commonality or difference that show your explanation of cause to be valid.

  3. Address the issue of correlation rather than cause, if appropriate. After presenting the results of a study of marriage that reveals many benefits (emotional, physical, financial) of marriage, you might wish to examine the question that skeptical readers may have: Does marriage cause the benefits, or is the relationship one of correlation only—that is, do the benefits of marriage just happen to come with being married instead of being caused by being married? As you try to determine the main cause of a trend or phenomenon, you will need to admit if there is a possibility for correlation. This demonstrates to your reader that you are a logical writer and creates credibility for your work.

We've all waited for an elevator with someone who pushes the button repeatedly just prior to the doors opening. But does pushing the button repeatedly make the elevator come faster? The answer is clearly no. While there may be a correlation between the two events, the first does not cause the second. Watch for this common error while constructing your causal essay.

4. Conclude by discussing the implications of the causal pattern you have argued for, if appropriate. If, for example, in explaining the causes of teen vandalism, you see one cause as "group behavior," a gang looking for something to do, it then follows that you can advise young readers to stay out of gangs. Often with arguments about cause, there are personal or public-policy implications in accepting the causal explanation. Just be careful not to spend the majority of your essay on solutions rather than arguments for your claim.

Counterarguments in Causal Essays

Counterarguments play a very important role in the causal essay. They can help you eliminate alternate potential causes, which will help lead your reader to the conclusion that your cause is the most logical or acceptable. By refuting what others believe is causing the trend or phenomenon, you can build support for your own argument. But be careful! You don't have to completely dismiss the validity of every alternate cause. You can acknowledge their effects on the trend, while still building a case for your cause being the primary cause. For example, imagine writing a causal essay focusing on the state of the education system in America.

> Your writing purpose: Statistics suggest that America is falling far behind many other nations in producing well-educated and globally prepared citizens. What is the main cause of this trend?

> Tentative thesis: The central cause of the declining academic preparedness of American students is the lack of funding for public school systems that do not currently meet the "no child left behind" testing standards.

Imagine how this thesis might be received by your readers who believe that the "no child left behind" act is an effective program that promotes high standards. They may immediately reject your thesis (or your entire essay) based on the fact that your focus seems to ignore the complexity of this issue. If your entire essay simply goes on to provide negative information about the "no child left behind" program and then concludes that this is the main cause of the problem, your essay will fail to persuade your skeptical readers.

Instead, you will need to address the complexity of the issue by pointing to other potential causes (counterarguments) and then addressing why they are not contributing to the problem as much as is your chosen cause (rebuttal). For example, if your thesis was revised to read

> Although many factors contribute to declining student preparedness in America, including poor teacher education and a lack of parental involvement, the primary cause of this disturbing trend is the lack of funding for public school systems that do not currently meet the "no child left behind" testing standards.

This thesis demonstrates the complexity of the issue and forecasts that you will present those alternate possibilities but will ultimately rebut the idea that they are the most likely or plausible causes of the trend. Including alternate causes and points of view demonstrates that you have a deep understanding of your issue and that you are a credible and thoughtful writer.

A Checklist for Revision

As you revise your causal essay, you will need to ask yourself the following questions. Read through your essay with these in mind:

- Do I have a clear statement of my claim? Is it appropriately qualified and focused?

- Have I organized my argument so that readers can see my pattern for examining cause?

- Have I used the language for discussing causes correctly, distinguishing among conditions and influences and remote and proximate causes? Have I selected the correct word—either *affect* or *effect*—as needed?

- Have I avoided the post hoc fallacy and the confusing of correlation and cause? Have I engaged in other logical fallacies? (See Chapter 5 for more on fallacies.)

Many people are concerned about the state of America's educational system. In fact, a report by the Promise Alliance states that nearly 50 percent of students in America's largest cities fail to graduate from high school. A causal essay might argue that this is due to student apathy, poor teachers, a lack of funding for materials and curriculum development, or even a combination of all three. Can you think of other potential causes?

try it !

As you read the following excerpt from an article posted on Slate.com, see if you can identify how this author is using counterarguments to his advantage. Does he present alternate causes, but still manage to point to one as the most likely or plausible? Do you find his argument more compelling because of his use of counterargument? Why or why not? Is this author making a direct cause-and-effect claim? Or is his claim implied and more complicated than that? What do you think he believes causes autism? How do you know?

TV Really Might Cause Autism
A Slate *exclusive: Findings from a new Cornell study*
Gregg Easterbrook
Slate Magazine
October 16, 2006

Last month, I speculated in *Slate* that the mounting incidence of childhood autism may be related to increased television viewing among the very young. The autism rise began around 1980, about the same time cable television and VCRs became common, allowing children to watch television aimed at them any time. Since the brain is organizing during the first years of life and since human beings evolved responding to three-dimensional stimuli, I wondered if exposing toddlers to lots of colorful two-dimensional stimulation could be harmful to brain development.

continued

This was sheer speculation, since I knew of no researchers pursuing the question.

Today, Cornell University researchers are reporting what appears to be a statistically significant relationship between autism rates and television watching by children under the age of 3. The researchers studied autism incidence in California, Oregon, Pennsylvania, and Washington state. They found that as cable television became common in California and Pennsylvania beginning around 1980, childhood autism rose more in the counties that had cable than in the counties that did not. They further found that in all the western states, the more time toddlers spent in front of the television, the more likely they were to exhibit symptoms of autism disorders.

The Cornell study represents a potential bombshell in the autism debate. "We are not saying we have found the cause of autism, we're saying we have found a critical piece of evidence," Cornell researcher Michael Waldman told me. Because autism rates are increasing broadly across the country and across income and ethnic groups, it seems logical that the trigger is something to which children are broadly exposed. Vaccines were a leading suspect, but numerous studies have failed to show any definitive link between autism and vaccines, while the autism rise has continued since worrisome compounds in vaccines were banned. What if the malefactor is not a chemical? Studies suggest that American children now watch about four hours of television daily. Before 1980—the first kids-oriented channel, Nickelodeon, dates to 1979—the figure is believed to have been much lower.

[. . .]

But the fact that rising household access to cable television seems to associate with rising autism does not reveal anything about how viewing hours might link to the disorder. The Cornell team searched for some independent measure of increased television viewing. In recent years, leading behavioral economists such as Caroline Hoxby and Steven Levitt have used weather or geography to test assumptions about behavior. Bureau of Labor Statistics studies have found that when it rains or snows, television viewing by young children rises. So Waldman studied precipitation records for California, Oregon, and Washington State, which, because of climate and geography, experience big swings in precipitation levels both year-by-year and county-by-county. He found what appears to be a dramatic relationship between television viewing and autism onset. In counties or years when rain and snow were unusually high, and hence it is assumed children spent a lot of time watching television, autism rates shot up; in places or years of low precipitation, autism rates were low. Waldman [concludes] that "just under 40 percent of autism diagnoses in the three states studied is the result of television watching." Thus the study has two separate findings: that having cable television in the home increased autism rates in California and Pennsylvania somewhat, and that more hours of actually watching television increased autism in California, Oregon, and Washington by a lot.

[. . .]

There are many possible objections to the Cornell study. One is that time indoors, not television, may be the autism trigger. Generally, indoor air quality is much lower than outdoor air quality: Recently the Environmental Protection Agency warned, "Risks to health may be greater due to exposure to air pollution indoors than outdoors." Perhaps if rain and snow cause young children to spend more time indoors, added exposure to indoor air pollution harms them. It may be that families with children at risk for autism disorders are for some reason more likely to move to areas that get lots of rain and snow or to move to areas with high cable-television usage. Some other factor may explain what only appears to be a television-autism relationship.

[...]

Researchers might also turn new attention to study of the Amish. Autism is rare in Amish society, and the standing assumption has been that this is because most Amish refuse to vaccinate children. The Amish also do not watch television.

Gregg Easterbrook is a fellow at the Brookings Institution. His most recent book is *The Progress Paradox: How Life Gets Better While People Feel Worse.*

- Have I carefully examined my assumptions and convinced myself that they are reasonable and can be defended? Have I defended them when necessary to clarify and thus strengthen my argument?

- Have I found relevant facts and examples to support and develop my argument? Do I need more research, statistics, or visuals to support my claims?

- Have I used the basic checklist for revision in Chapter 4 (see page 82)?

Guidelines for Analyzing Causal Arguments

When analyzing causal arguments, what should you look for? The basics of good argument apply to all arguments: a clear statement of claim, qualified if appropriate, a clear explanation of reasons and evidence, and enough relevant evidence to support the claim. How do we recognize these qualities in a causal argument? Use the following points as guides to analyzing:

- **Does the writer carefully distinguish among types of causes?** Word choice is crucial. Is the argument that A and A alone caused B, or that A was one of several contributing causes?

- **Does the writer recognize the complexity of causation and not rush to assert only one cause for a complex event or situation?** The credibility of an

argument about cause is quickly lost if readers find the argument oversimplified.

- **Is the argument's claim clearly stated, with qualifications as appropriate?** If the writer wants to argue for one cause, not the only cause, of an event or situation, then the claim's wording must make this limited goal clear to readers. For example, one can perhaps build the case for heavy television viewing as one cause of stereotyping, loss of sensitivity to violence, and increased fearfulness. But we know that the home environment and neighborhood and school environments also do much to shape attitudes.

- **What reasons and evidence are given to support the argument?** Can you see the writer's pattern of development? Does the reasoning seem logical? Are the data relevant? Is the reasoning presented in a clear manner? Does the author use visuals to make statistical data easier to comprehend? This kind of analysis of the argument's support will help you evaluate it.

- **Does the argument demonstrate causality, not just a time relationship or correlation?** A causal argument needs to prove agency: A is the cause of B, not just something that happened before B or something that is present when B is present. March precedes April, but March does not cause April to arrive.

- **Does the writer present believable and plausible causal agents, agents consistent with our knowledge of human behavior and scientific laws?** Most educated people do not believe that personalities are shaped by astrological signs or that scientific laws are suspended in the Bermuda Triangle, allowing planes and ships to vanish or enter a fourth dimension.

- **What are the implications for accepting the causal argument?** If A and B clearly are the causes of C, and we don't want C to occur, then we presumably must do something about A and B—or at least we must do something about either A or B and see if reducing or eliminating one of the causes significantly reduces the incidence of C.

- **Is the argument convincing?** After analyzing the argument and answering the preceding questions, you need to decide if, finally, the argument works.

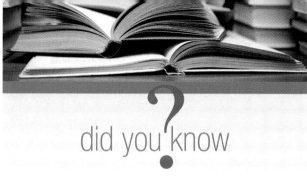

making connections

let's review

After reading this chapter, you should understand:

- How to write an argument that asserts what you believe to be the main causes of the trend, event, or phenomenon and that supports that assertion with logical reasons and evidence.

- This type of argument can not only lead to a better understanding of the world around us, but also to specific remedies that allow for positive change. We must, after all, understand what is causing something before we can make effective changes.

- Some causal arguments are about a particular situation; others seek explanations for a general state of affairs. However, in either case there may be one or several causes.

- It can often be tricky to identify the cause-effect relationship between two events or issues. Just because one event follows another, does not necessarily mean that the first caused the second.

- Before you begin drafting your causal argument, you will want to spend a significant amount of time working through your ideas.

- Oftentimes, causal essays depend heavily on the presentation of research and statistical data. Visual representations such as charts and graphs can be very helpful in causal essays. Visuals allow readers to quickly and easily understand trends, statistics, and complex information about cause-effect relationships.

- Counterarguments play a very important role in the causal essay. They can help you eliminate alternate potential causes, which will help lead your reader to the conclusion that your cause is the most logical or acceptable.

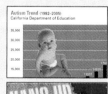

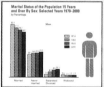

Read and study the following annotated argument. See if you can recognize the features of a causal argument as you read. Answer the questions that follow and discuss your analysis with your class.

A Specious "Experiment"

Eugene Robinson

A graduate of the University of Michigan where he was the first black student to be co-editor-in-chief of the university's student newspaper, Eugene Robinson joined The Washington Post *in 1980. He has served as city reporter, foreign correspondent, and managing editor in charge of the paper's style section. He is now an associate editor and twice-weekly columnist. Robinson focuses on the mix of culture and politics as the following column, published October 4, 2005, reveals. In this piece, Robinson attempts to discover why William Bennett, a talk-radio host, made inflammatory comments on the air.*

There's no need to pillory William Bennett for his "thought experiment" about how aborting all black children would affect the crime rate. I believe him when he says he wasn't actually advocating genocide, just musing about it to make a point. Instead of going into high-dudgeon mode, let's put him on the couch.

Attention-getting opening. How the author will deal with the issue.

Bennett, the former education secretary and anti-drug czar who has found a new calling in talk radio, told his audience last week that "if you wanted to reduce crime, you could—if that were your sole purpose—you could abort every black baby in this country, and your crime rate would go down." He quickly added that doing so would be "impossible, ridiculous and morally reprehensible," which is certainly true.

Explanation of the situation—what Bennett did and how he defended his actions.

So why would such a horrible idea even cross his mind? How could such an evil notion ever pass his lips?

Bennett was referring to research done by Steven D. Levitt, a University of Chicago economist and lead author of the best-selling book *Freakonomics*. The iconoclastic Levitt, something of an academic rock star, argues that the steep drop in crime in the United States over the past 15 years resulted in part from the *Roe v. Wade* decision legalizing abortion. In defending his words, Bennett has said he was citing *Freakonomics*. So why did his "thought experiment" refer only to black children?

Possible cause for Bennett's "experiment" and Robinson's rejection of this cause.

Levitt's thesis is essentially that unwanted children who grow up poor in single-parent households are more likely than other children to become criminals, and that *Roe v. Wade* resulted in fewer of these children being born. What he doesn't do in the book is single out black children.

Perhaps the ostentatiously intellectual Bennett went back and read Levitt's original 2001 paper on the subject, co-authored with John J. Donohue III. The authors do mention race briefly, in a discussion of the falling homicide rate, but attribute most of the decline to those race-neutral factors that Levitt later cited in *Freakonomics*. To bolster their argument, they cite research on abortion and lowered crime rates in Scandinavia and Eastern Europe—not places where you're likely to find a lot of black people.

If he was citing Levitt's work, Bennett could have said that to lower the crime rate "you could abort every white baby" or "you could abort every Hispanic baby" or "you could abort every Asian baby," since every group has unwanted, poor children being raised by single mothers.

Another possible cause for Bennett's "experiment" and Robinson's rejection of this cause.

So now that we have Bennett on the couch, shouldn't we conclude that he mentioned only black children because, perhaps on a subconscious level, he associates "black" with "criminal"?

That's what it sounds like to me. I grew up in the South in the days when we had to drink at "colored" water fountains and gas stations had separate "colored" restrooms; I know what a real racist is like, and Bennett certainly doesn't fit the description. But that's what's so troubling about his race-specific "thought experiment"—that such a smart, well-meaning opinion maker would so casually say something that translates, to African American ears, as "blacks are criminals."

Robinson's assertion of the "true" cause of Bennett's "thought experiment."

What makes it worse is that his words came in the context of abortion. That Bennett staunchly opposes abortion is beside the point. He should know enough history to understand why black Americans would react strongly when whites start imagining experiments to limit black reproduction. For hundreds of years, this country was obsessed with the supposed menace of black sexuality and fertility. Bennett's remarks have to make you wonder

Historical cause for the reactions of Blacks to Bennett's remarks.

whether that obsession has really vanished or just been deemed off-limits in polite discourse.

I've heard people argue—mostly in discussions of affirmative action—that the nation's problem of racial discrimination has mostly been solved. The issue now is class, they say, not race. I'd like to believe that, but I don't.

Bennett is too intelligent not to understand why many of us would take his mental experiment as a glimpse behind the curtain—an indication that old assumptions, now unspoken, still survive. He ought to understand how his words would be taken as validation by the rapper Kanye West, who told a television audience that "George Bush doesn't care about black people," or by the New Orleans survivors who keep calling me with theories of how "they" dynamited selected levees to flood the poor, black Lower Ninth Ward and save the wealthy French Quarter and Garden District.

I have a thought experiment of my own: If we put our racial baggage on the table and talk about it, we'll begin to take care of a lot of unfinished business.

QUESTIONS FOR REFLECTING AND WRITING

1. What is Robinson's claim? What does he assert about Bennett? About America?

2. How does the author support his claim? What Mill strategy does he use?

3. How would you describe the essay's tone? How does the tone help Robinson with readers?

4. Can you think of any other reasonable cause for Bennett's "thought experiment"?

5. Evaluate the argument's effectiveness. Does it ultimately work? Why or why not?

WITHOUT

the problem/
solution essay

c h a p t e r 9

Problem/solution arguments are extremely common and can be seen throughout your daily life. Think about the last billboard you saw for a local charity, the last pamphlet you received in the mail regarding an election, or even the last television commercial you watched. It is almost certain that each of these mentioned some sort of problem or issue and offered a specific solution or remedy. In fact, most (if not all) advertisements and arguments about public policy can be understood as arguments that propose solutions to problems. This type of argument asks its readers to examine a current problem and accept the writer's solution (or solutions) as valid, feasible, and logical. It is very important, then, for the writer to clearly identify and explain the problem, state the proposed solution, and then to support the validity of that solution. Sometimes, the writer even encourages the reader to take specific action in order to implement the proposed solution. This type of argument hinges on a clear, workable, and feasible claim or thesis. For example, consider the following claim:

> Drunk drivers should receive mandatory two-year suspensions of their licenses.

This claim attempts to solve a specific problem—drunk driving. After all, fewer people will drink and drive (and potentially cause injury accidents) if they know they will lose their licenses. This would be an ideal claim (or thesis) for a problem/solution argument.

Characteristics of Problem/ Solution Arguments

Problem/solution arguments are often easy to spot. They are typically straightforward in stating their

Other examples of claims that attempt to solve problems include the following. See if you can identify the problem each is attempting to solve.

We need to spend whatever is necessary to stop the flow of drugs into this country.

The school year in the United States should be extended by at least thirty days.

All college textbooks should be made available online at half the cost of the printed versions.

All American citizens should be required to pass a citizenship test before they are permitted to vote in an election.

SEEING

THE ARGUMENT

SEEING THE ARGUMENT

Consider this box of Cheerios breakfast cereal and the problem/solution argument it presents. What is the problem it identifies? What is the solution? What is its claim (or thesis)? As you look at advertisements in magazines, on television, on billboards, and even on products themselves, begin to think about the problem/solution arguments they present and about the validity of the claims they assert.

claim and present clear suggestions for change. However, even the most obvious arguments are carefully organized and contain elements of persuasion that

This is an ad for a vegetarian restaurant. How does this ad define the problem it is offering a solution for? What might be the author's proposed solution?

readers may not immediately recognize. Consider the following strategies writers often use as they craft this type of argument.

- Problem/solution arguments usually focus on the nature or definition of the problem, for the kind of problem has much to do with the kinds of solutions that are appropriate. For example, some people are concerned about our ability to feed a growing world population. But many argue that the problem is not as much an agricultural one (how much food we can produce) as a political one (to whom will the food be distributed and at what cost). If the problem is agricultural, we need to worry about available farmland, water supply, and farming technology. If the problem is political, we need to worry about price supports, distribution to poor countries, and grain embar-

goes imposed for political leverage. To support a solution claim, you will first need to define the problem for your readers.

- How you define the problem also is related to what you think are the causes of the problem. Cause is often a part of the debate and may need to be addressed, particularly if solutions are tied to eliminating what you consider to be the causes.

- Successful problem/solution arguments present viable solutions that are connected to what can realistically be accomplished. Consider Prohibition in the United States (1920–1933), for example. This was a solution to what many at the time perceived to be a huge social problem—alcohol abuse. This solution didn't work and couldn't be enforced, however, because the majority of Americans wouldn't accept the law as valid or fair.

This ad for Maredo's Steakhouse accurately identifies one of the causes of global warming. How is the proposed solution tied to the stated cause? Do you think this is an effective argument?

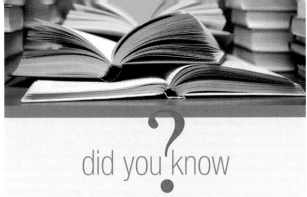

did you know ?

During Prohibition in the United States, illegal establishments called *speakeasies*, where patrons would order in soft voices in order to avoid suspicion, rapidly grew in popularity. Patrons typically brought their own alcohol in their coat pockets, purses, or even in their garters. The solution of completely outlawing alcohol in order to solve the problems associated with drinking was not plausible or workable. Be careful not to propose solutions to problems that will be unworkable or completely rejected by your audience. Can you think of a solution that may have been more workable than Prohibition? Why do you believe that your solution would be more viable?

- Problem/solution arguments must be targeted to a specific and clearly defined audience. Knowing your audience's expectations and preconceived notions plays a large role in determining what strategy you will use in your argument. Consider, for example, arguing for a smoking ban in order to solve the problem of illnesses related to secondhand smoke. Would your strategy change if you were presenting your solution to local bar owners as opposed to parents of small children in the community? Might you use different points of support? Different statistics or research? Knowing how your audience may react to your solution will help guide your argument.

Planning and Writing a Problem/Solution Argument

As with any argument, having a clear plan is key. In addition to the guidelines for writing arguments presented in Chapter 4, use the following advice specific to problem/solution arguments as you think about and begin drafting your essay.

- **What should be the focus and limits of your argument?** There's a big difference between presenting solutions to the problem of physical abuse of women by men and presenting solutions to the problem of date rape on your college campus. Select a topic that you know something about and that you can realistically handle in your paper.

- **What reasons and evidence do you have to support your tentative claim?** Think through what you already know that has led you to select your particular topic. Suppose you decide to write on the issue of campus rapes. Is this choice due to a recent event on campus? Was this event the first in many years, or the latest in a trend? Where and when are they occurring? A brainstorming list may be helpful.

- **Is there additional evidence that you need to obtain to develop your argument?** If so, where can you look for this evidence? Does the library have past issues of the campus paper? Will the campus police grant you an interview?

- **What about the feasibility of each solution you plan to present?** Your readers will want to know that your solutions can be put into action. Are you thinking of one solution with several parts or several separate solutions, perhaps to be implemented by different people? Will coordination be necessary to achieve success? How will this be accomplished? For the problem of campus rape,

As you begin to look for a topic for your problem/solution essay, try surveying your local or campus newspaper's Web site for current controversies in your area. You don't always have to take on large, global issues in order to have an impact. In fact, sometimes the most engaging and effective problem/solution arguments are about problems that are close to you. For example, look at the campus newspaper site here. Do you see any potential issues or problems that you might attempt to solve? If so, what are some feasible and plausible solutions to these problems?

you might want to consider several solutions as a package to be coordinated by the counseling service or an administrative vice president. Whatever solution or combination of solutions you present, make sure that they are doable and that your readers understand how they could be put into action.

Drafting

While there is no right or wrong organization for a problem/solution essay, you will want to make sure that you accomplish the following tasks as you write your argument:

- **Define the importance of the problem.** Begin by either reminding readers of an existing problem or arguing that a current situation should be rec-

ognized as a problem. Often, you can count on an audience who sees the world as you do and recognizes the problem you will address. But in some cases, your first task will be to convince readers that a problem exists that should worry them. If they are not concerned, they won't be interested in your solutions.

- **Define the problem.** Be sure, early in your essay, to define the problem—as you see it—for readers. Do not assume that they will necessarily accept your way of seeing the issue. You may need to defend your assessment of the nature of the problem before moving on to solutions.

- **Explain the causes of the problem (if appropriate).** If your proposed solution is tied to removing the cause or causes of the problem, then you need to establish cause and prove it early in your argument.

GOOD ADVICE

Remember to organize your essay in the most persuasive way possible. For example, while addressing the problem of campus rape, you may want to suggest better lighting on campus paths at night plus an escort service for women who are afraid to walk home alone plus sensitivity training for male students. Presenting the solutions in that order might be best. If you present your most plausible solutions first, you are more likely to create credibility with your readers.

If cause is important, argue for it; if it is irrelevant, move to your solution.

- **Explain your solution.** If you have several solutions, think about how best to order them. If several need to be developed in a sequence, then present them in that sequence. If you are presenting a package of diverse actions that together will solve the problem, then consider presenting them from the simplest to the most complex.

- **Explain the process for achieving your solution.** If you have not thought through the political or legal steps necessary to implement your solution, then this step cannot be part of your purpose in writing. However, a skeptical audience is likely to ask, "How are we going to do that?" so you would be wise to have precise steps to offer. You might obtain an estimate of costs for new lighting on your campus and suggest specific paths that need the lights. You might investigate escort services at other colleges and spell out how such a service can be implemented on your campus. Showing readers that you have thought about

the next steps in the process and that you have answers to potential objections can be an effective method of persuasion.

- **Support the feasibility of your solution.** Be able to estimate costs. Show that you know who would be responsible for implementing the solution. Explain how your solution can be sold to people who may be unwilling to accommodate your proposals. All this information will strengthen your argument.

- **Show how your solution is better than others.** Anticipate challenges (or counterarguments) by including in your paper reasons for adopting your program rather than another program. Explain how your solution will be more easily adopted or more effective when implemented than other possibilities. Of course, a less practical but still viable defense is that your solution is the right thing to do. Whatever strategy you choose, be sure to acknowledge and address potential counterarguments your readers may have. Ignoring other solutions, especially those already publicly known, will hurt the credibility of your argument.

- **Use visuals to your advantage.** If you are attempting to demonstrate a serious problem and propose a solution, it might be useful to show the problem. If you are focusing on the problem of obesity in America, for example, think about including a chart or graph showing the rate of obesity or even a photograph that demonstrates the problem.

GOOD ADVICE

As you draft your solutions essay, be careful not to commit one of these common errors in logic.

AD POPULUM FALLACY "In order to solve the problem of domestic violence in America, we need to lock up these maniacs and throw away the key!"

BEGGING THE QUESTION "Kids work hard when they know they will be tested, so standardized exit exams should become mandatory for all grade levels."

A Checklist for Revision

As you revise your essay, ask yourself the following questions:

- Do I have a clear statement of my policy claim? Is it appropriately qualified and focused?

- Have I clearly explained how the problem can be solved? If necessary, have I argued for seeing the problem that way?

- Have I presented my solutions—and argued for them—in a clear and logical structure? Have I explained how these solutions can be implemented and why they are better than other solutions that have been suggested?

- Have I used data that are relevant and current?

- Have I included visuals that are engaging and persuasive and that help support my claim?

- Have I used the basic checklist for revision in Chapter 4? (See page 82.)

Consider the following argument made by an editor of *The New York Times*. See if you can point to the elements of a problem/solution argument, including response to readers' possible counterarguments. Do you think this argument is ultimately successful? Why or why not?

The New York Times
Editorial
March 30, 2009
Reviewing Criminal Justice

America's criminal justice system needs repair. Prisons are overcrowded, sentencing policies are uneven and often unfair, ex-convicts are poorly integrated into society, and the growing problem of gang violence has not received the attention it deserves. For these and other reasons, a bill introduced last week by Senator Jim Webb, Democrat of Virginia, should be given high priority on the Congressional calendar.

The bill, which has strong bipartisan support, would establish a national commission to review the system from top to bottom. It is long overdue, and should be up and running as soon as possible.

The United States has the highest reported incarceration rate in the world. More than 1 in 100 adults are now behind bars, for the first time in history. The incarceration rate has been rising faster than the crime rate, driven by harsh sentencing policies like "three strikes and you're out," which impose long sentences that are often out of proportion to the seriousness of the offense.

Keeping people in prison who do not need to be there is not only unjust but also enormously expensive, which makes the problem a priority right now. Hard-pressed states and localities that reduce prison costs will have more money to help the unemployed, avert layoffs of teachers and police officers, and keep hospitals operating. In the last two decades, according to a Pew Charitable Trusts report, state corrections spending soared 127 percent, while spending on higher education increased only 21 percent.

Meanwhile, as governments waste money putting the wrong people behind bars, gang activity has been escalating, accounting for as much as 80 percent of the crime in some parts of the country.

The commission would be made up of recognized criminal justice experts, and charged with examining a range of policies that have emerged haphazardly across the country and recommending reforms. In addition to obvious problems like sentencing, the commission would bring much-needed scrutiny to issues like the special obstacles faced by the mentally ill in the system, as well as the shameful problem of prison violence.

Prison management and inmate treatment need special attention now that the Prison Litigation Reform Act has drastically scaled back prisoners' ability to vindicate their rights in court. Indeed, the commission should consider recommending that the law be modified or repealed.

Mr. Webb has enlisted the support of not only the Senate's top-ranking Democrats, including the majority leader, Harry Reid, but also influential Republicans like Arlen Specter, the ranking minority member on the Judiciary Committee, and Lindsey Graham, the ranking member of the crime and drugs subcommittee.

There is no companion bill in the House, and one needs to be written. Judging by the bipartisan support in the Senate, a national consensus has emerged that the criminal justice system is broken.

Consider the billboard here, which proposes a very clear solution to a problem. Some people might claim that the campaign in favor of abstinence in order to solve the problems of teen pregnancy and sexually transmitted disease is an oversimplified solution to a complicated problem and that it ignores many of the important issues that teens currently face. Do you agree? Why or why not?

Guidelines for Analyzing Problem/Solution Arguments

When analyzing problem/solution arguments, what should you look for? In addition to the basics of good argument, use the following points as guides to analyzing:

- **Is the writer's claim not only clear but also appropriately qualified and focused?** For example, if the school board in the writer's community is not doing a good job of communicating its goals for its funding proposal, the writer needs to focus on that particular school board, not on school boards in general.

- **Does the writer show an awareness of the complexity of most public policy issues?** There are many different kinds of problems with American schools and many more causes for those problems. A simple solution—a longer school year, more money spent, vouchers—is not likely to solve the mixed bag of problems. Oversimplified arguments quickly lose credibility.

- **How does the writer define and explain the problem?** Is the problem stated clearly? Does it make sense to you? If the problem is defined differently than most people define it, has the writer argued convincingly for looking at the problem in this new way?

- **What reasons and evidence are given to support the writer's solutions?** Can you see how the writer develops the argument? Does the reasoning seem logical? Is the data relevant? This kind of analysis will help you evaluate the proposed solutions.

- **Does the writer address the feasibility of the proposed solutions?** Does the writer make a convincing case for the realistic possibility of achieving the proposed solutions?

- **Is the argument convincing?** Will the solutions solve the problem as it has been defined? Has the problem been defined accurately? Can the solutions be achieved?

making connections

let's review

After reading this chapter, you should understand:

- Problem/solution arguments are extremely common and can be seen throughout daily life. This type of argument asks readers to examine a current problem and accept the writer's solution (or solutions) as valid, feasible, and logical.

- Problem/solution arguments usually focus on the nature or definition of the problem, for how we define a problem has much to do with the kinds of solutions that are appropriate.

- Successful problem/solution arguments present viable solutions, solutions that can realistically be accomplished.

- Problem/solution arguments must be targeted to a specific and clearly defined audience. Knowing your audience's expectations and preconceived notions will help you determine what strategy to use in your argument.

- While there is no right or wrong organization for a problem/solution essay, you should accomplish the following tasks as you write your argument:

  - Define the problem and its importance.
  - Explain the causes of the problem.
  - Explain your solutions fully.
  - Explain the process for achieving your solution.
  - Support the feasibility of your solution.
  - Show how your solution is better than others.
  - Use visuals to your advantage.

connect

Read and study the annotated argument on page 160. Then analyze and respond to the essay by answering the questions that follow.

A New Strategy for the War on Drugs

James Q. Wilson

Author of The Moral Sense, *James Q. Wilson is a professor of public policy at Pepperdine University. His solution to America's drug problem was published on April 13, 2000, in the* Wall Street Journal.

The current Senate deliberation over aid to Colombia aimed at fighting narcotics reminds us that there are two debates over how the government ought to deal with dangerous drugs. The first is about their illegality and the second is about their control. People who wish to legalize drugs and those who wish to curtail their supply believe that their methods will reduce crime. Both these views are mistaken, but there is a third way.

Opening presents two solutions that Wilson will challenge.

Advocates of legalization think that both buyers and sellers would benefit. People who can buy drugs freely and at something like free-market prices would no longer have to steal to afford cocaine or heroin; dealers would no longer have to use violence and corruption to maintain their market share. Though drugs may harm people, reducing this harm would be a medical problem not a criminal-justice one. Crime would drop sharply.

Prices Would Fall

But there is an error in this calculation. Legalizing drugs means letting the price fall to its competitive rate (plus taxes and advertising costs). That market price would probably be somewhere between one-third and one-twentieth of the illegal price. And more than the market price would fall. As Harvard's Mark Moore has pointed out, the "risk price"—that is, all the hazards associated with buying drugs, from being arrested to being ripped off—would also fall, and this decline might be more important than the lower purchase price.

Wilson rebuts first solution.

Under a legal regime, the consumption of low-priced, low-risk drugs would increase dramatically. We do not know by how much, but the little evidence we have suggests a sharp rise. Until 1968 Britain allowed doctors to prescribe heroin. Some doctors cheated, and their medically unnecessary prescriptions helped increase the number of known heroin addicts by a factor of 40. As a result, the government abandoned the prescription policy in favor of administering heroin in clinics and later replacing heroin with methadone.

When the Netherlands ceased enforcing laws against the purchase or possession of marijuana, the result was a sharp increase in its use. Cocaine and heroin create much greater dependency, and so the increase in their use would probably be even greater.

The average user would probably commit fewer crimes if these drugs were sold legally. But the total number of users would increase sharply. A large fraction of these new users would be unable to keep a steady job. Unless we were prepared to support them with welfare payments, crime would be one of their main sources of income. That is, the number of drug-related crimes per user might fall even as the total number of drug-related crimes increased. Add to the list of harms more deaths from overdose, more babies born to addicted mothers, more accidents by drug-influenced automobile drivers, and fewer people able to hold jobs or act as competent parents.

Treating such people would become far more difficult. As psychiatrist Sally Satel has written, many drug users will not enter and stay in treatment unless they are compelled to do so. Phoenix House, the largest national residential drug treatment program, rarely admits patients who admit they have a problem and need help. The great majority are coerced by somebody—a judge, probation officer or school official—into attending. Phoenix House CEO Mitchell Rosenthal opposes legalization, and for good reason. Legalization means less coercion, and that means more addicts and addicts who are harder to treat.

Douglas Anglin, drawing on experiences in California and elsewhere, has shown that people compelled to stay in treatment do at least as well as those who volunteer for it, and they tend (of necessity) to stay in the program longer. If we legalize drugs, the chances of treatment making a difference are greatly reduced. And as for drug-use prevention, forget it. Try telling your children not to use a legal substance.

But people who want to keep drugs illegal have problems of their own. The major thrust of government spending has been to reduce the supply of drugs by cutting their production overseas, intercepting their transfer into the United States and arresting dealers. Because of severe criminal penalties, especially on handlers of crack cocaine, our prisons have experienced a huge increase in persons sentenced on drug charges. In the early 1980s, about one-twelfth of all prison inmates were in for drug convictions; now well over one-third are.

Wilson rebuts second solution.

No one can be certain how imprisoning drug suppliers affects drug use, but we do know that an arrested drug dealer is easily replaced. Moreover, the government can never seize more than a small fraction of the drugs entering the country, a fraction that is easily replaced.

Emphasizing supply over treatment is dangerous. Not only do we spend huge sums on it; not only do we drag a reluctant U.S. military into the campaign; we also heighten corruption and violence in countries such as Colombia and Mexico. The essential fact is this: Demand will produce supply.

We can do much more to reduce demand. Some four million Americans are currently on probation or parole. From tests done on them when they are jailed, we know that half or more had a drug problem when arrested. Though a lot of drug users otherwise obey the law (or at least avoid getting arrested), probationers and parolees constitute the hard core of dangerous addicts. Reducing their demand for drugs ought to be our highest priority.

Wilson presents his solution.

Mark Kleiman of UCLA has suggested a program of "testing and control": Probationers and parolees would be required to take frequent drug tests—say, twice weekly—as a condition of remaining on the street. If you failed the test, you would spend more time in jail; if you passed it, you would remain free. This approach would be an inducement for people to enter and stay in treatment.

Challenges of implementing his solution are presented.

This would require some big changes in how we handle offenders. Police, probation, and parole officers would be responsible for conducting these tests, and more officers would have to be hired. Probation and parole authorities would have to be willing to sanction a test failure by immediate incarceration, initially for a short period (possibly a weekend), and then for longer periods if the initial failure were repeated. Treatment programs at little or no cost to the user would have to be available not only in every prison, but for every drug-dependent probationer and parolee.

These things are not easily done. Almost every state claims to have an intensive community supervision program, but few offenders are involved in them, the frequency with which they are contacted is low, and most were released from supervision without undergoing any punishment for violating its conditions.

But there is some hope. Our experience with drug courts suggests that the procedural problems

How solution can work.

can be overcome. In such courts, several hundred of which now exist, special judges oversee drug-dependent offenders, insisting that they work to overcome their habits. While under drug-court supervision, offenders reduce drug consumption and, at least for a while after leaving the court, offenders are less likely to be arrested.

Our goal ought to be to extend meaningful community supervision to all probationers and parolees, especially those who have a serious drug or alcohol problem. Efforts to test Mr. Kleiman's proposals are under way in Connecticut and Maryland.

If this demand-reduction strategy works, it can be expanded. Drug tests can be given to people who apply for government benefits, such as welfare and public housing. Some critics will think this is an objectionable intrusion. But giving benefits without conditions weakens the character-building responsibility of society.

Prevent Harm to Others

John Stuart Mill, the great libertarian thinker, argued that the only justifiable reason for restricting human liberty is to prevent harm to others. Serious drug abuse does harm others. We could, of course, limit government action to remedying those harms without addressing their causes, but that is an uphill struggle, especially when the harms fall on unborn children. Fetal drug syndrome imposes large costs on infants who have had no voice in choosing their fate.

Defense of his solution based on practicality and shared values.

Even Mill was clear that full liberty cannot be given to children or barbarians. By *barbarians* he meant people who are incapable of being improved by free and equal discussion. The life of a serious drug addict—the life of someone driven by drug dependency to prostitution and crime—is the life of a barbarian.

QUESTIONS FOR REFLECTING AND WRITING

1. What are the two solutions to the drug problem presented by others?

2. Why, according to Wilson, is legalizing drugs not a good solution? What are the specific negative consequences of legalization? Is his argument against the supply-reduction approach convincing? Why or why not?

3. What is Wilson's proposed solution? Explain the details of his solution.

4. What are some of the difficulties with the author's solution? What does he gain by bringing up possible difficulties?

5. What does Wilson seek to accomplish in his concluding two paragraphs? What potential counterargument does he seek to rebut in his conclusion?

6. Has Wilson convinced you that legalizing drugs will not reduce crime? Why or why not?

planning the researched argument

We do research all the time. You would not select a college or buy a car without doing research: gathering relevant information, analyzing that information, and drawing conclusions from your study. You may already have done some research in this course: using sources in this text or finding data online to strengthen an argument—and then acknowledging your sources informally in your essay. And if your instructor has required formal documentation for even one source, then you have already explored this section for documentation guidelines.

When you are assigned a more formal research essay, you will need to use a number of sources and to document them according to a specific style. You may be required to produce a longer essay and to demonstrate skill in finding a variety of sources. Remember that you have been doing research, in some ways, all along, so use this section to guide you to success in the particular demands of your research essay assignment.

Before beginning a major argumentative researched essay, it is important to understand what tools, or argumentative strategies, are available to you. There are many different types of arguments that you might choose to make, each with its own distinct writing purpose and its own writing strategy. The essay types featured in Chapters 6–9 offer some suggestions for four types of arguments and strategies for writing each one. (See Figure 10.1.)

figure 10.1 Argument Essay Types

It is crucial that you understand your writing purpose before you begin your research, prewriting, or drafting. This writing purpose, along with clear ideas about your audience's needs and expectations, will guide every step of your writing process.

Finding a Workable and Manageable Topic

A major challenge as you begin a researched essay is to select and limit a topic. One key to success is finding a workable topic. After all, no matter how interesting or clever a topic may seem, it is not workable if it does not meet the guidelines of your assignment. Begin with a thorough understanding of the writing context created by the assignment. In considering the context for your assignment, you will want to fully analyze the following considerations.

Who Is My Audience?

If you are writing a research essay in a specific discipline, imagine your instructor as a representative of that field, a reader with knowledge of the subject area. If you are learning about the research process in a composition course, your instructor may advise you to write to a general reader, someone who reads newspapers or magazines but may not have the exact information and perspective you have. For a general reader, specialized terms and concepts may need to be defined. Within the category of general reader, you can identify specific traits, beliefs, values, and experiences that you imagine your reader might hold. For example, if you are writing on the topic of making birth control available in public schools, who might be the most likely readers for your essay? People who might be interested in the topic could include parents of teenagers, teenagers themselves, and even people who work for the local school district. Narrowing your audience in this way will help you figure out what information, types of sources, and approaches your readers will expect from you on your chosen topic. Remember, too, that you cannot address all potential audiences for any given topic. You will need to narrow your topic in order to specifically address your chosen audience.

GOOD ADV!CE

You may want to conduct an audience needs-and-values analysis as part of your prewriting process in order to effectively narrow and refine your topic choice. Ask yourself the following questions:

- Will my readers already have ideas about or opinions on my topic? If so, does my approach provide a new or interesting perspective? If not, will my essay seem repetitive or unnecessary in this debate?

- Will my readers accept me as a credible source of information on this topic? Do I have a special perspective or experience that will allow me to write with authority on this subject? What types of sources will my readers want or need to see in order to trust my perspective?

- How might my readers' values (what they believe is worthwhile and important) affect their views on this subject? Are they likely to agree with my point of view? Are there minor points on which we may disagree? How will I bridge these gaps?

Whether you are writing for a specialized, knowledgeable reader or a more general audience, you will need to consider the values those readers hold, what they already know about your subject, and what they will expect you to provide as convincing evidence for your thesis.

Who is the intended audience for this ad from Population Services International designed to increase AIDS awareness? Do you think the ad will appeal to its intended audience?

Remember that if, after analyzing your audience's expectations, values, and needs, you decide that any of the following are true, you may want to consider changing your topic choice.

- **Your topic is so common or overly debated that your audience will view your essay as redundant or unnecessary.** If your readers can anticipate your main points and see your essay as a run-of-the-mill perspective on a heavily argued topic, you will most likely not succeed in gaining their attention or respect. If you are writing on a commonly debated topic, try to find a new or unique angle from which to approach it.

- **You don't have any authority on the subject.** This does not mean that you must be an expert on a topic in order to write about it. However, if you are attempting to persuade readers to accept your point of view as valid, you must have a thoughtful and well-informed opinion from which to start your writing process. Do not attempt to form your opinion on the subject as you write. Make sure you research your topic first and come to your writing with some measure of confidence and authority on your topic.

Analyze the intended audience for the advertisement here.

- Who do you think this author is trying to reach? How do you know?
- Do you think this audience will have preconceived ideas about this subject that might affect their attitude toward the author's position?
- Does this author attempt to approach this subject in a new way?
- Will readers accept PETA as a credible source on this issue?
- Do you think this ad ultimately does an effective job of reaching its intended audience with its message?

S
EE
ING
THE ARGUMENT

SEEING THE ARGUMENT

try it !

Consider the following issues that are typically considered overdone and run-of-the-mill. In a group or on your own, write a potential thesis statement that moves each topic in a new, engaging, and controversial direction. The first one has been done for you. Can you think of other overworked issues that might need to be moved in a new direction in order to become engaging research topics?

- Gun control

    Example: "Parents who keep guns in the house and whose children ultimately use those guns to commit a crime should receive a mandatory 10-year prison sentence."

- Television violence
- Teen pregnancy
- The drinking age
- Speed limits
- The death penalty
- Childhood obesity
- Prayer in public schools

Examine the billboard here. What argument is the author making? Would this be a good topic for a research essay aimed at parents of toddlers? Or might your readers simply agree with your main point that buckling up their children is a safe and wise choice? If your argument's claim (in this case, that children should use seatbelts) will be accepted without question, you may want to search for a new topic.

S
E E
I N G
THE ARGUMENT
SEEING THE ARGUMENT

- **Your readers will most likely agree with you.** This may seem like an odd statement, but if your chosen audience will most likely agree with every point you make, you may want to either choose a new topic or choose a new audience. After all, what is the point of working to persuade someone who values the same things you do and will automatically agree with every statement you make?

What Are the Assignment's Time and Length Constraints?

The required length of the paper, the time you have to complete the assignment, and the availability of sources are three constraints you must consider when selecting a research topic. Most instructors will establish guidelines regarding length. Knowing the expected length of the paper is crucial to selecting an appropriate topic, so if an instructor does not specify, be sure to ask.

Suppose, for example, that you must argue for solutions to either an educational or environmental problem. Your paper needs to be about six pages and is due in three weeks. Do you have the space or the time to explore solutions to all the problems caused by overpopulation? Definitely not. Limit your study to one issue such as coping with trash. You could further limit this topic by exploring waste management solutions for your particular city or county.

What Kinds of Topics Should I Avoid?

Here are several kinds of topics that are best avoided because they usually result in uninspired, irrelevant,

or disorganized essays, no matter how well researched they are.

1. **Topics that are irrelevant to your interests.** If you are not interested in your topic, you will not produce a lively, informative paper.

2. **Topics that are too broad.** These result in general surveys that lack appropriate detail and support. For example, it would be impossible to solve the issue of poverty in the space of eight pages. Be sure to narrow your topic sufficiently.

3. **Topics that can be fully researched with only one source.** You will produce a summary, not a research paper. For example, the issue of whether your neighbor should install a privacy fence would not sustain a fully documented research essay assignment. Topics can be too narrow, as well as too broad.

4. **Biographical studies.** Short undergraduate papers on a person's life usually turn out to be summaries of one or two major biographies.

5. **Topics that produce a strong emotional response in you.** If, in your mind, there is only one right answer to the abortion issue and you cannot accept counterarguments, don't choose to write on abortion. Probably most religious topics are also best avoided.

6. **Topics that are too technical for you at this point in your college work.** If you do not understand the complexities of the federal tax code, then arguing for a reduction in the capital gains tax may be an unwise topic choice.

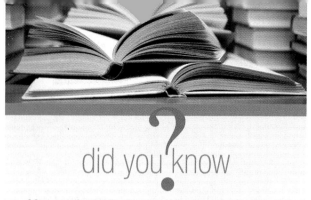

did you know

Many online resources can help you choose and refine research essay topics or turn "overdone" issues into relevant and engaging paper topics.

Just be sure that the site you are using is a credible idea-generating site and not a site that sells or distributes plagiarized work from other authors. Plagiarism is a serious academic offense. Simply browsing Web sites for possible essay topics is not considered academically dishonest, however.

Try these sites for starters:

http://collegeuniversity.suite101.com/article
.cfm/good_persuasive_essay_topics

www.goodessaytopics.com/argumentative-
essay-topics.html

Choosing a topic from which you have a difficult time distancing your emotions can often be dangerous in a research essay. You must be able to understand and appreciate all the complexities of an issue if you are to conduct reliable research and write with authority and credibility. If you cannot do unbiased research, you may want to consider changing topics.

How Can I Select a Good Topic?

Choosing from Assigned Topics

At times, students are unhappy with topic restriction. Looked at another way, however, your instructor has eliminated a difficult step in the research process

and has helped you avoid the problem of selecting an unworkable topic. If your professor gives you a list of possible topics, you will still have to choose well and develop your own claim and approach.

How Do I Get Started When There Are Few Restrictions?

When you are free to write on any course-related topic or any topic at all, you may need to use some strategies for topic selection. Here are some strategies to consider:

- Look through your text's table of contents or index for subject areas that can be narrowed or focused.
- Look over your class notes for topics that have particularly interested you.
- Consider college-based or local issues.
- Do a subject search in an electronic database to see how a large topic can be narrowed—for example, *dinosaur* may have subheadings such as *dinosaur behavior* and *dinosaur extinction*.
- To focus a broad topic, use one or more invention strategies:
  - Freewriting
  - Brainstorming
  - Asking questions about a broad subject, using the reporter's questions of who, what, where, when, and why.

Is My Topic Manageable?

Part of selecting a workable topic is making sure that the topic is sufficiently narrowed and focused. Students sometimes have trouble narrowing topics. Somehow it seems easier to write on a broad subject, such as education. You know there will be enough sources, all easy to find. But this line of thinking overlooks your purpose in doing research and what you know about good writing. Consider the following list of increasingly narrower topics about education:

1. Education
2. Problems in education today
3. Problems in K–12 education today
4. Problems with testing students
5. Why standardized tests aren't fair for all students

The first three items are clearly too broad for a short research project. Do you recognize that topic 4 is also too broad? Remember that the more limited and focused your topic, the more concrete and detailed—and thus convincing and engaging—your research essay will be.

http://www.mhhe.argument/fromtheauthor

GOOD ADV!CE

Oftentimes, you will find inspiration for your research essay topics by examining current issues on your campus or in your hometown or the city where you currently live. For example, the photo here shows a campus demonstration arguing for lower tuition rates. If you saw this image in your campus paper, it could be the start to forming an intriguing and relevant research essay topic. You could interview the participants in the rally, read local newspaper articles on the controversy, and then broaden your research to include national college tuition trends, student reactions, and governmental responses. You could then argue a position on this issue, propose possible solutions to the problem, and even speculate about the causes of the trend.

did you know?

A basic Google search for "No Child Left Behind Act" yields over 1 million search results. A Google Scholar search for "No Child Left Behind Act failure rate public schools New York 2009" yields about 500 hits. While this is still far too many sources to use in a single research project, you can see that refining your search can significantly narrow the number of articles or Web sites you must consider on your way to finding the most effective and relevant sources.

Writing a Tentative Claim or Research Proposal

Once you have selected and narrowed a topic, you need to write a tentative claim, research question, or research proposal. Some instructors will ask to see a statement—from one sentence to a paragraph long—to be approved before you proceed. Others may require as much as a one-page proposal that includes a tentative claim, a basic organizational plan, and a description of types of sources to be used. Even if your instructor does not require anything in writing, you need to write a plan for your own benefit—to direct your reading and thinking. Here are three student samples of research proposals, each of which takes a slightly different approach.

Subject: Computers

Topic: The impact of computers on the twentieth century

Claim: Computers had the greatest impact of any technological development in the twentieth century.

Research Proposal: I propose to show that computers had the greatest impact of any technological development in the twentieth century. I will show the influence of computers at work, in daily living, and in play

continued

> to emphasize the breadth of influence. I will argue that other possibilities (such as cars) did not have the same impact as computers. I will check the library's book catalog and databases for sources on technological developments and on computers specifically. I will also interview a family friend who works with computers at the Pentagon.

This example illustrates several key points. First, the initial subject, computers, is too broad and too unfocused. Second, the claim is more focused than the topic statement because it asserts a position, a claim the student must support. Third, the research proposal is more helpful than the claim only because it includes some thoughts on developing the thesis and finding sources.

Less sure of your topic? Then write a research question or a more open-ended research proposal. Take, for example, a history student studying the effects of Prohibition. She is not ready to write a thesis, but she can write a research proposal that suggests some possible approaches to the topic:

> **Topic:** The effect of Prohibition
>
> **Research Question:** What were the effects of Prohibition on the United States?
>
> **Research Proposal:** I will examine the effects of Prohibition on the United States in the 1920s (and possibly consider some long-term effects, depending on the amount of material on the topic). Specifically, I will look at the varying effects on urban and rural areas and on different classes in society. Ultimately, I would like to argue that Prohibition has had lasting negative effects on American society and that the lower socioeconomic classes feel these effects most profoundly.

Asking questions and working with fields of study (think of college departments) is a third approach. Suppose your assignment is to defend a position on a current social issue. You think you want to do something about television. Using an electronic database to search for a narrowed topic, you decide on the following:

> **Draft**
>
> **Topic:** Television and violence
>
> **Research Proposal:** I will explore the problem of violence on TV. I will read articles in current magazines and newspapers and see what's on the Internet.

Do you have a focused topic and a proposal that will guide your thinking and research? Not yet. Raise questions by field of study. This will help you narrow your focus and identify the direction you wish to take your research. For example, you may look at research questions raised in the following fields of study:

> **Literature/Humanities:** What kinds of violence are found on TV? children's cartoons? cop and mystery shows? the news? How are they alike? How are they different?
>
> **Sociology:** What are the consequences to our society of a continual and heavy dose of violence on television?
>
> **Psychology:** What are the effects of television violence on children? Why are we drawn to violent shows?
>
> **Politics/Government:** Should violence on TV be controlled in any way? If so, how?
>
> **Education:** What is the impact on the classroom when children grow up watching a lot of violence on TV? Does it impede social skills? learning?

Now your thinking is more focused. After reflecting, you choose a more specific topic:

> **Final draft—after conducting field-of-study preliminary research**
>
> **Topic:** The negative effects of television violence on children and some solutions
>
> **Research Proposal:** I will demonstrate that children suffer from their exposure to so much violence on TV and propose some solutions. Until I read more, I am not certain of the solutions I will propose; I want to read arguments for and against the V-chip and ratings and other possibilities.

Locating Effective Print and Online Sources

After you have refined your topic choice, identified your target audience, and written a tentative thesis or claim, it is time to begin your research. You will want to find relevant, up-to-date, and well-written sources so that you can learn what experts and other writers are saying about your issue, what counterarguments your readers might raise, and ultimately what you think about your issue. Research is a discovery process. It is not simply gathering quotes from experts who agree with you. It is part of the writing process and a way to think about your issue in new and interesting ways. The keys to conducting solid research are to target your searches effectively, to remain organized in collecting and citing your data, and to evaluate each source's relevance and importance to your writing goals. There are many effective strategies for finding, organizing, and evaluating your research, including the following.

Preparing a Working Bibliography

When you begin to gather important and relevant research for your topic, construct a working bibliography. This is a comprehensive list of all your potential sources, along with a brief note or explanation of why and how each source might help you in making your argument. By constructing a working bibliography, you will come to see your topic and your argument more clearly. Once you begin to write your essay, you will also be able to easily find your sources and what they have to offer in support of your argument.

To begin this stage of your research, you need to have made three decisions:

1. **Your search strategy.** If you are writing on a course-related topic, your research may start with your textbook, looking for relevant sections and possible sources (if the text contains a bibliography). In this text, for example, you may find some potential sources among the readings. Think about what you already know or have in hand as you plan your search strategy.

2. **A method for recording bibliographic information.** You have two choices: the always-reliable 3 X 5 index cards or a bibliography file in your personal computer. You might simply start a Word document and keep a running list of your sources as you read them.

3. **The documentation format you will be using.** You may be assigned the Modern Language Association (MLA) format or perhaps given a choice between MLA and the American Psychological Association (APA) documentation styles. Once you select the documentation style, skim the appropriate pages in either your textbook or a college writing handbook to get an overview of both format and the information you will need about your sources.

http://www.mhhe.argument/fromtheauthor

GOOD ADVICE

You will discover that online article indexes rarely present information in MLA format. The screen shows an example of a source on animal rights found in an online database.

If you read the article in the journal itself, then the citation in MLA style would look like this:

Vines, Gail. "Planet of the Free Apes?" *New Scientist* 5 June 1993: 39–42. Print.

However, if you obtain a full-text copy of the article from the electronic database, your citation will require additional information about the database. (See pages 177–178 for guidelines and examples.)

Do not be fooled into thinking that because the information is presented in a certain way on your computer screen, it will be in the correct order for your citations page. Be sure to check your handbook or textbook for correct citation conventions as you move from your working bibliography to your formal citations.

A list of possible sources is called a *working bibliography* because you do not yet know which sources you will use. (Your final bibliography will include only those sources you cite—actually refer to—in your paper.) Remember that a working bibliography will help you see what is available on your topic and where to locate each source; it will also contain the information needed to document your paper. Whether you are using cards or computer files, follow these guidelines:

1. Check all reasonable catalogues and indexes for possible sources. (Use more than one reference source even if you locate enough information in the first one; you are looking for the best sources, not the first ones you find.)

2. Complete a card or prepare an entry for every potentially useful source. You won't know what to reject until you start a close reading of sources.

3. Copy (or download from an online catalogue) all information needed to complete a citation and to locate the source. (When using an index that does not give all needed information, leave a space to be filled in when you read the source.)

4. Put bibliographic information in the correct format for every possible source; you will save time and make fewer errors. Do not mix or blend styles. When searching for sources, have your text or handbook handy and use the model citations as guides.

5. Make a brief note about each source. Why did you choose it? What information might it contain that will help you as you write? Is the author an expert in a certain field? What point do you think it will support in your essay?

Using correct documentation as you keep track of your sources in your working bibliography will help you later in the writing process as you construct your Works Cited or References page.

The following brief guide to correct form will get you started. Guidelines are for MLA style only; use Chapter 13 if you have selected a different style.

Basic Form for Books

The basic MLA form for books includes the following information in this pattern:

1. The author's full name, last name first.
   Smith, James.

2. The title (and subtitle if there is one) of the book, italicized.
   The First of Many Improbable Questions.

3. The facts of publication: the city of publication (followed by a colon), the publisher (followed by a comma), the date of publication (followed by a period), and the medium of publication.
   London: Royal Press, 2008. Print.

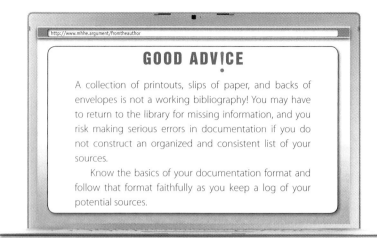

GOOD ADVICE

A collection of printouts, slips of paper, and backs of envelopes is not a working bibliography! You may have to return to the library for missing information, and you risk making serious errors in documentation if you do not construct an organized and consistent list of your sources.

Know the basics of your documentation format and follow that format faithfully as you keep a log of your potential sources.

Note that periods are placed after the author's name, after the title, after the year, and at the end of the citation. Other information, when appropriate (for example, the number of volumes), is added to this basic pattern. (See pages 229–231 for many sample citations.) In your working bibliography, include the book's classification number so that you can find it in the library.

Basic Form for Articles

This is the simplest form for magazine articles. Include the following information, in this pattern:

1. The author's full name, last name first.
   Morrell, Virginia.

2. The title of the article, in quotation marks.
   "A Cold, Hard Look at Dinosaurs."

3. The facts of publication: the title of the periodical (italicized), the volume number (if the article is from a scholarly journal), the date (followed by a colon), inclusive page numbers (followed by a period), and the medium of publication.
   Discover Dec. 1996: 98–108. Print.

Knowing Your Library

All libraries contain books and periodicals and a system for accessing them. A *book collection* contains the *general collection* (books that circulate), the *reference collection* (books of a general nature essential to research), and the *reserve book collection*. The library's *periodicals collection* consists of popular magazines, scholarly journals, and newspapers. Electronic databases with full texts of articles provide alternatives to the print periodicals collection.

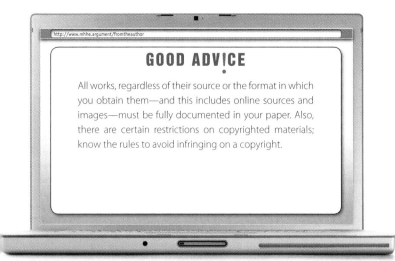

GOOD ADVICE

All works, regardless of their source or the format in which you obtain them—and this includes online sources and images—must be fully documented in your paper. Also, there are certain restrictions on copyrighted materials; know the rules to avoid infringing on a copyright.

Locating Books

Your chief guide to the book (and audiovisual) collection is the catalogue, probably a computer database (see the figure below for an example).

In a catalogue there are at least three entries for each book: the author entry, the title entry, and one or more subject entries. Online catalogues use these same access points plus a keyword option and possibly others, such as the book's International Standard Book Number (ISBN). When you go to your library's home screen and select the catalogue, you will come to the search screen.

Usually, *keyword* is the default.

SEARCH: Gatsby

If you know the exact title, switch to *Title*, type in the title (without the initial article *a, an, the*), and click on Submit Search.

SEARCH: Great Gatsby

If you want a list of all of the library's books by a certain author (in this case, F. Scott Fitzgerald), click on *Author* and type in the author's last name.

SEARCH: Fitzgerald

Keep in mind:

- Use correct spelling. If you are unsure of a spelling, use a keyword search instead of an author or title search.
- If you are looking for a list of books on your subject, do a keyword or subject search.

Reading Entries: Brief and Long View Screens

If you do an author search by last name only, you will get a list of all the library's books written by writers with that last name. A keyword search will provide a list of all book titles containing your keyword. These "brief view" lists provide enough information to locate a book in the library: author, title, and classification number—the number by which the book is shelved.

For books that look promising for your research, click on View Record (or similar command icon) to obtain the "long view" screen. The screen, as shown in the example below, provides additional information about the book, including its length, publication information, and status. For potentially useful books, copy all needed information into your working bibliography.

The book and periodicals collections are supplemented by audiovisual materials, including works on CD, tape, microfilm or microfiche, and online. Many

Online Catalogue Entry—Long View of One Book

Catalog screen from University of Texas at Dallas Libraries, using the Voyager Integrated System from Ex Libris. Reprinted with permission.

libraries store back issues of periodicals on microfilm, so learn where the microfilm readers are and how to use them. In addition, articles from electronic databases and Internet sources can be printed or, in many cases, e-mailed directly to your own PC.

Using the Reference Collection

The research process often begins with the reference collection. You will find atlases, dictionaries, encyclopedias, general histories, critical studies, and biographies. In addition, reference tools such as bibliographies and indexes are part of the reference collection.

Many tools in the reference collection once only in print form are now also online. Some are now only online. Yet online is not always the way to go. The table compares advantages of each of the formats.

Reasons to Use the Print Reference Collection	Reasons to Use Online Reference Materials
1. The reference tool is only in print—use it.	1. Online databases are likely to provide the most up-to-date information.
2. Only the print form covers the period you are studying. (Most online indexes and abstracts cover only from 1980 to the present.)	2. You can usually search all years covered at one time. (Some print references have separate volumes for each year.)
3. In a book, with a little scanning of pages, you can often find what you need without getting spelling or commands exactly right.	3. Full texts (with graphics) are sometimes available, as well as indexes with detailed summaries of articles. Both can be printed or e-mailed to your PC.
4. If you know the best reference source to use and are looking for only a few items, the print source can be faster than the online source.	4. Through links to the Internet, you have access to an amazing amount of material. (Unless you focus your keyword search, however, you may be overwhelmed.)
5. All computer terminals are in use—or down—open a book!	

Before using any reference work, take a few minutes to check its date, purpose, and organization. If you are new to online searching, take a few minutes to learn about each reference tool by working through the online tutorial. (Go to the Help screen.) These strategies can supplement the following brief review of some key reference tools.

Basic Reference Tools

Use your library's reference collection for facts, for background information, and for indexes to possible sources.

Dictionaries

For the spelling of specialized words not in your PC's dictionary, consult an appropriate subject dictionary; for foreign words, the appropriate foreign-language dictionary. If you need a word's origin or its definition from an earlier time, use an unabridged dictionary. Here are two to know:

Webster's Encyclopedic Unabridged Dictionary of the English Language. 1996.

The Oxford English Dictionary. 20 volumes in print.

Both of these resources offer online subscriptions. This may be more convenient if you have access to the Internet as you write.

General Encyclopedias

Two multivolume encyclopedias to know are the *Encyclopedia Americana* and the *Encyclopedia Britannica.* The *Britannica,* the *World Book,* and other encyclopedias are available online as well as in print, which again, may be more convenient if you have access to the Internet as you write (see figure on page 175).

Atlases

Atlases provide much more than maps showing capital cities and the names of rivers. Historical atlases show changes in politics, economics, and culture. Topographical atlases support studies in the earth sciences and many environmental issues. Here are two:

Historical Atlas of the United States. National Geographic Society, 1988.

The Times Atlas of the World, 9th ed. 1992.

Check to see what atlases your library has on CD-ROM.

Quotations, Mythology, and Folklore

If in your research you encounter unfamiliar quotations, myths, or references that seem to be common cultural knowledge or that you feel you should become more familiar with, you can use references such as the following:

Bartlett's Familiar Quotations, 16th ed. 1992. In print and online versions. (See page 176 for an example of the online version.)

Funk and Wagnall's Standard Dictionary of Folklore, Mythology, and Legend.

Almanacs and Yearbooks

These annually published references answer all kinds of questions about current events and provide statistical information on many topics. Many of these works are both in print and online. Check to see which format your library offers.

Congressional Record. 1873 to date. Issued daily during sessions. Online.

Facts on File. 1940 to date. Digest of important news events. Online.

Statistical Abstract of the United States. 1978 to date. Annual publication of the Bureau of the Census. Online.

Biographical Dictionaries

Most libraries have an array of biographical dictionaries, important tools for investigating authors with whom you are unfamiliar.

Contemporary Authors. 1962 to date. A multivolume guide to current fiction and nonfiction writers and their books. Online.

International Who's Who. 1935 to date. Brief biographies of important people from almost every country.

American Men and Women of Science. Brief sketches of more than 150,000 scientists. Lists degrees held and fields of specialization. Regularly updated.

Who's Who. 1849 to date. English men and women.

Who's Who in America. 1899 to date.

Who's Who in American Women. 1958 to date.

Using Indexes to Periodicals: In Print and Online

Periodicals (magazines, journals, and newspapers) are excellent sources for research projects, especially for projects on current issues. The best way to access articles on your topic is to use one or more periodical indexes. To be efficient, you want to select the most useful indexes for your particular study. Your library will maintain some print indexes to popular magazines,

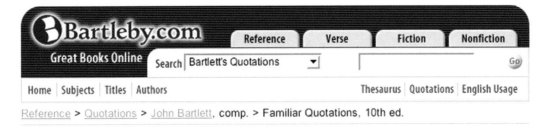

Reference > Quotations > John Bartlett, comp. > Familiar Quotations, 10th ed.

I have gathered a posie of other men's flowers. and nothing but the thread that binds them is mine own.

John Bartlett

Familiar Quotations

A Collection of Passages, Phrases, and Proverbs Traced to Their Sources in Ancient and Modern Literature

Compiled by John Bartlett

This tenth edition of 1919 contains over 11,000 searchable quotations and was the first new edition of John Bartlett's corpus to be published after his death in 1905—the new editor, however, choosing more to supplement than revise the work of the first name in quotations.

Search:

Bartlett's Quotations ▾ [   ] Go

CONTENTS

Bibliographic Record   Preface

TENTH EDITION
REVISED AND ENLARGED BY NATHAN HASKELL DOLE

BOSTON: LITTLE. BROWN. 1919
NEW YORK: BARTLEBY.COM. 2000

some for scholarly journals, and some to newspapers. In addition, your library probably provides many online databases. Online databases are more likely than older print indexes to blend magazines, journals, and newspaper articles, and many online databases include full texts of the articles. Learn which of the indexes provide full texts and which indexes provide only lists of articles that you must then locate in your library's paper collection of periodicals.

The Readers' Guide to Periodical Literature

Probably the most-used paper and online index, *The Readers' Guide to Periodical Literature* (1900 to date) combines author and subject headings that guide users to articles in about 200 popular magazines. Most college libraries have access to this database on their sites. Check with your librarian to see if your school offers this service. As the sample entries in Figure 10.2 show, the information is heavily abbreviated. When using

this index, study the explanation provided and check the list of periodicals found in the front of each volume for the complete title of each magazine. Use this index if you want articles written prior to 1980.

The New York Times Index

Newspapers are a good source of information about both contemporary topics and historical events and issues. Because it is one of the most thorough and respected newspapers, *The New York Times* is available in most libraries. So, when your topic warrants it, become familiar with *The New York Times Index*, for it can guide you to articles as far back as the mid-nineteenth century. (Back issues of the newspaper are on microfilm.) The print *NYT Index* is a subject index, cumulated and bound annually, with articles arranged chronologically under each subject heading. The *NYT Index* is also online, and articles in *The New York Times* are often indexed in other online databases.

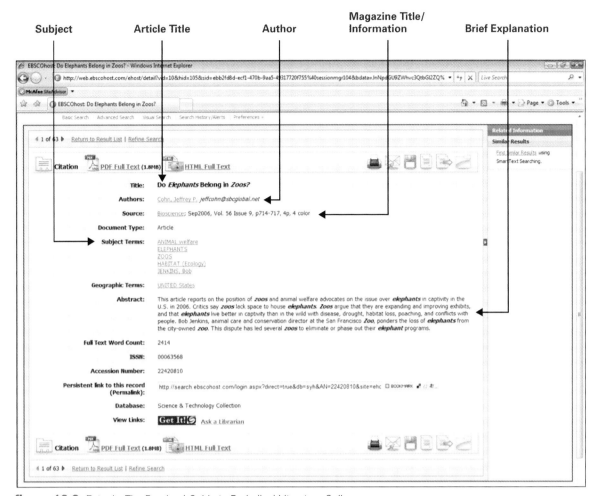

Subject   Article Title   Author   Magazine Title/Information   Brief Explanation

figure 10.2 Entry in *The Readers' Guide to Periodical Literature Online*

Reprinted with the permission of The H.W. Wilson Company (www.hwwilson.com).

Online Databases

You will probably access online databases by going to your library's home page and then clicking on the appropriate term or icon. (You may have found the book catalogue by clicking on Library Catalogue; you may find the databases by clicking on Library Resources or some other descriptive label.)

You will need to choose a particular database and then type in your keyword for a basic search or select Advanced Search to limit your search by date or periodical or to search for articles by a specific author. Each library has somewhat different screens, but the basic process of selecting among choices provided and then typing in your search commands is the same.

Figure 10.3 on page 178 shows the first screen in response to a search for magazine and newspaper articles in the library's research databases. The list of databases on this screen is one that the librarians have noted as being useful for undergraduate research projects. If you know which database you would like to work with, you can click on the alphabetical list of databases or search by subject. If you do not already know which database might work for your research, you may want to scroll through the options and select the database that seems most useful for your topic.

Suppose, after looking over your options, you select Academic Search Complete (EBSCO Host). The first screen is shown next (see Figure 10.4). You can do a basic keyword search or modify your search in a number of ways.

A basic keyword search for "zoos and animal rights" yielded 113 articles. Figure 10.5 on page 178 shows a partial list of those hits. You will want to try to narrow your search to a manageable number of hits. As a rule of thumb, if your keyword search returns more than 100 hits, you should try adding more keywords or using Boolean operators to narrow the search parameters. For more on how to effectively use Boolean operators in searches, see page 181 in this chapter.

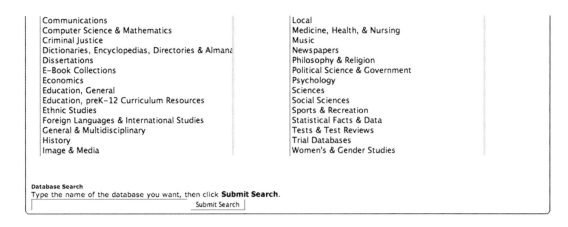

Communications	Local
Computer Science & Mathematics	Medicine, Health, & Nursing
Criminal Justice	Music
Dictionaries, Encyclopedias, Directories & Almana	Newspapers
Dissertations	Philosophy & Religion
E-Book Collections	Political Science & Government
Economics	Psychology
Education, General	Sciences
Education, preK–12 Curriculum Resources	Social Sciences
Ethnic Studies	Sports & Recreation
Foreign Languages & International Studies	Statistical Facts & Data
General & Multidisciplinary	Tests & Test Reviews
History	Trial Databases
Image & Media	Women's & Gender Studies

Database Search
Type the name of the database you want, then click **Submit Search**.

Submit Search

University Libraries | Contact Us at the University Libraries | Libraries Site Map

Bowling Green State University | Bowling Green, OH 43403-0001 | Contact Us | Campus Map | Site Map | Accessibility Policy (PDF Reader)

figure 10.3 Library search screen for online research databases

Used by permission, University Libraries, Bowling Green State University.

figure 10.4 Search screen in research database Academic Search Complete. Keyword search is the default for most online databases.

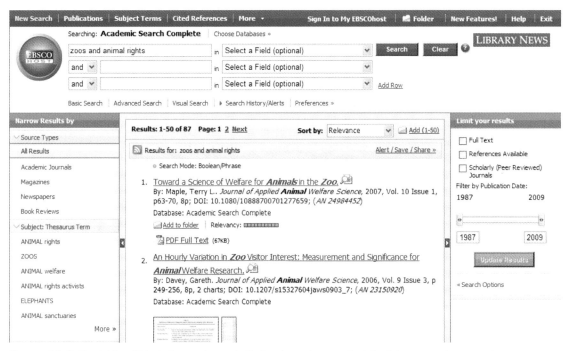

figure 10.5 Partial list of hits in keyword search. Notice the options on the left of the screen for narrowing this search. Notice also that the search results are listed in chronological order, not by relevance.

Using Indexes to Academic Journals: In Print and Online

The indexes to magazines and newspapers just described provide many good articles for undergraduate research. At times, though, you may need to use articles from scholarly journals. Many of the indexes to specialized journals began as print indexes but are now online as well. The following is a brief list of some of the academic indexes students frequently use. Your reference librarian can recommend others appropriate to your study.

Applied Science and Technology Index. An index to periodicals covering engineering, data processing, earth sciences, space science, and more. Online through FirstSearch.

Book Review Digest. Begun in 1905, this index is arranged by author of the book reviewed. It contains brief reviews of both fiction and nonfiction works. Online.

Essay and General Literature Index. From 1900, this author and subject index includes references to both biographical and critical materials. Its chief focus is literary criticism.

Educational Research Information Center (ERIC). In its print form, there are two sections, Current Index to Journals in Education and Resources in Education, a collection of unpublished reports on educational issues. ERIC is also online.

The GPO Publications Reference File or GPO Access (on the Web). The former has been replaced by the regularly updated index on the Internet. You can reach GPO Access at www.access.gpo.gov/su_docs.

Humanities Index. This index lists articles on art, literature, philosophy, folklore, history, and related topics. Online.

MLA International Bibliography. The annual listing by the Modern Language Association of books, articles, and dissertations on language and literature. Online.

Public Affairs Information Service (PAIS). This index covers books, pamphlets, reports, and articles on economics, government, social issues, and public affairs. It is international in scope and emphasizes works that are strong on facts and statistics. Online.

---

http://www.mhhe.argument/fromtheauthor

GOOD ADVICE

Guidelines for Using Online Databases

Keep these points in mind as you use online databases:

- Although some online databases provide full texts of all articles, others provide full texts of only some of the articles indexed. The articles not in full text will have to be located in a print collection of periodicals.

- Articles not available in full text often come with a brief summary or abstract. This allows you to decide whether the article looks useful for your project. Do not treat the abstract as the article. Do not use material from it and cite the author. If you want to use the article, find it in your library's print collection or obtain it from another library.

- The database's information about an article is not in the correct format for any of the standard documentation styles (such as MLA or APA). You will have to reorder the information and use the correct style. If your instructor wants to see a list of possible sources in MLA format, do not hand in a printout of articles from an online database.

- Although some search engines, like Google, order their results by relevance to your search terms, most academic research databases do not. Articles may be ordered in chronological order, for example. Do not assume that the first article on the list is the most useful or relevant to your research needs.

- Because no single database covers all magazines, you may want to search several databases that seem relevant to your project.

Science Citation Index. An index of more than 3,000 journals in mathematics and the natural, physical, and behavioral sciences. It includes an index to articles, a subject index based on keywords appearing in titles of articles indexed, and a citation index arranged by author that reveals which articles are referred to by other authors in their papers. The online version is SciSearch or through Web of Science.

Social Sciences Citation Index. Like the *Science Citation Index,* this index includes a source index, a subject index by keywords, and a citation index. The online version is Social SciSearch or through Web of Science.

Searching the Internet

In addition to using the online databases to find sources, you can search the Internet directly. Keep in mind, however, these facts about the Internet:

- The Internet is both disorganized and huge, so you can waste time trying to find information that is easily obtained in a reference book in your library.

- The Internet is best at providing current information, such as news and movie reviews. It is also a great source of government information.

- Because anyone can create a Web site and put anything on it, you will have to be especially careful in evaluating Internet sources. Remember that articles in magazines and journals have been selected by editors and are often peer reviewed as well, but no editor selects or rejects material on a personal Web site. (More on evaluating sources can be found in Chapter 11.)

If you are new to Internet searching, you may want to study online tutorials to be efficient in your search. Also, your college library may conduct workshops—check it out.

Access to the Internet provides information in a variety of ways, including:

- **E-mail.** E-mail can be used instead of a printed letter to request information from a government agency or company.

- **Mailing lists (listservs).** You can sign up to receive, via your e-mail, continually updated bulletins on a particular subject. Listservs are essentially organized mailing lists. If you find one relevant to your project, you can subscribe for a while and unsubscribe when you are no longer interested.

- **Newsgroups.** Newsgroups differ from listservs in that the discussions and exchanges are collected for you to retrieve; they are not sent to your e-mail address. Otherwise they are much the same: Both are a type of discussion group. To find newsgroups on a specific subject, go to http://groups.google.com, a research tool sponsored by the search engine Google, that surveys all Usenet newsgroups (see Figure 10.6).

- **World Wide Web.** To access the Web from your library terminal or on your own PC through a hookup with your college library, you will, as with the catalogue and online databases, start at your library's home page. Usually selecting Search the Internet will take you to a menu of search engines and subject directories. Not all search engines are the same, and people differ on which are the best. Here are some sites to visit for help in selecting an appropriate search engine:

  - *Librarians' Index to the Internet:* http://lii.org

  - *Greg R. Notess's search engine comparison pages:* www.notess.com/search

  - *Search Engine Watch:* www.searchenginewatch.com

Conducting Field Research

Field research (including conducting interviews, distributing surveys, and even firsthand observation of the issue) can enrich many projects. The following sections give some suggestions.

Federal, State, and Local Government Documents

In addition to federal documents you may obtain through *Public Affairs Information Services (PAIS)* or *GPO Access,* department and agency Web sites, or the Library of Congress's good legislative site, *Thomas* (http://thomas.loc.gov), consider state and county archives, maps, and other published materials. Instead of selecting a national or global topic, consider examining the debate over a controversial bill introduced in your state legislature. Use online databases to locate articles on the bill and the debate, and interview legislators and journalists who participated in or covered the debates or served on committees that worked with the bill.

You can also request specific documents on a topic from appropriate state or county agencies and

Google groups [voting_____] | Search Groups | Advanced Groups Search / Preferences

What can you do with groups?   Take the tour »

Discuss online or over email

Create rich, custom pages

Customize your look and graphics

Create a group in 3 steps

1 Create an account
2 Setup your group
3 Invite people

Create a group...

Explore groups

Find out what people are doing with Google Groups

[_____] Search for a group

Society & Humanities
alt.fan.letterman
talk.origins

Arts & Entertainment
...classical.recordings
rec.music.beatles

Sci/Tech
Epistemology
...electronics.misc

Computers
...java.programmer
...periphs.printers

Browse all group categories...

Popular groups

sci.math
sci.electronics.design
rec.gambling.poker
Random Conversation
Gmail Help Discussion
Videoblogging
misc.consumers.frugal-living
alt.sports.baseball.ny-yankees
Google Maps API
rec.food.cooking
more »

Create a group - Google Home - Terms of Service - Privacy Policy
©2009 Google

figure 10.6 Online newsgroups, like the ones on Google Groups, can be a useful tool in discovering what the current debates are in any given field of study. You can observe the conversation threads or even participate to gain a clearer understanding of your topic.

Google Brand Features are trademarks or distinctive brand features of Google Inc.

http://www.mhhe.argument/fromtheauthor

GOOD ADV!CE

Guidelines for Searching the Internet

1. Bookmark sites you expect to use often so that you do not have to remember Web addresses (uniform resource locators, or URLs).
2. Make your search as precise as possible to avoid getting overwhelmed with hits.
3. If you are searching for a specific phrase, put quotation marks around it. This will reduce the number of hits and lead to sites more useful to your research; for example, "Environmental Protection Agency" or "civil disobedience."
4. Use Boolean connectors to make your search more precise.
   - AND: This connector limits results to sites that contain both terms; for example, "zoos AND animal rights."
   - OR: This connector extends the hits to include all sites that contain one or the other search term. So "zoos OR animal rights" will generate a list of sites containing either term.
   - NOT: This connector limits the search to only the first term and excludes the second. Thus, "animal rights NOT zoos" will give you sites about animal rights issues not involving zoos.
5. If you are not successful with one search engine, try a different one. Remember that each search engine searches only a part of the Internet.
6. To get the best sites for most college research projects, try a directory of evaluated sites or subject guides rather than, say, Yahoo! (Yahoo! is better for news, people searches, and commercial sites.) Some of the best academic subject guides are:

   • The University of California's Infomine (http://infomine.ucr.edu)

   • Internet Scout Project (http://scout.cs.wisc.edu)
7. Be certain to complete a bibliography card—including the date you accessed the material—for each site from which you take information. All sources must be documented, including Internet sources. (See pages 171–172 for documentation guidelines.)

nonprofit organizations. For example, one student, given the assignment of arguing for specific solutions to an ecological problem, decided to study the local problem of preserving the Chesapeake Bay. After visiting the Web site for the nonprofit group Chesapeake Bay Foundation (see Figure 10.7) and using the Contact Us link, she obtained issues of their newsletters and brochures advising homeowners about hazardous household waste materials that end up in the bay.

She was able to add bulletins on soil conservation and landscaping tips for improving the area's water quality to her sources. Local problems can lead to interesting research topics because they are current and relevant to you and because they involve uncovering different kinds of source materials.

Correspondence

Business and government officials are usually willing to respond to written requests for information. Make your letter brief and well written. Either include a self-addressed, stamped envelope for the person's convenience or e-mail your request. If you are not e-mailing, write as soon as you discover the need for information and be prepared to wait several weeks for a reply. It is appropriate to indicate your deadline and ask for a timely response. Whether you write or e-mail, consider these guidelines:

1. Explain precisely what information you need. Don't just ask, "Please send me anything you have on this topic." Busy professionals are more likely to respond to requests that are specific and reveal knowledge of the topic.

2. Do not request information that can be easily found in your library's reference collection.

3. Explain how you plan to use the information. Businesses are understandably concerned with their public image and will be disinclined to provide information that you intend to use in an attack on them.

Consult reference guides to companies and government agencies or their Web sites to obtain addresses and the person to whom your letter or e-mail should be addressed. For companies, address your request to the public information officer. For e-mail addresses, check the organization's homepage.

figure 10.7 Web sites for nonprofit or county agencies can be useful sources of information on local topics and can often lead to interviews with those involved with the issues.

Interviews

Some experts are available for personal interviews. Call or write for an appointment as soon as you recognize the value of an interview. Remember that you are more likely to be able to schedule an interview with state and local officials than with the president of General Motors. If you are studying a local problem, also consider leaders of civic associations with an interest in the issue. In many communities, the local historian or a librarian will be a storehouse of information about the community. Former teachers can be interviewed for papers on education. Interviews with doctors or nurses can add a special dimension to papers on medical issues.

If an interview is appropriate for your topic, follow these guidelines:

1. Prepare specific questions in advance.

2. Arrive on time, appropriately dressed, and behave in a polite, professional manner.

3. Take notes, asking the interviewee to repeat key statements so that your notes are accurate.

4. Take a tape recorder with you but ask permission to use it before taping.

5. If you quote any statements in your paper, quote accurately, eliminating only such minor speech habits as "you know" and "um." (See Chapter 13 for proper documentation of interviews.)

6. Direct the interview with your prepared questions, but also give the interviewee the chance to approach the topic in his or her own way. You may obtain information or views that had not occurred to you.

7. Do not get into a debate with the interviewee. You are there to learn, not to try to change the interviewee's thinking.

Lectures

Check the appropriate information sources at your school to learn about visiting speakers. If you are fortunate enough to attend a lecture relevant to a current project, take careful, detailed notes. Because a lecture is a source, use of information or ideas from it must be presented accurately and then documented. (See Chapter 13 for documentation format.)

Films, Tapes, Television, Online Multimedia Sources

Your library and the Internet will have audiovisual materials that provide good sources for some kinds of topics. For example, if you are studying *Death of a Salesman*, you might view a videotaped or online version of the play.

Also pay attention to documentaries on public television and to the many news and political talk shows on both public and commercial channels. In many cases, transcripts of shows can be obtained from the TV station. Alternatively, tape or DVR the program while watching it so that you can view it several times and obtain accurate quotes, if necessary. (The documentation format for such nonprint sources is illustrated in Chapter 13.)

Surveys, Questionnaires, and Original Research

Depending on your paper, you may want to conduct a simple survey or write and administer a questionnaire. Surveys can be used for many campus and local issues, for topics on behavior and attitudes of college students or faculty, and for topics on consumer habits. Prepare a brief list of questions with space for answers. Poll faculty through their mailboxes or e-mail and students individually on campus or in your classes. Be aware, however, that many universities and colleges require special approval for research studies involving human subjects. Be sure to ask your instructor about gaining subject approval or university approval prior to conducting any surveys.

When writing survey questions, keep these guidelines in mind:

- Use simple, clear language.

- Devise a series of short questions rather than only a few multipart questions. (You want to separate information for better analysis.)

- Phrase questions to avoid wording that seeks to control the answer. For example, do not ask, How did you survive the horrors of the Depression? Do not write, Did you perform your civic duty by voting in the last election? These are loaded questions that prejudge the respondent's answers.

In addition to surveys and questionnaires, you can incorporate some original research. As you read sources on your topic, be alert to reports of studies that you could redo and update in part or on a smaller scale. Many topics on advertising and television give opportunities for your own analysis. Local-issue topics may offer good opportunities for gathering information on your own, not just from your reading.

For example, one student, examining the controversy over a proposed new shopping mall on part of the Manassas Civil War Battlefield in Virginia, made the argument that the mall served no practical need in the community. He supported his position by describing existing malls, including the number and types of stores each contained and the number of miles each was from the proposed new mall. How did he obtain this information? He drove around the area, counting miles and stores. Sometimes a seemingly unglamorous approach to a topic turns out to be an imaginative one.

making connections

let's review

After reading this chapter, you should understand the following:

- Before beginning a major researched argumentative essay, it is important to understand what tools, or argumentative strategies, are available. The essay types featured in Chapters 6–9 offer some suggestions for four specific types of arguments and strategies for writing each.

- It is crucial that you understand your writing purpose before you begin your research, prewriting, or drafting. This writing purpose, along with clear ideas about your audience's needs and expectations, will guide every step of your writing process.

- One key to success is finding a workable topic. After all, no matter how interesting or clever a topic may seem, it is not workable if it does not meet the guidelines of your assignment. The required length of the paper, the time you have to complete the assignment, and the availability of sources are three constraints you must consider when selecting a workable research topic.

- Once you have selected and narrowed a topic, you need to write a tentative claim, research question, or research proposal.

- After you have refined your topic, identified your target audience, and written a tentative thesis or claim, it is time to begin your actual research. You will want to find the most relevant, up-to-date, and well-written sources available to you so that you can learn what experts and other writers are saying about your issue, what potential counterarguments your readers may raise, and ultimately what you think about your issue.

- One way to begin to gather important and relevant research for your topic is to construct a working bibliography. This is a list of all of your potential sources, along with a brief note or explanation of why and how each source will help you in making your argument.

- Your library is a valuable resource during your research process. There you can find books, articles, reference materials, newspapers, and access to online research databases.

- In addition to using the online databases to find sources, you can search the Internet directly. Keep in mind, however, that there are special challenges to searching for credible research sources online.

- Field research (including interviews, surveys, and even firsthand observation of the issue) can enrich many projects.

evaluating and utilizing sources

In Chapter 10, you began the processes of finding a workable and manageable topic for your research essay and of finding appropriate and credible sources that support your thesis. The next step in this process involves two very important tasks: evaluating the sources you have found and figuring out where and how you will most effectively use them in your essay. After all, you will surely not be able to (or want to) use every single source you find regarding your topic, nor will every credible source fit with your particular argumentative strategy. Think, for example, of every article you might find on the topic of legalizing music downloading. Some might be written in favor of the idea, some might be opposed, some might be from noncredible sources, some might be too old to be relevant, some might be too technical, and some might be completely biased or full of logical fallacies. It is up to you as the researcher to figure out which sources will be credible, reliable, and useful to you as you construct your own argument. This is not an easy or quick task. It will involve careful research, reading and rereading your sources, evaluating each one as it relates to your thesis, and making an organized plan for where and how you will use each source. As you study your sources and your working bibliography, you will need to keep rethinking your purpose, audience, and approach. You should also test your research proposal or tentative claim against what you are learning. Remember: You can always change the direction and focus of your paper as new approaches occur to you, and you can even change your position as you reflect on what you are learning.

Finding Sources

You will work with sources more effectively if you keep in mind why you are using them. What you are looking for will depend on your topic and purpose, but there are several basic approaches to finding sources:

1. **Acquiring information and viewpoints firsthand.** Suppose that you are concerned about the mistreatment of animals kept in zoos. You do not want to just read what others have to say on this issue. Visit a zoo, taking notes on what you see. Before you go, arrange to interview at least one person on the zoo staff, preferably a veterinarian who can explain the zoo's guidelines for animal care. Only after gathering and thinking about these _primary sources_ do you want to add to your knowledge by reading articles and books—_secondary sources_. Many kinds of topics require the use of both primary and secondary sources. If you want to study violence in children's TV shows, for example, you should first spend some time watching specific shows and taking notes.

2. **Acquiring new knowledge.** Suppose you are interested in breast cancer research and treatment, but you do not know much about the choices of treatment and, in general, where we are with this medical problem. You will need to turn to sources first to learn about the topic. You should begin with sources that will give you an overview, perhaps a historical perspective of how knowledge

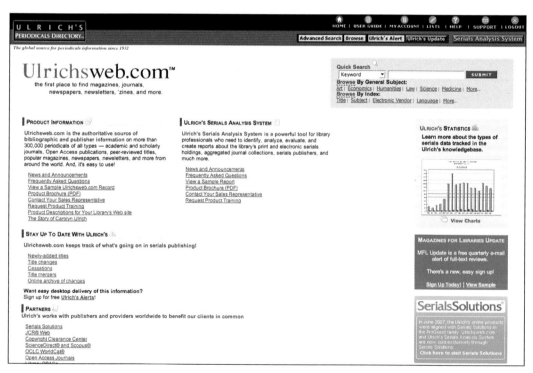

Ulrichsweb.com provides publisher information for more than 300,000 periodicals of all types—academic and scholarly journals, open access publications, peer-reviewed titles, popular magazines, newspapers, newsletters, and more—from around the world. It's a great starting point for finding sources.

GOOD ADV!CE

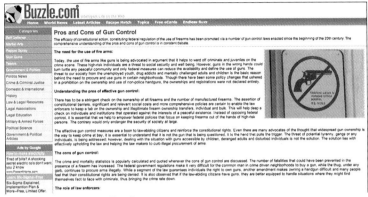

Buzzle.com is a dynamic network of authors and content contributors whom the site creators refer to as "Intelligent Life on the Web." As subject experts, these authors and content contributors create an informative, yet comfortable place for finding information about everything from animals to tourism. With current news in the What's the Buzz? section, thousands of interesting categories, an interactive online community, and thought-provoking polls, Buzzle .com offers a medium through which to share knowledge of the world. This would be an excellent place to search for a current and relevant topic or to begin your research process on your chosen issue. As with any online source, however, you will need to analyze and evaluate the credibility and authorship of each article. Be sure to click on the author's name in order to find out more about his or her specific qualifications, background, and organizational associations.

Reprinted by permission of Buzzle.com.

and treatment have progressed in the last thirty years. Similarly, if your topic is the effects of Prohibition in the 1920s, you will need to read first for knowledge but also with an eye to ways to focus the topic and organize your paper.

3. **Understanding the issues.** Suppose you think that you know your views on gun control or immigration, so you intend to read only to obtain some useful statistical information to support your argument. Should you scan sources quickly, looking for facts you can use? This approach may be too hasty. As explained in Chapter 4, good arguments rely on a writer's knowledge of counterarguments and opposing positions. You are wise to study sources presenting a variety of attitudes on your issue so that you understand—and can refute—the arguments of others.

   With controversial issues, often the best argument is a conciliatory one that presents a middle ground and seeks to bring people together. In order to fully understand all sides of your chosen issue, you may want to visit sites, read articles, or even collect survey responses in order to expose yourself to multiple points of view. This is a good way to educate yourself about the current debate so that you better understand your audience's values and potential counterarguments.

Evaluating Sources and Maintaining Credibility

When you use facts and opinions from sources, you are saying to readers that the facts are accurate and the ideas credible. If you do not evaluate your sources before using them, you risk losing your credibility as a writer. (Remember Aristotle's idea of *ethos*, or how your character is judged.) Just because they are in print or online does not mean that a writer's "facts" are reliable or ideas worthwhile. Judging the usefulness and reliability of potential sources is an essential part of the research process.

Today, with access to so much material on the Internet, the need to evaluate is even more crucial. Here are some strategies for evaluating sources, with special attention to Internet sources:

- **Locate the author's credentials.** Periodicals often list their writers' degrees, current position, and other publications; books, similarly, contain an "about the author" section. If you do not see this information, check biographical dictionaries (such as Biography Index, Contemporary Authors) for information about the author. For articles on the Web, look for the author's e-mail address or a

Online sources credited to authors with few or no credentials related to the subject matter, like the author of this blog, are not generally reliable for research essays. Although the information may seem accurate, it's best to try to find it in a source that comes from an author with credentials that relate to the information presented. Compare this blog to the article that follows. Based on authorship alone, which source seems more credible? Why? Which would you choose to use as a potential source for your research essay?

© 2003–2009 Diet-Blog. Reprinted with permission.

Medicinenet.com Web page reprinted with permission, 2009.

S

EE

ING

THE ARGUMENT

SEEING THE ARGUMENT

On the Web page shown here:

GOOD ADVICE

Although many online sources may not be excellent for research purposes, don't give up! You can find credible academic and journalistic articles online. Just be sure that the source is a reputable one and that the author supports his or her points with documented statistics and facts. On the Web page shown here, for example, the author cites a U.S. Justice Department research study and even provides a link to his source at the end of the article.

link to a homepage. Never use a Web source that does not identify the author or the organization responsible for the material. Critical question: Is this author qualified to write on this topic? How do I know?

- **Judge the credibility of the writing.** For books, read how reviewers evaluated the book when it was first published. For articles, judge the respectability of the magazine or journal. Study the author's use of documentation as one measure of credibility. Scholarly works cite sources. Well-researched and reliable pieces in quality popular magazines will also make clear the sources of any statistics used and the credentials of any authority who is quoted. One good rule: Never use undocumented or unreferenced statistical information. Another sign of credibility is the quality of writing. Do not use sources filled with grammatical and mechanical errors. For Web sources, find out what institution hosts the site. If you have not heard of the company or organization, find out more about it. The critical question to ask is, Why should I believe information/ideas from this source?

- **Select only sources that are at an appropriate level for your research.** Avoid works that are either too specialized or too elementary for college research.

You may not understand the former (and thus could misrepresent them in your paper), and you gain nothing from the latter. The critical question to ask is, Will this source provide a sophisticated discussion for educated adults?

- **Understand the writer's purpose.** Consider the writer's intended audience. Be cautious using works that reinforce biases already shared by the intended audience. Is the work written to persuade rather than to inform and analyze? Examine the writing for emotionally charged language. For Internet sources, ask yourself why this person or institution decided to have a Web site or contribute to a newsgroup. Critical question: Can I trust the information from this source, given the apparent purpose of the work?

- **In general, choose current sources.** Some studies published years ago remain classics, but many older works have become outdated. In scientific and technical fields, the "information revolution" has outdated some works published only five years ago. So look at publication dates (When was the Web site page last updated?) and pass over outdated sources in favor of current studies. Critical question: Is this information still accurate?

When evaluating your sources for an academic research essay, it is important to examine whether the piece is at the appropriate level (in both its writing and research) for an educated audience who has a serious investment in your argument. Consider this piece about eating disorders from *People* magazine. Would an academic audience accept this writer's writing style and research as credible and reliable? Would the visuals add to or detract from the perceived level of this article? Would you use this article as an academic source? Why or why not?

S
E E
I N G
THE ARGUMENT

SEEING THE ARGUMENT

EXTREME MEASURES

Drastic thinness has become the reigning beauty ideal from runways to the red carpet—and it's having an alarming effect on girls everywhere

At a party for designer Zac Posen in New York City on Sept. 14, the scene was fashion meets young Hollywood. There was Kate Bosworth looking whisper-thin in a black dress, dancing to Justin Timberlake's "SexyBack" and smoking cigarettes. There was the always misseudle Mary-Kate Olsen, who stopped by just long enough to puff a cigarette and pose for a few photos. At the center was Posen, 25, a current red-carpet favorite who has dressed a range of young actresses, from the plus-size Marissa Jaret Winokur to the sub-zero Bosworth. "I like women's bodies—I emphasize them in my clothing," Posen told PEOPLE on Sept. 21. "Healthy women are much sexier."

And yet the questions of who is healthy and what is sexy cut to the heart of a renewed debate that is currently raging everywhere from message boards to movie sets to modeling agencies. What makes this controversy new is that for the first time both designers and stars have been put on the defen-

sive: In Hollywood, stylemakers like Bosworth, 23, and Nicole Richie, 25, are setting troubling new standards for thinness, while in the fashion world, frail-looking runway models drew gasps at New York City's Fashion Week. "In the past, some young models have had issues with eating disorders—but they were rapidly singled out and left with very little options other than to address their problem," says David Bonnouvrier, head of DNA Model Management. "The latest trend of skinny models, however, has allowed many of these young women to continue working, living in total denial." Adds Dr. Ira Sacker, a Manhattan-based eating disorder specialist and the coauthor of *Dying to Be Thin*: "I have alot of A-list celebrities as clients, both actresses and models, and what they are telling me is that the pressure to be thin has never been greater. Why? Because whoever is thinner gets the job, and the competition is enormous."

To be sure, scrutiny of the thinnest stars is more

PEOPLE October 9, 2006

In interviews with PEOPLE at malls across the country, most teenage girls rejected Richie's body as "nasty" and "too skinny" but acknowledged that she and other stars serve as style role models. "Nicole's body is gross because her skeleton shows," says Kailey Koepplin, 17, of Eden Prairie, Minn. Other teens said they admire healthier-looking stars like Jessica Simpson ("She has cute clothes and she doesn't show too much"), Beyoncé and Jessica Alba ("She's tiny, but she's not too tiny").

GOOD ADVICE

MLA documentation requires that precise page references be given for all ideas, opinions, and information taken from sources—except for common knowledge. Author and page references provided in the text are supported by complete bibliographic citations on the Works Cited page. You are required to document direct quotations from sources; paraphrased ideas and opinions from sources; summaries of ideas from sources; and factual information, except common knowledge, from sources.

Documenting Sources to Avoid Plagiarism

Documenting sources accurately and fully is required of all researchers. Proper documentation distinguishes between the work of others and your ideas, shows readers the breadth of your research, and strengthens your credibility. In Western culture, copyright laws support the ethic that ideas, new information, and wording belong to their author. To borrow these without acknowledgment is against the law and has led to many celebrated lawsuits. For students who plagiarize, the consequences range from an F on the paper to suspension from college. Be certain, then, that you know the requirements for correct documentation; accidental plagiarism is still plagiarism and will be punished.

Putting an author's ideas in your own words in a paraphrase or summary does not eliminate the requirement of documentation. To illustrate, compare the following excerpt from Thomas R. Schueler's report

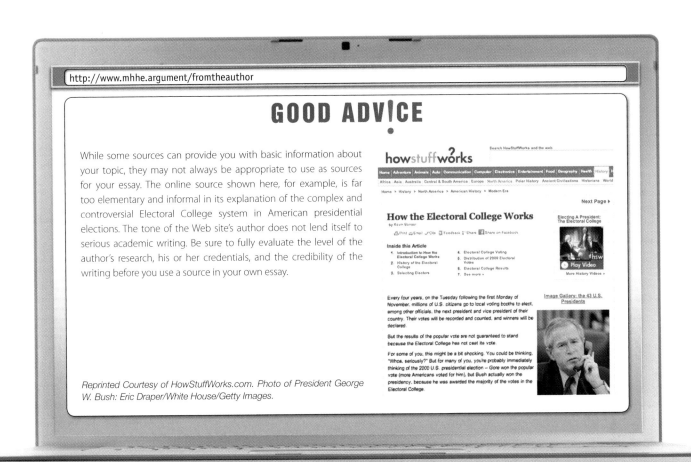

GOOD ADVICE

While some sources can provide you with basic information about your topic, they may not always be appropriate to use as sources for your essay. The online source shown here, for example, is far too elementary and informal in its explanation of the complex and controversial Electoral College system in American presidential elections. The tone of the Web site's author does not lend itself to serious academic writing. Be sure to fully evaluate the level of the author's research, his or her credentials, and the credibility of the writing before you use a source in your own essay.

Reprinted Courtesy of HowStuffWorks.com. Photo of President George W. Bush: Eric Draper/White House/Getty Images.

Many students have heard of sites such as Turnitin.com, where instructors can check students' work against large databases in order to catch suspected plagiarists. But there are also sites such as WriteCheck (powered by the same technology as Turnitin) designed specifically for students to allow them to check their work in order to prevent accidental or unintentional plagiarism. For more information on WriteCheck, go to http://writecheck.turnitin.com.

did you know

Controlling Urban Runoff (Washington Metropolitan Water Resources Planning Board, 1987: 3–4) and a student paragraph based on the report.

Original Source

The aquatic ecosystems in urban headwater streams are particularly susceptible to the impacts of urbanization. . . . Dietemann (1975), Ragan and Dietemann (1976), Klein (1979), and WMCOG (1982) have all tracked trends in fish diversity and abundance over time in local urbanizing streams. Each of the studies has shown that fish communities become less diverse and are composed of more tolerant species after the surrounding watershed is developed. Sensitive fish species either disappear or occur very rarely. In most cases, the total number of fish in urbanizing streams may also decline.

Similar trends have been noted among aquatic insects which are the major food resource for fish. . . . Higher post-development sediment and trace metals can interfere in their efforts to gather food. Changes in water temperature, oxygen levels, and substrate composition can further reduce the species diversity and abundance of the aquatic insect community.

Plagarized Student Paragraph

Studies have shown that fish communities become less diverse as the amount of runoff increases. Sensitive fish species either disappear or occur very rarely, and, in most cases, the total number of fish declines. Aquatic insects, a major source of food for fish, also decline because sediment and trace metals interfere with their food-gathering efforts. Increased water temperature and lower oxygen levels can further reduce the species diversity and abundance of the aquatic insect community.

The student's opening words establish a reader's expectation that the student has taken information from a source, as indeed the student has. But where is the documentation? The student's paraphrase is an obvious example of plagiarism: an unacknowledged paraphrase of borrowed information that even copies the source's exact wording in two places. For MLA style, the author's name and the page numbers are needed throughout the paragraph. Additionally, most of the first sentence and the final phrase must be put into the student's own words or be placed within quotation marks. The revised paragraph in Try It! shows appropriate acknowledgment of the source.

try it !

Rewrite the plagiarized student paragraph to remove the plagiarism concern. Then check with the sample revision here to see how you did.

Revised Student Paragraph to Remove Plagiarism

In *Controlling Urban Runoff,* Thomas Schueler explains that studies have shown "that fish communities become less diverse as the amount of runoff increases" (3). Sensitive fish species either disappear or occur very rarely and, in most cases, the total number of fish declines. Aquatic insects, a major source of food for fish, also decline because sediment and trace metals interfere with their food-gathering efforts. Increased water temperature and lower oxygen levels, Schueler concludes, "can further reduce the species diversity and abundance of the aquatic insect community" (4).

What Is Common Knowledge?

In general, common knowledge includes

- undisputed dates
- well-known facts
- generally known facts, terms, and concepts in the field of study in which you are writing

So do not cite a source for the dates of the American Revolution. If you are writing a paper for a psychology class, do not cite your text when using terms such as *ego* or *sublimation*. However, you must cite a historian who analyzes the causes of England's loss to the colonies or a psychologist who disputes Freud's ideas. Opinions about well-known facts must be documented. Discussions of debatable dates, terms, or concepts must be documented. When in doubt, defend your integrity and document.

Taking Notes on Sources

How are you going to keep track of information and ideas from your study? You have three possibilities: handwritten notes on cards, keyboarded notes in PC files, and annotations on photocopies of sources. How

GOOD ADV!CE

Hints for Effective Note-Taking

ON CARDS

1. Use either 4 x 6 cards or half sheets of letter-size paper.
2. Write in ink.
3. Write only one item on each card. Each card should contain only one idea, piece of information, or group of related facts. The flexibility of cards is lost if you do not follow this procedure. You want to be able to group cards according to your outline when you are ready to draft the paper.

WITH A COMPUTER

1. Make a file titled "Notes" or make a separate file for each note.
2. Use clear headings and subheadings for notes so that you can find each note easily.
3. Consider printing copies of your notes and cutting them into separate "cards" for organizing prior to drafting. (When drafting, do not re-keyboard. Just use your printed notes as a guide to placement in the draft.) Use the Cut and Paste or Move features of your word processor to rearrange notes into the order you want.

ANNOTATING PHOTOCOPIES

1. Do not endlessly highlight your photocopies. Instead, carefully bracket the passages that contain information you want to use.
2. Write a note in the margin next to bracketed passages indicating how and where you think you want to use that material. Use the language of your informal outline to annotate marked passages (such as "causes," "effects," "rebuttal to counterargument," "solutions").
3. Keep in mind that you will have to paraphrase the marked passages before using the material in your draft.

---

to choose? Most likely, your decision will be a matter of personal preference. However, if your instructor requires you to hand in notes, then you must use the first or second strategy. (Just print out your files and cut pages into separate "note cards.")

You will want to follow these guidelines as you begin to take notes on your potential sources. Remember that taking effective notes will help you remain organized as you later incorporate your sources into your research essay.

1. **Study first; take notes later.** First, do background reading. Second, skim what appear to be your chief sources. Prepare summary notes and annotate photocopies of sources. Read so that you can develop your preliminary outline. Learn what the writers on your topic consider to be important facts, issues, and arguments. Keep in mind that taking too many useless notes is a frustrating, time-wasting activity.

2. **Before preparing any note, identify the source of the note.** Write or type the author's name, a shortened title if necessary, and the page number from which the material comes. Remember: All borrowed information and ideas must be documented with precise page numbers if you are using MLA style—and for all direct quotations if you are using APA style.

3. **Type or write an identifying word or phrase for each note.** Identifying words or phrases will help you sort cards or find notes when you are ready to draft. Select words carefully to correspond to the sections of your preliminary outline.

4. **Record the information accurately and clearly.** Be sure to put all directly quoted passages within quotation marks. To treat a direct quotation as a paraphrase in your paper is to plagiarize.

5. **Distinguish between fact and opinion.** Notes that contain opinion should be identified with such phrases as "Smith believes that" or "Smith asserts that." Or, label the note "opinion."

6. **Distinguish between information from sources and your own opinions, questions, and reactions to the recorded information.** Write notes to yourself so that you do not forget good ideas that come to you as you are reading. Just be certain to label your notes "my notes"—or draw (or type) a line between information from a source and your response.

GOOD ADVICE

Should I Quote or Paraphrase Notes or Use Photocopies of Sources?

Knowing what type of notes to take is very important. Some argue that copying the exact quotation from the original source is best. Others believe that you should put the idea into your words. Here are the arguments:

Most of your paper should be in your own words, so most of your notes should be paraphrases or summaries. Putting off paraphrasing means having to do it when you are under the pressure of writing the paper.

However, taking direct-quotation notes will give you the exact wording of passages to think about when you draft your paper. At the drafting stage, you can turn the quoted passages into paraphrases. The previous point, along with the valid point of convenience, justifies using copies of sources that you annotate to show what passages you want to use.

In the end, probably some combination of strategies is a good choice. Photocopy (or download or e-mail to yourself) key articles so that you have the entire article to work with. Initially flag passages in books with Post-It notes or slips of paper. Then, as you get close to finishing your study of sources, make at least some paraphrased notes to start the process of moving away from the language of original sources. The more sources you are using, the more convenient and efficient notes will be when you are ready to draft your paper.

Using "Tags" or "Signal Phrases" to Avoid Misleading Documentation

If you are an honest student, you do not want to submit a paper that is plagiarized, even though the plagiarism was unintentional. What leads to unintentional plagiarism?

- A researcher takes careless notes, neglecting to include precise page numbers on the notes, but uses the information anyway, without any documentation.

- A researcher works in material from sources in such a way that, even with page references, readers cannot tell what has been taken from the sources.

Good note-taking strategies will keep you from the first pitfall. Avoiding the second problem means becoming skilled in ways to include source material in your writing while still making your indebtedness to sources absolutely clear to readers. The way to do this: Give the author's name in the essay. You can also include, when appropriate, the author's credentials ("According to Dr. Hays, a geologist with the Department of Interior, . . .").

These introductory tags or signal phrases give readers a context for the borrowed material, as well as serving as part of the required documentation of sources. Make sure that each tag clarifies rather than distorts an author's relationship to his or her ideas and your relationship to the source. Be aware, also, that simply introducing a source with a tag does not give your reader all of the information he or she may need about your source. Be sure to go on to explain the source's relevance to your argument, define key concepts or terms in the quote, or even explain the meaning of the source material if necessary.

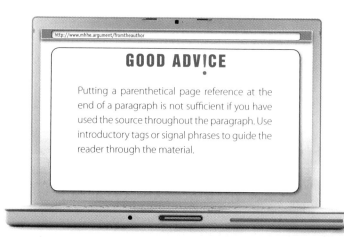

GOOD ADVICE

Putting a parenthetical page reference at the end of a paragraph is not sufficient if you have used the source throughout the paragraph. Use introductory tags or signal phrases to guide the reader through the material.

GOOD ADV!CE

Here are three guidelines to follow to avoid misrepresenting borrowed material:

Pay attention to verb choice in tags. When you vary such standard wording as "Smith says" or "Jones states," be careful that you do not select verbs that misrepresent Smith's or Jones's attitude toward his or her own work. Do not write "Jones wonders" when in fact Jones has strongly asserted her views.

Pay attention to the location of tags. If you mention Jones after you have presented her views, be sure that your reader can tell precisely which ideas in the passage belong to Jones. If your entire paragraph is a paraphrase of Jones's work, you are plagiarizing if you conclude with "This idea is presented by Jones." Which of the several ideas in your paragraph comes from Jones? Your reader will assume that only the last idea comes from Jones.

Paraphrase properly. Be sure that paraphrases are truly in your own words. To use Smith's words and sentence style in your writing is to plagiarize.

try it !

Acknowledging Sources

The following paragraph (from page 54 of Franklin E. Zimring's "Firearms, Violence and Public Policy" [*Scientific American*, Nov. 1991]) is the source material for the three student examples of adequate and inadequate acknowledgment of sources. After reading Zimring's paragraph, study the three examples and answer these questions:

(1) Which example represents adequate acknowledgment?

(2) Which examples do not represent adequate acknowledgment?

(3) In what ways is each plagiarized paragraph flawed?

ORIGINAL SOURCE

Although most citizens support such measures as owner screening, public opinion is sharply divided on laws that would restrict the ownership of handguns to persons with special needs. If the United States does not reduce handguns and current trends continue, it faces the prospect that the number of handguns in circulation will grow from 35 million to more than 50 million within 50 years. A national program limiting the availability of handguns would cost many billions of dollars and meet much resistance from citizens. These costs would likely be greatest in the early years of the program. The benefits of supply reduction would emerge slowly because efforts to diminish the availability of handguns would probably have a cumulative impact over time. [page 54]

continued

STUDENT PARAGRAPH 1

One approach to the problem of handgun violence in America is to severely limit handgun ownership. If we don't restrict ownership and start the costly task of removing handguns from our society, we may end up with around 50 million handguns in the country by 2040. The benefits will not be apparent right away but will eventually appear. This idea is emphasized by Franklin Zimring (54).

STUDENT PARAGRAPH 2

One approach to the problem of handgun violence in America is to restrict the ownership of handguns except in special circumstances. If we do not begin to reduce the number of handguns in this country, the number will grow from 35 million to more than 50 million within 50 years. We can agree with Franklin Zimring that a program limiting handguns will cost billions and meet resistance from citizens (54).

STUDENT PARAGRAPH 3

According to law professor Franklin Zimring, the United States needs to severely limit handgun ownership or face the possibility of seeing handgun ownership increase "from 35 million to more than 50 million within 50 years" (54). Zimring points out that Americans disagree significantly on restricting handguns and that enforcing such laws would be very expensive. He concludes that the benefits would not be seen immediately but that the restrictions "would probably have a cumulative impact over time" (54). Although Zimring paints a gloomy picture of high costs and little immediate relief from gun violence, he also presents the shocking possibility of 50 million guns by the year 2040. Can our society survive so much fire power?

Clearly, only the third student paragraph demonstrates adequate acknowledgment of the writer's indebtedness to Zimring. Notice that the placement of the last parenthetical page reference acts as a visual closure to the student's borrowing; then she turns to her response to Zimring and her own views on handguns.

making connections

let's review

- It is up to you as the researcher to figure out which sources will be <u>credible, reliable, and useful</u> to you as you construct your own argument. This is not an easy or quick task. It will involve careful research, reading and rereading your sources, evaluating each one as it relates to your thesis, and making an organized plan for where and how you will use each source.

- When you use facts and opinions from sources, you are saying to readers that the facts are accurate and the ideas credible. <u>If you do not evaluate your sources before using them, you risk losing your credibility as a writer</u>.

- Today, with access to so much material on the Internet, the need to evaluate is even more crucial. Effective strategies for evaluating sources include the following:

  - Locate the author's credentials.
  - Judge the credibility of the writing.
  - Select only sources that are at an appropriate level for your research.
  - Understand the writer's purpose.
  - In general, choose current sources.

- Documenting sources accurately and fully is required of all researchers. Proper documentation distinguishes between the work of others and your ideas, shows readers the breadth of your research, and strengthens your credibility.

- You do not need to document material that is common knowledge. In general, common knowledge includes

  - undisputed dates
  - well-known facts
  - generally known facts, terms, and concepts in the field of study in which you are writing

- The three basic possibilities for keeping track of information and ideas as you conduct your research are handwritten notes on cards, keyboarded notes in PC files, and annotations of photocopies of sources. The choice is most often a matter of personal preference.

- Using introductory tags or signal phrases gives readers a context for the borrowed material, as well as serving as part of the required documentation of sources. Make sure that each tag clarifies rather than distorts an author's relationship to his or her ideas and your relationship to the source.

connect

Evaluate the following online magazine article based on the criteria presented in the first part of this chapter. (See full article at www.time.com/time/health/article/0,8599,1889469,00.html.)

- Can you determine its authorship? Does the author and/or sponsoring organization seem reliable? How do you know?

- Does the author seem to have a particular bias? Does he ignore potential counterarguments or opposing positions?

- Does the article seem to be written at a level appropriate for educated audiences?

- Does the writing seem credible to you? Does the writer use credible sources and give proper attribution to those sources?

- Is the article current? How do you know?

Write a brief analysis of this source and explain why you would or would not use it as a source for an academic essay.

drafting and revising the researched argument

Now that you have chosen a workable topic and located sources that you think might be helpful in supporting your thesis, it's time to begin to construct your researched essay. As you organize and draft, keep in mind that your argument skills apply to the research paper as well. Do not let documenting of multiple sources distract you from your best use of critical thinking and writing skills.

Organizing the Paper

To make decisions about your paper's organization, a good place to begin is with the identifying phrases at the top of your notes or the list of support you developed as you studied sources (see Chapters 10 and 11 for more on locating and taking notes on sources). These phrases represent subsections of your topic that emerged as you studied sources. They will now help you organize your paper, as well as figure out where and how sources may be synthesized with each other and with your own ideas. Here are some guidelines for getting organized to write:

1. **Arrange notes by identifying phrases and read them through.** Read personal notes as well. Work all notes into one possible order as suggested by the identifying phrases or themes. In reading through all notes at one time, you may discover that some now seem irrelevant. Set them aside, but do not throw them away yet. Some additional note-taking may be necessary to fill in gaps that have become apparent. You know your sources well enough by now to be able to find the additional material that you need.

2. **Re-examine your tentative claim or research proposal and the preliminary list that guided your research.** As a result of reading and reflection, do you need to alter or modify your claim in any way? Or if you began with a research question, what now is your answer to the question? What, for example, was the impact of Prohibition on the 1920s? Or is TV violence harmful to children? You need to decide. Remember that the final thesis or claim in a research argument cannot be a question. Rather, it must be your answer to the research question.

3. **Decide on a final claim.** To produce a unified and coherent essay with a clear central idea and a reason for being, you need a claim that meets the following criteria:

   • *It is a complete sentence, not a topic or statement of purpose.*

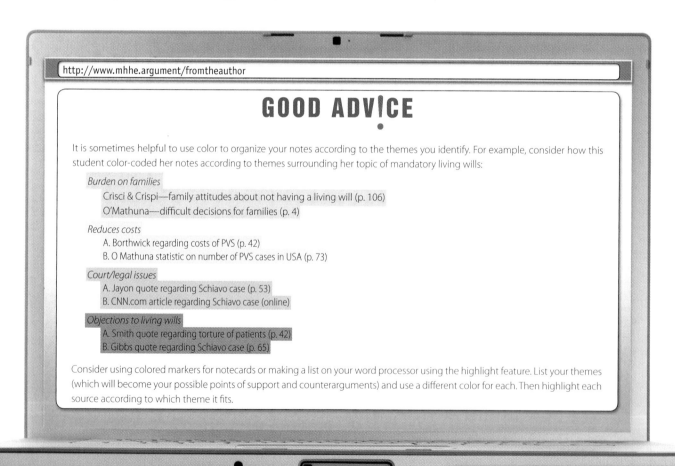

http://www.mhhe.argument/fromtheauthor

GOOD ADVICE

It is sometimes helpful to use color to organize your notes according to the themes you identify. For example, consider how this student color-coded her notes according to themes surrounding her topic of mandatory living wills:

Burden on families
    Crisci & Crispi—family attitudes about not having a living will (p. 106)
    O'Mathuna—difficult decisions for families (p. 4)

Reduces costs
    A. Borthwick regarding costs of PVS (p. 42)
    B. O Mathuna statistic on number of PVS cases in USA (p. 73)

Court/legal issues
    A. Jayon quote regarding Schiavo case (p. 53)
    B. CNN.com article regarding Schiavo case (online)

Objections to living wills
    A. Smith quote regarding torture of patients (p. 42)
    B. Gibbs quote regarding Schiavo case (p. 65)

Consider using colored markers for notecards or making a list on your word processor using the highlight feature. List your themes (which will become your possible points of support and counterarguments) and use a different color for each. Then highlight each source according to which theme it fits.

There are several Web sites dedicated to providing free help and advice for writers. The OWL (Online Writing Lab) at Purdue University is one of them. The site offers advice on how to outline and organize your research among other topics. Check it out!

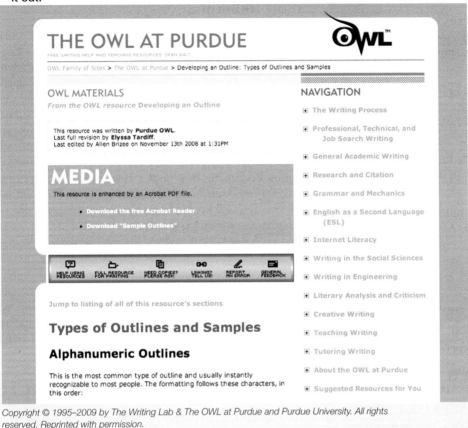

THE OWL AT PURDUE

FREE WRITING HELP AND TEACHING RESOURCES OPEN 24/7

OWL Family of Sites > The OWL at Purdue > Developing an Outline: Types of Outlines and Samples

OWL MATERIALS

From the OWL resource Developing an Outline

This resource was written by **Purdue OWL.**
Last full revision by **Elyssa Tardiff.**
Last edited by Allen Brizee on November 13th 2008 at 1:31PM

MEDIA

This resource is enhanced by an Acrobat PDF file.

- Download the free Acrobat Reader
- Download "Sample Outlines"

HELP USING RESOURCES | FULL RESOURCE FOR PRINTING | NEED COPIES? PLEASE ASK | LEMONS? TELL US! | REPORT AN ERROR | GENERAL FEEDBACK

Jump to listing of all of this resource's sections

Types of Outlines and Samples

Alphanumeric Outlines

This is the most common type of outline and usually instantly recognizable to most people. The formatting follows these characters, in this order:

NAVIGATION

⊕ The Writing Process

⊕ Professional, Technical, and Job Search Writing

⊕ General Academic Writing

⊕ Research and Citation

⊕ Grammar and Mechanics

⊕ English as a Second Language (ESL)

⊕ Internet Literacy

⊕ Writing in the Social Sciences

⊕ Writing in Engineering

⊕ Literary Analysis and Criticism

⊕ Creative Writing

⊕ Teaching Writing

⊕ Tutoring Writing

⊕ About the OWL at Purdue

⊕ Suggested Resources for You

TOPIC: Rape on college campuses.
CLAIM/THESIS: There are specific steps that both students and administrators should take to reduce incidents of campus rape.

- *It is limited and focused.*
  UNFOCUSED AND NONLIMITED THESIS: Drunk driving violators should be punished.
  FOCUSED AND LIMITED THESIS: Drunk driving, even as a first offense, should be treated as an extremely serious criminal offense and should carry a mandatory sentence of five years in prison.

- *It can be supported by your research.*
  UNSUPPORTABLE THESIS: *Time* magazine does not like George Bush.
  SUPPORTABLE THESIS: A study of *Time*'s coverage of President Bush during the 1990–91 winter months reveals a strong negative bias against the President beginning at the start of the Persian Gulf War.

- *It establishes a new or interesting approach to the topic that makes your research worthwhile.*
  NON-INVENTIVE THESIS: A regional shopping mall should not be built adjacent to the Manassas Battlefield.
  INVENTIVE THESIS: Putting aside an appeal to our national heritage made by local historians, the building of a regional shopping mall adjacent to the Manassas Battlefield has no economic justification and should not be completed.

4. Write down the organization revealed by the way you have grouped notes and compare this organization with your preliminary plan. If you have deleted sections or reordered them, justify those changes in your own mind. Does the new, fuller plan now provide a complete and logical development of your claim?

The Formal Outline

Some instructors expect a formal outline with research essays. Preparing a formal outline requires that you think through the entire structure of your paper and see the relationship of parts. Remember that the more you analyze your topic, the fuller and therefore more useful your outline will be. But do not expect more out of an outline than it can provide. A logical and clear organization does not result from a detailed outline; rather, a detailed outline results from a logical analysis of your topic.

Remember the following points as you construct your outline:

- The formal outline uses a combination of numbers and letters to show headings and subheadings.
- The parts of the paper indicated by the same types of numbers or letters should be equally important.
- Headings and subheadings indicated by the same types of numbers or letters should have the same structure (for example, A. Obtain*ing* Good Equipment; B. Tak*ing* Lessons; C. Practic*ing*).
- Headings that are subdivided must contain at least two subsections (that is, if there is a 1 under A, there has to be a 2).
- You can choose to write a full-sentence outline or a briefer, topical outline. Ask your instructor which is required.

Consider this topical outline for a student's research essay. Then convert this outline into a full-sentence outline that allows you to clearly see the writer's direction and purpose. Compare your outline to a classmate's. Are they the same? Or do they differ?

What would be some potential benefits to a full-sentence outline as opposed to this brief topical outline? Be sure to check with your instructor regarding which type of outline is required for your course.

OUTLINE

Introduction	Introduce controversy and issue
Thesis:	A law should be created that makes having a living will mandatory
I. First point of support	Burden
II. Second point	Cost
III. Third point	Court
IV. Counterargument(s)	Might be torture
V. Rebuttal	But no feeling
VI. Conclusion	

Drafting the Paper

Plan Your Time

Effective time-management skills are crucial to any research essay project. Be sure you know your deadlines and leave yourself sufficient time to complete your tasks. One of the easiest ways to produce a poorly written research essay is to rush the process. Cramming weeks worth of work into a single night or two will not produce a thoughtful, well-crafted argument.

Consider how much time you will need to draft your essay. Working with notes and being careful about documentation make research paper writing more time-consuming than writing undocumented essays. You will probably **need two or three afternoons or evenings to complete a draft**. You should start writing, then, **at least five days before your paper is due** to **allow time between drafting and revising.** Don't throw away weeks of study by trying to draft, revise, and proof your paper in one day. The good news is that there are specific strategies that can help you and effectively utilize your time. The goal is to minimize the number of times you must revise by doing it **right on your first draft**.

Handle Documentation As You Draft

Although you may believe that stopping to include parenthetical documentation as you write will cramp your writing, you should not wait until you complete your draft to add the documentation. The risk of failing to document accurately is too great. Parenthetical documentation is brief; take the time to include it as you compose. Then, when your paper is finished and you are preparing your list of works cited, go through your paper carefully to make certain that a work is listed for every parenthetical reference.

Choose and Maintain an Appropriate Writing Style

Specific suggestions for composing the parts of your paper will follow, but first here are some general guidelines for research paper style.

Use the Proper Person

Research papers are written primarily in the third person (*she, he, it, they*) to create objectivity and to direct attention to the content of the paper. You are not likely to use the second person (*you*) at all, for the second person often creates an informal and conversational tone that isn't appropriate for research papers. The usual question is about the appropriateness of the first person (*I, we*). Although you want to avoid writing "as you can see," do not try to skirt around the use of *I* if you need to distinguish your position from the views of others. It is better to write "I" than "it is the opinion of this writer" or "the researcher learned" or "this project analyzed." On the other hand, avoid qualifiers such as "I think." Just state your ideas.

Use the Proper Tense

When you are writing about people, ideas, or events of the past, the appropriate tense is the past tense. When writing about current times, the appropriate tense is the present. Both may occur in the same paragraph, as the following paragraph illustrates.

> Twenty-five years ago "personal" computers were all but unheard of. Computers were regarded as unknowable, building-sized, mechanized monsters that required a precise 68 degree air-conditioned environment and eggheaded technicians with thick glasses and white lab coats scurrying about to keep the temperamental and fragile egos of the electronic brains mollified. Today's generation of computers is accessible, affordable, commonplace, and much less mysterious. A computer that used to require two rooms to house is now smaller than a briefcase. A computer that cost hundreds of thousands of dollars twenty-five years ago now has a price tag in the hundreds. The astonishing progress made in computer technology in the last few years has made computers practical, attainable, and indispensable. Personal computers are here to stay.

In this example, when the student moves from computers in the past to computers in the present, he shifts tenses accurately.

When writing about sources, the convention is to use the present tense even for works or authors from the past. The idea is that the source, or the author, continues to make the point or use the technique into the present—that is, every time there is a reader. Use of the *historical present tense* requires that you write "Lincoln selects the biblical expression 'Fourscore and seven years ago'" and "King echoes Lincoln when he writes 'five score years ago.'"

Avoid Excessive Quoting

Many students use too many direct quotations. Plan to use your own words most of the time for these good reasons:

- Constantly shifting between your words and the language of your sources (not to mention all those quotation marks) makes reading your essay difficult.

- This is your paper and should sound like you.

- When you take a passage out of its larger context, you face the danger of misrepresenting the writer's views.

- When you quote endlessly, readers may begin to think either that you are lazy or that you don't really understand the issues well enough to put them in your own words. You don't want to present either image to your readers.

- You do not prove any point by quoting another person's opinion. All you indicate is that there is someone else who shares your views. Even if that person is an expert on the topic, your quoted material still represents the view of only one person. You support a claim with reasons and evidence, both of which can usually be presented in your own words.

When you must quote, keep the quotations brief, weave them carefully into your own sentences, and be sure to identify the author in a signal phrase. (For more on using direct quotations, see Chapter 11 or page 209 later in this chapter.)

Avoid Ineffective Openings

Follow these rules for avoiding openings that most readers find ineffective or annoying.

1. **Do not restate the title** or use the title as the first sentence in paragraph 1. First, the title of the paper appears at the top of the first page of text. Second, it is a convention of writing to have the first paragraph stand independent of the title.

2. **Do not begin with "clever" visuals** such as artwork or fancy lettering.

3. **Do not begin with humor** unless it is part of your topic.

4. **Do not begin with a question that is just a gimmick,** or one that a reader may answer in a way you do not intend. Asking "What are the advantages of solar energy?" may lead a reader to answer "None that I can think of." However, a straightforward research question ("Is *Death of a Salesman* a tragedy?") is appropriate.

5. **Do not open with an unnecessary definition quoted from a dictionary.** "According to Webster, solar energy means . . ." is a tired, overworked beginning that does not engage readers.

6. **Do not start with a purpose statement:** "This paper will examine . . ." Although a statement of purpose

Consider the following opening for a student's research paper on mandatory drug testing for college professors. What tone is the author setting by using this particular font and visual? Do you find it effective? Do you think an educated audience will take this research argument seriously? Be sure to consider how your choice of visuals (especially in your opening paragraphs) can affect your essay's effectiveness. A good rule when using visuals is "just because you can, doesn't necessarily mean you should." Make sure that each visual has a clear purpose and helps to support your claim. Otherwise, leave it out.

Jake Tebron
Professor Canton
Research Essay

20 March 2009

The Fast and the Furious: Professors on Drugs

is necessary in a report of empirical research, the report still needs an interesting introduction.

Write Effective Openings

The best introduction is one that presents your subject in an interesting way to gain the reader's attention, states your claim, and gives the reader an indication of the scope and limits of your paper. In a short research essay, you may be able to combine an attention-getter, a statement of subject, and a claim in one paragraph. Typically in longer papers, the introduction will be two or three paragraphs. In the physical and social sciences, the claim may be withheld until the conclusion, but the opening introduces the subject and presents the researcher's hypothesis, often posed as a question. Since students sometimes have trouble with research paper introductions in spite of knowing these general guidelines, several approaches are illustrated in the following examples.

Begin with a brief example or anecdote to dramatize your topic. One student introduced her argument on the quality of America's nightly news with this attention-getter:

When I watched television in the first weeks after moving to the United States, I was delighted by the relaxing display of the news programs. It was different from what I was used to on German television, where one finds a stern-looking man reading the news without any emotion. Here the commentators laugh without showing distress; their tone with each other is amiable. Watching the news in this country was a new and entertaining experience for me initially, but as my English reading and speaking skills improved, I found that I was a bit disturbed by their ability to deliver negative, if not horrendous information with smiles on their faces. After reading Neil Postman's attack

> on television news shows in "Television News Narcosis," I was reminded of this odd disconnect. I wondered if American news programs were not somehow being irresponsible in their presentation of world events.

In the paragraph that follows this introductory paragraph, the student completes her introduction by explaining the procedures she used for analyzing network news programs and presents her thesis that American news programs are indeed being negligent in their duty to present accurate and important information to the masses.

In the opening to her study of car advertisements, a student, relating her topic to what readers know, reminds readers of the culture's concern with image:

> Many Americans are highly image conscious. Because the right look is essential to a prosperous life, no detail is too small to overlook. Clichés about first impressions remind us that "you never get a second chance to make a first impression," so we obsessively watch our weight, firm our muscles, sculpt our hair, select our friends, find the perfect houses, and buy our automobiles. Realizing the importance of image, companies compete to make the "right" products, that is, those that will complete the "right" image. Then advertisers direct specific products to targeted groups of consumers. Although targeting may be labeled as stereotyping, it has been an effective strategy in advertising.

Challenging a popular attitude or assumption is an effective attention-getting opening. For a paper on the advantages of solar energy, a student began:

> America's energy problems are serious, despite the popular belief that difficulties vanished with the end of the Arab oil embargo in 1974. Our problems remain because the world's supply of fossil fuels is not limitless.

Begin with a thought-provoking question. A student who was arguing that the media both reflect and shape reality started with these questions:

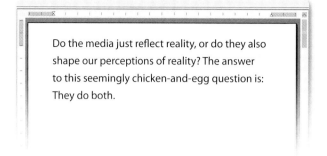

> Do the media just reflect reality, or do they also shape our perceptions of reality? The answer to this seemingly chicken-and-egg question is: They do both.

Beginning with important, perhaps startling, facts, evidence, or statistics is an effective way to introduce a topic, provided the details are relevant to the topic. Observe the following example:

> Teenagers are working again, but not on their homework. Over 40 percent of teenagers have jobs by the time they are juniors (Samuelson A22). And their jobs do not support academic learning since almost two-thirds of teenagers are employed in sales and service jobs that entail mostly carrying, cleaning, and wrapping (Greenberger and Steinberg 62–67), not reading, writing, and computing. Unfortunately, the negative effect on learning is not offset by improved opportunities for future careers.

Compose Solid, Unified Paragraphs

As you compose the body of your paper, keep in mind that you want to (1) maintain unity and coherence, (2) guide readers clearly through source material, and (3) synthesize source material and your own ideas. Do not settle for paragraphs in which facts from notes are just loosely strung together. Review the following discussion and study the examples to see how to craft effective body paragraphs.

Provide Unity and Coherence

You achieve paragraph unity when every sentence in a paragraph relates to and develops the paragraph's main idea. If you have a logical organization, composing unified paragraphs is not a problem. Unity, however, does not automatically produce coherence; that takes attention to wording. Coherence is achieved when readers can follow the connection between one sentence and another and between each sentence and the main idea. Strategies for achieving coherence include repetition of

You might want to include in your introductory paragraph a compelling visual that helps to clarify your issue or provides background information for your reader. While cartoons or visuals meant simply to be eye-catching may not set the correct tone for a research essay, persuasive and informative visuals can be a great way to get your reader invested in your issue. Consider the following opening to a student essay on reforming the way in which animals are slaughtered in America. What does it provide for the reader that words might not? Do you think that this author is using an effective strategy by including this visual? Why or why not? Might it backfire in some way?

Emily Davis
Professor Yaska
Research Essay

12 March 2008

Cruelty to Feed the Masses

There is no easy answer to the question of whether slaughtering animals for food is right or wrong. There are clear arguments on both sides of the issue. However, one fact that is undeniable is that far too many animals are dying unnecessarily horrible and inhumane deaths in this process. Consider, for example, the chickens shown in Figure 1. These animals are dipped into boiling water (while still alive), then tied upside down for hours prior to slaughter while machines beat the feathers from their bodies, causing them excruciating pain before their throats are finally slashed.

Figure 1. Chickens being tortured before slaughter

key words, the use of pronouns that refer to those key words, and the use of transition and connecting words and sentences (also called *metadiscourse*). The following student paragraph is unified (all of the sentences relate to the same topic), but it is not coherent. Compare the student's revision of the paragraph to provide better coherence or "flow."

Original "unified" paragraph

Many authors agree that blind obedience to authority is a bad thing. The most important difference between the ideas of Robinson and Biff is that Robinson only focuses on how blind obedience can devastate an individual's childhood and cause the child to become depressed and withdrawn. Biff discusses how he learned about adulthood—and entered adulthood—piecemeal and without support. This ultimately led him to a life filled with unquestioned obedience to poor authority figures. Both authors agree that when an individual is taught to follow direction without thinking critically about the situation, the outcome is usually a negative one.

Revised "unified and coherent" paragraph

Many **authors** agree on the basic fact that blind obedience to authority is a bad thing. Two such **authors**, Barry Robinson, a noted child psychologist, and Randall Biff, a best-selling author on the subject, provide slightly different perspectives on the issue, but ultimately arrive at the same notion: that teaching children to **blindly** "follow the leader" can be a dangerous practice. The most important difference between the ideas of Robinson and Biff, however, is that Robinson primarily focuses on how **blind obedience** can devastate an individual's childhood and cause the **child to become depressed and withdrawn.** Biff moves beyond the **effects on the child,** and discusses how he personally learned about adulthood—and entered adulthood—piecemeal and without support. This ultimately **led him** to a life filled with **unquestioned obedience** to poor authority figures, including his first "real" boss, who forced him to commit unethical acts as part of his job. While, clearly, these **perspectives** differ slightly, both authors agree that when an individual is taught to follow direction without thinking critically about the situation, the outcome is usually a negative one.

Coherence is needed not only within paragraphs, but also between paragraphs. You need to guide readers through your paper, connecting paragraphs and showing relationships by the use of transitions and effective metadiscourse. The following opening sentences of four paragraphs from a paper on solutions to rape on the college campus illustrate smooth transitions:

¶ 3 Specialists have provided a number of reasons why men rape.

¶ 4 Some of the causes of rape on the college campus originate with the colleges themselves and with how they handle the problem.

¶ 5 Just as there are a number of causes for campus rapes, there are also a number of ways to help solve the problem of these rapes.

¶ 6 If these seem like common-sense solutions, why, then, is it so difficult to significantly reduce the number of campus rapes?

Without awkwardly writing "Here are some of the causes" and "Here are some of the solutions," the student guides her readers through a discussion of causes for and solutions to the problem of campus rape.

Guide Readers through Source Material

To understand the importance of guiding readers through source material, consider first the following paragraph from a paper on the British coal strike in the 1970s:

> The social status of the coal miners was far from good. The country blamed them for the dimmed lights and the three-day work week. They had been placed in the position of social outcasts and were beginning to "consider themselves another country." Some businesses and shops had even gone so far as to refuse service to coal miners (Jones 32).

The student has presented information and given Jones the credit for it. But who is Jones and how can we be sure that this information is reliable? Readers cannot begin to judge the validity of these assertions without some context provided by the writer. Most readers are put off by an unattached direct quotation or some startling observation that is documented correctly but given no context within the paper. Using introductory tags that identify the author of the source and, when useful, the author's credentials helps guide readers through the source material. The following revision of the paragraph above provides not only context but also sentence variety:

> The social acceptance of coal miners, according to Peter Jones, **British correspondent** for *Newsweek*, was far from good. From interviews both in London shops and in pubs near Birmingham, Jones concluded that Britishers blamed the miners for the dimmed lights and three-day work week. Several striking **miners**, in a pub on the outskirts of Birmingham, **asserted** that some of their friends had been denied service by shopkeepers and that they "consider[ed] themselves another country" (32).

When you use introductory tags, try to vary both the words you use and their place in the sentence. Look, for example, at the first sentence in the sample paragraph above. The tag is placed in the middle of the sentence and is set off by commas. The sentence could have been written two other ways:

> The social acceptance of coal miners was far from good, according to Peter Jones, British correspondent for *Newsweek*.

OR

> According to Peter Jones, British correspondent for *Newsweek*, the social acceptance of coal miners was far from good.

GOOD ADVICE

Whenever you provide a name and perhaps credentials for your source, you have three sentence patterns to choose from (as discussed on page 209) . Make a point to use all three options in your paper. Word choice can be varied as well. Instead of writing "Peter Jones says" throughout your paper, consider some of the many options you have:

Jones asserts	Jones contends	Jones attests to
Jones states	Jones thinks	Jones points out
Jones concludes	Jones stresses	Jones believes
Jones presents	Jones emphasizes	Jones agrees with
Jones argues	Jones confirms	Jones speculates

But be careful! Not all the words in this list are synonyms; you cannot substitute *confirms* for *believes*. First, select the term that most accurately conveys the writer's relationship to his or her material. Then, when appropriate, vary word choice as well as sentence structure.

Readers need to be told how they are to respond to the sources used. They need to know which sources you accept as reliable and which you disagree with, and they need to see you distinguish between fact and opinion. Ideas and opinions from sources need introductory tags and then some discussion from you.

Synthesize Source Material and Your Own Ideas

As you write an academic researched argument, you will need to demonstrate the ability to synthesize, or smoothly combine, various authors' opinions, research findings, and quotations into your work. The ability to synthesize the ideas of others into your work requires much more than simply dropping quotations into your essay at appropriate points. It requires a critical understanding of your sources' meanings and how the ideas of other authors connect both to each other and to your own argument. Your goal is to develop the connections between your sources—to show how their ideas relate to each other and to the larger debate as a whole—and also to clarify for your reader how the ideas presented in your sources relate to your own thesis.

Synthesis is an exercise in both critical reading and critical thinking. It requires you to read, annotate, and fully understand each of your sources in order to find common themes, points of contention, or other connections that can be made with other readings on your topic.

A smooth synthesis of source material is aided by introductory tags and parenthetical documentation because they mark the beginning and ending of material taken from a source. But a complete synthesis requires something more: your ideas about the source and the topic. To illustrate, consider the following paragraph from a student's essay on the "skinny trend" in the media:

With television and magazines glamorizing skin and bones, it's no wonder that anorexia and bulimia are becoming problems with teenage girls. Author Jennifer Wulff states, "Surrounded by images of young celebrities who are painfully thin—or very slender with improbably large breasts—girls growing up can feel immense pressure to meet the same standard. Trying hard to look like their idols, some fall prey to eating disorders, and some abuse drugs to help them lose weight" (25). In another article, Dr. Helga Dittmar states, "Women and girls cannot help being exposed to ultra-thin models in advertising, whose body sizes are unrealistic and unhealthy. There is good evidence already that exposure to these unhealthy models leads a large proportion of women to feel dissatisfied with their own bodies" (16). Celebrities should

> take control and stop feeding this vicious cycle and instead start feeding themselves. Magazine editors should refuse to pander to this trend and should begin showing real women with healthy bodies.

This paragraph is a good example of random details strung together for no apparent purpose. How do we know that these sources are credible? And what purpose do these quotes serve in the paper's development? Note that the entire paragraph is developed with material from the two sources rather than from the author. This paragraph is weak for several reasons: (1) it lacks a controlling idea (topic sentence) to give it purpose and direction; (2) it relies for development entirely on its sources; (3) it lacks any discussion or analysis by the writer.

By contrast, the following paragraph demonstrates a successful synthesis:

Sample synthesis paragraph

Source is fully introduced to lend credibility.

Remember to use present tense when discussing quotes.

Synthesis connection is clear—shows how these sources are related to each other.

Author's discussion of how sources help her cause and support her main point. This explains to the reader why these sources were included in this essay.

With television and magazines glamorizing skin and bones, it's no wonder that anorexia and bulimia are becoming problems with teenage girls. Extremely thin celebrity "role models" are even driving young girls toward drugs like cocaine in order to shed the pounds. The results of this trend can be devastating. In an article in a leading women's magazine titled "Pressure to Be Perfect," author Jennifer Wulff states, "Surrounded by images of young celebrities who are painfully thin—or very slender with improbably large breasts—girls growing up can feel immense pressure to meet the same standard. Trying hard to look like their idols, some fall prey to eating disorders, and some abuse drugs to help them lose weight" (25). In another article titled "Research Backs Normal Size Models in Ads," Dr. Helga Dittmar of the University of Sussex expresses the same awareness of this dangerous trend. She conveys the message that young female fans feel extremely self-conscious about their bodies because of the images they constantly see being advertised as "normal." Dittmar states, "Women and girls cannot help being exposed to ultra-thin models in advertising, whose body sizes are unrealistic and unhealthy. There is good evidence already that exposure to these unhealthy models leads a large proportion of women to feel dissatisfied with their own bodies" (16). It is clear that current researchers and authors agree that ultra-thin celebrities and models are causing young girls to resort to eating disorders or drugs and to become insecure with their body image. More should be done to stop these images from permeating our media. Celebrities should take control and stop feeding this vicious cycle and instead start feeding themselves. Magazine editors should refuse to pander to this trend and should begin showing real women with healthy bodies.

Paragraph begins with author's own voice and opinions. One reason these images are bad is that they can cause eating disorders/drug use.

Only page number is included since source was introduced before quote.

Gives brief explanation of how source connects to main idea.

Paragraph ends with a return to the main idea proposed in the topic sentence—eating disorders/drug use.

This paragraph's synthesis is accomplished by several strategies: (1) the paragraph has a controlling idea; (2) the paragraph combines information from several sources, but does not let it overwhelm the voice of the writer; (3) information from the different sources is clearly indicated to readers; and (4) the student explains and discusses the information.

You might have noticed the very different lengths of the two sample paragraphs just presented. Although the second paragraph is long, it is not unwieldy because it achieves unity and coherence. By contrast, body paragraphs of only three sentences are probably too short.

To sum up, good body paragraphs need

- a controlling idea,
- in most cases, information from more than one source, and
- analysis and discussion from the writer.

Avoid Ineffective Conclusions

Follow these rules to avoid conclusions that most readers consider ineffective and annoying:

1. **Do not introduce a new idea.** If the point belongs in your paper, you should have introduced it earlier.

2. **Do not just stop or trail off,** even if you feel you have run out of steam. A simple, clear restatement of the claim is better than no conclusion.

3. **Do not tell your reader what you have accomplished:** "In this paper I have explained the advantages of solar energy by examining the costs . . ." If you have written well, your reader knows what you have accomplished.

4. **Do not offer apologies or expressions of hope.** "Although I wasn't able to find as much on this topic as I wanted, I have tried to explain the advantages of solar energy, and I hope that you will now understand why we need to use it more" is a disastrous ending.

5. **Do not end with a vague or confusing one- or two-sentence summary of complex ideas.** The following sentences make little sense: "These authors have similar and different attitudes and ideals concerning American desires. Faulkner writes with the concerns of man toward man whereas most of the other writers are more concerned with man toward money."

Write Effective Conclusions

Sometimes, ending a paper seems even more difficult than beginning one. You know you are not supposed to just stop, but every ending that comes to mind sounds corny, not clever. If you have trouble, try one of these types of endings:

1. Do not just repeat your claim **exactly as it was stated in paragraph 1,** but **expand** on the original wording and emphasize the claim's significance. Here is the conclusion of the solar energy paper:

> The idea of using solar energy is not as far-fetched as it seemed years ago. With the continued support of government plus the enthusiasm of research groups, environmentalists, and private industry, solar energy may become a household word quite soon. With the increasing cost of fossil fuel, the time could not be better for exploring this use of the sun.

2. End with a **quotation that** effectively **summarizes** and drives home the point of your paper. Researchers are not always lucky enough to find the ideal quotation for ending a paper. If you find a good one, use it. Better yet, present the quotation and then add your comment in a sentence or two. The conclusion to a paper on the dilemma of defective newborns is a good example:

> Dr. Joseph Fletcher is correct when he says that "every advance in medical capabilities is an increase in our moral responsibility" (48). In a world of many gray areas, one point is clear: From an ethical point of view, medicine is a victim of its own success.

3. If you have researched an issue or a problem, emphasize your **proposed** solutions in the concluding paragraph. The student opposing a mall adjacent to the Manassas Battlefield concluded with several solutions:

> Whether the proposed mall will be built is clearly in doubt at the moment. What are the solutions to this controversy? One approach is, of course, not to build the mall at all. To accomplish this solution, now, with the rezoning having been approved, probably requires an act of Congress to buy the land and make it part of the National Park. Another solution, one that would please the County and the developer and satisfy citizens objecting to traffic problems, is to build the needed roads before the mall is completed. A third approach is to allow the office park of the original plan to be built, but

not the mall. The local preservationists had agreed to this original development proposal, but now that the issue has received national attention, they may no longer be willing to compromise. Whatever the future of the William Center, the present plan for a new regional mall is not acceptable.

Choose an Effective Title

Give some thought to your paper's title since that is what your reader sees first and what your work will be known by. A good title provides information and creates interest. Make your title informative by making it specific. If you can create interest through clever wording, so much the better. But do not confuse cutesiness with clever wording. Better to be just straightforward than to demean a serious effort with a cutesy title.

The Completed Paper

Your research paper should be double-spaced throughout (including the works cited page) with 1-inch margins on all sides. Your project will contain the following parts, in this order:

1. **A title page,** with the paper's title, your name, the course name or number, your instructor's name, and the date, centered, if an outline follows. If you do not include an outline, place this information at the top left of the first page. Check with your instructor regarding his or her preference.

2. **An outline,** or statement of purpose, if required.

3. **The body or text of your paper.** Number all pages consecutively, including pages of works cited, using arabic numerals. Place numbers in the upper right-hand corner of each page. Include your last name before each page number.

4. **A list of works cited** starting on a separate page after the text. Title the first page "Works Cited." (Do not use the title "Bibliography.")

Revising the Paper: A Checklist

After completing a first draft, catch your breath and then gear up for the next step in the writing process: revision. Revision involves three separate steps. *Revising,* Step 1, means rewriting—adding or deleting text,

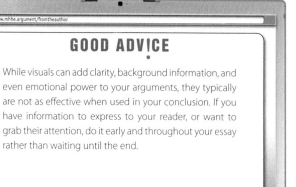

GOOD ADVICE

While visuals can add clarity, background information, and even emotional power to your arguments, they typically are not as effective when used in your conclusion. If you have information to express to your reader, or want to grab their attention, do it early and throughout your essay rather than waiting until the end.

try it !

Review the following essay titles. Within each set, decide which one you would choose to use for your own essay. Discuss your results with your classmates. Why did you choose the one you chose? What about it seemed better or more effective than the other option?

A Perennial Issue Uncovered

The Perennial Issue of Press Freedom versus Press Responsibility Uncovered at Last!

Press Freedom versus Press Responsibility: The Perennial Issue

Earthquakes

The Need for Earthquake Prediction

Quake!!!!!!

Babes in Trouble

The Dilemma of Defective Newborns and What Can Be Done to Help

A Difficult Dilemma

A Call for Mercy: Euthanasia in America

Mercy for All

Euthanasia and Its Benefits

or moving parts of the draft around. Next comes *editing,* a rereading to correct errors from misspellings to incorrect documentation format. Finally, you need to *proofread* the typed copy. If you treat these as separate steps, you will do a more complete job of revision—and get a better grade on the completed paper!

Rewriting

Read your draft through and make changes as a result of answering the following questions:

Purpose and Audience

- Is my draft long enough to meet assignment requirements and my purpose?
- Are terms defined and concepts explained appropriately for my audience?

Content

- Do I have a clearly stated thesis—the claim of my argument?
- Have I presented sufficient evidence to support my claim?
- Are there any irrelevant sections that should be deleted?

Structure

- Are paragraphs ordered to develop my topic logically?
- Does the content of each paragraph help develop my claim?
- Is everything in each paragraph on the same sub-topic to create paragraph unity?
- Do body paragraphs have a balance of information and analysis, of source material and my own ideas?
- Are there any paragraphs that should be combined? Are there any very long paragraphs that should be divided? (Check for unity.)

Editing

Make revisions guided by your responses to the questions, make a clean copy, and read again. This time, pay close attention to sentences, words, and documentation format. Use the following questions to guide revisions.

Coherence

- Have connecting words been used and key terms repeated to produce paragraph coherence?
- Have transitions been used to show connections between paragraphs?

Sources

- Have I paraphrased instead of quoted whenever possible?
- Have I used signal phrases to create a context for source material?
- Have I documented all borrowed material, whether quoted or paraphrased?
- Are parenthetical references properly placed after borrowed material?

Style

- Have I varied sentence length and structure?
- Have I used my own words instead of quotations whenever possible?
- Have I avoided long quotations?
- Do I have correct form for quotations? For titles?
- Is my language specific and descriptive?
- Have I avoided inappropriate shifts in tense or person?
- Have I removed any wordiness, trite expressions, and clichés?
- Have I used specialized terms correctly?
- Have I avoided contractions as too informal for most research papers?
- Have I maintained an appropriate style and tone for academic work?

Proofreading

When your editing is finished, prepare a completed draft of your paper according to the format described and illustrated at the end of this chapter. Then proofread the completed copy, making any corrections neatly in ink. If a page has several errors, print a corrected copy. Be sure to make a copy of the paper for yourself before submitting the original to your instructor.

making connections

let's review

After reading this chapter, you should know the following:

- To make decisions about your paper's organization, you need to begin with the identifying phrases at the top of your notes or the list of support you developed as you studied sources. They will now help you organize your paper as well as figure out where and how sources may be synthesized with each other and with your own ideas.

- To produce a unified and coherent essay with a clear central idea and a reason for being, you need a claim that meets the following criteria:

  - It is a complete sentence, not a topic or statement of purpose.

  - It is limited and focused.

  - It can be supported by your research.

  - It establishes a new or interesting approach to the topic that makes your research worthwhile.

- Some instructors expect a formal outline with research essays. Preparing a formal outline requires you to think through the entire structure of your paper and see the relationship of parts. But do not expect more out of an outline than it can provide. A logical and clear organization does not result from a detailed outline; rather, a detailed outline results from a logical analysis of your topic.

- Effective time management skills are crucial to any research essay project. Be sure you know your deadlines and leave yourself sufficient time to complete your tasks.

- Take the time to include parenthetical documentation as you compose. Then, when your paper is finished and you are preparing your list of works cited, go through your paper carefully to make certain that there is a work listed for every parenthetical citation.

- The best introduction is one that presents your subject in an interesting way to gain the reader's attention, states your claim, and gives the reader an indication of the scope and limits of your paper.

- As you compose the body of your paper, keep in mind that you want to (1) maintain unity and coherence, (2) guide readers clearly through source material, and (3) synthesize source material and your own ideas.

- Coherence is needed not only within paragraphs but also between paragraphs. You need to guide readers through your paper, connecting paragraphs and showing relationships by the use of transitions and effective metadiscourse.

- Readers need to be told how they are to respond to the sources used. They need to know which sources you accept as reliable and which you disagree with, and they need to see you distinguish clearly between fact and opinion. Ideas and opinions from sources need introductory tags and then some discussion from you.

- As you write an academic researched argument, you will need to demonstrate the ability to synthesize, or smoothly combine, various authors' opinions, research findings, and quotations into your work. Your goal is to develop the connections between your sources—to show how their ideas relate to each other and to the larger debate as a whole—and also to clarify for your reader how the ideas presented in your sources relate to your own thesis.

connect

SAMPLE STUDENT RESEARCH ESSAY

The following paper illustrates MLA style of documentation for an argument that is developed using sources. The paper shows a separate title page and outline, though these may not be required by your instructor. Study how the student blends information and arguments from sources with her views on this issue to build her argument.

Living Wills:

Your Right or Your Duty?

Laura Lee

English 112

Professor Lane

20 April 2010

Outline

Thesis: To alleviate all these problems, and despite arguments claiming that this type of law is a violation of civil rights, it is clear that a law should be created that makes having a living will mandatory for everyone over the age of eighteen in the United States.

I.   What exactly is a living will?

II.   One reason why a living will should be mandatory is so that patients in a persistent vegetative state (PVS) do not put a burden on their families and make them try to decide what would really be best for their loved one.

  A. Crisci and Crispi report that "[t]he relatives described their own quality of life as 'poor, miserable.'"

  B. O'Mathuna quote regarding difficult family decisions states that "[m]odern medicine has provided people with many great benefits, but it has also forced families to make difficult decisions."

III. A second reason as to why everyone over the age of eighteen should create their own living will is because it would help reduce some of the cost it would take to provide medical care for someone experiencing PVS.

  A. Borthwick article regarding costs of PVS gives estimate of the total annual costs in the United States for the care of adults and children in a persistent vegetative state to be $1 billion to $7 billion.

  B. O'Mathuna's statistic estimates that 10,000 to 25,000 adults and 4,000 to 10,000 children live in PVS in the United States.

IV.   The final reason why those over the age of eighteen should be mandated to create their own living will is that if one was created, then a legal battle could easily be avoided.

  A. Jayson quote regarding Schiavo case states that "[t]he battle between Terri Schiavo's husband and parents is a call to action for the two-thirds of adult Americans who, like Schiavo, have not prepared living wills that help direct their care in terminal circumstances."

  B. CNN.com article regarding Schiavo case states, "Terri Schiavo did not leave anything in writing about what she would want if she ever became incapacitated. Over the years, courts have sided with her husband in more than a dozen cases."

V.   Many people don't fully understand the realities of having a living will. They often believe that it means a person will be actively and possibly painfully killed in the event of an accident or injury.

  A. Smith quote regarding torture of patients claims, "Some might even argue that refusing Terri any chance to live would be a non-voluntary euthanasia homicide."

  B. Gibbs quote regarding Schiavo's case demonstrates negative attitude and says, "Terri is in the process of being starved to death."

VI.   Rebuttal

      However, I believe that these authors are missing an important point: A person who is in a vegetative state is said to not experience any sensation or sentiment.

Living Wills:

Your Right or Your Duty?

Many people do not realize that if they do not have a living will, they will not have any say in what decisions will be made if something tragic happens to them. Every day in this country, laws are made to help protect our society and to benefit the greater good. We have laws against speeding, abusing others, and even against public intoxication. Each of these ensures (even at the risk of a loss of absolute personal freedom) that society remains safe and that people protect themselves from harm. But there is currently no law that ensures that people legally express their personal medical wishes in case of a life-threatening injury or illness. As a result, family members and friends are not protected from making gut-wrenching life and death decisions for the injured person, and the patient is not protected from having painful life-extending treatments forced upon him or her against his or her wishes.

Beyond the emotional and physical pain involved, other serious problems arise when a person does not have a living will. For example, people who do not legally express their wishes run the risk of losing all their assets and inheritance to a medical facility rather than having the ability to pass those on to their family. This situation also creates a financial burden on our government. For those who cannot pay their medical bills, Medicaid (a last-resort program that picks up a patient's medical costs at the expense of the taxpayers) must take over. To alleviate all of these problems, and despite opponents' arguments that living wills amount to a sort of assisted suicide (or even homicide), it is clear that a law should, in fact, be created that makes a living will mandatory for everyone over the age of eighteen in the United States. A mandatory living will statute will help eliminate emotional controversies and legal battles, ease financial burdens on families and the government, and will greatly benefit the American people.

What exactly is a living will? A living will is simply a written document defining a person's "right to die." Despite the negative image some have created for the term, it is not a document that allows medical personnel or anyone else to "pull the plug" or kill a patient against their wishes. Instead, it simply means that a person gets to predetermine what happens in a medical emergency and has the right to die with dignity if he or she so chooses. The living will usually states to what extent he or she wishes to have his or her life artificially prolonged by all of the modern technology that hospitals now possess. Many people do not believe that it is desirable to be kept alive when there is no hope for curing them or for them to live normal lives. The living will instructs doctors whether or not a person wishes to die naturally, explains the patient's decisions regarding whether life-support equipment should be used, whether CPR should be administered, and about how much medicine should be used to relieve pain. It also typically names the person who is authorized to make all their care decisions for them when they are unable. In short, the living will is the document that can help to express a patient's personal, medical, and emotional or spiritual wishes.

One reason why a living will should be mandatory is so that patients' families do not bear the burden of making highly emotional decisions for their loved ones. If a person is in a persistent vegetative state (PVS), it is said that they do not experience any sensation or sentiment. According to some experts, "They are not even considered as persons [. . .] because their internal organs work automatically while their cortex is shut off, not engaged in even minimal social interaction" (Crisci and Crispi). Patients who are in a persistent vegetative state require a large amount of medical and nursing attention. As a result, complex family interactions and conflicts can occur. In one important study, several relatives of those who have a loved one in a PVS were asked what their attitudes and feelings were toward the situation. According to C. Crisci and F. Crispi, authors of the article "Patients in Persistent Vegetative State . . . and What of Their Relatives?" "The relatives described their own quality of life as poor, miserable. None of the relatives would ever clearly admit that death would have been better, but all admitted that this event would not have been more distressing than their present situation" (534). Dr. Donald O'Mathuna, a noted author on this subject, agrees with Crisci and Crispi that families often bear a huge burden in these situations, saying, "Modern medicine has provided people with many great benefits, but it has also forced families to make difficult decisions. People must now decide if and when they would want certain treatments withheld or withdrawn from themselves or others." It seems clear that if everyone over the age of eighteen were to create their own living will, then the families of those in a PVS would not have to deal with the pressure of making the correct decisions for their loved ones. A living will would also help to clarify their loved ones' wishes and what, exactly, they want regarding their personal care, medication, and resuscitation, even if they are only temporarily unable to make their wishes known.

This benefit would be most applicable to families of patients who are unable to make decisions for themselves over long periods of time, that is, who are in a persistent vegetative state. Most relatives of those who are in a PVS understand the meaning of the illness, but often do not realize that the prognosis is generally poor. The relatives usually maintain hope for some months, praying that a miracle will happen and that their loved one will eventually respond. At four to six months after the beginning of PVS, however, the size of the group of relatives accepting involvement decreases and, typically, only one (usually the mother or a sister) remains as the "deputy of the family" to assist the patient (Crisci and Crispi). If a living will were mandatory for all of those over eighteen years of age, then the family of the loved one dealing with PVS would not ever have to face this awful situation. The strain of dealing with a situation like this can become very stressful to those involved and often can cause problems or even legal battles within the family. Creating a living will would help to eliminate all these problems, letting the family enjoy their last few moments with their loved one in peace instead of worrying about what decisions must be made.

Not only would a living-will mandate allow families to avoid difficult emotional decisions, it would also help to reduce some of the cost of medical care for someone in a PVS. Patients who are in a persistent vegetative state typically require intensive physical care, including respirators, feeding tubes, and round-the-clock supervision. The care given by a family member to someone who is in a persistent vegetative state is most often not enough. PVS patients must usually be either hospitalized or put in nursing homes for the constant care they must receive. According to Chris Borthwick, author of "The Permanent Vegetative State: Ethical Crux, Medical Fiction?" this type of care is extremely expensive:

> A previous survey of care costs for PVS patients that did at least refer to recorded costs in actual cases suggested a range from a low of $18,000 to a high of $120,000 with an average of around $60,000. The Consensus Statement refers to a single case study to reach an estimate of cost of care for the PVS patient in a nursing facility as costing from $126,000 to $180,000 per year, on average two and a half times the previous estimate. A rough approximation of the total annual costs in the United States for the care of adults and children in a persistent vegetative state is $1 billion to $7 billion.

Donald O'Mathuna brings new light to these shocking figures by stating that "a review of the medical information concerning PVS was published in 1994 by the Multi-Society Task Force on PVS. They estimated that 10,000 to 25,000 adults and 4,000 to 10,000 children live in PVS in the United States." The figures presented by these authors, when taken in conjunction, show a shocking truth: there are large numbers of people in our country who are in a PVS and the cost is extremely high to keep those patients alive. The conditions of those who are considered long-term patients are more than likely never going to change. And inevitably, over time, the patient's resources and ability to pay run out. It then very often becomes either the family or the government that ends up paying these astoundingly high bills. Medicaid, funded by the U.S. taxpayers, will pay hundreds of thousands of dollars a year to keep a patient alive who may very well have wished to die given the option. And while cost alone is never a good reason to end a human life, it seems wrong to force families into bankruptcy or force taxpayers to foot the bill for care that the patient himself or herself would have chosen to refuse.

Finally, a living-will statute would prevent legal battles between family members, hospitals, and insurance companies. Often, when the patient's wishes cannot be determined and when different family members believe that they each "know" what the patient would want, a long, expensive, and emotional court battle ensues. Other times, hospitals and insurance companies must get involved in order to assert what medical professionals believe is appropriate care when family members refuse certain treatments. A perfect example of a fairly recent and very public legal battle over a patient's right to die is the Terri Schiavo case, which was waged in the nation's courts for several years until her feeding tube was ultimately removed in 2005. The battle between Terri Schiavo's husband and parents is evidence enough why a living will should be created by those over the age of eighteen. The CNN.com article "Schiavo's Feeding Tube Removed" provides some important background on this case:

> The disconnecting of the feeding tube was the latest step in a contentious family saga that began 15 years ago, when Terri Schiavo collapsed from heart failure that resulted in severe brain damage. [. . .] Michael Schiavo contends his wife would not want to be kept alive artificially. But her parents argue she had no such death wish and believe she could get better with rehabilitation. Terri Schiavo did not leave anything in writing about what she would want if she ever became incapacitated. Over the years, courts have sided with her husband in more than a dozen cases.

According to Sharon Jayson, who covered the story for *USA Today,* "The battle between Terri Schiavo's husband and parents is a call to action for the two-thirds of adult Americans who, like Schiavo, have not prepared living wills that help direct their care in terminal circumstances." The struggles involved in this case clearly support the idea of a mandatory living-will statute. If a patient has a living will, parents and loved ones will not have to make it a legal issue or get anyone other than family involved because they will already know the wishes of their loved one. If Terri Schiavo had had a living will, her family would have better understood what her wishes were and they would not have had to fight with her husband about what to do.

Many people don't fully understand the realities of having a living will. They often believe that it means that a person will be actively (and possibly painfully) killed in the event of an accident or injury. They may believe that when the feeding tube of someone in a persistent vegetative state is disconnected, the person will suffer and face a death that they should not have to face. Referencing the Terry Schiavo case, Wesley Smith seems to believe that this amounts to torture:

> Terri should be allowed reasonable rehabilitation attempts before Judge Greer (judge of the Sixth Judicial Circuit, in Clearwater, Florida) orders her dehydration to death. Refusing this clearly humane and merciful request would be to intentionally cause Terri harm. Some might even argue that refusing Terri any chance to live would be a non-voluntary euthanasia homicide.

In the article "Schiavo's Feeding Tube Removed," David Gibbs agrees with Smith by stating, "We're now up against a very tight clock because Terri is in the process of being starved to death. It is looking more and more like Washington, D.C., or Tallahassee is going to have to step forward and save Terri's life." Both of these authors seem to believe that when someone is in a persistent vegetative state, they should be preserved at all costs. However, these authors are missing an important point. According to medical professionals and experts, a person who is in a vegetative state does not experience any sensation or sentiment. If someone who is in a PVS is unaware of what is happening, or even whether he or she is being fed, then disconnecting the feeding tube does not cause any pain or suffering. Quite the opposite, in fact, is true. Allowing someone in a persistent vegetative state to linger between life and death rather than letting him or her die in peace is punishment for both the patient and the family members and causes the true pain and suffering for all involved.

As the battles between family members wage on, and as those in persistent vegetative states are forced to hover between life and death without any clear directives as to their own wishes, hopefully government officials and voters alike will begin to become more aware of the benefits of having a living-will statute. A living will is one of the most important documents in our society. It clearly instructs not only the doctors and nurses but also family members what a person's wishes are regarding personal care in the event of a tragic accident or illness. And, even more importantly, it ultimately upholds a person's most sacred right to leave this world in the manner he or she feels is most dignified.

Works Cited

Borthwick, Chris. "The Permanent Vegetative State: Ethical Crux, Medical Fiction?" *Issues in Law and Medicine* 12.2 (1996): n. pag. Web. 12 Apr. 2005.

Crisci, C., and F. Crispi. "Patients in Persistent Vegetative State . . . and What of Their Relatives?" *Nursing Ethics* 7.6 (2000): n. pag. Web. 14 Apr. 2005.

Jayson, Sharon. "A Living Will Clarifies Your Wishes." *USA Today.com.* USA Today, 24 Mar. 2005. Web. 5 Apr. 2005.

O'Mathuna, Donald P. "Responding to Patients in the Persistent Vegetative State." *Philosophia Christi* 19.2 (1996). n. pag. Web. 14 Apr. 2005.

"Schiavo's Feeding Tube Removed." *CNN.com.* Cable News Network, 18 Mar. 2005. Web. 31 Mar. 2005.

Smith, Wesley J. "Terri Schiavo's Life and Death." *National Review Online.* National Review Online, 16 Sept. 2003. Web. 31 Mar. 2005.

documenting sources (MLA, APA, and more)

Although the research process is much the same regardless of the area of study, documentation varies from one discipline to another. The common styles of documentation include MLA, author/year or APA style, and the footnote or endnote style.

MLA Style

The MLA style is favored by those in the humanities and is fully detailed in the *MLA Handbook for Writers of Research Papers* (7th edition, 2009). The following guidelines are drawn from this publication and provide an overview for in-text citations and works cited pages.

MLA In-Text (Parenthetical) Documentation

The most common form of parenthetical documentation in MLA style is parenthetical references to author and page number, or just to page number if the author has been mentioned in an introductory tag. Because a reference only to author and page number is an incomplete citation (readers could not find the source with such limited information), whatever is cited this way in the essay must refer to a specific source presented fully in a Works Cited list that follows the text of the paper. General guidelines for citing are given below, followed by examples and explanations of the required patterns of documentation.

Guidelines for Using Parenthetical Documentation

- The purpose of documentation is to make clear exactly what material in a passage has been borrowed and from what source the borrowed material has come.

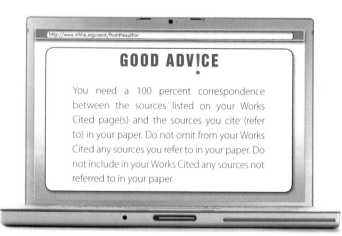

GOOD ADVICE

You need a 100 percent correspondence between the sources listed on your Works Cited page(s) and the sources you cite (refer to) in your paper. Do not omit from your Works Cited any sources you refer to in your paper. Do not include in your Works Cited any sources not referred to in your paper.

- Parenthetical documentation requires specific page references for borrowed material.
- Parenthetical documentation is required for both quoted and paraphrased material.
- Parenthetical documentation provides as brief a citation as possible consistent with accuracy and clarity.

The Simplest Patterns of Parenthetical Documentation

The simplest parenthetical reference can be prepared in one of three ways:

1. Give the author's last name (full name in the first reference) in the text of your paper, and place the relevant page number(s) in parentheses following the borrowed material.

   Frederick Lewis Allen observes that, during the 1920s, urban tastes spread to the country (146).

2. Place the author's last name and the relevant page number(s) in parentheses following the borrowed material.

   During the 1920s, "not only the drinks were mixed, but the company as well" (Allen 82).

3. On the rare occasion that you cite an entire work rather than borrowing from a specific passage, give the author's name in the text and omit any page numbers.

   Barbara Tuchman argues that there are significant parallels between the fourteenth century and our time.

Each one of these in-text references is complete *only* when the full citation is found in the Works Cited section of your paper.

   Allen, Frederick Lewis. *Only Yesterday: An Informal History of the Nineteen-Twenties*. New York: Harper, 1931. Print.

   Tuchman, Barbara W. *A Distant Mirror: The Calamitous 14th Century*. New York: Knopf, 1978. Print.

The three patterns just illustrated should be used in each of the following situations:

1. The work is not anonymous—the author is known.
2. The work is by one author.
3. The work cited is the only work used by that author.
4. No other author in your bibliography has the same last name.

Placement of Parenthetical Documentation

The simplest placing of a parenthetical reference is at the end of the appropriate sentence ~~before~~ the period, but, when you are quoting, *after* the quotation mark.

> During the 1920s, "not only the drinks were mixed, but the company as well" (Allen 82).

Do not put any punctuation between the author's name and the page number.

If the borrowed material ends before the end of your sentence, place the parenthetical reference at the first natural pause *after* the borrowed material and before any subsequent punctuation. This placement more accurately shows what is borrowed and what is your own work without interrupting the sentence.

> Sport, Allen observes about the 1920s, had developed into an obsession (66), another similarity between the 1920s and the 1980s.

If a quoted passage is long enough to require setting off in display form (block quotation), then place the parenthetical reference at the end of the passage, *after* the last period. (Remember that long quotations in display form do not have quotation marks.)

> It is hard to believe that when he writes about the influence of science, Allen is describing the 1920s, not the 1980s:
>
>> The prestige of science was colossal. The man in the street and the woman in the kitchen, confronted on every hand with new machines and devices which they owed to the laboratory, were ready to believe that science could accomplish almost anything. (164)

And to complete the documentation for all three examples:

Works Cited

Allen, Frederick Lewis. *Only Yesterday: An Informal History of the Nineteen-Twenties*. New York: Harper, 1931. Print.

Parenthetical Citations of Complex Sources

Not all sources can be cited in one of the three simplest forms described above, for not all meet the four criteria listed on page 226. Works by two or more authors, for example, will need somewhat fuller references. Each sample form of parenthetical documentation below would be completed with a full Works Cited reference, as illustrated above and in the next section of this chapter.

Two Authors, Mentioned in the Text

> Richard Herrnstein and Charles Murray contend that it is "consistently . . . advantageous to be smart" (25).

Two Authors, Not Mentioned in the Text

> The advantaged smart group form a "cognitive elite" in our society (Herrnstein and Murray 26–27).

A Book in Two or More Volumes

> Sewall analyzes the role of Judge Lord in Dickinson's life (2: 642–47).

> *OR*

> Judge Lord was also one of Dickinson's preceptors (Sewall 2: 642–47).

Note: The number before the colon always signifies the volume number: the number(s) after the colon represents the page number(s).

A Book or Article Listed by Title (Author Unknown)

> According to the *Concise Dictionary of American Biography*, William Jennings Bryan's 1896 campaign stressed social and sectional conflicts (117).

> The *Times*'s editors are not pleased with some of the changes in welfare programs ("Where Welfare Stands" 4:16).

Always cite the title of the article, not the title of the journal, if the author is unknown.

A Work by a Corporate Author

> According to the report of the Institute of Ecology's Global Ecological Problems Workshop, the civilization of the city can lull us into forgetting our relationship to the total ecological system on which we depend (13).

Although corporate authors may be cited with the page number within the parentheses, your presentation will be more graceful if corporate authors are introduced in the text. Then only page numbers go in parentheses.

Two or More Works by the Same Author

> During the 1920s, "not only the drinks were mixed, but the company as well" (Allen, *Only Yesterday* 82).

> According to Frederick Lewis Allen, the early 1900s were a period of complacency in America (*The Big Change* 4–5).

> In *The Big Change*, Allen asserts that the early 1900s were a period of complacency (4–5).

If your Works Cited list contains two or more works by the same author, the fullest parenthetical citation will include the author's last name, followed by a comma, the work's title, shortened if possible, and the page number(s). If the author's name appears in the text—or the author and title both, as in the third example above—omit these items from the parenthetical citation. When you have to include the title, it is best to simplify the citation by including the author's last name in the text.

Two or More Works in One Parenthetical Reference

> Several writers about the future agree that big changes will take place in work patterns (Toffler 384–87; Naisbitt 35–36).

Separate each author cited with a semicolon. But if the parenthetical citation would be disruptively long, cite the works in a "See also" note rather than in the text.

Complete Publication Information in Parenthetical Reference

Occasionally you may want to give complete information about a source within parentheses in the text of your paper. Then a Works Cited list is not used. Square brackets are used for parenthetical information within parentheses. This approach may be appropriate when you use only one or two sources, even if many references are made to those sources. Literary analyses are one type of paper for which this approach to citation may be a good choice. For example:

> Edith Wharton establishes the bleakness of her setting, Starkfield, not just through description of place but also through her main character, Ethan, who is described as "bleak and unapproachable"

(*Ethan Frome* [New York: Scribner's, 1911; print] 3. All subsequent references are to this edition.). Later Wharton describes winter as "shut[ting] down on Starkfield" and negating life there (7).

Additional Information Footnotes or Endnotes

At times you may need to provide additional useful information, explanation, or commentary about your ideas or a source that is not central to the development of your paper. These additions belong in footnotes or endnotes. However, use these sparingly and never as a way of advancing your thesis. Some instructors object to content footnotes or endnotes and prefer only parenthetical citations in student papers.

> Chekhov's debt to Ibsen should be recognized, as should his debt to Maeterlinck and other playwrights of the 1890s who were concerned with the inner life of their characters.[1]
>
> 1. For further discussion of this point, see Bentley 330; Bruford 45; and Williams 126–29.

Preparing MLA Citations for a "Works Cited" Page

Parenthetical (in-text) citations are completed by a full reference to each source in a list presented at the end of the paper. To prepare your Works Cited page(s), alphabetize, by the author's last name, the sources you have cited and complete each citation according

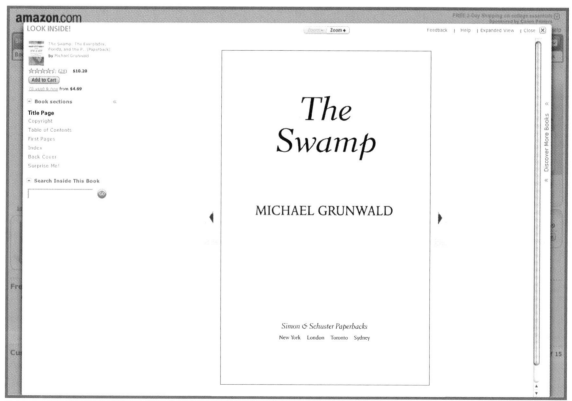

to the forms illustrated and explained in the following pages. The basic information for each citation includes the author, the title, publication information, and also the medium of the source (print, Web, DVD, etc.). The key is to find the appropriate model for each of your sources and then follow the model exactly.

Forms for Books: Citing the Complete Book

A Book by a Single Author

Silver, Lee M. *Remaking Eden: Cloning and Beyond in a Brave New World*. New York: Avon, 1997. Print.

The subtitle is included, preceded by a colon, even if there is no colon on the book's title page.

A Book by Two or Three Authors

Adkins, Lesley, and Ray Adkins. *The Keys of Egypt: The Race to Crack the Hieroglyph Code*. New York: HarperCollins, 2000. Print.

Second (and third) authors' names appear in signature form.

A Book with More Than Three Authors

Baker, Susan P., et al. *The Injury Fact Book*. Oxford: Oxford UP, 1992. Print.

You may use the name of the first author listed on the title page, followed by "et al." (which means "and others"), or you may list all authors in the order their names appear on the title page. Shorten "University Press" to "UP."

Two or More Works by the Same Author

Goodall, Jane. *In the Shadow of Man*. Boston: Houghton, 1971. Print.

---. *Through a Window: My Thirty Years with the Chimpanzees of Gombe*. Boston: Houghton, 1990. Print.

Give the author's full name with the first entry. For the second (and additional works), begin the citation with three hyphens followed by a period. Alphabetize the entries by the books' titles.

A Book Written under a Pseudonym with Name Supplied

Wrighter, Carl P. [Paul Stevens]. *I Can Sell You Anything*. New York: Ballantine, 1972. Print.

Supply the author's name in square brackets.

An Anonymous Book

Beowulf: A New Verse Translation. Trans. Seamus Heaney. New York: Farrar, 2000. Print.

Do not use "anon." Alphabetize by the book's title.

An Edited Book

Hamilton, Alexander, James Madison, and John Jay. *The Federalist Papers*. Ed. Isaac Kramnick. New York: Viking-Penguin, 1987. Print.

Lynn, Kenneth S., ed. *Huckleberry Finn: Text, Sources, and Critics*. New York: Harcourt, 1961. Print.

If you cite the author's work, put the author's name first and the editor's name after the title, preceded by "Ed." If you cite the editor's work (an introduction or notes), then place the editor's name first, followed by a comma and "ed."

A Translation

Schulze, Hagen. *Germany: A New History*. Trans. Deborah Lucas Schneider. Cambridge: Harvard UP, 1998. Print.

Cornford, Francis MacDonald, trans. *The Republic of Plato*. New York: Oxford UP, 1945. Print.

Fagels, Robert, trans. *The Odyssey*. By Homer. New York: Viking, 1996. Print.

If the author's work is being cited, place the author's name first and the translator's name after the title, preceded by "Trans." If the translator's work is the important element, place the translator's name first, as in the second example above. If the author's name does not appear in the title, give it after the title, as in the third example.

A Book in Two or More Volumes

Spielvogel, Jackson J. *Western Civilization*. 2 vols. Minneapolis: West, 1991. Print.

Blotner, Joseph. *Faulkner: A Biography*. Vol. 2. New York: Random House, 1974. Print.

When using two or more volumes of a multivolume work, note the total number of volumes in the work after the title. But cite a specific volume when referring to only one of the volumes.

A Book within One Volume of a Multivolume Work

James, Henry. *The American*. New York: Scribner's, 1907. Print. Vol. 2 of *The Novels and Tales of Henry James*. 26 vols. 1907–17.

Cite the author and title of the single work used and the facts of publication for that work, then the volume number and title of the complete work. Then give the total number of volumes, followed by the inclusive publication dates for the work.

A Book in Its Second or Subsequent Edition

O'Brien, David M. *Storm Center: The Supreme Court and American Politics.* 2nd ed. New York: Norton, 1990. Print.

Sundqist, James L. *Dynamics of the Party System.* Rev. ed. Washington: Brookings, 1983. Print.

Always include the number of the edition you have used, abbreviated as shown, if it is not the first edition.

A Book in a Series

Parkinson, Richard. *The Rosetta Stone.* British Museum Objects in Focus. London: British Museum Press, 2005. Print.

The series title—and number, if there is one—follows the book's title but is not italicized.

A Reprint of an Earlier Work

Cuppy, Will. *How to Become Extinct.* 1941. Chicago: U of Chicago P, 1983. Print.

Twain, Mark. *Adventures of Huckleberry Finn.* 1885. Centennial Facsimile Edition. Introd. Hamlin Hill. New York: Harper, 1962. Print.

Faulkner, William. *As I Lay Dying.* 1930. New York: Vintage-Random, 1964. Print.

Since the date of a work is often important, cite the original date of publication as well as the facts of publication for the reprinted version. Indicate any new material that is part of the reprinted book, as in the second example. The third example shows how to cite a book reprinted, by the same publisher, in a paperback version. (Vintage is a paperback imprint of the publisher Random House.)

A Book with Two or More Publishers

Green, Mark J., James M. Fallows, and David R. Zwick. *Who Runs Congress?* Ralph Nader Congress Project. New York: Bantam; New York: Grossman, 1972. Print.

If the title page lists two or more publishers, give all as part of the facts of publication, placing a semicolon between them, as illustrated above.

A Corporate or Governmental Author

California State Department of Education. *American Indian Education Handbook.* Sacramento: California State Department of Education, Indian Education Unit, 1991. Print.

Hispanic Market Connections. *The National Hispanic Database: A Los Angeles Preview.* Los Altos, CA: Hispanic Market Connections, 1992. Print.

List the institution as the author even when it is also the publisher.

A Book in a Foreign Language

Blanchard, Gerard. *Images de la musique au cinéma.* Paris: Edilig, 1984. Print.

Capitalize only the first word of titles and subtitles and words normally capitalized in that language (e.g., proper nouns in French, all nouns in German). A translation in square brackets may be provided. Check your work carefully for spelling and accent marks.

The Bible

The Reader's Bible: A Narrative. Ed. with intro. Roland Mushat Frye. Princeton: Princeton UP, 1965. Print.

Although scriptural works such as the Bible, Talmud, or Koran are not italicized like other titles within the text of your paper, the versions of the works usually have specific names, which are italicized.

A Book with a Title in Its Title

Piper, Henry Dan, ed. *Fitzgerald's* The Great Gatsby: *The Novel, the Critics, the Background.* Scribner Research Anthologies. Ed. Martin Steinmann, Jr. New York: Scribner's, 1970. Print.

Forms for Books: Citing Part of a Book

A Preface, Introduction, Foreword, or Afterword

Sagan, Carl. Introduction. *A Brief History of Time: From the Big Bang to Black Holes.* By Stephen W. Hawking. New York: Bantam, 1988. ix–x. Print.

Use this form if you are citing the author of the preface, etc. Provide the appropriate identifying phrase after the author's name and give inclusive page numbers for the part of the book by that author at the end of the citation.

An Encyclopedia Article

Ostrom, John H. "Dinosaurs." *McGraw-Hill Encyclopedia of Science and Technology.* 1987 ed. Print.

"Benjamin Franklin." *Concise Dictionary of American Biography.* Ed. Joseph G. E. Hopkins. New York: Scribner's, 1964. Print.

When articles are signed or initialed, give the author's name. Complete the name of the author of an initialed article thus: K[enny], E[dward] J. Identify well-known encyclopedias and dictionaries by the year of the edition only. Give the complete facts of publication for less well-known works or those in only one edition.

A Work in an Anthology or Collection

> Hurston, Zora Neale. "The First One." *Black Female Playwrights: An Anthology of Plays Before 1950*. Ed. Kathy A. Perkins. Bloomington: Indiana UP, 1989. 80–88. Print.

> Comstock, George. "The Medium and the Society: The Role of Television in American Life." *Children and Television: Images in a Changing Sociocultural World*. Eds. Gordon L. Berry and Joy Keiko Asamen. Newbury Park, CA: Sage, 1993. 117–31. Print.

Cite the author and title of the work you have used. Then give the title, the editor(s), and the facts of publication of the anthology or collection. Conclude by providing inclusive page numbers for the work used and the publication medium.

An Article in a Collection, Casebook, or Sourcebook

> Welsch, Roger. "The Cornstalk Fiddle." *Journal of American Folklore* 77.305 (1964): 262–63. Rpt. in *Readings in American Folklore*. Ed. Jan Harold Brunvand. New York: Norton, 1979. 106–07. Print.

> MacKenzie, James J. "The Decline of Nuclear Power." *engage/social* April 1986. Rpt. as "America Does Not Need More Nuclear Power Plants" in *The Environmental Crisis: Opposing Viewpoints*. Eds. Julie S. Bach and Lynn Hall. Opposing Viewpoints Series. St. Paul: Greenhaven, 1986. 136–41. Print.

Most articles in collections have been previously published, so a complete citation needs to include the original facts of publication (excluding page numbers if they are unavailable) as well as the facts of publication for the collection. End the citation with inclusive page numbers for the article used and the publication medium.

Cross-References

If you are citing several articles from one collection, you can cite the collection and then provide only the author and title of specific articles used, with a cross-reference to the editor(s) of the collection:

> Head, Suzanne, and Robert Heinzman, eds. *Lessons of the Rainforest*. San Francisco: Sierra Club, 1990. Print.

> Bandyopadhyay, J., and Vandana Shiva. "Asia's Forest, Asia's Cultures." Head and Heinzman 66–77. Print.

> Head, Suzanne. "The Consumer Connection: Psychology and Politics." Head and Heinzman 156–67. Print.

Forms for Print Periodicals: Articles in Journals

Article in a Journal

> Truman, Dana M., David M. Tokar, and Ann R. Fischer. "Dimensions of Masculinity: Relations to Date Rape, Supportive Attitudes, and Sexual Aggression in Dating Situations." *Journal of Counseling and Development* 76 (1996): 555–62. Print.

Give the volume and issue number, separated by a period; followed by the year only, in parentheses; followed by a colon and inclusive page numbers; followed by the medium of publication.

Article in a Journal That Uses Issue Numbers Only

> Keen, Ralph. "Thomas More and Geometry." *Moreana* 86 (1985): 151–66. Print.

If the journal uses only issue numbers, not volume numbers, cite the issue number alone.

Forms for Print Periodicals: Articles in Magazines

Article in a Monthly Magazine

> Norell, Mark A., and Xu Xing. "The Varieties of Tyrannosaurs." *Natural History* May 2005: 35–39. Print.

Do not use volume or issue number. Instead, cite the month(s) and year after the title, followed by a colon and inclusive page numbers. If page numbers are not consecutive, cite the first page number followed by the plus sign. Abbreviate all months except May, June, and July.

Article in a Weekly Magazine

> Stein, Joel. "Eat This, Low Carbers." *Time* 15 Aug. 2005: 78. Print.

Provide the complete date, using the order of day, month, and year.

An Anonymous Article

> "Death of Perestroika." *Economist* 2 Feb. 1991: 12–13. Print.

The missing name indicates that the article is anonymous. Alphabetize under D.

A Published Interview

> Angier, Natalie. "Ernst Mayr at 93." Interview. *Natural History* May 1997: 8–11. Print.

Follow the pattern for a published article, but add the descriptive label "Interview" (followed by a period) after the article's title.

A Review

Bardsley, Tim. "Eliciting Science's Best." Rev. of *Frontiers of Illusion: Science, Technology, and the Politics of Progress*, by Daniel Sarewitz. *Scientific American* June 1997: 142. Print.

Shales, Tom. "A Chilling Stop in 'Nuremberg.'" Rev. of the movie *Nuremberg*, TNT 16 July 2000. *Washington Post* 16 July 2000: G1. Print.

If the review is signed, begin with the author's name, then the title of the review article. Give the title of the work being reviewed, a comma, and its author, preceded by "Rev. of." Alphabetize unsigned reviews by the title of the review. For reviews of art shows, videos, or computer software, provide place and date or descriptive label to make the citation clear.

Forms for Print Periodicals: Newspapers

An Article from a Newspaper

Wilford, John Noble. "Astronauts Land on Plain; Collect Rocks, Plant Flag." *New York Times* 21 July 1969, late city ed.: 1. Print.

A newspaper's title should be cited as it appears on the masthead, excluding any initial article; thus *New York Times*, not *The New York Times*. If there is a specific edition listed in the masthead (late ed., nat'l ed.), include it after the date.

An Article from a Newspaper with Lettered Sections

Diehl, Jackson. "Inhuman: Yes or No?" *Washington Post* 12 Sept. 2005: A19. Print.

Place the section letter immediately before the page number, without any spacing.

An Article from a Newspaper with Numbered Sections

Roberts, Sam. "Another Kind of Middle-Class Squeeze." *New York Times* 18 May 1997, sec. 4: 1+. Print.

Place the section number after the date, preceded by a comma and the abbreviation "sec."

An Editorial

"Japan's Two Nationalisms." Editorial. *Washington Post* 4 June 2000: B6. Print.

Add the descriptive label "Editorial" after the article title.

A Letter to the Editor

Wiles, Yoko A. "Thoughts of a New Citizen." Letter. *Washington Post* 27 Dec. 1995: A22. Print.

If the letter is titled, use the descriptive label "Letter" after the title. If the letter is untitled, place "Letter" after the author's name.

Citing Other Print and Nonprint Sources

The materials in this section, although often important to research projects, do not always lend themselves to documentation by the forms illustrated above. Follow the basic order of author, title, facts, and medium of publication as much as possible, and add whatever information is needed to make the citation clear and useful to a reader.

Cartoons and Advertisements

Schulz, Charles M. "Peanuts." Comic strip. *Washington Post* 10 Dec. 1985: D8. Print.

Give the cartoon title, if there is one; add the descriptive label such as "Cartoon"; then give the facts of publication. The pattern is similar for advertisements.

Halleyscope. "Halleyscopes Are for Night Owls." Advertisement. *Natural History* Dec. 1985: 15. Print.

Computer Software

"Aardvark." *The Oxford English Dictionary*. 2nd ed. Oxford: Oxford UP, 1992. CD-ROM.

Give author, title, edition or version, publisher, year of issue, and publication medium (CD-ROM or DVD-ROM).

Dissertation—Unpublished

Brotton, Joyce D. "Illuminating the Present Through Literary Dialogism: From the Reformation Through Postmodernism." Diss. George Mason U, 2002. Print.

Dissertation—Published

Brotton, Joyce D. *Illuminating the Present Through Literary Dialogism: From the Reformation Through Postmodernism*. Diss. George Mason U, 2002. Ann Arbor: UMI, 2002. Print.

Films or Videos

Coen, Ethan, and Joel Coen, dir. *No Country for Old Men*. Perf. Javier Bardem, Josh Brolin, and Tommy Lee Jones. Miramax, 2008. DVD.

Slumdog Millionaire. Dir. Danny Boyle. Perf. Dev Patel, Anil Dapoor, and Freida Pinto. Fox Searchlight Pictures, 2008. Film.

Begin a film or video entry with the title of the work, unless you are citing a particular individual's contribution. A title can be followed by relevant information like the director, screenwriter, and/or performers (unless already mentioned); then include the distributor, the release date, and the format. For video recordings, you may include the original film's release date before the distributor if pertinent.

Government Documents

> U.S. President. *Public Papers of the Presidents of the United States*. Washington: Office of the Federal Register, 1961. Print.

> United States. Senate. Committee on Energy and Natural Resources. Subcommittee on Energy Research and Development. *Advanced Reactor Development Program: Hearing*. 24 May, 1988. Washington: GPO, 1988. Print.

> ---. Environmental Protection Agency. *The Challenge of the Environment: A Primer on EPA's Statutory Authority*. Washington: GPO, 1972. Print.

Observe the pattern illustrated here. If the author of the document is not given, cite the name of the government first followed by the name of the department or agency. If you cite more than one document published by the United States government, do not repeat the name but use the standard three hyphens followed by a period instead. If you cite a second document prepared by the Environmental Protection Agency, use the following pattern:

> United States. Cong. House. . . .

> ---. Environmental Protection Agency . . .

> ---.---. [second source from EPA]

If the author is known, follow this pattern:

> Geller, William. *Deadly Force*. U.S. Dept of Justice National Institute of Justice Crime File Study Guide. Washington: U.S. Dept. of Justice, n.d. Print.

If the document contains no date, use the abbreviation "n.d."

> Hays, W. W., ed. *Facing Geologic and Hydrologic Hazards*. Geological Survey Professional Paper 1240-B. Washington: GPO, 1981. Print.

Abbreviate the U.S. Government Printing Office thus: GPO.

An Interview

> Plum, Kenneth. Personal Interview. 5 Mar. 1995.

A Lecture, Reading, or Address

> Whitman, Christine Todd, and Bill McKibben. "Containing Carbon: Markets, Morals, and Mobilization." Amherst College. Johnson Chapel, Amherst. 4 Feb. 2009. Address.

Legal Documents

> U.S. Const. Art. 1, sec. 3.

The Constitution is referred to by article and section. Abbreviations are used; do not italicize.

> Turner v. Arkansas. 407 U.S. 366. 1972. Print.

In citing a court case, give the name of the case (the plaintiff and defendant); the volume, name, and page of the report cited; and the date. The name of a court case is italicized in the text but not in the Works Cited.

> Federal Highway Act, as amended. 23 U.S. Code 109. 1970. Print.

> Labor Management Relations Act (Taft-Hartley Act). Statutes at Large. 61. 1947. Print.

> 34 U.S. Code. 1952. Print.

Citing laws is complicated, and lawyers use many abbreviations that may not be clear to nonexperts. Bills that become law are published annually in *Statutes at Large* (Stat.) and later in the *U.S. Code* (USC). Provide the title of the bill and the source, volume, and year. References to both *Statutes at Large* and the *U.S. Code* can be given as a convenience to readers.

Unpublished Letter/E-Mail

> Usick, Patricia. Message to the author. 26 June 2005. E-mail.

Treat a published letter as a work in a collection.

Maps and Charts

> *Hampshire and Dorset*. Map. Kent, Eng.: Geographers' A-Z Map, n.d. Print.

The format is similar to that for an anonymous book but add the appropriate descriptive label.

Plays or Concerts

> *Mourning Becomes Electra*. By Eugene O'Neill. Shakespeare Theater, Washington, DC. 16 May 1997. Performance.

Include title, author, theater, city, and date of performance. Principal actors, singers, musicians, and/or the director can be added as appropriate after the author.

Recordings

> Holiday, Billie, perf. "All of You." By Cole Porter. Rec. 11 Mar. 1959. *Last Recording*. Cond. Ray Ellis. Polygram, 1990. CD.

The order of the entry depends upon the focus of the interest; composer, conductor, group, or performer may come first, followed by the title, the artists, or composer (if different from the first information), the manufacturer, the year, and the medium (CD, LP). You may also include the date of the recording.

A Report

> *Environment and Development: Breaking the Ideological Deadlock*. Report of the Twenty-first United Nations Issues Conference, 23–25 Feb. 1990. Muscatine, Iowa: Stanley Foundation, n.d. Print.

Television or Radio Program

> "The Wolf That Changed America." *Nature*. PBS. WNET, New York, 23 Nov. 2008. Television.

Additional information, such as directors, narrators, or performers, follow the title of the episode or the series, depending on which it describes.

Citing Web Publications

Remember that the purpose of a citation is to provide readers with the information they need to obtain the source you have used. Most sources on the Web have the same basic elements—author, title, and publication information—that print sources do. However, works on the Web can be changed or updated at any point, or they may be located in several places online. Citing Web sources requires that you provide more information than is usually needed for print sources in order to document the precise source you used. The citation formats for Web sources fall into three basic categories: sources with only Web publication information, sources with additional print publication information, and sources retrieved through online databases.

Works from the Web

Articles cited with only Web publication information can include articles in online magazines, reference databases, professional Web sites, or homepages. The basic pattern for the citation includes:

1. Author (or editor or translator, as appropriate), if there is one

2. Title of the work, if there is a title separate from the larger page

3. Online publication information including title of the Web page—italicized—the version used (if available), the publisher or sponsor (or n.p.

if unavailable); the date of publication (or n.d. if unavailable); and the medium of publication (Web)

4. Date you accessed the source

> Coyne, Amanda. "Palin and the Wolves." *Newsweek .com.* Newsweek, 10 Apr. 2009. Web. 12 Apr. 2009.
>
> Rosner, Shmuel. "Too Busy to Save Darfur: The Obama Administration Has Very Few Options for Solving the Crisis in Sudan." *Slate.* Slate Magazine, 9 Apr. 2009. Web. 13 Apr. 2009.
>
> "Governor's Blue Ribbon Panel on Child Protection." *CNN.com.* Cable News Network, 27 May 2002. Web. 10 Apr. 2009.
>
> "Prohibition." *Encyclopedia Britannica Online.* Encyclopedia Britannica, 1998. Web. 24 Jan. 1998.
>
> Vachss, Andrew. "How Journalism Abuses Children." *The Zero—The Official Site of Andrew Vachss.* Ed. The Zero Collective, Aug. 1996. Web. 2 Aug. 2003.

Works from the Web with Previous Print Publication

For books, articles, poems, or other items that have been published previously and are also available online, you may include additional information about the original publication. Include the following information in your citation:

1. Citation for the original source: author, title, original publication information
2. Title of the Web site, italicized
3. Medium of publication
4. Date you accessed the source

> "Failed States and Failed Policies: How to Stop the Drug Wars." *The Economist* 5 Mar. 2009. *Economist .com.* Web. 7 Apr. 2009.
>
> Douglass, Frederick. *Life and Times of Frederick Douglass: His Early Life as a Slave, His Escape from Bondage, and His Complete History to the Present Time.* Hartford: Park Publishing, 1881. *Documenting the American South.* Web. 6 Apr. 2009.

Articles from Online Databases

To cite a journal article retrieved through a database, begin as you would if you had accessed the article in its print form, including the inclusive page numbers if possible (or n. pag. if unavailable). Then include the online access information.

1. Cite the source: author, title, journal, volume and issue, and page numbers
2. Title of the database

3. Medium of publication
4. Date you accessed the source

> Adams, Terri M., and Douglas B. Fuller. "The Words Have Changed But the Ideology Remains the Same: Misogynistic Lyrics in Rap Music." *Journal of Black Studies* 36.6 (2006): 938–57. *CSA Illumina.* 6 Apr. 2009.
>
> "The Bulls and Bears: A Tremendous Crash in the Wall Street Menagerie." *Washington Post* 22 Nov. 1879. *ProQuest.* Web. 10 Apr. 2009.

Author/Year or APA Style

The *author/year system* identifies a source by placing the author's last name and the publication year of the source within parentheses at the point in the text where the source is cited. The in-text citations are supported by complete citations in a list of sources at the end of the paper. Most disciplines in the social sciences, biological sciences, and earth sciences use some version of the author/year style. Of the various style manuals presenting this style, the most frequently used is the *Publication Manual of the American Psychological Association* (6th ed., 2009), supplemented by the *APA Style Guide to Electronic References* (pdf, 2009).

APA Style: In-Text Citations

The simplest parenthetical reference can be presented in one of three ways:

1. Place the year of publication within parentheses immediately following the author's name in the text.

> In a typical study of preference for motherese, Fernald (1985) used an operant auditory preference procedure.

Within the same paragraph, additional references to the source do not need to repeat the year, if the researcher clearly establishes that the same source is being cited.

> Because the speakers were unfamiliar subjects Fernald's work eliminates the possibility that it is the mother's voice per se that accounts for the preference.

2. If the author is not mentioned in the text, place the author's last name followed by a comma and the year of publication within parentheses after the borrowed information.

> The majority of working women are employed in jobs that are at least 75 percent female (Lawrence & Matsuda, 1997).

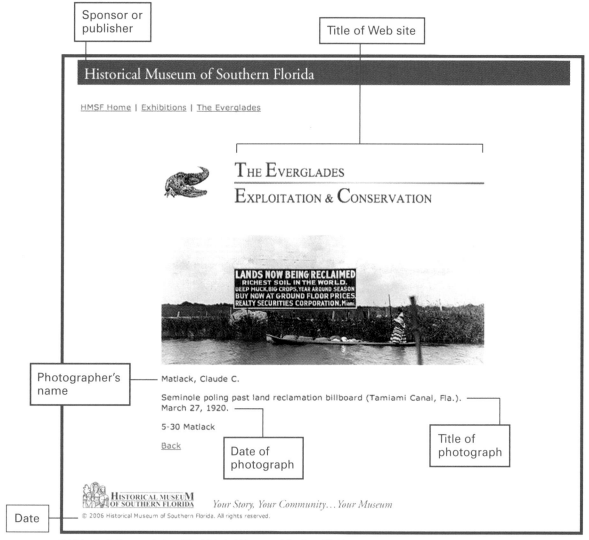

Sponsor or publisher

Title of Web site

Historical Museum of Southern Florida

HMSF Home | Exhibitions | The Everglades

THE EVERGLADES

EXPLOITATION & CONSERVATION

LANDS NOW BEING RECLAIMED
RICHEST SOIL IN THE WORLD.
DEEP MUCK, BIG CROPS, YEAR AROUND SEASON
BUY NOW AT GROUND FLOOR PRICES.
REALTY SECURITIES CORPORATION, Miami

Photographer's name

Matlack, Claude C.

Seminole poling past land reclamation billboard (Tamiami Canal, Fla.). March 27, 1920.

5-30 Matlack

Back

Date of photograph

Title of photograph

HISTORICAL MUSEUM OF SOUTHERN FLORIDA   *Your Story, Your Community…Your Museum*

Date

Published with the permission of the Historical Museum of Southern Florida.

try it !

Presenting and Documenting Borrowed Information and Preparing Citations

Read the following passage and then the three plagiarized uses of the passage. Explain why each one is plagiarized and how it can be corrected.

Original Text: Stanley Karnow, *Vietnam, A History. The First Complete Account of Vietnam at War.* New York: Viking, 1983, 319.

Lyndon Baines Johnson, a consummate politician, was a kaleidoscopic personality, forever changing as he sought to dominate or persuade or placate or frighten his friends and foes. A gigantic figure whose extravagant moods matched his size, he could be cruel and kind, violent and gentle, petty, generous, cunning, naïve, crude, candid, and frankly dishonest. He commanded the blind loy-alty of his aides, some of whom worshipped him, and he sparked bitter derision or fierce hatred that he never quite fathomed.

1. LBJ's vibrant and changing personality filled some people with adoration and others with bitter derision that he never quite fathomed (Karnow 319).

2. LBJ, a supreme politician, had a personality like a kaleidoscope, continually changing as he tried to control, sway, appease, or intimidate his enemies and supporters (Karnow 319).

3. Often, figures who have had great impact on America's history have been dynamic people with powerful personalities and vibrant physical presence. LBJ, for example, was a huge figure who polarized those who worked for and with

him. "He commanded the blind loyalty of his aides, some of whom worshipped him, and he sparked bitter derision or fierce hatred" from many others (Karnow 319).

Read the following passage and then each of the four sample uses of the passage. Judge each of the uses for how well it avoids plagiarism and if it is documented correctly. Make corrections as needed.

Original Text: Stanley Karnow, *Vietnam, A History. The First Complete Account of Vietnam at War.* New York: Viking, 1983, 327.

On July 27, 1965, in a last-ditch attempt to change Johnson's mind, Mansfield and Russell were to press him again to "concentrate on finding a way out" of Vietnam—"a place where we ought not be," and where "the situation is rapidly going out of control." But the next day, Johnson announced his decision to add forty-four American combat battalions to the relatively small U.S. contingents already there. He had not been deaf to Mansfield's pleas, nor had he simply swallowed the Pentagon's plans. He had waffled and agonized during his nineteen months in the White House, but eventually this was his final judgment. As he would later explain: "There are many, many people who can recommend and advise, and a few of them consent. But there is only one who has been chosen by the American people to decide."

1. Karnow writes that Senators Mansfield and Russell continued to try to convince President Johnson to avoid further involvement in Vietnam, "a place where we ought not be" they felt. (327).

2. Though Johnson received advice from many, in particular Senators Mansfield and Russell, he believed the weight of the decision to become further engaged in Vietnam was solely his as the one "'chosen by the American people to decide'" (Karnow 327).

3. On July 28, 1965, Johnson announced his decision to add forty-four battalions to the troops already in Vietnam, ending his waffling and agonizing of the past nineteen months of his presidency. (Karnow 357).

4. Karnow explains that LBJ took his responsibility to make decisions about Vietnam seriously (327). Although Johnson knew that many would offer suggestions, only he had "'been chosen by the American people to decide'" (Karnow 327).

Turn the information printed below into correct bibliographic citations for each of the works. Pay attention to the order of information, the handling of titles, and punctuation. Write each cita-tion on a separate index card, or, if your instructor requests, prepare the citations as an alphabetical listing of works.**

1. On July 14, 1997, Newsweek magazine printed Robert J. Samuelson's article titled Don't Hold Your Breath on page 40.

2. Richard B. Sewell's book The Life of Emily Dickinson was published in 1974. His book was published in two volumes by the New York City publisher Farrar, Straus, & Giroux.

3. Richard D. Heffner has edited an abridged version of Democracy in America by Alexis De Tocqueville. This is a Mentor Book paperback, a division of (New York City's) New American Library. The book was published in 1956.

4. The Object Stares Back: On the Nature of Seeing by James Elkins is reviewed in an article titled Vision Reviewed by Luciano da F. Costa. The review appeared on pages 124 and 125 in the March 1997 issue of Scientific American.

5. Arthur Whimbey wrote the article Something Better Than Binet for the Saturday Review on June 1, 1974. Joseph Rubinstein and Brent D. Slife reprinted the article on pages 102–108 in the third edition of the edited collection Taking Sides. Taking Sides was published in 1984 by the Dushkin Publishing Company located in Guilford, Connecticut.

6. The Discovery of Superconductivity appeared in Physics Today on pages 40–42. The author of the article is Jacobus de Nobel. The article appeared in the September 1996 issue, volume 49, number 9.

7. You used a biographical article, titled Marc Chagall (1887–1985), from Britannica Online which you found on the Internet September 25, 1999. You used the 1998 version, published by Encyclopaedia Britannica and available at <http://www.eb.com:180>.

8. An editorial appeared in the New York Times, on Sunday, September 7, 1997, with the title Protecting Children from Guns. The editorial could be found on page 16 of section 4.

9. Anthony Bozza's article "Moby Porn" appeared in the magazine Rolling Stone on June 26, 1977, on page 26. You obtained the text of the article from the September 1997 "edition" of General Periodicals Ondisc. The vendor is UMI-ProQuest.

10. A Letter to the Editor titled What Can We Do about Global Warming? appeared in the Washington Post on July 24, 1997. The letter was written by S. Fred Singer and printed on page A24.

3. Cite a specific passage by providing the page, chapter, or figure number following the borrowed material. *Always* give specific page references for quoted material.

- A brief quotation:

Deuzen-Smith (1988) believes that counselors must be involved with clients and "deeply interested in piecing the puzzle of life together" (p. 29).

- A quotation in display form:

Bartlett (1932) explains the cyclic process of perception:

> Suppose I am making a stroke in a quick game, such as tennis or cricket. How I make the stroke depends on the relating of certain new experiences, most of them visual, to other immediately preceding visual experiences, and to my posture, or balance of posture, at the moment. (p. 201)

Indent a block quotation of 40 words or more by 0.5″ from the left margin, do not use quotation marks, and double-space throughout. To show a new paragraph within the block quotation, indent the first line of the new paragraph an additional 0.5″. Note the placing of the year after the author's name and the page number at the end of the direct quotation.

If the author is not mentioned in the text, place the author's last name followed by a comma, the year followed by a comma, and the page number at the end of the direct quotation: (Bartlett, 1932, p. 201).

More complicated in-text citations should be handled as follows.

Two Authors, Mentioned in the Text

Kuhl and Meltzoff (1984) tested 4- to 5-month-olds in an experiment . . .

Two Authors, Not Mentioned in the Text

. . . but are unable to show preference in the presence of two mismatched modalities (e.g., a face and a voice; see Kuhl & Meltzoff, 1984).

Give both authors' last names each time you refer to the source. Connect their names with "and" in the text. Use an ampersand (&) in the parenthetical citation.

More Than Two Authors

For works coauthored by three, four, or five people, provide all last names in the first reference to the source. Thereafter, cite only the first author's name followed by "et al."

As Price-Williams, Gordon, and Ramirez have shown (1969), . . .

OR

Studies of these children have shown (Price-Williams, Gordon, & Ramirez, 1969) . . .

THEN

Price-Williams et al. (1969) also found that . . .

If a source has six or more authors, use only the first author's last name followed by "et al." every time the source is cited.

Corporate Authors

In general, spell out the name of a corporate author each time it is used. If a corporate author has well-known initials, the name can be abbreviated after the first citation.

FIRST IN-TEXT CITATION: (National Institutes of Health [NIH], 1989)

SUBSEQUENT CITATIONS: (NIH, 1989)

Two or More Works Within the Same Parentheses

When citing more than one work by the same author in a parenthetical reference, use the author's name only once and arrange the years mentioned in order, thus:

Several studies of ego identity formation (Marcia, 1966, 1983) . . .

When an author, or the same group of coauthors, has more than one work published in the same year, distinguish the works by adding the letters *a*, *b*, *c*, and so on, as needed, to the year. Give the last name only once, but repeat the year, each one with its identifying letters; thus:

Several studies (Smith, 1990a, 1990b, 1990c) . . .

When citing several works by different authors within the same parenthesis, list the authors in the order in which they appear in the list of references. Separate authors or groups of coauthors with semicolons; thus:

Although many researchers (Archer & Waterman, 1983; Grotevant, 1983; Grotevant & Cooper, 1986; Sabatelli & Mazor, 1985) study identity formation . . .

APA Style: Preparing a List of References

Every source cited parenthetically in your paper needs a complete bibliographic citation. These complete citations are placed on a separate page (or pages) after the text of the paper and before any appendices included in the paper. Sources are arranged alphabetically by author's last name, and the first page is titled "References." Begin each source flush with the left margin and indent second and subsequent lines five spaces. Double-space throughout the list of references. Follow these rules for alphabetizing:

1. Organize two or more works by the same author, or the same group of coauthors, chronologically.

   Beck, A. T. (1991).

   Beck, A. T. (1993).

2. Place single-author entries before multiple-author entries when the first of the multiple authors is the same as the single author.

   Grotevant, H. D. (1983).

   Grotevant, H. D., & Cooper, C. R. (1986).

3. Organize multiple-author entries that have the same first author but different second or third authors alphabetically by the name of the second author or third and so on.

   Gerbner, G., & Gross, L.

   Gerbner, G., Gross, L., Jackson-Beeck, M., Jeffries-Fox, S., & Signorielli, N.

   Gerbner G., Gross, L., Morgan, M., & Signorielli, N.

4. Organize two or more works by the same author(s) published in the same year alphabetically by title and add a letter (a, b, c) to the year to distinguish each entry in your in-text citation.

Form for Books

A book citation contains these elements in this form:

Seligman, M. E. P. (1991). *Learned optimism*. New York: Knopf.

Weiner, B. (Ed.). (1974). *Achievement motivation and attribution theory*. Morristown, NJ: General Learning Press.

Authors

Give up to and including six authors' names, last name first, and initials. For more than seven authors, list the first six, three ellipses, and the final author. Separate authors with commas, use the ampersand (&) before the last author's name, and end with a period. For edited books, place the abbreviation "Ed." or "Eds." in parentheses following the last editor's name.

Date of Publication

Place the year of publication in parentheses followed by a period.

Title

Capitalize only the first word of the title and of the subtitle, if there is one, and any proper nouns. Italicize

the title and end with a period. Place additional information such as number of volumes or an edition in parentheses after the title, before the period.

Butler, R., & Lewis, M. (1982). *Aging and mental health* (3rd ed.).

Publication Information

Cite the city of publication; add the state (using the Postal Service abbreviation) or country if necessary to avoid confusion; then give the publisher's name, after a colon, eliminating unnecessary terms such as *Publisher, Co.*, and *Inc.* End the citation with a period.

Newton, D. E. (1996). *Violence and the media*. Santa Barbara: ABC-Clio.

Mitchell, J. V. (Ed.). (1985). *The ninth mental measurements yearbook*. Lincoln: University of Nebraska Press.

National Institute of Drug Abuse. (1993, April 13). *Annual national high school senior survey*. Rockville, MD: Author.

Give a corporate author's name in full. When the organization is both author and publisher, place the word *Author* after the place of publication.

Form for Articles

An article citation contains these elements in this form:

Changeaux, J-P. (1993). Chemical signaling in the brain. *Scientific American, 269,* 58–62.

Date of Publication

Place the year of publication for articles in scholarly journals in parentheses, followed by a period. For articles in newspapers and popular magazines, give the year followed by month and day (if appropriate).

(1997, March).

See also example below.

Title of Article

Capitalize only the title's first word, the first word of any subtitle, and any proper nouns. Place any necessary descriptive information in square brackets immediately after the title.

Scott, S. S. (1984, December 12). Smokers get a raw deal [Letter to the Editor].

Publication Information

Cite the title of the journal in full, capitalizing according to conventions for titles. Italicize the title and follow it with a comma. Give the volume number, italicized, followed by a comma, and then inclusive page numbers followed by a period. *If* a journal begins each issue with a new page 1, then also cite the issue number in parentheses immediately following the volume number. Do not use "p." or "pp." before page numbers when citing articles from scholarly journals and magazine articles; do use "p." or "pp." in citations to newspaper articles.

> Martin, C. L., Wood, C. H., & Little, J. K. (1990). The development of gender stereotype components. *Child Development, 61,* 1891–1904.

> Leakey, R. (2000, April–May). Extinctions past and present. *Time,* 35.

Form for an Article or Chapter in an Edited Book

> Goodall, J. (1993). Chimpanzees—Bridging the gap. In P. Cavalieri & P. Singer (Eds.), *The great ape project: Equality beyond humanity* (pp. 10–18). New York: St. Martin's.

Cite the author(s), date, and title of the article or chapter. Then cite the name(s) of the editor(s) in signature order after "In," followed by "Ed." or "Eds." in parentheses; the title of the book; the inclusive page numbers of the article or chapter, in parentheses, followed by a period. End with the place of publication and the publisher of the book.

A Report

> U.S. Merit Systems Protection Board. (1988). *Sexual harassment in the federal workplace: An update.* Washington, DC: U.S. Government Printing Office.

Electronic Sources

Many types of electronic sources are available on the Internet, and the variety can make documenting these sources complex. Generally, you should include the same information in the same order that you would for a print source; you replace the publication information, which no longer applies, with information on where to access the materials online. At minimum, an APA reference for any type of Internet source should include the following information: an author name, whenever possible; the date of publication or latest update (use n.d. for "no date" when a publication date is not available); a document title or description; and a Digital Object Identifier (DOI) or Internet address (URL).

The DOI is an alpha-numeric string that many scholarly publishers now assign to articles to connect them to their locations online. APA style uses this DOI instead of a URL whenever possible. Within your citation, do not place the DOI or URL in angle brackets (<>). Also, do not place a period at the end of a reference when the DOI or URL concludes it. If the DOI or URL falls across a line break, you should break the string or address before a punctuation mark.

Provide a retrieval date only for material that is likely to be moved or changed; otherwise, the DOI or URL is sufficient. Similarly, you should provide the database where you retrieved material only if the document has limited circulation and would be hard to find without the information. If you do include the database name, you do not need to include the URL. Finally, when a document is available only by subscription (like a journal article) or is available by search (like an entry in an online dictionary or an article on a magazine's Web site), you need give only the URL of the home or menu page for the document's source.

Journal Article with a DOI

> Hussain, M. (2008). Freedom of speech and adolescent public school students. *Journal of the American Academy of Child & Adolescent Psychiatry, 47,* 614–618. doi: 10.1097/CHI.0b013e31816c42ac

Journal Article with No DOI

> Michael, M. (2005). Is it natural to drive species to extinction? *Ethics and the Environment, 10*(1), 49–66. Retrieved from http://www.phil.uga.edu/eande/

Electronic Daily Newspaper Article Available by Search

> Schwartz, J. (2002, September 13). Air pollution con game. *Washington Times.* Retrieved from http://www.washtimes.com

U.S. Government Report on a Government Web Site

> U.S. General Accounting Office. (2002, March). Identity theft: Prevalence and cost appear to be growing. Retrieved February 23, 2009, from http://www.gao.gov/new.items/d2363.pdf

Document from a Web Site

> McDermott, M. (2009, February 26). Pedestrian-friendly improvements coming to NYC's Herald and Times Squares. [Online exclusive]. *Treehugger.* Retrieved February 26, 2009, from http://www.treehugger.com/files/2009/02/pedestrian-friendly-improvements-coming-to-new-york-city-herald-square-times-square.php

Citing information that has been archived and is available for retrieval, such as posts to newsgroups or electronic mailing lists, in the references lists. However, e-mails, like personal interviews or letters, should be cited as "personal communication" only in the essay and not in the list of references.

Sample Student Essay in APA Style

The following essay illustrates APA style. Use 1-inch margins and double-space throughout, including any block quotations. Block quotations should be indented *five spaces* or ½ inch from the left margin (in contrast to the ten spaces required by MLA style). The paper illustrates the following elements of papers in APA style: title page, running head, abstract, author/year in-text citations, subheadings within the text, and a list of references.

Transracial Adoptions   1

Sample title page for a paper in APA style.

Adoptions: An Issue of Love, Not Race

Connie Childress

Anthropology 314

Professor Murals

May 15, 2008

Observe placement of running head and page number.

Papers in APA style usually begin with an abstract of the paper which should not exceed 150 to 200 words.

Abstract

Over 400,000 children are in foster care in the United States. The majority of these children are nonwhite. However, the majority of couples wanting to adopt children are white. While matching race or ethnic background when arranging adoptions may be the ideal, the mixing of race or ethnic background should not be avoided, or delayed, when the matching of race is not possible. Children need homes, and studies of racial adoptees show that they are as adjusted as adoptees with new parents of their own race or ethnicity. Legislation should support speedier adoptions of children, regardless of race or ethnic background.

Adoption: An Issue of Love, Not Race

Nine years ago when my daughter, Ashley, was placed in my arms, it marked the happy ending to a long, exhausting, and, at times, heartbreaking journey through endless fertility treatments and the red tape of adoption procedures. Ironically, she had not been in our home a day before we received a call from another adoption agency that specialized in foreign adoptions. The agency stated that it was ready to begin our home study. As I look at Ashley, with her brown hair, hazel eyes, and fair complexion, I have trouble imagining not having her in my life. I know in my heart that I would have this feeling about my daughter whether she came to us from the domestic agency or the agency bringing us a child from a foreign country. To us the issue was only the child, not his or her race or ethnic background. The issue of race or ethnicity should be considered by adoptive parents along with all the other issues needing thought when they make the decision to adopt. But race or ethnicity alone should not be a roadblock to adoption. It is not society's place to decide for parents if they are capable of parenting a child of a different race or ethnic background.

Transracial adoptions are those adoptions involving a family and a child of a different race or ethnic background. Cultural differences occur when the family is of one racial or ethnic background and the adoptive child is of another. Amy Kuebelbeck (1996) reports that, according to the U.S. Department of Health and Human Services, "about 52 percent of children awaiting adoption through state placement services around the country are black." On average, Black children wait longer to be adopted than White, Asian, or Hispanic children. Why should it be more difficult for a White family to adopt an African American child than a child from China or Russia? Or a Hispanic American or mixed-race child? Any of these combinations still results in a mixed-race adoption.

Student introduces her paper by referring to her adoption experience.

The first paragraph concludes with her thesis.

Observe form of author/year citations.

Adoption Issues and Problems

Although interracial adoptions are "statistically rare in the United States,"
according to Robert S. Bausch and Richard T. Serpe (1997), who cite a 1990 study
by Bachrach et al., the issue continues to receive attention from both social
workers and the public (p. 137). A *New Republic* editorial (1994) lists several
articles, including a cover story in *The Atlantic* in 1992, to illustrate the attention
given to transracial adoptions. All of the popular-press articles as well as those
in scholarly journals, the editors explain, describe the country's adoption and
foster-care problems. While the great majority of families wanting to adopt are
White, about half of the children in foster care waiting to be adopted are Black.
Robert Jackson (1995) estimates that, in 1995, about 440,000 children are being
cared for in foster families. The *New Republic* editorial reports on a 1993 study
revealing that "a black child in California's foster care system is three times less
likely to be adopted than a white child" (p. 6). In some cases minority children
have been in a single foster home with parents of a different race their entire
life. They have bonded as a family. Yet, often when the foster parents apply to
adopt these children, their petitions are denied and the children are removed
from their care. For example, Beverly and David Cox, a White couple in Wisconsin,
were asked to be foster parents to two young sisters, both African American.
The Coxes provided love and nurturing for five years, but when they petitioned
to adopt the two girls, not only was their request denied, but the girls were
removed from their home. Can removing the children from the only home they
have ever known just because of their skin color really be in the best interest of
the children? Cole, Drummond, and Epperson (1995) quote Hillary Clinton as
saying that "skin color [should] not outweigh the more important gift of love
that adoptive parents want to offer" (p. 50).

The argument against transracial adoption has rested on the concern that
children adopted by parents of a different race or ethnic background will lose

Page numbers
must be given
for direct
quotations.

Words added
to a quotation
for clarity
are placed
in square
brackets.

their cultural heritage and racial identity, and that these losses may result in adjustment problems for the children (Bausch & Serpe, 1997). The loudest voice against mixed-race adoptions has been the National Association of Black Social Workers (NABSW), who passed a resolution in 1972 stating their "vehement opposition to the practice of placing Black children with white families" and reaffirmed their position in 1994 (Harnack, 1995, p. 188). Audrey T. Russell (1995), speaking at the 1972 conference, described White adoption of Black children as "a practice of genocide" (p. 189). Fortunately, for both children and families wanting to adopt, the NABSW has now reversed its position and concedes that placement in a home of a different race is far more beneficial to the child than keeping the child in foster care (Jackson, 1995). The NABSW's new position may have come in response to the passage of the Multiethnic Placement Act of 1994, legislation designed to facilitate the placement of minority children into adoptive homes. As Randall Kennedy (1995) explains, while this legislation continues to allow agencies to consider "the child's cultural, ethnic and racial background and the capacity of prospective foster or adoptive parents to meet the needs of a child of this background" (p. 44), it prohibits the delaying of an adoption solely for the purpose of racial matching. Kennedy objects to the law's allowing for even some consideration of race matching because he believes that this results in some children never being adopted, as agencies search for a race match. Sandra Haun (personal communication, Sept. 30, 1997), a social worker from Fairfax County, Virginia, said in an interview that she does not oppose transracial adoptions but that the best choice for a child is with a family of the same race, if the choice exists. Providing that both adoptive homes could offer the child the same environment in every aspect, then clearly the same-race home may be the best choice. More often than not, however, placing a child in a home of the same race is not an option. How can we worry about a child's cultural identity when the child doesn't have a home to call his or her own? In the cases of minority children who have been with a foster family of a different race for most of their young lives, the benefits of remaining in a stable home far outweigh the benefits of moving to a family of the same race.

Good transition into discussion of movie.

The emotional effects of removing a child from a home that he or she has lived in for an extended period of time is well illustrated in the movie *Losing Isaiah*. In the film, a Black child is adopted by a White social worker and her husband after the child's birth mother has placed him in the garbage when he is three days old so that she can be free to search for drugs. When Isaiah is three, the courts return him to his birth mother, who is now off drugs. Is it fair to Isaiah for her reward to be at the expense of his emotional health? The attorney representing the adoptive parents sums up the plight of these children in one sentence: "The child is then wrenched from the only family they've ever known and turned over to strangers because of the color of their skin." In the end, Isaiah's birth mother realizes that this system is unfair to him. She appeals to his adoptive parents to assist him in his adjustment to his new home.

Subheadings are often used in papers in the social sciences.

Some Consequences of Negative Attitudes Toward Transracial Adoptions

To protect themselves from heartbreaking situations such as the one depicted in *Losing Isaiah,* potential adoptive couples in this country are seeking other alternatives. We know that many couples seeking to adopt often adopt children from foreign countries. One of the reasons for this is the assumed shortage of children in the United States available for adoption. What may be less widely known is that many American children of mixed race or African American are placed with adoptive families overseas. One of the reasons for this situation is the continued unwillingness of social workers to place Black or mixed-race children with White couples. The NABSW's years of resistance to placing Black children with White parents has left its mark, although Edmund Blair Bolles (1984) speculates that the rare placing of Black—or American Indian—children with White couples may reflect racial prejudices rather than a great concern to preserve Black or Indian identities. Whatever the explanation, it is ironic that American babies are being "exported" to adoptive homes in other countries while babies from other countries are being "imported" to American adoptive homes. The child social services system needs to be overhauled to remove the stigmas or concerns that keep American children from being adopted in the country of their birth. If one of the arguments against transracial adoptions is the possible loss of cultural identity, how can we tolerate a system which appears to prefer placing African American children outside their own country—their own cultural heritage?

The argument that adopted children may lose their cultural identity is no longer a justifiable objection to transracial adoptions. As Randall Kennedy (1995) asserts, "there exists no credible empirical support that substantiates" the idea that "adults of the same race as the child will be better able to raise that child than adults of a different race" (p. 44). Bausch and Serpe (1997) cite four studies done between 1972 and 1992 that show that "most children of color adopted by white parents appear to be as well adjusted as children of color adopted by same-race parents" (p. 137). Perhaps the most important study is one conducted over twenty years by Rita Simon, American University sociologist. Davis (1995) reports that she studied 204 interracial adoptees over the twenty-year period and found that many of the adoptees supported transracial adoptions. Some did report that they felt isolated from other people of their own race, but we need to remember that those who participated in this study were adopted when adoptions were more secretive (and when races were more separated). At that time, most adoptees, regardless of race, may have felt isolated because of this lack of openness. Simon (1995), in her book (with Howard Altstein and Marygold S. Melli), draws these conclusions:

> Transracial adoptees do not lose their racial identities, they do not appear
> to be racially unaware of who they are, and they do not display negative
> or indifferent racial attitudes about themselves. On the contrary, . . .
> transracially placed children and their families have as high a success rate
> as all other adoptees and their families. (p. 204)

With open adoptions becoming increasingly popular, more adoptees today are aware of their adopted state and often have knowledge of one or both of their birth parents. It is not only possible, but probably easier, to provide opportunities for today's adoptee to learn about his or her racial and cultural background. The fact that the child is being raised by a family of a different race or ethnic background does not condemn that child to a life of ignorance concerning his or her own racial and cultural identity.

Conclusion

There can be only one logical solution to the issues surrounding mixed-race adoptions. Children and their adoptive parents should be united as a family because they have passed the background investigations and screening interviews that show they are emotionally and financially able to provide loving and nurturing environments for the children. To keep children needing homes and loving parents apart because they are of different races or ethnic backgrounds is not fair to the children or the adoptive parents. Preventing or delaying such adoptions is detrimental to each child's development. Children require a consistent home environment to flourish, to grow to be productive members of society. Legislation needs to support speedier adoptive placements for minority children to give them the same quality of life afforded other adoptees. Society needs to protect the right of adoptive parents by not denying transracial adoptions as an option for couples seeking to adopt.

Student restates her position in a concluding paragraph.

References

All in the family. (1994, January). *The New Republic, 210*(4), 6. Retrieved from
    http://www.tnr.com

Bausch, R. S., and Serpe, R. T. (1997). Negative outcomes of interethnic adoptions
    of Mexican American children. *Social Work 42*(2), 136–143. Retrieved from
    http://naswpressonline.org

Bolles, E. B. (1984). *The Penguin adoption handbook: A guide to creating your new
    family*. New York: Viking.

Cole, W., Drummond, T., & Epperson, S. E. (1995, August 14). Adoption in black
    and white. *Time*. Retrieved from http://www.time.com

Davis, R. (1995, Apr. 13). Suits back interracial adoptions. *USA Today*, p. A3.
    Retrieved from http://www.usatoday.com

Gyllenhaal, S. (Director). (1995). *Losing Isaiah* [Motion Picture]. United States:
    Paramount Pictures.

Harnack, A. (Ed.). (1995). *Adoption: Opposing viewpoints*. San Diego: Greenhaven.

Jackson, R. L. (1995, April 25). U.S. stresses no race bias in adoptions. *Los Angeles
    Times*, p. A6. Retrieved from http://www.latimes.com

Kennedy, R., & Moseley-Braun, C. (1995). At issue: Interracial adoption—Is the
    multiethnic placement act flawed? *ABA Journal, 81*, pp. 44–45. Retrieved
    from http://abajournal.com

Kuebelbeck, A. (1996, December 31). Interracial adoption debated. *AP US
    and World*. Retrieved October 10, 1999, from http://www.donet
    .com/~brandyjc/p6at111.htm

Russell, A. T. (1995). Transracial adoptions should be forbidden. In A. Harnack
    (Ed.), *Adoption: Opposing viewpoints* (pp. 189–96). San Diego: Greenhaven.

Simon, R. J., Altstein, H., & Melli, M. S. (1995). Transracial adoptions should be en-
    couraged. In A. Harnack (Ed.), *Adoption: Opposing viewpoints* (pp. 198–204).
    San Diego: Greenhaven.

Title the page
"References."

Double-space
throughout. In
each citation
indent all lines,
after the first,
five spaces.
Note APA style
placement of
date and for-
mat for titles.

Footnote or Endnote Style

Instructors in history, philosophy, and art history frequently prefer the footnote or endnote form of documentation to any pattern using parenthetical documentation. The chief guide for this pattern is the *Chicago Manual of Style* (15th ed., 2003). Chicago style states a preference for endnotes (citations placed at the end of the paper) rather than footnotes (citations placed at the bottom of appropriate pages), but some instructors may want to see footnotes, so always be sure to determine the precise guidelines for your assignment. Further learn your instructor's expectations with regard to a bibliography in addition to footnotes or endnotes. If the first footnote (or endnote) reference to a source contains complete bibliographic information, a list of works cited may not be necessary. Still, some instructors want both complete documentation notes and the alphabetized Bibliography following the text (with footnotes) or after the endnotes.

In-Text Citations

Notes can be easily made with the footnote or endnote function on a word processor. Use a raised (superscript, such as this [2]) arabic numeral immediately following all material from a source, whether the borrowed material is quoted or paraphrased. The number follows all punctuation except the dash, and it always follows material needing documentation at the end of a sentence or clause. Number footnotes or endnotes consecutively throughout the paper, beginning with "1." Use care to present material from sources with introductory tags and to place superscript numbers so that readers can tell where borrowed material begins and where it ends. Regularly placing citation numbers only at the ends of paragraphs will not result in accurate documentation.

Location and Presentation of Footnotes

1. Place footnotes on the same page as the borrowed material.

2. Begin the first footnote four lines (two double-spaces) below the last line of text.

3. Indent the first line of each footnote five spaces. Type the online, full-size numeral that corresponds to the superscript numeral in the text, followed by a period.

4. If a footnote runs to more than one line of text, single-space between lines and begin the second line flush with the left margin.

5. If more than one footnote appears on a page, double-space between notes.

Location and Presentation of Endnotes

1. Start endnotes on a new page titled "Notes." Endnotes follow the text and precede a list of works cited, if such a list is included.

2. List endnotes in consecutive order corresponding to the superscript numbers in the text.

3. Indent the first line of each endnote five spaces. Type the online number followed by a period, leave one space, and then type the reference.

4. If an endnote runs to more than one line, double-space between lines and begin the second line flush with the left margin.

5. Double-space between endnotes.

Footnote/Endnote Form: First (Primary) Reference

Each first reference to a source contains all the necessary author, title, and publication information that would be found in a list of works cited or list of references. Subsequent references to the same source use a shortened form. Prepare all first-reference notes according to the following guidelines.

Form for Books

1. Cite the author's full name in signature order, followed by a comma.

2. Cite the title of the book in italics. Include the complete subtitle, if there is one, unless a list of works cited is also provided. No punctuation follows the title.

3. Give the facts of publication in parentheses: city of publication followed by a colon, publisher followed by a comma, and year of publication.

4. Give the precise page reference. Do not use "p." or "pp." Place a comma after the closing parenthesis, before the page number. All notes end with a period.

> 1. Daniel J. Boorstin, *The Americans: The Colonial Experience* (New York: Vintage-Random, 1958), 46.

Form for Articles

1. Cite the author's full name in signature order, followed by a comma.

2. Cite the title of the article in quotation marks, and place a comma *inside* the closing quotation mark.

3. Give the facts of publication: the title of the journal, italicized; the volume in arabic numerals; the issue preceded by "no."; and the date followed by a colon. Citations of scholarly journals require the volume number followed by

the date including month or season if desired in parentheses; citations of popular magazines and newspapers eliminate the volume number, giving the date only, not in parentheses. In the past, issue numbers have been required only when a journal paginates each issue separately rather than continuously throughout a volume. *The Chicago Manual of Style* now suggests including issue numbers whenever available to help locate a source. The month or season of an issue, sometimes given with the year, may also be included, but it is not required.

4.   Provide a precise page reference following the colon, without using "p." or "pp." All notes end with a period.

> 2. Everard H. Smith, "Chambersburg: Anatomy of a Confederate Reprisal," *American Historical Review* 96, no. 2 (1991): 434.

Sample Footnotes/Endnotes

Additional information must be added as necessary. Some of the common variations are illustrated here. Note that the examples are presented as endnotes; that is, the lines of each note are double-spaced. Remember that footnotes are single-spaced *within* each note but double-spaced *between* notes. For materials that are accessed online, generally follow the guidelines given for print materials. Then, following a comma, provide a URL. If you retrieved the article through a subscription database (like LexisNexis or JSTOR), you may include the URL of the entry page only (http://jstor .org) rather than the entire URL.

A Work by Two or Three Authors

> 3. Charles A. Beard and Mary R. Beard, T*he American Spirit* (New York: Macmillan, 1942), 63.

A Work by More Than Three Authors

> 4. Lester R. Brown et al., *State of the World 1990: A Worldwatch Institute Report on Progress Toward a Sustainable Society* (New York: Norton, 1990), 17.

(The phrase "and others" may be used in place of "et al.")

An Edited Work

> 5. *The Autobiography of Benjamin Franklin*, ed. Max Farrand (Berkeley: University of California Press, 1949), 6–8.

(Begin with the title—or the editor's name—if the author's name appears in the title.)

> 6. Bentley Glass, Owsei Temkin, and William L. Straus, Jr., eds., *Forerunners of Darwin: 1745–1859* (Baltimore: Johns Hopkins Press paperback edition, 1968), 326.

A Translation

> 7. Allan Gilbert, trans. and ed., *The Letters of Machiavelli* (New York: Capricorn Books, 1961), 120.

A Preface, Introduction, or Afterword

> 8. Ernest Barker, introduction to *The Politics of Aristotle* (New York: Oxford University Press, 1962), xiii.

A Book in Two or More Volumes

> 9. Paul Tillich, *Systematic Theology*, 3 vols. (Chicago: University of Chicago Press, 1951–63), 1:52.

(Make the page reference first to the volume number, followed by a colon, and then the page number.)

A Book in Its Second or Subsequent Edition

> 10. Frank J. Sorauf and Paul Allen Beck, *Party Politics in America*, 6th ed. (Glenview, IL: Scott, Foresman/Little, Brown, 1988), 326.

A Book in a Series

> 11. Charles L. Sanford, ed., *Benjamin Franklin and the American Character*, Problems in American Civilization (Lexington, MA: D.C. Heath, 1955), 4.

A Work in a Collection

> 12. George Washington, "Farewell Address, 1796," in *A Documentary History of the United States*, ed. Richard D. Heffner (New York: New American Library, 1965), 64–65.

An Encyclopedia Article

> 13. *The Concise Dictionary of American Biography*, 1964 ed., s.v. "Anthony, Susan Brownell."

(Do not cite a page number for reference works arranged alphabetically; rather, cite the entry in quotation marks after "s.v." [*sub verbo*—"under the word"]. The edition number or year is needed, but no other facts of publication are required for well-known reference works.)

An Article in a Scholarly Journal

> 14. Ellen Fitzpatrick, "Rethinking the Intellectual Origins of American Labor History," *American Historical Review* 96, no. 2 (1991): 426.

OR

> 14. Ellen Fitzpatrick, "Rethinking the Intellectual Origins of American Labor History," *American Historical Review* 96, no. 2 (1991): 426, http://www .proquest.com.

An Article in a Popular Magazine

     15. Richard Leakey, "Extinctions Past and Present," *Time,* April 26, 2000: 35.

OR

     15. Richard Leakey, "Extinctions Past and Present," *Time,* April 26, 2000, http://www.time.com/time/magazine/article/0,9171,996748,00.html.

An Editorial

     16. "Means of Atonement," editorial, *Wall Street Journal,* 22 May 2000: A38.

OR

     16. "Means of Atonement," editorial, *Wall Street Journal,* 22 May 2000: A38, http://www.lexis-nexis.com.

A Review

     17. Gabriel P. Weisberg, "French Art Nouveau," review of *Art Nouveau in Fin-de-Siècle France: Politics, Psychology, and Style* by Deborah Silverman, *Art Journal* 49 (Winter 1990): 427.

OR

     17. Gabriel P. Weisberg, "French Art Nouveau," review of *Art Nouveau in Fin-de-Siècle France: Politics, Psychology, and Style* by Deborah Silverman, *Art Journal* 49, no. 4 (1990): 427, http://www.jstor.org/stable/777145.

An Online News Service

     18. Leslie Gevirtz, "US Leads 100-Year Game of Economic Development," *Reuters,* Nov./Dec. 1999, http://www.reuters.com/magazine.

An Article from a Reference Database

     19. *Encyclopaedia Britannica Online,* s.v. "Prohibition," http://search.eb.com.

An Article from a Web Page

     20. Alice C. Hudson, "Heading West: Mapping the Territory," Heading West: Touring West, The New York Public Library, http://www.nypl.org/west/hw_subhome.shtml.

A Document from a Web Site

     21. Annie Page, Interview by Bernice Bowden, "Born in Slavery: Slave Narratives from the Federal Writers' Project 1936–1938," American Memory, Library of Congress, http://memory.loc.gov/cgi-bin/ampage?collId=mesn&fileName=025/mesn025.db&recNum=241&itemLink=D?mesnbib:1:./temp/~ammem_m1Zu:.

(Neither break a URL across a line after a hyphen, nor insert a hyphen to a URL to indicate a line break. You should make the break after a slash; before a tilde (~), a period, a comma, a hyphen, an underline (_), a question mark, a number sign, or a percent symbol; or before or after an equals sign or an ampersand.)

Footnote/Endnote Form: Short Forms

After the first full documentary footnote or endnote, subsequent references to the same source should be shortened forms. The simplest short form for any source with an author or editor is the author's or editor's last name followed by a comma and a precise page reference; thus: 20. Fitzgerald, 425. If there is no author cited, use a short title and page number. If two sources are written by authors with the same last name, then add first names or initials to distinguish between them.

     21. Henry Adams, 16.
     22. James T. Adams, 252.

     If you use two or more sources by the same author, then add a short title to the note; thus:

     23. Boorstin, *American Politics,* 167.
     24. Boorstin, *The Americans,* 65–66.

     The Latin abbreviations *loc. cit.* and *op. cit.* are no longer recommended, and ibid. is almost as obsolete, usually replaced now by the simple short form of author's last name and page number. Remember that ibid. can be used only to refer to the source cited in the immediately preceding note. The following footnotes, appearing at the bottom of a page from a history paper, illustrate the various short forms.

Sample Footnotes from a History Paper

    While mid-twentieth-century historians may be more accurate, they may have lost the flavor of earlier American historians who had a clear ideology that shaped their writing.[20]

     11. William Bradford, *Of Plymouth Plantation,* in *The American Puritans: Their Prose and Poetry,* ed. Perry Miller (New York: Anchor-Doubleday, 1956), 5.
     12. Daniel J. Boorstin, *The Americans: The Colonial Experience* (New York: Vintage-Random, 1958), 16.
     13. Ibid., 155.
     14. James T. Adams, 136.
     15. Henry Adams, *The Education of Henry Adams,* ed. D. W. Brogan (Boston: Houghton Mifflin, 1961), 342.
     16. Boorstin, *American Politics,* 167.
     17. Henry Adams, "The Tendency of History," 16.
     18. Ibid., 71.
     19. Henry Adams, *Education,* 408.
     20. John Higham, "The Cult of the 'American Consensus': Homogenizing Our History," *Commentary* 27 (Feb. 1959): 94–96.

Sample Bibliography

A bibliography would include all cited works and may include additional works relevant to the paper's research or topic. The list is arranged in alphabetical order by the first word in the entry, usually the author's last name or the first significant word in a title. The first line of each entry begins at the far left, and additional lines are indented two or three spaces. Double-space the entire list. Bibliographies are not necessary in the note system since the notes contain complete bibliographic information. However, since they list all sources in one place, they provide a good overview of a paper's sources and may be required by an instructor. Entries in a bibliography differ from the information provided in the notes only in the inversion of the author's name (last name first), the use of periods instead of commas to separate elements in the entry, and the inclusion of the page range of articles rather than identifying the single page where a quotation or reference is located. Items from daily newspapers or reference books or databases are rarely given in the bibliography. Some of the common variations, based on earlier sample notes, are illustrated here.

Bibliography

Barker, Ernest. Introduction to *The Politics of Aristotle*. New York: Oxford University Press, 1962.

Beard, Charles A., and, Mary R. Beard. *The American Spirit*. New York: Macmillan, 1942.

Boorstin, Daniel J. *The Americans: The Colonial Experience*. New York: Vintage-Random, 1958.

Brown, Lester R., and others. *State of the World 1990: A Worldwatch Institute Report on Progress Toward a Sustainable Society*. New York: Norton, 1990.

Fitzpatrick, Ellen. "Rethinking the Intellectual Origins of American Labor History." *American Historical Review* 96, no. 2 (1991): 422–428. http://www.proquest.com.

Franklin, Benjamin. *The Autobiography of Benjamin Franklin*. Edited by Max Farrand. Berkeley: University of California Press, 1949.

Gilbert, Allan, trans. and ed. *The Letters of Machiavelli*. New York: Capricorn Books, 1961.

Glass, Bentley, Owsei Temkin, and William L. Straus, Jr., eds. *Forerunners of Darwin: 1745–1859*.

Paperback. Baltimore: Johns Hopkins Press, 1968.

Hudson, Alice C. "Heading West: Mapping the Territory." Heading West: Touring West. The New York Public Library. http://www.nypl.org/west/hw_subhome.shtml.

Leakey, Richard. "Extinctions Past and Present." *Time* April 26, 2000: 35. http://www.time.com/time/magazine/article/0,9171,996748,00.html.

Page, Annie. Interview by Bernice Bowden. "Born in Slavery: Slave Narratives from the Federal Writers' Project 1936–1938." American Memory. Library of Congress. http://memory.loc.gov/cgi-bin/ampage?collId=mesn&fileName=025/mesn025.db&recNum=241&itemLink=D?mesnbib:1:./temp/~ammem_m1Zu:.

Sanford, Charles L., ed. *Benjamin Franklin and the American Character*. Problems in American Civilization. Lexington, MA: D. C. Heath, 1955.

Smith, Everard H. "Chambersburg: Anatomy of a Confederate Reprisal." *American Historical Review* 96, no. 2 (1991): 432–455.

Sorauf, Frank J., and Paul Allen Beck. *Party Politics in America*. 6th ed. Glenview, IL: Scott, Foresman/Little, Brown, 1988.

Tillich, Paul. *Systematic Theology*. 3 vols. Chicago: University of Chicago Press, 1951–1963.

Washington, George. "Farewell Address, 1796." In *A Documentary History of the United States*, edited by Richard D. Heffner. New York: New American Library, 1965.

Weisberg, Gabriel P. "French Art." Review of *Art Nouveau in Fin-de-Siècle France: Politics, Psychology, and Style* by Deborah Silverman. *Art Journal* 49, no. 4 (1990): 426–429. http://www.jstor.org/stable/777145.

the myth and
reality of the
image in american
consumer culture

c h a p t e r 14

Media and advertising images bombard us all the time, pressuring us to buy a multitude of products and services. We encounter the omnipresent consumer culture whenever we watch television, go to the movies, play videogames, look at magazines, or even drive on an interstate highway. Advertising images from billboards, television commercials, and the World Wide Web are virtually inescapable. This chapter's selections address the impact of advertising images as part of consumer culture as well as the rise of product placement in videogames, popular television series, and big-budget films. The pervasiveness of images contributes significantly to creating a culture of consumerism, so it is important for us as citizens to understand the reality underlying the myths sometimes perpetuated by advertising and media.

---

prereading questions

1. How are new forms of media forcing changes in entertainment industry practices?

2. Do advertising images succeed in encouraging people to buy products? Why or why not?

3. How have companies become more concerned with marketing an image than marketing a product?

4. Product placement is becoming pervasive in movies, television shows, and videogames. Is this increasing pervasiveness a problem? Why or why not?

---

web sites related to this chapter's topic

THE NADER PAGE
www.nader.org
Web page of consumer advocate Ralph Nader.

CENTER FOR MEDIA LITERACY
www.medialit.org
Web site for the Center for Media Literacy offering several links and resources.

CAMPAIGN FOR A COMMERCIAL-FREE CHILDHOOD
www.commercialfreechildhood.org
Organization dedicated to minimizing the effect of commercials on children.

---

web site essay

prereading question } **What does it mean to "sell the sizzle and not the steak"?**

The End of Consumer Culture?

Should designers work toward the end of aspirational consumer culture? Can the design industry, broadly defined, reposition and reinvent itself to provide value and sustainability while still creating desire?

Hugh Graham

Hugh Graham published this essay on his company's Web site on January 30, 2008. Hugh Graham Creative "provides design strategy, research, and storytelling for corporations, nonprofits, and community organizations" (Hugh Graham Creative Web site).

When I was at Northwestern, I took some classes from a professor of philosophy, David Michael Levin, who once asked us whether having a choice was important in our lives. Specifically, he was asking about the difference between choice and the appearance of choice. For instance, he asked, is it important to be able to choose between Crest and Colgate?

I think of Professor Levin from time to time, and often when I'm walking down the personal care aisle of the supermarket. Looking at all the variations of toothpaste and related products (Whitestrips, anyone?), I wonder whether it's possible that our society in general may have gone just a bit too far, and that the designers and product managers and marketers are spending too much of their creative resources on selling products with limited value and without any real differentiation.

I'm not arguing that there isn't valuable product innovation going on, but I tend to doubt the big change involves one of the 50 swirly paste/gel combos on every American supermarket aisle. Think of the improved efficiencies we'll see just as soon as all the rest of you realize that Tom's of Maine Peppermint is plenty good enough for everyone.

Innovation, or Variation?

Okay, that's probably not going to be happening any time soon. And if there were only one kind of toothpaste, I'd likely never have gotten the chance to try out Tom's products, or the cool toothpaste that combines gel, paste, and some crazy sparkly bits. I do love the crazy sparkly bits.

I'm not recommending some sort of centralized control of the means of production; it wouldn't work anyhow, not in the fast-moving consumer goods market, and certainly not in the broader markets. But there's still something decadent and even unethical about the way we sell the aspirational in consumer goods.

Of course, if people didn't want it, we wouldn't sell it, and the invisible hand of the market will ultimately level everything out, right? Well, maybe.

The toothpaste reference is pretty trivial, but it points to a bigger question about designer culture. Designer culture is still about the aspirational, and it's well established in mainstream markets.

Rob Horning wrote an article on *PopMatters* called "The Design Imperative." In it, he considers both the historical underpinnings and the current nature of our consumer culture. Historically,

> the consumer revolution depended on the sudden availability of things, which allowed ordinary people to buy ready-made objects that once were inherited or self-produced.

And in our current world,

> We are consigned to communicating through design, but it's an impoverished language that can only say one thing: "That's cool." Design ceases to serve our needs, and the superficial qualities of useful things end up cannibalizing their functionality.

The problem ultimately is that all this consumption fills some sort of void in our lives, at least temporarily. And by feeding the void in our lives, designers are providing the stimulus that keeps the modern economy moving.

It's the Economy, Stupid

According to the news reports I've been reading, the economy of the United States has a pretty good chance of heading into a recession for most if not all of 2008. One of the primary causes, resulting in part from the rocking of the financial markets due to sub-prime lending, is decreased consumer spending. Consumer spending, which accounts for two thirds of economic activity, weakened in the month of December.

But for those of us who would like to see a decrease in consumption, is this necessarily bad news?

After the terrorist attacks in 2001, I remember being slightly horrified by Bush the 43rd admonishing the people of America to "go shopping" to fight back against terrorism. Of course, there was an important idea in there somewhere, that we shouldn't allow our lives to be controlled by a few fundamentalist wackos. But I found it hard to believe that a trip to Wal-mart was the best way to fight back against Osama bin Laden. It's a long way from the Victory Gardens our grandparents planted to help win World War II.

I was thinking about this when I came across an excellent article by Madeleine Bunting, published in the *Guardian*, called "Eat, drink and be miserable: The true cost of our addiction to shopping."

As Ms. Bunting points out:

We have a political system built on economic growth as measured by gross domestic product, and that is driven by ever-rising consumer spending. Economic growth is needed to service public debt and pay for the welfare state. If people stopped shopping, the economy would ultimately collapse. No wonder, then, that one of the politicians' tasks after a terrorist outrage is to reassure the public and urge them to keep shopping (as both George Bush and Ken Livingstone did). Advertising and marketing, huge sectors of the economy, are entirely devoted to ensuring that we keep shopping and that our children follow in our footsteps.

The question that I have been wrestling with regarding this question is how we can both decrease our rampant disposable consumerism while still continuing to have a reasonably robust economy. How am I supposed to continue pushing the economy forward while cutting my carbon footprint by 60 percent?

Happy Now?

In her article, Ms. Bunting discusses the work of Tim Kasser, an American psychologist concerned with materialism, values, and goals. Kasser has created an aspirational index which helps to distinguish between two types of goals:

Extrinsic, materialistic goals (e.g., financial success, image, popularity) are those focused on attaining rewards and praise, and are usually means to some other end. Intrinsic goals (e.g., personal growth, affiliation, community feeling) are, in contrast, more focused on pursuits that are supportive of intrinsic need satisfaction.

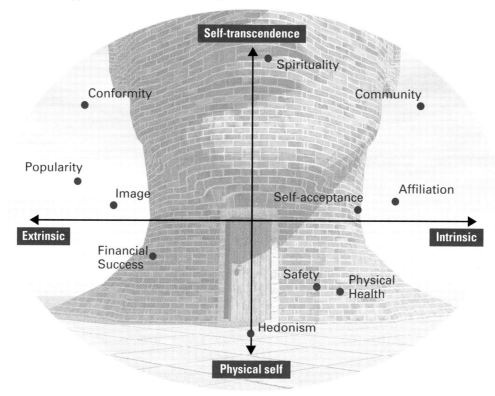

According to Kasser, he would like to "help individuals and society move away from materialism and consumerism and towards more intrinsically satisfying pursuits that promote personal well-being, social justice, and ecological sustainability."

Personally, I'm not quite sure where I fall on the Aspirational Index.

I try to be mindful of what I'm consuming, where it comes from, and where it ends up. Still, I have a couple pair of shoes that I bought on a whim, and a jacket I didn't wear more than a few times. I don't get a whole lot of joy out of going shopping, whether for clothes or anything else, but I'm sure there are many, many ways I could do more with less.

It occurs to me that there needs to be a new paradigm of consumption, one that will work for business, community, and environment. I don't know what form this new paradigm will take, but I believe it has something to do with learning to appreciate the real value of things and their place in our world.

Designers have an opportunity to engage in this paradigm shift. Part of the story lies in creating products that have intrinsic and lasting value, products that I like to call artisanal. And part of the story lies in better communicating the value of the artisanal. I believe that designers have an ethical duty to work toward the end of disposable culture. Of course, this isn't going to happen overnight, and it's not going to happen in vacuum. But it is going to happen, whether we choose to be a part of the process or not. Better to engage the future rather than have it thrust upon us.

Toward a Moral Equivalent of Consumerism

The subtitle of Madeleine Bunting's *Guardian* article is "Today it seems politically unpalatable, but soon the state will have to turn to rationing to halt hyper-frantic consumerism." She speaks to the inevitability of changing our behaviors, and believes that the change will not happen without intervention from the state. Whether it is rationing, or taxes, or other means, the change, ultimately, will have to come.

But change is never easy or simple. In *The Moral Equivalent of War* (1906), William James explained the difficulties of advocating pacifism:

> So far, war has been the only force that can discipline a whole community, and until an equivalent discipline is organized, I believe that war must have its way.

War, like consumer capitalism, offers a way of getting people motivated and organized. Adam Smith, in *The Wealth of Nations,* argues that "It is not from the benevolence of the butcher, the brewer, or the baker, that we expect our dinner, but from their regard to their own self-interest." Self-interest is a strong motivational force, and unless and until there is a "Moral Equivalent of Consumerism" it may well be impossible to create an alternative solution.

It will likely be necessary for government to engage in rationing or taxation to decrease our impact on the environment. But there is also an important component that should not be ignored, and one that can and should be engaged in by the designers of our products and communications. A new aspiration, perhaps focused on the intrinsic and self-transcendent as Tim Kasser explains. An aspiration toward what is valuable, an experience where less is truly more.

In *The Moral Equivalent of War,* James argues that:

> Great indeed is Fear; but it is not, as our military enthusiasts believe and try to make us believe, the only stimulus known for awakening the higher ranges of men's spiritual energy.

In seeking a moral equivalent of consumerism it is our challenge to use our capabilities to awaken the higher ranges of each person's spiritual energy, and to produce objects and communications that are filled with value.

Should designers work toward the end of aspirational consumer culture? Ultimately, I'm not sure there is any other choice.

http://hughgrahamcreative.com/2008/01/30/toward-a-moral-equivalent-of-consumerism

QUESTIONS FOR READING

1. What is "aspirational consumer culture"?
2. To what "bigger question" does the article's toothpaste example point?
3. What two types of goals does Tim Kasser's aspirational index distinguish between?

QUESTIONS FOR REASONING AND ANALYSIS

1. What is Graham's thesis? Is it explicit or implicit? If explicit, what sentence reflects his thesis? If implicit, how would you summarize his thesis in your own words?
2. Why does Graham include Kasser's aspirational index in his essay? What point does it support? Does providing the visual depiction of Kasser's index help support Graham's argument? Why or why not?
3. How does Graham define "artisanal" products? What problem will artisanal products address?
4. Who do you think is the primary audience for Graham's essay? Why does this group represent his primary audience?

QUESTIONS FOR REFLECTING AND WRITING

1. How do you view the impact of disposable consumerism or disposable culture? Do you agree with Graham regarding disposable consumerism? Why or why not?
2. With regard to your own buying habits, why do you purchase one product over another? Do you usually purchase a product based on its intrinsic value, the way Graham explains it, or because you prefer the color of the packaging, for instance?
3. How would you respond to Graham? Do you agree or disagree? Why or why not?

Turning Goys into Girls

Michelle Cottle

A graduate of Vanderbilt University, Michelle Cottle was an editor for two years at the *Washington Monthly* prior to becoming a senior editor, in 1999, at *The New Republic*. She is also a panelist on the PBS political talk show *Tucker Carlson Unfiltered*. Her essay on men's magazines was published in the May 1998 issue of the *Washington Monthly*.

I love *Men's Health* magazine. There, I'm out of the closet, and I'm not ashamed. Sure, I know what some of you are thinking: What self-respecting 90s women could embrace a publication that runs such enlightened articles as "Turn Your Good Girl Bad" and "How to Wake Up Next to a One-Night Stand"? Or maybe you'll smile and wink knowingly: What red-blooded hetero chick wouldn't love all those glossy photo spreads of buff young beefcake in various states of undress, ripped abs and glutes flexed so tightly you could bounce a check on them? Either way you've got the wrong idea. My affection for *Men's Health* is driven by pure gender politics—by the realization that this magazine, and a handful of others like it, are leveling the playing field in a way that *Ms.* can only dream of. With page after page of bulging biceps and Gillette jaws, robust hairlines and silken skin, *Men's Health* is peddling a standard of male beauty as unforgiving and unrealistic as the female version sold by those dewy-eyed pre-teen waifs draped across the covers of *Glamour* and *Elle*. And with a variety of helpful features on "Foods That Fight Fat," "Banish Your Potbelly," and "Save Your Hair (Before It's Too Late)," *Men's Health* is well on its way to making the male species as insane, insecure, and irrational about physical appearance as any Cosmo girl.

Don't you see, ladies? We've been going about this equality business all wrong. Instead of battling to get society fixated on something besides our breast size, we should have been fighting spandex with spandex. Bra burning was a nice gesture, but the greater justice is in convincing our male counterparts that the key to their happiness lies in a pair of made-for-him Super Shaper Briefs with the optional "fly front endowment pad" (as advertised in *Men's Journal*, $29.95 plus shipping and handling). Make the men as neurotic about the circumference of their waists and the whiteness of their smiles as the women, and at least the burden of vanity and self-loathing will be shared by all.

This is precisely what lads' mags like *Men's Health* are accomplishing. The rugged John-Wayne days when men scrubbed their faces with deodorant soap and viewed gray hair and wrinkles as a badge of honor are fading. Last year, international market analyst Euromonitor placed the U.S. men's toiletries market—hair color, skin moisturizer, tooth whiteners, etc.—at $3.5 billion. According to a survey conducted by DYG researchers for *Men's Health* in November 1996, approximately 20 percent of American men get manicures or pedicures, 18 percent use skin treatments such as masks or mud packs, and 10 percent enjoy professional facials. That same month, *Psychology Today* reported that a poll by Roper Starch Worldwide showed that "6 percent of men nationwide actually use such traditionally female products as bronzers and foundation to create the illusion of a youthful appearance."

What men are putting on their bodies, however, is nothing compared to what they're doing to their bodies: While in the 1980s only an estimated one in 10 plastic surgery patients were men, as of 1996, that ratio had shrunk to one in five. The American Academy of Cosmetic Surgery estimates that nationwide more than 690,000 men had cosmetic procedures performed in 1996, the most recent year for which figures are available. And we're not just talking "hair restoration" here, though such procedures do command the lion's share of the male market. We're also seeing an increasing number of men shelling out mucho dinero for face peels, liposuction, collagen injections, eyelid lifts, chin tucks, and of course, the real man's answer to breast implants: penile enlargements (now available to increase both length and diameter).

Granted, *Men's Health* and its journalistic cousins (*Men's Journal*, *Details*, *GQ*, etc.) cannot take all the credit for this breakthrough in gender parity. The fashion and glamour industries have perfected the art of creating consumer "needs," and with the women's market pretty much saturated, men have become the obvious target for the purveyors of everything from lip balm to lycra. Meanwhile, advances in medical science have made cosmetic surgery a quicker, cleaner option for busy executives (just as the tight fiscal leash of managed care is driving more and more doctors toward this cash-based specialty). Don't have several weeks to recover from a full-blown facelift? No problem. For a few hundred bucks you can get a microdermabrasion face peel on your lunch hour.

Then there are the underlying social factors. With women growing ever more financially independent, aspiring suitors are discovering that they must bring more to the table than a well-endowed wallet if they expect to win (and keep) the fair maiden. Nor should we overlook the increased market power of the gay population—in general a more image-conscious lot than straight guys. But perhaps most significant is the ongoing, ungraceful descent into middle age by legions of narcissistic baby boomers. Gone are the days when the elder statesmen of this demographic bulge could see themselves in the relatively youthful faces of those insipid yuppies on *Thirtysomething*. Increasingly, boomers are finding they have more in common with the parents of today's TV, movie, and sports stars. Everywhere they turn some upstart Gen Xer is flaunting his youthful vitality, threatening boomer dominance on both the social and professional fronts. (Don't think even Hollywood didn't shudder when the Oscar for best original screenplay this year went to a couple of guys barely old enough to shave.) With whippersnappers looking to steal everything from their jobs to their women, post-pubescent men have at long last discovered the terror of losing their springtime radiance.

Whatever combo of factors is feeding the frenzy of male vanity, magazines such as *Men's Health* provide the ideal meeting place for men's insecurities and marketers' greed. Like its more established female counterparts, *Men's Health* is an affordable, efficient delivery vehicle for the message that physical imperfection, age, and an underdeveloped fashion sense are potentially crippling disabilities. And as with women's mags, this cycle of insanity is self-perpetuating: The more men obsess about growing old or unattractive, the more marketers will exploit and expand that fear; the more marketers bombard men with messages about the need to be beautiful, the more they will obsess. Younger and younger men will be sucked into the vortex of self-doubt. Since 1990, *Men's Health* has seen its paid circulation rise from 250,000 to more than 1.5 million; the magazine estimates that half of its 5.3 million readers are under age 35 and 46 percent are married. And while most major magazines have suffered sluggish growth or even a decline in circulation in recent years, during the first half of 1997, *Men's Health* saw its paid circulation increase 14 percent over its 1996 figures. (Likewise, its smaller, more outdoorsy relative, Wenner Media's *Men's Journal*, enjoyed an even bigger jump of 26.5 percent.) At this rate, one day soon, that farcical TV commercial featuring men hanging out in bars, whining about having inherited their mothers' thighs will be a reality. Now that's progress.

Vanity, Thy Name Is Man

Everyone wants to be considered attractive and desirable. And most of us are aware that, no matter how guilty and shallow we feel about it, there are certain broad cultural norms that define attractive. Not surprisingly, both men's and women's magazines have argued that, far from playing on human insecurities, they are merely helping readers be all that they can be—a kind of training camp for the image impaired. In recent years, such publications have embraced the tenets of "evolutionary biology," which argue that, no matter how often we're told that beauty is only skin deep, men and women are hardwired to prefer the Jack Kennedys and Sharon Stones to the Rodney Dangerfields and Janet Renos. Continuation of the species demands that specimens with shiny coats, bright eyes, even features, and other visible signs of ruddy good health and fertility automatically kick-start our most basic instinct. Of course, the glamour mags' editors have yet to explain why, in evolutionary terms, we would ever desire adult women to stand 5 ft. 10 in. and weigh 100 pounds. Stories abound of women starving themselves to the point that their bodies shut down and they stop menstruating—hardly conducive to reproduction—yet Kate Moss remains the dish du jour and millions of Moss wannabes still struggle to subsist on a diet of Dexatrim and Perrier.

Similarly, despite its title, *Men's Health* is hawking far more than general fitness or a healthful lifestyle. For every half page of advice on how to cut your stress level, there are a dozen pages on how to build your biceps. For every update on the dangers of cholesterol, there are multiple warnings on the horrors of flabby abs. Now, without question, gorging on Cheetos and Budweiser while your rump takes root on the sofa is no way to treat your body if you plan on living past 50. But chugging protein drinks, agonizing over fat grams, and counting the minutes until your next Stairmaster session is equally unbalanced. The line between taking pride in one's physical appearance and being obsessed by it is a fine one—and one that disappeared for many women long ago.

Now with the lads' mags taking men in that direction as well, in many cases it's almost impossible to tell whether you're reading a copy of *Men's Health* or of *Mademoiselle*: "April 8. To commemorate Buddha's birthday, hit a Japanese restaurant. Stick to low-fat selections. Choose foods described as yakimono, which means grilled," advised the monthly "to do list" in the April *Men's Health*. (Why readers should go Japanese in honor of the most famous

continued

religious leader in India's history remains unclear.) The January/February list was equally thought provoking: "January 28. It's Chinese New Year, so make a resolution to custom-order your next takeout. Ask that they substitute wonton soup broth for oil. Try the soba noodles instead of plain noodles. They're richer in nutrients and contain much less fat." The issue also featured a "Total Body Workout Poster" and one of those handy little "substitution" charts (loathed by women everywhere), showing men how to slash their calorie intake by making a few minor dietary substitutions: mustard for mayo, popcorn for peanuts, seltzer water for soda, pretzels for potato chips. . . .

As in women's magazines, fast results with minimum inconvenience is a central theme. Among *Men's Health's* March highlights were a guide to "Bigger Biceps in 2 Weeks," and "20 Fast Fixes" for a bad diet; April offered "A Better Body in Half the Time," along with a colorful four-page spread on "50 Snacks That Won't Make You Fat." And you can forget carrot sticks—this think-thin eating guide celebrated the wonders of Reduced Fat Cheez-its, Munch 'Ems, Fiddle Faddle, Oreos, Teddy Grahams, Milky Ways, Bugles, Starburst Fruit Twists, and Klondike's Fat Free Big Bear Ice Cream Sandwiches. Better nutrition is not the primary issue. A better butt is. To this end, also found in the pages of *Men's Health*, is the occasional, tasteful ad for liposuction—just in case nature doesn't cooperate.

But a blueprint to rock-hard buns is only part of what makes *Men's Health* the preeminent "men's lifestyle" magazine. Nice teeth, nice skin, nice hair, and a red-hot wardrobe are now required to round out the ultimate alpha male package, and *Men's Health* is there to help on all fronts. In recent months it has run articles on how to select, among other items, the perfect necktie and belt, the hippest wallet, the chicest running gear, the best "hair-thickening" shampoo, and the cutest golfing apparel. It has also offered advice on how to retard baldness, how to keep your footwear looking sharp, how to achieve different "looks" with a patterned blazer, even how to keep your lips from chapping at the dentist's office: "[B]efore you start all that 'rinse and spit' business, apply some moisturizer to your face and some lip balm to your lips. Your face and lips won't have that stretched-out dry feeling. . . . Plus, you'll look positively radiant!"

While a desire to look good for their hygienists may be enough to spur some men to heed the magazine's advice (and keep 'em coming back for more), fear and insecurity about the alternatives are generally more effective motivators. For those who don't get with the *Men's Health* program, there must be the threat of ridicule. By far the least subtle example of this is the free subscriptions for "guys who need our help" periodically announced in the front section of the magazine. April's dubious honoree was actor Christopher Walken:

Chris, we love the way you've perfected that psycho persona. But now you're taking your role in "Things to Do in Denver When You're Dead" way too seriously with that ghostly pale face, the "where's the funeral?" black clothes, and a haircut that looks like the work of a hasty undertaker. . . . Dab on a little Murad Murasun Self-Tanner ($21). . . . For those creases in your face, try Ortho Dermatologicals' Renova, a prescription antiwrinkle cream that contains tretinoin, a form of vitamin A. Then, find a barber.

Or how about the March "winner," basketball coach Bobby Knight: "Bob, your trademark red sweater is just a billboard for your potbelly. A darker solid color would make you look slimmer. Also, see 'The Tale of Two Bellies' in our February 1998 issue, and try to drop a few pounds. Then the next time you throw a sideline tantrum, at least people won't say, 'Look at the crazy fat man.'"

Just as intense as the obsession with appearance that men's (and women's) magazines breed are the sexual neuroses they feed. And if one of the ostensible goals of women's mags is to help women drive men wild, what is the obvious corollary objective for men's magazines? To get guys laid—well and often. As if men needed any encouragement to fixate on the subject, *Men's Health* is chock full of helpful "how-tos" such as "Have Great Sex Every Day Until You Die" and "What I Learned from My Sex Coach," as well as more cursory explorations of why men with larger testicles have more sex ("Why Big Boys Don't Cry"), how to maintain orgasm intensity as you age ("Be one of the geysers"), and how to achieve stronger erections by eating certain foods ("Bean counters make better lovers"). And for those having trouble even getting to the starting line, last month's issue offered readers a chance to "Win free love lessons."

The High Price of Perfection

Having elevated men's physical and sexual insecurities to the level of grand paranoia, lads' mags can then get down to what really matters: moving merchandise. On the cover of *Men's Health* each month, in small type just above the magazine's title, appears the phrase "Tons of useful stuff." Thumbing through an issue or two, however, one quickly realizes that a more accurate description would read: "Tons of expensive stuff." They're all there: Ralph Lauren, Tommy Hilfiger, Paul Mitchell, Calvin Klein, Clinique, Armani, Versace, Burberrys, Nautica, Nike, Omega, Rogaine, The Better Sex Video Series. . . . The magazine even has those annoying little perfume strips guaranteed to make your nose run and to alienate everyone within a five-mile radius of you.

Masters of psychology, marketers wheel out their sexiest pitches and hottest male models to tempt/intimidate the readership of *Men's Health*. Not since the last casting call for *Baywatch* has a more impressive display of firm, tanned, young flesh appeared in one spot. And just like in women's magazines, the articles themselves are designed to sell stuff. All those helpful tips on choosing blazers, ties, and belts come complete with info on the who, where, and how much. The strategy is brilliant: Make men understand exactly how far short of the ideal they fall, and they too become vulnerable to the lure of high-priced underwear, cologne, running shoes, workout gear, hair dye, hair straightener, skin softener, body-fat monitors, suits, boots, energy bars, and sex aids. As Mark Jannot, the grooming and health editor for *Men's Journal*, told *Today* show host Matt Lauer in January, "This is a huge, booming market. I mean, the marketers have found a group of people that are ripe for the picking. Men are finally learning that aging is a disease." Considering how effectively *Men's Health* fosters this belief, it's hardly surprising that the magazine has seen its ad pages grow 510 percent since 1991 and has made it onto *Adweek*'s 10 Hottest Magazines list three of the last five years.

To make all this "girly" image obsession palatable to their audience, lads' mags employ all their creative energies to transform appearance issues into "a guy thing." *Men's Health* tries to cultivate a joking, macho tone throughout ("Eat Like Brando and Look Like Rambo" or "Is my tallywhacker shrinking?") and tosses in a handful of Y-chromosome teasers such as "How to Stay Out of Jail," "How to Clean Your Whole Apartment in One Hour or Less," and my personal favorite, "Let's Play Squash," an illustrated guide to identifying the bug-splat patterns on your windshield. Instead of a regular advice columnist, which would smack too much of chicks' magazines, *Men's Health* recently introduced "Jimmy the Bartender," a monthly column on "women, sex, and other stuff that screws up men's lives."

It appears that, no matter how much clarifying lotion and hair gel you're trying to sell them, men must never suspect that you think they share women's insecurities. If you want a man to buy wrinkle cream, marketers have learned, you better pitch it as part of a comfortingly macho shaving regime. Aramis, for example, assures men that its popular Lift Off! Moisture Formula with alpha hydroxy will help cut their shave time by one-third. "The biggest challenge for products started for women is how to transfer them to men," explained George Schaeffer, the president of OPI cosmetics, in the November issue of SoapCosmetics-Chemical Specialties. Schaeffer's Los Angeles based company is the maker of Matte Nail Envy, an unobtrusive nail polish that's proved a hit with men. And for the more adventuresome shopper, last year Hard Candy cosmetics introduced a line of men's nail enamel, called Candy Man, that targets guys with such studly colors as Gigolo (metallic black) and Testosterone (gun-metal silver).

On a larger scale, positioning a makeover or trip to the liposuction clinic as a smart career move seems to help men rationalize their image obsession. "Whatever a man's cosmetic shortcoming, it's apt to be a career liability," noted Alan Farnham in a September 1996 issue of *Fortune*. "The business world is prejudiced against the ugly." Or how about *Forbes*' sad attempt to differentiate between male and female vanity in its Dec. 1 piece on cosmetic surgery: "Plastic surgery is more of a cosmetic thing for women. They have a thing about aging. For men's it's an investment that pays a pretty good dividend." Whatever you say, guys.

The irony is rich and bittersweet. Gender equity is at last headed our way—not in the form of women being less obsessed with looking like Calvin Klein models, but of men becoming hysterical over the first signs of crows-feet. Gradually, guys are no longer pumping up and primping simply to get babes, but because they feel it's something everyone expects them to do. Women, after all, do not spend $400 on Dolce & Gabbana sandals to impress their boyfriends, most of whom don't know Dolce & Gabbana from Beavis & Butthead (yet). They buy them to impress other women—and because that's what society says they should want to do. Most guys haven't yet achieved this level of insanity, but with grown men catcalling the skin tone and wardrobe of other grown men (Christopher Walken, Bobby Knight) for a readership of still more grown men, can the gender's complete surrender to the vanity industry be far behind?

The ad for *Men's Health*'s Web site says it all: "Don't click here unless you want to look a decade younger . . . lose that beer belly . . . be a better lover . . . and more! *Men's Health* Online: The Internet Site For Regular Guys." Of course, between the magazine's covers there's not a "regular guy" to be found, save for the occasional snapshot of one of the publication's writers or editors—usually taken from a respectable distance. The moist young bucks in the Gap jeans ads and the electric-eyed Armani models have exactly as much in common with the average American man as Tyra Banks does with the average American woman. Which would be fine, if everyone seemed to understand this distinction. Until they do, however, I guess my consolation will have to be the image of thousands of once-proud men, having long scorned women's insecurities, lining up for their laser peels and trying to squeeze their middle-aged asses into a snug set of Super Shaper Briefs—with the optional fly front endowment pad, naturally.

QUESTIONS FOR READING

1. What is Cottle's subject?
2. What are men's magazines doing to men?
3. How are women achieving "gender equity," according to Cottle?
4. What anxieties do the men's magazines feed?
5. What are the magazines ultimately seeking to accomplish?

QUESTIONS FOR REASONING AND ANALYSIS

1. What is the author's claim?
2. What kind of evidence does Cottle provide? Is it convincing?
3. Examine the author's word choice. What "voice" does she create? What is the essay's tone?

QUESTIONS FOR REFLECTING AND WRITING

1. Does Cottle's analysis of men's magazines surprise you with new information and ideas? If so, what is most surprising to you? If you are not surprised, why not?
2. Has the author convinced you with her details and analysis of strategies in the men's magazines? Why or why not?
3. Does Cottle actually believe that women have achieved gender equity? Is she pleased with what the men's magazines are doing? Support your answer.
4. How do we resist the anxieties created by advertising—or the unnecessary purchases? What advice do you have?

advertisement

prereading question } **Does advertising succeed in encouraging people to buy products?**

Nissan Advertisement

1. What does this advertisement say to potential consumers of cars and SUVs? Does it effectively communicate its message? Why or why not?
2. What comparisons are being made in this advertisement? What is the overall effect of those comparisons?

3. How have the advertisers made use of the light and dark contrast in this advertisement? Why have they chosen to use light and dark in this way?
4. What other observations can you make about this advertisement?

QUESTIONS FOR REFLECTING AND WRITING

1. The advertisement promotes the Nissan Armada, a sport-utility vehicle or SUV. Is driving such a vehicle financially and environmentally responsible? Why or why not?
2. Do you think advertising succeeds in encouraging people to buy products? Why or why not?

3. Is it ethical for advertisers to encourage people to buy products they do not need? Should advertisers emphasize only positive aspects of a product without mentioning the negative? Why or why not?

---

magazine column

prereading questions } **Have you seen any of the Dove ads? If not, look for them and think about what you find. If yes, what was your initial reaction to the ads?**

Social Lubricant: How a Marketing Campaign Became the Catalyst for a Societal Debate

Rob Walker

Rob Walker is a contributing writer to *Inc.* magazine, the author of *Letters from New Orleans* (2005), and the author of a weekly column, "Consumed," in *The New York Times Magazine*. In his "Consumed" column, Walker seeks meaning in the consumer culture, that is, what it has to tell us about ourselves. The following column appeared September 4, 2005.

"Fat or Fabulous?" asked a line on the cover of a recent issue of *People* magazine, underneath a small photograph of some of the "Dove Girls." These are the young women appearing on billboards and other advertising on behalf of Dove Body Nourishers Intensive Firming Lotion and related products; they are not the ultra-thin fashion-model types common to advertising, and they are dressed only in underwear. They have become a minor sensation, sparking opinion articles in major publications (including a *New York Times* editorial) and showing up as guests on the *Today* show. This is a rare thing and pretty clearly a publicity bonanza for the Dove brand.

The debate over whether these images of women are positive (because they are more "real" than many marketing or media depictions of women) or negative (because they are all well within typical beauty norms, practically naked and pushing a product) has offered few surprises. But lurking behind it is the more intrigu-ing fact that it is a marketing campaign—not a political figure, or a major news organization, or even a film—that "opened a dialogue" (as one of the young women said to *People*). The buzziest pop artifact to dwell on the unthin female form in recent memory was the Showtime series *Fat Actress*; the Dove Girls ads seem almost intellectual in comparison.

Dove's marketing director, Philippe Harousseau, says the campaign has been in the works for a couple of years. It began with a "global study," commissioned by Dove (which is owned by Unilever) that posed questions about beauty to thousands of women in many countries. Among other things, the women tended to agree that "the media and advertising" were push-ing "unrealistic" beauty standards. It seems likely that if this same not-so-original conclusion were reached by a university or a think tank, the impact would have been minimal. But a giant corporation with a huge marketing

continued

budget is not so easily ignored. Early pieces of the campaign, which actually started last year, included images of older women and women with stretch marks and such. But it was challenging the only-thin-is-beautiful stereotype that "really hit a nerve," Harousseau says. "Women were ready to hear this."

Why they were ready to hear it from marketers is the puzzle. Maybe it is somehow inevitable that marketing, which caused much of the underlying anxiety in the first place, can offer up a point of view that blithely tries to resolve that anxiety. Moreover, as the entertainment side of the media fragments, marketing becomes the one form of communication that permeates everywhere—and is just as effective whether you've actually seen the campaign or you simply have an opinion about it based on what you've heard.

Finally, perhaps there is something here that's a backlash against not just the waifing of American media culture but also the self-improvement imperative: enough counting carbs, enough lectures from Dr. Phil, enough pressure to learn to dress well enough for the *Queer Eye* crew and achieve Martha-like aesthetic perfection in bathroom décor. The flip side of "Don't you care enough to do better?" could be "Stop telling me how to live."

Unilever will not get specific about the campaign's effect on sales, but ultimately Dove products aren't really the point. The Dove Girls could be selling pretty much anything, since what people are really responding to is the attitude they symbolize: an unapologetic self-confidence so appealing that we're basically willing to overlook the shaky intellectual consistency of linking it to Firming Lotions. In fact, maybe the Dove Girls' next move should be to show up in a Burger King ad, enjoying an Enormous Omelet Sandwich, daring anyone to criticize them for it.

Dove's survey is available on its *Campaign for Real Beauty* Web site, and among its other findings is that the top "attributes of making a woman beautiful" are happiness and kindness. In other words, they had nothing to do with physical appearance at all. But these encouraging insights would not have given Dove much of an opportunity to sell—and would have left everyone else very little to debate and nothing at all to buy.

QUESTIONS FOR READING

1. Who are the Dove Girls?
2. What is the debate over them?
3. What is the most "intriguing fact" about the Dove Girls, in Walker's view?
4. What reasons does Walker give for the positive response to the Dove ads?
5. What do the ads encourage us to overlook?

QUESTIONS FOR REASONING AND ANALYSIS

1. What is Walker's purpose in writing? What is his claim?
2. Analyze the author's list of causes; do they make sense to you?

QUESTIONS FOR REFLECTING AND WRITING

1. Do you agree with Dove's survey result that beauty is not based on physical traits? If you disagree, how do you account for this survey finding? And how do you explain all the money spent on beauty products?
2. What is your reaction to the Dove ads?

Why have companies made greater efforts in recent years to incorporate product placement in videogames as well as movies and popular television series?

Product Placement

The following image reflects product placement in an episode of the NBC television series *30 Rock*. However, Tina Fey, creator of *30 Rock*, has denied this scene was a deliberate attempt at product placement, saying that the show's producers "received no money from the McDonald's Corporation" (http://hollywoodinsider.ew.com/2009/02/tina-fey-respon.html).

QUESTIONS FOR REASONING AND ANALYSIS

1. Tina Fey, creator of *30 Rock*, claims that the show's producers were in no way attempting product placement in this scene. Does it matter whether the inclusion of McDonald's food products was intentional product placement? Why or why not?

2. What other factors, besides the mere appearance of McDonald's food products, contribute to product placement in this *30 Rock* scene?

QUESTIONS FOR REFLECTING AND WRITING

1. Can you think of other instances of product placement from popular films, television shows, or videogames? Why are these instances examples of product placement?

2. Do you think product placement attempts succeed in encouraging people to buy products? Why or why not?

3. Does product placement diminish the quality of movies and other media? In other words, do some movies, for example, simply become marketing tools for products? Why or why not?

prereading questions } How are new forms of media bringing about changes in music industry practices? How will new media continue to affect the way people purchase and consume music?

Why the Music Industry Hates *Guitar Hero*

Jeff Howe

This essay, by contributing editor Jeff Howe, appeared in *Wired* magazine on February 23, 2009. Mr. Howe is also the author of *Crowdsourcing: Why the Power of the Crowd Is Driving the Future of Business*, published in 2008.

Nobody expected the number-one-with-a-bullet rise of the music videogame—least of all the music industry. Armed with little more than crappy graphics, plastic guitars, and epic hooks, play-along titles like *Guitar Hero* and *Rock Band* have become an industry in their own right, raking in more than $2.3 billion over the past three years. Album sales fell 19 percent this past holiday season, but the thrill isn't gone—it just moved to a different platform.

The success of these games is good news for the music biz. They're breathing new life into old bands (Weezer, anyone?) and helping popularize new ones. They're even becoming a significant distribution outlet for new releases. So the record labels ought to be ecstatic, right? Nope. They're whining over licensing fees.

"The amount being paid to the music industry, even though [these] games are entirely dependent on the content we own and control, is far too small," Warner Music Group CEO Edgar Bronfman told analysts last summer. The money Warner receives for the use of its songs is "paltry," he said, and if the gamemakers don't pony up more cash, "we will not license to those games." In response, *Rock Band* publisher MTV Games is now boycotting Warner artists, according to a source close to the negotiations.

This is a fight no one can win. Putting the brakes on music gaming would hurt everyone in the ailing music industry. Instead of demanding greater profit participation, Warner should be angling for creative participation. Thirty years ago, Hollywood took a similar threat—the VCR—and turned it into a new source of revenue, building customer loyalty in the process. The music industry could use new games the same way—but its track record suggests that it won't.

How does this play out? Gamemakers could respond by using cover versions of songs from the Warner catalog, but Bronfman already has that move blocked. He also runs the giant music publisher Warner/Chappell, and he could deny the game companies access there, too. From Bronfman's perspective, the record labels got ripped off when MTV was sold in 1985 for $690 mil-

lion ($1.4 billion in today's dollars) on the strength of videos it received for free, and then ripped off again when Apple initially denied the labels control over pricing on iTunes. He won't get fooled again.

To be fair, Bronfman has a point. Game publishers generally sign low-cost synchronization licenses—as if the music were being used incidentally, in the background. Compare this to Electronic Arts' *Madden NFL* franchise, from which the football league collects some 30 percent of gross revenue, and you can begin to feel his pain.

But there's better money to be made by playing together. Music games are proven earners—Aerosmith has reportedly earned more from *Guitar Hero: Aerosmith* than from *any single album* in the band's history. The labels ought to push for more such titles and integrate them into their promotional strategies. They might not maximize profit on the licensing, but who cares? With more entries to come in the play-along genre, and networked hardware to play them on, the games themselves could even become an online music retail channel to rival iTunes. Or what about a game for turntable artists? Labels could provide the stem tracks for songs (in which each instrument's recording is isolated) and let players mix their own versions. Users could vote for their favorites through online services like Xbox Live, and Warner could sell the winning mixes back to customers using the very platform on which they were created. Call it Wii-Mix.

If the company wants a case study, it need look no further than Universal Music Group. Rather than cavil over licensing fees, Universal parent company Vivendi simply bought *Guitar Hero's* publisher, Activision. Look, the labels know that recorded music is in irreversible decline. Warner has actually led the industry with a policy of signing bands to so-called 360 deals, in which artists give the label a cut of everything they sell, be it ringtones, merchandise, or concert tickets. On the strength of such foresight, Bronfman has styled himself as the man who will reinvent the music industry. But part of that reinvention must be an end to petty haggling over fees. Going PvP [player versus player] against gamemakers isn't going to solve the industry's problems. At this point, Bronfman still seems intent on dragging his business kicking and screaming back to the 20th century.

www.wired.com/culture/culturereviews/
magazine/17–03/st_essay

QUESTIONS FOR READING

1. What are record labels "whining over," according to Howe?
2. How should record labels, like Warner, use music videogames to their advantage?
3. What does Howe suggest record labels should do to offset declining revenues?

QUESTIONS FOR REASONING AND ANALYSIS

1. How does Howe organize his article like a problem-solution essay? What is the problem as he defines it? What is Howe's solution?
2. The photograph preceding the essay shows someone holding a deflated electric guitar. What does this image suggest? Why do you think the *Wired* editors chose this image to introduce Howe's piece?
3. Howe suggests "Wii-Mix" as one possible answer to the music industry's declining revenues. What is "Wii-Mix"? Do you agree that "Wii-Mix" represents a plausible solution for the music industry? Why or why not?
4. Howe's last sentence suggests Bronfman, the Warner Music Group CEO, refuses to adapt to a changing business environment. How do you think Howe conceives of doing business in the twenty-first century?

QUESTIONS FOR REFLECTING AND WRITING

1. What does the future hold for music consumers? Will the sale of CDs, for example, eventually become a thing of the past? Why or why not?
2. Do you think record labels are entitled to more money from companies using music tracks in other media (such as music videogames)? Why or why not?
3. Have you considered another compromise solution different from "Wii-Mix"? If so, what is your solution?

the challenges of living in a high-tech, multimedia world

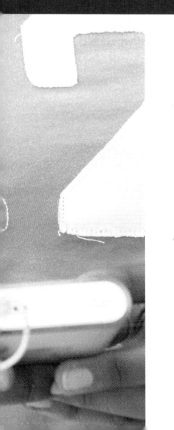

chapter 15

Every day, we find ourselves increasingly immersed in a media environment and constantly engaged in use of new and innovative communication and digital technologies. Media is literally everywhere; we cannot even walk into some fast-food restaurants without encountering a digital television mounted to the wall of a dining area. News updates from CNN, MSNBC, or Fox News resonate while restaurant patrons feast on hamburgers and french fries. We have become so accustomed to our high-tech and multimedia world that some of us may find it difficult to remember a time when media was somewhat less pervasive. Some authors of this chapter's selections, however, are less than optimistic concerning the ubiquitousness of technology, media, and information. They cite potential problems with diminished social relations and threats to privacy that people should take very seriously.

prereading questions

1. Even though we are all now a part of the global economy, that seems an abstract concept to many people. How does technology affect your life in more immediate ways? Try listing the ways that technology affects our daily lives.

2. Do you miss any of the "older" ways of doing things? If so, what? If not, why not?

3. How do you envision technology and media affecting your life in the next 20 years? In the next 50 years? Will the effects be good or bad—or both? Why?

4. Are you concerned about your privacy online or as a member of a social networking site like Facebook? Why or why not?

web sites related to this chapter's topic

WIRED NEWS
www.wired.com
Site for *Wired* magazine as well as links to other technology and media resources.

SOCIAL NETWORKING SITES: SAFETY TIPS FOR TWEENS AND TEENS
www.ftc.gov/bcp/edu/pubs/consumer/tech/tec14.shtm
Federal Trade Commission's "Facts for Consumers" site providing information concerning online safety.

PRESIDENT OBAMA'S AGENDA FOR TECHNOLOGY
www.whitehouse.gov/agenda/technology
White House site explaining the Obama Administration's agenda for technology.

"Accident" Advertisement from Apple (Mac vs. PC)

To view the commercial go to: http://link.brightcove.com/services/player/
bcpid1315793544?bctid=1317865847

QUESTIONS FOR REASONING AND ANALYSIS

1. In your own words, how would you explain the claim of this advertisement?
2. What are the advertisers communicating by presenting "PC" sitting in a wheelchair with casts on his arms and legs?

3. Besides depicting "PC" with injuries, what other observations can you make with regard to the appearance of "PC" and "Mac"? What do you think these observations mean to an audience? What are the advertisers attempting to communicate by presenting the two characters in certain ways?

QUESTIONS FOR REFLECTING AND WRITING

1. In a short essay, convince an audience of potential computer buyers that they should purchase a Mac rather than a PC or vice versa. What reasons support one computer over another as the best choice?

2. The advertising campaign depicting two characters representing Mac and PC has apparently been very successful for the Apple Corporation. Why might these ads continue to receive a positive response from potential consumers?

prereading questions } Do you think that PowerPoint improves presentations? If so, why?
What objections to PowerPoint presentations might someone have?

PowerPoint: Killer App?

Ruth Marcus

Ruth Marcus is a member of *The Washington Post* editorial board, and she occasionally has a column on the op-ed page of the *Post*. The following column was published August 30, 2005.

Did PowerPoint make the space shuttle crash? Could it doom another mission? Preposterous as this may sound, the ubiquitous Microsoft "presentation software" has twice been singled out for special criticism by task forces reviewing the space shuttle disaster.

Perhaps I've sat through too many PowerPoint presentations lately, but I think the trouble with these critics is that they don't go far enough: The software may be as much of a mind-numbing menace to those of us who intend to remain earthbound as it is to astronauts.

PowerPoint's failings have been outlined most vividly by Yale political scientist Edward Tufte, a specialist in the visual display of information. In a 2003 *Wired* magazine article headlined "PowerPoint Is Evil" and a less dramatically titled pamphlet, "The Cognitive Style of PowerPoint," Tufte argued that the program encourages "faux-analytical" thinking that favors the slickly produced "sales pitch" over the sober exchange of information.

Exhibit A in Tufte's analysis is a PowerPoint slide presented to NASA senior managers in January 2003, while the space shuttle *Columbia* was in the air and the agency was weighing the risk posed by the tile damage on the shuttle wings. Key information was so buried and condensed in the rigid PowerPoint format as to be useless.

"It is easy to understand how a senior manager might read this PowerPoint slide and not realize that it addresses a life-threatening situation," the Columbia Accident Investigation Board concluded, citing Tufte's work. The board devoted a full page of its 2003 report to the issue, criticizing a space agency culture in which, it said, "the endemic use of PowerPoint" substituted for rigorous technical analysis.

But NASA—like the rest of corporate and bureaucratic America—seems powerless to resist PowerPoint. Just this month a minority report by the latest shuttle safety task force echoed the earlier concerns: Often, the group said, when it asked for data it ended up with PowerPoints—without supporting documentation.

These critiques are, pardon the phrase, on point, but I suspect that the insidious influence of PowerPoint goes beyond the way it frustrates scientific analysis. The deeper problem with the PowerPointing of America—the PowerPointing of the planet, actually—is that the program tends to flatten the most complex, subtle, even beautiful, ideas into tedious, bullet-pointed bureaucratese.

I experienced a particularly dreary example of this under a starry Hawaiian sky this year, listening to a talk on astronomy. It was the perfect moment for magical images of distant stars and newly discovered planets. Yet, instead of using technology to transport, the lecturer plodded point-by-point through cookie-cutter slides.

The soul-sapping essence of PowerPoint was captured perfectly in a spoof on the Gettysburg Address by computer whiz Peter Norvig of Google. It featured Abe Lincoln fumbling with his computer ("Just a second while I get this connection to work. Do I press this button here? Function-F7?") and collapsing his speech into six slides, complete with a bar chart depicting four score and seven years.

For example, slide 4:

Review of Key Objective & Critical Success Factors

- What makes nation unique
  - Conceived in liberty
  - Men are equal
- Shared vision
  - New birth of freedom
  - Gov't of/by/for the people

If NASA managers didn't recognize the safety problem, perhaps it's because they were dazed from having to endure too many presentations like this—the inevitable computer balkiness, the robotic recitation of bullet points, the truncated language of a marketing pitch. Hence the

New Yorker cartoon in which the devil, seated at his desk in Hell, interviews a potential assistant: "I need someone well versed in the art of torture—do you know PowerPoint?"

Like all forms of torture, though, PowerPoint degrades its practitioners as well as its victims. Yes, boring slides were plentiful in the pre-PowerPoint era—remember the overhead projector? Yes, it can help the intellectually inept organize their thoughts. But the seductive availability of PowerPoint and the built-in drive to reduce all subjects to a series of short-handed bullet points eliminates nuances and enables, even encourages, the absence of serious thinking. Really, why think at all when the auto-content wizard can do it for you?

The most disturbing development in the world of PowerPoint is its migration to the schools—like sex and drugs, at earlier and earlier ages. Now we have second-graders being tutored in PowerPoint. No matter that students who compose at the keyboard already spend more energy perfecting their fonts than polishing their sentences—PowerPoint dispenses with the need to write any sentences at all. Perhaps the politicians who are so worked up about the ill effects of violent video games should turn their attention to PowerPoint instead.

In the meantime, Tufte, who's now doing consulting work for NASA, has a modest proposal for its new administrator: Ban the use of PowerPoint. Sounds good to me. After all, you don't have to be a rocket scientist to see the perils of PowerPoint.

QUESTIONS FOR READING

1. What is Marcus's subject?
2. What is Tufte's objection to the slide used during a discussion of *Columbia*'s damaged tiles?
3. What is "seductive" about PowerPoint?
4. What, in the author's view, does PowerPoint allow people to avoid doing?

QUESTIONS FOR REASONING AND ANALYSIS

1. What is Marcus's claim; that is, what is the problem with PowerPoint?
2. Analyze her use of examples, considering their range and effectiveness. Do they provide good support for her claim?
3. Find examples of the author's clever use of language. How does her cleverness serve her purpose?

QUESTIONS FOR REFLECTING AND WRITING

1. Have you ever heard/read anyone objecting to PowerPoint—or is this a new idea for you? Does it make sense, on reflection?
2. On what assumption about the nature or role of language does this argument rest? What do you think Marcus means by the assertion that PowerPoint "flatten[s]" ideas?

Obama: "It is unacceptable that the United States ranks 15th in the world in broadband adoption"

Sam Diaz

Sam Diaz, a blogger, made this post to ZDNet on December 6, 2008.
http://blogs.zdnet.com/BTL/?p=11115

The 21st century Tech President said Saturday morning that the United States will launch new investments in its infrastructure—including a boost of broadband accessibility—as part of a larger strategy to revitalize the economy and create jobs. Specifically, President-elect Barack Obama said broadband connections need to be made widely available to schoolchildren and hospitals. Hospitals should be able to connect to each other via the Internet. He said:

> It is unacceptable that the United States ranks 15th in the world in broadband adoption. Here, in the country that invented the Internet, every child should have the chance to get online, and they'll get that chance when I'm president—because that's how we'll strengthen America's competitiveness in the world.

Bravo! It was just days ago that a coalition of technology and telecom companies, along with public interest and other groups, called on Washington to establish a National Broadband Strategy for 2009. It was also just days ago that the government declared that the United States has been in a recession since December 2007. According to a report by Agence France-Presse, 533,000 jobs in the United States were lost in November, sending the jobless rate to 6.7 percent, the highest since October 1993. The report notes that 2.7 million people have become jobless since the recession began.

"We will create millions of jobs by making the single largest new investment in our national infrastructure since the creation of the federal highway system in the 1950s," Obama said in his weekly radio and YouTube address. He said the plan, which includes making public buildings more energy-efficient and building new roads and bridges, will "save or create" 2.5 million jobs.

YouTube is a trademark of Google Inc.

QUESTIONS FOR REASONING AND ANALYSIS

1. President Obama states, "Here, in the country that invented the Internet, every child should have the chance to get online, and they'll get that chance when I'm president—because that's how we'll strengthen America's competitiveness in the world." What are the assumptions behind his arguments? In other words, what is the assumption, for example, underlying the contention that "every child should have the chance to get online"? How will enabling greater student access to the Internet strengthen America's competitiveness?

2. What is the advantage of increasing broadband in hospitals? Why should hospitals be able to connect to one another via the Internet?

3. Why do you think President Obama addressed the broadband issue, national infrastructure, and the ailing economy in the same Internet broadcast?

QUESTIONS FOR REFLECTING AND WRITING

1. Besides the potential benefits to education and the health care establishment, what are other advantages of greater broadband access? What other groups and organizations might benefit from greater investment in broadband access? Why might these groups and organizations benefit?

2. Does simply expanding broadband access result in greater global competitiveness? Why or why not? What other steps must the United States take to become more competitive in a global economy?

---

newspaper column

prereading questions } How do you spend your playing time—using electronic "toys" or exercising or playing sports or enjoying the outdoors? Do you think you have a good balance of activities in your life? Do you think most American young people do?

Out of the Woods: Today's Kids Can't See the Forest for the MTV

Joel Achenbach

For years the author of "Rough Draft," a *Washington Post* Sunday magazine column of humor and ideas, Joel Achenbach now writes for the paper's style section and maintains a blog, *achenblog,* on Washingtonpost.com. The following "Rough Draft" column was published May 29, 2005.

Because we need more to worry about, here comes a new ailment: Nature-Deficit Disorder. It's the subject of a new book, by Richard Louv, called *Last Child in the Woods,* which basically says our children stay indoors too much, are alienated from nature, and are going a little crazy.

Certainly every parent today has had the experience of begging a child to go outside. The child always asks, "And do what?" And we always say, "Climb a tree!" From the way we talk about it, all we did as children was climb trees, build treehouses and swing on vines. We are arboreal. But these days, when you ask a child to climb a tree, there's a pause while the child tries to figure out a tactful way to point out that people don't do that anymore. It's like you've asked the kid to churn butter or boil up a vat of lye.

At some point you'll deliver the entire canned speech how, as a child, you were always building forts, exploring forest trails, roasting squirrels over a fire, and so on, the classic Huck Finn sort of existence, and the only thing you'll forget to mention is that you were nearly fatally bored.

Face it, we had no choice but to play in the woods, because civilization hadn't yet invented Nintendo. Kids today don't know the crippling intensity of stupefaction that afflicted young people before the coming of personal computers and MTV. The boredom was like the ocean, and we were all at the bottom, our entire corpuscular beings compressed to 1/100th the normal size. Those "lazy summer days" were lazy for the reason that our blood had stopped circulating altogether.

continued

During summer we had nothing to do all day other than eat Fritos and watch that zany Richard Dawson host *Family Feud.* Or maybe it was Gene Rayburn over on *Match Game.* Our parents' generation survived the Great Depression and World War II, but we survived *Love, American Style.* Back then you got three channels, and a fourth if you could pull in that snowy station on the UHF band. The dreadfulness of the programs was commensurate with the absurd measures taken to improve their reception—tinfoil on the rabbit-ear antennae, someone climbing on the roof to adjust the aerial, turning the broken TV knob with pliers. (Younger readers: Whaaa??)

Our toys were also dysfunctional, particularly the electric race cars, which invariably fishtailed out of control and off the track entirely. We also had Hot Wheels cars that could roll down a plastic track, over and over, demonstrating for anyone who might doubt it the amazing force of gravity. We would try to filibuster away the boredom with Risk or Stratego or Clue, but eventually even that got dull, and we'd soon be digging up ant beds, trying to get red ants and black ants to fight one another.

I would use a metal curtain rod to whack a plastic ball around the yard as though I were Arnold Palmer. Once I decided to dig a swimming pool. It took me hours of hacking through the roots of pine trees and excavating the sandy Florida soil. Finally, I had my pool. I added water from a hose and got into it, and for a moment had a sense of the good life, of living it up, of being the kind of person who owns a pool.

And then I was just a boy up to his neck in muddy water.

My own kids are going to know what nature is about. I take them on long hikes. "Is this going to be a long hike?" they ask with trepidation. "A death march," I assure them. This may be one reason they associate nature with torture. Sometimes I ask them to help me work in the yard, and they always say, "Doing what?" and I say, "Maybe a little weeding," and they react as though I said we were going to skin and gut a rabbit. Children don't weed, which is just as well, because when you do persuade them to weed, they do it slower than the weeds actually grow.

They love the outdoors when it's sunny and the temperature is between 67 and 73 degrees and there are no bugs other than butterflies. They would prefer that there be less dirt, less earth, maybe Astro Turf instead of a lawn.

Ultimately it's our fault, as parents, that we've let our kids get so soft and indoorsy. We overprotect. We hint, constantly, that the outside world is dangerous, that it's the land of speeding cars, heatstroke, lightning, and creepy strangers. We've got to stop sending a message that says, in essence, "Go play outside, and watch out for serial killers."

Children need to get in touch with their inner animals. They need to go wild. As soon as I'm done typing this column, I'm ordering my critters outside to climb a tree. But, you know, not too high up.

From *The Washington Post*, May 29, 2005. p. W9.

QUESTIONS FOR READING

1. What is Achenbach's subject?
2. What is the author's view of childhood activities from the past?
3. What does he want his children to experience?
4. What anxieties are faced by today's parents?

QUESTIONS FOR REASONING AND ANALYSIS

1. What is the author's claim? Does he agree with Richard Louv that children are alienated from nature? How do you know?
2. Why is it perhaps difficult to know what Achenbach's position is? Note all points in the essay at which Achenbach seems to shift perspectives. Why does he do this? What does it accomplish?
3. What elements of humor are most amusing? Why?

QUESTIONS FOR REFLECTING AND WRITING

1. How do we get more children to love the outdoors and sports activities? What advice do you have for parents?
2. What are the advantages of activities in the outdoors? What are the disadvantages of playing electronic games and watching TV?

prereading questions } Do you frequently "plug in" to a Walkman or iPod? If so, do you think that you may be missing something?

Society Is Dead: We Have Retreated into the iWorld

Andrew Sullivan

A native of England with a doctorate in political science from Harvard, Andrew Sullivan is editor of *Andrewsullivan.com,* an online source of commentary on current issues; a *Time* magazine essayist; and a columnist for the *Sunday Times* of London. He also lectures widely and appears frequently on both radio and television programs. The following appeared on *TimesOnline* on February 20, 2005.

I was visiting New York last week and noticed something I'd never thought I'd say about the city. Yes, nightlife is pretty much dead (and I'm in no way the first to notice that). But daylife—that insane mishmash of yells, chatter, clatter, hustle and chutzpah that makes New York the urban equivalent of methamphetamine—was also a little different. It was quieter.

Manhattan's downtown is now a Disney-like string of malls, riverside parks and pretty upper-middle-class villages. But there was something else. And as I looked across the throngs on the pavements, I began to see why.

There were little white wires hanging down from their ears, or tucked into pockets, purses or jackets. The eyes were a little vacant. Each was in his or her own musical world, walking to their soundtrack, stars in their own music video, almost oblivious to the world around them. These are the iPod people.

Even without the white wires you can tell who they are. They walk down the street in their own MP3 cocoon, bumping into others, deaf to small social cues, shutting out anyone not in their bubble.

Every now and again some start unconsciously emitting strange tuneless squawks, like a badly tuned radio, and their fingers snap or their arms twitch to some strange soundless rhythm. When others say "Excuse me" there's no response. "Hi," ditto. It's strange to be among so many people and hear so little. Except that each one is hearing so much.

Yes, I might as well own up. I'm one of them. I witnessed the glazed New York looks through my own glazed pupils, my white wires peeping out of my ears. I joined the cult a few years ago: the sect of the little white box worshippers.

Every now and again I go to church—those huge, luminous Apple stores, pews in the rear, the clerics in their monastic uniforms all bustling around or sitting behind the "Genius Bars," like priests waiting to hear confessions.

Others began, as I did, with a Walkman—and then a kind of clunkier MP3 player. But the sleekness of the iPod won me over. Unlike other models it gave me my entire music collection to rearrange as I saw fit—on the fly, in my pocket.

What was once an occasional musical diversion became a compulsive obsession. Now I have my iTunes in my iMac for my iPod in my iWorld. It's Narcissus heaven: we've finally put the "i" into Me.

And, like all addictive cults, it's spreading. There are now 22 million iPod owners in the United States and Apple is becoming a mass-market company for the first time.

Walk through any airport in the United States these days and you will see person after person gliding through the social ether as if on autopilot. Get on a subway and you're surrounded by a bunch of Stepford commuters staring into mid-space as if anesthetized by technology. Don't ask, don't tell, don't overhear, don't observe. Just tune in and tune out.

It wouldn't be so worrying if it weren't part of something even bigger. Americans are beginning to narrow their lives.

You get your news from your favorite blogs, the ones that won't challenge your view of the world. You tune into a satellite radio service that also aims directly at a small market—for new age fanatics, liberal talk, or Christian rock. Television is all cable. Culture is all subculture. Your cell phones can receive e-mail feeds of your favorite blogger's latest thoughts—seconds after he has posted them—or get sports scores for your team or stock quotes of your portfolio.

Technology has given us a universe entirely for ourselves—where the serendipity of meeting a new stranger, hearing a piece of music we would never choose for ourselves or an opinion that might force us to change our mind about something are all effectively banished.

continued

Atomization by little white boxes and cell phones. Society without the social. Others who are chosen—not met at random. Human beings have never lived like this before. Yes, we have always had homes, retreats, or places where we went to relax, unwind, or shut out the world. But we didn't walk around the world like hermit crabs with our isolation surgically attached.

Music was once the preserve of the living room or the concert hall. It was sometimes solitary but it was primarily a shared experience, something that brought people together, gave them the comfort of knowing that others too understood the pleasure of a Brahms symphony or that Beatles album.

But music is as atomized now as living is. And it's secret. That bloke next to you on the bus could be listening to heavy metal or a Gregorian chant. You'll never know. And so, bit by bit, you'll never really know him. And by his white wires, he is indicating he doesn't really want to know you.

What do we get from this? The awareness of more music, more often. The chance to slip away for a while from everydayness, to give our lives its own soundtrack, to still the monotony of the commute, to listen more closely and carefully to music that can lift you up and keep you going.

We become masters of our own interests, more connected to people like us over the Internet, more instantly in touch with anything we want, need, or think we want and think we need. Ever tried a Stairmaster in silence? But what are we missing? That hilarious shard of an overheard conversation that stays with you all day; the child whose chatter on the pavement takes you back to your early memories; birdsong; weather; accents; the laughter of others. And those thoughts that come not by filling your head with selected diversion, but by allowing your mind to wander aimlessly through the regular background noise of human and mechanical life.

External stimulation can crowd out the interior mind. Even the boredom that we flee has its uses. We are forced to find our own means to overcome it.

And so we enrich our life from within, rather than from white wires. It's hard to give up, though, isn't it?

Not so long ago I was on a trip and realized I had left my iPod behind. Panic. But then something else. I noticed the rhythms of others again, the sound of the airplane, the opinions of the taxi driver, the small social cues that had been obscured before. I noticed how others related to each other. And I felt just a little bit connected again and a little more aware.

Try it. There's a world out there. And it has a soundtrack all its own.

© Andrew Sullivan/NI Syndication, February 20, 2005.

QUESTIONS FOR READING

1. What is the "addictive cult" that Sullivan writes about?
2. How has the iPod changed New York City?
3. How has it changed people's lives?
4. How did humans experience music in the past? How has this changed?

QUESTIONS FOR REASONING AND ANALYSIS

1. What is Sullivan's claim? State it as a problem.
2. Why, according to the author, do people choose to be wired into a private musical world? What are they seeking? Is his argument convincing?
3. Sullivan develops his claim in large part by creating pictures and reflecting on causes and consequences. Analyze his writing strategies, considering examples, figurative language, sentence patterns, and word choice.
4. How would you describe the tone of the essay?

QUESTIONS FOR REFLECTING AND WRITING

1. On a recent trip to New York City, I saw many people walking with little white wires; I also saw many, often together, talking on cell phones. I even saw tourists on Fifth Avenue taking pictures of people walking and talking on their phones. Sullivan is troubled by such images. Are you? Why or why not?
2. Sullivan concludes by inviting readers to turn off their iPods and listen to the "soundtrack" of the world around them. Does he mean this literally? Does he mean it *only* literally? Should we take his advice? Why or why not?

Is MySpace Good for Society?
A Freakonomics Quorum

Stephen J. Dubner

Stephen J. Dubner is a journalist and author from New York City. He and Steven D. Levitt, an economics professor at the University of Chicago, published *Freakonomics: A Rogue Economist Explores the Hidden Side of Everything* in 2006. On February 15, 2008, the following post appeared on *The New York Times* Web site (http://freakonomics.blogs .nytimes.com/2008/02/15/is-myspace-good-for-society-a-freakonomics-quorum).

http://freakonomics.blogs.nytimes.com

Two little words—*social networking*—have become a giant buzzphrase over the past couple of years, what with the worldwide march of Facebook and headline-ready stories about Web-assisted suicides. So what's the net effect of social networking?

We gathered a group of wise people who spend their days thinking about this issue—**Martin Baily, danah boyd, Steve Chazin, Judith Donath, Nicole Ellison,** and **William Reader**—and asked them this question:

> Has social networking technology (blog-friendly phones, Facebook, Twitter, etc.) made us better or worse off as a society, either from an economic, psychological, or sociological perspective?

Here are their replies.

NICOLE ELLISON, assistant professor of Telecommunication, Information Studies and Media at Michigan State University:

I believe the benefits provided by social network sites such as Facebook have made us better off as a society and as individuals, and that, as they continue to be adopted by more diverse populations, we will see an increase in their utility. Anecdotal evidence of positive outcomes from these technologies—such as political activities organized via Facebook or jobs found through LinkedIn—is well-known, but now a growing corpus of academic research on social networks sites supports this view as well.

Over the last three years, our research team at Michigan State University has examined the use of Facebook by undergraduate students. Charles Steinfield, Cliff Lampe, and I have used surveys, interviews, and automated capture of the MSU Facebook site to try to understand how and why students use Facebook.

Our original motivation was to better understand why individuals would voluntarily use a site that, based on media reports, offered them only a way to disclose information they shouldn't disclose, collect hundreds of "friends" they didn't know, and waste time better spent studying. What we found surprised us. Our survey included questions designed to assess students' "social capital," a concept that describes the benefits individuals receive from their relationships with others. Undergraduates who used Facebook intensively had higher bridging social capital scores than those who didn't, and our longitudinal data show that Facebook use preceded these social capital gains.

Bridging social capital reflects the benefits we receive from our "weak ties"—people we don't know very well but who provide us with useful information and ideas. These students were using Facebook to increase the size of their social network, and therefore their access to more information and diverse perspectives. Our interview data confirmed these findings, with participants commenting on how the affordances of Facebook helped them maintain or strengthen relationships: they used the site to look up old high school acquaintances, to find out information about people in their classes or dorms that might be used to strike up a conversation, to get contact information for friends, and many other activities.

continued

These aren't the kinds of Facebook activities you are likely to read about in the media, which have encouraged widespread public concern about Facebook use by young people. Yes, there have been cases in which students have shown poor judgment regarding their profile disclosures. However, tools that enable us to engage in online self-presentation and connect with others will be increasingly part of our social and professional landscape, as social network sites continue to be embraced by businesses, nonprofits, civic groups, and political organizations that value the connections these tools support. IBM, for instance, has created an internal social network site, "Beehive," to encourage more collaboration and communication across teams. In India, "Babajob" harnesses social networking tools to pair employers with those who seek work. We will continue to see these trends grow as social networking features are employed for fun, profit, and social good.

Social technologies never have predictable and absolute positive or negative effects, which is why social scientists dread questions like these. In considering the effects of social network sites, it is clear that there are many challenges to work through—the increasing commercialization of this space, the need to construct strong privacy protections for users, and safety issues—but I believe the benefits we receive as a society provided by these tools far outweigh the risks.

WILLIAM READER, professor of psychology at Sheffield Hallam University and social networking site researcher:

From a psychological point of view, it is difficult to answer the question with any degree of certainty; the technology is simply too new and the research too equivocal. However, some (such as Barry Wellman) have suggested that social capital hasn't really declined, but has simply moved online. As our social networks are becoming increasingly more geographically fragmented, social network sites are a useful way for us to keep in touch and seek social contact with our friends.

Some doom-mongers have suggested that social networking technologies will eventually lead to a society in which we no longer engage in face-to-face contact with people. I don't see it. Face-to-face contact is, I believe, very important for the formation of intimate relationships (and most of us crave those). The reason for this is that friendships represent a considerable burden on our time, and our physical and emotional resources. Friends are, therefore, a big investment, and we want to be pretty sure that any friend is prepared to invest as much in us as we are in them. We therefore monitor potential friends for signals of their investment in us, and some of the best indicators of people's investment in us are those that we experience face to face.

Shared attitudes are important for friendship. We know that people like to associate with people who are like them, a predilection termed "homophily" (love of the same). The more similar we are to our friends, the less room there is for conflicts of interest. This is why I believe that social networking will never replace face-to-face communication in the formation of close friendships. Talk is cheap. Anyone can post "u r cool" on someone's "wall," or "poke" them on Facebook, but genuine smiles and laughs are much more reliable indicators of someone's suitability as a faithful friend.

To return to the notion of social capital, we know that people are increasingly "meeting" people on social network sites before they meet them face to face. As a result of this, when many students begin university, they find themselves with a group of ready-made acquaintances. Given people's preferences for people who are like them, it could be that friendship networks become increasingly homogeneous. Is this a bad thing? It might be if, by choosing potential friends via their Facebook profiles, it means that folk cut themselves off from serendipitous encounters with those who are superficially different from them, ethnically, socio-economically, and even in terms of musical taste.

So has social networking technology made us better or worse off? My view is neither utopian nor dystopian: social networking technologies are doubtless changing society. But like anything—apart from motherhood and apple pie—whether this is good or bad depends upon what kind of society you value.

STEVE CHAZIN, former Apple marketing director and current chief marketing officer at DimDim.com:

I believe social networking technology has changed our lives for the better, but at a cost. Social networking tools have made it nearly effortless for me to keep in touch with friends, family and colleagues. I can know what's on their minds (MySpace), who else they know (Facebook/LinkedIn), and even what they are doing at this very moment (Twitter). On the other hand, I'm not sure I need to know any of that.

Instant messaging, e-mail, and voice-over-Internet-protocol has made it possible for me to be in touch with more people than I will ever meet in person, yet each one of those contacts often requires me to return a call, respond to an e-mail, or reply to an IM. The Outlook "Out of Office" flag doesn't stop the mail from coming, it just postpones the response. And there will come a time when we'll hold all our meetings on the Web, have truly immersive face-to-face video conversations, and experience a fusion of our real and cyber worlds when Second Life becomes second nature. We're just not there yet.

While all humans need to feel connected to each other or to some cause, there are also times when we simply want to disconnect, and disconnecting is becoming increasingly hard thanks to social networking technology. As one who was bitten early by the Blackberry bug, I can attest that the pull of these wireless electronic leashes is often too strong to resist. Today, we experience a feeling of isolation when our Internet connections go down, revealing just how dependent we've become on the connective power of the Web.

I remember one day a few years ago when our office phones and Internet stopped working. No e-mail, no voicemail, no Facebook, no Skype, and no Twitter. People came out of their offices and talked. I enjoyed that day.

MARTIN BAILY, a senior fellow at the Brookings Institution and an adviser to the McKinsey Global Institute:

Powerful new technologies provide great benefits, but they also change the way we live, and not always in ways that everyone likes. An example is the spread of air conditioning, which makes us more comfortable, but those who grew up before its invention speak fondly of a time when everyone sat on the front porch and talked to their neighbors rather than going indoors to stay cool and watch TV. The declining cost of information processing and communication represents a powerful new technology, with social networking as the most recent service to be provided at modest cost. It can be expected to bring pluses and minuses.

New social networking services are counted in our measure of GDP, and will likely show up as an increase in productivity. Their effect is not large enough yet to move the needle by much, but it will be in the data, although in a rather strange way. Sites such as Facebook are free to users, with the "price" of using the service being the online ads viewed. This is, of course, the same way we "pay for" most television programming. This approach provides only a rough estimate of the economic value of the service.

But will social networking sites really improve the quality of people's lives? The pluses include easier contacts with friends, and increased chances to make new friends and create a community, as well as find romantic relationships. Even the advertising may be a plus, because it is targeted to the particular interests of the user.

The minuses are that all of this sharing can be dangerous, through gossip and potential abuse of the services. Examples include reported suicides linked to malicious gossip circulated on a social network. Some people become addicted to life on the computer screen, and withdraw from personal contact—it's a long way from people sitting on the porch talking to friends and neighbors.

Social networking sites are affecting the labor market as well, because recruiters evaluating young professionals applying for jobs are now hacking into applicants' profiles, and making hiring decisions based on profile photos in which applicants are drunk or inappropriately dressed.

I am by inclination a technology optimist, believing that the bad things will be filtered out over time and net benefits will emerge. But in the early stages of any new technology, the buyer must beware.

JUDITH DONATH, associate professor at the M.I.T. Media Lab:

The good: social networking technologies make it easier to keep up with a large circle of acquaintances and meet new people. They provide a venue for online socializing, as well as for coordinating in-person meetings.

The bad: they devalue the meaning of "friend." Our traditional notion of friendship embraces trust, support, compatible values, etc. On social network sites, a "friend" may simply be someone on whose link you have clicked.

The ugly: for teens, who can be viciously competitive, networking sites that feature a list of one's best friends and space for everyone to comment about you can be an unpleasant venue for social humiliation and bullying. These sites can make the emotional landmines of adolescence concrete and explicit.

The big picture: social networking technologies support and enable a new model of social life, in which people's social circles will consist of many more, but weaker, ties. Though we will continue to have some strong ties (i.e., family and close friends), demographic changes, such as frequent household moves and the replacement of friends and family with market services for tasks such as daycare, are diminishing the role of social ties in everyday life. Weak ties (e.g., casual acquaintances, colleagues) may not be reliable for long-term support; their strength instead is in providing a wide range of perspectives, information, and opportunities. As society becomes increasingly dynamic, with access to information playing a growing role, having many diverse connections will be key.

Social networking technologies provide people with a low cost (in terms of time and effort) way of making and keeping social connections, enabling a social scenario in which people have huge numbers of diverse, but not very close, acquaintances. Does this make us better as a society? Perhaps not—we can imagine this being a selfish and media-driven world in which everyone vies for attention and no one takes responsibility for one another. But perhaps it does—we can also imagine this being a world in which people are far more accepting of diverse ways and beliefs, one in which people are willing to embrace the new and different.

continued

DANAH BOYD, Ph.D. candidate at the School of Information, University of California–Berkeley, and fellow at the Harvard University Berkman Center for Internet and Society:

Social media (including social network sites, blog tools, mobile technologies, etc.) offer mechanisms by which people can communicate, share information, and hang out. As an ethnographer traipsing across the U.S., I have heard innumerable stories of how social media has been used to bring people together, support learning, and provide an outlet for creative expression.

These sites are tools. They can and have been used for both positive and negative purposes. For homosexual teens in rural America, they can be tools for self-realization in the battle against depression. Thanks to such tools, many teens have chosen not to take the path of suicide, knowing that there are others like them. For teens who are unable to see friends and family due to social and physical mobility restrictions, social media provides a venue to build and maintain always-on intimate communities. For parents whose kids have gone off to college, social media can provide a means by which the family can stay in meaningful contact through this period of change.

This is not to say that all of the products of social media are positive. We can all point to negative consequences: bullying, gossip mongering, increased procrastination, etc. Our news media loves to focus on these. Even the positive stories that do run often have a negative or sensationalist angle, such as those who used Twitter to track the California fires. Unfortunately, those who do not understand social media look to the news, see the negative coverage, and declare all social media evil.

It's easy to look at a lot of elements of today's society and cry foul. It's equally easy to look at the new technology that we don't understand and blame it as the cause for all social ills. It's a lot harder to accept that social media is mirroring and magnifying all of the good, bad, and ugly about today's society, shoving it right back in our faces in the hopes that we might face the underlying problems. Technology does not create bullying; it simply makes it more visible and much harder for adults to ignore.

QUESTIONS FOR READING

1. What is "social capital"?
2. How does Baily explain the effect of social networking sites (SNS) on the domestic economy?
3. What are some negative consequences of SNS the various experts describe?

QUESTIONS FOR REASONING AND ANALYSIS

1. Do you agree that certain "challenges" exist as SNS becomes more prevalent? If so, what are those challenges? Do you believe the experts are overstating or underestimating the challenges? Why or why not?
2. Reader argues that SNS will never replace face-to-face communication in the formation of close friendships. Do you agree? Why or why not?
3. What do you think Chazin is implying in the last paragraph of his response?
4. Overall, how would you describe the organization and structure of each expert's response to the question? In other words, how has he or she organized his or her argument? Does a pattern emerge from all the responses?

QUESTIONS FOR REFLECTING AND WRITING

1. How would you respond to the question "What is the net effect of social networking?"
2. In a broader sense, why do you think so many people have joined Facebook, MySpace, and Twitter? Aside from connecting and reconnecting with other people, why might a person feel compelled to join an SNS and create his or her own page?
3. Are you concerned that too much personal information is available on Facebook? Why or why not?

prereading question } Should people exercise more caution when revealing information about themselves on social networking sites?

On Facebook, Biggest Threat to Your Private Data May Be You

Jacquielynn Floyd

Jacquielynn Floyd has written for the *Dallas Morning News* since 1990. This article appeared in the February 21, 2009 edition of that newspaper.

Don't friend me! I mean it.

While we're talking about this, I don't want to be Twittered, blasted, poked or super-poked, either. Kindly refrain from telling me What You're Doing Right Now, and I'll return the favor. Don't confide that you have two spleens or that you threw up at your junior prom, and I won't burden you with my secret passion for the late Paul Henreid.

It's not that I don't like you. It's just that, if I want you to know that stuff, maybe it would be nicer to tell you in person over a glass of wine than to send out a buckshot bulletin to 200 people online.

Look, there's not a thing wrong with Facebook. But all this hysteria and hand-wringing over privacy could readily be sidestepped by not posting private information on the Internet.

The big alarm went off this week when alert bloggers noted a change in the micro-print "terms of service" agreement that goes with signing up for the ubiquitous social-network site. "Facebook *owns* you!" angry critics howled.

Opinions seem divided over whether the change in language actually constitutes a threat. Some saw a resurgence of the company's ill-fated "Beacon" experiment, when it devised the idea of essentially alerting everybody you know every time you buy something.

Others say it was nothing more than standard, self-protecting legal language. No matter: The bad-publicity deluge put Facebook's CEO (How old is that guy, anyway? Seventeen?) on the defensive, and the change was—for the moment—abandoned.

But people are surely fooling themselves if they depend on a company—any company—to guarantee privacy for information voluntarily posted in a place that, by definition, is extremely public.

Face this: You are your own front line of defense in maintaining your privacy. This extends to vetting personal information on the Internet. In the same way, it means exercising discretion over allowing people to take hilarious party pictures of you that might wind up being published as the Bong Hit Heard 'Round the World.

Sites like Facebook work from an oddly inverted social premise of starting with the whole of cyberspace and winnowing your way down, through a series of blocks and filters. Don't want that creepy guy from the mailroom to be your "friend"? You have to reject him. Don't want embarrassing pictures of you posted to your "wall"? Make sure you trust your friends.

Some people seem to plant the flag with a minimum of information: no picture, no bio, no recitation of favorite bands or (God help us) astrological sign. They bypass the rather juvenile, one-size-fits-all personality template the site provides.

But others "share" in an odd stream-of-consciousness broadcast about what they wore today, how they feel, what time they need to be at the dentist, and leave it to their friends to sift through the information for what's relevant. Their friends do the same to them—there's no boundary between what goes on inside and outside their skulls.

And that's what's really, deeply, seriously frightening.

What if, in our addiction to the temporary rush of joy that we all experience in talking about ourselves, we lose the ability to distinguish between our public and our private selves?

If we don't have enough sense not to "friend" somebody we haven't seen in 20 years and we didn't really know that well in the first place, what business do we have getting all huffy over Facebook's terms of service?

How can we expect somebody we don't know to safeguard our privacy if we think so little of it ourselves?

Sure, Facebook has an obligation to its users. But long before that, users have obligations to themselves.

QUESTIONS FOR READING

1. What is the answer to the "hand-wringing over privacy," according to Floyd?
2. What recent event had angered Facebook users?
3. What ability does Floyd think is dangerous to lose?

QUESTIONS FOR REASONING AND ANALYSIS

1. What is Floyd's thesis or major claim? Do you agree or disagree? Why or why not?
2. How does Floyd defend her argument? Through evidence? Through reasons and logic? Has she effectively substantiated her claims? Why or why not?
3. Should Facebook users exercise greater discretion with regard to how much they reveal about themselves? Why or why not? Do you agree with Floyd that losing the ability to distinguish between our public and private selves is a serious concern? Why or why not?

QUESTIONS FOR REFLECTING AND WRITING

1. What kinds of information have you divulged about yourself on MySpace, Facebook, or Twitter? Are you concerned that you have made too much information available—even to your friends and people you know well? Why or why not? If you have never joined one or more of these social networking sites (SNS), then why have you chosen not to do so?
2. What are the possible consequences of revealing too much about oneself on an SNS? Are you concerned about such consequences? Why or why not?
3. How can a person best determine what information to make publicly available and what information to keep private?

POLICE LINE DO NOT CROSS

violent media or violent society?

chapter 16

Many people see societal violence as a problem growing rapidly out of control in this country. In recent years, for example, we have seen a dramatic increase in incidents of school violence on both high school and college campuses. Several experts believe that violence as depicted in videogames and in popular television programs and movies encourages young people to commit heinous acts. They hold media responsible as the major cause for violence in society. Others, however, argue that Americans' love affair with guns fosters a violent culture. In this chapter, readings as well as visual rhetoric examples capture not only the debate over causes of societal violence but also the debate over solutions—solutions that may mean greater restrictions for some individuals and groups.

magazine essay

Supremacy Crimes

Gloria Steinem

Editor, writer, and lecturer, Gloria Steinem has been cited in World Almanac as one of the 25 most influential women in America. She is the cofounder of *Ms.* magazine and of the National Women's Political Caucus and is the author of a number of books and many articles. The following article appeared in the August/September 1999 issue of *Ms.*

You've seen the ocean of television coverage, you've read the headlines: "How to Spot a Troubled Kid," "Twisted Teens," "When Teens Fall Apart." After the slaughter in Colorado that inspired those phrases, dozens of copycat threats were reported in the same generalized way: "Junior high students charged with conspiracy to kill students and teachers" (in Texas); "Five honor students overheard planning a June graduation bombing" (in New York); "More than 100 minor threats reported statewide" (in Pennsylvania). In response, the White House held an emergency strategy session titled "Children, Violence, and Responsibility." Nonetheless, another attack was soon reported: "Youth With 2 Guns Shoots 6 at Georgia School."

I don't know about you, but I've been talking back to the television set, waiting for someone to tell us the obvious: it's not "youth," "our children," or "our teens." It's our sons—and "our" can usually be read as "white," "middle class," and "heterosexual."

We know that hate crimes, violent and otherwise, are overwhelmingly committed by white men who are apparently straight. The same is true for an even higher percentage of impersonal, resentment-driven, mass killings like those in Colorado; the sort committed for no economic or rational gain except the need to say, "I'm superior because I can kill." Think of Charles Starkweather, who reported feeling powerful and serene after murdering ten women and men in the 1950s; or the shooter who climbed the University of Texas Tower in 1966, raining down death to gain celebrity. Think of the engineering student at the University of Montreal who resented females' ability to study that subject, and so shot to death 14 women students in 1989, while saying, "I'm against feminism." Think of nearly all those who have killed impersonally in the workplace, the post office, McDonald's.

White males—usually intelligent, middle class, and heterosexual, or trying desperately to appear so—also account for virtually all the serial, sexually motivated, sadistic killings, those characterized by stalking, imprisoning, torturing, and "owning" victims in death. Think of Edmund Kemper, who began by killing animals, then murdered his grandparents, yet was released to sexually torture and dismember college students and other young women until he himself decided he "didn't want to kill all the coeds in the world." Or David Berkowitz, the Son of Sam, who murdered some women in order to feel in control of all women. Or consider Ted Bundy, the charming, snobbish young would-be lawyer who tortured and murdered as many as 40 women, usually beautiful students who were symbols of the economic class he longed to join. As for John Wayne Gacy, he was obsessed with maintaining the public mask of masculinity, and so hid his homosexuality by killing and burying men and boys with whom he had had sex.

These "senseless" killings begin to seem less mysterious when you consider that they were committed disproportionately by white, non-poor males, the group most likely to become hooked on the drug of superiority. It's a drug pushed by a male-dominant culture that presents dominance as a natural right; a racist hierarchy that falsely elevates whiteness; a materialist society that equates superiority with possessions; and a homophobic one that empowers only one form of sexuality.

As Elliott Leyton reports in *Hunting Humans: The Rise of the Modern Multiple Murderer*, these killers see their behavior as "an appropriate—even 'manly'—response to the frustrations and disappointments that are a normal part of life."

In other words, it's not their life experiences that are the problem, it's the impossible expectation of dominance to which they've become addicted.

This is not about blame. This is about causation. If anything, ending the massive cultural cover-up of supremacy crimes should make heroes out of boys and men who reject violence, especially those who reject the notion of superiority altogether. Even if one believes in a biogenetic component of male aggression, the very existence of gentle men proves that socialization can override it.

Nor is this about attributing such crimes to a single cause. Addiction to the drug of supremacy is not their only root, just the deepest and most ignored one. Additional reasons why this country has such a high rate of violence include the plentiful guns that make killing seem as unreal as a video game; male violence in the media that desensitized viewers in much the same way that combat killers are desensitized in training; affluence that allows maximum access to violence-as-entertainment; a national history of genocide and slavery; the romanticizing of frontier violence and organized crime; not to mention extremes of wealth and poverty and the illusion that both are deserved.

But it is truly remarkable, given the relative reasons for anger at injustice in this country, that white, non-poor men have a near-monopoly on multiple killings of strangers, whether serial and sadistic or mass and random. How can we ignore this obvious fact? Others may kill to improve their own condition, in self-defense, or for money or drugs; to eliminate enemies; to declare turf in drive-by shootings; even for a jacket or a pair of sneakers—but white males addicted to supremacy kill even when it worsens their condition or ends in suicide.

Men of color and females are capable of serial and mass killing, and commit just enough to prove it. Think of Colin Ferguson, the crazed black man on the Long Island Railroad, or Wayne Williams, the young black man in Atlanta who kidnapped and killed black boys, apparently to conceal his homosexuality. Think of Aileen Carol Wuornos, the white prostitute in Florida who killed abusive johns "in self-defense," or Waneta Hoyt, the upstate New York woman who strangled her five infant children between 1965 and 1971, disguising their cause of death as sudden infant death syndrome. Such crimes are rare enough to leave a haunting refrain of disbelief as evoked in Pat Parker's poem "jonestown": "Black folks do not/Black folks do not/Black folks do not commit suicide." And yet they did.

Nonetheless, the proportion of serial killings that are not committed by white males is about the same as the proportion of anorexics who are not female. Yet we discuss the gender, race, and class components of anorexia, but not the role of the same factors in producing epidemics among the powerful.

continued

The reasons are buried deep in the culture, so invisible that only by reversing our assumptions can we reveal them.

Suppose, for instance, that young black males—or any other men of color—had carried out the slaughter in Colorado. Would the media reports be so willing to describe the murderers as "our children"? Would there be so little discussion about the boys' race? Would experts be calling the motive a mystery, or condemning the high school cliques for making those young men feel like "outsiders"? Would there be the same empathy for parents who gave the murderers luxurious homes, expensive cars, even rescued them from brushes with the law? Would there be as much attention to generalized causes, such as the dangers of violent videogames and recipes for bombs on the Internet?

As for the victims, if racial identities had been reversed, would racism remain so little discussed? In fact, the killers themselves said they were targeting blacks and athletes. They used a racial epithet, shot a black male student in the head, and then laughed over the fact that they could see his brain. What if that had been reversed?

What if these two young murderers, who were called "fags" by some of the jocks at Columbine High School, actually had been gay? Would they have got the same sympathy for being gay-baited? What if they had been lovers? Would we hear as little about their sexuality as we now do, even though only their own homophobia could have given the word "fag" such power to humiliate them?

Take one more leap of the imagination: suppose these killings had been planned and executed by young women—of any race, sexuality, or class. Would the media still be so disinterested in the role played by gender-conditioning? Would journalists assume that female murderers had suffered from being shut out of access to power in high school, so much so that they were pushed beyond their limits? What if dozens, even hundreds of young women around the country had made imitative threats—as young men have done—expressing admiration for a well-planned massacre and promising to do the same? Would we be discussing their youth more than their gender, as is the case so far with these male killers?

I think we begin to see that our national self-examination is ignoring something fundamental, precisely because it's like the air we breathe: the white male factor, the middle-class and heterosexual one, and the promise of superiority it carries. Yet this denial is self-defeating—to say the least. We will never reduce the number of violent Americans, from bullies to killers, without challenging the assumptions on which masculinity is based: that males are superior to females, that they must find a place in a male hierarchy, and that the ability to dominate someone is so important that even a mere insult can justify lethal revenge. There are plenty of studies to support this view. As Dr. James Gilligan concluded in *Violence: Reflections on a National Epidemic*, "If humanity is to evolve beyond the propensity toward violence . . . then it can only do so by recognizing the extent to which the patriarchal code of honor and shame generates and obligates male violence."

I think the way out can only be found through a deeper reversal: just as we as a society have begun to raise our daughters more like our sons—more like whole people—we must begin to raise our sons more like our daughters—that is, to value empathy as well as hierarchy; to measure success by other people's welfare as well as their own.

But first, we have to admit and name the truth about supremacy crimes.

QUESTIONS FOR READING

1. What kinds of crimes is Steinem examining? What kinds of crimes is she excluding from her discussion?

2. What messages, according to Steinem, is our culture sending to white, nonpoor males?

3. How does Elliott Leyton explain these killers' behavior?

4. What is the primary reason we have not examined serial and random killings correctly, in the author's view? What is keeping us from seeing what we need to see?

5. What do we need to do to reduce "the number of violent Americans, from bullies to killers"?

QUESTIONS FOR REASONING AND ANALYSIS

1. What is Steinem's claim? Where does she state it?
2. What kind of argument is this; that is, what *type* of claim is the author presenting?
3. What is her primary type of evidence?
4. How does Steinem qualify her claim and thereby anticipate and answer counterarguments? In what paragraphs does she present qualifiers and counterarguments to possible rebuttals?
5. How does the author seek to get her readers to understand that we are not thinking soundly about the mass killings at Columbine High School? Is her strategy an effective one? Why or why not?

QUESTIONS FOR REFLECTING AND WRITING

1. Steinem concludes by writing that we must first "name the truth" about supremacy violence before we can begin to address the problem. Does this make sense to you? How can this be good advice for coping with most problems? Think of other kinds of problems that this approach might help solve.
2. Do you agree with Steinem's analysis of the causes of serial and random killings? If yes, how would you add to her argument? If no, how would you refute her argument?

---

drawing/illustration

prereading questions } **At first glance, what do you think this picture says? What is your general impression?**

Kids, Guns, and Television

QUESTIONS FOR READING

1. What images appear in this picture?
2. How are the different images arranged in the picture?
3. Which images from the picture stand out in the foreground?

QUESTIONS FOR REASONING AND ANALYSIS

1. In viewing this picture, on what image did you focus first? Why?
2. In the picture, it is probably safe to assume the handgun represents violence on television. What does the picture suggest about the relationship between violence on television and children? Or the relationship between violence on TV and school shootings, for instance?
3. The boy in the picture appears standing upright with his arms folded. Does his pose signify anything important or noteworthy?
4. How would you explain the claim or thesis of this picture?

QUESTIONS FOR REFLECTING AND WRITING

1. On April 16, 2007, a Virginia Tech student shot and either wounded or killed several faculty and students in one of the worst campus tragedies in American history. Do you think exposure to violent images in the media (such as TV, movies, videogames) possibly influenced this student's behavior? Why or why not?
2. The words "the TV made me do it" appear in the backdrop of the picture. Do you think a causal relationship exists between violence on TV and violence in society? Do violent images encourage violent behavior? Why or why not?
3. What are some other possible causes of school violence or violence in society in general? Why might one cause supersede another or exist as a primary cause of violence?

editorial cartoon

prereading questions } **Do you remember your initial reactions to the Virginia Tech shooting? If so, what were those reactions?**

Bill Richards

Redandblack.com, an independent student newspaper of the University of Georgia, published this cartoon on April 17, 2007.

Bill Richards, The Red & Black, *April 17, 2007. Reprinted with permission.*

1. What is this cartoon about?

2. What is the context of this cartoon?

QUESTIONS FOR REASONING AND ANALYSIS

1. What claim do you think the cartoonist is trying to make?

2. How would you describe the visual effect of changing the *T* in the Virginia Tech logo to a smoking gun?

3. The cartoonist has positioned the image in the center with a black background surrounding the image. What might be the intended effect of this contrast?

QUESTIONS FOR REFLECTING AND WRITING

1. In April 2007, this cartoon was met with negative reaction from the readers of the Virginia Tech newspaper. What was your first reaction to the cartoon? Negative? Indifferent? Why?

2. If you knew nothing of the context or nothing of the events at Virginia Tech, how might your reaction be different? How might you *interpret* this cartoon differently?

3. In response to negative reaction, Bill Richards, the cartoonist, issued an explanation for his work. While explaining he never intended to make light of the tragedy, Richards said that he meant his cartoon as a symbol for "senseless gun violence that takes place in this country day after day" (*The Red and Black*, 17 April 2007). Do you agree that the cartoon functions effectively the way the cartoonist intended? Why or why not?

---

newspaper column

prereading questions } Do you use the internet for "fun": games, porn, violent cartoons? Do you see a problem with such Internet sites?

What's Up Doc? A Bloody Outrage, That's What

Katherine Ellison

A Pulitzer Prize–winning former foreign correspondent for Knight-Ridder Newspapers, Katherine Ellison is the author of three nonfiction books. Her latest is *The Mommy Brain: How Motherhood Makes Us Smarter* (2005). Her reaction to violent Internet cartoons appeared on October 23, 2005 in *The Washington Post*.

The other day I found my 6-year-old son watching an Internet cartoon called *Happy Tree Friends*.

Purple daisies danced, high-pitched voices sang and animals with heart-shaped noses waved cheerily. But then the music changed, and a previously merry green bear, wearing dog tags and camouflage, suffered an apparent psychotic breakdown.

Crrrrrack!! went the neck of a purple badger, as the bear snapped off its head. Blood splashed and continued flowing as the bear gleefully garroted a hedgehog, then finished off a whimpering squirrel already impaled on metal spikes by placing a hand grenade in its paw.

Joshua turned to me with a sheepish grin. He clearly had a sense that I wasn't happy about his new friends, but he couldn't have known what I was really thinking. Which was this: I'm a longtime journalist who reveres the First Amendment, and I live in California's liberal bastion of Marin County. Yet I would readily skip my next yoga class to march with right-wing fundamentalists in a cultural war against *Happy Tree Friends*.

Just when parents thought we knew who our electronic enemies were—the shoot-'em-up video games, the TVs hawking trans fats, the pedophile e-mail stalkers and teenage-boobs Web sites—here comes this new swamp-thing mass entertainment: the Internet "Flash cartoon," pared down to pure shock value. Its music and animation are tuned to the Teletubbies set—that's its "joke." Its faux warning, "Cartoon Violence: Not for Small Children or Big Babies," is pure come-on—for those who can read. And it's easy to watch over and over again, reinforcing its empathy-dulling impact. That makes it particularly harmful to young psyches, UCLA neuroscientist Marco

continued

Iacoboni told me, because children are prompted to copy what they see—especially what they see over and over again. "Not only do you get exposed and desensitized; you're primed, facilitated, almost invited to act that way," maintains Iacoboni, whose expertise in the brain dynamics of imitation makes him an outspoken critic of media mayhem.

Happy Tree Friends appears tailor-made to sneak under the radar of blocking software (which can't filter images), unless parents are somehow Internet-savvy enough to know about the site and specifically ban it in advance. And it's certainly suited for the kind of viral contagion that caught up with my 6-year-old, who learned of the site from his 9-year-old brother, who first saw it over the shoulder of a teenage summer camp counselor.

But the bottom line is, well, the bottom line. In its Web-cartoon class, *Happy Tree Friends* is a humongous moneymaker, as irresistible to big advertisers as it is to 6-year-olds. At last count, the site was drawing 15 million unique viewers a month, reaping $300,000 or more in ads for each new episode. It recently snagged a place on cable TV, while spawning DVDs, trademark mints, T-shirts and, inevitably, a planned video game.

Internet cartoons had their defining moment with the hilarious "This Land Is Your Land" 2004 election-year parody, featuring George W. Bush calling John Kerry a "liberal wiener" and Kerry calling Bush a "right-wing nut job" to the famous Woody Guthrie tune. By then, the beaten-down Web ad industry was already starting to ride a dramatic recovery, thanks to burgeoning new content and the increasing prevalence of high-quality, high-speed connections. The trend has brought some truly interesting material—and also such savage fare as the graphic cartoon "Gonads & Strife" and another inviting you to repeatedly electrocute a gerbil in a light socket. The Bush-Kerry feature by some reports was the most popular cartoon ever. *Happy Tree Friends,* now in its fifth, most successful, year may well be the most lucrative.

Its narrative is as primitive as its business plan. In every episode, the cute creatures are introduced, after which something awful happens to them, either by gruesome accident, or at the paws of the psychopathic bear. The wordless content appeals to a global audience, enhancing an already remarkably efficient delivery system for advertising. There's a running ad before each episode, while banners flash below and beside the cartoons.

The show itself reportedly began as a potential ad—ironically, against media violence according to Kenn Navarro, its co-creator. Navarro came up with the idea while designing an eight-second spot for an educational company, to illustrate what kids shouldn't be watching. Indeed, 30 years of extensive research underscores the link between TV violence and increased violent behavior among viewers. One study equates the impact as larger than that of asbestos exposure to cancer—a health risk that certainly moved our society to act. But try telling that to *Happy Tree Friends* executive producer John Evershed, CEO of Mondo Media in San Francisco.

Evershed, the father of three children, the youngest aged 2, told me during a phone conversation that he wouldn't let them watch *Happy Tree Friends.* But then he argued that the cartoon wasn't really harmful. "It's like *Tom & Jerry*," he said. "I grew up on *Tom & Jerry,* and I don't think I'm particularly aggressive."

Aggressive? AGGRESSIVE? Much as I'd like to, I can't fairly speak for Evershed on this point, but I certainly do worry about the impact on my children. As for *Tom & Jerry,* I know *Tom & Jerry,* and this is no *Tom & Jerry. Tom & Jerry* never pulled knives or tore heads off or used someone's intestines to strangle a third party, just for starters.

Tom & Jerry also had creativity, with surprising plot twists and a richly emotive score. Most importantly, *Tom & Jerry* had a conscience. Routinely, Tom attacks Jerry and is punished for his aggression. In terms of human evolution, the 1940s classic is light-years ahead of *Happy Tree Friends,* whose authors, Navarro and Rhode Montijo, have been quoted as saying, "If we are in a room brainstorming episodes and end up laughing at the death scene, then it's all good!"

Mad as I am, I'm actually not suggesting that the feds step in and ban this cartoon. The basic freedom of the Internet is too precious, and government censorship too risky and probably not even feasible. The current rules—restrictions on the major airwaves, but anything goes on the Web—will have to do.

But what about the big mainstream advertisers who've made *Happy Tree Friends* such a wild success? I was startled, while watching the cartoon, to see banner ads for companies including Toyota and Kaiser Permanente (which has a new campaign they call "Thrive." Thrive, indeed!). Consumers ought to be able to raise a stink, threaten a reputation, even wage boycotts in the face of such irresponsibility. But many Internet ads enjoy the escape clause of being random and ephemeral, as I found out when I called Hilary Weber, Kaiser's San Francisco-based head of Internet marketing. Weber said she couldn't even confirm that her company's ad had appeared.

"I can't replicate it," she said, adding that it would "take a lot of research" to establish whether Kaiser indeed had purchased such an ad. That, she explained, is because Kaiser, like many other big corporations, buys bulk ads through third parties—saving money, yet relinquishing control over where the ads end up.

Weber said she was concerned about Kaiser's reputation and planned to investigate further, yet declined to tell me the names of the third-party companies placing the firm's ads. So I then turned to Mika Salmi, CEO of Atom-Shockwave, which manages the ads on *Happy Tree Friends*. Salmi, on his cell phone, said he couldn't, with confidence, name the third-party companies with whom he contracts, though he thought one "might" be Advertising.com. But when I contacted Lisa Jacobson, Advertising.com's spokeswoman, she declined to name advertisers not already listed on her firm's Web page. "We actually don't think we're the best fit for this piece," Jacobson wrote me by e-mail. "You'll probably need to speak with companies like Kaiser and Toyota directly. But thanks for thinking of us . . ."

In our brief telephone conversation, Evershed told me he thinks parents have the ultimate responsibility to shield their kids from media violence. In the abstract, I certainly agree with that, but I admit I sometimes wonder if I'm actually doing my kids a disservice by spending so much time and energy chasing them off the Internet, while coaching them in empathy, manners and the Golden Rule. Because if most of their peers, who lack the luxury of moms with time to meddle, are gorging on *Happy Tree Friends*, it would probably serve them better to be trained to defend themselves with firearms and karate.

Still, for now at least, I refuse to be overwhelmed by the sheer magnitude of what society expects from parents, with so little support in return.

So I'd like to offer just two public suggestions. Why can't summer camps and afterschool programs more closely supervise Internet use? And why can't Kaiser and other big companies start crafting contracts that specifically stipulate that their ads never, ever end up on sites like *Happy Tree Friends*?

Meanwhile, I'm talking to other parents because the first step in this peaceful war is to realize we're not alone. Together, we may even manage to subvert our culture's embrace of shock for shock's sake, one gory excess at a time.

QUESTIONS FOR READING

1. *Happy Tree Friends* is Ellison's primary example; what is her subject?
2. What is the problem with *Happy Tree Friends*? How does it differ from *Tom & Jerry*?
3. How did the author's 6-year-old discover the cartoon?
4. What did the author's research reveal about the Web site's advertisers?
5. What suggestions for change does Ellison propose?

QUESTIONS FOR REASONING AND ANALYSIS

1. What does Ellison *not* want to happen to the Internet? Why?
2. What is her claim?
3. Near the end of her column, Ellison writes that her sons might be better off with "firearms and karate" than encouragement in empathy and the Golden Rule. Does she really mean this? Why does she write it?

QUESTIONS FOR REFLECTING AND WRITING

1. Do you think that Ellison's suggestions will be helpful? Why or why not?
2. Should there be federal controls on Internet content? Why or why not?
3. If there are no controls, how will we protect youngsters from unhealthy sites? Or, should we not worry about protecting them? Explain and defend your position.

The Boondocks

Aaron McGruder

QUESTIONS FOR REASONING AND ANALYSIS

1. The boy in the second frame asks why "they" do not "go after gun manufacturers and gun dealers instead of people who make video games?" The character claims it does not make sense. What is the cartoonist saying in this frame about the causes of violent behavior?
2. What is the other character—in the third frame of this comic strip—implying when he says, "Who would you rather start a beef with—some nerd who makes video games or some dude with a warehouse full of AK-47s?" In a different sense, what is the cartoonist implying?
3. How would you explain the claim or thesis of this comic strip? In other words, what is the cartoonist attempting to argue?

QUESTIONS FOR REFLECTING AND WRITING

1. In your view, do media-related activities, like watching movies or playing videogames, contribute to the causes of violent behavior in society? Why or why not?
2. Those arguing that violent videogames contribute to violence in society basically assume that some people will most likely mimic behaviors they have seen acted out on screen (that is, "copycat" behavior). Is this warrant (implicit assumption) in their argument valid? Why or why not?
3. Do violent videogames contribute to any societal ills at all? Are videogames completely innocuous? Why or why not?

prereading questions } Do you listen to hip-hop music? If yes, what is its appeal for you? If no, why not? Whether yes or no, are you ever bothered by either the lyrics or the public personas of some of the rappers?

How Hip-Hop Music Lost Its Way and Betrayed Its Fans

Brent Staples

Holding a doctorate in psychology from the University of Chicago, Brent Staples is currently an editorial writer, specializing in politics and culture, for *The New York Times*. He has written a memoir, *Parallel Time: Growing Up in Black and White* (1994), and his essays and columns are widely published. The following column appeared on nytimes.com on May 12, 2005.

African American teenagers are beset on all sides by dangerous myths about race. The most poisonous one defines middle-class normalcy and achievement as "white," while embracing violence, illiteracy and drug dealing as "authentically" black. This fiction rears its head from time to time in films and literature. But it finds its most virulent expression in rap music, which started out with a broad palette of themes but has increasingly evolved into a medium for worshiping misogyny, materialism and murder.

This dangerous narrowing of hip-hop music would be reason for concern in any case. But it is especially troubling against the backdrop of the 1990's, when rappers provoked a real-world gang war by using recordings and music videos to insult and threaten rivals. Two of the music's biggest stars—Tupac Shakur and the Notorious B.I.G.—were eventually shot to death.

People who pay only minimal attention to the rap world may have thought the killings would sober up the rap community. Not quite. The May cover of the hip-hop magazine *Vibe* was on the mark when it depicted fallen rappers standing among tombstones under the headline: "Hip-Hop Murders: Why Haven't We Learned Anything?"

The cover may have been prompted in part by a rivalry between two rappers that culminated in a shoot-out at a New York radio station, Hot 97, earlier this spring. The events that led up to the shooting show how recording labels now exploit violence to make and sell recordings.

At the center of that Hot 97 shootout was none other than 50 Cent, whose given name is Curtis Jackson III. Mr. Jackson is a confessed former drug dealer who seems to revel in the fact that he was shot several times while dealing in Queens. He has also made a career of "beef" recordings, in which he whips up controversy and heightens tension by insulting rival artists.

He was following this pattern in a radio interview in March when a rival showed up at the station. The story's murky, but it appears that the rival's entourage met Mr. Jackson's on the street, resulting in gunfire.

Mr. Jackson's on-air agitation was clearly timed to coincide with the release of *The Massacre*, his grotesquely violent and misogynist compact disc. The CD cover depicts the artist standing before a wall adorned with weapons, pointing what appears to be a shotgun at the camera. The photographs in the liner notes depict every ghetto stereotype—the artist selling drugs, the artist in a gunfight—and include a mock autopsy report that has been seen as a covert threat aimed at some of his critics.

The Massacre promotion raises the ante in a most destructive way. New artists, desperate for stardom, will say or do anything to win notice—and buzz—for their next projects. As the trend escalates, inner-city listeners who are already at risk of dying prematurely are being fed a toxic diet of rap cuts that glorify murder and make it seem perfectly normal to spend your life in prison.

Critics who have been angered by this trend have pointed at Jimmy Iovine, the music impresario whose Interscope Records reaped millions on gangster rap in the 90s. Mr. Iovine makes a convenient target as a white man who is lording over an essentially black art form. But also listed on *The Massacre* as an executive producer is the legendary rapper Dr. Dre, a black man who happens to be one of the most powerful people in the business. Dr. Dre has a unique vantage point on rap-related violence. He was co-founder of Death Row Records, an infamous California company that marketed West Coast rap in the 1990s and had a front-row seat for the feud that led to so much bloodshed back then.

continued

The music business hopes to make a financial killing on a recently announced summer concert tour that is set to feature 50 Cent and the mega-selling rap star Eminem. But promoters will need to make heavy use of metal detectors to suppress the kind of gun-related violence that gangster artists celebrate. That this lethal genre of art has grown speaks volumes about the industry's greed and lack of self-control.

But trends like this reach a tipping point, when business as usual becomes unacceptable to the public as a whole. Judging from the rising hue and cry, hip-hop is just about there.

QUESTIONS FOR READING

1. What seems to be the dominant message of today's hip-hop music?
2. What continues to go on in the rap world? How does this affect the studios? How are some rappers contributing to the situation?
3. How is the public reacting to rappers' behavior and their music, in Staples's view?

QUESTIONS FOR REASONING AND ANALYSIS

1. What is Staples's claim?
2. Staples's argument rests upon a key assumption; what is that assumption? Is it one that Staples can expect readers to accept?
3. What is to be gained by not addressing a perhaps controversial assumption upon which your argument rests? What is risked by this strategy?

QUESTIONS FOR REFLECTING AND WRITING

1. Staples blames the music industry along with specific rappers for "greed and lack of self-control." Ellison blames companies for providing ad money for violent Internet cartoons. Is there any way to reduce violent media by going after the companies that make money off of this violence? What suggestions do you have?
2. Some would argue that the world created by rap music is a fantasy, and listeners know this. Thus the violence has no real impact on listeners. What is your position on the impact of violent rap on listeners? Explain and defend your position.

america in the age of obama

chapter 17

On November 4, 2008, Americans voted, by a significant margin, to elect Barack Obama 44th President of the United States. His election is historic for several reasons, not the least of which is an African American will sit in the Oval Office for the first time in U.S. history. Several of the following selections explore how race affected Obama becoming president as well as the significance of his becoming the nation's first black president. Other selections highlight images of the new president as an iconic figure. A November 2008 issue of *The Amazing Spider-Man*, for example, relates how many Americans see Obama as a hero, or perhaps even a "superhero."

prereading questions

1. How has President Obama's staff used several mediums of communication to reach the American people?

2. What makes President Obama an effective communicator? Is it his speaking style? The ideas he conveys?

3. What has made President Obama so popular among so many Americans? Why did some prominent Republicans cross party lines to support him?

4. What challenges does President Obama face in his presidency?

web sites related to this chapter's topic

FORMER CAMPAIGN WEB SITE FOR BARACK OBAMA NOW SITE SUPPORTING THE PRESIDENT. INCLUDES MULTIPLE LINKS AND RESOURCES
www.barackobama.com/index.php

LINK TO THE OBAMA WHITE HOUSE
www.whitehouse.gov

FACEBOOK PAGE FOR OBAMA SUPPORTERS
www.facebook.com/barackobama?ref=s

talk show transcript

prereading question } What reasons and issues lead you to choose one political candidate over another?

Meet the Press transcript for October 19, 2008

On October 19, 2008, Colin Powell, secretary of state for the first George W. Bush administration, formally endorsed Democratic presidential candidate Barack Obama on *Meet the Press*.

MR. TOM BROKAW: Our issues this Sunday: He served as President George W. Bush's secretary of state and was once called the man most likely to become the nation's first African American president. He has been courted by both the Obama and McCain presidential campaigns and said this last month:

(Videotape)

GEN. COLIN POWELL (RET.): I have been watching both of these individuals. I know them both extremely well, and I have not decided who I'm going to vote for yet.

(End videotape)

MR. BROKAW: Is he now ready to make an endorsement in this presidential race? What are his thoughts on the major issues facing the country and the world? Our exclusive guest this Sunday, former Secretary of State General Colin Powell. . . . Welcome back to *Meet the Press*.

GEN. POWELL: Thank you, Tom.

MR. BROKAW: We indicated in that opening, there is a lot of anticipation and speculation about your take on this presidential campaign. We'll get to that in a moment. But in your old business we might call this a tour of the horizon. Whoever's elected president of the United States, that first day in the Oval Office on January 21st will face this: an American economy that's in a near paralytic state at this time; we're at war in two different countries, Afghanistan and Iraq; we have an energy crisis; we have big decisions to make about health care and about global climate change. The president of the United States and the Congress of the United States now have the highest disapproval ratings that we have seen in many years. In all your years of public service, have you ever seen an incoming president face such daunting challenges?

GEN. POWELL: No. I have seen more difficult times in our history. I think about the early 70s when we were going through Watergate–

Spiro Agnew–Nixon period, that was not a good time. But right now we're also facing a very daunting period. And I think the number one issue the president's going to have to deal with is the economy. That's what the American people are worried about. And, frankly, it's not just an American problem, it's an international problem. We can see how all of these economies are now linked in this globalized system. And I think that'll be number one. The president will also have to make decisions quickly as to how to deal with Iraq and Afghanistan. And also I think the president has to reach out to the world and show that there is a new president, a new administration that is looking forward to working with our friends and allies. And in my judgment, also willing to talk to people who we have not been willing to talk to before. Because this is a time for outreach.

MR. BROKAW: Given the state of the American economy, can we continue our military commitments around the world at the level that they now exist?

GEN. POWELL: We can. I think we have to look as to whether they have to be at that level. But we have the wealth, we have the wherewithal to do that. We have the ability to do that. And so, first and foremost, we have to review those commitments, see what they are, see what else is needed, and make sure we give our troops what they need to get the job done as we have defined the job. We have that ability.

MR. BROKAW: If you were called into the Oval Office on January 21st by the new president, whoever it happens to be, and he said to you, "General Powell, I need from you your recommendation on where I begin. What should be my priorities?" Where would you start?

GEN. POWELL: I would start with talking to the American people and talking to the world, and conveying a new image of American leadership, a new image of America's role in the world.

The problems will always be there, and there's going to be a crisis come along in the 21st or 22nd of January that we don't even know about right now. And so I think what the president has to do is to start using the power of the Oval Office and the power of his personality to convince the American people and to convince the world that America is solid, America is going to move forward, and we're going to fix our economic problems, we're going to meet our overseas obligations. But restoring a sense of purpose, a sense of confidence in the American people and, in the international community, in America.

MR. BROKAW: What's not on the screen right now that concerns you that should be more prominent in the minds of the American people and the people running for president?

GEN. POWELL: I think the American people and the gentlemen running for president will have to, early on, focus on education more than we have seen in the campaign so far.

America has a terrible educational problem in the sense that we have too many youngsters not finishing school. A third of our kids don't finish high school, 50 percent of minorities don't finish high school. We've got to work on this, and my wife and I are leading a campaign with this purpose.

Also, I think, the new president has to realize that the world looks to America for leadership, and so we have to show leadership on some issues that the world is expecting us to, whether it's energy, global warming and the environment. And I think we have to do a lot more with respect to poverty alleviation and helping the needy people of the world. We need to increase the amount of resources we put into our development programs to help the rest of the world. Because when you help the poorest in the world, you start to move them up an economic and social ladder, and they're not going to be moving toward violence or terrorism of the kind that we worry about.

MR. BROKAW: Well, let's move to the American presidential campaign now, if we can. We saw at the beginning of this broadcast a short tease of what you had to say just a month ago. Let's share with our viewers now a little more of Colin Powell on these two candidates and your position.

(Videotape, September 20, 2008)

GEN. POWELL: I'm an American, first and foremost, and I'm very proud—I've said to my beloved friend and colleague John McCain, a friend of 25 years, "John, I love you, but I'm not just going to vote for you on the basis of our affection or friendship." And I've said to Barack Obama, "I admire you. I'll give you all the advice I can. But I'm not going to vote for you just because you're black." We have to move beyond this.

(End videotape)

MR. BROKAW: General Powell, actually you gave a campaign contribution to Senator McCain. You have met twice at least with Barack Obama. Are you prepared to make a public declaration of which of these two candidates that you're prepared to support?

GEN. POWELL: Yes, but let me lead into it this way. I know both of these individuals very well now. I've known John for 25 years as your setup said. And I've gotten to know Mr. Obama quite well over the past two years. Both of them are distinguished Americans who are patriotic, who are dedicated to the welfare of our country. Either one of them, I think, would be a good president. I have said to Mr. McCain that I admire all he has done. I have some concerns about the direction that the party has taken in recent years. It has moved more to the right than I would like to see it, but that's a choice the party makes. And I've said to Mr. Obama, "You have to pass a test of do you have enough experience, and do you bring the

continued

judgment to the table that would give us confidence that you would be a good president."

And I've watched him over the past two years, frankly, and I've had this conversation with him. I have especially watched over the last six of seven weeks as both of them have really taken a final exam with respect to this economic crisis that we are in and coming out of the conventions. And I must say that I've gotten a good measure of both. In the case of Mr. McCain, I found that he was a little unsure as to deal with the economic problems that we were having and almost every day there was a different approach to the problem. And that concerned me, sensing that he didn't have a complete grasp of the economic problems that we had. And I was also concerned at the selection of Governor Palin. She's a very distinguished woman, and she's to be admired; but at the same time, now that we have had a chance to watch her for some seven weeks, I don't believe she's ready to be president of the United States, which is the job of the vice president. And so that raised some question in my mind as to the judgment that Senator McCain made.

On the Obama side, I watched Mr. Obama and I watched him during this seven-week period. And he displayed a steadiness, an intellectual curiosity, a depth of knowledge and an approach to looking at problems like this and picking a vice president that, I think, is ready to be president on day one. And also, in not just jumping in and changing every day, but showing intellectual vigor. I think that he has a, a definitive way of doing business that would serve us well. I also believe that on the Republican side over the last seven weeks, the approach of the Republican Party and Mr. McCain has become narrower and narrower. Mr. Obama, at the same time, has given us a more inclusive, broader reach into the needs and aspirations of our people. He's crossing lines—ethnic lines, racial lines, generational lines. He's thinking about all villages have values, all towns have values, not just small towns have values.

And I've also been disappointed, frankly, by some of the approaches that Senator McCain has taken recently, or his campaign ads, on issues that are not really central to the problems that the American people are worried about. This Bill Ayers situation that's been going on for weeks became something of a central point of the campaign. But Mr. McCain says that he's a washed-out terrorist. Well, then, why do we keep talking about him? And why do we have these robocalls going on around the country trying to suggest that, because of this very, very limited relationship that Senator Obama has had with Mr. Ayers, somehow, Mr. Obama is tainted. What they're trying to connect him to is some kind of terrorist feelings. And I think that's inappropriate.

Now, I understand what politics is all about. I know how you can go after one another, and that's good. But I think this goes too far. And I think it has made the McCain campaign look a little narrow. It's not what the American people are looking for. And I look at these kinds of

approaches to the campaign and they trouble me. And the party has moved even further to the right, and Governor Palin has indicated a further rightward shift. I would have difficulty with two more conservative appointments to the Supreme Court, but that's what we'd be looking at in a McCain administration. I'm also troubled by, not what Senator McCain says, but what members of the party say. And it is permitted to be said such things as, "Well, you know that Mr. Obama is a Muslim." Well, the correct answer is, he is not a Muslim, he's a Christian. He's always been a Christian. But the really right answer is, what if he is? Is there something wrong with being a Muslim in this country? The answer's no, that's not America. Is there something wrong with some seven-year-old Muslim-American kid believing that he or she could be president? Yet I have heard senior members of my own party drop the suggestion, "He's a Muslim and he might be associated with terrorists." This is not the way we should be doing it in America.

I feel strongly about this particular point because of a picture I saw in a magazine. It was a photo essay about troops who are serving in Iraq and Afghanistan. And one picture at the tail end of this photo essay was of a mother in Arlington Cemetery, and she had her head on the headstone of her son's grave. And as the picture focused in, you could see the writing on the headstone. And it gave his awards—Purple Heart, Bronze Star—showed that he died in Iraq, gave his date of birth, date of death. He was 20 years old. And then, at the very top of the headstone, it didn't have a Christian cross, it didn't have the Star of David, it had crescent and a star of the Islamic faith. And his name was Kareem Rashad Sultan Khan, and he was an American. He was born in New Jersey. He was 14 years old at the time of 9/11, and he waited until he could go serve his country, and he gave his life. Now, we have got to stop polarizing ourself in this way. And John McCain is as nondiscriminatory as anyone I know. But I'm troubled about the fact that, within the party, we have these kinds of expressions.

So, when I look at all of this and I think back to my Army career, we've got two individuals, either one of them could be a good president. But which is the president that we need now? Which is the individual that serves the needs of the nation for the next period of time? And I come to the conclusion that because of his ability to inspire, because of the inclusive nature of his campaign, because he is reaching out all across America, because of who he is and his rhetorical abilities—and we have to take that into account—as well as his substance—he has both style and substance—he has met the standard of being a successful president, being an exceptional president. I think he is a transformational figure. He is a new generation coming into the world—onto the world stage, onto the American stage, and for that reason I'll be voting for Senator Barack Obama.

MR. BROKAW: Will you be campaigning for him as well?

GEN. POWELL: I don't plan to. Two weeks left, let them go at each other in the finest tradition. But I will be voting for him.

MR. BROKAW: I can already anticipate some of the reaction to this. Let's begin with the charge that John McCain has continued to make against Barack Obama. You sit there, as a man who served in Vietnam, you commanded a battalion of 101st, you were chairman of the Joint Chiefs, you were a national security adviser and secretary of state. There is nothing in Barack Obama's history that nearly parallels any of the experiences that you've had. And while he has performed impressively in the context of the campaign, there's a vast difference between sitting in the Oval Office and making tough decisions and doing well in a campaign.

GEN. POWELL: And he knows that. And I have watched him over the last two years as he has educated himself, as he has become very familiar with these issues. He speaks authoritatively. He speaks with great insight into the challenges we're facing of a military and political and economic nature. And he is surrounding himself, I'm confident, with people who'll be able to give him the expertise that he, at the moment, does not have. And so I have watched an individual who has intellectual vigor and who dives deeply into issues and approaches issues with a very, very steady hand. And so I'm confident that he will be ready to take on these challenges on January 21st.

MR. BROKAW: And you are fully aware that there will be some—how many, no one can say for sure—but there will be some who will say this is an African American, distinguished American, supporting another African American because of race.

GEN. POWELL: If I had only had that in mind, I could have done this six, eight, 10 months ago. I really have been going back and forth between somebody I have the highest respect and regard for, John McCain, and somebody I was getting to know, Barack Obama. And it was only in the last couple of months that I settled on this. And I can't deny that it will be a historic event for an African American to become president. And should that happen, all Americans should be proud—not just African Americans, but all Americans—that we have reached this point in our national history where such a thing could happen. It will also not only electrify our country, I think it'll electrify the world.

MR. BROKAW: You have some differences with Barack Obama. He has said that once he takes office, he wants to begin removing American troops from Iraq. Here's what you had to say about that: "I have found in my many years of service, to set arbitrary dates that don't coincide with the situation on the ground or what actually is happening tends not to be a useful strategy. . . . Arbitrary deadlines that are snatched out of the air and are based on some

lunar calculation is not the way to run a military or a strategic operation of this type." That was on February 10th of this year on CNN. Now that you have Barack Obama's ear in a new fashion, will you say to him, "Drop your idea of setting a deadline of some kind to pull the troops out of Iraq"?

GEN. POWELL: First of all, I think that's a great line, and thanks for pulling it up. And I believe that. But as I watch what's happening right now, the United States is negotiating an agreement with the Iraqi government that will call for most major combat operations to cease by next June and for American forces to start withdrawing to their bases. And that agreement will also provide for all American troops to be gone by 2011, but conditioned on the situation as it exists at that time. So there already is a timeline that's being developed between the Iraqis and the United States government. So I think whoever becomes the president, whether it's John McCain or whether it's Barack Obama, we're going to see a continued drawdown. And when, you know, which day so many troops come out or what units come out, that'll be determined by the commanders and the new president. But I think we are on a glide path to reducing our presence in Iraq over the next couple of years. Increasingly, this problem's going to be solved by the Iraqis. They're going to make the political decisions, their security forces are going to take over, and they're going to have to create an environment of reconciliation where all the people can come together and make Iraq a much, much better place.

MR. BROKAW: Let me go back to something that you raised just a moment ago, and that's William Ayers, a former member of the Weathermen who's now active in school issues in Illinois. He had some past association with Barack Obama. Wouldn't it have been more helpful for William Ayers to, on his own, to have renounced his own past? Here was a man who was a part of the most radical group that existed in America at a time when you were serving in Vietnam, targeting the Pentagon, the Capitol. He wrote a book about it that came out on 2001, on September 11th that said, "We didn't bomb enough."

GEN. POWELL: It's despicable, and I have no truck for William Ayers. I think what he did was despicable, and to continue to talk about it in 2001 is also despicable. But to suggest that because Mr. Barack Obama had some contacts of a very casual nature—they sat on a educational board—over time is somehow connected to his thinking or his actions, I think, is a, a terrible stretch. It's demagoguery.

MR. BROKAW: I want to ask you about your own role in the decision to go to war in Iraq. Barack Obama has been critical of your appearance before the United Nations at that time. Bob Woodward has a new book out called *The War Within,* and here's what he had to say about Colin Powell and his place in the administration: "Powell . . . didn't think [Iraq] was a necessary war,

continued

and yet he had gone along in a hundred ways, large and small. He had resisted at times but had succumbed to the momentum and his own sense of deference—even obedience—to the president. . . . Perhaps more than anyone else in the administration, Powell had been the 'closer' for the president's case on war."

And then you were invited to appear before the Iraq Study Group. "'Why did we go into Iraq with so few people?' [former Secretary of State James] Baker asked. . . . 'Colin just exploded at that point,' [former Secretary of Defense William] Perry recalled later. 'He unloaded,' [former White House Chief of Staff] Leon Panetta added. 'He was angry. He was mad as hell.' . . . Powell left [the Study Group meeting]. Baker turned to Panetta and said solemnly, 'He's the one guy who could have perhaps prevented this from happening.'"

What's the lesson in all of that for a new secretary of state or for a new national security adviser, based on your own experience?

GEN. POWELL: Well, let's start at the beginning. I said to the president in 2002, we should try to solve this diplomatically and avoid war. The president accepted that recommendation; we took it to the U.N. But the president, by the end of 2002, believed that the U.N. was not going to solve the problem, and he made a decision that we had to prepare for military action. I fully supported that. And I have never said anything to suggest I did not support going to war. I thought the evidence was there. And it is not just my closing of the whole deal with my U.N. speech. I know the importance of that speech, and I regret a lot of the information that the intelligence community provided us was wrong. But three months before my speech, with a heavy majority, the United States Congress expressed its support to use military force if it was necessary. And so we went in and used military force. My unhappiness was that we didn't do it right. It was easy to get to Baghdad, but then we forgot that there was a lot more that had to be done. And we didn't have enough force to impose our will in the country or to deal with the insurgency when it broke out, and that I regret.

MR. BROKAW: Removing the weapons of mass destruction from the equation . . .

GEN. POWELL: I also assure you that it was not a correct assessment by anybody that my statements or my leaving the administration would have stopped it.

MR. BROKAW: Removing the weapons of mass destruction from the equation, because we now know that they did not exist, was it then a war of necessity or just a war of choice?

GEN. POWELL: Without the weapons of mass destruction present, as conveyed to us by the intelligence community in the most powerful way, I don't think there would have been a war. It was the reason we took it to the public; it was the reason we took it to the American people to

the Congress, who supported it on that basis; and it's the presentation I made to the United Nations. Without those weapons of mass destruction then Iraq did not present to the world the kind of threat that it did if it had weapons of mass destruction.

MR. BROKAW: You do know that there are supporters of Barack Obama who feel very strongly about his candidacy because he was opposed to the war from the beginning, and they're going to say, "Who needs Colin Powell? He was the guy who helped get us into this mess."

GEN. POWELL: I'm not here to get their approval or lack of approval. I am here to express my view as to who I'm going to vote for.

MR. BROKAW: There's a summing up going on now as, as the Bush/Cheney administration winds down. We'd like to share with our audience some of what you had to say about the two men who are at the top of the administration. At the convention in 2000, this is Colin Powell on President Bush and Dick Cheney at that time.

(Videotape, July 31, 2000)

GEN. POWELL: Dick Cheney is one of the most distinguished and dedicated public servants this nation has ever had. He will be a superb vice president.

The Bush/Cheney team will be a great team for America. They will put our nation on a course of hope and optimism for this new century.

(End videotape)

MR. BROKAW: Was that prophetic or wrong?

GEN. POWELL: It's what I believed. It reflected the agenda of the new president, compassionate conservatism. And some of it worked out. I think we have advanced our freedom agenda; I think we've done a lot to help people around the world with our programs of development. I think we've done a lot to solve some conflicts such as in Liberia and elsewhere. But, at the same time, we have managed to convey to the world that we are more unilateral than we really are. We have not explained ourself well enough. And we, unfortunately, have left an impression with the world that is not a good one. And the new president is going to have to fix the reputation that we've left with the rest of the world.

Now, let me make a point here. The United States is still seen as the leader at the world that wants to be free. Even though the numbers are down with respect to favorability ratings, at every embassy and consular office tomorrow morning that we have, people will be lined up, and they'll all say the same thing, "We want to go to America." So we're still the leader of the world that wants to be free. We are still the inspiration of the rest of the world. And we can come back. In 2000, it was moment where I believed that the new administration coming in would be able to achieve the agenda that President-elect Bush had set out of compassionate conservatism.

MR. BROKAW: But it failed?

GEN. POWELL: I don't think it was as successful as it might have been. And, as you see from the presidential approval ratings, the American people have found the administration wanting.

MR. BROKAW: Let me ask you a couple of questions—quick questions as we wrap all of this up. I know you're very close to President Bush 41. Are you still in touch with him on a regular basis? And what do you think he'll think about you this morning endorsing Barack Obama?

GEN. POWELL: I will let President Bush 41 speak for himself and let others speak for themselves, just as I have spoken for myself. Let me make one point, Tom: Both Senator McCain and Senator Obama will be good presidents. It isn't easy for me to disappoint Senator McCain in the way that I have this morning, and I regret that. But I strongly believe that at this point in America's history, we need a president that will not just continue, even with a new face and with some changes and with some maverick aspects, who will not just continue, basically, the policies that we have been following in recent years. I think we need a transformational figure. I think we need a president who is a generational change. And that's why I'm supporting Barack Obama. Not out of any lack of respect or admiration for Senator John McCain.

MR. BROKAW: And finally, how much of a factor do you think race will be when voters go into that booth on November 4th?

GEN. POWELL: I don't know the answer to that question. One may say that it's going to be a big factor, and a lot of people say they will vote for Senator Obama but they won't pull a lever. Others might say that has already happened. People are already finding other reasons to say they're not voting for him. "Well, he's a Muslim." "He's this." So we have already seen the so-called "Bradley factor" in the current spread between the candidates. And so that remains to be seen. I hope it is not the case. I think we have advanced considerably in this country since the days of Tom Bradley. And I hope that is not the case. It would be very unfortunate if it were the case.

MR. BROKAW: Finally, if Senator Obama is elected president, will there be a place for Colin Powell in that administration? Maybe as the ambassador at large in Africa or to take on the daunting task of resolving the Israeli/Palestinian issue?

GEN. POWELL: I served 40 years in government, and I'm not looking forward to a position or an assignment. Of course, I have always said if a president asks you to do something, you have to consider it. But I am in no way interested in returning to government. But I, of course, would sit and talk to any president who wishes to talk to me.

MR. BROKAW: You're not ruling it out?

GEN. POWELL: I would sit and talk to any president who wishes to talk to me, but I'm not anxious to rule it in.

MR. BROKAW: General Colin Powell, thank you very much for being with us this morning. Appreciate it.

GEN. POWELL: Thank you, Tom.

www.msnbc.msn.com/id/27266223

QUESTIONS FOR READING

1. Why did Powell choose to support Obama over McCain?
2. What problems does Powell cite as major concerns for the next U.S. president? What does he say is the number-one issue?
3. What does Powell say in response to Brokaw's question concerning priorities for the next president?
4. What does Powell say that he admires about Barack Obama?

QUESTIONS FOR REASONING AND ANALYSIS

1. Why does Powell describe this period of history as "daunting"? What call does he make for addressing this "daunting period"? In your view, does he have the right answer? Why or why not?
2. Why do you think Brokaw plays a videotape from September 20, 2008 in which Powell expressed his support for McCain? How does Powell respond? Is his response effective or ineffective? Why?
3. How would you summarize Powell's argument concerning Barack Obama's association with political radical William Ayers? Do you agree with Powell? Why or why not?
4. Powell relates the story of a young Muslim American serviceman who died fighting in Iraq. What argument is he supporting by relating this narrative? Is this narrative effective in communicating his point? If so, in what way? If not, then why not?
5. Do you perceive Powell as credible? Why or why not? What reasons, aside from his credentials, support that he is credible?

1. As Powell explains, he and John McCain have been close friends for several years. Do you think the interview transcript conveys any regret or remorse from Powell in his choosing to support Obama over McCain? If so, what evidence suggests remorse? Do you see Powell as disloyal to his party or his friend in making this decision? Why or why not?

2. Imagine that your close friend is running for president of the student government at your university. You believe based on strong evidence, however, that his or her opponent—someone you know only casually—could perform more effectively in the job. Would you vote for that person based on that reason? Would you remain loyal to your friend? Why would you choose one person over the other?

3. Do you align yourself with one political party over another? Are you a die-hard Republican or a loyal Democrat? Can you see yourself voting for someone outside your political party affiliation? Why or why not?

political cartoon

prereading question } **Is it fair to cast aspersions on President Obama's character because he has ancestors of the Islamic faith?**

Steve Benson

This political cartoon first appeared during the 2008 presidential campaign.

By permission of Steve Benson and Creators Syndicate, Inc.

QUESTIONS FOR REASONING AND ANALYSIS

1. Overall, what is the cartoon saying? In other words, what is the cartoon's major premise or claim?

2. Does suggesting that Obama is sympathetic to terrorists necessarily mean his opponents are only attempting to smear him? Why or why not?

3. Assuming that Obama does maintain "ties" to Islam, does it necessarily mean he is aligning himself with terrorists? Is the cartoonist pointing to flawed logic in the arguments of Obama's opponents? In your view, is their logic flawed? Why or why not?

4. What other observations can you make with regard to this cartoon? Do you notice anything else significant or noteworthy?

QUESTIONS FOR REFLECTING AND WRITING

1. Write a response to this cartoon. Do you agree or disagree with its premise? Why or why not?

2. Is terrorism still a major threat? Why or why not? What evidence suggests the threat remains present even almost 10 years after 9/11? Does evidence suggest the threat has subsided?

prereading question } **What role did race play in Obama becoming the country's first African American President?**

What Obama's Election Really Means to Black America

Steven Gray / Chicago, November 6, 2008

Steven Gray, a contributor for *Time*, published this piece on November 6, 2008, two days after Obama's election.

Much of black America is still struggling to grasp the full meaning of Barack Obama's election to the presidency. The overall mood is awash with pride but shaded with angst and the larger question: Now what?

On Wednesday, the Harvard University scholar Henry Louis Gates Jr. appeared on Oprah Winfrey's celebratory post-election special. After learning the news, Gates says, "we jumped up, we wept, we hooped and hollered." It is hard to overestimate the historical significance of the election of the first black U.S. President. For many blacks, and certainly for much of the country and world, Obama's victory is an extraordinary step toward the redemption of America's original 400-year-old sin. It is astonishing not least for its quickness, coming just 145 years after President Abraham Lincoln issued the Emancipation Proclamation effectively ending slavery and four decades after the assassination of Martin Luther King Jr. And it is even more astonishing for its decisiveness—Obama carried Virginia, once the home of the Confederacy, a place whose laws just five decades ago would have made the interracial union of his parents illegal.

"Just a little more than 10 years ago," Atlanta mayor Shirley Franklin told *Time* this week, "it was inconceivable to any of us that we would see an African American win a national party's ticket and then compete effectively. It's mind-boggling," she continued, "how much this means about the opportunities available to all people—Asians, Latinos and other people who've historically been locked out of the system."

What is perhaps most surprising about many blacks' support of Obama is that it was not immediate or easy. Many African Americans were initially skeptical about Obama's candidacy, partly because they regarded him as somehow inauthentically black due to his upbringing in Hawaii and Indonesia, as well as his last name, which even the President-elect has described as "funny sounding."

Black support of Obama soared after he won last winter's Iowa caucuses. But there were moments in this campaign when Obama was forced to manage the issue of race deftly and explain the unexplainable to a largely white electorate. Consider the case of his former pastor, the Rev. Jeremiah Wright Jr. Obama joined Wright's Trinity United Church of Christ in Chicago in the 1980s, when Obama was an obscure community organizer. Trinity gave Obama an entrée to the city's thriving black middle class, and Obama came to view Wright in particular as a mentor. Yet earlier this year, Obama was compelled for political reasons to leave the church. The public criticism stemmed from controversial comments about the U.S. by Wright that proved too harsh to the ears of outsiders, many who are not aware of the nuances of the black religious-cultural experience, or of the fact that black churches have traditionally been a place for coping with the legacy of racism in this country. When Obama left Trinity, he suggested that the scrutiny he faced because of Wright's sermons would follow him to whatever church he and his family chose to attend as the First Family. That will be especially true if the Obamas choose another traditional black church, where the rhetoric on matters of social policy and everyday life—not just on racism—may sound radical to much of the country.

Obama's candidacy inspired scores of blacks like Michael Johnson, 33, to vote for the first time. At about noon on Nov. 4, Johnson showed up at his Gary, Indiana, polling station to cast his vote. But he was turned away. The reason: his name appeared on a list of people who had already cast absentee votes. Johnson left the station dismayed. He spent the next five hours driving across Lake County, Indiana, sorting out the mess with election authorities in Crown Point, the county's seat, before eventually returning to the Gary polling station. He says the polling station's managers applauded when they saw him. "They didn't think I was coming back," the hotel dishwasher said late Tuesday. "But this election was just too important for me to miss."

Meanwhile, Barbara Gray, 65, a retiree who is also from Gary, said she voted

continued

for Obama partly because she hoped he would take interest in improving conditions in urban areas—like Obama's adopted hometown neighborhood, Hyde Park, a leafy Chicago enclave surrounded by some of the city's bleakest communities. She said Obama may be the first President with a firsthand understanding of life in neighborhoods like hers. Gray said she wants the basics: cracked sidewalks repaved, enough funding so that largely black and Latino urban public schools can compete with the predominately white schools in affluent suburbs. "Just look around," she said on Election Day, pointing to a long row of blighted buildings along one of Gary's main boulevards, Broadway Street. "There's 101 things that need to be done."

In an interview with *Time* this week, the Reverend Jesse Jackson said that Obama's election "shows that there's nothing else we can't be. There's no university we can't be seriously considered to lead. There's no bank we can't be considered in if we have the right credentials."

There's no doubting that Obama's candidacy represents the shattering of many of the racial barriers that have long been entrenched in America. But it is also worth tempering those expectations. Standing in the crisp breeze along Chicago's Michigan Avenue, on the night of Obama's election, Freddie Arnett, a 51-year-old maintenance supervisor, expressed hope that Obama would show concern for urban affairs. But Arnett acknowledged, "I know it's going to take time."

Shortly after Obama's election, a throng of people stood outside the Chicago headquarters of two of the country's leading chronicles of black life, *Jet* and *Ebony* magazines, and beamed at a row of covers featuring Barack and Michelle Obama.

"Our country is showing its forward evolution, that the color of one's skin cannot inhibit one's ability, and that's worthy of celebration," said Corey Booker, mayor of Newark, New Jersey.

QUESTIONS FOR READING

1. What was one moment in which Obama was forced to "explain the unexplainable," according to Gray?
2. Why was Michael Johnson turned away from the polling station in Gary, Indiana?
3. Why did Barbara Gray and Freddie Arnett vote for Obama?

QUESTIONS FOR REASONING AND ANALYSIS

1. How would you summarize Gray's thesis or major claim?
2. Gray explains that many African Americans were skeptical of Obama at first, but he eventually won many of them over. Why were they skeptical at first? Do you think Obama can honestly identify himself as "African American"? What arguments might challenge his status as an African American person? Are these arguments valid? Why or why not?
3. Why do you think Gray says Americans should "temper expectations" when it comes to shattering racial barriers? Do you agree? Why or why not?

1. Gray tells stories of black people who voted for Obama not because he represents the African American race but because of his stances on social issues, such as urban renewal. In doing so, Gray suggests not every African American supported Obama simply because of his race. Why was Obama elected president? Was race as significant a factor in his election as some believe? Why or why not?

2. Many writers, pundits, and politicians have noted the historical significance that marks Obama becoming the first African American president. What is your view of Obama becoming the first African American president and, moreover, the first non-Anglo president? Do you think the country is destined to see a trend? Will Obama's election pave the way for future presidents of minority races? Why or why not?

3. What issues strongly influence your decision to vote for one political candidate over another? What issues least influence your decision? Why are certain issues and concerns more significant than others?

magazine cover

prereading question } Is President Obama's race an important factor in his becoming President as well as carrying out his duties as President?

The following is an October 2008 cover of *Time* magazine.

1. What does the image of Obama's face, depicted in this way, communicate? What does the line dividing his face into black and white halves signify?
2. What do you think the picture of Obama's face means in relation to the caption "Why the economy is trumping race"? Why do you think the *Time* editors chose this image to highlight the major focus of this issue?
3. The black half of Obama's face, when one looks closely, is slightly greater than the white half. Is this slight disproportion significant? Why or why not?

1. Is the United States still a racially divided nation? Do you think the country has become more unified? Is it as racially divided as it was during the civil rights movement of the 1960s? Why or why not?
2. Many believe race was an important factor in Obama's election. Has race remained an important factor during his presidency? Why or why not?

magazine essay

prereading questions } **Will Obama be an effective President? What might keep him from becoming an effective President?**

The Age of Obama

Obama will need the spirits of Kennedy, FDR and Lincoln, and also a patient public

Jon Meacham

This article appeared in *Newsweek* on November 5, 2008, the day after the election of Barack Obama. Jon Meacham is a contributor to that publication.

He was, once, the consummate outsider. The first time Barack Obama saw the White House was a quarter century ago, in 1984, when he was working as a community organizer based at the Harlem campus of the City College of New York. President Reagan was proposing reductions in student aid. The young Obama, just out of Columbia, got together with student leaders—"most of them black, Puerto Rican, or of Eastern European descent, almost all of them the first in their families to attend college"—to take petitions protesting the cuts to the New York delegation on Capitol Hill. Afterward, Obama wrote in *The Audacity of Hope*, the group wandered down Pennsylvania Avenue to the Washington Monument and then to the White House, where they stood outside the gates, looking in.

The glib literary move at this point would be to note how Obama, who will become the 44th president of the United States on January 20, 2009, will now return to that house to undo the work that was unfolding inside all those years ago—the work of the Republican Party of Nixon, Reagan, and George W. Bush. But the story, like Obama himself, is more complicated than one might think. The Democratic Party's success in 2008 is not a straightforward revenge-of-the-left drama. Many true believers say this is the dawn of a new progressive era, a time of resurgent (and in many ways rethought) liberalism. The highly caffeinated have high hopes. At the same time, many conservatives—most, it seems, with a show on Fox News—see things the same way, and believe an Age of Obama will be a grim hour of redistribution at home and weakness abroad.

But if Obama governs as he ran—from the center—then there will be disappointed liberals and conservatives. The left may feel somehow cheated, and the right, eager to launch perpetual assaults on the new administration, could well find Obama as elusive and frustrating as the opposition found Reagan.

Parallels from the past risk seeming irrelevant and antique given the enormity of the historical moment. A nation whose Constitution enshrined slavery has elected an African American president within living memory of days when blacks were denied fundamental human rights—including the right to vote. Hyperbole around elections comes easy and cheap, but this is a moment—a year—when even superlatives cannot capture the magnitude of the change that the country voted for last Tuesday. "If there is anyone out there who doubts that America is a place where all things are possible; who still wonders if the dream of our Founders is alive in our time; who still questions the power of our democracy, tonight is your answer," Obama told an adoring yet serious throng in Chicago's Grant Park. He alluded to the historic nature of the victory only indirectly. "This election had many firsts and many stories that will be told for generations," he said. He did not need, really, to add anything to that: that he was saying the words was testament enough.

Obama ran, in part, by arguing that his candidacy transcended race. Perhaps it did; many of us believed that his skin color, unusual name and unfamiliar background might well cost him the election. As it turned out, he won decisively, a rare feat for a Democratic presidential nominee. Does this mean that America is now beyond black and white? No, but we are much further ahead than we were a week ago. Obama's victory, no matter what one's politics, is a redemptive moment in the life of a nation for which race has been called, simply and starkly, "the American dilemma."

John McCain is a man of honor, a patriot who has lived a life of service and devotion to country. He was, however, on the wrong side of history in 2008. Like Hillary Clinton, also a formidable American and public servant, he had the great personal misfortune to be standing in the path of an unstoppable political force. (One of the riddles of the age will be what might have happened had he survived the South Carolina primary in 2000 and defeated Bush for the Republican nomination eight years ago.) External forces, chiefly the economic collapse in the autumn and President Bush's stubbornly low approval ratings, created an environment that made a GOP victory virtually impossible. With a man of Obama's undeniable political gifts on the other side, the task became actually impossible.

Like Franklin D. Roosevelt in 1932 and Reagan in 1980, the Obama win of 2008 marks a real shift in real time. It is early yet, but it is not difficult to imagine that we will, for years to come, think of American politics in terms of Before Obama and After Obama. Certainly many of his voters already see the world this way. Exit polls suggest that one of every 10 voters was casting a ballot for the first time, and they were overwhelmingly minority or young. Eighteen- to 24-year-olds accounted for roughly the same percentage of the electorate—17 percent—as they did in 2004, but while the split four years ago was 54–40 percent for John Kerry, it was 68–30 percent for Obama, a net swing of 24 points in Obama's favor, which was by far the biggest shift in any age group.

Their battles are not the battles of their fathers and mothers. Why, Obama once asked someone he identified only as "an old Washington hand," did the capital of the first decade of the 21st century feel so much harsher than the postwar era? "It's generational," the man replied. "Back then, almost everybody with any power in Washington had served in World War II. We might've fought like cats and dogs on issues. A lot of us came from different backgrounds, different neighborhoods, different political philosophies. But with the war, we all had something in common. That shared experience developed a certain trust and respect. It helped to work through our differences and get things done." That version of the past was heavily edited: Joe McCarthy was a veteran, too.

Still, the point stands. Shared experiences tend to create shared values. Even the epic events of recent years— September 11, Iraq, the economic crisis—cannot begin to give the Obama coalition anything like World War II to smooth the rough edges of partisanship. His voters share convictions, not experiences. Chief among these convictions is a passion for a change from the rule of George W. Bush and an unabashed love for Barack Obama.

In this light, Obama has more in common with Reagan than appearances might suggest. Reagan's loyalists believed in his issues, or at least one of his issues, and they believed in him. They were anxious for a change from the incumbent administration at a time of shattered confidence and economic turmoil. The comparison is revealing, for it may foreshadow the nature of the next four or eight years. Like Reagan, Obama is an astute performer, a maker of myths and a teller of stories. Like Reagan, he is popularly seen, by friend and foe alike, as an ideological purist—but has demonstrated a tendency toward the pragmatic. Like Reagan, he is the leader of a core of believers so convinced he is on their side that they are likely to forgive him his compromises.

Obama gets the Gipper. "Reagan spoke to America's longing for order," he has written, "our need to believe that we are not simply subject to blind, impersonal forces but that we can shape our individual and collective destinies, so long as we rediscover the traditional virtues of hard work, patriotism, personal responsibility, optimism and faith."

A man with a vivid literary and historical imagination, Obama is something of a dreamer, if a down-to-earth one. As a senator, he saw things that are not there, but once were. "Sometimes, standing there in the chamber, I can imagine Paul Douglas or Hubert Humphrey at one of these desks, urging yet again the adoption of civil-rights legislation; or Joe McCarthy, a few desks over, thumbing through lists, preparing to name names; or LBJ prowling the aisles, grabbing lapels and gathering votes. Sometimes I will wander

continued

chapter 17 America in the age of Obama | **315**

over to the desk where Daniel Webster once sat and imagine him rising before the packed gallery and his colleagues, his eyes blazing as he thunderously defends the Union against the forces of secession."

Visiting the White House when he arrived in Washington as a senator, Obama mused: "The inside of the White House doesn't have the luminous quality that you might expect from TV or film; it seems well kept but worn, a big old house that one imagines might be a bit drafty on cold winter nights. Still, as I stood in the foyer and let my eyes wander down the corridors, it was impossible to forget the history that had been made there—John and Bobby Kennedy huddling over the Cuban missile crisis; FDR making last-minute changes to a radio address; Lincoln alone, pacing the halls and shouldering the weight of a nation."

It is telling that his visions ended before the middle of the 1960s, a decade that has disproportionately shaped subsequent decades. Obama's campaign was about moving beyond the wars of the baby-boom generation. In this he is a contradictory figure. Pressing a centrist message in the presidential campaign, he had a reliably liberal and not terribly interesting voting record in the Senate. Which Obama will show up for work in the White House? The New New Democrat, or the safely liberal former community organizer from Chicago? It seems safe to say that he would not have won as he did if he had appeared to be an eloquent Walter Mondale, or a tactically brilliant Michael Dukakis. He ran as a more practical kind of center-left politician—not a Great Society liberal, but one who, in the tradition of Bill Clinton, believes in pursuing progressive goals through centrist means and with an occasionally conservative cultural message. The "socialist" attacks of the McCain-Palin ticket failed in part because they stretched credulity.

Liberals who have thrilled to Obama could grow disenchanted with him if he fails to deliver a progressive Valhalla by, say, Valentine's Day. But the Reagan example offers a different—and more likely—possibility. Given Obama's popularity with his base, he may be that rare politician who can get away with making a deal without being seen as selling out. Reagan raised taxes and nobody held it against him, or even noticed all that much. Obama could be a Teflon man for the new century.

One thing is certain: Obama knows the Washington game he disdains, and he knows it well. He confounded virtually every prognostication in the campaign, and he knows politics, psychology and history. He understands that patience is a rare American virtue, and that it is easy to lose one's perspective. "When Democrats rush up to me at events and insist that we live in the worst of political times, that a creeping fascism is closing its grip around our throats, I may mention the internment of Japanese Americans under FDR, the Alien and Sedition Acts under John Adams, or a hundred years of lynching under several dozen administrations as having been possibly worse, and suggest that we all take a deep breath," he wrote.

There will not be much time for deep breathing between now and January. Before the crowd in Grant Park, Obama acknowledged the difficulties: "two wars, a planet in peril, the worst financial crisis in a century." In characteristically serious tones, he downplayed expectations, trying an all-too-novel approach in American politics: he was (basically) honest about what awaits us. "The road ahead will be long," he said. "Our climb will be steep. We may not get there in one year or even one term, but America, I have never been more hopeful than I am tonight that we will get there." But he quickly came back to earth. "There will be setbacks and false starts," he said, promising that "I will always be honest with you about the challenges we face."

To govern well, Obama will need all those spirits he once evoked—FDR, Kennedy, Lincoln—and he will need an understanding public. Two years ago, on the eve of his campaign for president, Obama said this about the American people: "I imagine they are waiting for a politics with the maturity to balance idealism and realism, to distinguish between what can and cannot be compromised, to admit the possibility that the other side might sometimes have a point."

Now he has the chance to help make such a politics a reality. On the night before the election, en route from Akron, Ohio, home to Chicago, Obama wandered back into the press section of his campaign plane, thanking reporters—especially those who had been with him from the beginning. "It will be fun to see how the story ends," said Obama, as he headed to the front of the plane. Yes, Mr. President-elect, it will.

QUESTIONS FOR READING

1. What does Meacham identify as the "American dilemma"?
2. Why, according to Meacham, did John McCain lose the election?
3. Why did politicians after World War II succeed in "getting things done" more so than politicians in the first decade of the 21st century?
4. According to Meacham, how are Obama and former President Ronald Regan, who was a conservative Republican, similar?
5. What does Meacham say Obama will need to govern well?

QUESTIONS FOR REASONING AND ANALYSIS

1. What is the thesis of Meacham's article? How would you express his thesis in your own words?
2. What does Meacham mean when he calls it a "glib literary move" to describe "how Obama, who will become the 44th president of the United States on January 20, 2009, will now return to that house to undo the work that was unfolding inside all those years ago"? What is he saying about the way in which Obama will govern?
3. Why does Meacham make so many historical references throughout this piece? What is he communicating to an audience by making such references?
4. How would you describe Meacham's attitude toward Obama? Hopeful? Optimistic? Pessimistic? Why would you use one term over another to describe his attitude toward the new president?

QUESTIONS FOR REFLECTING AND WRITING

1. What does Meacham mean when he says Obama's voters "share convictions, not experiences"? Do you agree? Why or why not?
2. Why does a president need a strong sense of a nation's history in order to govern well? For Obama, what makes this time in U.S. history different from others? How might it be similar to other periods?
3. Some of Obama's opponents have argued that he lacks experience to sit in the Oval Office. Do you agree or disagree? In what ways could Obama compensate for a possible lack of experience?

The Amazing Spider-Man, Inaugural Day edition

Story by Zeb Wells, Todd Nauck, and Frank D'Armata

Barack Obama makes a guest appearance in the November 2008 issue of *The Amazing Spider-Man* (#583, Marvel Comics).

Spider-Man: TM & © 2010 Marvel Characters, Inc. Used with permission.

QUESTIONS FOR REASONING AND ANALYSIS

1. In this story, the arch villain known as the Chameleon makes an attempt on Obama's life during his inauguration. After Spider-Man saves Obama, Obama remarks that he was actually more dismayed over the Chameleon's failure to understand the electoral process. Is a broader and more significant statement being made here? If so, what is that statement?

2. Although Spider-Man is the superhero in these stories, does he, in this issue, represent something or someone else? If so, what does he represent? Consider for a moment the frame in which Obama gives Spidey a "fist bump" and then calls him "partner." What is the message of this frame?

3. Is it important that the villain for this issue is the Chameleon? Why or why not? How is the Chameleon dressed? Who is he pretending to be?

QUESTIONS FOR REFLECTING AND WRITING

1. Is Barack Obama a superhero to some people? Can any one person or leader be characterized as a "superhero"? Why or why not?

2. What characteristics, virtues, and skills might cause people to think of one person as "super"? Is it realistic to elevate one person to this status?

3. In the comics, superheroes come to the rescue in times of crisis. The American people, some might argue, elected Barack Obama because they felt he could save the country from disaster. Can Barack Obama, as one man, lead the United States out of financial crisis, effectively protect the country from terrorists, and improve the overall state of the nation? Why or why not?

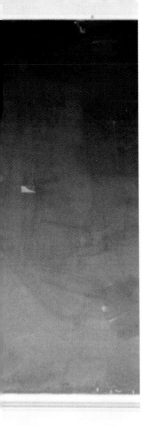

students, teachers, and schools in the 21st century

chapter | 18

Issues in education reflect numerous and serious concerns for teachers, school administrators, politicians, and, last but not least, parents and students. The federal government and state legislatures as well as local school districts constantly struggle with the best way to finance schools and educational programs and, at the same time, constantly deliberate the best methods for evaluating teacher job performance and assessing student learning. The examples in this chapter highlight those challenges, revealing different sides of arguments over quality and fairness of our educational system. On a slightly different note, however, the last two readings address the new and connected issue of the digital library.

prereading question

The topics of these selections are connected to one another and to the questions about U.S. education in general. Think about each author's particular argument, but also reflect on the ways that each one contributes to the larger debate about quality and fairness in America's schools.

web sites related to this chapter's topic

U.S. DEPARTMENT OF EDUCATION
www.ed.gov
This government site contains links to many resources on educational issues.

AMERICAN FEDERATION OF TEACHERS
www.aft.org
This union's site contains many resources and links. Go to their higher education page for resources on college issues, including distance learning.

PRESIDENT OBAMA'S AGENDA FOR EDUCATION
www.whitehouse.gov/agenda/education
This Web page explains President Barack Obama's agenda for education.

web site

prereading question } **What do you think is the most significant problem U.S. education faces today?**

National Education Association

The National Education Association (NEA) boasts a membership of 3.2 million with affiliate organizations in every state and in over 14,000 communities across the United States. Its major goal is to advance public education at every level (preschool through graduate education).

QUESTIONS FOR REASONING AND ANALYSIS

1. What do you find persuasive and compelling about the NEA home page? Why do you find certain features more compelling than others?
2. Under the "Take Action on NCLB" page, what is the major argument or claim? Are adequate reasons given to support the claim? Why or why not? If so, what are those reasons?
3. The "Research" layer, which is associated with the NCLB section, provides a synopsis of performance for each state. A user can select a specific state from the drop-down menu. How would you assess the performance of your state? What evidence suggests positive performance? Negative performance? Neither?
4. Overall, do you think the site (these layers, specifically) depends more upon emotional or logical appeal? Why? How has the association attempted to establish credibility for audiences?

QUESTIONS FOR REFLECTING AND WRITING

1. Conduct some additional research on the No Child Left Behind (NCLB) Act. What are the provisions of this legislation? In your view, is the NCLB Act a solid piece of legislation? Why or why not?
2. What should be the priorities of the U.S. educational system? Why should the system set these priorities as priorities per se?
3. How would you improve education in your home state? What actions would you take and why?

prereading question } Is a high school education too oriented toward standardized testing?

Daryl Cagle

This cartoon originally appeared on MSNBC.com.

© 2007 Daryl Cagle and PoliticalCartoons.com.

QUESTIONS FOR REASONING AND ANALYSIS

1. In your view, what is the cartoonist's point?
2. How would you describe the character applying for the job? Is it significant that the cartoonist has depicted the character in a certain way? Why or why not?
3. Would the cartoon communicate the point more effectively if a college admissions officer was interviewing the high school graduate? How so? If not, why not?

QUESTIONS FOR REFLECTING AND WRITING

1. Many claim that high school teachers are required all too often to "teach to the test." As a person who recently graduated from high school, do you see that claim as valid? Why?
2. If high school teachers do "teach to the test," then why is their doing so problematic, assuming that standardized tests effectively assess a student's basic skills and competencies? Are standardized tests an accurate measure, in your view? Why or why not?
3. How would you assess and evaluate students' mastery of skills and concepts in high school? Why would you choose one particular assessment over another?

Are schools failing our students? Are school administrators misguided in their priorities?

Gary Varvel

This cartoon appeared in the Union Leader.com on May 2, 2006 ("State of Education" section).

By permission of Gary Varvel and Creators Syndicate, Inc.

QUESTIONS FOR REASONING AND ANALYSIS

1. In your own words, what is the cartoonist's thesis or claim?
2. With whom are the parents in the cartoon meeting? A teacher or a principal? What evidence suggests one over the other? Is the identity of the character important? Why or why not?
3. The cartoonist suggests something about emphasis on athletics, but more specifically, do you think the cartoonist is suggesting something about funding for schools? If so, what is the cartoonist trying to say? What evidence or reasoning from the cartoon supports the idea that the cartoonist is making a statement about the allocation of funds in schools (that is, the way schools and school districts spend money)?

QUESTIONS FOR REFLECTING AND WRITING

1. Is a strong emphasis on athletics in public schools contrary to a school's academic mission? Do you agree with what this cartoon implies about the relationship between the two? Why or why not?
2. In many instances, public school teachers must express a willingness to coach athletics to fulfill job expectations regardless of whether or not they wish to do so. Does it make sense to hire teachers more for their ability or willingness to coach athletics rather than for their ability or willingness to teach a subject? Why or why not?
3. How might schools achieve a better balance between supporting athletic programs and stressing academics?

Left Behind, Way Behind

Bob Herbert

An op-ed columnist for *The New York Times* since 1993, Bob Herbert has also been a national correspondent for NBC and a founding panelist for *Sunday Edition*. He writes on politics, urban issues, and social trends, as we see in the following column from the August 29, 2005 nytimes.com.

First the bad news: Only about two-thirds of American teenagers (and just half of all black, Latino and Native American teens) graduate with a regular diploma four years after they enter high school.

Now the worse news: Of those who graduate, only about half read well enough to succeed in college.

Don't even bother to ask how many are proficient enough in math and science to handle college-level work. It's not pretty.

Of all the factors combining to shape the future of the U.S., this is one of the most important. Millions of American kids are not even making it through high school in an era in which a four-year college degree is becoming a prerequisite for achieving (or maintaining) a middle-class lifestyle.

The Program for International Assessment, which compiles reports on the reading and math skills of 15-year-olds, found that the U.S. ranked 24th out of 29 nations surveyed in math literacy. The same result for the U.S.—24th out of 29—was found when the problem-solving abilities of 15-year-olds were tested.

If academic performance were an international athletic event, spectators would be watching American kids falling embarrassingly behind in a number of crucial categories. A new report from a pair of Washington think tanks—the Center for American Progress and the Institute for America's Future—says an urgent new commitment to public education, much stronger than the No Child Left Behind law, must be made if that slide is to be reversed.

This would not be a minor task. In much of the nation the public education system is in shambles. And the kids who need the most help—poor children from inner cities and rural areas—often attend the worst schools.

An education task force established by the center and the institute noted the following:

Young low-income and minority children are more likely to start school without having gained important school readiness skills, such as recognizing letters and counting. . . . By the fourth grade, low-income students read about three grade levels behind nonpoor students. Across the nation, only 15 percent of low-income fourth graders achieved proficiency in reading in 2003, compared to 41 percent of nonpoor students.

How's that for a disturbing passage? Not only is the picture horribly bleak for low-income and minority kids, but we find that only 41 percent of nonpoor fourth graders can read proficiently.

I respectfully suggest that we may be looking at a crisis here.

The report, titled *Getting Smarter, Becoming Fairer,* restates a point that by now should be clear to most thoughtful Americans: too many American kids are ill equipped educationally to compete successfully in an ever-more competitive global environment.

Cartoonish characters like Snoop Dogg and Paris Hilton may be good for a laugh, but they're useless as role models. It's the kids who are logging long hours in the college labs, libraries and lecture halls who will most easily remain afloat in the tremendous waves of competition that have already engulfed large segments of the American work force.

The report makes several recommendations. It says the amount of time that children spend in school should be substantially increased by lengthening the school day and, in some cases, the school year. It calls for the development of voluntary, rigorous national curriculum standards in core subject areas and a consensus on what students should know and be able to do by the time they graduate from high school.

The report also urges, as many have before, that the nation take seriously the daunting (and expensive) task of getting highly qualified teachers into all classrooms. And it suggests that an effort be made to connect schools in low-income areas more closely with the surrounding communities. (Where necessary, the missions of such schools would be extended to provide additional services for children whose schooling is affected by such problems

continued

as inadequate health care, poor housing, or a lack of parental support.)

The task force's recommendations are points of departure that can be discussed, argued about and improved upon by people who sincerely want to ramp up the quality of public education in the U.S. What is most important about the report is the fact that it sounds an alarm about a critical problem that is not getting nearly enough serious attention.

QUESTIONS FOR READING

1. What is the source of Herbert's data?
2. In what three ways are American students "behind"? (That is, who is most behind, whom do we trail, and what other standards are we not meeting?)
3. What solutions are suggested in the report?

QUESTIONS FOR REASONING AND ANALYSIS

1. What is the author's view of the report's proposed solutions? What must be the first step to improvement, implied by Herbert?
2. State the author's claim.
3. What is clever about the opening two paragraphs?
4. How would you describe Herbert's tone? How does it contribute to his argument?

QUESTIONS FOR REFLECTING AND WRITING

1. What statistic is most surprising to you? Why?
2. Do you agree with Herbert that the report presents a crisis in American education? Why or why not?
3. If you agree that we have a problem, what solutions would you propose? Do you embrace any of the report's solutions? Do you object to any of them? Be prepared to explain and defend your position.

magazine essay

preading question } **How should we fund education in the United States?**

Education Funding: Follow the Money
How tax deals short schools, and what you can do about it.

Cynthia Kopkowski McCabe

Cynthia Kopkowski McCabe writes for the *NEA Today*. This article appeared in the January/February 2009 issue of that publication.

Every day in this country, big businesses are getting a sweetheart deal paid for by our public school children. And no, we're not talking high-interest lunch money loans.

It's common practice in most states and municipalities to let businesses off the hook for paying taxes, in the vague hope of stimulating economic development. But that practice regularly shortchanges the schools where you work and send your children. Maybe *shortchanges* isn't the best term, actually. Try *shortbillions*. Over the past 20 years, the percentage of profits corporations paid in state and local taxes dropped 50 percent. Have your taxes gone down 50 percent in the last 20 years? Didn't think so.

Yet, after decades of watching such incentives weaken the financial footing of the nation's schools, many people still don't understand the relationship between tax breaks and things like class size and salaries. "We have a wonderful antenna that goes up when we hear a politician talk about public schools and testing and pay and pensions," says NEA Vice President Lily Eskelsen. "We need that same antenna to start vibrating when we hear a politician talk about economic development."

Here's how it works: A large corporation comes to state legislators, county commissioners, or city council members and offers to set up shop in their area, creating jobs and boosting the local economy. In exchange, they ask for tax breaks. Lots of them. Well-meaning government officials agree, seeing the business's arrival as the quickest way to spur development in the area. The problem is that many of these deals spell years of lost tax revenues.

"People don't see the other side of it," says Bruce Nissen, the director of research at the Center for Labor Research and Studies at Florida International University. "Tax cuts mean cuts to necessary services from government." Taxes not paid by the corporation can hit local residents twice: Their local schools are shorted and, on top of that, local governments are forced to shift the tax obligation to residents to stanch the bleeding.

Add this to the growing list of things about which educators now have to be concerned, knowledgeable, and energized. But what's the solution to this tax break bonanza? That would be "TEF," an economic theory whose acronym is shorthand for tax structure, economic development policies, and funding for schools. Essentially, TEF is a call for fair taxation—both personal and corporate—and economic development that invests in education, rather than cripples it.

Right now, the nation's schools are at the mercy of misguided policies around these three elements, says Associate Project Director Michael Kahn of NEA Research. "Unfortunately, these things have been going in the wrong direction for the last 30 years." (If you're wondering about the multi-billion-dollar bailouts for the banking and credit industries, that's a separate issue, says Dawn Addy, director of the Center for Labor Research and Studies. "We're talking about money that goes directly into the community and certainly that's different from giving buyouts to the big guys.")

Let's look at personal taxation first. American workers on average pay $12 in taxes for every $100 they earn. Anyone making more than $1 million annually pays only $5 out of every $100. "We can't achieve adequate schools if the tax responsibility is being shifted to those who have the least amount of money," says Kahn.

Unfair economic development is just as troublesome. Consider Sykes Enterprises, Inc., a call center company. In 1999, the company located in Pikeville, Kentucky,

after the local government gave it a multimillion-dollar package that included a five-year pass on property tax, which would have helped fund schools. In 2004, the company shuttered the facility and eliminated 324 jobs.

Similar stories come from Colorado, Oregon, North Dakota, Kansas, Nebraska, Minnesota, and Florida. Nationwide, state tax subsidies, cuts, incentives, and abatements offered to businesses and corporations have an annual price tag of more than $50 billion. Michigan alone estimates its state and local giveaways hover around $929 million annually. Decades ago, education activists didn't pay much attention to these tax breaks, NEA's Eskelsen says. "Now we've all seen what can happen to school dollars when some slick snake oil salesman with a PowerPoint presentation talks about economic development," she says. (Oddly enough, these companies examine the quality of the local schools—the same schools that any tax breaks they might get would end up hurting—as they mull whether to locate their employees there.)

And nowhere are the current failed system's misplaced priorities more apparent than school funding. In recent years, District of Columbia taxpayers footed a $611 million bill for a new stadium for the Washington Nationals baseball team. That amount of money could have built 61 brand new elementary schools, 36 middle schools, or 32 high schools, or refurbished hundreds of crumbling facilities in the District.

As the country's economy continues to stumble, TEF proponents want local and state leaders to understand that a country's fiscal health is directly related to a fair and equitable tax system, a level economic development playing field for large and small businesses, and adequate and equitable funding for public education. The underlying premise is simple: In the new global, knowledge-based economy, investing in public education—our human capital—provides a greater return on investment than tax cuts and subsidies for big business and sports stadiums.

Included in these TEF proponents are members of the Mississippi Association of Educators. After watching for years as businesses came into the state and received deals that let them escape local taxes for as long as a decade in some cases, state and local Association leaders began fighting back. Why? Cuts to school supplies and equipment, eroding facilities that had no relief coming in the form of repairs or renovations, ballooning class sizes, stagnant salaries, and staff layoffs. When it was finally time for the corporations to start paying their taxes, "they would up and leave," says Frank Yates, the Association's executive director. Nobody is anti-business, Yates says. "The idea here now is that yes, we want the local

continued

governments to recruit economic development, but they need to pay their fair share of taxes, otherwise the local citizens have to have their taxes raised," to pay for essential services like schools and educator salaries and pensions, he says.

With the help of NEA, the Mississippi affiliate trained 25 members and UniServ directors to talk to colleagues, parents, and others about the importance of supporting fair taxation and economic development, and increased school funding. They're heading out into their communities, holding forums and giving people "a true picture of our economic future," says Yates.

David Odom, a high school algebra teacher in DeSoto County, Mississippi, is a member of that team. He travels the state in his free time, explaining in cafeterias and church halls how, in some cases, educators pay a higher percentage of their salaries in taxes than big businesses do. Adding insult to injury, they're then forced to dig into their own pockets to pay for essential supplies when schools don't get the money they need. "If these businesses were paying their fair share, we wouldn't have that problem," Odom says. "Most people don't realize what is actually going on. You get mad when you do."

There is hope on the horizon. Efforts like Odom's and similar ones in other states are paying off as concern about corporate tax breaks is starting to take root among the general public. A study this fall by the Wisconsin Education Association Council found that nearly seven out of 10 voters think changes are needed in school funding, and a majority strongly favor eliminating corporate tax loopholes. "Public opinion is very much in tune with our beliefs," says Council President Mary Bell. "We need a better school funding system—one that is accountable to the people who pay for it and depend on it."

But it can't be just a handful of states that tackle big business opportunism and the legislators who enable it. Grassroots activists are needed across the country to point out how educators and students are being hurt by unfair taxes, underfunded schools, and corrosive economic development. And there's no better spokesperson to talk with parents, community members, and legislators about the damage being done in schools than the very people on the frontlines. "In order for TEF to work," says Odom, "everyone needs to get on the bandwagon."

www.nea.org/home/20750.htm

QUESTIONS FOR READING

1. How much have corporate taxes on profits dropped in the last 20 years?

2. According to McCabe, what is the overall effect on schools of corporate tax breaks or cuts?

3. What is TEF? What are its goals?

QUESTIONS FOR REASONING AND ANALYSIS

1. How would you summarize McCabe's thesis or claim in this article?

2. Consider the argument McCabe makes in these sentences: "Let's look at personal taxation first. American workers on average pay $12 in taxes for every $100 they earn. Anyone making more than $1 million annually pays only $5 out of every $100. 'We can't achieve adequate schools if the tax responsibility is being shifted to those who have the least amount of money,' says Kahn." What is the warrant, or implicit assumption, linking her evidence to the claim here?

3. What are some examples of logical appeal from this article? Why are these appeals logical rather than emotional?

4. How might McCabe's essay reflect a problem-solution argument?

5. Has McCabe made a convincing case? Why or why not?

QUESTIONS FOR REFLECTING AND WRITING

1. If you were to post a comment in response to McCabe, what would you say? Would you defend corporate tax breaks? Why or why not?

2. In one paragraph, McCabe claims that the District of Columbia spent $611 million of taxpayer money to build a new baseball stadium. She argues that a trade-off occurred; in other words, the District could have spent that money on infrastructure for schools. What argument can one make in response? What reasons might defend the District's decision to build a new baseball stadium?

3. What is your answer to the problem of funding public education? Higher corporate taxes? Measures to encourage economic development? Budget cuts for other programs?

prereading question } What are your views on digital libraries? Reflect on the pros and cons on your own and then read both arguments.

The Digital Library Plan: Riches We Must Share

Mary Sue Coleman

A professor of biochemistry for many years, Mary Sue Coleman has been president of the University of Michigan since 2002. She led the university to a successful case in the Supreme Court defending college affirmative action policies. Her university is now one of the five working with Google to digitize its holdings. Her argument and its counter by Nick Taylor that follows were published in *The Washington Post* on October 22, 2005.

Some authors and publishers have cried foul regarding Google's digital library initiative, sparking debate about intellectual property rights in an online age. Beyond the specific legal challenges emerging in the wake of such a sea change, there are deeply important public policy issues at stake. We must not lose sight of the transformative nature of Google's plan or the public good that can come from it.

Throughout history, most of the world's printed knowledge has been created, preserved and used only by society's elites—those for whom education and power meant access to the great research libraries. Now, groundbreaking tools for mass digitization are poised to change that paradigm. We believe the result can be a widening of human conversation comparable to the emergence of mass literacy itself.

Google plans to make its index searchable to every person in the world who enjoys access to the Internet. For those works that remain in copyright, a search will reveal brief excerpts along with information about how to buy the work or borrow it from a public library. Searches of work in the public domain will yield access to complete texts online.

Imagine what this means for scholars and the general public, who, until now, might have discovered only a fraction of the material written on a subject. Or picture a small, impoverished school—in America or anywhere in the world—that does not have access to a substantial library but does have an Internet connection.

This enormous shift is already upon us. Students coming to my campus today belong to the Net Generation. By the time they were in middle school, the Internet was a part of their daily lives. As we watch the way our students search for and use information, this much is clear: If information is not digitized, it will not be found.

Libraries and educational institutions are the only entities whose mission is to preserve knowledge through the centuries. It is a crucial role, one outside the inter-

est of corporate entities and separate from the whims of the market. If libraries do not archive and curate, there is substantial risk that entire bodies of work will be lost.

Universities and the knowledge they offer should be accessible by all.

We must continue to ensure access to the vast intellectual opportunity and knowledge we generate and preserve. The digitization of information is a profound gesture that holds open our doors. Limiting access to information is tantamount to limiting the opportunities of our citizens.

Criticism of the Google library project revolves around questions of intellectual property. Universities are no strangers to the responsible management of complex copyright, permission and security issues; we deal with them every day in our classrooms, libraries, laboratories and performance halls. We will continue to work within the current criteria for fair use as we move ahead with digitization.

But we believe deeply that this endeavor exemplifies the spirit under which our nation's copyright law was developed: to encourage the free exchange of ideas in the service of innovation and societal progress. The protections of copyright are designed to balance the rights of the creator with the rights of the public. At its core is the most important principle of all: to facilitate the sharing of knowledge, not to stifle such exchange.

No one believed more fervently in the diffusion of knowledge than Thomas Jefferson, who resurrected the Library of Congress, using his own books, after its predecessor was destroyed by fire. We must continue to heed his message:

> And it cannot be but that each generation succeeding to the knowledge acquired by all those who preceded it, adding to it their own acquisitions and discoveries, and handing the mass down for

continued

successive and constant accumulation, must advance the knowledge and well-being of mankind, not infinitely, as some have said, but indefinitely, and to a term which no one can fix and foresee.

I worry that we are unnecessarily fearful of a world where our libraries can be widely accessed and that our fear will strangle the exchange of ideas so critical to our Founders. As these technologies are developed, our policies must help ensure that people can find information and that printed works are preserved for future generations.

QUESTIONS FOR READING

1. What is Coleman's subject?
2. What change will the Google digital library produce?
3. How will Google handle works under copyright?

4. What is the ultimate goal of copyright laws, according to the author?
5. What role does the university have that bears on this issue?

QUESTIONS FOR REASONING AND ANALYSIS

1. What is Coleman's claim?
2. What are her primary reasons? State them in your own words.

3. How does she counter the copyright issue?

QUESTIONS FOR REFLECTING AND WRITING

1. Coleman suggests that our "online age" has made a difference in the debate on copyright. Has it? That is, just because we can digitize books, does that mean that it is right to ignore intellectual property rights? Can this argument be defended? Why or why not?

2. What is your position on this debate? Why? Has Coleman influenced your position? If so, how? If not, why not?

newspaper column

prereading questions } **What potential problems can you identify in plans to digitize large numbers of books? Are these problems avoidable?**

The Digital Library Plan: But Not at Writers' Expense

Nick Taylor

Nick Taylor is president of the Authors Guild, a member of PEN, and the author of many articles and nonfiction books, including a memoir of astronaut and Senator John Glenn. He is currently working on a book about the Depression-era public works program. His argument was published with the previous one in *The Washington Post* on October 22, 2005.

I am a writer.

For some time now—too much time, I suspect my editor believes—I have been working on a history of the Works Progress Administration. This has taken me to states from Maine to California, into archives and libraries, and on long and occasionally fruitful searches for survivors of the Depression-era program.

I have invested a small fortune in books chronicling the period and copies of old newspapers, spent count-

less hours on Internet searches, paid assistants to dig up obscure bits of information, and then sat at my keyboard trying to spin a mountain of facts into a compelling narrative. Money advanced by my publisher has made this possible.

Except for a few big-name authors, publishers roll the dice and hope that a book's sales will return their investment. Because of this, readers have a wealth of wonderful books to choose from. Most authors do not live high on their advances; my hourly return at this point is laughable.

Only if my book sells well enough to earn back its advance will I make additional money, but the law of copyright assures me of ongoing ownership. With luck, income will flow to my publisher and me for a long time, but if my publisher loses interest, I will still own my book and be able to make money from it.

So my question is this: When did we in this country decide that this kind of work and investment isn't worth paying for?

That is what Google, the powerful and extremely wealthy search engine, with co-founders ranking among the 20 richest people in the world, is saying by declining to license in-copyright works in its library scanning program, which has the otherwise admirable aim of making the world's books available for search by anyone with Web access.

Google says writers and publishers should be happy about this: It will increase their exposure and maybe lead to more book sales.

That's a devil's bargain.

We'd all like to have more exposure, obviously. But is that the only form of compensation Google can come up with when it makes huge profits on the ads it sells along the channels its users are compelled to navigate?

Now that the Authors Guild has objected, in the form of a lawsuit, to Google's appropriation of our books, we're getting heat for standing in the way of progress, again for thoughtlessly wanting to be paid. It's been tradition in this country to believe in property rights. When did we decide that socialism was the way to run the Internet?

The New York Public Library and Oxford University's Bodleian Library, two of the five libraries in the Google program, have recognized the problem. They are limiting the books scanned from their collections to those in the public domain, on which copyright protections have expired.

That is not the case with the others—the libraries of the University of Michigan, Harvard and Stanford. Michigan's librarian believes that the authors' insistence on their rights amounts to speed bumps in the road of progress. "We cannot lose sight of the tremendous benefits this project will bring to society," he said in a news release.

In other words, traffic is moving too slowly, so let's remove the stop signs. Google contends that the portions of books it will make available to searchers amount to "fair use," the provision under copyright that allows limited use of protected works without seeking permission. That makes a private company, which is profiting from the access it provides, the arbiter of a legal concept it has no right to interpret. And they're scanning the entire books, with who knows what result in the future.

There is no argument about the ultimate purpose of Google's initiative. Great value lies in a searchable, online "library at Alexandria" containing all the world's books, at least to that fraction of society that has computers, the electricity to run them and Internet connections. It would make human knowledge available on an unprecedented scale. But it must be done correctly, by acquiring the rights to the resources it wishes to exploit.

The value of Google's project notwithstanding, society has traditionally seen its greatest value in the rights of individuals, and particularly in the dignity of their work and just compensation for it.

The people who cry that information wants to be free don't address this dignity or this aspect of justice. They're more interested in ease of assembly. The alphabet ought to be free, most certainly, but the people who painstakingly arrange it into books deserve to be paid for their work. This, at the core, is what copyright is all about. It's about a just return for work and the dignity that goes with it.

QUESTIONS FOR READING

1. What must writers and publishers do to make money?
2. What is Google's response to writers?
3. What is the position of the New York Public and Bodleian libraries on copyrighted books?
4. What is Google doing in spite of the copyright lawsuit?

QUESTIONS FOR REASONING AND ANALYSIS

1. What is Taylor's claim?
2. What are his reasons? State them in your own words.
3. How does Taylor rebut Coleman's primary defense of the Google project?

4. What does Taylor seek to accomplish in his opening six paragraphs?

QUESTIONS FOR REFLECTING AND WRITING

1. How does Coleman depict Google? How does Taylor depict Google? Who seems more accurate and fair in your view? Why?
2. Who has the best argument? Why?

3. Do we, as a culture, fail to value the time, effort, and creativity that writing a book demands? If so, why? What is your view of the work of writers? Why do you hold that view?

freedom

of expression

in the 21st

century

This chapter explores controversies over First Amendment rights as related to censorship, obscenity, and freedom of speech on college campuses. Essays, Web sites, political cartoons, and photographs make arguments in favor of unequivocally supporting First Amendment rights, or they make arguments that certain forms of expression (pornography, for instance) are not protected under the Constitution. The themes and issues here remain timely and controversial, particularly considering that the U.S. Supreme Court continues to hand down rulings that shape interpretations of the First Amendment.

prereading questions

1. Have you considered positions between the extremes of absolutely no censorship of published materials (in any medium) and of laws prohibiting the publication of obscene, pornographic, or treasonable works or hate speech? What are some possible restrictions that may be agreed upon by most people?

2. What are some ways to control what is published (in any medium) without always resorting to legal restrictions? Are any of these possibilities feasible?

web sites related to this chapter's topic

NATIONAL COALITION AGAINST CENSORSHIP (NCAC)
www.ncac.org
Organization promoting free speech. Site contains articles and news alerts.

NATIONAL FREEDOM OF SPEECH WEEK
www.freespeechweek.org
Site promoting the annual National Freedom of Speech Week.

WE WILL STAND
www.wwstand.org
Nondenominational Christian organization that opposes pornography.

magazine essay

prereading question } Should school officials ever be able to censor a student's speech?

The Schools Are Destroying Freedom of Speech

John W. Whitehead

Constitutional attorney John W. Whitehead is founder and president of The Rutherford Institute. His most recent book, *The Change Manifesto*, was published in 2008 by Sourcebooks, Inc. This editorial appeared on *Right Side News* in March 2009.

"The Constitution makes clear there can be no religious test for holding office, and it is just as clear there can be no religious test for individual expression of free speech—or censorship thereof, including at a high school graduation."—*Nat Hentoff, author and journalist*

Looking at America's public schools, it is difficult to imagine that they were once considered the hope of freedom and democracy.

That dream is no longer true. The majority of students today have little knowledge of the freedoms they possess in the Constitution and, specifically, in the Bill of Rights.

For example, a national survey of high school students reveals that only 2% can identify the Chief Justice of the Supreme Court; 35% know the first three words of the U.S. Constitution; 1.8% know that James Madison is considered the father of the U.S. Constitution; and 25% know that the Fifth Amendment protects against double jeopardy and self incrimination, among other legal rights. Clearly, high school civics classes are failing to teach the importance of our constitutional liberties.

Public educators do not fare much better in understanding and implementing the

Constitution in the classroom. A study conducted by the University of Connecticut found that while public educators seem to support First Amendment rights in principle, they are reluctant to apply such rights in the schools. Consequently, the few students who do know and exercise their rights are forced to deal with school officials who, more often than not, fail to respect those rights.

Unfortunately, instead of being the guardians of freedom, the courts increasingly are upholding acts of censorship by government officials. As a result, the horrific lesson being taught to our young people is that the government has absolute power over its citizens and young people have very little freedom. Two incidents come to mind to illustrate this sad state of affairs, both having to do with school officials heavy-handedly silencing student expression at high school graduation ceremonies.

The first incident involves Nicholas Noel, the senior class president of his graduating class at Grand Rapids Union High School in Michigan. With more than 1,000 people in the audience listening to Noel deliver his commencement address, school officials turned off the microphone when he strayed from his approved speech and referred to the high school as a "prison." Noel said he described the school as a "prison" because it stressed conformity and students were "expected to act alike." His message was that high school paints an incomplete picture of life for students. "The colors of life are yet to come," Noel said. "It was really nice, nothing in bad taste. I tried to be different, and I was punished." Adding insult to injury, school officials even initially refused to award him his diploma.

The second incident, strikingly similar to Noel's, also involves a student whose microphone was cut off during her graduation speech simply because she voiced her personal convictions. Brittany McComb, the graduating valedictorian at Foothill High School in Nevada, was instructed by school officials to reflect over past experiences and lessons learned, say things that came from her heart and inject hope into her speech. Brittany adhered to the school's guidelines and wrote about the true meaning of success in her life—her religious beliefs. However, when she submitted her speech in advance to school administrators, they censored it, deleting several Bible verses and references to "the Lord" and one mention of "Christ."

Believing that the district's censorship amounted to a violation of her right to free speech, McComb attempted to deliver the original version of her speech at graduation. The moment school officials realized that she was straying from the approved text, they *unplugged* her microphone. The move drew extended jeers from the audience, with some people screaming, "Let her speak!"

School officials justified their actions by claiming that McComb's speech amounted to proselytizing. McComb disagrees. "I was telling my story," she said. "And if what I said was proselytizing, it was no more so than every other speaker who espoused his or her personal moral viewpoint about success. We're talking about life here: opinions about the means of success in life, from whatever source, are indeed forms of individual religious expression. It's also hard for me to believe that anyone at graduation could think I or any other speaker was speaking on behalf of the school system."

McComb filed a First Amendment lawsuit in federal court. But on March 19, 2009, a federal appeals court held that school officials did not violate her First Amendment rights by censoring her speech and unplugging the microphone. McComb, who is majoring in journalism at Biola University, plans to appeal to the U.S. Supreme Court.

She should not expect much help from the ACLU. Despite being a longtime champion of student expression, the ACLU actually condoned the school's act of censorship. As ACLU lawyer Allen Lichtenstein remarked about the case, "It's important for people to understand that a student was given a school-sponsored forum by a school and therefore, in essence, it was a school-sponsored speech."

Frankly, if the ACLU applied this logic consistently, then nowhere in the schools would students have the right to say anything that wasn't approved by their teachers or high-level school officials since every area in a public school is controlled and sponsored by the school.

Unfortunately, the trend in the federal courts is to agree with this type of skewed reasoning. However, this type of logic will only succeed in eradicating free expression by students in schools, and the ramifications are far-reaching. Eventually, it will mean that government officials can pull the plug on microphones when they disagree with whatever any citizen has to say. Yet the lessons of history are clear: every authoritarian regime from Hitler to Saddam Hussein has not only unplugged citizens' microphones but stopped those with whom the government disapproved from speaking.

Civil libertarians and the courts have long held that the First Amendment right to free speech applies to everyone, whatever their beliefs. This includes what many people consider offensive or deplorable speech. It also includes speech that persuades, as well as religious speech, non-religious speech or pointedly atheistic speech. Thus, unless we want free speech to end up in a totalitarian graveyard, no one, no matter their viewpoint or ideology, should be censored in any state institution.

1. What were the findings of the University of Connecticut study?
2. According to Whitehead, what "horrific lesson" are students learning?

3. Why did school officials unplug McComb's microphone, effactually censoring her graduation speech?

QUESTIONS FOR REASONING AND ANALYSIS

1. What is Whitehead's claim? What evidence does Whitehead marshal in support of his claim?
2. Does Whitehead rely more on emotional or logical appeal? How does he rely more on one than the other?

3. Why does Whitehead think that the ACLU, in supporting the school against McComb, has used faulty logic in support of its position? Do you agree with Whitehead? Why or why not?

QUESTIONS FOR REFLECTING AND WRITING

1. Should school officials ever restrict or censor a student's speech? Why or why not? If school officials are justified in sometimes censoring students, then under what circumstances should they do so?
2. Whitehead does not explain the federal appeals court's justification for ruling against McComb. Does this omission hurt his credibility or weaken his argument? Why or why not?

3. In relating the McComb example, Whitehead never mentions the possible objection to her actions based on the constitutional separation of church and state. How might someone argue that McComb's actions violated the separation of church and state? Should Whitehead have explicitly addressed the church and state issue? Why or why not?

scholarly journal essay

prereading questions } Should the government control content on the Internet?
Does the First Amendment protect flag burning?

Why the First Amendment (and Journalism) Might Be in Trouble

Ken Dautrich and John Bare

Ken Dautrich, chair of the Department of Public Policy at the University of Connecticut, directed the study *The Future of the First Amendment* with colleague David Yalof. They are coauthors of the book *The First Amendment and the Media in the Court of Public Opinion* (2002). John Bare, Dautrich's coauthor for this article, is vice president for strategic planning and evaluation at the Arthur M. Blank Family Foundation in Atlanta. Their article appeared in the Summer 2005 issue of *Nieman Reports*, published by Harvard University.

Our first-of-its-kind exploration of the future of the First Amendment among American high school students—a highly visible study of 112,000 students and 8,000 teachers in over 300 high schools—suggests a fragile future for key constitutional freedoms while also pointing us to potential remedies. This study, *The Future of the First Amendment,* which was released earlier this year, arrived at a timely moment in American history, on the heels of a national election and amid a war the President is using, by his account, to spread democratic freedoms. The results drew remarkable media attention, which tended to focus on one of the more fearful statistics to emerge from the study: Only 51 percent of 9th to 12th graders agree that newspapers should be allowed to publish freely without government approval of stories—in other words, nearly half entertain the idea of newspaper censorship.

Beyond that flashpoint finding, the study allows for a more thorough understanding of today's high school students and can point us to potential remedies. The research also suggests ways to improve support for the First Amendment. While many of the findings raise concern, some are not so bad. Some are even encouraging. Most of all, the results should be viewed within the context of the history of the First Amendment, which faced challenges—some would say it was compromised—as soon as it was adopted.

First Amendment Challenges

One of the first acts of the first Congress in 1789 was to append a bill of rights to the U.S. Constitution, which, among other things, explicitly denied Congress the ability to tamper with Americans' rights of free expression. Indeed, through the course of our history, Americans and their leaders have proclaimed a commitment to freedom and liberty. Most recently, President Bush, in his second inaugural address, justified the Iraqi and Afghani military operations as a vehicle to spread freedom and liberty throughout the world.

Despite a long history of veneration to these values, freedom of expression has met with a number of challenges. Not long after adoption of the First Amendment, President John Adams and the Federalist Congress passed the Alien and Sedition Acts, severely thwarting the freedom to speak out against government. Abraham Lincoln's suspension of habeas corpus, the internment of Japanese Americans during Franklin Roosevelt's administration after Pearl Harbor, Senator Joseph McCarthy's "red scare," and Attorney General John Ashcroft's aggressive implementation of the USA Patriot Act represent just a few of the more notable breaches to liberty in America.

Like any value in our society, the health and vitality of freedom and liberty are largely dependent upon the public's attention to, appreciation for, and support of them. When Americans are willing to compromise freedom of expression in return for a sense of being more secure, then government officials can more readily take action to curtail freedom. Public fear of Communism allowed McCarthy to tread on people's liberty, just as fear of terrorism allowed Ashcroft to curb freedoms.

The real protection of free expression rights lies not in the words of the First Amendment. Rather, it lies in the people's willingness to appreciate and support those rights. That idea led the Freedom Forum's First Amendment Center to commission an annual survey on public knowledge, appreciation and support for free expression rights since 1997 to gauge the health and well-being of the First Amendment.

If public opinion is a good measure of the First Amendment's well-being, then its annual checkup has been fraught with health problems.

- While more than 9 in 10 agree that "people should be allowed to express unpopular opinions," a paltry 4 in 10 believe that high school students should be able to report on controversial issues in school newspapers without the consent of school officials.

- More than one-third say the press has too much freedom.
- Fewer than 6 in 10 say that musicians should be able to sing songs with lyrics that may be offensive to some.

These annual checkups have shown over time that half of adults think that flag burning as a method of protest should not be tolerated. In general, the surveys have revealed that the public holds low support for, a lack of appreciation for, and dangerously low levels of knowledge of free expression rights. Is it no wonder, then, that the suspension of liberty in this land of freedom has been so readily accomplished by its leaders from time to time?

It was these rather anemic annual checkups that convinced the John S. and James L. Knight Foundation to commission this unique survey of American high school students and to begin a wider discussion about how to strengthen the polity's commitment to the democratic ideal of freedom and liberty.

What follows are some findings from the Knight Foundation survey of high school students that explain, in part, why Americans should be concerned about the First Amendment's future.

- Thirty-six percent of high school students openly admit that they take their First Amendment rights for granted and another 37 percent say they never thought enough about this to have an opinion.
- Seventy-five percent incorrectly believe that it is illegal to burn the flag as a means of political protest, and 49 percent wrongly think that government has the right to restrict indecent material on the Internet.
- A source of the lack of support for free press rights might be due to the fact that only four percent of students trust journalists to tell the truth all of the time.
- Thirty-five percent say the First Amendment goes too far in the rights it guarantees, and 32 percent think the press has too much freedom to do what it wants.

Proposing Some Remedies

This is a bleak picture of what may be in store for the First Amendment as this group matures into adulthood. More importantly, however, a number of findings from the study suggest policies or actions that might better prepare students to value and use their constitutional freedoms. While the suggestions below grow out of findings that are based on correlations, not causation, the logic of the policy ideas holds up against both our experience and our understanding of the data.

continued

1. Instruction on the First Amendment matters. Education works! Students who have taken classes that deal with journalism, the role of the media in society, and the First Amendment exhibit higher levels of knowledge and support for free expression rights than those who haven't. The problem, of course, is that the strong trend toward math and science and "teaching to the standardized test" has crowded out instruction that could help students develop good citizenship skills. The less the schools focus on developing strong citizens, the weaker our democracy becomes. The positive lesson to learn from this is that through enhancements to the high school curriculum, students can become better prepared to value and use their freedoms.

2. Use leads to greater appreciation. When students are given an opportunity to use their freedoms, they develop a better appreciation for them. The Knight project found that students who are engaged in extracurricular student media (such as school newspaper, Internet sites, etc.) are more aware and much more supportive of free expression rights.

3. School leaders need lessons, too. Most high school principals need to be reminded of the value of experiential learning and its implications for the future of the First Amendment. While 80 percent of principals agree that "newspapers should be allowed to publish freely without government approval of a story," only 39 percent say their students should be afforded the same rights for publishing in the school newspaper. Granted, principals have many issues to deal with (like parents and school board members calling and asking how they could have ever allowed a story to be printed in a school paper). But if we are to expect students to mature into responsible democratic citizens, they should be given the freedom to express themselves and act responsibly while in school.

4. Place the issues in the context of their daily lives. The project suggests that, as with most people, when issues affecting one's freedom are brought close to home, students are best able to discern the true meaning and value of freedom. When asked if they agreed or disagreed with this statement— "Musicians should be allowed to sing songs with lyrics that might be offensive to others"—70 percent agreed (only 43 percent of principals and 57 percent of adults agree with this). Music matters to many young people. When this form of free expression is challenged, most students come to its defense. The lesson, of course, is that in teaching students about the virtues of free expression, showing how it relates to things important to them will best instill in students why it is so important to the life of a democracy.

The future of the First Amendment is, at best, tenuous. As the current group of high school students takes on their important role as citizens in our democracy, their lack of appreciation and support for free expression rights will provide a ripe atmosphere for government to further intrude on these freedoms. Many institutions in society should shoulder part of the responsibility to ensure good citizenship skills for our youth. Parents, religious institutions, the media, as well as leadership from public officials, just to name a few. But the public schools play an especially important role in socializing youngsters in how to be responsible citizens, and through the schools the future health and vitality of the First Amendment might be restored.

QUESTIONS FOR READING

1. What is the occasion for the authors' article? What was the purpose of the study?
2. What is the primary source of protection for free expression? For what reason do Americans allow free expression to be restricted?
3. What views revealed in the nation's "annual checkup" put First Amendment rights at risk, according to the authors? What did the study reveal about high school students' views?
4. State the four remedies proposed by the authors in your own words.

QUESTIONS FOR REASONING AND ANALYSIS

1. What, specifically, is the essay's topic? What is the authors' claim?
2. What assumption about freedom is part of this argument?
3. Analyze the four proposals. Do they seem logical remedies to you? Do some seem more likely to produce change than others?

1. What statistic is most surprising to you? Why?

2. Do you share the authors' concerns for the tenuous state of free speech in the United States? If you disagree, how would you rebut them?

3. Can democracy survive without First Amendment rights? Be prepared to debate this issue.

newspaper column

prereading questions } The courts have established that schools have rights that would seem to violate students' First Amendment rights. Should schools have these rights? If so, in what areas? If not, why not?

A Little Civility, Please

Mark Davis

Mark Davis, a Texas native and graduate of the University of Maryland, is a popular radio talk show host (the *Mark Davis Show*) for WBAP Dallas-Fort Worth and has been writing for the *Dallas Morning News* since 2004. The following column was posted on Star-Telegram.com on March 5, 2003.

Try something for me.

Send your teenager to school wearing a T-shirt that says "Martin Luther King Jr. Was Evil" or "Jews Lie: There Was No Holocaust."

Then wait for supporters to suggest that your child was not engaged in the spread of hate but rather in the sparking of vigorous debates.

First, your kid would have been yanked from school so fast that his eyeballs would have popped out.

But just let him (or you) argue that all this does is get people talking about the civil rights era or anti-Semitism, and the shock will be replaced by laughter.

That is exactly the argument made by defenders of Bretton Barber, a Michigan high school junior. The intellectual opening salvo he offered in his school on February 17 was a T-shirt bearing the face of President Bush, framed by the words "International Terrorist."

A regular William F. Buckley, this kid. His intent was obviously not to start a constructive discussion. Conversely, the school did not seek to squelch debate by ordering young Barber to turn the shirt inside out or go home.

If his T-shirt was more generalized and less hateful, with a slogan such as "No War" or even the famous Steve Nash shirt, "Shoot for Peace," I'd say the school should relax.

In the 1960s, students wearing black armbands to protest the Vietnam War won U.S. Supreme Court approval. In the case of *Tinker v. Des Moines*, the court ruled that students "did not shed their constitutional rights to freedom of expression at the schoolhouse gate."

Well, not all of them, anyway. In the years since, we have properly learned that schools do indeed have the right to establish dress guidelines. Most people have shed the absurd notion that an 11th-grader in a public school has the exact same First Amendment rights as an adult in the outside world.

The student newspaper can be barred from calling for the principal's ouster. Student assemblies can be squelched if they feature racial or religious bigotry.

And T-shirts can be nixed if they are—here's the tough word—disruptive. Well, how exactly does a T-shirt disrupt? Do the words on the fabric leap from the wearer's chest and block the students' view of the teacher and blackboard?

No, but an atmosphere that fails to preserve a sense of order and decorum sends the message that various other behavioral extremes might also be tolerated. That is bad.

An armband is one thing. Hate speech, even under the guise of political discourse, is quite another.

How bizarre is it that most who would stand up for Barber's hamhanded "protest" condemning the president would recoil in shock if a kid wore a logo for Marlboro cigarettes or a Confederate flag emblem?

Gosh, wouldn't these be lost opportunities to discuss tobacco and the Civil War?

Passionate debate on controversial issues is good for students and should be encouraged. But within that exercise must be rules of decorous speech and behavior.

This should have nothing to do with whether we agree or disagree with the sentiment expressed. A student wearing a "Clinton Is a Pervert" shirt around 1999 or so would have received no argument from me with regard to content, but I would have supported any school banning it.

continued

The *Star-Telegram* is not the only newspaper to stick up for Bretton Barber. I would expect a certain First Amendment zeal from journalists, and I am not immune to it myself.

But his scolding is not, as an editorial stated, a missed opportunity for discussion. It is an opportunity far too rarely claimed, namely to teach a kid what is and is not permissible within the borders of civilized debate.

Young Barber should be welcome to suggest and participate in vigorous discussions on important issues on his own time or in an appropriate class.

QUESTIONS FOR READING

1. What is Davis's occasion for writing? That is, what student action has received media attention?
2. What are some of the controls that the courts have given to K–12 schools since the 1960s? What, specifically, can lead to a prohibiting of T-shirts?
3. What is Davis's newspaper's position on Bretton Barber? Why is Davis not surprised by his paper's position?

QUESTIONS FOR REASONING AND ANALYSIS

1. What is Davis's claim? Where does he state it?
2. What is Davis's evidence? How does he defend his position?
3. How does he rebut the potential counterargument that students should be encouraged to debate controversial issues?
4. Study the examples Davis gives of T-shirt slogans that would quickly be squelched. What do they have in common? What is Davis's point in using those examples?
5. What strategy does Davis use in paragraphs 7 and 18?

QUESTIONS FOR REFLECTING AND WRITING

1. Do you agree with Davis's position on T-shirt slogans? If so, why? If not, how would you rebut his argument?
2. Why have the courts defended the right of K–12 schools to limit the First Amendment rights of students? Is this different from the issue of controlling access to certain Web sites through a college server? (See Robert O'Neil, pages 344–346.) Should it be different? Why or why not?

---

newspaper column

prereading questions } Should pornography be restricted on the Internet? Should access to pornography be restricted at the office? Do you have a position on these issues?

What Limits Should Campus Networks Place on Pornography?

Robert O'Neil

A former president of the University of Wisconsin system and the University of Virginia, Robert O'Neil holds a law degree from Harvard University and currently teaches constitutional and commercial law at the University of Virginia. He is also the founding director of the Thomas Jefferson Center for the Protection of Free Expression and an authority on First Amendment issues. His article was published in the *Chronicle of Higher Education* on March 21, 2003.

What if you were about to present a PowerPoint lecture to a large undergraduate class, but found instead on your computer a series of sexually explicit ads and material from pornographic Web sites? That's essentially what happened recently to Mary Pedersen, a nutrition-science professor at California Polytechnic State University at San Luis Obispo. That incident and the increasing presence of such imagery at Cal Poly have led to a novel, although undoubtedly predictable, struggle over computer content—one that is quite likely to be replicated at countless campuses in the coming months.

A concerned faculty group at Cal Poly has announced its intention to bring before the Academic Senate, sometime this spring, a Resolution to Enhance Civility and Promote a Diversity-Friendly Campus Climate. Specifically, the measure would prohibit using the university's computers or network to access or download digital material generally described as "pornography." The resolution would also forbid the "transmission" of hate literature and obscenity on the Cal Poly network.

The sponsoring faculty members have offered several reasons for proposing such drastic action. First and foremost, they contend that the ready availability of sexually explicit imagery can create occasional but deeply disturbing encounters like Pedersen's discovery of unwelcome and unexpected material on her classroom computer. The pervasive presence of such images, proponents of the resolution argue, is inherently demeaning to female faculty members, administrators, and students.

Indeed, they suggest that the university might even be legally liable for creating and maintaining a "hostile workplace environment" if it fails to take steps to check the spread of such offensive material. That concern has been heightened by a putative link to a growing number of sexual assaults in the environs of the university.

Those who call for tighter regulation cite several other factors to support anti-pornography measures. In their view, a college or university must maintain the highest of standards, not only in regard to the integrity of scholarship and relations between teachers and students, but also in the range of material to which it provides electronic access. The clear implication is that the ready availability of sexually explicit and deeply offensive imagery falls below "the ethical standards that the university claims to uphold."

Critics of easy access to such material also claim that it can divert time, talent, and resources from the university's primary mission. Kimberly Daniels, a local lawyer who is advising the resolution's sponsors, told the student newspaper that "it is offensive that Cal Poly is taking the position that it is acceptable for professors to view pornography during work hours in their work office." That risk is not entirely conjectural. In fact, one professor left the institution last year after being convicted on misdemeanor charges for misusing a state-owned computer, specifically for the purpose of downloading in his office thousands of sexually explicit images. Local newspapers have also reported that the FBI is investigating another former Cal Poly professor who allegedly used a campus computer to view child pornography.

Finally, the concerned faculty group insists that the free flow of pornographic materials may expose the Cal Poly computer network to a greater risk of virus infection. They cite a student's recent experience in opening a salacious virus-bearing attachment that the student mistakenly believed had been sent by one of his professors.

The proposed Academic Senate resolution has touched off an intense debate. The university's existing computer-use policy presumes that access and choice of material are broadly protected, although it adds that "in exceptional cases, the university may decide that such material directed at individuals presents such a hostile environment under the law that certain restrictive actions are warranted." The new proposal would focus more sharply on sexually explicit imagery, and would require those who wish to view such material through the campus network to obtain the express permission of the university's president.

Defenders of the current approach, including the senior staff of the university's office of information technology, insist that a public university may not banish from its system material that is offensive, but legal, without violating First Amendment rights. Those familiar with the operations of such systems also cite practical difficulties in the enforcement of any such restrictions, given the immense volume of digital communications that circulate around the clock at such a complex institution.

The debate at Cal Poly echoes what occurred some six years ago in Virginia. The General Assembly enacted what remains as the nation's only ban on public employees' use of state-owned or state-leased computers to access sexually explicit material—at least without express permission of a "superior" for a "bona fide research purpose." Six state university professors immediately challenged the law on First Amendment grounds. A district judge struck down the statute, but the U.S. Court of Appeals for the Fourth Circuit reversed that ruling. The law had been modified before that judgment, and many Virginia professors have since received exemptions or dispensations, but the precedent created by the appeals-court decision remains troubling for advocates of free and open electronic communications.

The Virginia ruling complicates the Cal Poly situation. The First Amendment challenge of those who oppose the Academic Senate resolution is less clear than it might at first appear. Two premises underlying that resolution—the need to protect government-owned hardware and the imperative to combat sexual hostility in the public workplace—contributed both to the passage of the Virginia ban, and to its eventual success in the federal courts. What's more, the U.S. Equal Employment Opportunity Commission some months ago gave its blessing to a hostile-workplace complaint filed by Minneapolis Public Library staff members who were offended by persistent display of graphic sexual images on reading-room terminals.

continued

Thus, there is more than a superficial basis for the claims of Cal Poly's porn-banishers that (in the words of one faculty member) "the First Amendment doesn't protect . . . subjecting others to inappropriate material in the workplace." Even the information-technology consultant who has championed the current computer-use policy at the university has conceded that access to controversial material is fully protected only "as long as it isn't offending others."

Although the desire to reduce the potential for offense and affront to other users of a campus computer network seems unobjectionable, its implications deserve careful scrutiny. In the analogous situation of public terminals in a library reading room, it is one thing to ask a patron who wishes to access and display sexually explicit material—or racially hateful material, for that matter—to use a terminal facing away from other users and staff members. It is quite another matter to deny access to such material altogether on the plausible premise that, if it can be obtained at all, there is a palpable risk that its visible display will offend others. To invoke an analogy that is now before the U.S. Supreme Court in a challenge to the Children's Internet Protection Act: It is one thing for a library to provide—even be compelled to provide—filtered access for parents who wish it for their children, but quite another to deny all adult patrons any unfiltered access.

What Cal Poly should seek to do, without impairing free expression, is to protect people from being gratuitously assaulted by digital material that may be deeply offensive, without unduly restricting access of those who, for whatever reason, may wish to access and view such material without bothering others. The proposal in the resolution that permission may be obtained from the university's president, for bona-fide research purposes, is far too narrow. Among other flaws, such a precondition might well deter sensitive or conscientious scholars, whether faculty members or students, who are understandably reluctant to reveal publicly their reasons for wishing to access sexually explicit images or hate literature.

A responsible university, seeking to balance contending interests of a high order, might first revisit and make more explicit its policies that govern acceptable computer use and access, by which all campus users are presumably bound. Such policies could condemn the flaunting of thoughtless dissemination of sexually explicit material and digital hate literature, expressing institutional abhorrence of such postings, without seeking to ban either type of material. The computer network might also establish a better warning system through which to alert sensitive users to the occasional and inevitable presence of material that may offend. Finally, a broader disclaimer might be in order, recognizing the limited practical capacity of a university server to control (or even enable users to avoid) troubling material.

What is needed is a reasonable balance that avoids, as Justice William O. Douglas warned a half-century ago, "burning down the house to roast the pig." That aphorism has special felicity here; in the offensive flaunting of sexually explicit imagery, there is a "pig" that doubtless deserves to be roasted. But there is also a house of intellect that must remain free and open, even to those with aberrant tastes and interests.

QUESTIONS FOR READING

1. What is the occasion for O'Neil's article? What is he responding to?
2. What is the resolution some Cal Poly faculty want passed by their Academic Senate? How do they want to limit access?
3. List the arguments for their resolution in your own words.
4. What are the arguments of those supporting the current Cal Poly Internet guidelines?
5. What arguments were used to support the Virginia ban?
6. How do these First Amendment debates affect terminals in public libraries? What is the current ruling on public libraries?

QUESTIONS FOR REASONING AND ANALYSIS

1. What is O'Neil's claim? Where does he state it? What, specifically, does he think that a university's position or strategy should be regarding "offensive" materials obtained through the university's server?
2. What organizational pattern does O'Neil use in the development of his argument? (Note where he states his claim.) What does he gain by his approach?
3. Where, essentially, does the author stand on censorship versus First Amendment freedoms?
4. Examine O'Neil's conclusion. How does he use Justice Douglas's metaphor to conclude his argument effectively?

1. Evaluate O'Neil's argument. Is he clear and thorough in his analysis of the conflicting positions in this debate? Does he, in your view, have the stronger argument? If so, why? If not, why not?

2. Analyze the author's use of a conciliatory approach. Where does he acknowledge the merits of the opponents' views? How does his claim seek common ground? What might you conclude about the effectiveness of the conciliatory approach when engaged in First Amendment issues?

book excerpt

prereading questions } Does pornography pose a threat to society? To families? To individuals?

A Perfect Storm
Privacy. Neutrality. Free Expression.

Rick Santorum

Former U.S. Senator Rick Santorum (R-PA) now works as a senior fellow for the Ethics and Public Policy Center. He is currently authoring a book addressing the "gathering storm" of the 21st century—the challenges of Islamic radicalism and fundamentalism. "A Perfect Storm" is an excerpt from *It Takes a Family: Conservatism and the Common Good* (Intercollegiate Studies Institute, 2005).

> **EDITOR'S NOTE:** This is the fourth in a series of five excerpts from *It Takes a Family*, by Sen. Rick Santorum. Together they comprise Chapter 23, "The Rule of Judges."

I could go further and discuss the cases that touch on pornography and obscenity, also part of our moral ecology. For decades, communities in America have tried to shore up common decency, have tried to guard their collective moral capital, by regulating *smut*. Congress has likewise responded to Americans' moral sensibilities by attempting to regulate broadcast media and the Internet. But time and again over the past generation America's communities and Congress have run up against a Supreme Court intent to side *against* the American people and *with* the pornographers. The Court's doctrine has been that virtually all efforts to regulate smut run afoul of the First Amendment, which the Court says protects all individuals' "freedom of expression."

But let's look for a minute at what that First Amendment actually says about our freedoms: "Congress shall make no law ... abridging freedom of speech. ..." Since this amendment goes on to discuss the people's right to assemble and to petition the government, as well as freedom of the press, it is clear that the "speech" in question concerns, in the first instance, *political* speech—arguments about the public good. At the time this amendment was passed, the English Crown could and did regulate what could be published and said

about sensitive political questions; in America, things would be different.

But you may have noticed that in pornography the words aren't really the point, are they? *Speech* implies words, rationally intelligible discussion and argument, *communication*. Pictures also can be "worth a thousand words," of course: Sometimes images are central to a political or social cause. But America's huge porn industry is not about political debate; it is not about the communication of ideas. It's about the commercial production of objects of titillation for profit. Based on the text of the Constitution, the courts should have recognized a hierarchy of protected "speech," with political speech and writing receiving the greatest constitutional protection, commercial speech less protection, and mere titillation the least of all. Yet in the topsy-turvy world of the new court-approved morality, limits on political speech like the recently passed McCain-Feingold campaign finance bill are just fine, but congressional restrictions on Internet pornographers are seen as violating the First Amendment and are therefore struck down.

Privacy. Neutrality. Free Expression. None of these terms is in the Constitution. They "look like" terms that actually are there. Freedom from "unreasonable searches and seizures": That's in the Fifth Amendment. "Equal protection of the laws": That's in the Fourteenth Amendment. "Freedom of speech": That's in the First Amendment. That is why liberals

continued

believe what they are doing is merely refining the intentions of our founders, making explicit the underlying philosophical tenets of our Constitution. The problem is that these "philosophical" tenets are pure abstractions, fit only for those great abstractions, "liberal individuals." But the U.S. Constitution was the fruit of long experience in the great complexity and wisdom of English common law.

As Harvard's Mary Ann Glendon has written,

> [T]he peculiar excellence of the Anglo-American common-law tradition over centuries, that which distinguished it from continental "legal science," was its rejection of simplifying abstractions, its close attention to facts and patterns of facts. . . . It was this unique combination of common sense and modest . . . theory that enabled England and the United States to develop and maintain a legal order possessing the toughness to weather political and social upheavals. . . . When legal scholars distance themselves from those ways of thinking, they repudiate much of what is best in their professional tradition.

The Supreme Court of the United States in the past half-century has been a bad steward of its own jurisprudential traditions, preferring instead the neat abstractions of the latest "theories."

Privacy. Neutrality. Free Expression. These three abstractions together make for a perfect storm, a jurisprudential hurricane for wreaking havoc on a moral ecosystem. Together they make of our Constitution not a document for democratic self-governance, but instead describe a pure liberal society of isolated individuals each doing their own thing within the politically correct boundaries carefully crafted and enforced by the village elders.

The irony is that the tradition of common law had made marriage and family exactly a *privileged* institution; Supreme Court decisions originally based on this traditional conception (*Griswold*) eventually undermined that privileged status in the name of abstract privacy. Similarly, as Justice O'Connor observed, on its face the U.S. Constitution is not neutral between religion and irreligion. Religion is a specially protected category in the actual text of the Constitution: It gets a special mention as the "first freedom" of the First Amendment. Religion and the family were the two main agents for *moralizing* society, for generating new moral capital. The Court's decisions have undermined these institutions, creating in their place a society of atomized and de-moralized individuals, shielded by the village elders from the natural moral influences of faith and family.

National Review Online, June 21, 2005.
www.nationalreview.com/comment/
santorum200507210812.asp

QUESTIONS FOR READING

1. How does Santorum define "political speech"?
2. If not about "speech," what is pornography really about, according to Santorum?
3. What "philosophical tenets" does Santorum label "pure abstractions"?
4. In the last paragraph, what accusation does Santorum make of the U.S. Supreme Court?

QUESTIONS FOR REASONING AND ANALYSIS

1. What is Santorum's thesis?
2. Santorum uses the terms *privacy*, *neutrality*, and *free expression* to begin two paragraphs of this essay. He simply states the terms in sequence without using the terms in an actual sentence. What is the rhetorical effect of doing so? How does using the terms in this way become a strategy for organizing the essay?
3. Why does Santorum use textual evidence from Harvard professor Mary Ann Glendon? What point is he trying to support with use of her statement?
4. At the beginning of the piece, Santorum references "moral ecology," and near the end, he mentions the "moral ecosystem." What is he suggesting through use of such references? How do these references function as metaphors? How does the comparison support his thesis?

1. Do you agree with the way Santorum defines "free speech" or "free expression" in this essay? Why or why not?

2. "A Perfect Storm" appeared in the *National Review Online,* a far-right and conservative publication. In your view, does its appearance in *NRO* suggest bias? If an author arguing the opposite point of view published his or her article in *New Republic,* a far-left and liberal magazine, would its appearance there also suggest bias? Why or why not?

3. Does pornography indeed harm the institutions of marriage and family? If so, how so? Do you agree with what Santorum suggests by the end of the essay?

---

web site

prereading question } Should the government ever restrict First Amendment rights and freedoms?

Free Speech Coalition, Inc.: Protecting Nonprofits' First Amendment Rights

Free Speech Coalition, Inc.

Originally founded in 1993, Free Speech Coalition, Inc. protects the First Amendment rights of nonprofit organizations (freespeechcoalition.org).

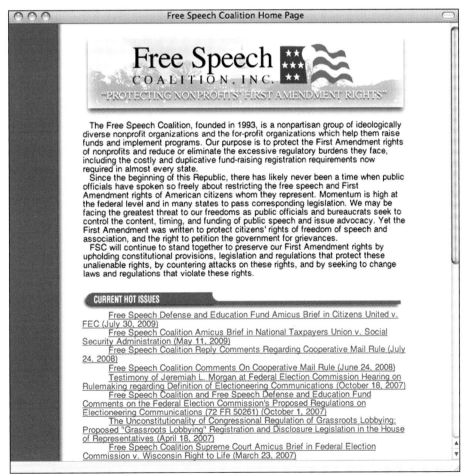

Reprinted by permission of Free Speech Coalition, Inc.

QUESTIONS FOR READING

1. What are some topics Free Speech Coalition, Inc. has chosen to highlight?
2. What sorts of information does this web site provide?
3. What threats to First Amendment rights does this organization cite?

QUESTIONS FOR REASONING AND ANALYSIS

1. What are some examples of persuasive appeals from the Free Speech Coalition, Inc. homepage? Does the site rely more on logical appeal or emotional appeal? Why?
2. Do you view this organization as credible based upon the homepage content? Why or why not?
3. Who is the primary audience for this web site? Why are they the primary audience? Does the organization wish to reach other audiences? If so, whom does it wish to reach?

QUESTIONS FOR REFLECTING AND WRITING

1. Does this web site persuade you to support the Free Speech Coalition, Inc. cause? What arguments from this site compel you the most? Compel you the least? Why?
2. Should the government restrict the freedom of speech in certain circumstances? Which circumstances? Why? If not, why not?
3. How do you view this organization's role and function? Is it important that this organization exists? Why or why not?

prereading question } Should individuals be permitted to say what they wish even if it insults the beliefs and values of most people?

In 2002, students held up a sign with the words "Bong Hits 4 Jesus" during the Olympic torch passing in Juneau, Alaska.

QUESTIONS FOR REASONING AND ANALYSIS

1. What statement are the students attempting to make with their banner? Are they attempting to make more than one statement? If so, what are those statements?
2. Why do you think the students have chosen this event for making this statement?

3. Who is the intended audience for this banner? Why are they the intended audience?
4. Which groups might find the words "Bong Hits 4 Jesus" offensive? For what reasons might they find the words offensive?

QUESTIONS FOR REFLECTING AND WRITING

1. If you were in charge of the Olympic torch passing event in Juneau, would you forbid these students to hold up this banner? Why or why not?
2. Could the students have made this statement in a more constructive and less offensive way? If so, in what way(s)? Would the students' words have the same

impact if they held up a banner that said "The American marijuana policy is illogical" or "Legalize drugs now!"? Why or why not?
3. Was the Olympic torch passing event the best venue for staging this protest? Why or why not?

Brian Fairrington

In September 2007, Senator John Kerry spoke at the University of Florida's Constitution Day, an event organized by the UF student government. Upon hearing the organizers would take only one more question for Senator Kerry, Andrew Meyer, a senior telecommunications major, grabbed a microphone and demanded to be heard. Meyer then became increasingly unruly, prompting the campus security to intervene; according to accounts, Meyer resisted UF police, who then resorted to Tasering him. The student's exclamation, "Don't taze me, bro!" pervaded media channels for several weeks, with people uploading numerous videos to YouTube spotlighting his plea. Brian Fairrington, the cartoonist, uses the incident to make a broader claim about free speech on college campuses.

© 2007 Brian Fairrington and PoliticalCartoons.com.

QUESTIONS FOR REASONING AND ANALYSIS

1. What is the point of the cartoon? What is the cartoonist attempting to say about freedom of expression on college campuses?
2. How does the cartoonist portray the two main characters (the student and the campus police officer)? What do the two characters signify?
3. What do the words on the warning sign imply? ("Warning: Colleges are free speech free zones.")
4. What does the acronym, P.C., on the back of the policeman's uniform suggest? Why has the cartoonist chosen to include this label?

QUESTIONS FOR REFLECTING AND WRITING

1. Can you think of any circumstances in which campus authorities might use force in response to a student's outspokenness? If so, what are those circumstances?
2. In 1917, Oliver Wendell Holmes, U.S. Supreme Court justice and legal scholar, argued that the government could suppress First Amendment rights in certain circumstances. He said that a person, for example, does not have the right to enter a crowded theater and shout, "Fire!" when no "fire" exists. Holmes's analogy has become famous as an argument for restricting freedom of expression in certain cases. Do you agree with the analogy? Why or why not? Would it necessarily apply to free speech on college campuses? Why or why not?
3. Are universities and colleges guilty of suppressing those who express "un-PC" opinions? Why or why not? Can you think of examples in which a college or university has censored a student because his or her opinion did not reflect a politically correct point of view?

enduring controversies in a new age

Abortion, Animal Rights, Capital Punishment, and Health Care

chapter 20

WHAT'S TO COME

In the first decade of the 21st century, people have continued to debate some of the same issues people debated in the 1970s, 1980s, and 1990s. Abortion, animal rights, capital punishment, and health care issues still evoke very strong emotions. Health care, for instance, is one of the most enduring crises because costs have spiraled seemingly out of control, with a number of people—particularly those living below the poverty line—finding themselves unable to receive adequate treatment because they cannot afford it. Selections in this chapter represent opposing viewpoints about such serious problems as funding for international organizations supporting abortion rights, the use of animals in medical and scientific research, the administration of the death penalty, and universal health care coverage.

prereading questions

1. Should the U.S. government fund organizations in other countries that perform abortions or provide counseling to women considering the option?

2. Do advances in medical research ever outweigh the cruelty associated with the use of animals to achieve those advances?

3. What are the current laws on the use of capital punishment? In capital cases, what kinds of evidence should be presented to decide on guilt beyond a reasonable doubt?

4. Is health care a right or a responsibility—an entitlement or the moral obligation of government to provide?

5. Should the free market determine the cost of health care? If not, should the government establish price controls to keep costs down?

6. If you wanted to change any of the current laws on these issues to make them reflect your views, how would you go about trying to get the laws changed?

web sites related to this chapter's topic

CORNELL LAW SCHOOL—CORNELL DEATH PENALTY PROJECT
http://library2.lawschool.cornell.edu/death
Information on court decisions and results of relevant studies.

ASSOCIATION OF THE BRITISH PHARMACEUTICAL INDUSTRY
www.abpi.org.uk/amric/amric.asp
Site of an association that supports the use of animals in medical research.

RELIGIOUS TOLERANCE.ORG, MEXICO CITY POLICY
www.religioustolerance.org/abo_wrld.htm
Site that explains the history of this policy as well as arguments for and against it.

PRESIDENT OBAMA'S AGENDA FOR HEALTH CARE
www.whitehouse.gov/agenda/health_care
White House Web site that explains the Obama-Biden plan for health care.

NATIONAL INSTITUTES OF HEALTH
www.nih.gov
Information from U.S. government agency and links to other resources on health issues and health research.

prereading question } **Should the U.S. government fund international organizations that support abortion rights?**

Under previous presidential administrations, the Mexico City Policy had banned funding to international organizations performing abortions and/or providing counseling to women considering the option. President Obama, however, rescinded the Mexico City Policy as one of his first presidential actions.

This Associated Press Photograph taken in February 2009 shows a man wearing a mask in the likeness of President Obama. The man is giving away fake money during an anti-abortion rally protesting the reversal of the Mexico City Policy.

1. In your own words, what is the claim of this visual depiction?
2. Does this visual depiction offer a fair assessment of President Obama's position? Why or why not?

3. Is it significant that the likeness of Obama's face is smiling? Why or why not? How does the smiling face of the mask contribute to the message?

1. Should the U.S. government fund organizations that support abortion rights, perform abortions, and/or counsel women regarding the option? Why or why not?
2. President Obama made the decision to rescind the Mexico City Policy less than one week after his inauguration. Should this measure have been one of his top priorities? Why or why not? Should other issues have taken precedence? If so, which ones?

3. Is it an obligation of the U.S. government to support or oppose controversial practices (such as abortion) in other countries? Should the U.S. government concern itself with issues affecting the citizens of other nations? Why or why not?

photo

prereading question } **Is animal research absolutely necessary for improving human health?**

A newly formed "pro-test" group marched in Oxford, England, in February 2006. The group was responding to an animal rights group that had targeted an Oxford University laboratory—a facility which at the time was still under construction.

1. The sign the person holds in this photograph makes a clear argument. In your own words, what is that argument?
2. What is the premise supporting the claim of the protest sign? In other words, what is the major reason why animal testing should receive support—as expressed by the protest sign, that is?
3. Why do you think the protesters have written the word *human* in red?
4. How would you explain the warrant, or implicit assumption, that links the claim and the reasoning offered by this protest sign?

QUESTIONS FOR REFLECTING AND WRITING

1. Is animal testing the only method for achieving advances in medical science? If not, what other methods exist? Are animal testing methods superior? Why or why not?
2. Assume for a moment that you stand opposed to animal testing for medical research purposes. (Understandably, you may already oppose animal testing, but take the opposite point of view in this instance.) If medical scientists, for example, argued that the *only* way to achieve a cure for cancer was through animal testing, would you then support such testing? Why or why not?
3. Should animals have rights per se? Why or why not?

web site

prereading question } **Should state governments restrict the rights of hunters?**

Stop Aerial Wolf Hunting in Alaska

Dorothy and Leo Keeler

The Stop Aerial Wolf Hunting in Alaska Web site encourages Alaskan citizens to help stop this practice. This site is hosted by Wilderness Inspirations (www.alaskawolfkill.com).

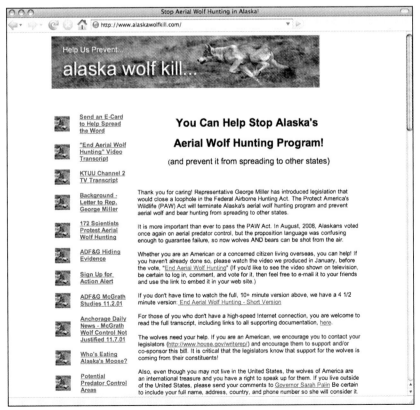

© Leo & Dorothy Keeler. Reprinted with permission.

1. According to the Web site, what act will prevent aerial wolf hunting?
2. What advice does the organization offer for those sending comments to Alaska's governor?
3. What arguments does the site suggest against aerial wolf hunting?

QUESTIONS FOR REASONING AND ANALYSIS

1. What audiences is the Web site attempting to reach? Is it just animal rights activists? What indications suggest that it is trying to communicate with other audiences besides animal rights activists?
2. What is the major purpose of the site? What are its creators trying to accomplish by communicating with audiences this way?
3. In what ways does this Web site (1) establish credibility with audiences and (2) advise audiences to establish ethos or credibility in communicating with public officials?
4. Does the site provide evidence to support the claim that adopting aerial wolf hunting programs in Alaska will lead to such programs in other states? If so, what evidence does the site offer? If not, does the lack of evidence for this claim undermine this site's credibility? Why or why not?

QUESTIONS FOR REFLECTING AND WRITING

1. Do attempts to prohibit the hunting of a species in a certain way restrict the freedoms of hunters? Why or why not?
2. Is aerial wolf hunting unique? In other words, would this group also oppose hunting wolves using ATVs (all-terrain vehicles) or on foot? Why or why not? Why is hunting wolves from helicopters especially controversial?
3. For additional information and background on this issue, read this article from Slate.com: www.slate.com/ id/2199140. Does knowing more about this practice make you feel more or less sympathetic toward efforts to stop it? What is your position after reviewing the Web site and reading the Slate.com article?

drawing/illustration

prereading questions } **Is the death penalty a suitable punishment for some crimes? If so, which ones?**

Michael Hogue

Michael Hogue's drawing appeared alongside Mike Hashimoto's April 15, 2007, *The Dallas Morning News* editorial "Capital Punishment Should Continue: Three Reasons Texas Should Not Repeal the Death Penalty" (www.dallasnews.com/sharedcontent/dws/dn/opinion/points/stories/ DN-deathhashimoto_15edi.ART.State.Edition1.42ce26c.html). Hogue is a senior illustrator for *The Dallas Morning News.*

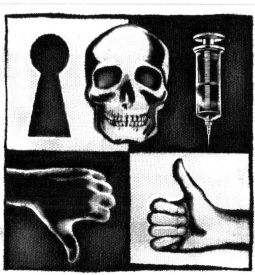

Michael Hogue/The Dallas Morning News

1. What do the different icons in this drawing signify or represent?
2. If the drawing represents an argument supporting the death penalty, then why might one interpret it as such? Could it also become an argument opposing the death penalty? Why or why not? Why do you interpret the drawing one way over another?

3. What is the purpose of the skull in the photograph? What does it represent? How does it contribute to the message of the drawing?
4. Does the black and white contrast serve any purpose in this photograph? If so, what is that purpose?

1. What are arguments and reasons opposing the death penalty? Do you find those arguments compelling? Why or why not?
2. Does this drawing, by itself, make a strong argument? Why or why not? Originally, it appeared alongside a newspaper editorial arguing in favor of the death

penalty. Does the drawing need the author's words to make it more compelling and effective? Why or why not?
3. Are you opposed to or in favor of the death penalty? For what reasons do you oppose or support the death penalty?

political cartoon

prereading question } **Is administration of the death penalty racially biased?**

Khalil Bendib

The following political cartoon appeared alongside an unsigned entry in *The Black Sentinel* on August 9, 2007, a blog devoted to issues facing African Americans (http://theblacksentinel.word-press.com). The cartoonist, Khalil Bendib, was born in North Africa and now lives in Berkeley, California. His cartoons appear in newspapers and online publications. This one first appeared in December 2005.

Reprinted by permission of Khalil Bendib. www.bendib.com.

QUESTIONS FOR REASONING AND ANALYSIS

1. In your own words, how would you summarize the thesis or claim of this cartoon?
2. What do the two major images (blind justice and the grim reaper) represent?
3. What does the cartoon imply or suggest about justice for accused people of different races?
4. Does the cartoon rely more on logical or emotional appeal? Why does it rely more on one than the other?

QUESTIONS FOR REFLECTING AND WRITING

1. The cartoon makes a very controversial statement in a very bold way. In your view, is the statement accurate? Do you agree or disagree? Why?
2. Many experts cite statistics showing that African American inmates outnumber Caucasians in U.S. prisons by a large margin. This cartoon, however, suggests, albeit implicitly, that more blacks await execution on death row than whites. If one accepts this condition as true, then why might this condition exist?

Why might more blacks receive the death penalty instead of a life sentence?

3. Some people remain opposed to the death penalty because they believe the judicial system fails to apply it fairly and equitably. Assuming the validity of their belief, would making changes to ensure fairness in sentencing make the death penalty a more effective punishment? Why or why not?

YouTube video

prereading questions } Is the death penalty inhumane? Is the death penalty a form of "cruel and unusual punishment" and therefore unconstitutional?

A YouTube user, "ATXgambino" (the "Italian stallion from Austin, Texas"), posted this video on April 11, 2008 (www.youtube.com/watch?v=qvFerSuoLhs&feature=channel_page). Through use of mostly images, and not voiceover or text, the video makes an argument opposing the death penalty.

Reprinted by permission of YouTube and YouTube user "ATXgambino". YouTube is a trademark of Google Inc.

(Stream the video before answering these questions.)

1. After the words "Texas Death Row Inmates" appear on the screen, the video then mostly becomes a series of photographs (headshots) of Texas death row inmates. What is the intended effect of showing these photographs this way? How does the approach reflect an emotional appeal?

2. What observations can you make regarding the photographs of inmates? Do you see any photographs of female death row inmates? Are the inmates all members of the same race? What race or races do these inmates represent? Is the race and gender of a death row inmate important? Why or why not?

3. In your own words, how would you explain the thesis or claim of this video? The video makes two supporting points using text—one in the first frame and one in the last frame. What are those two points? How do the points, as premises, support the claim of this video?

4. How would you describe the effects of the other visual and auditory techniques in the video? For example, each picture gradually zooms in before the frame changes, and during the entire video, the audience hears music being played on an acoustical guitar. As an audience member, do you react positively or negatively to these features? Why?

QUESTIONS FOR REFLECTING AND WRITING

1. Some have claimed that a relatively large percentage of death row inmates are actually *innocent* of the crimes that resulted in their incarceration. The last frame of this video basically argues that the wrongful execution of even *one* innocent death row inmate delegitimizes the use of capital punishment. Do you agree or disagree with this sentiment? Why or why not?

2. The Eighth Amendment of the U.S. Constitution says, "Excessive bail shall not be required, nor excessive fines imposed, nor cruel and unusual punishments inflicted." Some opponents of the death penalty argue that it represents a form of cruel and unusual punishment, thereby making the death penalty unconstitutional. Why might one consider the death penalty "cruel and unusual"? Why do you agree or disagree with this argument?

---

blog post

prereading question } Is universal health care coverage a realistic goal?

Elizabeth Edwards
Favors Clinton's Health Plan, Says Obama's "Not Universal," Slams McCain's as Ineffective

Jason Linkins

Elizabeth Edwards, wife of former senator and vice-presidential candidate John Edwards, was interviewed on *Morning Joe*, a daily program on MSNBC hosted by Mika Brzezinski and Joe Scarborough, a former congressman from Florida. In the video clip posted in this *Huffington Post* article from April 2, 2008, Edwards speaks to the differences between the health care plans of Barack Obama and Hillary Clinton and why she supports the Clinton proposal.

Elizabeth Edwards continued her passionate advocacy of universal health care on today's morning shows, appearing on both *The Today Show* and *Morning Joe*. Edwards noted her preference for the health care plan devised by Hillary Clinton, stating that its mandated coverage made it the only truly "universal" health plan between Clinton and Barack Obama: "It means every American has to be covered. Senator Obama means every child has to be covered. I think we need to go the full nine yards." Edwards also continued to criticize the health care plan put forth by John McCain, saying, "He's the beneficiary of some great government programs. But in terms of private insurance, he would not be guaranteed coverage under his own plan. Neither would I or anybody with a pre-existing condition."

EDWARDS: Senator McCain has a health care policy that frankly does not guarantee him or me or a lot of Americans, certainly the people I'm going to go see this morning to get my treatment

continued

next to this morning; those people are not guaranteed treatment, not guaranteed insurance coverage.

BRZEZINSKI: So you're saying that McCain wouldn't get coverage under his own plan?

EDWARDS: He's the beneficiary of some great government programs. But in terms of private insurance, he would not be guaranteed coverage under his own plan. Neither would I or anybody with a pre-existing condition. Imagine how many families that involves across this country. . . .

SCARBOROUGH: Which plan is better? Which plan covers more Americans? The Clinton plan or the Obama plan?

EDWARDS: In my view, the Clinton plan provides, because it provides a mandate. It means every American has to be covered. Senator Obama means every child has to be covered. I think we need to go the full nine yards and make certain we have—I'm not very good at clichés, is that the cliché. It ought to be ten yards, shouldn't it?

SCARBOROUGH: Well, not if it's fourth and nine.

EDWARDS: In any event, we want to make certain that every American is covered. In fact, Senator McCain does not cover every American. The way that you really keep down the costs of health insurance is that you have universality. You're still going to have everybody cost shifting, trying to cover the cost of the uninsured or cover the cost of people who have an exclusion that doesn't cover this particular condition. You're always going to have this cost shifting, and that keeps costs up—to keep costs down, you really need everybody covered.

When asked about the possibility of forthcoming endorsements from either her or husband John, Edwards begged off, saying, "We believe both of these candidates would make fine presidents and fine nominees for the party and certainly, particularly with respect to health care, a significant improvement over John McCain and we think our endorsement may be a little less important than y'all do." Edwards also disputed reports of lingering rancor between her, her husband, and Senator Obama: "I did not find him condescending. He was charming . . . as was Senator Clinton, and I have absolutely no idea where this report comes from."

www.huffingtonpost.com/2008/04/02/elizabeth-edwards-favors_n_94654.html

QUESTIONS FOR REASONING AND ANALYSIS

1. What is Edwards's argument against McCain's plan? What reasons support her argument?
2. According to Edwards, what is at issue between the health care plans of Hillary Clinton and Barack Obama? Why does she support the Clinton plan?
3. What do you think Edwards means by "cost shifting"? What argument is she attempting to make by referring to "cost shifting"?

QUESTIONS FOR REFLECTING AND WRITING

1. Do you agree or disagree with the idea of universal health care coverage? Why or why not?
2. Imagine for a moment that you are a member of the McCain camp. What would you argue in response to Edwards? What reasons would you use to support your claims?
3. Now imagine yourself as a member of the Obama camp. What would you argue in response to Edwards? What reasons would you use to support your claims?

prereading questions } How do you conceive of "rights"? What rights constitute human rights, civil rights, and so forth? Is universal health care a right?

Is Health Care a Right?

Maggie Mahar

Author and award-winning journalist Maggie Mahar is a contributor to *The Health Care Blog*. She also works as a fellow for the Century Foundation, a public policy think tank and research institute. The following article appeared on *THCB* on October 8, 2008.

I have to admit I often have found the language of health care "rights" off-putting. Yet the idea of health care as a "right" is usually pitted against the idea of health care as a "privilege." Given that choice, I'll circle "right" every time.

Still, when people claim something as a "right," they often sound shrill and demanding. Then someone comes along to remind us that people who have "rights" also have "responsibilities," and the next thing you know, we're off and running in the debate about health care as a "right" vs. health care as a matter of "individual responsibility."

As regular readers know, I believe that when would-be reformers emphasize "individual responsibilities," they shift the burden to the poorest and sickest among us. The numbers are irrefutable: low-income people are far more likely than other Americans to become obese, smoke, drink to excess, and abuse drugs, in part because a healthy lifestyle is expensive, and in part because the stress of being poor—and "having little control over your life"—leads many to self-medicate. This is a major reason why the poor are sicker than the rest of us, and die prematurely of treatable conditions.

Those conservatives and libertarians who put such emphasis on "individual responsibility" are saying, in effect, that low-income families should learn to take care of themselves.

At the same time I'm not entirely happy making the argument that the poor have a "right" to expect society to take care of them. It only reinforces the conservative image (so artfully drawn by President Reagan) of an aggrieved, resentful mob of freeloaders dunning the rest of us for having the simple good luck of being relatively healthy and relatively wealthy. "We didn't make them poor," libertarians say. "Why should they have the 'right' to demand so much from us?" Put simply, the language of "rights" doesn't seem the best way to build solidarity. And I believe that social solidarity is key to improving public health.

Given my unease with the language of rights, I was intrigued by a recent post by Shadowfax, an Emergency Department doctor from the Pacific Northwest

who writes a blog titled *Movin Meat*. (Many thanks to Kevin M.D. for calling my attention to this post.) Shadowfax believes in universal health care. Nevertheless, he argues that health care is not a "right," but rather a "moral responsibility for an industrialized country."

He begins his post provocatively: "Health care is not a right . . . I know this will piss off" many of my readers, "but I wanted to come out and say it for the record. . . . My objection may be more semantic than anything else, but words mean things and it is important to be clear in important matters like these."

Anyone who says that words are meaningful has captured my attention. I'm enthralled. After all, words shape how we think about things. Too often we automatically accept certain words and phrases, without realizing that they define the terms of the argument.

Shadowfax then quotes from a reader's comment on his blog: "Jim II said it well in the comments the other day: *'rights are limitations on government power.'*"

"Exactly," writes Shadowfax. "When we use the language of 'rights,' we are generally discussing very fundamental liberties, which are conferred on us at birth, and which no government is permitted to take away: free speech; religion and conscience; property; assembly and petition; bodily self-determination; self-defense; and the like. Freedoms. Nowhere in that list is there anything which must be given to you by others. These are freedoms which are yours, not obligations which you are due from somebody else. There is no right to an education, nor to a comfortable retirement, nor to otherwise profit by the sweat of someone else's labor."

Normally, I would object: Americans *do* have a right to an education. But Shadowfax is defining our "rights" in a very specific sense: our constitutional rights make us, as individuals, free *from* something—usually, interference by government, our neighbors, or the majority in our society.

Shadowfax then turns from the idea of rights to what people deserve: "some societies, ours included, from time to time decide

continued

that its citizens, or certain groups of them, should be *entitled* to certain benefits. Sometimes this [is] justified by the common good—a well-educated populace serves society well, so we guarantee an education to all children. Sometimes this is derived from humanitarian principles—children should not go hungry, so we create childhood nutrition programs. Health care would, in my estimation, fall into the category of an entitlement rather than a right. . . ."

Here, we are no longer talking about our rights as *individuals;* instead, Shadowfax is asking us to think *collectively* about what we all deserve simply by virtue of being human. These are what I would call our "human rights," which are quite different from our constitutional rights as individual citizens.

This is what Jim II is referring to when, after defining "rights" as "limitations on government power," he writes: "That said, I think it is immoral for someone's access to healthcare, politics, or justice to be dependent on how good a capitalist he or she is. And therefore, I think we should use the government to ensure that people from all economic classes are treated equally in this sense." In other words, a person's access to medical care should not turn on just how skilled he is as an economic creature. While some of us are smarter, taller, and quicker than others, as human beings we are equal.

In the economy, the swift will win the material prizes; but in society, humans possess certain "inalienable" rights to "life, liberty and the pursuit of happiness" simply by virtue of being human. These are different from a citizen's "right" to free speech—a right that no government can take away. The framers of the Declaration of Independence believed that these "inalienable rights" are bestowed upon us by God. To me, this means that we have moved from the rule of law in the public sphere to the private sphere and those moral rules which begin "Do unto others . . ."

When Jim II argues we should "use the government" to oversee health care, and to "ensure that people from all economic classes are treated equally in this sense," he is saying that government should oversee that moral compact among men and women who recognize each other as equals. Here I would add that, *when it comes to the necessities of life, a society that seeks stability and solidarity* strives for equality.

Shadowfax goes on to point out that "our nation has long defined health care as an entitlement for the elderly, the disabled, and the very young. We are now involved in a national debate whether this entitlement will be made universal. As you all know, I am an advocate for universal health care. Though there may be an argument for the societal benefit of universal health care, or for the relative cost-efficiency of universal health care, I support it almost entirely for humanitarian reasons. It needs to be paid for, of course, and that

will be a challenge, but as a social priority it ranks as absolutely critical in my estimation."

On this point, I don't entirely agree. In my view there is a very strong argument to be made for the societal benefit of universal health care; if people are not healthy, they cannot be productive and add to the wealth of the nation. And there is an argument for cost-efficiency—if we don't treat patients in a timely fashion, they become sicker, and charity care becomes more expensive. But I would add that even if we are talking about a person who cannot be expected to add to the economic wealth of the nation—say, a Down syndrome child who will need more care than he can "pay back" over the course of a lifetime—he is entitled to health care for humanitarian reasons. As health care economist Rashie Fein has said: "We live not just in an economy, but in a society." And as a human being, that child can contribute to society, by bringing joy to his family, or by being in a classroom with children who will learn from him.

What of the "Rights" and "Obligations" of Doctors?

Shadowfax's argument then takes a shocking turn. Without fanfare, he acknowledges that he has some sympathy for "the common line of argument against universal health care" which declares that, "with any good or service that is provided by some specific group of men, if you try to make its possession by all a right, you thereby enslave the providers of the service, wreck the service, and end up depriving the very consumers you are supposed to be helping. To call 'medical care' a right will merely enslave the doctors and thus destroy the quality of medical care in this country. It will deliver doctors bound hands and feet to the mercies of the bureaucracy."

Here, Shadowfax is quoting from a speech by Alan Greenspan's moral mentor, Ayn Rand, released by the Ayn Rand Institute in 1993 as a comment on the Clinton Health Plan.

In that speech, Rand denies that health care is either a right or an entitlement: "Under the American system you have a right to health care if you can pay for it, i.e., if you can earn it by your own action and effort. But nobody has the right to the services of any professional individual or group simply because he wants them and desperately needs them. The very fact that he needs these services so desperately is the proof that he had better respect the freedom, the integrity, and the rights of the people who provide them."

"You have a right to work," she continues, "not to rob others of the fruits of their work, not to turn others into sacrificial, rightless animals laboring to fulfill your needs."

If I find the language of "rights" troubling, I find Rand's language terrifying. Shadowfax admits "There's a lot not to like about this sentiment. But," he argues, "it has some limited validity."

Shadowfax then turns to the predicament of his cohort—emergency room doctors. Under law, they are required to at least stabilize patients—even if those patients cannot pay. And most often, physicians go well beyond stabilizing them, treating them and even admitting them to their hospitals.

"Only problem is," Shadowfax writes, "I and my colleagues are not caring for you out of the goodness of our heart, nor out of charity, but because we are obligated under federal law to do so. While this isn't exactly slavery, this coercion of our work product is essentially compulsory if you work in a U.S. hospital."

What I like about Shadowfax is that he then moves from complaint to a potential solution: *"Universal health care, or, more precisely, universal health insurance, might improve upon the current state of affairs by ensuring that doctors are always paid for the services we provide, rather than being obligated to give them away to 15–30% of their patients as we now are. . . .* The typical emergency physician provides about $180,000 of free services annually," he adds, "just for reference."

I'm not sure that the average ER doc should be paid $180,000 more than he is today. (I would agree that, when compared to many specialists, ER docs are not overpaid—and theirs is a very demanding job. But $180,000 seems a large sum; I don't know whether taxpayers could afford it.) Nevertheless, I agree that the current law regarding ER care is an unfunded mandate—and one that hospitals located in very poor neighborhoods cannot afford. Moreover, when ER doctors feel that they are being forced to deliver free care, many will be resentful. This is understandable, and does not lead to the best care.

On the other hand, in a society where so many are uninsured, I do believe that physicians have a moral obligation, as professionals, to provide some charity care. They have taken an oath to put patients' interests ahead of their own. The problem is that the burden falls unfairly on those who are willing to work in emergency rooms or neighborhood clinics while many doctors in private practice simply shun the poor. We need a system that is fairer, both for patients and for doctors.

The answer, as Shadowfax suggests, is universal health insurance that funds ER care for everyone who needs it—and, I would add, health reform that restructures the delivery system so that Americans don't have to go to an ER for non-emergency care.

In the end, I agree with Shadowfax that reformers need to think carefully about the language they use: "When advocates of universal health care misuse the language of universal rights to push for health care for all, we fall into the trap of over-reaching and provoke a justified pushback, even from some who might be inclined to agree with us. Universal health care is, however, a moral obligation for an industrialized society, and will not result in the apocalyptic consequences promised by the jeremiads."

What I like about calling health care a "moral obligation" is that it presents health care, not as a right that "the demanding poor" extort from an adversarial society—or even as an obligation that the poor impose upon us. Rather, Shadowfax is talking about members of a civilized society recognizing that all humans are vulnerable to disease—this is something we have in common—and so willingly pooling their resources to protect each of us against the hazards of fate.

QUESTIONS FOR READING

1. According to Mahar, what is Shadowfax's argument?
2. How does Mahar define "human rights"?

3. Why does Mahar say that physicians have a moral obligation to provide *some* charity care?

QUESTIONS FOR REASONING AND ANALYSIS

1. How do you think Mahar sees the distinction between "rights" and "responsibilities"? What passages from the text help define this distinction?
2. How does Mahar use Shadowfax in making her argument? How does Shadowfax provide support for her argument as well as a way to clarify how her position differs from his?
3. What do you think Mahar is implying in this passage from her post: "The framers of the Declaration of Independence believed that these "inalienable rights" are bestowed upon us by God. To me, this means that we have moved from the rule of law in the public sphere to the private sphere and those moral rules which begin "Do unto others . . ."?

4. In the end, how is Mahar defining "moral obligation"? How does she distinguish "moral obligation" from "right"?

1. If you were to post a comment, what would you say in response to Mahar? Would you agree or disagree with her position? With some aspects of her argument but not others? Why or why not?

2. What do you see as the "moral obligations" of the U.S. government? Why must the U.S. government meet these obligations under a moral imperative?

3. How do you view the distinction between "right" and "responsibility"? Why is one a "right" and another a "responsibility"?

web site essay

prereading question } Should the market—free of government regulation—determine the cost of health care?

The Right Vision of Health Care

Yaron Brook

Yaron Brook is managing director of BH Equity Research as well as executive director of the Ayn Rand Institute. This piece appeared on *Forbes.com*, January 8, 2008.

http://www.forbes.com/

With the primary season in full swing, the presidential candidates are fighting over what to do about the spiraling cost of health care—especially the cost of health insurance, which is becoming prohibitively expensive for millions of Americans.

The Democrats, not surprisingly, are proposing a massive increase in government control, with some even calling for the outright socialism of a single-payer system. Republicans are attacking this "solution." But although they claim to oppose the expansion of government interference in medicine, Republicans don't, in fact, have a good track record of fighting it.

Indeed, Republicans have been responsible for major expansions of government health care programs: As governor of Massachusetts, Mitt Romney oversaw the enactment of the nation's first "universal coverage" plan, initially estimated at $1.5 billion per year but already overrunning cost projections. Arnold Schwarzenegger, who pledged not to raise any new taxes, has just pushed through his own "universal coverage" measure, projected to cost Californians more than $14 billion. And President Bush's colossal prescription drug entitlement—expected to cost taxpayers more than $1.2 trillion over the next decade—was the largest expansion of government control over health care in 40 years.

Today, nearly half of all spending on health care in America is government spending. Why, despite their lip service to free markets, have Republicans actually helped fuel the growth of socialized medicine and erode what remains of free-market medicine in this country?

Consider the basic factor that has driven the expansion of government medicine in America.

Prior to the government's entrance into the medical field, health care was regarded as a product to be traded voluntarily on a free market—no different from food, clothing, or any other important good or service. Medical providers competed to provide the best quality services at the lowest possible prices. Virtually all Americans could afford basic health care, while those few who could not were able to rely on abundant private charity.

Had this freedom been allowed to endure, Americans' rising productivity would have allowed them to buy better and better health care, just as, today, we buy better and more varied food and clothing than people did a century ago. There would be no crisis of affordability, as there isn't for food or clothing.

But by the time Medicare and Medicaid were enacted in 1965, this view of health care as an economic product—for which each individual must assume responsibility—had given way to a view of health care as a "right," an unearned "entitlement," to be provided at others' expense.

This entitlement mentality fueled the rise of our current third-party-payer system, a blend of government programs, such as Medicare and Medicaid, together with government-controlled employer-based health insurance (itself spawned by perverse tax incentives during the wage and price controls of World War II).

Today, what we have is not a system grounded in American individualism, but a collectivist system that aims to relieve the individual of the "burden" of paying for his own health care by coercively imposing its costs on his neighbors. For every dollar's worth of hospital care a patient consumes, that patient pays only about 3 cents out-of-pocket; the rest is paid by third-party coverage. And for the health care system as a whole, patients pay only about 14 percent.

The result of shifting the responsibility for health care costs away from the individuals who accrue them was an explosion in spending.

In a system in which someone else is footing the bill, consumers, encouraged to regard health care as a "right," demand medical services without having to consider their real price. When, through the 1970s and 1980s, this artificially inflated consumer demand sent expenditures soaring out of control, the government cracked down by enacting further coercive measures: price controls on medical services, cuts to medical benefits, and a crushing burden of regulations on every aspect of the health care system.

As each new intervention further distorted the health care market, driving up costs and lowering quality, belligerent voices demanded still further interventions to preserve the "right" to health care. And Republican politicians—not daring to challenge the notion of such a "right"—have, like Romney, Schwarzenegger, and Bush, outdone even the Democrats in expanding government health care.

The solution to this ongoing crisis is to recognize that the very idea of a "right" to health care is a perversion. There can be no such thing as a "right" to products or services created by the effort of others, and this most definitely includes medical products and services. Rights, as our founding fathers conceived them, are not claims to economic goods, but freedoms of action.

You are free to see a doctor and pay him for his services—no one may forcibly prevent you from doing so. But you do not have a "right" to force the doctor to treat you without charge or to force others to pay for your treatment. The rights of some cannot require the coercion and sacrifice of others.

So long as Republicans fail to challenge the concept of a "right" to health care, their appeals to "market-based" solutions are worse than empty words. They will continue to abet the Democrats' expansion of government interference in medicine, right up to the dead end of a completely socialized system.

By contrast, the rejection of the entitlement mentality in favor of a proper conception of rights would provide the moral basis for real and lasting solutions to our health care problems—for breaking the regulatory chains stifling the medical industry; for lifting the government incentives that created our dysfunctional, employer-based insurance system; for inaugurating a gradual phase-out of all government health care programs, especially Medicare and Medicaid; and for restoring a true free market in medical care.

Such sweeping reforms would unleash the power of capitalism in the medical industry. They would provide the freedom for entrepreneurs motivated by profit to compete with each other to offer the best quality medical services at the lowest prices, driving innovation and bringing affordable medical care, once again, into the reach of all Americans.

Source: Yaron Brook, "The Right Vision Of Health Care," Forbes.com, January 8, 2008. Reprinted by Permission of Forbes.com © 2008 Forbes LLC.

www.forbes.com/2008/01/08/health-republican-plans-oped-cx_ybr_0108health.html

QUESTIONS FOR READING

1. According to Brook, who is responsible for expanding government health care programs?
2. What would be the result if health care had remained, in Brook's words, "a product to be traded voluntarily on a free market"?

3. What is Brook's solution to the health care crisis?

QUESTIONS FOR REASONING AND ANALYSIS

1. Brook refers to "rights" and "entitlements" throughout this piece. How does he define each term? Do you agree with his assessment that providing health care through a government program becomes an "entitlement"? Why or why not?
2. Brook argues that "what we have is not a system grounded in American individualism, but a collectivist system that aims to relieve the individual of the 'burden' of paying for his own health care by coercively imposing its costs on his neighbors." What does Brook

mean by a "collectivist system"? What evidence does he use in supporting this argument? Do you find the argument compelling? Why or why not?

3. Like Mahar, Brook argues that a "moral basis" should guide the implementation of solutions to this crisis. However, his conception of "moral basis" is very different from Mahar's conception of "moral obligation." By the end of the essay, how has Brook defined "moral basis" or "moral obligation" in solving the health care crisis?

QUESTIONS FOR REFLECTING AND WRITING

1. If you were to post a response to Brook, what would you say? Would you agree or disagree with his argument? Why or why not?
2. How could one possibly conceive of health care as a "right"? As an exercise, write an argument supporting health care as a "right," making certain to define "right" or "rights" in stating the position.

3. Is free-market capitalism the answer to the health care crisis? What problems might emerge in a completely free-market health care system? What problems can you see with a totally government-operated health care system (that is, socialized medicine)?

marriage and gender roles

Changing Attitudes vs. Traditional Values

chapter 21

The selections in this chapter represent two very different sides of a very controversial issue. Some argue vehemently in favor of permitting same-sex marriage and allowing for changing gender roles in subsequent family arrangements; others, however, argue passionately against the acceptance of same-sex marriage. In 2008, the controversy over Proposition 8 in California brought this issue to the forefront, with California voters passing the measure and thereby supporting a change in the state's constitution to recognize marriage as only between a man and a woman. Although a 1996 federal law known as DOMA, or the Defense of Marriage Act, essentially forbids gay marriage, two states, Massachusetts and Connecticut, now allow people of the same sex to marry, while several other states permit civil unions. As events of the 21st century continue to unfold, will we see more states follow Massachusetts and Connecticut?

prereading questions

1. What role, if any, should the government and the courts have in defining marriage?

2. What has been meant by the "traditional family"? How has it changed in the past thirty years?

3. Do you have a position on gay marriage? On partnership recognition and rights? If you have a position, what is it, and what is its source?

4. Is there anything that you can learn from arguments presenting opposing views on gay rights or acceptance of gay marriage? Why or why not?

web sites related to this chapter's topic

THE WHITE HOUSE
www.whitehouse.gov/agenda/civil_rights
President Obama's agenda for civil rights.

YAHOO NEWS
http://fullcoverage.yahoo.com/fc/us/same_sex_marriage
This Yahoo Full Coverage site contains news, opinions, and useful links.

THE HUFFINGTON POST
www.huffingtonpost.com/news/gay-marriage
News site about gay marriage.

drawing/illustration

prereading questions } Are people who live in certain regions or states more likely to oppose gay marriage? Does age become a major factor in determining the likelihood that a person will support gay marriage?

Todd Trumbull, *San Francisco Chronicle*, July 18, 2008

The following data was reproduced by Jay McDonough, a contributor to *Examiner.com*, an experiment in citizen journalism. McDonough posted this information on July 18, 2008.

Field Poll indicates divisions in regional, gender and age groups

Fifty-one percent of likely voters in the state oppose Proposition 8 on the November ballot, a constitutional amendment that bans same-sex marriage by defining marriage as only between a man and woman, according to a Field Poll released today. The poll shows voters are divided by where they live, their age, gender, and political party.

Results among all Californians likely to vote in the November general election:

Yes 42%
No 51%
Undecided 7%

The survey was conducted July 8–14 by telephone among a random sample of 672 Californians likely to vote in the November election. The poll has a margin of error of plus or minus 3.8 percentage points.
Source: Field Research Corp.

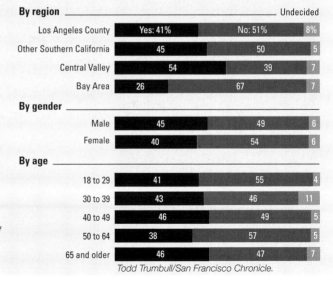

By region — Undecided

	Yes	No	Undecided
Los Angeles County	41%	51%	8%
Other Southern California	45	50	5
Central Valley	54	39	7
Bay Area	26	67	7

By gender

	Yes	No	Undecided
Male	45	49	6
Female	40	54	6

By age

	Yes	No	Undecided
18 to 29	41	55	4
30 to 39	43	46	11
40 to 49	46	49	5
50 to 64	38	57	5
65 and older	46	47	7

Todd Trumbull/San Francisco Chronicle.

1. What reasons might explain why the majority of survey respondents from California's Central Valley support Proposition 8, while the vast majority of Bay Area respondents oppose it?

2. Can you draw any conclusions about the age factor based on the bar graph? If so, what are those conclusions? If not, why not?

3. How would you restate in words the point that the pie chart and bar graph, as visual depictions, convey?

QUESTIONS FOR REFLECTING AND WRITING

1. Proposition 8 called for a change in the California state constitution that would define marriage as only between a man and a woman. In 2008, California voters passed Proposition 8 by a small margin (52 percent in favor to 48 percent opposed). Why do you think Proposition 8 passed? Conduct some additional research to learn more about the passage of Proposition 8.

2. Should a state government attempt to legislate who a person can and cannot marry? Why or why not? What role should the government play in such matters?

3. Would you support an amendment to the U.S. Constitution banning same-sex marriage? Why or why not?

---

blog post

prereading question } **What could have brought about the passage of Proposition 8 as opposed to its defeat?**

Gay Rights in California

Kevin Drum

Kevin Drum made this post to the *Mother Jones* blog on November 5, 2008.

The votes aren't quite fully counted yet, but with 95 percent of the precincts reporting it looks like Proposition 8 banning gay marriage in California is headed for passage, 52 percent–48 percent. In one sense, this might have been inevitable: this is precisely the margin I projected six months ago based on basic demographic trends. What's more, the voting trends are exactly what you'd expect: strong No votes in the liberal coastal counties, especially in the north, and Yes votes in the conservative inland counties. On the other hand, it only passed by *two points*. I really, really wonder if we could have beaten it if Barack Obama had been willing to step up and take a bit of a risk on behalf of defeating it.

Especially toward the end, when it was unlikely to hurt him in the national race. If he had cut an ad to run over the final weekend, would it have made the difference? Maybe.

Not the worst night ever for California initiatives, then, but not great either. The good news, I guess, is that the same demographic trends that doomed gay marriage this year also guarantee its eventual victory. We'll try this again in five or ten years and win easily.

www.motherjones.com/kevin-drum/
2008/11/gay-rights-california

1. What possible reason does Drum suggest for the passage of Proposition 8? Do you think this reason is valid? Why or why not?

2. In his last paragraph, Drum says, "The good news, I guess, is that the same demographic trends that doomed gay marriage this year also guarantee its eventual victory." What does he mean by "demographic trends"? How will these trends "guarantee its eventual victory"?

3. Who do you think Drum sees as his audience for this post? Why do you think a particular group represents his audience?

1. In which states would a measure like Proposition 8 fare the best? In which states would such a measure likely fail? Why?

2. How might the passage of Proposition 8 galvanize and unify its opponents?

3. If you were to write in response to Drum, what would you say? Would you agree or disagree with him? Why would you agree or disagree?

web site

prereading question } Is same-sex marriage threatening to children and, more broadly, the institution of marriage?

Protect Marriage: Vote "Yes" on Proposition 8

Protect Marriage: Vote "Yes" on Proposition 8 is a Web site campaigning for passage of this measure in California. In the November 2008 elections, California voters passed Proposition 8 by a very narrow margin of 52 percent to 48 percent. *Protectmarriage.com* is a project of a group calling itself California Renewal.

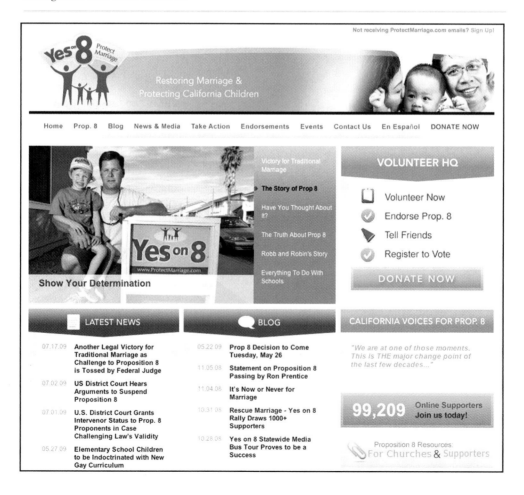

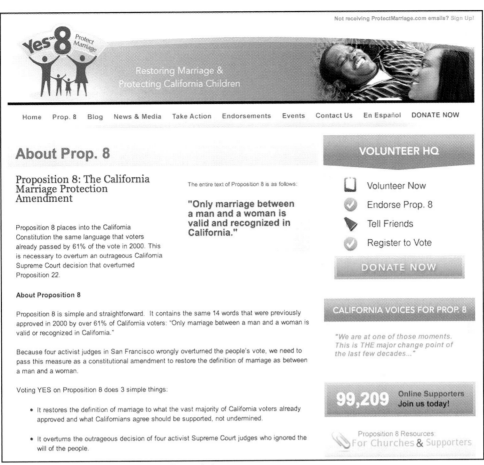

QUESTIONS FOR REASONING AND ANALYSIS

1. On the homepage, what actions does California Renewal want supporters of Proposition 8 to take? Which actions do you think the intended audience would most likely take? Why?

2. The "About Proposition 8" page indicates that the measure "does 3 simple things." How might one reword these statements to express "3 simple arguments"? In other words, how would you summarize the arguments made here in support of Proposition 8?

3. View the two short advertisements expressing opposition to legalizing gay marriage (see http://protectmarriage.com/video/view/7 and http://protectmarriage.com/video/view/8). What is the major argument made in both these videos? What evidence is cited in support of this major argument? Are the assumptions behind the argument valid? Why or why not?

4. Do the videos rely more on logical or emotional appeal? How might the videos rely on one more than another?

QUESTIONS FOR REFLECTING AND WRITING

1. Evaluate the Proposition 8 Web site as an argument. Does it achieve its purpose and communicate effectively with its intended audience? Why or why not? Are some arguments stronger than others? Weaker? If so, which ones? Overall, how could the site become more effective in persuading audiences and solidifying a support base for Proposition 8?

2. Do you agree or disagree that same-sex marriage poses a threat to children? If so, what is that threat? What is the ultimate consequence to children if persons of the same sex are permitted to marry? If you disagree, why is this concern over children misplaced?

3. Does same-sex marriage pose a threat to the institution of marriage? If so, what is that threat? If not, then why not?

prereading question } Are children hindered emotionally or developmentally when raised by two same-sex parents?

My Daughters Have No Mother

Max Mutchnick

Max Mutchnick was the co-creator of the television show *Will and Grace*, which aired on NBC from 1998 until 2006. A writer and producer in Hollywood, Mutchnick lives with his partner and their two daughters. He posted this argument on February 27, 2009, to *The Huffington Post* blog.

Some of you were annoyed. You didn't like that I referred to my daughters' surrogate as an oven. Truly I meant no disrespect. I love and admire the generous soul that carried my daughters for thirty-seven weeks. She went into labor as I sat in a theatre watching a preview of *9 to 5: The Musical*. I always wondered if she went into labor because she had sympathy pains for me. I have friends involved so I'll keep my review simple: Cute . . . with kinks. Mostly it brought back my repressed desire to own a silk work kimono like the one Lily Tomlin wore in the movie version.

Honey, I'm leaving for the office. Just gonna pour myself a cup of ambition, grab my purple work kimono and I'm out the door . . .

But I digress. Back to the oven, I mean, the surrogate. Here's what it's all about: It takes a village to make a *gaybie* (not my word). When a gay man realizes he wants to have a child, it forces him to face his own queerness, in the true sense of the word. And it's contrary to his life-long mantra: "I'm normal. I'm just like everyone else." So like it or not, it's back to the village. You're going to need everyone; especially the villagers with vaginas. You'll also need: money, support systems, time, lawyers, fertility specialists, location, and cashmere (don't ask). Homosexuals are not as fortunate as our heterosexual counterparts. We certainly don't have the luck on our side like, say, a Jamie Lynn Spears or a Palin daughter. Making children the gay way is like building a yacht.

Somewhere along the line I started to feel guilty or less than. As a result, I built up some defenses. You must want it so badly that you literally have to reach out your hand to virtual strangers for assistance. Of course they become real in the fullness of time, but when you're introduced at a Marie Callender's to the woman that's going to carry your children, it's impossible to think:

You're mommy.

So with key players, I found myself doing this thing I call "distance regulating." So much intimacy. So much vulnerability. So much need from others. I must save myself the only way I know how. Nicknames. Less eye-contact. Jokey banter. Let's keep it light . . . because it's *so not light*. And then there's the egg donor. You never even get to meet her.

It's hitting me now. My daughters have no mother.

So listen to this part. You log onto a secured Web site. (Octomom, if you're reading this, please skip to the next paragraph.) Page after page of girls—not women, girls. A headshot, a small video testimonial, and an extensive medical history. That's all you get. Fifty percent of my babies' DNA would be purchased online. Something about it depressed me. I must distance regulate.

Want a mom? She's three clicks away!

We quickly learned about the dearth of desirable donors. They're like diamonds; it's all good on the surface, but when you take a loupe to them, the difference between a flawless stone and an occluded one seems small, but looms large. Take the "Diamond" out of Lou Diamond Phillips and you're just stuck with a guy called Lou Phillips. (That almost makes sense.) I learned everything I know about diamonds from Suzanne Pleshette, may she rest in peace. She wore ten carats on her finger to work every day. A gift from a man, she told me.

Wow, that's quite a ring, Suzanne.

It's a piece of shit. You couldn't even cut the cheese with it. A zircon costs more.

So if and when you see a donor you like, it's a BUY NOW situation. Turn your head for a second and donors get scooped up by other gay couples competing from the same pool. We decided to go with V139K2 (not her real name). There was something very exciting and scary about it once the decision was made. We'll never know her. Our daughters will never kiss her. She is everything . . . and nothing. Oh my god, my daughters have no mother!

See that's what it is. I have to call our surrogate an oven because I can't call her their mother and I can't call V139K2 (not her real name) their mother. And it drives me crazy. I can't tell you how it drives me crazy.

But this is what saves me . . .
Here's a list of what they do have:

doting grandparents
lots of cousins
fifty gay uncles
two gay aunts
clean sheets
bubble baths
kisses from morning 'til night
walks in the park
laughter

dogs that lick their feet
and two adoring fathers.

And that's enough. And that's our family. And that's everything.

The Huffington Post, February 27, 2009. © 2009 Max Mutchnick. Reprinted with permission. www.huffingtonpost.com/max-mutchnick/ my-daughters-have-no-moth_b_170614 .html

QUESTIONS FOR REASONING AND ANALYSIS

1. What do you think Mutchnick means when he says, "Making children the gay way is like building a yacht"? In a latter passage, he refers to "distance regulating." What is he suggesting by using this term?

2. What is Mutchnick saying when he compares "desirable donors" to diamonds? He then proceeds to disparage "diamonds" (Suzanne Pleshette's ring, specifically). Why?

3. How would you describe the tone of Mutchnick's post? Is it playful, sarcastic, serious, or somber? Why is it one and not the other?

4. What argument is Mutchnick making by providing a list at the close of his post?

5. How would you summarize the thesis or claim of Mutchnick's post?

QUESTIONS FOR REFLECTING AND WRITING

1. Consider the opposing argument to Mutchnick's position. How would you express that opposing argument? What reasons or evidence would support that argument?

2. Can society dictate who can and cannot raise children? Why or why not? Under what circumstances might an authority prevent a person or couple from taking custody of and raising a child? Can such circumstances pertain to same-sex couples? If so, why?

3. Evaluate Mutchnick's claim in "My Daughters Have No Mother." Has he effectively made his argument? Are parts of his argument stronger than others? Weaker? If so, which ones? Regardless of whether or not you agree or disagree, do you take issue with any of his statements? Why or why not?

prereading question } Are racial discrimination and discrimination against someone for their sexual orientation the same thing?

Darrin Bell

This political cartoon appeared on Robyn Ochs's Web site (www.robynochs.com). Ochs is a professional author and public speaker.

Reprinted by permission of Darrin Bell. www.candorville.com.

QUESTIONS FOR REASONING AND ANALYSIS

1. How would you explain the thesis or claim of this cartoon?
2. What does it mean to "protect the sanctity of marriage"? What does the word *sanctity* mean?
3. What do you think of the portrayal of the male characters? What is the cartoonist attempting to say through this portrayal?

4. Is prohibiting gay marriage the same as prohibiting interracial marriage? Why or why not?

QUESTIONS FOR REFLECTING AND WRITING

1. What is the difference between marriage and legally recognized civil unions, life partnerships, and domestic partnerships? Do you oppose gay marriage but support civil unions? Why?

2. If you oppose gay marriage, why? If you support gay marriage, why?
3. Why do you think gay marriage has become such a controversial issue?

prereading question } Does permitting gay marriage erode the institution of marriage?

The Worst Thing About Gay Marriage

Sam Schulman

Sam Schulman, a writer in Virginia, was publishing director of the *American* and publisher of *Wigwag*. This article appeared in *The Weekly Standard*, Volume 14, Issue 35 on June 1, 2009.

There is a new consensus on gay marriage: not on whether it should be legalized but about the motives of those of us who oppose it. All agree that any and all opposition to gay marriage is explained either by biblical literalism or anti-homosexual bigotry. This consensus is brilliantly constructed to be so unflattering to those of us who will vote against gay marriage—if we are allowed to do so—that even biblical literalists and bigots are scrambling out of the trenches and throwing down their weapons.

But I think that the fundamental objection to gay marriage among most who oppose it has very little to do with one's feelings about the nature of homosexuality or what the Bible has to say about sodomy. The obstacle to wanting gay marriage is instead how we use and depend on marriage itself—and how little marriage, understood completely, affects or is relevant to gay people in love. Gay marriage is not so much wrong as unnecessary. But if it comes about, it will not be gay marriage that causes the harm I fear, as what will succeed its inevitable failure.

The embrace of homosexuality in Western culture has come about with unbelievable speed—far more rapidly than the feminist revolution or racial equality. Less than 50 years ago same-sex sexual intercourse was criminal. Now we are arguing about the term used to describe a committed relationship. Is the right to marry merely lagging behind the pace with which gays have attained the right to hold jobs—even as teachers and members of the clergy; to become elected officials, secret agents, and adoptive parents; and to live together in public, long-term relationships? And is the public, having accepted so rapidly all these rights that have made gays not just "free" but our neighbors, simply withholding this final right thanks to a stubborn residue of bigotry? I don't think so.

When a gay man becomes a professor or a gay woman becomes a police officer, he or she performs the same job as a heterosexual. But there is a difference between a married couple and a same-sex couple in a long-term relationship. The difference is not in the nature of their relationship, not in the fact that love-making between men and women is, as the Catholics say, open to life. The difference is between the duties that marriage imposes on married people—not rights, but rather onerous obligations—which do not apply to same-sex love.

The relationship between a same-sex couple, though it involves the enviable joy of living forever with one's soulmate, loyalty, fidelity, warmth, a happy home, shopping, and parenting, is not the same as marriage between a man and a woman, though they enjoy exactly the same cozy virtues. These qualities are awfully nice, but they are emphatically not what marriage fosters, and, even when they do exist, are only a small part of why marriage evolved and what it does.

The entity known as "gay marriage" only aspires to replicate a very limited, very modern, and very culture-bound version of marriage. Gay advocates have chosen wisely in this. They are replicating what we might call the "romantic marriage," a kind of marriage that is chosen, determined, and defined by the couple that enters into it. Romantic marriage is now dominant in the West and is becoming slightly more frequent in other parts of the world. But it is a luxury and even here has only existed (except among a few elites) for a couple of centuries—and in only a few countries. The fact is that marriage is part of a much larger institution, which defines the particular shape and character of marriage: the kinship system.

The role that marriage plays in kinship encompasses far more than arranging a happy home in which two hearts may beat as one—in fact marriage is actually pretty indifferent to that particular aim. Nor has marriage historically concerned itself with compelling the particular male and female who have created a child to live together and care for that child. It is not the "right to marry" that creates an enduring relationship between heterosexual lovers or a stable home for a child, but the more far-reaching kinship system that assigns every one of the vast array of marriage rules a set of duties and obligations to enforce. These duties and obligations impinge even on romantic

continued

marriage, and not always to its advantage. The obligations of kinship imposed on traditional marriage have nothing to do with the romantic ideals expressed in gay marriage.

Consider four of the most profound effects of marriage within the kinship system.

The first is the most important: It is that marriage is concerned above all with female sexuality. The very existence of kinship depends on the protection of females from rape, degradation, and concubinage. This is why marriage between men and women has been necessary in virtually every society ever known. Marriage, whatever its particular manifestation in a particular culture or epoch, is essentially about who may and who may not have sexual access to a woman when she becomes an adult, and is also about how her adulthood—and sexual accessibility—is defined. Again, until quite recently, the woman herself had little or nothing to say about this, while her parents and the community to which they answered had total control. The guardians of a female child or young woman had a duty to protect her virginity until the time came when marriage was permitted or, more frequently, insisted upon. This may seem a grim thing for the young woman—if you think of how the teenaged Natalie Wood was not permitted to go too far with Warren Beatty in *Splendor in the Grass*. But the duty of virginity can seem like a privilege, even a luxury, if you contrast it with the fate of child-prostitutes in brothels around the world. No wonder that weddings tend to be regarded as religious ceremonies in almost every culture: They celebrate the completion of a difficult task for the community as a whole.

This most profound aspect of marriage—protecting and controlling the sexuality of the child-bearing sex—is its only true reason for being, and it has no equivalent in same-sex marriage. Virginity until marriage, arranged marriages, the special status of the sexuality of one partner but not the other (and her protection from the other sex)—these motivating forces for marriage do not apply to same-sex lovers.

Second, kinship modifies marriage by imposing a set of rules that determines not only whom one may marry (someone from the right clan or family, of the right age, with proper abilities, wealth, or an adjoining vineyard), but, more important, whom one may not marry. Incest prohibition and other kinship rules that dictate one's few permissible and many impermissible sweethearts are part of traditional marriage. Gay marriage is blissfully free of these constraints. There is no particular reason to ban sexual intercourse between brothers, a father and a son of consenting age, or mother and daughter. There are no questions of ritual pollution: Will a hip Rabbi refuse to marry a Jewish man—even a Cohen—to a Gentile man? Do Irish women avoid Italian women? A same-sex marriage fails utterly to create forbidden relationships. If Tommy marries Bill, and they divorce, and Bill later marries a woman and has a daughter, no incest prohibition prevents Bill's daughter from marrying Tommy. The relationship between Bill and Tommy is a romantic fact, but it can't be fitted into the kinship system.

Third, marriage changes the nature of sexual relations between a man and a woman. Sexual intercourse between a married couple is licit; sexual intercourse before marriage, or adulterous sex during marriage, is not. Illicit sex is not necessarily a crime, but licit sexual intercourse enjoys a sanction in the moral universe, however we understand it, from which premarital and extramarital copulation is excluded. More important, the illicit or licit nature of heterosexual copulation is transmitted to the child, who is deemed legitimate or illegitimate based on the metaphysical category of its parents' coition.

Now to live in such a system, in which sexual intercourse can be illicit, is a great nuisance. Many of us feel that licit sexuality loses, moreover, a bit of its oomph. Gay lovers live merrily free of this system. Can we imagine Frank's family and friends warning him that "If Joe were serious, he would put a ring on your finger"? Do we ask Vera to stop stringing Sally along? Gay sexual practice is not sortable into these categories—licit-if-married but illicit-if-not (children adopted by a gay man or hygienically conceived by a lesbian mom can never be regarded as illegitimate). Neither does gay copulation become in any way more permissible, more noble after marriage. It is a scandal that homosexual intercourse should ever have been illegal, but having become legal, there remains no extra sanction—the kind which fathers with shotguns enforce upon heterosexual lovers. I am not aware of any gay marriage activist who suggests that gay men and women should create a new category of disapproval for their own sexual relationships, after so recently having been freed from the onerous and bigoted legal blight on homosexual acts. But without social disapproval of unmarried sex—what kind of madman would seek marriage?

Fourth, marriage defines the end of childhood, sets a boundary between generations within the same family and between families, and establishes the rules in any given society for crossing those boundaries. Marriage usually takes place at the beginning of adulthood; it changes the status of bride and groom from child in the birth family to adult in a new family. In many societies, such as village India and Jewish Chicagoland, a new bride becomes no more than an unpaid servant to her mother- and sisters-in-law. Even in modern romantic marriages, a groom becomes the hunting or business partner of his father-in-law and a member of his clubs; a bride becomes an ally of her mother-in-law in controlling her husband. There can, of course, be warm relations between families and their children's same-sex partners, but these come about because of liking, sympathy, and the inherent kindness of many people. A wedding between same-sex lovers does not create the fact (or even the feeling) of kinship between a man and his husband's family; a woman and her wife's kin. It will be nothing like the new kinship structure that a marriage imposes willy-nilly on two families who would otherwise loathe each other.

Marriage is also an initiation rite. Before World War II, high school graduation was accompanied by a burst of engagements; nowadays college graduation begins a season of weddings that go on every weekend for some years. In contrast, gay weddings are rather middle-aged affairs. My impression is borne out by the one available statistic, from the province of British Columbia, showing that the participants in first-time same-sex weddings are 13 years older, on average, than first-time brides-and-grooms. This feels about right. After all, declaring gay marriage legal will not produce the habit of saving oneself for marriage or create a culture which places a value on virginity or chastity (concepts that are frequently mocked in gay culture precisely because they are so irrelevant to gay romantic life). But virginity and chastity before marriage, license after—these are the burdens of real marriage, honored in spirit if not in letter, creating for women (women as modern as Beyoncé) the right to demand a tangible sacrifice from the men who would adore them.

These four aspects of marriage are not rights, but obligations. They are marriage's "a priori" because marriage is a part of the kinship system, and kinship depends on the protection, organization, and often the exploitation of female sexuality vis-à-vis males. None of these facts apply at all to love between people of the same sex, however solemn and profound that love may be. In gay marriage there are no virgins (actual or honorary), no incest, no illicit or licit sex, no merging of families, no creation of a new lineage. There's just my honey and me, and (in a rapidly increasing number of U.S. states) baby makes three.

What's wrong with this? In one sense, nothing at all. Gays who marry can be congratulated or regarded as foolish based on their individual choices, just as I might covet or lament the women my straight friends espouse. In fact, gay couples who marry enter into a relationship that married people might envy. Gay marriage may reside outside the kinship system, but it has all the wedding-planning, nest-building fun of marriage but none of its rules or obligations (except the duties that all lovers have toward one another). Gay spouses have none of our guilt about sex-before-marriage. They have no tedious obligations towards in-laws, need never worry about Oedipus or Electra, won't have to face a menacing set of brothers or aunts should they betray

their spouse. But without these obligations—why marry? Gay marriage is as good as no marriage at all.

Sooner rather than later, the substantial differences between marriage and gay marriage will cause gay marriage, as a meaningful and popular institution, to fail on its own terms. Since gay relationships exist perfectly well outside the kinship system, to assume the burdens of marriage—the legal formalities, the duty of fidelity (which is no easier for gays than it is for straights), the slavishly imitative wedding ritual—will come to seem a nuisance. People in gay marriages will discover that mimicking the cozy bits of romantic heterosexual marriage does not make relationships stronger; romantic partners more loving, faithful, or sexy; domestic life more serene or exciting. They will discover that it is not the wedding vow that maintains marriages, but the force of the kinship system. Kinship imposes duties, penalties, and retribution that champagne toasts, self-designed wedding rings, and thousands of dollars worth of flowers are powerless to effect.

Few men would ever bother to enter into a romantic heterosexual marriage—much less three, as I have done—were it not for the iron grip of necessity that falls upon us when we are unwise enough to fall in love with a woman other than our mom. There would be very few flowerings of domestic ecstasy were it not for the granite underpinnings of marriage. Gay couples who marry are bound to be disappointed in marriage's impotence without these ghosts of past authority. Marriage has a lineage more ancient than any divine revelation, and before any system of law existed, kinship crushed our ancestors with complex and pitiless rules about incest, family, tribe, and totem. Gay marriage, which can be created by any passel of state supreme court justices with degrees from middling law schools, lacking the authority and majesty of the kinship system, will be a letdown.

When, in spite of current enthusiasm, gay marriage turns out to disappoint or bore the couples now so eager for its creation, its failure will be utterly irrelevant for gay people. The happiness of gay relationships up to now has had nothing to do with being married or unmarried; nor will they in the future. I suspect that the gay marriage movement will be remembered as a faintly humorous, even embarrassing stage in the liberation saga of the gay minority. The archetypal gay wedding portrait—a pair of middle-aged women or paunchy men looking uncomfortable in rented outfits worn at the wrong time of day—is destined to be hung in the same gallery of dated images of social progress alongside snapshots of flappers defiantly puffing cigarettes and Kodachromes of African Americans wearing dashikis. The freedom of gays to live openly as they please will easily survive the death of gay marriage.

continued

So if the failure of gay marriage will not affect gay people, who will it hurt? Only everybody else.

As kinship fails to be relevant to gays, it will become fashionable to discredit it for everyone. The irrelevance of marriage to gay people will create a series of perfectly reasonable, perfectly unanswerable questions: If gays can aim at marriage, yet do without it equally well, who are we to demand it of one another? Who are women to demand it of men? Who are parents to demand it of their children's lovers—or to prohibit their children from taking lovers until parents decide arbitrarily they are "mature" or "ready"? By what right can government demand that citizens obey arbitrary and culturally specific kinship rules—rules about incest and the age of consent, rules that limit marriage to twosomes? Mediocre lawyers can create a fiction called gay marriage, but their idealism can't compel gay lovers to find it useful. But talented lawyers will be very efficient at challenging the complicated, incoherent, culturally relative survival from our most primitive social organization we call kinship. The whole set of fundamental, irrational assumptions that make marriage such a burden and such a civilizing force can easily be undone.

There is no doubt that women and children have suffered throughout human history from being over-protected and controlled. The consequences of under-protection and indifference will be immeasurably worse. In a world without kinship, women will lose their hard-earned status as sexual beings with personal autonomy and physical security. Children will lose their status as nonsexual beings.

Kinship creates these protections by adding the dimension of time, space, and thought to our sense of ourselves as food-eating, sex-having, child-rearing creatures. It makes us conscious not only of our parents and siblings but of their parents and siblings—our ancestors and our group identity. The family relations kinship creates—parents, godparents, uncles and sisters-in-law, cousins, clan, tribe, kingdom, nation—expand our sense of where we live and how we live. In our thought, kinship forces us to move beyond thoughtless obedience to instinct: It gives us a morality based on custom, "always adaptable and susceptible to the nuance of the situation." It makes past experience relevant to current behavior (I quote Michael Oakeshott and paraphrase Peter Winch) and gives us the ability to choose one way of conduct rather than another—the ability which Oakeshott says brings the moral life into being. The commonality of incest prohibitions and marriage rules from one community to another is a sign that we have moved from unselfconscious instinct-obedience (which works well enough to avoid parent-child incest in other species) to the elaboration of human kinship relationships in all their mutations and varieties—all of which have the same core (the organization of female sexuality, the avoidance of incest) but exist in glorious variety. Like the other great human determinant, language, kinship is infinitely variable in form but exists in some form everywhere.

Can gay men and women be as generous as we straight men are? Will you consider us as men who love, just as you do, and not merely as homophobes or Baptists? Every day thousands of ordinary heterosexual men surrender the dream of gratifying our immediate erotic desires. Instead, heroically, resignedly, we march up the aisle with our new brides, starting out upon what that cad poet Shelley called the longest journey, attired in the chains of the kinship system—a system from which you have been spared. Imitate our self-surrender. If gay men and women could see the price that humanity—particularly the women and children among us—will pay, simply in order that a gay person can say of someone she already loves with perfect competence, "Hey, meet the missus!"—no doubt they will think again. If not, we're about to see how well humanity will do without something as basic to our existence as gravity.

www.weeklystandard.com/Content/Public/Articles/000/000/016/533narty.asp?pg=1.

QUESTIONS FOR READING

1. According to Schulman, what is the difference between a heterosexual married couple and a homosexual couple in a long-term relationship?
2. What is only a "small part" of what marriage does, according to the author?
3. What are the four profound effects of marriage within the kinship system?
4. What is the most significant effect of marriage within the kinship system?

QUESTIONS FOR REASONING AND ANALYSIS

1. In your own words, how would you express Schulman's thesis?
2. The concept of *kinship* is integral to Schulman's argument. What does he mean by *kinship*? Why is kinship so important?
3. Why does Schulman believe gay marriage will negatively affect women? Do you agree or disagree? Why or why not?
4. According to Schulman, what impact will result if kinship becomes ultimately irrelevant? Do you believe that gay marriage will bring about these negative consequences? Why or why not?

QUESTIONS FOR REFLECTING AND WRITING

1. Do you take issue with the logic of Shulman's argument? What response might you offer to Schulman? If not, why do you agree with Schulman?
2. In your view, does gay marriage escape the constraints and obligations of kinship? Why or why not?
3. In your view, should homosexual couples be permitted to marry? Why or why not?

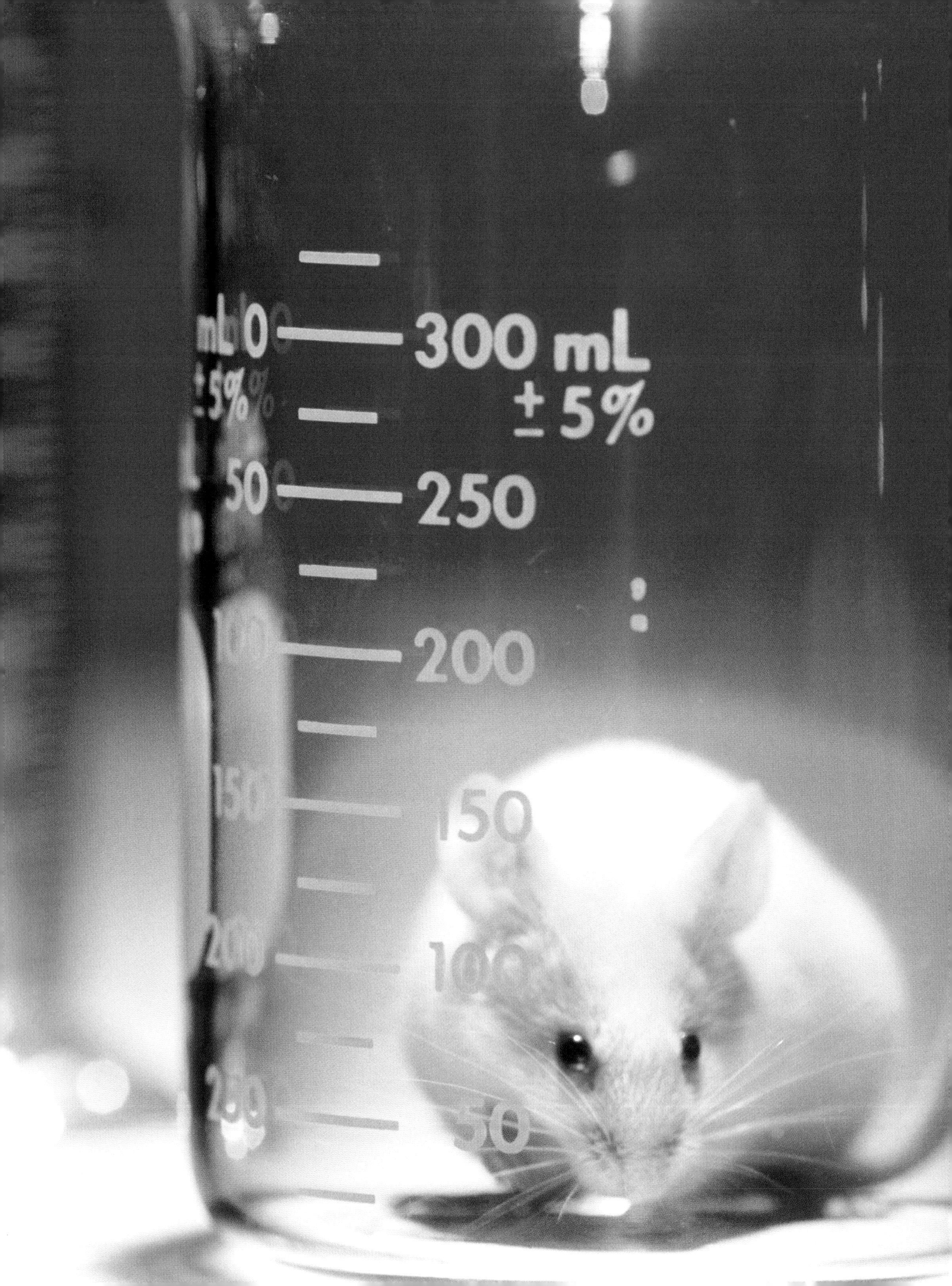
300 mL
± 5%
250
200
150
100
50

arguing about science

Policy, Politics, and Culture

chapter 22

Science does not just take place within the confines of a laboratory, with a solitary scientist performing experiments while surrounded by beakers, test tubes, and laboratory animals. Science's reach extends far beyond the laboratory by informing policy making and even, in some instances, by influencing popular culture. During the Cold War, for example, the government constantly made arguments using scientific evidence to support new weapons technologies as well as nuclear research. The selections from this chapter reveal how scientific debates permeate many aspects of our lives and shape our attitudes and beliefs toward aging, the origin of the universe, and the environment.

prereading questions

1. How well do you understand stem cell research and what is referred to as "cloning"? How important is it to understand the science involved in order to have a position on this research?

2. What is your position on global warming? Do you believe global warming is a legitimate threat to humans? Why or why not?

3. Are you more likely to listen to scientists or to politicians or religious leaders when exploring scientific questions? What is the reasoning behind your choice of expert?

web sites related to this chapter's topic

ENVIRONMENTAL PROTECTION AGENCY
www.epa.gov
U.S. government agency's Web site on environmental issues.

BIOETHICS RESOURCES ON THE WEB—NIH
www.nih.gov/sigs/bioethics
Bioethics resources from the National Institutes of Health, a U.S. government agency.

CENTER FOR BIOETHICS AND HUMAN DIGNITY
www.cbhd.org
Information from a perspective of Christian values.

scholarly journal essay

prereading questions } What are the scientist's ethical obligations to society? Do you think policy makers adequately adhere to scientific findings?

The Challenge for the Obama Administration Science Team

Michael M. Crow

Michael M. Crow is currently president of Arizona State University in Tempe, Arizona. This article appeared in *Issues in Science and Technology*, Spring 2009. Prior to becoming president of Arizona State, Dr. Crow was executive vice provost at Columbia University as well as professor of science and technology policy in the School of International and Public Affairs.

President Obama's choices for top government science positions have made a strong statement about the importance of science and technology (S&T) in our society. In choosing Nobel Prize–winning physicist Stephen Chu for Secretary of Energy, marine biologist Jane Lubchenko to run the National Oceanic and Atmospheric Administration (NOAA), and physicist and energy and arms control expert John Holdren to be his science advisor, Obama has assembled a team with not only impeccable technical credentials but considerable policy and administrative savvy as well.

Yet the ability of science policy leaders to contribute to the nation will not depend on technical expertise, or even effective advocacy on behalf of S&T in the new administration. Far more important will be the team's capacity to ensure that our scientific enterprise improves our environment, enhances our energy security, prepares us for global health risks, and—perhaps most important—brings new insights to the complex challenges associated with maintaining and improving the quality of life across this crowded planet.

President Obama was elected on the promise of change, and in science policy, effective change means, above all, breaching the firewall between science and policy that compromises the nation's ability to turn new knowledge into social benefit. Failure to acknowledge the critical interactions between science and policy has contributed to a scientific enterprise whose capacity to generate knowledge is matched by its inability to make that knowledge useful or usable. Consider, as but one example, that scientists have been able to deliver skillful predictions of the paths and effects of hurricanes while having virtually no impact on the nation's hurricane preparedness, as we saw in 2005 when Hurricane Katrina forever changed our perceptions of extreme weather events. Or that 15 years and $30 billion of research on the climate system are matched by no discernible progress in preparing for or preventing climate change. Or that our marvelous biomedical research capacity, funded at $30 billion per year, is matched by a health care system whose cost, inequity, and performance rank near the bottom among affluent nations.

So even as we applaud our new national science policy leaders, we should also encourage the Obama administration to make the necessary transition from a campaign posture focused on countering political interference in science to a governing posture that connects the $150 billion U.S. public investment in S&T to our most urgent problems.

One key obstacle to strengthening this connection is a culture that values "pure" research above other types, as if some invisible hand will steer scientists' curiosity toward socially useful inquiries. There is no such hand. We invest in the research necessary to refine hurricane forecasts, yet we neglect to develop new knowledge to support populations living in vulnerable areas. We spend 20 years refining our fundamental understanding of Earth's climate while disinvesting in energy technology research. We spend billions each year on the molecular genetic causes of cancer while generally neglecting research on the behavior that can enhance cancer prevention. Overall, we act as if the intellectual goals of scientists are automatically and inevitably aligned with our most important goals as a society. They are not.

This is not about basic versus applied research; both are crucial, and in many cases the boundary between them is so fuzzy as to be meaningless. Rather, it is about the capacity of our research institutions to create knowledge that is as socially useful as it is scientifically meritorious, in areas as broad and complex as social justice, poverty alleviation, access to clean water, sustainable land use, and technological innovation. This challenge is therefore about institutional design; about designing knowledge-producing enterprises that understand and respond to their constituents. Any corporation that imitated our federal science effort, spewing out wonderful products without regard to consumer needs or preferences, would deservedly go bankrupt. Yet we continue to support a public scientific enterprise whose chief measures of productivity—for example, the hundreds of thousands of disciplinary peer-reviewed papers churned out each year—have little if any connection to the public values they allegedly support.

How can we steer the vast capacity of our scientific enterprise toward better meeting the goals and values that justify the confidence and investment of the public? By increasing the level and quality of interaction between our institutions of science and the diverse constituents who have a stake in the outcomes of science; by changing the ethos of research from insular to engaged, from elitist to communitarian; by giving the scientific workforce incentives to broaden the way it selects problems and defines excellence.

We do not need to start from zero. We can tap as exemplary models some promising efforts that align research with the outcomes we would most like to see. For example, the agricultural sciences have a long history of building institutions that bring scientists and users together in the service of food security, productivity, and affordability, from the extension services and experiment stations first developed in the 19th century to the distributed research centers of the Consultative Group on International Agricultural Research that helped create the Green Revolution.

We can learn from the experiences of federal agencies such as the National Institute of Standards and Technology, whose effectiveness depends on its ability to interact with and learn from its complex network of constituents, mostly in the private sector. At NOAA, several innovative (and poorly funded) programs, such as the Regional Integrated Sciences and Assessment, bring scientists together with environmental managers to craft research agendas that are relevant to the needs of decisionmakers in areas such as the management of water supplies and fisheries. A radical expansion of this participatory approach is necessary if we are to avoid endless repetitions of the Katrina debacle. In another realm, the National

continued

Nanotechnology Initiative includes a vibrant research network coordinated across 23 agencies aimed at applying social science research to signal emerging risks and help guide nanoscale research and innovation toward socially desirable outcomes. Although funded far too modestly, this effort shows that fundamental scientific research can be fully integrated with research on societal, ethical, environmental, and economic concerns from the outset, rather than assuming that the invisible hand of scientific inquiry will automatically lead to the maximal social benefit. This type of integrated approach should be implemented across all areas of frontier research.

The nation's science policy leaders can lead the way here by tying R&D funds to institutional innovation of this sort. For example, universities, the site of much of the fundamental research sponsored by the federal government, should become much more aggressive and effective contributors to the solution of social problems. As a university president, I am only too well aware that the tenure process is still largely driven by counting grants, publications, and citations—a weak proxy for social value, and I would say even for scientific excellence. At my institution we try to encourage new modes of scientific success, but until the ability to attract federal funds is decoupled from outmoded notions of productivity and excellence, a process that must be led by the funding institutions themselves, this will be an uphill battle.

The success of President Obama's new science team should be measured by its ability to break down the historical disconnect between science and policy. Our scientific enterprise excels at creating knowledge, but it continues to embrace the myth that new knowledge, emerging from the stubbornly disciplinary channels of today's scientific programs, automatically and serendipitously turns into social benefit. A new administration facing a host of enormous challenges to human welfare can best unleash the power of S&T by rejecting this myth and building a government-wide knowledge-creating enterprise that strengthens the linkages between research and social need.

www.issues.org/25.3

QUESTIONS FOR READING

1. According to Crow, what does "effective change" mean in science policy?
2. What is Crow's answer for steering science toward the goals and values that justify the public's confidence?

3. What federal agencies does Crow cite as examples of scientists interacting effectively with various constituents? What problem does Crow cite that these agencies are facing?

QUESTIONS FOR REASONING AND ANALYSIS

1. What problem does Crow address?
2. Is Crow's thesis explicit or implicit? If explicit, which statement or statements capture Crow's thesis? If implicit, how would you summarize Crow's thesis?

3. What is the difference between "basic" and "applied" scientific research? Why do you think Crow raises this distinction in making his point?

QUESTIONS FOR REFLECTING AND WRITING

1. Do you agree or disagree that scientists are ethically and morally obligated to conduct research that will ultimately benefit society? Why or why not?
2. In your view, has science failed to address adequately certain problems facing society? If so, what are those problems? How has science failed to address these problems? If not, how has science succeeded in achieving the goals Crow describes?

3. If you became one of President Obama's scientific advisors, what recommendations would you make? Why would you make such recommendations? Would your recommendations address only one particular issue? More than one issue? Which issue or issues? Why?

Why would the creators and producers of *An Inconvenient Truth* choose to publish a Web site that complements the message of the film?

An Inconvenient Truth

In 2006, Paramount Classics (a division of Paramount Pictures) released a documentary film titled *An Inconvenient Truth*. The film is narrated by former Vice President and U.S. Senator Al Gore, and it describes the causes and potentially catastrophic effects of global warming. An official Web site was constructed to accompany the message of the film (www.climatecrisis.net).

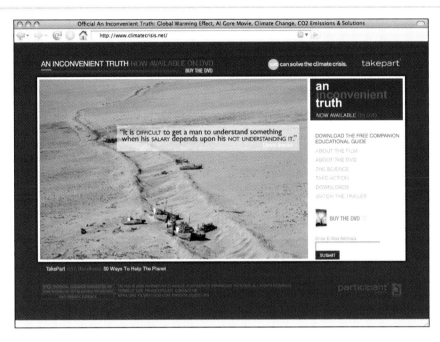

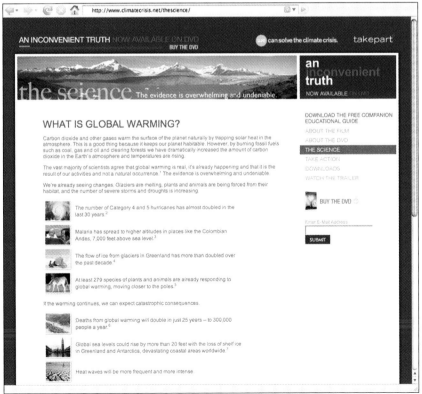

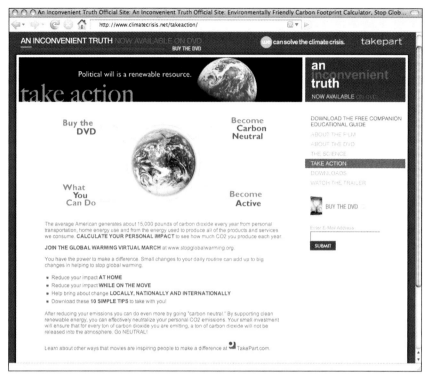

Screen shots courtesy of Participant Media, and Paramount Digital Entertainment, a division of Paramount Pictures Corporation.

QUESTIONS FOR READING

1. According to "The Science" layer of the climate crisis Web site, what is global warming?

2. What sources of carbon dioxide does the "Take Action" page or layer identify?

3. What are some likely consequences of global warming?

QUESTIONS FOR REASONING AND ANALYSIS

1. On the homepage, how do text and graphics work together to appeal to audiences? How do text and graphics function to persuade?

2. Who is the primary audience for this Web site? What is the overall purpose of the site? What other purposes might the site fulfill?

3. How do the writers and designers of this Web site establish credibility, or *ethos*?

4. How does "The Science" page differentiate between "consequences" and "catastrophic consequences"? In other words, the Web site lists an increase in the number of hurricanes as a consequence, but it identifies a probable increase in deaths as a "catastrophic consequence." What is the difference?

QUESTIONS FOR REFLECTING AND WRITING

1. Log onto the homepage for this site (www.climatecrisis .net) and navigate to the "Take Action" page. This page or layer has listed a number of actions a person can take to help reduce carbon dioxide emissions. What steps do you think are most viable? Are you persuaded to take certain actions more than others? Why?

2. People do not read a Web site like they read a print book. They select links and navigate the content to access information. Under both "The Science" and "Take Action," what links would you select? Why?

3. If you have not seen the movie, do you feel compelled to see *An Inconvenient Truth* after looking at this Web site? If you have seen the movie, do you think the site persuades others to see the film? Why or why not?

prereading questions } Have you ever heard of "intelligent design"? If not, what do you think it means? If so, what do you already know about intelligent design?

Trouble Ahead for Science

Kenneth R. Miller

Kenneth Miller is professor of biology at Brown University and author of *Only a Theory— Evolution and the Battle for America's Soul* (forthcoming). Dr. Miller earned a PhD in biology from the University of Colorado in 1974, and he has authored numerous journal articles and review essays. Dr. Miller currently lends his expertise as an advisor to *The NewsHour*, a nightly news program on PBS. This article was first published in *The Boston Globe* on May 8, 2008.

American science is in trouble, and if you wonder why, just go to the movies. Popular culture is gradually turning against science, and Ben Stein's new movie, *Expelled*, is helping to push it along.

"Intelligent Design," the relabeled, repackaged form of American creationism, has always had a problem. It just can't seem to produce any evidence. To scientists, the reasons for this are obvious. To conservative *Washington Post* columnist Charles Krauthammer, Intelligent Design is nothing more than a "phony theory." No data, no science, no experiments, just an attempt to sneak a narrow set of religious views into U.S. classrooms.

Advocates of Intelligent Design needed a story to explain why the idea has been a nonstarter within the scientific community, and Ben Stein has given it to them. The story line is that Intelligent Design advocates are persecuted and suppressed. *Expelled* tells of this terrible campaign against free expression, and mocks the pretensions of the closed-minded scientific elite supposedly behind it.

There are many things wrong with this movie. One example: Viewers are told that Dr. Richard Sternberg lost his job at the Smithsonian Institution because he edited a paper favorable to Intelligent Design. Wrong.

Sternberg wasn't even employed by the Smithsonian (he had no job to lose), and had resigned as journal editor six months before the paper was published. In fact, the irony is that neither Steinberg nor any of the other people featured as martyrs in *Expelled* lost jobs as a result of their advocacy of Intelligent Design, while many others who supported evolution have. In 2007, Chris Comer, the director of science education for Texas schools, was fired for having done nothing more than forwarding an e-mail announcing a pro-evolution seminar.

The movie also uses interviews with avowed atheists like Richard Dawkins, author of *The God Delusion*, to argue that the scientific establishment is vehemently anti-God. Never mind that 40 percent of the members of the American Association for the Advancement of Science profess belief in a personal God. Stein, avoiding these 50,000 people, tells viewers that "Darwinists" don't allow scientists to even think of God.

Puzzled, the editors of *Scientific American* asked Mark Mathis, the film's co-producer, why he and Stein didn't interview such people, like Francis Collins (head of the Human Genome Project), Francisco Ayala, or myself. Mathis cited me by name, saying "Ken Miller would have confused the film unnecessarily." In other words, showing a scientist who accepts both God and evolution would have confused their story line.

Despite these falsehoods, by far the film's most outlandish misrepresentation is its linkage of Darwin with the Holocaust. A concentration camp tour guide tells Stein that the Nazis were practicing "Darwinism," and that's that. Never mind those belt buckles proclaiming *Gott mit uns* (God is with us), the toxic anti-Semitism of Martin Luther, the ghettoes and murderous pogroms in Christian Europe centuries before Darwin's birth. No matter. It's all the fault of evolution.

Why is all this nonsense a threat to science? The reason is Stein's libelous conclusion that science is simply evil. In an April 21 interview on the Trinity Broadcast Network, Stein called the Nazi murder of children "horrifying beyond words." Indeed. But what led to such horrors? Stein explained: "that's where science in my opinion, this is just an opinion, that's where science leads you. Love of God and compassion and empathy leads you to a very glorious place. Science leads you to killing people."

According to Stein, science leads you to "killing people." Not to cures and vaccines, not to a deeper understanding of nature, not to wonders like computers and cellphones, and certainly not to a better life. Nope. Science is murder.

continued

Expelled is a shoddy piece of propaganda that props up the failures of Intelligent Design by playing the victim card. It deceives its audiences, slanders the scientific community, and contributes mightily to a climate of hostility to science itself. Stein is doing nothing less than helping turn a generation of American youth away from science. If we actually come to believe that science leads to murder, then we deserve to lose world leadership in science. In that sense, the word *expelled* may have a different and more tragic connotation for our country than Stein intended.

www.boston.com/bostonglobe/
editorial_opinion/oped/articles/
2008/05/08/trouble_ahead_for_science

QUESTIONS FOR READING

1. What is the premise of Ben Stein's movie *Expelled*, as Miller explains it?
2. According to Miller, why was Chris Comer fired from his teaching position?
3. By the end of the article, how does Miller label Stein's piece?

QUESTIONS FOR REASONING AND ANALYSIS

1. What does Miller's reference to intelligent design as a "repackaged form of American creationism" imply or suggest? How would you describe the tone of such a statement?
2. Why does Miller cite the evidence that "40 percent of the members of the American Association of the Advancement of Science profess belief in a personal God"? What point is he making in this paragraph?
3. Miller says that Stein and Mathis failed to interview experts in science like Francis Collins, Francisco Ayala, and himself—all of whom disagree with intelligent design. What indictment of *Expelled* does he level by pointing out this failure to readers?
4. In the last paragraph, how does Miller use the word *expelled* to support his own argument?

QUESTIONS FOR REFLECTING AND WRITING

1. Miller claims to believe in God and to support evolution as a theory. Are the two points of view mutually exclusive? Or is it possible for a person to profess belief in God and to agree with evolution? Explain your view.
2. Consider Miller's critique of Stein's arguments about the Nazis. Is an unwavering allegiance to science just as detrimental as an unquestioning belief in religion (or vice versa)? Why or why not?
3. What is your position on intelligent design (or creation) versus evolution? Why do you support one or the other?

prereading questions } Should a state government or school board mandate the teaching of one hypothesis or theory over another? Why or why not?

Florida's Darwinian Interlude

Ben Stein

Ben Stein, who, in recent years, has become a celebrity, is also a writer and economist. His piece "Florida's Darwinian Interlude" first appeared in *The American Spectator* on February 20, 2008.

Just a few tiny, insignificant little questions.

- How did the universe start?
- Where did matter come from?
- Where did energy come from?
- Where did the laws of motion, thermodynamics, physics, chemistry, come from?
- Where did gravity come from?
- How did inorganic matter, that is, lifeless matter such as dirt and rocks, become living beings?
- Has anyone ever observed beyond doubt the evolution of a new mammalian or aviary species, as opposed to changes within a species?

These teeny weeny little questions are just some of the issues as to which Darwin and Darwinism have absolutely no verifiable answers. Hypotheses.

Yes. Guesses. Yes. Proof? None.

To my little pea brain, these are some pretty big issues about evolution, the origins of life, and genetics that Darwinism cannot answer. Now, to be fair, does anyone else have verifiable answers either? Not as far as I know.

But if there are no answers that can be reproduced in the laboratory, isn't any theory about them a hypothesis or a guess? Isn't any hypothesis worth thinking about? And aren't these immense questions?

Yet the state of Florida, the glorious Sunshine State, was (I am told), until recently, considering legislation that would make it illegal to allow teachers or students in public schools to discuss any hypothesis about origins of life or the universe except that it all happened by accident without any prime mover or first cause or designer—allowing only, again, the hypothesis, which is considered Darwinian, that it all started by, well, by, something that Darwin never even mentioned.

That is, the state of Florida was considering mandating that only Darwinian-type suppositions can be allowed about scientific subjects that Darwin never studied. (This is not to mention that we know now that Darwin was wildly wrong about some subjects such as genetics, and, again, although he wrote about the evolution of species, never observed an entirely new species evolve.)

This was beyond Stalinism. Stalinism decreed that only Marx-Engels-Lenin-Stalin knew all the answers, but it did not say that subjects they never mentioned could only be studied if the student guessed at what they might have said. The proposed law in the state of Florida was an anti-knowledge, anti-freedom of inquiry law on a scale such as has rarely been encountered. Maybe in Pol Pot's Kampuchea there were such laws, but they have been unknown in the USA until now.

By an incredible miracle of good sense, at the last minute, the state of Florida changed the proposed regulations. They backed off powerfully saying that only Darwinism could possibly make sense and said they would allow discussion of differing theories about the origins of life. That's the current proposal as I write this on the afternoon of the 19th of February.

I suspect the now omitted proposals would have been unconstitutional in any event (although this always depends on the court you ask). Freedom of inquiry is part of freedom of speech. That is basic. That is what America is all about. Whatever the proposed—now discarded—regulations were, they have nothing to do with freedom, very little to do with science, and not even much to do with Darwin, who had a lot more respect for freedom of thought than his henchmen in Florida apparently do.

http://spectator.org/archives/2008/02/20/floridas-darwinian-interlude

1. What legislation was the state of Florida considering?
2. How did Florida change its proposed regulations?

3. With what does Stein compare the law in Florida?

QUESTIONS FOR REASONING AND ANALYSIS

1. What is Stein's thesis?
2. Why does Stein begin his piece with a series of questions? What is the rhetorical effect of these questions?

3. Is Stein's comparison between the Florida law and Stalinism, Leninism, and Marxism justifiable? Or fair? Why or why not? How does this comparison strengthen or weaken his argument?

QUESTIONS FOR REFLECTING AND WRITING

1. Conduct a Web search to find further information on this particular law in Florida. Has Stein offered an accurate assessment of it? How so? If not, why not?
2. Should teachers teach only one theory or hypothesis concerning the origins of the universe? How should teachers go about teaching this subject?

3. As a student, how do you wish to learn about the origin of species? Or the origin of the universe, for that matter?

newspaper column

prereading questions } **Should information on building bombs or biological warfare be kept from publication or Internet posting? Why or why not?**

Censoring Science Won't Make Us Any Safer

Laura K. Donohue

Laura Donohue is an Associate Professor of Law at Georgetown Law, and a faculty affiliate of Georgetown's Center on National Security and the Law. Professor Donohue has held fellowships at Stanford Law School's Center for Constitutional Law, Stanford University's Center for International Security and Cooperation, and Harvard University's John F. Kennedy School of Government. She is the author of numerous articles as well as *Counter-Terrorist Law and Emergency Powers in the United Kingdom 1922–2000* (2001). The following article was published in *The Washington Post* on June 26, 2005.

In 1920, the Irish Republican Army reportedly considered a terrifying new weapon: typhoid-contaminated milk. Reading from an IRA memo he claimed had been captured in a recent raid, Sir Hamar Greenwood described to Parliament the ease with which "fresh and virulent cultures" could be obtained and introduced into milk served to British soldiers. Although the plot would only target the military, the memo expressed concern that the disease might spread to the general population.

Although the IRA never used this weapon, the incident illustrates that poisoning a nation's milk supply with biological agents hardly ranks as a new concept. Yet just two weeks ago, the National Academy of Sciences' journal suspended publication of an article analyzing the vulnerability of the U.S. milk supply to botulinum toxin, because the Department of Health

and Human Services warned that information in the article provided a "road map for terrorists."

That approach may sound reasonable, but the effort to suppress scientific information reflects a dangerously outdated attitude. Today, information relating to microbiology is widely and instantly available, from the Internet to high school textbooks to doctoral theses. Our best defense against those who would use it as a weapon is to ensure that our own scientists have better information. That means encouraging publication.

The article in question, written by Stanford University professor Lawrence Wein and graduate student Yifan Liu, describes a theoretical terrorist who obtains a few grams of botulinum toxin on the black market and pours it into an unlocked milk tank. Transferred to giant dairy silos, the toxin contaminates a much larger supply. Because even a millionth of a gram may be enough to kill an adult, hundreds of thousands of people die. (Wein summarized the article in an op-ed he wrote for *The New York Times*.[1]) The scenario is frightening, and it is meant to be—the authors want the dairy industry and its federal regulators to take defensive action.

The national academy's suspension of the article reflects an increasing concern that publication of sensitive data can provide terrorists with a how-to manual, but it also brings to the fore an increasing anxiety in the scientific community that curbing the dissemination of research may impair our ability to counter biological threats. This dilemma reached national prominence in fall 2001, when 9/11 and the anthrax mailings drew attention to another controversial article. This one came from a team of Australian scientists.

Approximately every four years, Australia suffers a mouse infestation. In 1998, scientists in Canberra began examining the feasibility of using a highly contagious disease, mousepox, to alter the rodents' ability to reproduce. Their experiments yielded surprising results. Researchers working with mice naturally resistant to the disease found that combining a gene from the rodent's immune system (interleukin-4) with the pox virus and inserting the pathogen into the animals killed them—all of them. Plus 60 percent of the mice not naturally resistant who had been vaccinated against mousepox.

In February 2001 the American Society for Microbiologists' (ASM) *Journal of Virology* reported the findings. Alarm ensued. The mousepox virus is closely related to smallpox—one of the most dangerous pathogens known to humans. And the rudimentary nature of the experiment demonstrated how even basic, inexpensive microbiology can yield devastating results.

When the anthrax attacks burst into the news seven months later, the mousepox case became a lightning rod for deep-seated fears about biological weapons. *The Economist* reported rumors about the White House pressuring American microbiology journals to restrict publication of similar pieces. Samuel Kaplan, chair of the ASM publications board, convened a meeting of the editors in chief of the ASM's nine primary journals and two review journals. Hoping to head off government censorship, the organization— while affirming its earlier decision—ordered its peer reviewers to take national security and the society's code of ethics into account.

Not only publications came under pressure, but research itself. In spring 2002 the newly formed Department of Homeland Security developed an information-security policy to prevent certain foreign nationals from gaining access to a range of experimental data. New federal regulations required that particular universities and laboratories submit to unannounced inspections, register their supplies and obtain security clearances.

Legislation required that all genetic engineering experiments be cleared by the government.

On the mousepox front, however, important developments were transpiring. Because the Australian research had entered the public domain, scientists around the world began working on the problem. In November 2003, St. Louis University announced an effective medical defense against a pathogen similar to—but even more deadly than—the one created in Australia. This result would undoubtedly not have been achieved, or at least not as quickly, without the attention drawn by the ASM article.

The dissemination of nuclear technology presents an obvious comparison. The 1946 Atomic Energy Act classifies nuclear information "from birth." Strong arguments can be made in favor of such restrictions: The science involved in the construction of the bomb was complex and its application primarily limited to weapons. A short-term monopoly was possible. Secrecy bought the United States time to establish an international nonproliferation regime. And little public good would have been achieved by making the information widely available.

Biological information and the issues surrounding it are different. It is not possible to establish even a limited monopoly over microbiology. The field is too fundamental to the improvement of global public health, and too central to the development of important industries such as pharmaceuticals and plastics, to be isolated. Moreover, the list of diseases that pose a threat ranges from high-end bugs, like smallpox, to common viruses, such as influenza. Where does one draw the line for national security?

Experience suggests that the government errs on the side of caution. In 1951, the Invention Secrecy Act gave the government the authority to suppress any design it deemed detrimental to national defense. Certain areas of research—atomic energy and cryptography— consistently fell within its purview. But the state also placed secrecy orders on aspects of cold fusion, space technology, radar missile systems, citizens band radio voice scramblers, optical engineering and vacuum technology. Such caution, in the microbiology realm, may yield devastating results. It is not in the national interest to stunt research into biological threats.

In fact, the more likely menace comes from naturally occurring diseases. In 1918 a natural outbreak of the flu infected one-fifth of the world's population and 25 percent of the United States'. Within two years it killed more than 650,000 Americans, resulting in a 10-year drop in average lifespan. Despite constant research into emerging strains, the American Lung Association estimates that the flu and related complications kill 36,000 Americans each

continued

year. Another 5,000 die annually from food-borne pathogens—an extraordinarily large number of which have no known cure. The science involved in responding to these diseases is incremental, meaning that small steps taken by individual laboratories around the world need to be shared for larger progress to be made.

The idea that scientific freedom strengthens national security is not new. In the early 1980s, a joint Panel on Scientific Communication and National Security concluded security by secrecy was untenable. Its report called instead for security by accomplishment—ensuring strength through advancing research. Ironically, one of the three major institutions participating was the National Academy of Sciences—the body that suspended publication of the milk article earlier this month.

The government has a vested interest in creating a public conversation about ways in which our society is vulnerable to attack. Citizens are entitled to know when their milk, their water, their bridges, their hospitals lack security precautions. If discussion of these issues is censored, the state and private industry come under less pressure to alter behavior; indeed, powerful private interests may actively lobby against having to install expensive protections. And failure to act may be deadly.

Terrorists will obtain knowledge. Our best option is to blunt their efforts to exploit it. That means developing, producing and stockpiling effective vaccines. It means funding research into biosensors—devices that detect the presence of toxic substances in the environment—and creating more effective reporting requirements for early identification of disease outbreaks. And it means strengthening our public health system.

For better or worse, the cat is out of the bag—something brought home to me last weekend when I visited the Tech Museum of Innovation in San Jose. One hands-on exhibit allowed children to transfer genetic material from one species to another. I watched a 4-year-old girl take a red test tube whose contents included a gene that makes certain jellyfish glow green. Using a pipette, she transferred the material to a blue test tube containing bacteria. She cooled the solution, then heated it, allowing the gene to enter the bacteria. Following instructions on a touch-screen computer, she transferred the contents to a petridish, wrote her name on the bottom, and placed the dish in an incubator. The next day, she could log on to a Web site to view her experiment, and see her bacteria glowing a genetically modified green.

In other words, the pre-kindergartener (with a great deal of help from the museum) had conducted an experiment that echoed the Australian mousepox study. Obviously, this is not something the child could do in her basement. But just as obviously, the state of public knowledge is long past anyone's ability to censor it.

Allowing potentially harmful information to enter the public domain flies in the face of our traditional way of thinking about national security threats. But we have entered a new world. Keeping scientists from sharing information damages our ability to respond to terrorism and to natural disease, which is more likely and just as devastating. Our best hope to head off both threats may well be to stay one step ahead.

---

1. Actually the description of a theoretical terrorist obtaining a toxin on the black market appeared only in *The New York Times* article, not in the original article that the National Academy of Sciences refused to publish.

QUESTIONS FOR READING

1. What is the occasion for Donohue's article?
2. What other restrictions have been developed by Homeland Security?
3. How is the scientific community reacting to restrictions? What is their concern?
4. What is probably a greater threat than terrorism?
5. Is it possible to censor information on microbiology?

QUESTIONS FOR REASONING AND ANALYSIS

1. What is Donohue's claim? State it as a problem/solution type of argument.
2. To state her claim as a problem/solution type of argument is to suggest that her argument is more practical than philosophical; is that a fair assessment?
Why or why not? What are the two key points of her argument?
3. In paragraph 11, Donohue reminds readers that nuclear information is classified and asserts that it should be. Why does she include this paragraph?

QUESTIONS FOR REFLECTING AND WRITING

1. Donohue reminds readers that scientific knowledge is built up by many contributing a little bit to the knowledge base. And yet a scientific journal suppressed an article. Why? Does Homeland Security have too much power? Have we all become too fearful of terrorists?
2. Has the author convinced you that we are at greater risk by censoring knowledge than by publishing information? Why or why not?

Oil Consumption per Dollar

(January to May 2008)

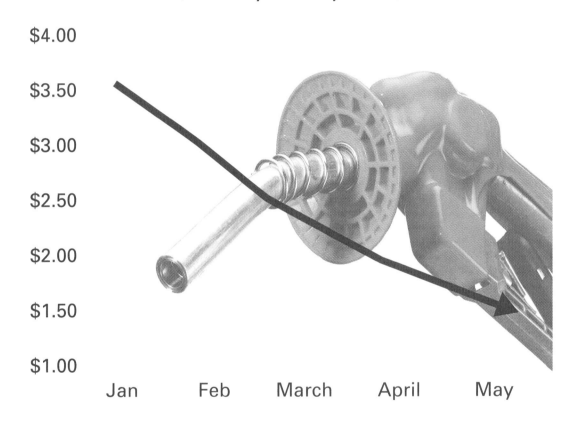

	Jan	Feb	March	April	May
$4.00					
$3.50					
$3.00					
$2.50					
$2.00					
$1.50					
$1.00					

competing perspectives on the american economic and financial crisis

chapter 23

Foreclosure. Bailout. Deficit. Recession. Depression. These terms have become all too familiar as our nation's leaders debate how to resolve the economic and financial crisis that began in 2008. This crisis has created a feeling of uncertainty in most Americans, many of whom lost their jobs, their homes, and their hope for the future. In response, the U.S. Congress passed almost $1 trillion of "economic stimulus," but some feared the measure would create more problems than it would solve by increasing deficits and eventually resulting in more taxes. Others feared our nation was on the brink of complete financial collapse, perhaps even worse than the Great Depression of the 1930s. The following selections capture these differing and competing perspectives, addressing, for example, the mortgage-lending debacle as well as President Obama's economic recovery plan for resolving one of the most serious crises in our nation's history.

prereading questions

1. What are the answers to the economic and financial crisis, which poses serious potential consequences for both the U.S. and the rest of the world?

2. What were the major causes of the economic crisis? Is any one party (political or otherwise) or group to blame for the crisis? Should politicians engage in finger-pointing in the midst of catastrophe? Why or why not?

3. Should the federal government bail out failing financial-lending institutions and major corporations? Why or why not?

4. Does President Obama's plan represent the right course of action for addressing the country's economic problems and financial woes? Why or why not?

5. How do you think this crisis will affect you as well as your family and friends in the next 10 to 20 years?

web sites related to this chapter's topic

AMERICANS UNITED FOR CHANGE
www.americansunitedforchange.com
Web site for the grassroots organization Americans United for Change, offering several links and multiple resources.

THE WORLD BANK
www.worldbank.org/html/extdr/financialcrisis
World Bank site addressing the global economic and financial crisis.

RELEVANT WHITE HOUSE LINKS
National Economic Council
www.whitehouse.gov/administration/eop/nec
Council of Economic Advisors
www.whitehouse.gov/administration/eop/cea
White House Agenda—Economy
www.whitehouse.gov/agenda/economy

newspaper editorial

prereading question } Is the federal government doing enough to resolve the financial crisis?

Behind the Curve

Paul Krugman

Paul Krugman, a professor of economics and international affairs at Princeton University, is also a columnist for *The New York Times* and recipient of the Nobel Prize for Economics. This editorial was published on March 8, 2009.

President Obama's plan to stimulate the economy was "massive," "giant," "enormous." So the American people were told, especially by TV news, during the run-up to the stimulus vote. Watching the news, you might have thought that the only question was whether the plan was too big, too ambitious.

Yet many economists, myself included, actually argued that the plan was too small and too cautious. The latest data confirm those worries—and suggest that the Obama administration's economic policies are already falling behind the curve.

To see how bad the numbers are, consider this: The administration's budget proposals, released less than two weeks ago, assumed an average unemployment rate of 8.1 percent for the whole of this year. In reality, unemployment hit that level in February—and it's rising fast.

Employment has already fallen more in this recession than in the 1981–82 slump, considered the worst since the Great Depression. As a result, Mr. Obama's promise that his plan will create or save 3.5 million jobs by the end of 2010 looks underwhelming, to say the least. It's a credible promise—his economists used solidly mainstream estimates of the impacts of tax and spending policies. But 3.5 million jobs almost two years from now isn't enough in the face of an economy that has already lost 4.4 million jobs, and is losing 600,000 more each month.

There are now three big questions about economic policy. First, does the administration realize that it isn't doing enough? Second, is it prepared to do more? Third, will Congress go along with stronger policies?

On the first two questions, I found Mr. Obama's latest interview with *The Times* anything but reassuring.

"Our belief and expectation is that we will get all the pillars in place for recovery this year," the president declared—a belief and expectation that isn't backed by any data or model I'm aware of. To be sure, leaders are supposed to sound calm and in control. But in the face of the dismal data, this remark sounded out of touch.

And there was no hint in the interview of readiness to do more.

A real fix for the troubles of the banking system might help make up for the inadequate size of the stimulus plan, so it was good to hear that Mr. Obama spends at least an hour each day with his economic advisors, "talking through how we are approaching the financial markets." But he went on to dismiss calls for decisive action as coming from "blogs" (actually, they're coming from many other places, including at least one president of a Federal Reserve bank), and suggested that critics want to "nationalize all the banks" (something nobody is proposing).

As I read it, this dismissal—together with the continuing failure to announce any broad plans for bank restructuring—means that the White House has decided to muddle through on the financial front, relying on economic recovery to rescue the banks rather than the other way around. And with the stimulus plan too small to deliver an economic recovery . . . well, you get the picture.

Sooner or later the administration will realize that more must be done. But when it comes back for more money, will Congress go along?

Republicans are now firmly committed to the view that we should do nothing to respond to the economic crisis, except cut taxes—which they always want to do regardless of circumstances. If Mr. Obama comes back for a second round of stimulus, they'll respond not by being helpful, but by claiming that his policies have failed.

The broader public, by contrast, favors strong action. According to a recent *Newsweek* poll, a majority of voters supports the stimulus, and, more surprisingly, a plurality believes that additional spending will be necessary. But will that support still be there, say, six months from now?

Also, an overwhelming majority believes that the government is spending too much to help large financial institutions. This suggests that the administration's money-for-nothing financial policy will eventually deplete its political capital.

So here's the picture that scares me: It's September 2009, the unemployment rate has passed 9 percent, and despite the early round of stimulus spending it's still headed up. Mr. Obama finally concedes that a bigger stimulus is needed.

But he can't get his new plan through Congress because approval for his economic policies has plummeted, partly because his policies are seen to have failed, partly because job-creation policies are conflated in the public mind with deeply unpopular bank bailouts. And as a result, the recession rages on, unchecked.

OK, that's a warning, not a prediction. But economic policy is falling behind the curve, and there's a real, growing danger that it will never catch up.

QUESTIONS FOR READING

1. What was the unemployment rate for February 2009?
2. What is Krugman's major concern with President Obama's plan?
3. What is the Republican answer to the crisis, according to Krugman?

1. What is Krugman's thesis?
2. What major problem associated with the financial crisis does Krugman suggest requires immediate government action? How does he explain the problem through use of evidence? Has he convinced you the government should take immediate action? Why or why not?
3. Does Krugman ever explain what a "bigger" stimulus should entail? If not, does his failure to specify the particulars of a bigger stimulus become a problem for you as a reader? Do you begin to doubt the validity of his argument? Why or why not?

1. In your view, what actions should the government take to resolve the financial crisis? Why do you think these actions will solve the problems?
2. What brought about the financial crisis? Do you believe one group (for example, politicians or bankers) shoulders more responsibility than another? Why?
3. Are you taking steps to become more financially responsible? If so, what are those steps?

web site essay

prereading question } **Should government assume a larger or smaller role in the midst of economic crisis?**

Bailout Politics

Thomas Sowell

Thomas Sowell, economist and Senior Fellow at Stanford University's Hoover Institution, wrote this editorial on September 30, 2008, for *National Review Online*.

http://www.nationalreview.com

The Congressional Dems who enabled this crisis are now being trusted to fix it?

Nothing could more painfully demonstrate what is wrong with Congress than the current financial crisis.

Among the Congressional "leaders" invited to the White House to devise a bailout "solution" are the very people who have for years created the risks that have now come home to roost.

Five years ago, Barney Frank vouched for the "soundness" of Fannie Mae and Freddie Mac, and said "I do not see" any "possibility of serious financial losses to the treasury."

Moreover, he said that the federal government has "probably done too little rather than too much to push them to meet the goals of affordable housing."

Earlier this year, Senator Christopher Dodd praised Fannie Mae and Freddie Mac for "riding to the rescue" when other financial institutions were cutting back on mortgage loans. He too said that they "need to do more" to help subprime borrowers get better loans.

In other words, Congressman Frank and Senator Dodd wanted the government to push financial institutions to lend to people they would not lend to otherwise, because of the risk of default.

The idea that politicians can assess risks better than people who have spent their whole careers assessing risks should have been so obviously absurd that no one would take it seriously.

But the magic words *affordable housing* and the ugly word *redlining* led to politicians directing where loans and investments should go, with such things as the Community Reinvestment Act and various other coercions and threats.

The roots of this problem go back many years, but since the crisis to which all this led happened on George W. Bush's watch, that is enough for those who think in terms of talking points, without wanting to be confused by the facts.

In reality, President Bush tried unsuccessfully, years ago, to get Congress to create some regulatory agency to oversee Fannie Mae and Freddie Mac.

N. Gregory Mankiw, his chairman of the Council of Economic Advisers, warned in February 2004 that expecting a government bailout if things go wrong "creates an incentive for a company to take on risk and enjoy the associated increase in return."

Since risky investments usually pay more than safer investments, the incentive is for a government-supported enterprise to take bigger risks, since they get more profit if the risks pay off and the taxpayers get stuck with the losses if not.

The government does not guarantee Fannie Mae or Freddie Mac, but the widespread assumption has been that the government would step in with a bailout to prevent chaos in financial markets.

Alan Greenspan, then head of the Federal Reserve System, made the same point in testifying before Congress in February 2004. He said: "The Federal Reserve is concerned" that Fannie Mae and Freddie Mac were using this implicit reliance on a government bailout in a crisis to take more risks, in order to "multiply the profitability of subsidized debt."

Chairman Greenspan added his voice to those urging Congress to create a "regulator with authority on a par with that of banking regulators" to reduce the riskiness of Fannie Mae and Freddie Mac, a riskiness ultimately borne by the taxpayers.

Fannie Mae and Freddie Mac do not deserve to be bailed out, but neither do workers, families and businesses deserve to be put through the economic wringer by a collapse of credit markets, such as occurred during the Great Depression of the 1930s.

Neither do the voters deserve to be deceived on the eve of an election by the notion that this is a failure of free markets that should be replaced by political micro-managing.

If Fannie Mae and Freddie Mac were free market institutions, they could not have gotten away with their risky financial practices because no one would have bought their securities without the implicit assumption that the politicians would bail them out.

It would be better if no such government-supported enterprises had been created in the first place and mortgages were in fact left to the free market. This bailout creates the expectation of future bailouts.

Phasing out Fannie Mae and Freddie Mac would make much more sense than letting politicians play politics with them again, with the risk and expense being again loaded onto the taxpayers.

National Review Online, September 30, 2008. © 2008 Creators Syndicate, Inc. By permission of Thomas Sowell and Creators Syndicate, Inc.

http://article.nationalreview.com/?q=OWE3OWU3OTExYzNINTUzMzY2YmJmOWZjMzcwN2M1NjU=

QUESTIONS FOR READING

1. What did former President George W. Bush attempt unsuccessfully to get Congress to do?
2. What did former Federal Reserve Chairman Alan Greenspan explain to Congress in February 2004?
3. Why did Fannie Mae and Freddie Mac get away with risky financial practices, according to Sowell?

QUESTIONS FOR REASONING AND ANALYSIS

1. How would you explain Sowell's thesis in your own words?
2. What does Sowell mean by *redlining*? How is he using this term in his essay? With a positive or negative connotation? Why one over the other?
3. By the end of the essay, has Sowell offered a solution to the housing loan crisis? How so? If not, why not?
4. How would you describe the tone of Sowell's essay? Cynical? Concerned? Optimistic? Why would you choose one descriptor over another?

QUESTIONS FOR REFLECTING AND WRITING

1. How would you respond to Sowell's essay? Do you agree or disagree with him? Why or why not?
2. What is your solution to the mortgage crisis? Why should the government and/or financial institutions take certain steps to resolve this crisis?
3. Should the government eliminate Fannie Mae and Freddie Mac? Why or why not?

Americans United for Change Advertisements

The grassroots organization Americans United for Change released these two videos in March 2009.

Reprinted by permission of Americans United for Change. YouTube is a trademark of Google Inc.
www.youtube.com/watch?v=j5_Wur3JFcg

Reprinted by permission of Americans United for Change. YouTube is a trademark of Google Inc.
www.youtube.com/watch?v=D-pLSdGa0M4&NR=1

(Watch the two videos on YouTube before answering these questions.)

1. What message is this group communicating by including the sound of the chirping crickets?
2. What effect is achieved by showing the several different key Republicans only saying the word *no*?

3. In the second video, what is Americans United for Change suggesting by presenting conservative radio talk show host Rush Limbaugh as the only person to whom Republicans say *yes*?

QUESTIONS FOR REFLECTING AND WRITING

1. Americans United for Change claims that the Republicans caused the financial crisis. Is their claim accurate? Why or why not? If not, who or what caused the financial crisis?
2. Is finger-pointing appropriate in the midst of this crisis? Why or why not?

3. What is your overall reaction to these two videos? Did you find humor in these videos? Were you offended? Why did you react one way over another?

political cartoon

prereading questions } **What does it mean to "redistribute wealth"? Is increasing taxes on the wealthiest Americans the answer to addressing the financial crisis?**

William Warren

The Barack the Plumber cartoon was originally published by William Warren of Warren Toons on October 16, 2008.

Reprinted by permission of William Warren. www.warrentoons.com.

QUESTIONS FOR REASONING AND ANALYSIS

1. What do you think is represented by the elaborate system of pipes leading from the worker's pocket to the "Federal Welfare State" bucket? What do you think Warren is suggesting by depicting the pipes in this way?

2. Is it important that Warren shows the American worker standing with a woman and a child who probably represent his wife and son? Why or why not?
3. Why do you think Warren chose to depict Obama as a plumber?

1. Is it fair to tax the wealthiest Americans more than others? Should the federal government raise their taxes? Why or why not?
2. President Obama has said he will not raise taxes on anyone making less than six figures a year. Do you believe him? Can he keep this promise? Why or why not?
3. Is raising taxes an appropriate response to the financial crisis? Why or why not?

blog post

prereading question } Should the federal government bail out failing major corporations and financial-lending institutions?

The Real Scandal of AIG

Robert Reich

Former Secretary of Labor Robert Reich made this post to *The Huffington Post* blog on March 15, 2009. In September 2008, the federal government seized control of American International Group (AIG), a major insurer of financial institutions, because the company was facing bankruptcy. AIG eventually received over $170 billion in federal loans and aid, but by early March 2009, it was reported that AIG intended to pay $165 million in bonuses to its executives, a decision that angered President Obama and his top aides as well as many members of Congress.

The real scandal of AIG isn't just that American taxpayers have so far committed $170 billion to the giant insurer because it is thought to be too big to fail—the most money ever funneled to a single company by a government since the dawn of capitalism—nor even that AIG's notoriously failing executives, at the very unit responsible for the catastrophic credit-default swaps at the very center of the debacle—are planning to give themselves $100 million in bonuses. It's that even at this late date, even in a new administration dedicated to doing it all differently, Americans still have so little say over what is happening with our money.

The administration is said to have been outraged when it heard of the bonus plan last week. Apparently, Secretary of the Treasury Tim Geithner told AIG's chairman, Edward Liddy (who was installed at the insistence of the Treasury, in the first place) that the bonuses should not be paid. But most will be paid anyway, because, according to AIG, the firm is legally obligated to do so. The bonuses are part of employee contracts negotiated before the bailouts. And, in any event, Liddy explained, AIG needed to be able to retain talent.

AIG's arguments are absurd on their face. Had AIG gone into Chapter 11 bankruptcy or been liquidated, as it would have without government aid, no bonuses would ever be paid; indeed, AIG's executives would have long ago been on the street. And any mention of the word *talent* in the same sentence as *AIG* or *credit default swaps* would be laughable if laughing weren't already so expensive.

Apart from AIG's sophistry is a much larger point. This sordid story of government helplessness in the face of massive taxpayer commitments illustrates better than anything to date why the government should take over any institution that's "too big to fail" and which has cost taxpayers dearly. Such institutions are no longer within the capitalist system because they are no longer accountable to the market. So to whom should they be accountable? When taxpayers have put up, and essentially own, a large portion of their assets, AIG and other behemoths should be accountable to taxpayers. When our very own Secretary of the Treasury cannot make stick his decision that AIG's bonuses should not be paid, only one conclusion can be drawn: AIG is accountable to no one. Our democracy is seriously broken.

www.huffingtonpost.com/robert-reich/
the-real-scandal-of-aig_b_175105.html

QUESTIONS FOR READING

1. What is the "real scandal of AIG," according to Reich?
2. Why should the government take over any institution "too big to fail"?
3. According to Reich, to whom should AIG and other "behemoths" be accountable?

QUESTIONS FOR REASONING AND ANALYSIS

1. How would you summarize or explain Reich's main point?
2. Why does Reich label AIG's arguments "absurd"? Do you agree with Reich that AIG is *not* legally obligated to pay bonuses? Why or why not?
3. Why does Reich claim that "our democracy is seriously broken"? Do you agree? Why or why not?

QUESTIONS FOR REFLECTING AND WRITING

1. How would you respond to Reich's post? Would you agree with him? Why or why not?
2. Should the federal government bail out failing financial institutions and major corporations with taxpayer money? Why or why not?

prereading question } **Is President Obama effectively addressing the economic and financial crisis?**

Jim Cramer hosts the CNBC financial program *Mad Money*. In this video clip, Matt Lauer of NBC's *Today Show* interviews Mr. Cramer and Erin Burnett, another CNBC financial commentator and analyst. The interview aired on March 3, 2009. As one who aligns himself with the Democratic Party, Mr. Cramer supported Barack Obama for president in 2008.

Reprinted with permission/NBC News Archives. YouTube is a trademark of Google Inc.
www.youtube.com/watch?v=JmAh8zQuAvc&NR=1

(Stream the video before answering these questions.)

1. What does Cramer mean by references to "wealth destruction" and "Garden Variety Depression"? Why does he think that President Obama has engaged in "wealth destruction"? Do you agree? Why or why not?

2. Why does Cramer accuse President Obama of advancing a "radical agenda"? Does Cramer substantiate or support this accusation? How so? If not, do you find Cramer's arguments less compelling? Why or why not?

3. Do you perceive Cramer as credible? Why or why not?

1. Do you support President Obama's plan for solving the economic and financial crisis in America? Is he taking the right steps to achieve economic stability? Why or why not?

2. What is your overall response to this video segment? If you were in a position to address Mr. Cramer face-to-face, what would you say?

3. What economic challenges do you think Americans will face in the next 10 to 20 years? Do you think, for example, that you will find yourself sacrificing some material comforts? If so, what do you think you might be forced to sacrifice? If not, why not?

---

newspaper column

prereading question } **Is the United States facing another Great Depression?**

The Shadow of Depression

Robert J. Samuelson

As a weekly columnist for *The Washington Post*, Robert J. Samuelson writes about economic, political, and social issues. *The Washington Post* published this piece on March 16, 2009.

We live in the shadow of the Great Depression. Americans' gloom does not reflect just 8.1 percent unemployment or the loss of $13 trillion worth of housing and stock market value since mid-2007. There is also an amorphous anxiety that we are falling into a deep economic ravine from which escape will be difficult. These worries may prove ill-founded. But until they do, they promote pessimism and the hoarding of cash, by consumers and companies alike, that further weaken the economy.

Our only frame of reference for this sort of breakdown is the Great Depression. Superficially, the comparison seems absurd. We are a long way from the 1930s, as Christina Romer, head of President Obama's Council of Economic Advisers, noted recently in a useful talk. Unemployment peaked at 25 percent in 1933. At its low point, the economy (gross domestic product) was down 25 percent from its 1929 high. So far, U.S. GDP has dropped only about 2 percent.

What's more, the Depression changed our thinking and institutions. The human misery of economic turmoil has diminished. "American workers [in the 1930s] had painfully few of the social safety nets that today help families," Romer said. Until 1935, there was no federal unemployment insurance. At last count, there were 32 million food stamp recipients and 49 million on Medicaid. These programs didn't exist in the 1930s.

Government also responds more quickly to slumps. Despite many New Deal programs, "fiscal policy"—in effect, deficit spending—was used only modestly in the 1930s, Romer argued. Some of Franklin Roosevelt's extra spending was offset by a tax increase enacted in Herbert Hoover's last year. The federal deficit went from 4.5 percent of GDP in 1933 to 5.9 percent in 1934, not a huge increase.

Contrast that with the present. In fiscal 2009, the budget deficit is projected at 12.3 percent of GDP, up from 3.2 percent in 2008. Some of the increase reflects "automatic stabilizers" (in downturns, government spending increases and taxes decrease); the rest stems from the massive "stimulus program." On top of this, the Federal Reserve has cut its overnight interest rate to about zero and is lending directly in markets where private investors have retreated, including housing.

Government's aggressive actions should reinforce some of the economy's normal mechanisms for recovery. As pent-up demand builds, so will the pressure for more spending. The repayment of loans, lowering debt burdens, sets the stage for more spending. Ditto for the runoff of surplus inventories.

So, are Depression analogies far-fetched, needlessly alarmist? Probably—but not inevitably. Even some Depression scholars, who once dismissed the possibility of a repetition, are less confident.

"Unfortunately, the similarities [between then and now] are growing more striking every day," says economic historian Barry Eichengreen of the University of California at Berkeley. "I never thought I'd say that in my lifetime." Argues economist Gary Richardson of UC Irvine: "This is the first business downturn since the 1930s that looks like the 1930s."

One parallel is that it's worldwide. In the 1930s, the gold standard transmitted the crisis from country to country. Governments raised interest rates to protect their gold reserves. Credit tightened, production and trade suffered, unemployment rose. Now, global investors and banks transmit the crisis. If they suffer losses in one country, they may sell stocks and bonds in other markets to raise cash. Or as they "deleverage"—reduce their own borrowing—they may curtail lending and investing in many countries.

The consequences are the same. In the fourth quarter of 2008, global industrial production fell at a 20 percent annual rate from the third quarter, says the World Bank. International trade may "register its largest decline in 80 years." Developing countries need to borrow at least $270 billion; if they can't, their economies will slow and that will hurt the advanced countries that export to them. It's a vicious circle.

Just as in the 1930s, there's a global implosion of credit. What's also reminiscent of the Depression are quarrels over who's to blame and what should be done. The Obama administration wants bigger stimulus packages from Europe and Japan. Europeans have rebuffed the proposal. The United States has also proposed greater lending by the International Monetary Fund to relieve stresses on poorer countries. Disputes could fuel protectionism and economic nationalism.

No one knows how this epic struggle will end—whether the forces pushing down the global economy will prevail over those trying to pull it up. "Depression" captures a general alarm. The vague fear that something bad is happening, by whatever label, causes consumers and business managers to protect themselves by conserving their cash and slashing their spending. They hope for the best and prepare for the worst. When people stop worrying about depression, when the shadow lifts, the crisis will be over.

QUESTIONS FOR READING

1. What did the Depression change, according to Samuelson?
2. What differences does he cite between the Depression of the 1930s and the present age? What are some similarities?
3. What does the "vague fear that something bad is happening" cause?

QUESTIONS FOR REASONING AND ANALYSIS

1. In your own words, what is Samuelson's thesis?
2. What does Samuelson mean by the "shadow of the Great Depression"? Why do you think he uses this imagery?
3. What type of evidence does Samuelson typically rely upon for supporting his point? Has he effectively used this evidence? Why or why not?
4. What does Samuelson mean when he states that "disputes could fuel protectionism and economic nationalism"? What is he suggesting might cause "disputes"?

QUESTIONS FOR REFLECTING AND WRITING

1. In your view, are fears of another Great Depression well founded? Why or why not? What evidence supports that we will face another Depression? If fears are unfounded, then what evidence supports that we will *not* face another Great Depression?
2. What are your concerns related to the current economic and financial crisis? Are you, for instance, worried about finding a job after earning your degree? Why or why not?
3. How would you respond to Samuelson? Would you agree with him? Why or why not?

Photos

Design Elements

Seeing the Argument feature: (glasses) © Murat Giray Kaya/iStockphoto. *Try It! feature:* (grass) © Eva Serrabassa/iStockphoto; (Stork) © Dirk Freder/iStockphoto; (umbrella) © Gary Blakeley/iStockphoto; (billboard) © Photodisc/Getty Images; (cow) © Erik de Graaf/iStockphoto; (temple) © Robert Churchill/iStockphoto. *Did You Know?* feature: (newspapers) © Kyle Maass/iStockphoto; (books) © Viorika Prikhodko/iStockphoto. *Collaborative Exercise* feature: (handshake) © Ben Blankenburg/iStockphoto; (students) © Jacob Wackerhausen/iStockphoto; (hands) © Jacob Wackerhausen/iStockphoto; (cd) © Tatiana Popova/iStockphoto.

Chapter 1

p. 2: Getty Images; **p. 4 (left):** © Reproduced by permission of The Economist Newspaper Ltd. All rights reserved. Reprinted with permission. Further reproduction prohibited. www.economist.com; **p. 4 (right):** Phrased & Confused - www.phrasedandconfused.co.uk; **p. 5 (top):** © Condé Nast Publications; **p. 5 (bottom):** Penguin Group (USA) Inc.; **p. 6 (left to right):** © Ingram Publishing / AGE Fotostock, © Stockdisc/PunchStock, © Comstock Images/Alamy; **p. 6 (bottom):** © Digital Vision/Getty Images; **p. 9:** Ryan McVay/Getty Images; **p. 10:** Photo by Time Life Pictures/Mansell/Time Life Pictures/Getty Images; **p. 12:** © Sophie Bassouls/ Sygma/Corbis; **p. 13:** Reprinted through the courtesy of the Editors of TIME Magazine © 2009 Time Inc.; **p. 14:** © U.S. Air Force photo by Airman 1st Class Jesse Shipps; **p. 15:** © Somos Images/Corbis; **p. 16:** Magnetic Poetry Photograph: Natalie Roberts, surrealmuse.com; **p. 17:** Library of Congress - Prints and Photographs Division; **p. 19 (top):** Lisa Haney/Getty Images; **p. 19 (bottom):** image100/Punchstock; **p. 20:** Photo by Justin Sullivan/Getty Images.

Chapter 2

p. 22: Bryce Newell / Alamy; **p. 24:** Library of Congress - Prints and Photographs Division / LC-USZ62-15984 (b&w film copy neg.); **p. 26:** © Brand X Pictures / Alamy; **p. 28:** 'Shakespeare's Romeo and Juliet' by Annaliese F. Connolly, 9780764585920/0764585924. © 2000. Reproduced with Permission of John Wiley & Sons, Inc.; **p. 29:** © Library of Congress - Prints and Photographs Division / LC-USZ62-105425 (b&w film copy neg.); **p. 30 (left):** Library of Congress - Prints and Photographs Division/LC-USZ62-111159 (b&w film copy neg.); **p. 30 (right):** Stan honda/AFP/Getty Images; **p. 31:** Photo by Frederick M. Brown/Getty Images; **p. 38:** Photo by Hulton Archive/Getty Images; **p. 41:** Library of Congress - Prints and Photographs Division Washington, D.C. 20540 US [LC-DIG-cwpb-07639].

Chapter 3

p. 46: © Lars Niki; **p. 48 (top):** Shah Marai/AFP/Getty Images; **p. 48 (bottom):** © Theo Westenberger/Corbis; **p. 50 (left):** Martha Stewart © 2008 America's Milk Processors/Lowe, NY; **p. 50 (right):** David Beckham © 2006 America's Milk Processors/Lowe, NY; **p. 51 (top):** © PETA.org.uk; **p. 51 (bottom):** The Bridgeman Art Library/Greek; **p. 52:** © Irene Fertik; **p. 54 (top):** Courtesy of www.askleap.com; **p. 54 (bottom):** © Brand X Pictures; **p. 55:** © Roy McMahon/Corbis; **p. 57:** Courtesy of Soulforce; **p. 59:** Royalty-Free/Corbis; **p. 60:** The McGraw-Hill Companies, Inc./John Flournoy, photographer; **p. 61:** AP Photo/Jae C. Hong.

Chapter 4

p. 66: BananaStock/PictureQuest; **p. 68:** Photo by Scott J. Ferrell/Congressional Quarterly/Getty Images; **p. 70 (top):** Arne Nævra/Naturbilder; **p. 70 (middle):** Stan Honda/AFP/Getty Images; **p. 70 (bottom, left to right):** © Royalty-Free/Corbis, © Ingram Publishing / Fotosearch, Big Cheese Photo / JupiterImages, © Royalty-Free/Corbis, **p. 71:** © Borders Perrin Norrander & Pollinate Media; **p. 72:** © Artwork by Rick Whitfield; **p. 73 (left to right):** (blackboard) © Digital Vision/PunchStock, (graphics) Ryan McVay/Getty Images, (presentation) © Corbis, (newspaper) © BananaStock / PunchStock, (magazine) © The McGraw-Hill Companies, Inc./John Flournoy, photographer, (protest) The McGraw-Hill Companies, Inc./John Flournoy, photographer, (laptop) © BananaStock/PunchStock, (argument) © BananaStock/PunchStock; **p. 75:** Ferdinand Daniel/Getty Images; **p. 77:** AP Photo/Alex Brandon; **p. 78 (left to right):** (drawing) © Stockbyte/PunchStock, (revising) Ryan McVay/Getty Images, (editing) © Photodisc Collection/Getty Images, (proofreading) © Photodisc Collection/Getty Images; **p. 81:** © Last Resort/PhotoDisc/

Chapter 16

p. 288: © Stockbyte/Getty Images; p. 293: © (gun) Stockbyte/Getty Images, (bus) © Lew Robertson / Corbis, (boy) © Digital Vision/ Getty Images, (tv) © Photodisc.

Chapter 17

p. 302: The McGraw-Hill Companies; p. 313: Reprinted through the courtesy of the Editors of TIME Magazine © 2009 Time Inc.; p. 318: SPIDER-MAN: TM & © 2010 Marvel Characters, Inc. Used with permission.

Chapter 18

p. 320: Ryan McVay/Getty Images.

Chapter 19

pp. 336, 351: © Clay Good/Zuma Press.

Chapter 20

p. 354: The McGraw-Hill Companies, Inc./ Andrew Resek, photographer; p. 357: AP Photo/Gregory Bull; p. 358: Reuters/Stephen Hird.

Chapter 21

p. 372: The McGraw-Hill Companies, Inc./Jill Braaten, photographer.

Chapter 22

p. 386: © Comstock Images/PictureQuest.

Chapter 23

p. 400: Don Farrall/Getty Images.

Figures/Text

Chapter 1

p. 7: www.unc.edu/writingcenter, The Writing Center, The University of North Carolina at Chapel Hill. Reprinted with permission; p. 11: Editorial, "Music Piracy: A New Tune," *The Los Angeles Times*, December 20, 2008. Copyright © 2008, The Los Angeles Times. All rights reserved. Reprinted with permission.

Chapter 2

p. 31: Dave Barry, excerpt from "In a Battle of Wits with Kitchen Appliances, I'm Toast," *Miami Herald*, February 27, 2000. Reprinted by permission of Dave Barry; p. 42: "Grim Warning for America's Fast Food Consumers Offered By 'Supersize Me' Mice Research," *Medical News Today*, May 29, 2007. Reprinted by permission of Medical News Today; pp. 43–44: Alyson Waite, "Beware of Facebook Danger," *Diamondback Online*, May 10, 2006. Reprinted by permission of The Diamondback, University of Maryland.

Chapter 3

p. 49: "Welcome to America, Now Speak English." © Opus, 2000. Reprinted by permission of Opus I Distributors; "If you can read this thank a teacher..." © Militaria 2005. Reprinted by permission of Militaria Inc.; Bicycle Evolution, © Microcosm Publishing 2002. Reprinted by permission of Microcosm Publishing; p. 54: Figure "Murder in America" from *Drug War Facts*, 6th ed., Douglas A. McVay, editor. Common Sense for Drug Policy, 2007, p. 21. http://www.drugwarfacts.org/ cms/?q=node/34. Reprinted by permission of Common Sense for Drug Policy.

Chapter 4

p. 75: Figure "The Long-Term Legacy of TV Violence" from *ISR Update*, vol. 1, no. 2 (Spring 2002), p. 7. Reprinted by permission of Institute for Social Research, University of Michigan; pp. 84–85: Deborah Tannen, "We Need Higher Quality Outrage," *The Christian Science Monitor*, October 22, 2004, p. 9, copyright Deborah Tannen. Reprinted by permission. This article is adapted from *The Argument Culture: Moving from Debate to Dialogue*. New York: Ballantine, 1999. This article first appeared in *The Christian Science Monitor* (www.csmonitor.com).

Chapter 5

p. 102: Stephen Heath, Letter to the Editor, "Legalization of Drugs Would Solve Many Problems for Government," *Collegiate Times*, February 8, 2005. Copyright © 2005 Educational Media Company at Virginia Tech Inc. Reprinted with permission; p. 103: Miles Haefner, Letter to the Editor, "Better Things to Worry about Than Smoking," *Reporter*, May

2, 2006. Reprinted by permission of Reporter, Minnesota State University, Mankato.

Chapter 6

pp. 107–108: David Sadker, "Gender Games," *The Washington Post*, July 31, 2000. Reprinted by permission of the author. David Sadker is professor emeritus, American University and currently teaching and writing in Tucson, Arizona. He is co-author of *Still Failing at Fairness* (Scribner's 2009); **pp. 109–110:** Mike Alleyway, "Response to Goth's Wan Stamina," *The Chronicle of Higher Education*, Chronicle Forums, posted June 13, 2007. Reprinted by permission of Mike Alleyway; **p. 113:** From "Cover Wars: the rebuttals," http://politicalirony.com/2008/07/15/cover-wars-the-response/. Reprinted by permission of politicalirony.com

Chapter 7

p. 123: Text about Common Ground, from Wikipedia. http://creativecommons.org/licenses/by-sa/3.0; **pp. 125–126:** Editorial, "Ultimately We Control Our Own Privacy Levels on Facebook," *Collegiate Times*, February 19, 2009. Copyright © 2009 Educational Media Company at Virginia Tech Inc. Reprinted with permission.

Chapter 8

pp. 143–145: Excerpts from Gregg Easterbrook, "TV Really Might Cause Autism. A *Slate* Exclusive: Findings from a New Cornell Study," *Slate*, October 16, 2006. Copyright 2006 by Gregg Easterbrook. Reprinted by permission of the author.

Chapter 9

pp. 160–161: James Q. Wilson, "A New Strategy for the War on Drugs." Reprinted from *The Wall Street Journal*, April 13, 2000. © 2000 Dow Jones & Company. All rights reserved.

Chapter 13

Chapter 13 is adapted from Dorothy U. Seyler, *Read, Reason, Write*, 8th ed., pp. 289–306, 310–312, 342–364. Copyright © 2008 by The McGraw-Hill Companies, Inc. Used with permission of the McGraw-Hill Companies.

Chapter 14

pp. 256–259: Hugh Graham, "The End of Consumer Culture?" hughgrahamcreative.com, January 30, 2008. Reprinted by permission of the author. The figure is from Grouzet, F. M. E., Kasser, T., Ahuvia, A., et al. (2005). The structure of goal contents across 15 cultures. *Journal of Personality and Social Psychology*, 89: 800–816 (Figure 1, p. 808). Copyright 2005 by the American Psychological Association. Reprinted with permission; **pp. 260–263:** Michelle Cottle, "Turning Goys into Girls." Reprinted with permission from the *Washington Monthly*, May 1998. Copyright by Washington Monthly Publishing, LLC, 1200 18th Street, NW, Suite 330, Washington, DC 20036, 202-955-9010. www.washingtonmonthly.com; **pp. 265–266:** Rob Walker, "Social Lubricant: How a Marketing Campaign Became the Catalyst for a Societal Debate," *The New York Times Magazine*, September 4, 2005. © 2005, The New York Times. Reprinted by permission; **pp. 268–269:** Jeff Howe, "Why the Music Industry Hates *Guitar Hero*," *Wired*, February 23, 2009. Reprinted by permission of Jeff Howe, Contributing Editor, *Wired* magazine. Originally published in *Wired*.

Chapter 16

pp. 290–292: Gloria Steinem, "Supremacy Crimes," *Ms.* magazine, August/September 1999. Reprinted by permission of Gloria Steinem, feminist activist and writer; **pp. 295–297:** Katherine Ellison, "What's Up, Doc? A Bloody Outrage, That's What," *The Washington Post*, October 23, 2005, p. B1. Reprinted by permission of the author.

Chapter 17

pp. 304–309: Tom Brokaw and Gen. Colin Powell (ret.), *Meet the Press*, October 19, 2008. Reprinted with permission/NBC News Archives.

Chapter 18

pp. 328–330: Cynthia Kopkowski McCabe, "Education Funding: Follow the Money," *NEA Today*, January/February 2009. Reprinted by permission of the National Education Association. nea.org; **pp. 331–332:** Mary Sue

Coleman, "The Digital Library Plan: Riches We Must Share," *The Washington Post*, October 22, 2005, p. A21. Reprinted by permission of the author; **pp. 332–333:** Nick Taylor, "The Digital Library Plan: But Not at Writers' Expense," *The Washington Post*, October 22, 2005, p. A21. Reprinted by permission of the author.

Chapter 19

pp. 338–339: John W. Whitehead, "The Schools Are Destroying Freedom of Speech," *Right Side News*, March 25, 2009. Reprinted by permission of the author; **pp. 340–342:** Ken Dautrich and John Bare, "Why the First Amendment (and Journalism) Might Be in Trouble." This article was published in the Summer 2005 issue of *Nieman Reports*. Reprint is courtesy of Nieman Reports; **pp. 343–344:** Mark Davis, "A Little Civility, Please," *Fort Worth Star-Telegram*, March 5, 2003. Reprinted by permission of the author; **pp. 344–346:** Robert O'Neil, "What Limits Should Campus Networks Place on Pornography?" *Chronicle of Higher Education*, March 21, 2003. Reprinted by permission of the author; **pp. 347–348:** Rick Santorum, excerpt from Chapter 23 from *It Takes a Family*. Copyright © 2005 ISI Books, Wilmington, Delaware. Reprinted with permission.

Chapter 20

pp. 363–364: Introduction from *The Huffington Post*, April 2, 2008. Reprinted by permission of The Huffington Post. Excerpts from *Morning Joe*, April 2, 2008. Reprinted with permission/NBC News Archives; **pp. 365–367:** Maggie Mahar, "Is Healthcare a 'Right' or a 'Moral Obligation'?" *Health Beat*, October 8, 2008. Reprinted by permission of Maggie Mahar, The Century Foundation. www.healthbeatblog.org. Maggie Mahar is the author of *Money-Driven Medicine*, HarperCollins, 2006; film 2009.

Chapter 21

p. 375: Kevin Drum, "Gay Rights in California," Motherjones.com, November 5, 2008. © 2008, Foundation for National Progress. Reprinted with permission; **pp. 381–384:** Sam Schulman, "The Worst Thing About Gay Marriage, It Isn't Going to Work," *The Weekly Standard*, Vol. 014, Issue 35 (June 1, 2009). Reprinted by permission of The Weekly Standard.

Chapter 22

pp. 388–390: Reprinted with permission from *Issues in Science and Technology*, Michael M. Crow, "The Challenge for the Obama Administration Science Team," Spring 2009, pp. 29–30, Copyright © 2009 by the University of Texas at Dallas, Richardson, TX; **pp. 393–394:** Kenneth R. Miller, "Trouble Ahead for Science," *The Boston Globe*, May 8, 2008. Opinion – OpEd. Reprinted by permission of the author; **p. 395:** Ben Stein, "Florida's Darwinian Interlude," *American Spectator*, February 20, 2008. Reprinted by permission of The American Spectator, Spectator.org; **pp. 396–398:** Laura K. Donohue, "Censoring Science Won't Make Us Any Safer," *The Washington Post*, June 26, 2005, p. B5. Reprinted by permission of the author.

Chapter 23

p. 408: Robert Reich, "The Real Scandal of AIG," *The Huffington Post*, March 15, 2009. Reprinted by permission of the author. Robert Reich is Professor of Public Policy, University of California at Berkeley, and former U.S. Secretary of Labor.